THE CITRUS INDUSTRY

VOLUME IV

Crop Protection

EDITED BY:

Walter Reuther

E. Clair Calavan

Glenn E. Carman

Professor of Horticulture, Emeritus;
Professor of Plant Pathology; and
Professor of Entomology, respectively.
University of California, Riverside, California

WITH THE COLLABORATION OF:

Leo J. Klotz • James W. Wallace • E. Clair Calavan • Stanley M. Mather
E. H. McEachern • Dan Y. Rosenberg • F. Louis Blanc • Daniel W. Robinson
H. Len Foote • Maynard W. Cummings • Rex E. Marsh • C. P. Clausen
R. C. Baines • S. D. Van Gundy • E. P. DuCharme

Revised Edition

University of California

Division of Agricultural Sciences

1978

Library of Congress Catalog Card Number: 67-63041
Printed in the United States of America

International Standard Book Number: 0-931876-24-9

DEDICATED TO

HOWARD SAMUEL FAWCETT (1877-1948)

★◆◆◆★

HOWARD SAMUEL FAWCETT

(1877–1948)

"Let us learn to dream, gentlemen; then perhaps we shall find the truth. . . . But let us beware of publishing our dreams before they have been put to proof by waking understanding."

—AUGUST KEKULÉ

On the morning of May 15, 1933, Howard Samuel Fawcett stood beneath an orange tree in a grove affected with a mysterious disease that had baffled plant pathologists for decades. Suddenly a group of leaves hanging in just the right light against the sky caught his attention. Eleven years earlier, Fawcett had discovered a therapeutic treatment for the disease, but the cause still eluded him. Now he was "seized with a sensation as if the eyes of the scientific workers in this subject for the preceeding eleven years were looking through mine." The illuminated flecked markings on the leaves broke upon Fawcett as a light of instantaneous understanding. Years later he could recall the exact instant—eight o'clock—that he reached a completely new hypothesis about the cause of psorosis. From that moment of prescience, he proceeded methodically to gather the data leading to the first discovery of a virus disease in citrus.

Sudden creative insights, always subject to rigid experimental scrutiny, were characteristic of Fawcett. He often spoke of the need for "constructive dreaming" in research, citing as an example August Kekulé, the organic chemist, who had formulated the benzene ring structure as the result of a dream. Fawcett's coworkers were continually amazed at how often his hunches directed him toward productive areas of investigation that other researchers had ignored. As a pioneer in citrus pathology, Fawcett was one of those rare scientists most often found on the frontiers of a developing new discipline who blaze a path for other researchers to follow through every uncharted area on which their attention focuses. His discoveries far outweigh those of any other citrus pathologist of his era, and he was the founder of citrus virology. His contributions were surpassed only by the inspiration and stimulation he gave to colleagues throughout the world.

Of slight stature, quiet and soft spoken, he endeared himself to his colleagues by his good fellowship, enthusiasm, and willingness to help. The adjectives most often used by his friends in describing him were "kind," "patient," "fair," and "understanding." His surviving close associates in plant pathology pay lavish tribute to his genius as a scientist, and to the inspiration and leadership he gave to his discipline. They also delight in telling humorous anecdotes involving Fawcett's monumental absentmindedness; without doubt, many of these stories lose nothing in retelling over the years.

Howard Samuel Fawcett was born of Quaker parents on a farm near Salem, Ohio, on April 12, 1877. He completed the local high school curriculum and then attended a Friends' preparatory school in Westtown, Pennsylvania, graduating in 1899. After teaching science for a year in a preparatory school in Le Grande, Iowa, Fawcett enrolled at Iowa State College, where he majored in botany and received his B.S. degree in 1905.

Following graduation, Fawcett accepted a post as assistant in botany and horticulture at the University of Florida, where he carried out research in association with three distinguished pioneers in citrus investigation, Herbert John Webber, Walter T. Swingle, and P. H. Rolfs. He was appointed assistant plant pathologist in 1907 and plant pathologist in 1908. During seven years at the University of Florida, Fawcett made many significant contributions on scaly bark and gummosis diseases of citrus trees, on stem-end rot of citrus fruits, and on fungus diseases of citrus insects. While in Florida, Fawcett married T. Helen Tostenson in 1909. They had one daughter, Rosamond Annette Fawcett.

In 1912, Fawcett accepted an assignment with the California State Commission of Horticulture to investigate the brown rot gummosis which was ravaging the citrus trees of the state. In that same year, Herbert John Webber became the first director of the University of California Citrus Experiment Station (now the Citrus Research Center and Agricultural Experiment Station) at Riverside, California. Webber immediately began building a staff of outstanding citrus scientists. The state agreed to release Fawcett to join Webber's staff with the understanding that his research on gummosis be continued. During the next three years, Fawcett single-handedly isolated the causal fungi, proved their relationship to the disease, and developed effective treatment methods.

For two years, beginning in 1916, Fawcett was on leave at John Hopkins University, where he received his Ph.D. in 1918. During that period he worked under Dr. Burton E. Livingston, investigating the temperature relations of certain fungi parasitic on citrus trees and pioneering development of temperature control apparatus for botanical studies.

From 1918 until his retirement in 1947, Fawcett was a professor of plant pathology for the University of California and a plant pathologist for the Citrus Experiment Station at Riverside. He also served as chairman of the department of plant pathology from 1920 until 1946, when he relinquished the post to devote full time to research.

From 1922 to 1923, Fawcett was on sabbatical leave with a mission sent by the American Friends Service Committee to assist the famine-stricken area of southeastern Russia. Throughout his life, he worked quietly and persistently in many ways for the advancement of peace and goodwill among men. His humanitarianism permeated his nonscientific writings, including an insightful publication that explores the workings of the scientific mind, *Adventures in the Plant-Disease World*, first presented as a Faculty Research Lecture in 1940 at the University of California, Los Angeles.

As a collaborator with the U. S. Department of Agriculture from 1929 to 1930, Fawcett studied citrus and date diseases in the Mediterranean countries, North Africa, and Palestine. In 1936-37, he investigated citrus problems in Brazil and Argentina. His findings during these travels appeared in technical papers and later in his authoritative textbook *Citrus Diseases and Their Control*. This landmark work, considered the classic reference on citrus diseases, first appeared in 1926 with Dr. H. A. Lee, who wrote several chapters, serving as junior author. Subsequently, it was greatly revised and expanded under the sole authorship of Fawcett in 1936 and 1947.

During his long career in plant pathology, Fawcett studied numerous citrus diseases and various diseases of walnuts, dates, cotton, and avocados. He contributed upwards of 300 articles to scientific and industrial journals and published two books. His second book, *Color Handbook of Citrus Diseases*, coauthored with L. J. Klotz, was a practical guide to identification and control of citrus diseases. His name was starred in the fifth edition of *American Men of Science* (1933), which meant that he was then considered one of the 250 leading scientists in the United States and one of twenty-five leading botanists.

Fawcett's discovery of the psorosis virus opened up a new field of research in citrus diseases and placed the Citrus Experiment Station in the forefront of virology research. Shortly before his death in 1948, Fawcett demonstrated the virus origin of tristeza disease with J. M. Wallace, which provided the key for dealing with a disease that threatened much of the world's citrus industry. Another major research contribution was his demonstration that stubborn disease was caused by a virus which could be transmitted by vegetative propagation. A review of early literature on citrus diseases clearly indicates the massive influence that Fawcett had on our knowledge of the cause, biology, and control of almost all of the major diseases affecting citrus.

Fawcett was a charter member of the American Phytopathological Society founded in 1909, and received its highest honor with his election to president of that national group in 1930. He was a member of Phi Beta Kappa, Sigma Xi, the Botanical Society of America, the Mycological Society of America, Societa Internazionale di Microbiologia (Milano), and a Fellow of the American Association for the Advancement of Science.

PREFACE

Since each volume of the revised and new edition of THE CITRUS INDUSTRY is complete in itself, the general plan of the work must be restated in each volume. The first volume of the revised edition, *History, World Distribution, Botany, and Varieties,* was published by the University of California Division of Agricultural Sciences in 1967. The second volume, *Anatomy, Physiology, Genetics,* and *Reproduction,* followed in 1968. These first two volumes covered much of the subject matter originally presented in Volume I of the first edition, plus some additional material. The third volume, *Production Technology,* published in 1973, encompasses orchard management portions of the subject matter originally covered in Volume II of the first edition. This fourth volume, *Crop Protection,* covers portions of Volume II of the first edition that were concerned with the biology and control of pests and diseases. Because many Crop Protection chapters exceeded original estimates of length, it was necessary to divide them into two volumes. Thus, a fifth volume, also concerned with crop protection, will appear soon. None of the chapters in these volumes are revisions of chapters in Volume II of the first edition; all are completely new treatments of the subject matter by a new generation of authors.

The first edition of *The Citrus Industry* served for more than two decades as the classic reference work on the biology and culture of citrus throughout the world. The first volume, *History, Botany,* and *Breeding,* edited by H. J. Webber and L. D. Batchelor, was published by the University of California Press in 1943, and was followed by two later reprintings. A larger printing of the second volume, *Production of the Crop,* edited by L. D. Batchelor and H. J. Webber, was published in 1948 by the University of California Press. In the decades following World War II, an increased tempo of citrus research has provided a much broader base of information and experience than was available to the original authors of the first edition. Thus, the chapters presented in this and the other revised volumes reflect a substantial expansion of coverage and, thus, pages.

Most of the chapters in this volume were prepared by members of the staff of the University of California who are affiliated either with the Citrus Research Center and Agricultural Experiment Station (CRC-AES) at Riverside or with the University of California Agricultural Extension Service. Chapter 3 was prepared in collaboration with staff members of the State of California Department of Food and Agriculture, and Chapter 4 was written entirely by staff of this agency. Professor E. P. DuCharme of the University of Florida collaborated in the preparation of Chapter 7. Authors' treatment of subjects, therefore, tends to exhibit a regional perspective, although improved communications and transportation in the past few decades have made it possible for citrus researchers and specialists to be more cognizant of developments in other regions than was the case for contributors to the original volumes.

Taxonomic usage in this and other volumes of THE CITRUS INDUSTRY varies among chapters. No attempt was made to standardize the systematics since diversity in usage is common among technical citrus publications. A majority now accept W. T. Swingle's system, with seven species in the genus *Citrus,* for example, but some follow R. W. Hodgson, T. Tanaka, and others with many more species (see Volume I, Chapter 3 of THE CITRUS INDUSTRY, pp. 358–369).

The five volumes of the new revised and expanded edition of *The Citrus Industry* are intended to present a comprehensive view of all the production phases of the industry to a broad readership of researchers, administrators, advisors, teachers, students, and knowledgeable growers. An effort has been made to present all material clearly, yet scientifically, so that it might be understood by an intelligent and informed readership. The editors, however, considered it essential that scientific principles on which various practices are based also should be explained. Some parts of this volume, therefore, may present material of a highly technical nature best followed by specialists. Literature reviews for most chapters in the volume were completed with 1976 citations.

Tables for converting units of measurement from the English to the metric system and vice-versa are presented in Table I-1 of Appendix I.

Chapter 1, "Fungal, Bacterial, and Nonpapasitic Diseases and Injuries Originating in the Seedbed, Nursery, and Orchard," by Leo J. Klotz, is a comprehensive review of the biology and control of the known diseases (except viruses) which afflict citrus seedlings as well as nursery and orchard trees. Also included are descriptions of various physiological and other nonparasitic disorders and injuries common in citrus orchards, together with the available preventative or therapeutic measures. This chapter is the most authoritative and up-to-date treatment of citrus diseases now available.

Chapter 2, "Virus and Viruslike Diseases" by James M. Wallace concerns the virus and viruslike diseases of citrus which have caused such serious losses to citrus growers throughout the world in the last half-century. The author, taking advantage of the great strides that have been made in the field of citrus virology in the past quarter century, provides a scholarly review of the subject. Included are descriptions of the symptoms, the nature of and structure of the organism when known, as well as modes of transmission, vector and host relations, rootstock-scion effects, detection methods, and avoidance procedures. Unfortunately, very little concerning practical therapeutic methods for infected orchard trees is included because of the lack of progress in field control methods for virus diseases of crop plants in general. This chapter is the first complete and up-to-date treatment to be written about this relatively new group of citrus diseases.

Chapter 3, "Registration, Certification, and Indexing of Citrus Trees" by E. Clair Calavan, Stanley M. Mather and E. H. McEachern, outlines the objectives of registration and certification programs and the historical evolution of the present day California program. Details of the legal basis, organization, and procedure used in California for ensuring the production of disease-free, true-to-name nursery stock are reviewed, along with description of programs in other states. Also, the methods used for virus and viruslike pathogen detection are described. This chapter will be of special interest not only to those interested in virus detection methodology, but also to regulatory people in other regions wishing to establish a citrus registration and certification program, or to improve an existing program.

Chapter 4, "Regulatory Measures For Pest and Disease Control" by Dan Y. Rosenberg, Eley H. McEachern, F. Louis Blanc, Daniel W. Robinson, and H. Len Foote is concerned with the role of public regulatory agencies in pest and disease control in California and the United States. The philosophy, objectives, legal aspects, procedures and difficulties involved in quarantine, nursery inspection, pest and disease detection and eradication are discussed. Special emphasis is given to the problems of protecting the California citrus industry from the introduction of pests and diseases, and minimizing their spread within the state once they are established.

Chapter 5, "Vertebrate Pests of Citrus" by Maynard W. Cummings and Rex E. Marsh places greatest emphasis on the biology, damage, and control or management of the major vertebrate pest species. In the United States, rodents and lagomorphs (rabbits and hares) cause the most economic damage, while birds cause only minor economic losses. Also included are brief discussions of minor and potential pests. The depredations of birds, bats, and other pests in citrus orchards in some other citrus countries are discussed, but the information available is limited. Control measures are discussed from three viewpoints: (1) population reduction by use of lethal or sterilizing chemical agents, or by physical methods such as trapping or shooting; (2) habitat manipulation or modification to reduce orchard population by cultural practices and other means of altering the environment in a way unfavorable to the pests; and (3) behavioral manipulation by use of techniques which reduce damage by modifying or altering some behavior pattern, such as by use of chemical or physical repellents or barriers.

Chapter 6, "Biological Control of Citrus Insects" by C. P. Clausen is a basic treatment of the essentials of biological control of citrus pests throughout the world. Included are general discussions of the historical background, biotic control agents and procedures, biology of parasitic insects, microbial pathogens of insects, mass production of parasites, interactions with insecticides, and the time framework. The greater portion of the chapter is concerned with the biological control of specific insects parasitizing citrus.

Chapter 7, "Nematodes Attacking Citrus" by Richard C. Baines, Seymour D. Van Gundy, and Ernest P. DuCharme is a comprehensive treatment of the nematodes of citrus species. A majority of the chapter deals with the details of the biology and control of specific nematode species which parasitize the roots of citrus species. Included are discussions of the influence of soil temperature and other soil factors, host plants, varietal tolerance, resistant strains, soil sterilization, and biological and chemical control measures.

The editors wish to express their deep appreciation to their colleagues too numerous to list at Riverside and elsewhere around the world who so generously assisted by reviewing all or part of the text dealing with their particular fields of specialization.

WALTER REUTHER
Riverside, California
September 15, 1977

CONTENTS

CHAPTER 3. Registration, Certification, and Indexing of Citrus Trees 185

E. Clair Calavan, Stanley M. Mather, and E. H. McEachern

CHAPTER 4. Regulatory Measures for Pest and Disease Control 223

Dan. Y. Rosenberg, Eley H. McEachern, F. Louis Blanc, Daniel W. Robinson, and H. Len Foote

CHAPTER 5. Vertebrate Pests of Citrus ... 237

Maynard W. Cummings and Rex E. Marsh

CHAPTER 6. Biological Control of Citrus Insects ... 274

C. P. Clausen

CHAPTER 1

Fungal, Bacterial, and Nonparasitic Diseases and Injuries Originating in the Seedbed, Nursery, and Orchard

LEO J. KLOTZ

THE CITRUS NURSERYMAN, grower, and packinghouse manager are, of necessity, greatly concerned with the prevention and control of maladies to which citrus is subject. If the grower had to combat all the numerous disorders of the world's citrus, he would soon be discouraged. Fortunately, however, only a few diseases in any citrus-growing locality are sufficiently important to require drastic control measures. Quarantine vigilance and local or worldwide differences in climate and soil conditions largely determine which disorders are present in a citrus area. For example, the dry climates of California, Arizona, and North Africa are unfavorable for citrus canker, scab, and melanose diseases which thrive near the equator and in environments such as those of Florida, Japan, and the West Indies. Septoria spot, brown rot, and water spot of citrus fruit, which cause great losses in California, are of minor or no significance in Florida. Northern California navel orchards suffer from blast, a disease which is of very minor importance in southern California.

In its broadest sense, plant disease is a deviation from the normal, healthy condition of a plant that threatens its usefulness or well being. Any one of many agencies can cause disease: (1) parasitic higher plants, algae, fungi, and bacteria; (2) nonparasitic factors such as malnutrition, physical condition of environment, and inherited genetic weaknesses; (3) animal organisms, such as higher animals, insects, mites, and nematodes; and the very important group of agencies, including (4) viruses, mycoplasmalike and viroid organisms (Semancik and Weathers, 1971). This chapter, with minor exceptions, deals with diseases and injuries of citrus under the first two categories. Other chapters in this volume, in Volumes 2 and 3, and in Volume 5 (in press) discuss virus, mycoplasmalike, viroid, and postharvest diseases, nutritional deficiencies and excesses, and injury by insects, nematodes, rodents, and adverse climatic factors.

In general, the discussions of this chapter are arranged in groups corresponding to the parts of the citrus tree affected: (1) soil-borne diseases of roots and rootstocks; (2) diseases of trunk and scaffold branches; and (3) diseases of small branches, twigs, leaves, and fruit in the orchard.

In the prevention and treatment of diseases, three factors must always be considered: effectiveness of the methods of treatment, cost of treatments, and possible injury to the plants. Obviously, the cost of control measures used must be less than the losses the disease could cause. In the control of diseases caused by parasitic organisms, various means are employed: (1) removing or restricting the sources of infections; (2) avoiding or decreasing the effects of conditions that promote the infection; (3) preventing entrance of the parasite by treating susceptible parts of plants with fungicides or disinfectants; (4) using resistant species and varieties; and (5) when the disease has not yet appeared or become established, excluding parasites from the orchard, locality, or even the entire country by quarantine measures.

Limitations of space for this chapter require that emphasis be given to brief descriptions of the diseases and means for control. More detailed discussion of history, geographic distribution, and the nature of causes of citrus diseases, and conditions contributing to their occurrence, together with literature references, have been presented in earlier publications.

The first edition of the classic publication *Citrus Diseases and Their Control* was written by Howard S. Fawcett and H. Atherton Lee (1926). The second edition with Dr. Fawcett (1936) as sole author recorded results of experiments and observations on citrus diseases up to 1936. Material up to 1948 was collected by H. S. Fawcett and L. J. Klotz (1948) in Chapter XI of Volume 2 of *The Citrus Industry*. The University of California Press in 1941 and 1948 published the first and second (revised) editions of a *Color Handbook of Citrus Diseases*, which by color photographs and descriptions gave the essential symptoms or means of recognizing all the diseases, injuries, and nutritional troubles of citrus considered important at that time. Control measures were also presented. The Division of Agricultural Sciences of the University of California published the third revised and enlarged edition of the handbook in 1961. Since 1948, many investigators have entered the field and made valuable contributions to our knowledge of citrus maladies caused by fungi, viruses, and unfavorable environmental conditions. Much of their material was abstracted and used in the fourth revised and enlarged edition of the color handbook (Klotz, 1973). Other useful compilations on citrus diseases have been published by Bondar (1929); Rhoads and DeBusk (1931); Rose *et al.* (1943); Suit (1949); Knorr, Suit, and DuCharme (1957); Pratt (1958); Chapot and Delucchi (1964); Scaramuzzi (1965); Del Rosario (1968); and Knorr (1965, 1973).

FACTORS AFFECTING INCIDENCE OF DISEASE

Although conditions and operations influencing the occurrence and severity of diseases in seedbed, nursery, and orchard are discussed in more detail in later sections, a general statement may be made concerning such factors. Assuming first of all that a grower has secured trees free of diseases and pests and suitable to climatic and other conditions of his locale, there are several factors that can be controlled to keep his orchard healthy and productive. Soils and water with excessive or toxic salts or which harbor parasites of citrus obviously will be detrimental to the health and growth of trees. Excessive watering and poor drainage will promote root rot at all stages of growth. Crowding of seedlings and nursery and orchard trees will increase humidity in orchards and favor development and rapid spread of diseases such as damping-off, fruit and leaf spots, and decays. Injury from cold, even when tissues are not directly killed, provides conditions for bark- and wood-rotting fungi and weak parasites which ordinarily do not attack sound fruit or other parts of a tree. Damage by wind, hail, and lightning (see p. 58) also provides openings for disease-producing fungi and bacteria.

Avoidance or control of these unfavorable factors is the objective of the successful orchardist. Injuries to roots resulting from deep cultivation and concentrated fertilizers can be minimized by careful cultivation methods or the so-called noncultivation method and uniform application of recommended amounts of fertilizers. Quality of soil and water is a primary consideration. Soils and water harboring citrus parasites can be disinfested by treatment with certain chemicals. By close attention to irrigation, which should be guided by tensiometers, damage from overwatering can be avoided. Approved seeding and planting distances and pruning obviate dangers from overcrowding. Severe injury by cold weather usually can be avoided or lessened by careful selection of the orchard site to provide good air drainage and by use of heaters, air mixers, and certain plant-growth regulators. Again, it must be emphasized that since parasitism of citrus by several fungi is favored by cold injury, protection of trees from frost is also important in avoiding disease. The trees, moreover, can be protected from many maladies by timely application of fungicides.

THE MAJOR BACTERIAL AND FUNGAL DISEASES

The four most important bacterial and fungal diseases in world citrus orchards both in terms of destructiveness and difficulty or expense in achieving control, are citrus canker, mal secco, black spot, and infections caused by *Phytophthora* spp. In certain areas, various other diseases, such as Armillaria root rot, blast, and scab are extremely serious, but the first four diseases mentioned are generally the most destructive.

The only successful method for control of citrus canker, a bacterial disease, is a campaign of thorough eradication, which involves the expense of frequent surveys, the use of a large amount of labor, and the destruction of affected trees. Mal secco is most severe in lemon orchards of the Mediterranean basin. This fungal disease requires almost daily observance and control measures by orchardists to remove affected parts of trees. Black spot is most damaging to the fruit of lemons and Valencia oranges in South Africa, Australia, and the Far East, requiring three or four well-timed sprays per crop to reduce enormous losses from fruit spoilage. *Phytophthora* spp. attack all organs of citrus trees and can destroy them at any growth stage. Great losses are caused, particularly through fruit decay.

It is evident that control measures in the orchard, including avoidance of mechanical injuries due to chemical and climatic factors are required not only for protection of trees and fruit but also for many of the fruit maladies that may develop after harvest.

SEEDBED DISORDERS

Damping-Off Disease

The general occurrence and seriousness of the damping-off disease of citrus seedlings (figs. 1-1 and 1-2) make it an important concern of nurserymen and growers. The disease wreaks havoc in seedbeds where excessive soil moisture accompanies favorable temperatures for the causal fungi (Klotz *et al.*, 1966).

Symptoms.—Two phases of the disorder are recognized: (1) the pre-emergence phase, during which the fungi attack the young embryo before it reaches the soil surface; and (2) the post-emergence phase, in which fungi attack the seedling stem at ground level. The former results in a sparse stand and the latter in many toppled seedlings.

A soil-borne fungus, *Rhizoctonia solani* Kuhn, is the principal cause of this malady with citrus seedlings. *Pythium aphanidermatum (Eds.) Fitz.* and other *Pythium* spp. may occasionally cause some damage (DeWolfe, Calavan, and Sufficool, 1954). Where present, *Phytophthora citrophthora* (Sm. & Sm.) Leonian and *P. nicotianae*

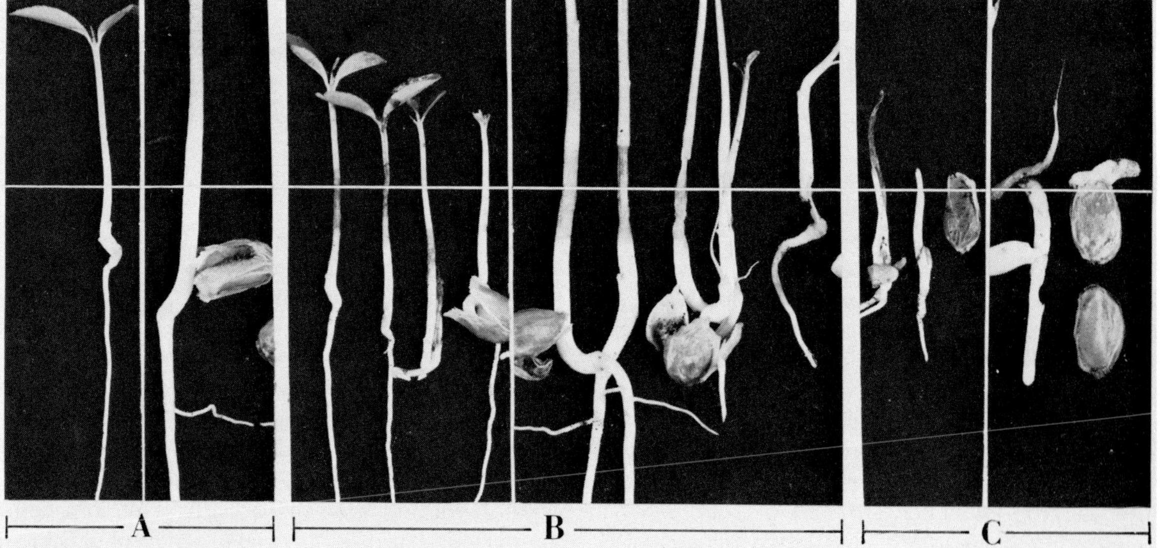

Fig. 1–1. Damping-off disease of citrus seedlings. *A*, **healthy seedlings.** *B*, **post emergence damping off.** *C*, **preemergence damping off. White line indicates soil surface. (Photos courtesy of T. A. DeWolfe).**

Fig. 1–2. A demonstration of effective control of damping-off disease with chemicals. The control citrus seedlings in the front row were not treated.

B. de Haan var. *parasitica* (Dastur) Waterk can ruin many plants if temperature and moisture are favorable.

Control.—The best features of several recommendations for damping-off control may be summarized as follows. Prepare the seedbed with uninfested virgin soil, if available. If such soil is not available, disinfest each 1,000 square feet of the seedbed by sprinkling with 17 gallons of a solution containing 3 ounces of Special Semesan. Disinfestation also can be accomplished with other chemicals, such as methyl bromide (400 pounds per acre, tarped), D-D or Vidden D (260 gallons per acre), Vapam (100 gallons per acre), and Vorlex (70 gallons per acre). Waiting periods between treatment and seeding range from as short as one month to as long as a year, depending upon the chemical used (tables 1–1 and 1–2) and the soil type. A mixture of one-third chloropicrin and two-thirds methyl bromide also has been found very effective as a soil disinfestant (Baines *et al.*, 1962). Allow seedbed to dry to a depth of 2 to 3 inches (5 to 7.5 cm) and acidify the surface inch of soil by applying 1-1/4 ounces (35 gm) of aluminum sulfate per square foot and raking it into the top inch of soil (Weindling and Fawcett, 1936).

One large nursery has found that on sandy loam application of 5,000 pounds of ferrous sulfate with 10,000 pounds of sulfur per acre, rototilled into the top 6 inches (15 cm) of soil, gives a long-lasting, favorable acid reaction between pH 4.5 and 6.0. Larger dosages may be necessary in heavier soils (Klotz *et al.*, 1966).

Picking fruit directly from trees above a height of 4 feet generally precludes infection of seed by *Phytophthora* spp., but to be safe one should assume that even high fruit may be infected, either directly by *Phytophthora hibernalis* Carne or by *P. citrophthora* and *P. parasitica* when fruit comes in contact with soil or contaminated picking bags, boxes, and seed extractors. To destroy Phytophthora fungi that may thus reach fruit and seed, immerse seed in agitated water at 125° F (51.7° C) for 10 minutes (Klotz *et al.*, 1960*a*).

If treated seeds are to be used at once, distribute them over the seedbed, placing about 30-50 seeds per square foot, and press them into the surface with a board. Cover with a ¾-inch layer of sand or the same depth of an acid peat moss.

If seeds are to be stored for future use, coat with a slurry of Arasan (a pint of Arasan powder in 4 pints of water), surface dry, and store in polyethylene bags at 40° F to 50° F; or place surface-dried seeds in polyethylene bags with dry Arasan powder, shake to cover thoroughly, and store at 40° F to 50° F. If the slurry is used, it is quite necessary to dry only the seed surface before bagging and storage. Further drying can reduce or destroy seed germinability. A one per cent solution of 8-hydroxyquinoline sulfate can be used in place of Arasan. Immerse seed for three minutes, shake off excess liquid, and plant at once or store in polyethylene bags at 40° F to 50° F.

Although a recent study showed that damping-off can occur at all concentrations of moisture from 15 to 28.5 per cent used in Ramona soil, 15 to 17 per cent moisture was most favorable for the disease and germination of seeds. Wet soil, high humidity, excessive shading, and crowding of seedlings should be avoided. Under such conditions, the leaves and stems of seedlings may be attacked by *Phytophthora* spp., which cause a firm, leathery decay.

If seedlings to be sold or budded by a commercial nursery appear unthrifty and examination reveals Phytophthora infection on leaves, stems, or roots, it is advisable to destroy seedlings and not try to salvage apparently uninfected ones. Growers who wish to try to salvage for their own use apparently uninfected seedlings in a bed containing some diseased plants may do some good by spraying at once with 3-2-6-100 zinc sulfate-copper sulfate-hydrated lime or its equivalent in a commercial one-package material or a pound of Captan (active ingredient) per 100 gallons. Pull out and dispose of obviously affected seedlings.

Most citrus seedlings will not tolerate the hot

water treatment of immersion in water at 125° F for 10 minutes, and no surface application of a chemical fungicide can disinfect an already-infected plant.

A soil pH range of 4.0 to 5.5 has been found to be most favorable for avoiding damping-off disease. This also is the most favorable acidity for parasitism by *Trichoderma* spp. of the most important damping-off fungus of citrus, *Rhizoctonia solani* (Weindling and Fawcett, 1936). The acidifying action of aluminum sulfate and peat also favors this biological method of control (see fig. 1-2).

Where it is possible to maintain the soil temperature in the range of 87° F to 90° F by electricity or steam during germination, much of the loss from damping-off can be avoided because that temperature range is above optimum for the fungi. After seedlings are 5 inches high they are less susceptible to the disease. The temperature may then be dropped to 75° F to 80° F, which is a more favorable range for growth.

Water from canals and reservoirs can be a source of contamination of seedbeds. *Phytophthora* spp. were isolated from 13 of 15 canals and reservoirs tested, but not from well water (Klotz, Wong, and DeWolfe, 1959). Runoff water from citrus orchards is particularly dangerous. Contaminated water can be treated with copper sulfate (20.0 ppm of $CuSO_4 \cdot 5H_2O$) or chlorine (1.0 ppm of Cl_2) to destroy these fungi

The application of large quantities of nitrogenous fertilizers to force growth should be discouraged. High concentrations of ammonia and nitrate nitrogen that form from the concentrates injure or kill small plants (Carpenter *et al.*, 1959).

To protect seedbed areas from infestation by animals and shoes carrying soil, fence the seedbeds and treat shoes with one-package Bordeaux powder. Treat tools with a suitable noncorrosive disinfectant such as 5 per cent Formalin.

Albinism

Albinism, another disorder of citrus seedlings, often causes large losses. The complete or partial failure of the leaves to manufacture chlorophyll eventually causes seedlings to die.

The factor responsible for albinism was a matter of conjecture for many years. Perlberger and Reichert (1938) found that immersion of seeds for 20 minutes in any of several disinfectant solutions largely obviated the problem, but soil disinfestation did not. Solutions of copper sulfate pentahydrate (1 in 5,000 to 1 in 1,000) gave good control. Ryan (1958) showed that dusting seeds with ferric dimethyldithiocarbamate (76 per cent active), tetramethylthiuram disulfide (50 per cent), or 2,3-dichloro-1,4,naphthoquinone (50 per cent), or dipping them in 1 per cent solution of 8-hydroxyquinoline sulfate for 1 minute prevented albinism in Cleopatra mandarin seedlings. Tager and Cameron (1957) found that removing the seed coat prevented the malady. Koehler and Woodworth (1938) demonstrated that the fungi *Aspergillus flavus* Link and *A. tamarii* Kita can cause the malady in corn. The findings induced Durbin (1959) to try *A. flavus* on citrus seed. He showed that this fungus, which grows mainly on the seed coat, can definitely be a factor in causing albinism, either directly or indirectly.

DISEASES AND INJURIES IN THE NURSERY AND YOUNG ORCHARD

Since many diseases that affect small trees of the nursery and young orchards also attack older trees, detailed discussion is given under diseases and injuries of the latter. Maladies common to young and old trees include scab, canker, injury by dodder, gummosis, and root rots caused by *Phytophthora* spp., *Armillaria mellea* Vahl. ex Fr., *Botrytis cinerea* Pers. ex Fr., *Sclerotinia sclerotiorum* (Lib.) d'By., *Thielaviopsis basicola* (Berk. & Br.) Ferr., and by overwatering.

Some of the suggestions for combating seedbed troubles apply to those encountered in the nursery and young orchard. The soil should be virgin to citrus or disinfested of citrus pathogens such as *Armillaria mellea* (Vahl.) Quel., and so chosen to avoid contamination from runoff. If feasible, irrigation water should be free or freed of *Phytophthora* spp. which cause gummosis and destroy feeder roots. Because of excessive cost it may be impractical to disinfest the entire area of an infested orchard site for the proposed planting. However, it will usually be found economically beneficial to treat individual tree sites (Klotz *et al.*, 1960*b*). These are surrounded by 8-foot circular or 7-foot square earth-ridged basins into which Vapam is introduced. A pint of Vapam for each basin is placed in a pail at the center of the site and water added to the pail until the overflow is 4 to 6 inches deep in the basin. This method ensures disinfestation from the surface to a depth of 3 or 4 feet (fig. 1–3). Planting should be delayed one month to allow toxic chemicals to dissipate. See also table 1-1 (p. 6) for other materials effective in disinfesting soils.

Table 1-1.
CONTROL OF FUNGUS AND BACTERIAL DISEASES OF CITRUS IN CALIFORNIA

Disease or Disorder	Formulation to Use	Time and Method of Application	Coverage per Tree (Gal.)	Crops
Bacterial blast (northern California)	Bordeaux 10-10-100	Spray Oct.-Nov., before 1st rain.	Complete: 10-25	Oranges, mandarins,* grapefruit
Phytophthora brown rot	Bordeaux 3-4½-100 where no history of copper injury; zinc sulfate-copper sulfate-hydrated lime 3-2-6-100 or Captan 50W 2-100 where danger of copper injury.† Single package neutral copper and copper-zinc spray dried materials to give equivalent metal content of above home-made sprays may also be used if 4 oz of casein spreader-sticker are added per 100 gal water. More concentrated formulations of some materials may be applied at low volumes.‡	Spray Nov.-Dec., just before or just after 1st rain. In severe brown rot season, apply second application Jan.-Feb. In average season, one application is sufficient.	Six gal. skirt of tree- 3-4 ft. high; also 2-4 gal. on trunk and ground under tree. Low volumes (0.35 to 1.0 gal/tree) of concentrated formulations of some fungicides may be used.‡ Complete: 10-25, only if *P. hibernalis* present.	Lemons, oranges, grapefruit

Phytophthora gummosis	Neutral spray dried, one package copper spray materials stirred into water to make consistency of house paint.	Apply as paint or spray on trunk and crown right after excision of diseased bark.	Treat excised area.	All susceptible *citrus* spp., varieties, and hybrids
Septoria fruit and leaf spot, particularly central Calif., and brown rot, and zinc and copper deficiencies.	Zinc sulfate-copper sulfate-hydrated lime 3-2-6-100[10]	Spray Oct., Nov., or Dec., before or just after 1st rain.	Complete: 10-25	Grapefruit, oranges, lemons
Leafhopper injury to fruit in central California; Septoria, brown rot, and zinc and copper deficiencies.	Zinc sulfate-copper sulfate-hydrated lime 3-2-20-100 and ½ lb. casein spreader. Use only 15 lb. hydrated lime on navels.	Spray navels and early maturing mandarins by Oct. 15; Valencias in Nov.	Complete: 10-25	Oranges, mandarins

*Bordeaux 10-10-100 contains 10 pounds of copper sulfate ($CuSO_4 \cdot 5H_2O$) with 25% metallic copper and 10 pounds of hydrated lime. $Ca(OH)_2$ in 100 gallons of water. Because of the undesirable residue left on mandarin fruit by this formulation, it should be applied after picking. If protection of mandarin fruit from brown rot is necessary, a low residue spray such as ammoniacal copper carbonate or Burgundy mixture may be applied. After picking, the trees should be protected from blast by an application of 10-10-100 bordeaux.

†Zinc sulfate-copper sulfate-hydrated lime 3-2-6-100 contains 3 pounds of zinc sulfate ($ZnSO_4 \cdot 1H_20$) with 36% metallic zinc, 2 pounds of blue-stone, 6 pounds of hydrated lime in 100 gallons of water. Captan residue on fruit must not exceed 100 ppm of the whole fruit. Do not feed treated raw fruits to dairy animals or to those being finished for slaughter.

‡See Klotz, L. J. *et al.* 1971. New orchard methods for brown rot control. *Citrograph* 56(7):220–22.

Source: Anon. 1976-1978. Treatment Guide for California Citrus Crops. Leaflet 2903. University of California Division of Agricultural Sciences, Berkeley, Calif. 94720.

Table 1-2
FUMIGATION OF PHYTOPTHORA-INFESTED SOIL TO BE PLANTED TO SUSCEPTIBLE CITRUS*

Chemicals	Gallons per acre		Method of Application	Months Before Planting‡	For 8-ft Diameter Tree Site (Fl. Oz.)
	Sandy Loam	Heavier Soils			
D-D, Vidden D	150	260	Inject 12″-14″; 18″ apart.	6-12	42
Telone	120	210	Inject 12″-14″; 18″ apart	6-12	34
Vapam	100	100	In water 4″-8″ deep.	1½	16
Vorlex	70	140	Inject 12″-14″; 18″ apart.	4-8	22
Methyl bromide† (tarped)	200 lb	400 lb	Inject 7″-8″; 12″-18″ apart; tarp immediately§	1	8 (avoir oz)
Chloropicrin†	400 lb	800 lb	Inject 7″-8″; 18″ apart tarp immediately§	3	16 (avoir oz)

NOTE:
D-D and Vidden D contain chlorinated C_3 hydrocarbons, including 1,3-dichloropropene and 1,2-dichloropropane.

Telone contains chlorinated C_3 hydrocarbons, including 1,3-dichloropropene.

Vapam contains 4 lb. per gallon of sodium n-methyl dithiocarbamate.

Vorlex contains 80 per cent chlorinated C_3 hydrocarbons, including 1,3-dichloropropene and 20 per cent methyl isothiocyanate.

*For additional information on Phytophthora diseases see University of California, Division of Agricultural Sciences leaflet 2593, *Gum diseases of citrus in California*.

†These chemicals also will control citrus nematode (see *II Nematodes*, page 70).

‡Periods suggested are for average soil conditions; heavy soils, especially when cold and wet, may require more time before trees can be safely grown. Trees should not be planted before the soil is free of the odor of the chemical used.

§Minimum thickness of polyethylene tarp should be 0.0004 inch (4.0 mils) to retain effective concentration of fumigant.

Source: Same as Table 1-1.

In balling and planting nursery trees, care should be taken to avoid infection. Tools should be clean and disinfested with a 5.0 per cent Formalin solution or 1.0 per cent of potassium permanganate. Making smooth cuts of the roots in balling, avoiding injuries to the stem and crown bark, and lightly spraying the exterior of the ball with 2-2-100 Bordeaux mixture will aid in minimizing infections. Since root bark is more resistant than stem bark to gummosis (Klotz and Calavan, 1969), the tree should be planted so that when it has settled, its main lateral roots are just below the soil surface. This can be accomplished by planting in soil ridges about 6 inches above the general soil surface, and removing the ridge as the tree settles. Shortly after planting, paint or spray the bases of susceptible rootstocks from ground level up 10 to 12 inches with a water suspension of one-package, reacted, spray-dried, neutral Bordeaux or other neutral noninjurious copper spray materials of about the consistency of house paint. Bare root trees may be cleaned of infection caused by the common brown-rot gummosis fungus, *P. citrophthora*, before planting by immersion in hot water since citrus nursery trees will tolerate higher temperatures than the fungus. The water temperature must be accurately controlled, however, to avoid injuring the nursery tree. Immersion of the rootstock and the entire root system in agitated water at one of the following temperature-time periods will stop the disease:

Water Temperature		Immersion Time
(°F)	(°C)	(Min.)
110	43.2	10
111	43.8	8
112	44.3	6

Irrigation of young trees in the nursery and orchard should be done so that water penetrates to

Fig. 1–3. Lisbon lemons on Cleopatra mandarin rootstock. Left, tree from 7 x 7 foot site treated with a pint of Vapam in 6 inches of water one month prior to planting. Right, tree from untreated site six months after planting.

the roots in the nursery row and to the balls of the transplanted trees. To minimize Phytophthora gummosis infections, water should not be allowed to remain in contact with the stem or to waterlog soil for long periods. In an irrigation experiment (Klotz, Richards, and DeWolfe, 1967) with 72 Lisbon lemon and 96 Washington navel orange trees on sweet orange rootstocks, half the number of each variety were irrigated with one furrow down the line of trees with water contacting the trunks, and the other half were irrigated with two furrows so that water did not stand in contact with tree stems. The trees under the one-furrow regime had much more gummosis and root rot than those watered with two furrows. During the first year, the rate of increase of trunk diameter of the navels was the same under both watering systems, but lemon trunks under the two-furrow system grew twice as rapidly as those irrigated with one furrow.

When a young tree requires water between regular irrigations, make a 3-foot earthen basin around it and from a tank wagon fill the basin with a weak Bordeaux suspension containing a pound of copper sulfate ($CuSO_4 \cdot 5H_2O$) and a pound of hydrated lime per 100 gallons or with an equivalent amount of a one-package Bordeaux or other neutralized copper fungicide, if the tank is equipped with agitators. If the tank has no agitators, use an ounce of copper sulfate and no lime in 400 gallons of water. Do not fertilize with large amounts of nitrogenous fertilizers or pile animal manures against the trunks. Examine the crowns of young trees every four months during the two years following planting, every six months from the second to fifth years, and once a year thereafter.

Recontamination from surrounding untreated soil by runoff water from rains or irrigation can be minimized during the first year by dusting the surface of sites with single-package, spray-dried (reacted) Bordeaux (Klotz *et al.*, 1960*b*) or other neutralized copper spray material as soon as the water with the disinfestant has penetrated the soil; keep the surface of sites slightly blue by repeated dustings during this period. The young tree, unhampered by root parasites, makes a rapid growth and becomes well established. Thereafter, even with the sites recontaminated, the trees, given good cultural care, should be able to grow roots fast enough to establish a successful orchard.

DISEASES AND INJURIES OF THE ROOT SYSTEM, TRUNK, AND SCAFFOLD BRANCHES

Any general damage to roots and trunk of the citrus tree has an adverse effect on the entire tree and is more apt to be fatal than damage to branches and foliage. A striking example is the mal secco disease of lemon trees in Sicily caused by the fungus *Deuterophoma tracheiphila* Petri (Klotz, 1956). Growers there combat the disease in the tops rather effectively by removing affected twigs and limbs; but when the root system becomes infected, disease spreads rapidly upward and kills the tree. Girdling of trunk or crown by such agencies as *Phytophthora* spp. or destruction of bark sieve tubes near the bud union by tristeza, a virus disease, results in starvation of roots and death of the tree.

Diseases Caused by Phytophthora spp.

Phytophthora spp., including *P. citrophthora*, *P. nicotianae* var. *parasitica*, *P. syringae* Kleb., and *P. hibernalis* Carne, cause the most important fungus diseases of citrus (fig. 1–4). All have been found damaging citrus in California (Klotz, Stolzy, and DeWolfe, 1963). While these fungi attack all organs of the tree, their occurrence on roots, crown, and trunk causes a rapidly fatal infection. This form of the disease was known in Spain as early as the tenth century A.D. (Sirag-el-Din, 1931, 1934). Fawcett (1936) mentioned other early writers who described the disease more fully, citing Ferrari in 1646, Sterbeeck in 1682, Feuille in 1714, Clarici in 1726, and Corrado in 1787. The malady appeared in the Azores Islands in 1832 and in France in 1851. In Italy, it appeared at Messina, 1863; Reggio Calabria, 1864; and Palermo, 1865 (Fawcett, 1936). All citrus trees in Sicily are said to have been destroyed by the disease between 1863 and 1870. By 1878, all Mediterranean countries growing citrus had reported the disease. It was noted in South Africa in 1891. Australia recorded its appearance during the period from 1860 to 1885 (Alderton, 1884; McAlpine, 1899). In the western hemisphere, Phytophthora disease was first noted in California in 1875; Florida, 1876; Cuba, 1906; Paraguay, 1911; Brazil, 1917; Puerto Rico, 1918; Mexico, 1920; and Trinidad, 1935 (Fawcett, 1936). Most present-day citrus nurserymen and growers are acquainted with the great destructiveness of the disease.

Symptoms.—Symptoms of *Phytophthora* gummosis above ground are: (1) dead areas of bark that remain firm; (2) exudation of small or large amounts of gum, depending on citrus variety and weather; (3) infiltration with gum and brown staining of a thin layer of wood; (4) a yellow gummous zone at the cambium beyond the dead invaded area; and (5) a subsequent drying and vertical cracking of bark.

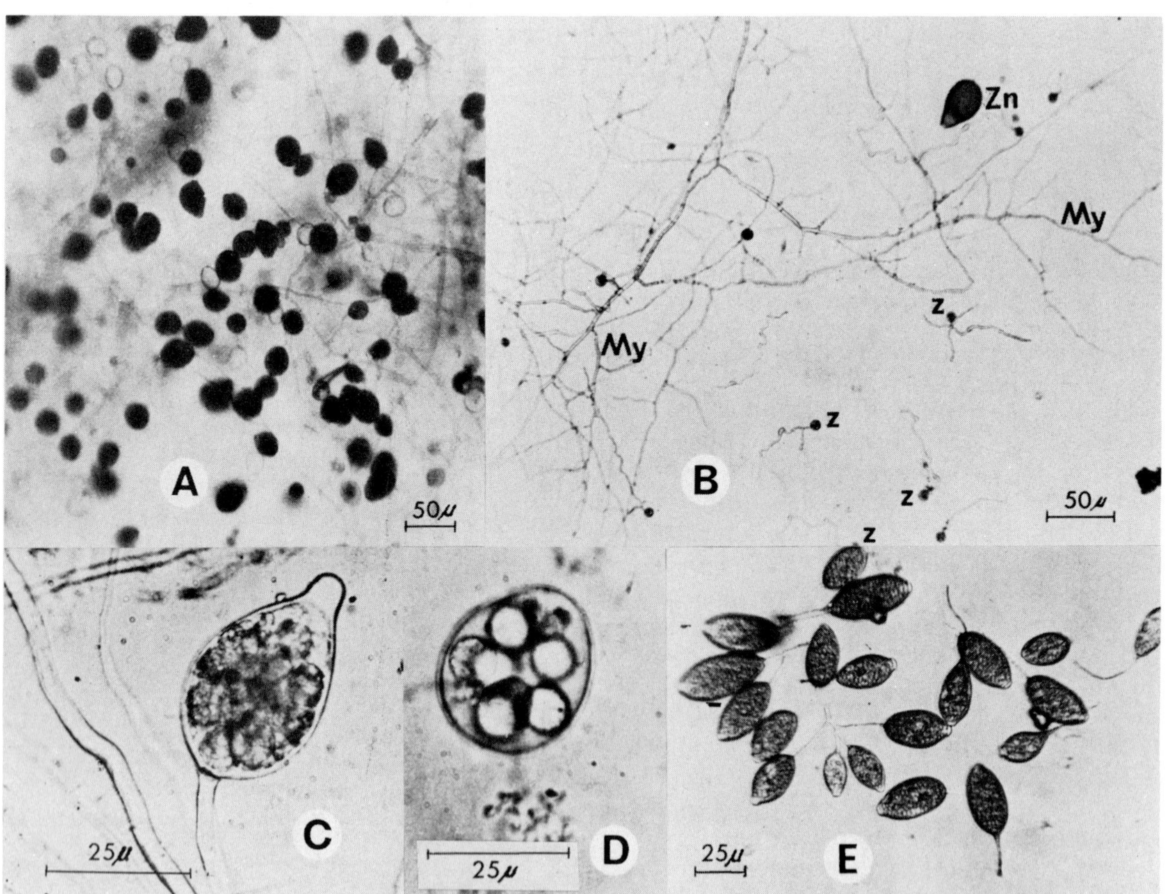

Fig. 1–4. Zoosporangia of *Phytophthora citrophthora* (A-D) and *P. hibernalis* (E). *A*, zoosporangia some of which have discharged zoospores (mount was teeming with zoospores which do not show in photo because of their motility). *B*, a discharged zoosporangium (Zn) and germinating zoospores (Z) from it; My, mycelium. *C*, zoosporangium about ready to discharge. *D*, motile zoospores in zoosporangium. *E*, deciduous zoosporangia of *P. hibernalis*.

Symptoms known as foot rot occur below ground under moist conditions. They include: (1) dead areas that remain firm; (2) less noticeable gum, since it is usually absorbed by water in the soil; (3) the entrance of secondary organisms that kill and discolor wood to a greater depth than the above ground form of the disease; and (4) usually a greater lateral extension of the lesions producing the foot rot form of the disease. This type of infection by *Phytophthora* spp. also supplies an entrance for the so-called dry root rot, a disease in which the wood is invaded by one or more of several fungi, yeasts, and bacteria.

Injury and destruction of small fibrous feeder roots by *Phytophthora* spp. are revealed by a fewer number of rootlets as compared with uninfected root systems and by sloughing bark on some that have not been completely rotted. The decaying bark is easily slid off the stele by a slight pinching pressure. Attraction of zoöspores of the fungus by small roots has been noted for a number of years (fig. 1–5). Qualitative evidence of chemotaxy of motile zoöspores and chemotropism of germ tubes were recorded with a movie camera (see fig. 1-5) in March, 1960 (Klotz and DeWolfe, unpublished). Zentmyer (1961) obtained quantitative data on the phenomena. Broadbent (1969) demonstrated that zoöspores of *P. citrophthora* are chemotactically attracted to the region of root elongation and to wounds of both susceptible and resistant roots. Materials responsible for chemotaxis are denatured by boiling.

Tsao and his associates extensively studied the mycology, ecology, population, and parasitism of *Phytophthora parasitica* and *P. citrophthora* on citrus plantings (Tsao, 1959, 1960, and 1969; Tsao and Garber, 1960; and Holdaway and Tsao, 1971, 1972).

Large roots frequently show so-called frog-eye lesions from which *Phytophthora* spp. are isolatable (fig. 1–6).

To the grower, the most startling and obvious symptom is gummosis of the bark and cambium of the crown and trunk, since this infection can girdle and kill trees. Gummosis is characterized by a profuse exudation of dark, amber-colored gum on the bark surface. *P. citrophthora* and *P. parasitica* are chiefly responsible for gummosis and for killing fibrous feeder roots when temperature and moisture conditions are favorable (Klotz, DeWolfe, and Miller, 1969).

P. citrophthora grows fastest when the temperature is near 77° F, and is operative mainly

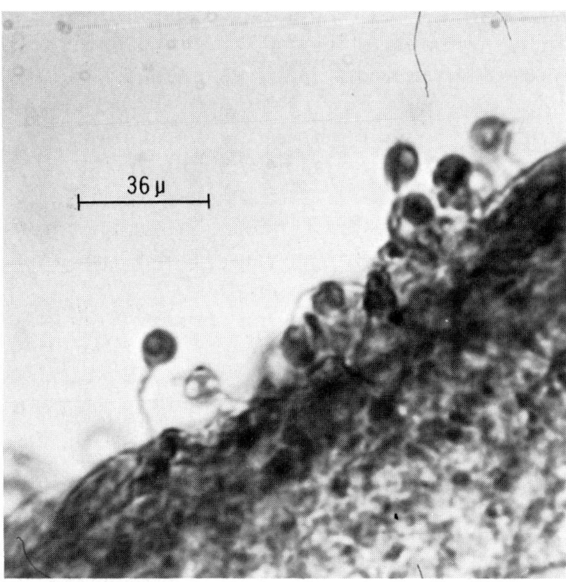

Fig. 1–5. Zoospores of *Phytophthora parasitica* infecting primary root of lemon seedling. (Photo by T. A. DeWolfe.)

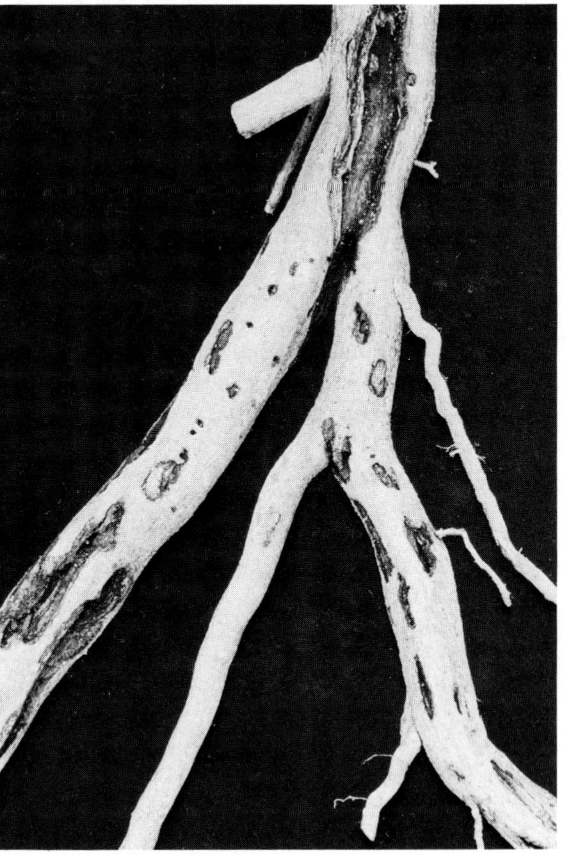

Fig. 1–6. "Frog-eye" lesions caused by *Photophthora parasitica*.

during winter and early spring. *P. parasitica* has a higher optimum of near 90° F. It is frequently recoverable from gummosis lesions and from diseased roots and infested soil during late spring and summer. The high temperature of California summers will inactivate and even kill the fungi in exposed lesions.

Control.—Considerable protection from gummosis can be provided by removing soil from the base of the trunk down to the first main lateral roots. The trunk and trunk crown should be painted with a safe Carbolineum† (containing not more than 0.7 per cent phenols) or with a suspension of one-package, spray-dried, neutral Bordeaux powder in water. This should be at about the consistency of house paint. Soil should be prevented from accumulating around the base of the tree and covering the bud union. Such accumulation is particularly troublesome on terraces or slopes and at the end of irrigation runs. The soil should be removed from an area 1 foot to 18 inches out from the trunk to barely expose the tops of main lateral roots. The larger the basin, the less frequently it is necessary to repeat the operation. An outlet ditch should be dug to provide drainage from this basin surrounding the base of the tree.

Each tree should be inspected once or twice a year. Tree wraps on young trees should be lifted or removed for the inspection. If infected, the bark lesion should be excised and the exposed bark edge and wood painted with Carbolineum, Bordeaux mixture, or a one per cent solution of potassium permanganate before replacing the wraps (fig. 1–7). Where the disease is detected on the trunk or crown, soil should be removed to determine the extent of bark infection. The margin of the lesion can be determined by lightly scraping the bark surface. Diseased bark has a dusky appearance. The gummosis lesion is then excised, and the dark-brown, diseased bark is removed to a line that includes a ¼ inch width of healthy bark surrounding the lesion (see fig. 1-8). It is not necessary to remove any strained wood or the dried, hard, gummy bark in the central part of old lesions (fig. 1–9).

In the dry climate of interior plantings, no further treatment is required to stop this form of disease, but in moister, coastal orchards the exposed cambium surface of the wood should be

Fig. 1–7. Tools and chemicals used in treatment of Phytophthora gummosis.

treated with a disinfectant such as one per cent potassium permanganate† solution or a safe Carbolineum.† After the surface of the wood has dried, it and the exposed edges of the healthy bark may be covered with nontoxic pruning paint. Young trees should be replaced if the circumference of the trunk or crown bark is half or more involved by disease.

Other manifestations of damage caused by *P. citrophthora* and *P. parasitica* are poor growth and production which are often attributable to destruction of small, fibrous feeder roots by either these fungi or nematodes, or by suffocation from overwatering. Infested planting sites and areas to be used for nurseries can be disinfested with one of the recommended chemicals (see table 1–1, p. 6).

The following chemicals are effective in killing fungi or nematodes: D-D or Vidden D at a rate of 150 gallons per acre in light soil or up to 260 gallons per acre on heavy soils; Telone at a rate of 120 to 210 gallons per acre; Trizone (tarped) at 20 to 40 gallons per acre; Vapam at 100 gallons per acre on both soil types; Vorlex at 70 to 140 gallons per acre; methyl bromide (tarped) at 200 to 400 pounds per acre; and chloropicrin at 400 to 800 pounds per acre. Where expense precludes disinfestation of an entire orchard area, tree sites and smaller areas to be occupied by seedlings and nursery trees should be treated. While small tree site areas of about 50 square feet eventually become reinfested, the reinfection of the root system by the parasites can thus be sufficiently delayed to enable young trees to become well established.

†This chemical or chemical formulation is not currently registered with or recommended for usage by the United States Environmental Protection Agency for this particular pest of citrus. Citrus producers in other countries are advised to check their country's regulations for using such treatment methods.

Fig. 1–8. Phytophthora gummosis and treatment. Left, infected grapefruit trunk. Center, infected lemon trunk. Right, infected lemon trunk after treatment.

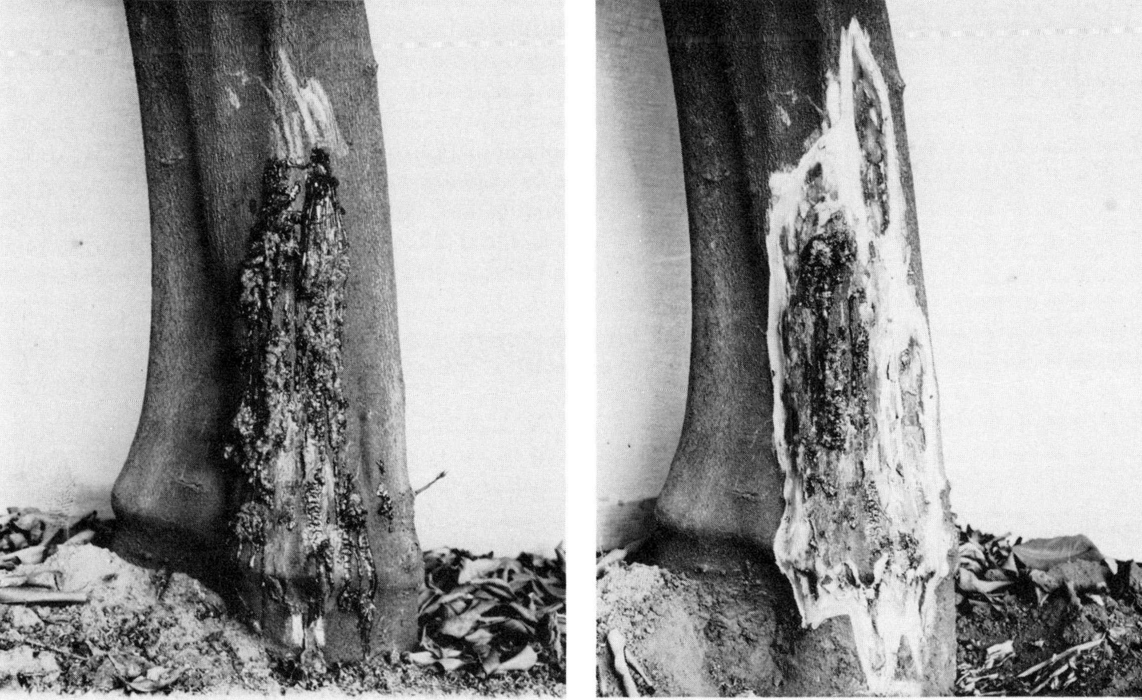

Fig. 1–9. Old orange tree with Phytophthora gummosis before treatment (left) and after treatment (right). Note that the treatment does not require removing the hard, dried diseased bark in the center of the lesion.

For disinfestation of a basined, circular site, eight feet in diameter, 16 fluid ounces of Vapam or 8 avoirdupois ounces of methyl bromide (tarped) are used. The waiting period between treatments and planting should be six to twelve months for D-D, Vidden D, and Vorlex; for chloropicrin, three months; and for Vapam and methyl bromide, one and one-half months (see table 1–1, p. 6).

Following such preparation, trees under a good cultural regime can produce roots sufficiently fast to keep well ahead of the destruction by parasites. Good culture includes the proper use of tensiometers to avoid overwatering, which favors destruction of feeder roots by fungi and by suffocation (Loest, 1950). The use of rootstocks resistant to *Phytophthora* spp., such as some varieties of trifoliate orange and citrange, some mandarins, citremon, Ichang lemon, and Nanshôdaidai should be an important consideration (see table 1–3 and fig. 1-10).

Table 1-3
APPROXIMATE INTEGRATED RESPONSE OF CITRUS SPP. TO NATURAL AND ARTIFICIAL INOCULATION WITH *PHYTOPHTHORA* SPP.

Level of Susceptibility	Varieties
Highly susceptible	Lemons *(Citrus limon)* Some citranges *(Poncirus trifoliata* X *C. sinensis)*, except Troyer and Carrizo
Susceptible—order of susceptibility, highest to lowest	Sweet orange *(C. sinensis)* Limes *(C. aurantifolia)* Sampson tangelo *(C. reticulata* X *C. paradisi)* Rough lemon *(C. jambhiri)* Grapefruit *(C. paradisi)* Mandarins *(C. reticulata)* Troyer and Carrizo citranges Citremon *(P. trifoliata* X *C. limon)* Nanshôdaidai *(C. taiwanica)* Siamelo *(C. reticulata* X *C. sinensis* X *C. paradisi)* Most selections of trifoliate orange *(P. trifoliata)*, including USDA and Pomeroy
Resistant	Ichang lemon 1219 *(C. ichangensis* X *C. grandis)* Alemow *(C. macrophylla)* Sour orange *(C. aurantium)* Texas, Barnes, English, Rubidoux, and Davis B. trifoliates Kumquat *(Fortunella spp.)* Severinia *(S. buxifolia)*

Growth, production, and longevity of trees also depend primarily on the choice of rootstocks horticulturally compatible with the tops as well as on their resistance to disease (Klotz *et al.*, 1967; Klotz, DeWolfe, and Baines, 1969; Whiteside, 1971, 1974*b*).

Since fruit and foliage can be attacked by all four species of *Phytophthora*, trees should be protected from brown rot by fungicidal sprays. *P. syringae* with an optimum growth requirement near 68° F and *P. hibernalis*, growth optimum near 62° F, have been found attacking fruit and foliage during cool weather. In orchards where *P. hibernalis* is present, complete coverage of the entire tree with spray is necessary because spore cases of this species are easily detached and distributed throughout the tree by wind-driven rains. For protection against brown rot infection by the other three species, a thorough skirt spray to a height of 4 feet is sufficient (see "Brown Rot and Phytophthora Blight," pp. 36 to 39 and table 1–1, p. 6).

To sum up, control of Phytophthora gummosis and root rot of susceptible citrus rootstocks can be effected by (1) using uncontaminated or disinfected seed together with planting in disinfested seedbed, nursery, and orchard sites; (2) irrigating with disinfested water; (3) protecting planting sites during the first one or two years from contamination by orchard runoff water; (4) regularly inspecting crowns and trunks of trees for signs of infection and promptly surgically treating the infected bark areas; and (5) practicing the best cultural methods.

Fig. 1–10. Method of testing for resistance to Phytophthora gummosis.

Bark Rots Caused by Other Fungi

Other fungi which attack citrus bark primarily are *Thielaviopsis basicola* (Berk. & Br.) Ferr., *Sclerotinia sclerotiorum* (Lib.) Mass., *Botrytis cinerea* Pers., and *Ascochyta corticola* McAlp. Since 1948, De Wolfe (verbal communication) has isolated *T. basicola* from many citrus soils, but has not recovered it from some orchards. While Tsao (1962) found this fungus in 69 of 126 orchard soils, its importance there as a pathogen of citrus has been questioned.

Chapman and Brown (1942) showed that high phosphate levels promoted growth and parasitism by *Thielaviopsis basicola*, reducing the growth rate of citrus pot cultures. Martin *et al.* (1956) found that the addition of the fungus, *T. basicola*, to pot cultures markedly reduced growth rate. Tsao and Van Gundy (1960*a*, 1960*b*, 1962) found that the organism can produce discrete lesions on the bark of citrus rootlets. In a temperature range of 15-20° C, it caused chlorosis of sweet orange seedlings and reduced their growth rate 89 to 95 per cent. This indicated it may cause more damage in orchards from November to April than during other periods.

In pot cultures, the fungus reduced seedling growth rate at all moisture levels tested (Tsao, 1963*b*).

Citrus species and relatives varied in their susceptibility to *T. basicola* in this descending order: Cleopatra mandarin (very susceptible), West Indian lime and Carrizo citrange, Troyer citrange, Homosassa sweet orange, siamelo, and New Mexican trifoliate orange (least susceptible of those tested) (Tsao, 1963*a*).

Chlamydospores, not the endoconidia or mycelium, are important for survival of the fungus in soil (Tsao and Bricker, 1966).

The presence of soil organic matter may not only stimulate germination of the propagules of *T. basicola* but also growth of lytic microorganisms. The latter reduce inoculum density of the fungus by lysing its germ tubes, thus reducing viability of its spores (Hawthorne and Tsao, 1970).

Klotz, Stolzy, and DeWolfe (1962, 1963) found that *T. basicola* had a much higher oxygen requirement than *Phytophthora citrophthora* and *P. nicotianae* var. *parasitica*, species parasitic probably at all soil levels reached by roots. *Phytophthora* spp. were isolatable from frogeye lesions on deeply lying large roots (see fig. 1-6). *T. basicola* is generally present only in the upper, more aerated soil levels. These findings may partially explain the limited effect of this fungus as a root pathogen in citrus orchards. While investigations with pot cultures suggest that the fungus could cause damage to citrus in the orchard, doubt of its importance there has not been dispelled by the data now available.

Waterlogged and poorly drained soils and injuries by rodents, insects, and cultivation tools open the way for attack of roots by *S. sclerotiorum*. Roots and branches of any size may be attacked, but the fungus enters wood much less readily than bark (fig. 1–11). Bark is softened and gum is usually produced. Healing callus begins to form as gum appears, and the lesion becomes self-limiting. As the affected part dries, bark is left in a characteristically shredded condition. Black sclerotia measuring up to ½ inch (1.2 cm) in length form in and on the bark and on the wood. Injury by sunburn or cold favors infection of twigs by *S. sclerotiorum* and *B. cinerea*. Sclerotia produced by the latter fungus are much smaller than those of the former.

Bark Blotch

McAlpine (1899) reported a disease in Australia which he named bark blotch; later, Cunningham (1921) found it in New Zealand.

Areas of bark of various sizes are killed to the wood, producing dark-brown gummy lesions with slightly raised margins. Small, black fruiting bodies (pycnidia) of the fungus *Ascochyta corticola* later appear. The causal relationship of this fungus to the disease was demonstrated by Brien (1931*a*, 1931*b*).

For control, Cunningham (1921) suggests removing diseased bark and applying Bordeaux paste; after the paste dries, paint with a watertight material such as asphalt.

Rio Grande Gummosis

Rio Grande gummosis is the common name for a disease that Godfrey (1946) has called infectious wood necrosis and gummosis. It is one of the most serious citrus tree diseases in Texas, and is also found in Florida. Godfrey (1946) and Childs (1953) have attributed the disease to an actinomycete, while Olson (1952) attributed it to a *Diplodia* sp. In California, the disease is called both Rio Grande gummosis and ferment gum, and is widespread on grapefruit trees of all ages, especially in the Coachella and Imperial Valleys. Calavan and Christiansen (1958) and Calavan (1961) described the symptoms of the disease and injuries that favor its development, and attributed the cause to an unidentified basidiomycetous fungus. Calavan *et al.* (1962-63) found two fungi commonly associated

Fig. 1–11. Sclerotinia or cottony rot and twig blight. Left, the fungus *Sclerotinia sclerotiorum* showing the apothecium growing out of the sclerotium. Center, damage to twigs. Right, damage to fruit.

with the trouble. One, the unidentified fungus isolated by Calavan and Christiansen (1958), enters through pruning wounds and other injuries and invades the pith and heart wood; the other, *Hendersonula toruloidea* Nattrass, invades wounds and heat- and frost-injured areas, and grows throughout the wood from the surface inward (Calavan and Wallace, 1954).

Symptoms.—The most evident effect of the disease is the profuse exudation of clear, sometimes frothy, amber-brown gum from gum pockets under the bark over the affected wood (fig. 1–12).

The wood attacked by the unidentified fungus ranges in color from a vinaceous buff through buff brown to olive brown, while that invaded by *H. toruloidea* is light grayish-olive to light brownish-olive (Ridgway, 1912). Under the bark, *H. toruloidea* produces a powdery, brownish-black deposit of spores. Frequently at the margin of the decayed wood is an orange- to pink-colored line from 1- to 3-mm (1/25 to ⅛ inch) wide. Wood of affected branches may eventually become completely invaded and killed resulting in branch wilt and dieback (fig. 1–13).

Control.—Prevention, rather than treatment of trees after they have become infected, should be the primary objective. Orchard heating for protection against frost injury, and whitewashing of exposed bark immediately after pruning with a zinc-copper-lime spray to protect it from sunburn, should markedly lower the incidence of infection. Pruning cuts should be disinfected and when dry, covered with asphalt. Between cuts, tools should be disinfested with a solution of 4 per cent Formalin or 1 per cent potassium permanganate† in water. Affected limbs should be cut off well below the advancing margin of decay. According to Godfrey (1946), healthy exposed wood resulting from pruning should be treated with a penetrating disinfectant such as Carbolineum† having 2 per cent phenols. The final coating on the exposed wood should be a low-melting-point asphalt mixed with an equal quantity of Carbolineum. Once infection invades the trunk, it is practically impossible to eliminate by surgery. Trees beyond hope of successful treatment should be kept only as long as they produce profitable crops.

†This chemical or chemical formulation is not currently registered with or recommended for usage by the United States Environmental Protection Agency for this particular pest of citrus. Citrus producers in other countries are advised to check their country's regulations for using such treatment methods.

Fig. 1–12. Rio Grande gummosis or ferment gum disease. Left, disease induced by natural infection. Right, disease induced by manual inoculation. (Photos by T. A. DeWolfe.)

Fig. 1–13. Hendersonula branch wilt. Left, infection of tree trunk. Center, closer view of trunk showing black, powdery spores. Right, gum exudation from infection on branch.

Branch Wilt

Fawcett (1936) observed a fungus resembling *Torula dimidiata* Penzig damaging frost-injured oranges and grapefruit trees in Tulare County, California. Fawcett also reported that A. J. Olson found a similar organism, *Hendersonula toruloidea* Nattrass, attacking citrus trees following the 1931 freeze in northern California. Penzig (1887) and Nattrass (1933) described these fungi they found on citrus and deciduous trees in Mediterranean countries. Olson showed that the fungus caused gumming and wood rot of orange and lemon trees. Wilson (1952) demonstrated that this fungus also causes branch wilt of Persian walnut and, because it also forms pycnidia, should be placed in the genus *Hendersonula*. Calavan and Wallace (1954) confirmed the findings of Fawcett and Olson and suggested that the organism sometimes plays a role in Rio Grande gummosis. Symptoms and suggested control measures for branch wilt are described under "Rio Grande Gummosis."

Bark Rot

Bark rot of mandarin, kabuyao, and calamondin has been seen only in the Orient (Lee, 1923). A white foamy exudate from cracks in the bark is the characteristic symptom. In this froth, one finds yeast cells and fungal hyphae of several species, all believed to be secondary agents. The cracks apparently form as a result of a dissolution of the soft cells of the bark. Insects are attracted by the foam and enter the cracks. Bark tissues are killed in all directions and limbs or trunk may be girdled. Since outbreaks of the trouble follow periods of dry weather, it is believed that drought is the inciting cause. According to Toxopeus, the trouble can be prevented by good irrigation practices (Fawcett, 1936).

Diplodia Gummosis

The fungus *Diplodia natalensis* Pole-Evans [*Physalospora rhodina* (B. & C.) Cooke] can invade both the bark and wood of citrus and cause formation of gum and death of the parts (Fawcett and Burger, 1911). The disease has been reported in all citrus-growing areas of both North and South America, all Mediterranean citrus countries, South Africa (Loest, 1950), Japan, China, India, Australia, Indonesia, and the Philippines. While important, it is decidedly less so than gummosis caused by *Phytophthora* spp., since the latter is fatal if affected trees are not treated.

Symptoms.—The involvement of bark by *D. natalensis* is usually self-limiting and confined to small patches of mature or weakened tissues, but wood may be much more extensively invaded. The decayed parts have a dusky color. Trees injured by cold and heat are particularly susceptible, with large areas of bark and even larger branches being killed.

Control.—Control consists in drastically cutting back affected parts well below the apparent involvement and disinfecting and covering the exposed healthy parts as in the treatment for Rio Grande gummosis (pp. 15–16).

Dothiorella Gummosis

The fungus *Dothiorella gregaria* Sacc. [*Botryosphaeria ribis* (Tode ex Fr.) Gross. & Dug.] caused a gummosis disease resembling that caused by *Diplodia natalensis* in occurrence and external symptoms. The disease, also called pocket gum, is less severe and more self-limiting than that caused by *D. natalensis*. The invaded inner bark and wood surface are colored chocolate brown. As in *Phytophthora* gummosis, a tan-colored zone of gummous influence extends beyond the margin of invasion. The same control measures used in Diplodia gummosis should be employed.

Phomopsis Gummosis

Phomopsis gummosis caused by *Phomopsis citri* Faw. [*Diaporthe citri* (Faw.) Wolf] has been seen in American and Japanese plantings. As in some of the previously described diseases, injury by cold favors infection. The same control measures used for Rio Grande, Diplodia, and Dothiorella gummoses apply.

The fungus also causes melanose of fruit, foliage, and twigs described on page 34. Together with *Diplodia natalensis*, *Dothiorella gregaria*, and *Alternaria citri*, it causes stem-end rots of citrus fruits. Orchard practices for lessening losses from stem-end rots are thorough elimination of dead wood by pruning and spraying with copper fungicides as for melanose (p. 34). In the packinghouse, immersion in fungicidal solutions, gassing with nitrogen trichloride (Littauer, 1947), and keeping temperatures below 50° F further help reduce loss.

Armillaria Root Rot

Although it is not of general or frequent occurrence in citrus orchards, Armillaria root rot,

Fig. 1–14. Armillaria root rot. Left, fungus fans and rhizomorphs. Right, mushroom bodies of *A. mellea* growing on Valencia roots.

caused by *Armillaria mellea* (Vahl.) Quel., is a very serious disease where it does occur. It is also called fungus or mushroom root rot, oak root fungus disease, and, in Australia, honey fungus. It has been found on citrus in the United States, Australia, Cyprus, Malta, Corsica, Tunisia, and Italy.

Symptoms.—The onset of the disease is insidious, since the fungus has already become well established on the roots before the aboveground parts of the tree show any evidence of trouble (fig. 1–14). The disease is evidenced either by slow decline, indicated by yellowing and dropping of leaves of the whole or part of the tree, or by the sudden wilt and collapse of the tree. The acute form indicates girdling of the crown or most of the larger roots with resulting starvation of the root system. The affected bark swells and has a spongy waterlogged feeling. White, fan-shaped mycelial mats are found only on the under bark surface and into the wood. The purple-to-black rhizomorphs ("cords" or "shoestrings") are found on the outer bark surface and in the surrounding soil. At the ground surface adjacent to the infected tree trunks or shallow-lying roots light brown mushrooms, the fruiting bodies of the fungus, appear in clumps. They have a ring or veil close under the cap and produce white spores. Trouble from this disease in new plantings in California frequently starts from infected roots of native chaparral and on land that has grown oaks, sycamores, and pepper trees (*Schinus molle* L.), all of which are susceptible hosts of Armillaria.

Control.—Prevention and control of Armillaria root rot require great effort and care. In clearing land of native trees or land known to be infested, remove, dry, and burn all the roots possible. Infected roots should be burned in place and, insofar as feasible, not dragged over noninfested areas by plowing and tillage. To eradicate the fungus in infested soil, fumigation with methyl bromide[1] (CH_3Br) has largely replaced the use of carbon disulfide[2] (Rackham *et al.*, 1968; Kolbezen *et al.*, 1974). Before application of the chemical and to permit its thorough diffusion, soil should first be dried to a depth of 8 feet. This is accomplished in California by growing deep-rooted plants such as

[1]Methyl bromide is a colorless, odorless, poisonous gas which should not be inhaled for long periods.

[2]For previous investigations with carbon disulfide, see Bliss (1944).

Sudan grass or safflower on the area. Sudan grass is planted in early spring and irrigated until well established. It receives no more water and is mowed in midsummer to retard its going into dormancy. The second crop of the grass is mowed in early fall, and the area is subsoiled to 24 inches and disked to provide a loose texture.

Methyl bromide may be applied by machine or by hand. On large areas suitable for tractor-drawn equipment, the gas is injected as deeply as possible (fig. 1–15). The chisels of this rig are 5 feet apart and the delivery tubes behind them deliver the gas at the 30-inch level. Smaller areas and dooryards are injected by hand, using an adapter to puncture 1-pound cans and a lead-in tube to place the chemical at the 18-inch depth. Another commercial method for tree site treatment that may gain usage is the injection of 2 pounds of methyl bromide at the 5-foot depth of freshly mixed and dried soil, thus eliminating the necessity of using a tarpaulin. However, best results are had by covering the treated area immediately with a tarpaulin of 1.0 to 2.0 mil thickness. These treatments in dry, open soils have been found effective in killing fungus down to 8-foot depths.

Fig. 1–15. Machine for applying and covering soil disinfestant. (Photos courtesy of Wesley Wilbur.)

The method has been tested in several soil types (Kolbezen *et al.*, 1974).

To isolate an infested area in an orchard, diseased trees are pulled and the root system of apparently healthy trees surrounding the area are carefully examined. Thorough detection of infections requires 3-foot deep inspection trenches along the side of the root system adjacent to the infested area. Trees showing roots infected by *A. mellea* are also pulled.

The grower may wish to retain old, infected trees that still produce profitable crops. Extension of the useful life of such trees and prevention of spread of the disease into noninfested areas can be effected by removing the soil around the trunk crown and crown roots. Exposure of roots to air stops progress of the fungus into the parts of the root system not yet invaded. When affected trees no longer pay for their care, they are removed and the area is fumigated, allowed to aerate for three months, and replanted.

The fungus *Clitocybe tabescens* (Scop. ex Fr.) Bres. causes a root rot resembling that due to *A. mellea*. Like the latter, it attacks ornamentals, shrubs, and fruit trees. It has been reported from several southern states including Florida, the Carolinas, Texas, Oklahoma, and Missouri. In Florida, it has been found on Rough lemon rootstocks but not on sour orange.

Although the onset and symptoms of the disease are similar to Armillaria root rot, the former can be distinguished from the latter by the absence in *C. tabescens* of rhizomorphs and of an annulus and veil on the mushroom fruiting body. Control measures are the same as those described for *A. mellea*.

Rosellinia Root Rot

Root rot caused by *Rosellinia* spp. has been particularly troublesome in tropical plantings of many kinds of plants including citrus (limes, sour orange, and sweet orange). However, since the species *R. necatrix* (Hart.) Berl. has been reported attacking citrus roots, mainly sour orange, in semitropical countries of the Mediterranean basin and South America, one should be aware of the possibility of a serious outbreak in important areas of citrus production. In plantings of the wet, humid tropics, development of the disease may be very rapid.

Symptoms.—As with the two previously described diseases, a gradual yellowing of leaves and defoliation indicate a more or less gradual infection of the tree's root system, while setting of a large crop of fruit and sudden wilting or shedding of leaves indicate girdling at the crown or stem. Roots are covered by dark brown-to-black mycelium of the fungus. Whitish, fan-shaped mycelial growth is found in the cambium region and dark brown-to-black spherical perithecia—the sexual fruiting structures—are generally in crowded groups on the bark surface.

Control.—Control in tropical countries (Nowell, 1917) consists of removing stumps of forest trees, which are common hosts of *Rosellinia* spp., from land to be planted to citrus. Since the fungi do not tolerate drought, the land should be allowed to dry out thoroughly and tree sites should be separated by trench drains. If it is not feasible to remove stumps of infected forest trees, they should be isolated with trenches. It seems reasonable to assume that the measures outlined for control of Armillaria root rot would be effective against root rot caused by *Rosellinia* spp.

Phymatotrichum Root Rot

A comprehensive monograph on Phymatotrichum root rot by Streets and Bloss (1973) covers many reports on this destructive disease of dicotyledonous plants. This malady, caused by *Phymatotrichum omnivorum* (Shear) Dugger, also called Texas root rot and ozonium root rot, occurs on citrus and other dicots in Texas, western Arizona, along the southern border of New Mexico and Oklahoma, the northern third of Baja California, and along the upper third of the western coastal area of Mexico. It is also present in isolated locations in southeastern California.

Symptoms.—Yellowing or bronzing and increased falling of leaves are the first top symptoms of the disease seen on citrus. In summer, following a rain or irrigation, whitish-yellow, cottony, flat spore mats, 3 to 9 inches in diameter, appear on the soil surface under susceptible hosts. The white-to-yellow-buff colored hyphae of the fungus grow on the host roots and in the soil. Under high power magnification, the hyphae are identifiable by their anastomoses and right-angled branches with a light constriction at their places of origin. Small chains of sclerotia resembling radish seed may with some difficulty be found near the host roots.

Control.—Inoculations by Bach (1929, 1931) in Texas indicated that sour orange was "fairly resistant"; trifoliate orange, Cleopatra mandarin, Rusk citrange, and citrangequat were "very susceptible." Taubenhaus and Ezekiel (1936), basing disease resistance-susceptibility ratings on the relative incidence and severity of the disease on its hosts, concluded that of the Rutaceae, round kumquat, oval kumquat, sour orange, and trifoliate orange are "resistant"; lemon, citron, and Satsuma orange are "moderately susceptible"; and lime, grapefruit, tangerine, orange are "highly susceptible." Streets states that 95 per cent of citrus in Arizona are on resistant sour orange rootstock and have had no commerical losses due to Phymatotrichum root rot. Even lemon on Rough lemon rootstock in deep sandy soils has experienced no real problem from this disease.[3]

Streets and Bloss (1973) state that crop rotation with monocots, even for four or more years, has not been satisfactorily effective, reducing the disease incidence in cotton only up to 60 per cent in many instances due to the longevity of the fungus propagules and their persistence at depths below the plow sole of the soil. However, since the parasite is inhibited by anaerobic conditions of 25 to 100 per cent carbon dioxide or 100 per cent nitrogen, green manure crops, such as alfalfa, cowpeas, guar, and seshania, have proven effective in reducing root rot incidence as much as 90 per cent after four years of incorporating them in infested soils. Competitive microorganisms such as *Trichoderma* spp., *Rhizoctonia solani*, *Actinomyces* spp., and bacteria flourish on the green manures and reduce the incidence of the disease.

In the Arizona experiments, the parasite did not penetrate barriers of sulfur. Many substances including ammonia, formaldehyde, and aluminum sulfate prevented germination. Fumigants of chloropicrin, Mylone, Vapam, and methyl bromide have been tried in preplant eradication of the fungus. Methyl bromide in 1-pound cans released at depths of 6 to 8 feet was an effective eradicant. According to Streets,[4] however, avoiding losses from root rot is more practical than direct control measures. Losses from general infestation of soil by this persistent fungus are so severe on susceptible hosts like cotton, alfalfa, stone fruit

[3]Personal communication from Dr. Streets.

[4]See footnote 3.

trees, pomegranates, grapes, and figs that prospective sites should not be planted until the area has been tested for freedom from the fungus by growing a susceptible crop like cotton or alfalfa on the site for at least two years.

Hard Root Rot

Root rots of citrus trees under waterlogged conditions have been subjects of investigations and speculation regarding the responsible microorganisms. In the early stages of trouble in the presence of excess water, trees appear thin and chlorotic as a result of twig dieback and mineral nutrient deficiencies. Hard root rot was found by Hopkins (1933*a*) in Rhodesia to be caused by *Rhizoctonia lamellifera* Small.

Symptoms.—The fungus attacks the roots and trunk of sweet oranges on Rough lemon rootstocks, causing the bark just above the bud union to crack, slough off, and occasionally gum. The surface of exposed wood is light buff in color. In section, it shows three distinct layers: an outer thin (1.6 mm) layer of white wood; a layer of hard gum-infiltrated wood of the same thickness; and finally, a thicker layer of gray wood if a secondary fungus, *Diplodia natalensis* Pole-Evans, has invaded the region. The affected roots are light in color, dry, brittle, and contain many small (0.8 mm) black sclerotia. The black-colored bark of roots forms a loose cover which readily breaks away in shreds and powder.

Control.—Care in planting to avoid causing unnecessary wounds and provision for optimum watering and good drainage are the recommended control measures.

Macrophomina Root Rot

Macrophomina phaseoli (Maubl.) Ashby [*Rhizoctonia Bataticola* (Taub.) Butl.] has been associated with a citrus root rot in California, Arizona, Israel, the West Indies, Rhodesia, Tanzania, and Sri Lanka.

Symptoms.—On heavily watered young grapefruit trees on Rough lemon rootstocks, Fawcett (1936) found soft, watery lesions caused by this fungus on bark of main lateral roots. Klotz (Fawcett, 1936) found the parasite on roots of young citrus trees near Riverside, California. The surface of the wood and cambial surface of the bark darkened as the lesions dried. The attack differed from that by *R. lamellifera* in not penetrating as far into the wood.

Control.—Drying out the crown and root surfaces near the crown and careful control of irrigation and drainage to avoid excessive wetting of the crown are the control measures.

In Spain, Italy, and Malta, *Rhizoctonia violaceae* Tul. causes a similar rot of the bark of citrus roots (Penzig, 1887). The lesions, which at first are dark red in color, darken further and the bark loosens in shreds. The same precautions on watering should apply in prevention and control of this malady.

Dry Root Rot

Dry root rot can be found wherever citrus is grown because the most important condition contributing to its occurrence is, anomalously, excessive moisture (Klotz, DeWolfe, and Miller, 1967). Bark and wood of the crown and larger roots are affected.

Symptoms.—As first noticed by the grower, leaves have either wilted suddenly and dried in place, or some of them have dropped, giving the tree an open, thin appearance, with more dead twigs than usual. These symptoms are common to any disorder caused by an agency which kills roots or girdles the tree in whole or in part.

Further examination discloses that some or all of the bark at the crown of the tree first shows a moist decay, which later dries, cracks, and shreds. This may suggest gummosis, but lack of gumming, together with a dusky-to-black discoloration of the wood below its surface, revealed by cutting, precludes gummosis as the main cause. Phytophthora gummosis fungi do not invade citrus wood beneath the cambium layers.

Occasionally, the affected part has a fishy odor. The appearance of the tree above ground depends upon the number of roots affected and the extent to which the wood of the crown is involved. In terminal cases, the decaying wood becomes punky in texture (fig. 1–16).

All common rootstocks are susceptible, including trifoliate orange and Troyer citrange (which have considerable resistance to brown rot gummosis).

While all of the factors and sequence of disease development may not be evident, damage to the root or crown tissue by one or more of several agencies apparently opens the way for initiation of the disease. Suffocation of the fibrous feeder roots by overwatering, infection of the bark of feeder roots or larger roots or crown by gummosis fungi, or damage of the roots by strong inorganic or organic fertilizers or by herbicides,

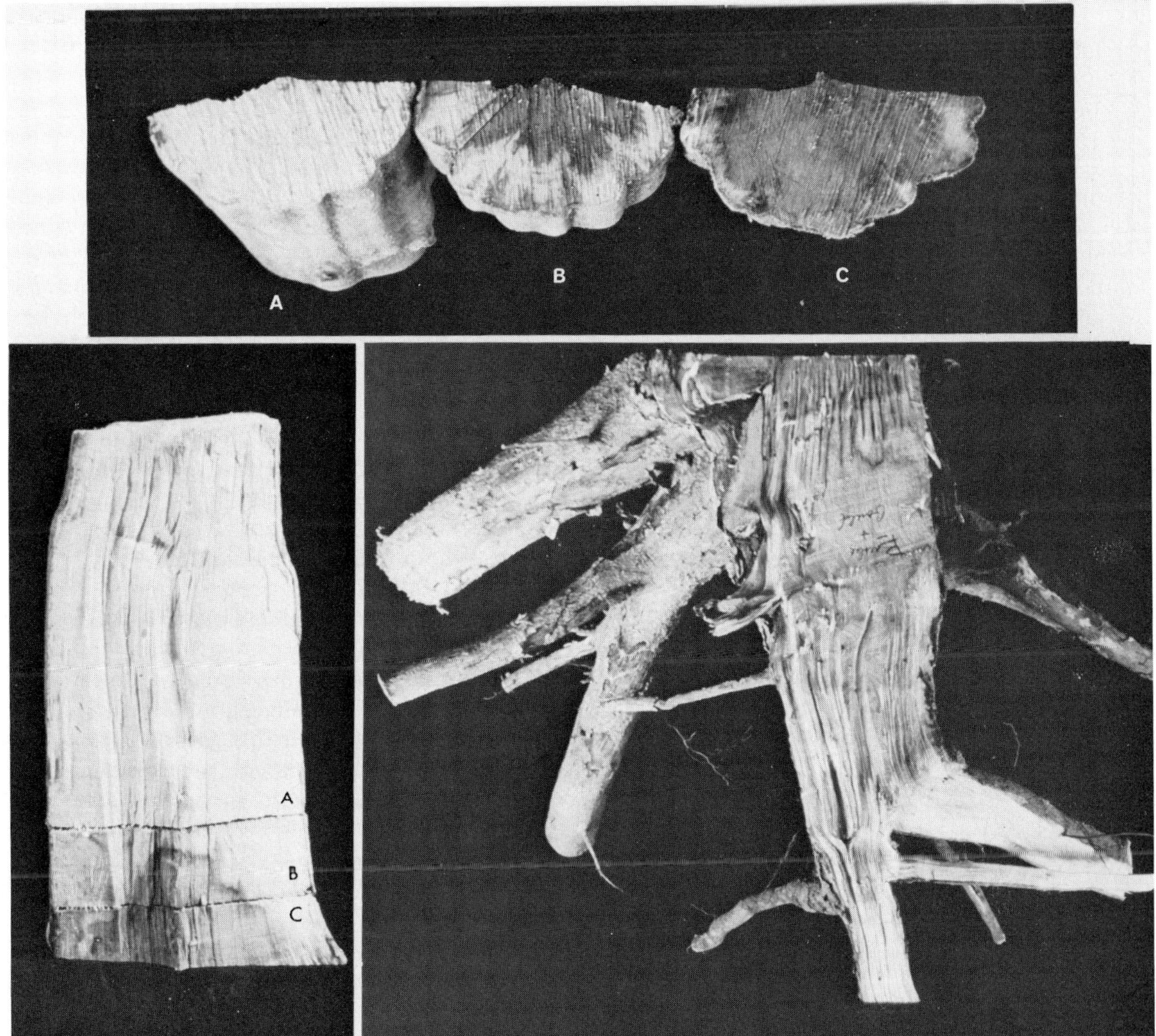

Fig. 1–16. Dry root rot of Troyer citrange. Left, longitudinal section of trunk showing progress of rot from roots to crown. Top, cross-section of areas A, B, and C shown at left. Right, longitudinal section through crown and subtending roots, showing staining and decay. (Photos by T. A. DeWolfe.)

nematocides, tillage, kerosene sprays, gophers, and other rodents (see chap. 5) may provide entrance for dry root rot.

The initial damage to the tree may occur shortly after planting or at any period in its life, and may require several years before the disease causes visible symptoms in the aboveground parts.

As revealed by longitudinal and cross sections (fig. 1–16), dry root rot may start in rotting fibrous feeder roots or larger roots, progress into still larger roots, and ultimately reach into the crown and trunk of the tree. It may also appear first at the crown, if the injury occurs there. Staining and decay may also work from the crown into the larger subtending roots.

Bark beyond the places of entrance of the disease remains intact until the wood cambium immediately beneath it becomes involved. Then the bark dies. In collapsed trees, most or all of the woody cylinder of the crown may be diseased.

Cultures from affected wood generally yield one or more species of *Fusarium* and bacteria, and occasionally yield low-grade citrus parasites found in soils such as *Macrophomina* sp. or saprophytes such as *Chaetomium* sp. Eventually, other wood-destroying fungi enter and reduce the wood to punk. In microscopic sections of the wood, *Fusarium* spp. are seen to progress through the living cells of medullary rays and into soil solution-conducting vessels. Fortunately, in most cases of damage to fibrous roots, *Fusarium* spp., bacteria, and other low grade parasites fail to become established and active in the wood.

Control.—To decrease incidence of dry root rot, avoid excessive watering; do not permit water to stand in contact with the tree crown. The precautions suggested to prevent and combat gummosis in young trees apply to dry root rot, since gummosis lesions favor early development of the disease. Follow manufacturers' instructions carefully for dosages and methods of application of herbicides, nematocides, and other pesticides. Inspect regularly for gummosis and gopher activity and take prompt control measures.

Fertilizers applied in the hole, around roots, or next to the trunk of young trees during planting have at times caused severe injury (Carpenter *et al.*, 1959). Wait at least six weeks or until the young tree has put out new growth and becomes established before applying fertilizers.

In advanced stages when fruit production no longer justifies keeping the tree, it should be removed and the site replanted.

Wood Rots

As noted in the discussion of various gummosis diseases, injury by cold, sunburn, insects, and various mechanical agencies expose wood to invasion by fungi. Most of these wood invaders are Basidiomycetes, species of the genera *Daldinia*, *Ganoderma*, *Polyporus*, *Stereum*, *Fomes*, and *Schizophyllum* (fig. 1–17). Several of the fungi are worldwide in distribution. The prevention and control measures outlined for Rio Grande gummosis are applicable.

Fig. 1–17. Wood rot of orange tree caused by *Schizophyllum commune*.

DISEASES AND INJURIES OF BRANCHES, TWIGS, LEAVES, AND PREHARVEST FRUIT

Pink Disease

Citrus trees of all varieties in eastern tropical countries have a widespread and very destructive malady of the trunk, limbs, and twigs called pink disease (Lee and Yates, 1919). The color of the causal parasite has provided a name for the disease. It is caused by the fungus *Corticium salmonicolor* Berk. & Broome, and is found to a much less extent in Central America and the West Indies than in the tropics of the western hemisphere.

Symptoms.—The first evidence of pink disease is a small amount of gum appearing in vertical cracks. At this stage the bark is dry and hard and removable from the wood only with difficulty. Then, in the form of minute (1.0 mm) gray-to-pink pustules, the fungus pushes through the bark surface and mycelium forms over the entire affected area, producing the characteristic pink covering (fig. 1-19). Basidia of the fungus have not been found on citrus. Healthy bark adjacent to the pink area is invaded by the mycelium which first appears as smooth, fragile, fanlike growth. The lesion cover, which is at first smooth, eventually breaks up into disconnected areas and fades to a gray color. The invaded bark is discolored a light brown. Wood is also attacked, and thus transport of xylem solution is impeded. Once the disease girdles the trunk, the tree is quickly killed. Since the disease requires extended periods of warm, wet weather typical of the tropics, it has not become a problem in drier, subtropical plantings.

Control.—Control consists in removing affected bark of the trunk and pruning off diseased limbs. Sterilize tools between cuts and spray trees with lime sulfur to prevent the disease.

Thread Blight

The cause of thread blight has been attributed by some investigators to *Corticium koleroga* (Cooke) Hohn and to *C. stevensii* Burt by others. According to Rogers and Jackson (1943), both would be *Pellicularia koleroga* Cooke; later, Donk (1956) renamed the fungus *Thanatephorus*. The disease occurs on citrus in Florida, the West Indies, and Argentina. It also attacks coffee in Puerto Rico, Cuba, the Lesser Antilles, Jamaica, Trinidad, Surinam, Venezuela, Colombia, Guatemala, Brazil, India, Java, Malaysia, Queensland, and Zaire.

Fig. 1–18. Two types of leaf spot. Left, lemon leaf spots caused by *Mycosphaerella* **spp. Right, areolate spots caused by** *Pellicularia filamentosa* **(Pat.) Rogers.**

Symptoms and Control.—The fungus forms mycelium in slender strands which are nearly uniform in diameter. The strands are whitish at first and finally become dark brown. They extend along branches, twigs, and the midrib and veins of leaves, branch out between cells of leaf parenchyma, and spread to the upper leaf surface where they form minute pustules with a speckled appearance. The pustules grow to form a thin smoke-gray-colored membrane which covers the leaf surface,[5] followed by the death of leaves and twigs. Nowell (1923) reported a spray of Bordeaux mixture with an excess of lime to be an effective control; he noted that lime sulfur is ineffective. Rhoads and DeBusk (1931) controlled thread blight with an application of Bordeaux-oil emulsion at the beginning of the rainy season.

Areolate Spot or Mancha Areolada

This is a leaf spot of striking appearance found in Brazil, Venezuela, and Surinam. It is produced by a fungus judged by Rogers (1943) and Rogers and Jackson (1943) to be *Pellicularia filamentosa* (Pat.) Rogers, originally described by

[5]Ridgway (1912).

Fig. 1–19. Pink disease caused by *Corticium salmonicolor*. *A*, showing pink color and advancing white mycelium. *B*, sterile pustules and gum formation during early stage of disease. *C* and *D*, orange-colored, spore-bearing sporodochia.

Stahel (1940) in Venezuela as *Corticium areolatum* Stahel.[6]

Symptoms.—The affected areas are light-colored, with concentric partial rings or bands (fig. 1-18, right). Often along the darker rings, numerous fruiting structures occur of the common saprophytic fungus, *Leptosphaeria bondari* Jenkins and Bitancourt, which was at first mistakenly considered by Bondar (1929) to be the causal organism. Bondar (1929), however, mentioned another fungus in association with the spot, which he called *Oidium citri* Bondar. This is probably the pathogen. The disease is known in Brazil as *Mancha areolada*.

According to Stahel (1940), the sour orange used as a rootstock suffers most; grapefruit, mandarin, and some kinds of sweet oranges are also susceptible. The common sweet orange is fairly resistant, except when grown in heavy shade. Spots may be found on young twigs, but have not been seen on fruits. In Surinam no spots have been seen on lemon, lime, and kumquat.

Control.—In Surinam nurseries, the disease was effectively suppressed by collecting and burning all spotted leaves. In both Surinam and Brazil, a spray of Bordeaux mixture is suggested for control.

Corticium Blight in Panama

On sour orange seedlings collected in Panama in May, 1937, a fungus later judged to be a variety of *Corticium solani* Prill. & Del.[7] was found producing a mildew-like growth on leaves and causing dead spots. The spots did not show the concentric rings characteristic of areolate spot. In examining the fungus, Stahel[8] reported that the hyphae were similar to those on areolate spot, but that the side branches were strangely curled and not so heavily swollen as those of the South American fungus. Because of these differences and a striking difference in symptoms, it is believed to be a fungus different from, but closely related to, *Pellicularia filamentosa*.

Citrus Canker

Citrus canker, cancrosis A, caused by the bacterium *Xanthomonas citri* (Haase) Dowson is a very destructive disease which originated in oriental citrus orchards, probably in northwest India. It arrived in the Gulf States in 1911 on trifoliate orange seedlings from Japan, and in South Africa a few years prior to 1916 on Japanese shipments. The eradication of canker in Florida, South Africa, and Australia, after it had become well established and in spite of great difficulties and expense, is one of the most remarkable achievements in plant disease control on record.

Symptoms.—The bacterium attacks all young developing parts of the citrus plant. On young twigs, leaves, and fruit, the lesions start as yellow and later become white pinhead-sized eruptions, change to tan, and finally turn brown. The margin becomes watery, glazed, and greasy, and is greenish to yellow-brown in color, producing a halolike effect. Lesions resembling small craters attain a size of 3 to 5 mm (fig. 1–20).

[6]This name had previously been used by Bresadola (1925) for a different fungus on *Alnus*.

[7]Identified by Miss Wakefield, Kew Gardens, London, in a letter of April 4, 1939, to H. S. Fawcett. Rogers (1943) identified this fungus as the same species, *Pellicularia filamentosa* (Pat.) as that causing aerolate spot. The spots, however, were very different in appearance from aerolate spots.

[8]Letter from G. Stahel to H. S. Fawcett.

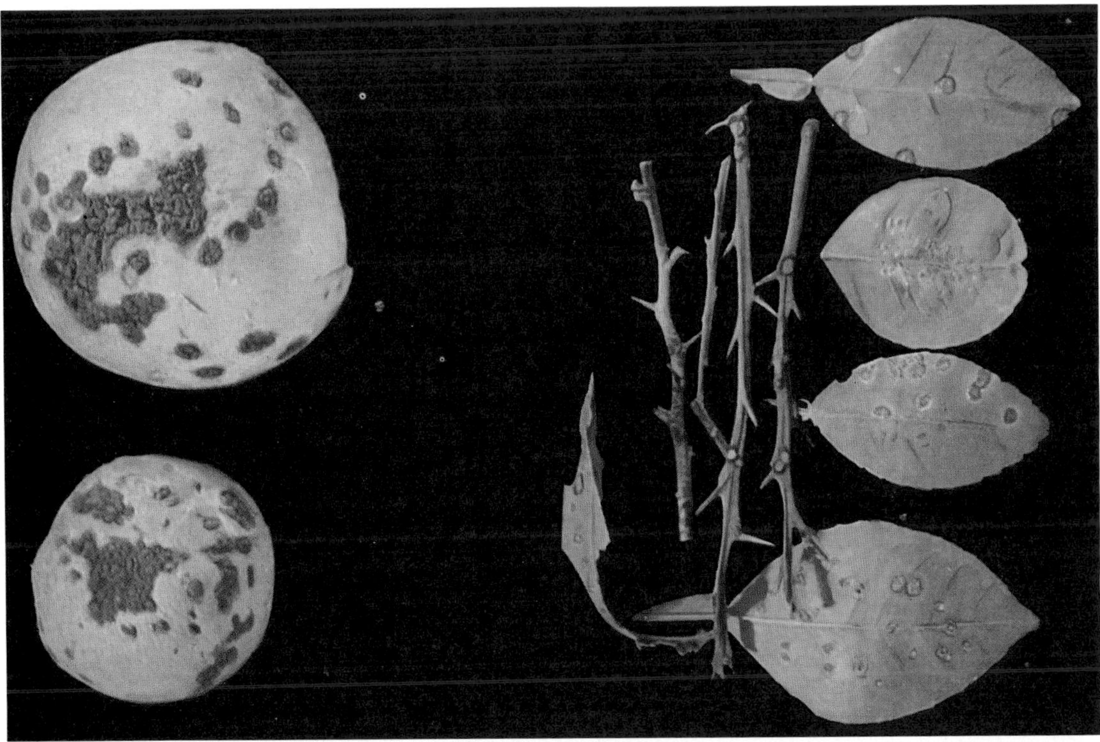

Fig. 1–20. Citrus canker of fruit, leaves, and twigs caused by the bacterium *Xanthomonas citri* (Haase) Dowson. (Photographed from preserved specimens loaned by W. B. Tisdale, University of Florida.)

Fig. 1–21. Citrus blast of twig and leaves and black pit of lemon fruit.

Control.—Eradication is, as already mentioned, the most effective control measure. Trees in Florida were sprayed with a mixture of kerosene and petroleum oil and burned. Clothes, shoes, and tools of workmen were disinfested and washed before removal from a contaminated location. Where eradication is not feasible, advantage may be taken of the resistance of some species and varieties to the disease. Susceptibility from most to least is as follows: grapefruit, trifoliate orange, limes, sweet oranges, lemons, and Satsuma mandarin. Tangerines, citron, calamondin, and kumquats are commercially resistant. However, the approximate order of susceptibility to another form of canker called cancrosis B is: lemon, citron, limes, sour orange, sweet orange, and grapefruit. A Bordeaux mixture spray (8-8-100) protects young fruit and growth if applied during the first three months of their development. For cancrosis B, in addition to spraying, diseased shoots should be pruned and removed from the orchard. Since canker requires a well-distributed rainfall during which the temperature is in the range of 68° F to 90° F, it is thought that it cannot become a threat in regions like Arizona and California where rainfall is sparse or lacking during periods of high temperatures.

Citrus Blast and Black Pit

Blast of twigs and leaves and black pit of fruit are caused by the bacterium *Pseudomonas syringae* van Hall (Lee, 1917). These diseases have been reported in all citrus areas except Brazil, Florida, Caribbean countries, and Central America and other hot tropical regions. Grapefruit and oranges are most susceptible to blast and lemons are most susceptible to black pit. The bacterium readily invades injuries to leaves, petioles, and fruit caused by thorns, hail, insects, or any other agency (fig. 1–21).

Symptoms.—Blast lesions most frequently start in a slight break on the wing of a petiole and extend rapidly to the base edge of the leaf and the subtending twig. Callus is formed at the edge of the twig lesion and the diseased area is covered by a reddish-brown to chestnut-colored scab or crust. Leaves wilt rapidly and either fall off or dry in place. In severe attacks, many twigs are girdled and killed.

Control.—In the northern California counties of Butte, Glenn, and Tehama, blast is sufficiently important to warrant control measures (Coit, 1916; Hodgson, 1917; Fawcett, Horne, and Camp, 1923). Injury is lessened by: (1) using such cultural methods as to prevent untimely and excessive foliage growth in the fall which would not harden before cold, wet weather sets in; (2) locating the orchard on the leeward side of slopes and planting windbreaks; (3) planting citrus varieties of a bushy compact form with relatively few thorns; (4) pruning out dead and diseased twigs; and (5) spraying during the first week in November with 10-10-100 Bordeaux mixture (DeWolfe *et al.*, 1966).

Black pit lesions may be small pits or specks or sunken spots measuring ¼ to ½ inch in diameter and affecting the flavedo and albedo of the fruit. The infections start in injuries and may enlarge during fruit storage (Smith and Klotz, 1945), especially where the fungus *Alternaria citri* Ellis & Pierce is also present (Klotz, DeWolfe, and Desjardins, 1955). While the disease is usually not of sufficient importance to justify the expense of control measures, those outlined for blast would be effective.

Bacterial Spot of South Africa

While blast and black pit are present in South Africa, another different bacterial disease also is known there. It is caused by *Erwinia citrimaculans* (Doidge) Magrou, first described by Doidge (1917) as *Bacillus citrimaculans*. It attacks all commercial varieties of citrus and produces symptoms on fruit and twigs much resembling those caused by *Pseudomonas syringae*. Presumably, the control measures suggested for blast-black pit would apply.

Bacterial Leaf Spot of Sour Orange

This leaf spot was first found in sour orange nursery trees in Uruguay in the vicinity of Salto in 1937 by Fawcett and Bitancourt (1940). Later, it was reported in Argentina. Its effect on some trees appeared to be injurious. The spots were usually in places where the leaf tissue was injured by scratching. Along a small thorn scratch on the epidermis a series of spots occurs, each with its center on the line of injury. The spots are 0.5 mm to 6 mm in diameter, more or less round, with definite, slightly wavy margins. They are raised somewhat at the periphery and depressed in the center. The smaller ones are waxy, and have an amber color; the larger ones show concentric regions as if they had enlarged in two or three stages. A chlorotic halo surrounds the spots. In transverse sections, Fawcett and Bitancourt (1940) found that the tissues in the spots are full of bacterial aggregations which occupy the much enlarged intercellular spaces of the spongy parenchyma.

Mal Secco

Mal secco, a highly destructive disease of sour orange, lemon, citron, and sometimes other citrus, is caused by the fungus *Phoma tracheiphila* Petri (Petri, 1929; Savastano and Fawcett, 1930; Ruggieri and Goidanich, 1953; Scrivani, 1954; Graniti, 1955; Klotz, 1956; Ciccarone, 1957; Bugiani, Scrivani, and Loprieno, 1959; Catara, Todaro, and Scaramuzzi, 1971). Lemon plantings in Italy (including Sicily), Turkey, Greece, and Israel have been severely damaged by the disease.

Symptoms.—Leaves and twigs suddenly wilt and dry, frequently on one side or section of the tree. Leaves either fall or remain attached and dry before the twigs die back. Large branches and finally the whole tree may die back in one to two years. If the sour orange rootstock of a tree becomes generally infected, the disease is soon fatal because the fungus spreads rapidly upward in the trunk and branches. Twig infection is less serious because affected parts can be pruned out. Wood of infected green twigs usually shows a pinkish or reddish color on a slanting cut (fig. 1–22). The pigmented isolates of *P. tracheiphila* were shown to be more pathogenic than nonpigmented isolates, but the pigment was not the toxic principle (Quilico *et al.*, 1952). Mal secco developed more slowly in sour orange seedlings having infectious variegation virus than in virus-free seedlings. This was thought attributable to the greater content of phenolic substances of the former (Catara, Todaro, and Scaramuzzi, 1971). Hail injury and wind-driven rains provide favorable conditions for infection.

Control.—In Sicily a spray of 1 per cent copper oxychloride applied every fifteen days during October to January inclusive was recommended by Ruggieri (1948). Resistant sweet orange and mandarin varieties may be used for replanting where trees on sour orange rootstocks have been killed. The Italian lemon varieties, Interdonato and Monachello, have high resistance but produce less fruit and inferior fruit to that of the susceptible Femminello variety. As formerly applied, the old *verdelli* method of producing summer fruit, which consisted of removing soil near the large roots and allowing trees to dry to wilting before supplying water and fertilizer, caused many injuries and fatal mal secco infections in the roots. With the method now practiced, the roots are not exposed and injured. Water is simply withheld until the trees wilt, then two applications of water and nitrogenous fertilizer are made one week apart. The treatment induces blooming and fruiting, and fruit matures the following summer when prices are favorable. The main control measure is removing diseased twigs and branches, cutting in the uninfected parts several inches back of the invading fungus.

Citrus Blight

Citrus blight, also called wilt, is known with certainty only in Florida where it is a very important cause of loss. The disease is somewhat more common on trees older than fourteen years of age, and in no particular patterns of spread from tree to tree, although it is more commonly seen along roadsides (fig. 1–23).

Symptoms.—The first apparent symptom is a general wilting or wilting on one side of the tree during hot, dry weather. Trees at first alternately wilt in daytime and revive at night, but ultimately reach a more or less permanently wilted state regardless of dry or moist conditions (Garnsey and Young, 1975). They have delayed blooming, reduced spring growth, and small acid fruit. Twigs show zinc deficiency symptoms and branches defoliate and die back, and the trunk and large limbs send out many water sprouts.

The cause of blight is unknown. Species of *Fusarium*, *Phoma*, and *Actinomyces* isolated from roots of affected trees have not been shown capable of causing the disease. Childs (1954) and Childs and Carlysle (1974) found many of the wood vessels that conduct soil solution plugged by material that could interfere with flow and thus cause wilting and decline symptoms. In Texas, Mortensen (1947) studied a decline of Satsuma mandarin and sweet orange trees that some investigators think resembles blight, and compared the incidence of the trouble in trees on sixteen different rootstocks.

Control.—At present, beyond providing the best cultural conditions in the orchard and pulling affected trees when fruit production is insufficient to justify keeping them, no other control measures can be suggested.

Fig. 1–22. Top left, sour orange twig infected by mal secco fungus *(Phoma tracheiphila)*. Pycnidia (spore cases) have formed on twig 6 at *D*. Pink discoloration of wood may be seen at *D* on twig 7; area L is uninvaded wood. Twig 8 shows acervuli of the secondary fungus, *Colletotrichum gloeosporioides* at *C*. Top right, dead limbs on a lemon tree attached by mal secco fungus. Bottom left, acervuli of secondary fungus, *C. gloeosporioides* and pycnidia of *P. tracheiphila*. Bottom Right, an enlargement of pycnidia of the causal fungus. (Top left illustration after Petri, 1930.)

Fig. 1–23. Citrus blight. Top left, early wilt stage of citrus blight of tangerine on Rough lemon rootstock. Top right, third stage of citrus blight of Valencia on Rough lemon. Bottom left, final stage in Valencia on Rough lemon. Bottom right, plugging of vessels in branches by the blight. (Photos courtesy of J. F. L. Childs.)

Diplodia Twig Blight

Various fungi kill twigs. *Diplodia natalensis* was found to cause death of citrus twigs in Florida and the islands of the West Indies (Fawcett and Burger, 1911). The fungus apparently advances until stopped by the formation of gum in the twig. Where no gum forms, the fungus may even invade and kill large limbs and the trunk.

Symptoms.—A reddish-brown discoloration of the dead bark and dusky gray color of the wood, together with presence of pycnidia, indicate presence of the fungus. As in Diplodia gummosis (see p. 18), injury by heat or cold opens the way to infection. Nowell (1923) reported that lime trees injured or weakened by insects, wind, mineral nutrient deficiencies, and drought are most readily attacked.

Fig. 1–24. Branch and twigs of lemon tree invaded by Botrytis fungus after injury by freezing.

Control.—Control is achieved by employing the best cultural methods and removing affected twigs at least three inches beyond the margin of invasion, disinfecting cuts with 2 per cent mercuric chloride† in 25 per cent wood alcohol or denatured alcohol, and, after drying, covering cuts with white lead paint or tree seal.

Sclerotinia Twig Blight

Sclerotinia sclerotiorum attacks twigs after freezing or near freezing weather. Root rot and gummosis caused by this fungus have already been described. The fungus also is the cause of a fruit rot commonly called cottony rot.

Symptoms.—Although the fungus usually kills back only a few twigs for short distances, it may attack further back on a twig or limb, lead to girdling, and thus kill everything to the distal end. Mature blossoms whose petals are beginning to fall may be attacked and the twig entered (see fig. 1-11, p. 16). Affected bark softens and exudes gum. As infection becomes self-limiting, the bark dries and turns a light buff color (Ridgway, 1912). Later, on weathering, the bark becomes shredded in longitudinal strips among which the fungus produces dark brown-to-black, seedlike sclerotia. When the sclerotia fall to the soil they produce small cuplike apothecia which bear the spores. Although damage caused by the disease is generally minor, the killed terminals worry growers. Affected parts may be pruned and burned. Heavy cover cropping and organic manuring favor growth and dissemination of the fungus; clean cultivation practically eliminates it. In soils with a meager amount of organic material, the advantages to be had from organic fertilizers and a cover crop outweigh the disadvantage of the small amount of injury to trees from this disease. However, if fruit from a lemon orchard has a history of serious losses from cottony rot in storage, control of the disease by clean cultivation becomes more important. Orchards adjacent to fields of vegetables or flowers affected by this fungus may show much Sclerotinia twig blight.

Botrytis Twig Blight

Much of the discussion of the disease caused by *S. sclerotiorum* applies to twig blight caused by *Botrytis cinerea*. Injury to bark by cold favors both fungi (fig. 1–23). In addition, the fungus in moist cool weather grows and sporulates on lemon blossoms (fig. 1–24), lowering fruit set, and eventually causing serious fruit rots in the packinghouse (Klotz, Calavan, and Zentmyer, 1946). Another effect originating in the orchard from infected blossom parts lying in contact with young fruit is the stimulation of their cells to form ridges (fig. 1–25), thus lowering the grade of the fruit (Jeppson, 1951; Calavan *et al.*, 1952).

Control.—Control in coastal areas where the trouble occurs is difficult because blossoms develop almost continuously and cool fogs are frequent, providing the best conditions for invasion by the fungus. It would be necessary to spray every few days to give adequate protection. However, if it is desirable to protect a particular fruit set, a Zineb spray† (2 pounds in 100 gallons with 2 ounces of a spreader-sticker) or a 2-4½-100 Bordeaux mixture may be applied (Weathers, 1957). The fungus also damages twigs, branches, and the trunks of trees previously injured by cold, shell bark-dry bark, and other agencies.

Fusarium Twig Disease

Wilting and dying back of the twigs of citron, orange, and mandarin were reported by

†This chemical or chemical formulation is not currently registered with or recommended for usage by the United States Environmental Protection Agency for this particular pest of citrus. Citrus producers in other countries are advised to check their country's regulations for using such treatment methods.

Sirag-el-Din (1931) to be caused by a strain of *Fusarium solani* (Mart) Appel & Wr. The disease occurs in Egypt, South Africa, the Philippines, and Honduras.

Symptoms and Control.—Leaves wilt and abscise and gum forms in the abscission scars. Twigs wither and die, bark splits, and gumming occurs at the margin of dead and dying tissues. Removing affected twigs and disinfecting cuts and injuries are recommended.

Citrus Scab

Scab on citrus occurs in three forms: (1) sour orange scab caused by the fungus *Elsinöe fawcetti* Bitancourt & Jenkins; (2) Tryon's scab (Australian citrus scab) due to *Sphaceloma fawcetti* var. *scabiosa* (McAlp. & Tryon) Jenkins; and (3) sweet orange fruit scab caused by *E. australis* Bitancourt & Jenkins.

Sour orange scab is widely distributed in the Orient, South Africa, the South Pacific, the Gulf States, the West Indies, and South America. Arriving in Florida in 1876 on Satsuma oranges from Japan, it spread to those citrus-growing areas of the United States where humidity and temperature conditions were favorable. Apparently the climates of Arizona and California are not conducive to the disease; although it was introduced in these states on early plantings of sour orange from Florida, it never became established. It has not been reported from Mediterranean basin countries. It occurs most severely on sour orange, lemon, Temple orange, calamondin, and tangelo; less severely on grapefruit, Tahiti lime, and mandarin varieties; rarely on some sweet oranges and one variety of kumquat; and not at all on other sweet oranges and kumquats, citron, and Mexican lime.

Tyron's scab occurs on lemons, satsumas, tangerines, and sweet and sour oranges in Australia and New Zealand. It is severe on lemons and uncommon on mandarins.

Sweet orange fruit scab until recently was found only in South American orchards where it is most severe on sweet oranges and mandarins. In 1957, it was discovered in Sicily (Ciccarone, 1957) on lemon fruit of trees growing in shaded or partially shaded locations.

Symptoms.—On leaves, small young lesions of sour orange scab are semi-translucent dots that become sharply defined pustules which sometimes are flat or somewhat depressed at the center. Leaves are often stunted, wrinkled, and otherwise distorted. Lesion surfaces become a dusky color with age. On fruit and leaves of sour orange and some other varieties, conical growths develop and bear lesions at their apices. Melanose causes a similar effect. On succulent twigs of the most susceptible varieties scab lesions form like those on leaves (fig. 1–26).

The lesions of Tryon's scab and sweet orange fruit scab are more nearly rounded and less spongy than those of sour orange scab and become so numerous and confluent as to cover the scab surface with a corky layer of buff-to-black elevations. Leaf lesions are also slightly larger and more regularly craterlike than those of sour orange scab.

Control.—The three scab forms can be controlled by: (1) spraying before growth starts in the spring with copper fungicide (0.75 pound metallic copper per 100 gallons water) or Ferbam (1.5 pound 75 per cent wettable powder per 100 gallons water); and (2) spraying a second time when two-thirds of the blossoms have fallen (Knorr, 1973). The second spraying will also control early melanose. When melanose is not a factor and scab is unlikely to be severe, one should spray before growth starts with 1½ pounds of Ferbam † per 100 gallons. Young, nonbearing trees also may be protected by spraying with the Ferbam spray. For decreasing the incidence of sour orange scab, remove susceptible sour orange or Rough lemon trees near orchards of susceptible varieties. Ferbam is registered for use four times a year on all trees. In Brazil, growers use a prebloom neutral copper spray followed by a petal-fall Zineb spray for sweet orange scab.

Melanose

Melanose caused by the fungus *Diaporthe citri* (Faw.) Wolf occurs in nearly all citrus-growing areas of the world and is most serious in regions which are moist during the early formative periods of leaves and fruit. In central Florida, melanose is a prime factor in lowering the grade of fruit. In drier areas, such as California or Arizona, it is of slight importance, rarely seen, and merits no control measures.

† This chemical or chemical formulation is not currently registered with or recommended for usage by the United States Environmental Protection Agency for this particular pest of citrus. Citrus producers in other countries are advised to check their country's regulations for using such treatment methods.

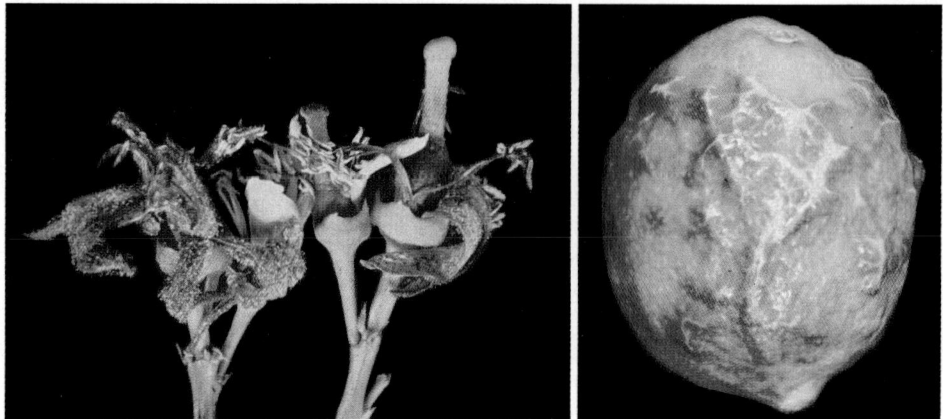

Fig. 1–25. Left, Botrytis blossom blight. Right, ridging of fruit.

Symptoms.—Melanose attacks small twigs, leaves, and fruit, producing small, raised pustules of gum-filled cells, frequently arranged in lines and irregularly shaped spots (fig. 1–27). Around the margin and across the surface, an extensive involvement and small cracks produce a mudcake effect. Continuous crusts may form from areas crowded together. The waxlike lesions are amber brown to dark brown or nearly black. They are like coarse sandpaper to the touch. Rain and dew may distribute the fungus in a tear-streaking pattern. Defoliation may result from extensive infections.

Control.—To control melanose, the foliage and fruit are thoroughly sprayed with 3-4-100 Bor-

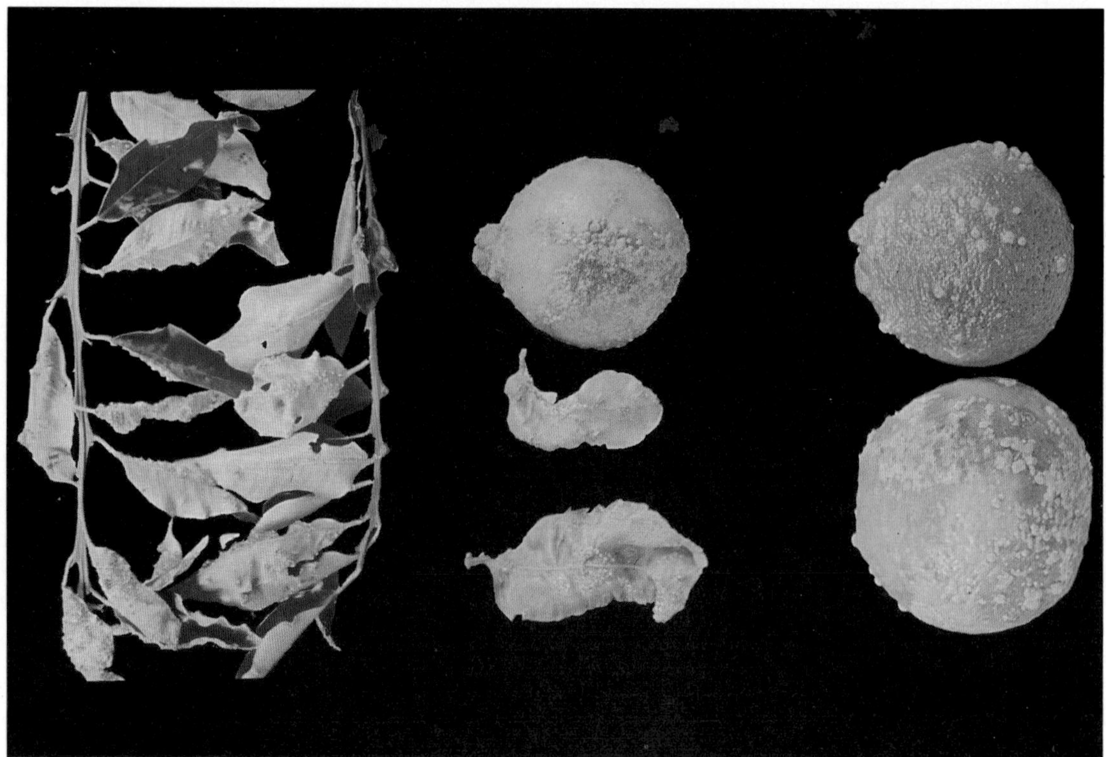

Fig. 1–26. Sour orange scab. Left, on Temple orange leaves. Center, on Sampson tangelo. Right, on Temple orange fruit.

Fig. 1–27. Melanose. Left, small, raised, superficial dots or pustules made up of gum-filled cells on sour orange leaves. Center, mud-cake type of melanose on fruit. Right, tear staining caused by dew or rain drops flowing down over the fruit surface and carrying spores.

deaux or neutral copper (0.75 pound per 100 gallons) soon after the fruit is set in April or 10 to 20 days after blossom drop. In seasons of above-normal rainfall, a second application is made one month to six weeks later. Infection is reduced if diseased and dead twigs are removed.

Greasy Spot

Dr. J. O. Whiteside (1970*b*, 1970*c*, 1972*a*, 1972*b*, 1973*a*, 1973*b*, 1974*a*) reports that, "Greasy spot is widespread in those citrus-growing areas of the world with hot, humid climates. In Florida, the disease frequently causes serious premature defoliation during the fall and winter as a result of the infection that occurred during the previous summer. The greasy spot fungus also causes a fruit rind blemish on some varieties.

"**Symptoms.**—Greasy spot has a long incubation period. Infection occurs mostly in the summer, but symptoms do not appear until 2 to 9 months later, the incubation period depending partly on the variety affected. On the leaves, early symptoms appear as a slight blistering on the underside of the leaves and at this time slight yellowing of the tissue may be visible when the leaves are viewed from above. The blistered area becomes light orange and later turns brown or black, suggesting a spot of grease. Infection of small twigs can occur, but injury is negligible and seldom visible.

"On the rind, the causal organism attacks the guard cells of stomata and varying numbers of the underlying cells. Usually the specks remain small, thereby producing a fine stippling effect between the oil glands. On grapefruit, however, the specks are sometimes large enough to coalesce with neighboring specks thereby causing a more unsightly blemish. Living cells adjacent to the specks retain a green color for longer than normal and such areas of the rind often fail to respond to ethylene degreening treatment. The disease on grapefruit previously described as pink pitting is now known to be caused by the greasy spot fungus (fig. 1–28, *A*).

"**Cause.**—For many years, greasy spot was considered to be caused by mites. After it was discovered in Japan that the disease could be controlled by copper fungicide sprays, a search began for a fungus as the causal agent. In Japan, greasy spot was subsequently attributed to the previously known citrus leaf spotting fungus, *Mycosphaerella horii* Hara. In Florida, a fungus named as *Cercospora citri-grisea* Fisher was reported to cause greasy spot. In both cases, the fungi described as causing greasy spot were found only in small, round brown spots. Such spots were thought to represent merely another expression of injury caused by greasy spot. Recent work in Florida has established that a previously unknown fungus causes greasy spot and that small, round brown spots are not a part of the greasy spot syndrome. The fungus discovered in Florida as the cause of greasy spot has been named *Mycosphaerella citri* Whiteside. Perithecia are produced only after the leaves have fallen and have reached a sufficiently advanced stage of decomposition. *M. citri* has an imperfect fungus form called *Stenella* which differs from *Cercospora* in the manner in which the conidia are produced. *M. citri* produces conidia only from hyphae growing externally over the surface of the leaf. These conidia are produced in very small numbers compared with ascospores and are therefore of minor importance epidemiologically. The external hyphae persist for only a few weeks after the initial leaf colonization and no conidia are likely to be seen by the time disease symptoms start to appear.

"**Epidemiology.**—In Florida, ascospore production and release from fallen leaves reaches a peak shortly after the summer rainy period commences. The inoculum supply decreases as the leaf litter decomposes further and there is little leaf drop during the summer to replenish this supply. Therefore, the period of major infection generally lasts only until August, but it can be prolonged if leaf decomposition is delayed by dry weather. A combination of prolonged high humidity and high temperature is required for infection. Substantial infection therefore occurs in Florida only from June to September and mostly at night.

"**Control.**—In Florida, greasy spot is controlled by spraying citrus trees in June or July with copper fungicides at rates equivalent to 1.25 to 2.5 pounds metallic copper per 500 gallons or with benomyl† at 0.5 pound of active ingredient per 500 gallons or with 1 per cent spray oil. Sprays, so timed, control greasy spot on the fruit and on leaves that have fully expanded prior to spraying. If disease pressure is heavy, an additional spray is sometimes required in August or September to control the disease on later summer growth flushes. Postbloom copper sprays applied primarily for melanose control also help to control greasy spot on the leaves. Because infection of leaves occurs almost entirely through the lower leaf surface, good spray coverage of the underside of the leaves is essential for effective greasy spot control." (See also Fisher (1961, 1966) on greasy spot and tar spot.)

Tar Spot

Tar spot is found to a very limited extent in Florida. It is distinguishable from greasy spot in late stages in having a mahogany-red circle within the margin of the spot and appearing tan to orange instead of yellow in the early stages (fig. 1–28, *B*). The cause has been attributed to a fungus *Cercospora gigantea* Fisher.

Phyllosticta Leaf Spots

Several leaf spotting fungi, *Phyllosticta* spp., have been causes of partial defoliation. With the exception of California and Arizona they are distributed worldwide. While they are not usually of much importance, *P. citricola* Hori has caused serious leaf drop in some localities in Japan (Hara, 1917).

As leaves mature, the fungi produce light colored areas surrounded by a dark green region which appears suffused with water. Brownish discolorations develop in the affected portions of the leaves, which then fall before healthy leaves normally drop. Cool, moist weather favors infection. Should the disease become important, a foliar spray could be used.

Brown Rot and Phytophthora Blight

As already noted (p. 3), all parts of the citrus plant are attacked by one or more *Phytophthora* spp. The fungi are soil inhabitants and the diseases they cause are known wherever citrus is grown. The most prevalent species attacking citrus fruit is *P. citrophthora*, which has been found along with

†This chemical or chemical formulation is not currently registered with or recommended for usage by the United States Environmental Protection Agency for this particular pest of citrus. Citrus producers in other countries are advised to check their country's regulations for using such treatment methods.

Fig. 1–28. Greasy spot and tar spot. *A*, **greasy spot of Valencia orange leaves. (Photos by Dr. J. O. Whiteside.)** *B*, **tar spot of pineapple orange leaf and fruit. (Photos by Dr. F. E. Fisher.)**

P. parasitica, *P. syringae*, and *P. hibernalis* in California (Klotz, DeWolfe, Roistacher *et al.*, 1960; Klotz, DeWolfe, and Miller, 1969). *P. parasitica* (*P. terrestis*) and *P. citrophthora* occur in Florida (Whiteside, 1970*a*). *P. palmivora* Butl. has been reported on citrus in India, Sri Lanka, Java, Malaysia, the Philippines, the West Indies, South America, Trinidad, and Tanzania. *P. citricola* Sawada attacks fruit in Japan and South Africa.

Symptoms.—On fruit, infections first appear as small dusky spots resembling peteca (p. 52). These soon enlarge rapidly and become firm, leathery, decaying areas of various shades of brown (fig. 1–29).

Control.—(See table 1-1.) In California coastal orchards and other areas where only minor or no copper injury has been noted, brown rot is prevented by spraying just before the start of the rainy season. All fruit and foliage within 3 or 4 feet of the soil is sprayed with 3-4½-100 Bordeaux mixture having 3 pounds of powdered copper sulfate pentahydrate and 4½ pounds of hydrated lime per 100 gallons; with proprietary mixtures with an equivalent amount of copper; or a zinc-copper-lime mixture (3-2-6-100) containing 3 pounds of zinc sulfate monohydrate (or 5 pounds of the heptahydrate), 2 pounds of powdered copper sulfate pentahydrate, and 6 pounds of hydrated lime in 100 gallons of water. In orchards where copper may accumulate in toxic amounts in soil (e.g., the sandy soils of Florida) (Reuther and Smith, 1954), or where it would increase the injury from cyanide fumigation, or in locations where copper sprays are causing direct injury to fruit and leaves and leaf drop, either the 3-2-6-100 zinc-copper-lime formula or Captan 50W, 2 pounds per 100 gallons, may be used (Calavan *et al.*, 1955). (See also "Damage to Leaves and Fruit by Copper Sprays," p. 58.) The 3-2-6-100 formula will also control mottle leaf (zinc deficiency), and Septoria spotting if used over the entire tree. In central California, it is usually desirable to use a formulation with a high lime content (15 to 30 pounds of hydrated lime per 100 gallons) to repel leafhoppers which cause oleocellosis injury by liberating rind oil. Full coverage should also be practiced where *P. hibernalis* is known to be common, since that species with its detachable sporangia can be distributed throughout the entire tree. The most satisfactory substitutes for copper sprays found thus far for use

Fig. 1–29. Brown rot of citrus fruit. Left, infected lemons. Right, infected navel oranges on the ground.

against these fungi are Captan 50W and its derivatives. Since they weather away more rapidly than copper materials, a second application should be made about ten weeks after the first. In years of heavy rainfall, a second spraying with even the copper sprays is needed.

Some of the same *Phytophthora* spp. that cause gummosis and brown rot may attack fruit, twigs, leaves, and blossoms high in the trees and produce the effect called blight. This occurs when strong wind gusts transport moisture with zoospores *(P. citrophthora, P. parasitica, P. syringae)* or with sporangia and zoospores *(P. hibernalis)* above the 3- or 4-foot height usually reached when raindrops splash from soil onto low-hanging fruits. Thorough coverage of the entire tree with the spray materials mentioned will control Phytophthora blight.

Various Leaf Spots

Leaf spots caused by various fungi, including *Cercospora* spp., *Mycosphaerella* spp. (fig. 1-18, left), *Ascochyta* spp., *Alternaria citri* Ellis & Pierce, and *Pleospora* spp., have been responsible for some leaf drop. In South Africa, A. *citri* caused enough defoliation of Rough lemon to justify control with a lime sulfur spray (2 gallons of commercial lime sulfur in 100 gallons of water), according to Hopkins (1933*b*).

Sooty Mold

On the surface of leaves and fruit, a conspicuous black coating known as sooty mold may occur. It is composed of a weft of microscopic fungus threads of several species of fungi, including *Capnodium citri* B. & Desm. It occurs wherever honeydew-secreting insects are found, such as white fly larvae in Florida, and black scale, cottony-cushion scale, and aphis in California. Although sooty mold does not attack tissue, it interferes with the normal function of leaves and is a sign of the presence of some insect pest.

Since sooty mold occurs merely concomitant to the presence of some honeydew-secreting insect, prevention and treatment consist not in fighting the mold itself, but in exclusion and control of the insects which bring it about. Soon after the insects are eliminated, sooty mold disappears.

Smoky Blotch and Flyspeck

Smoky blotch in Florida, Rhodesia, South Africa, and South America, was previously known as sooty blotch. It appears as smoky or sooty areas caused by a branching network of dark hyphae on the surface of the rind. In Brazil, this has been found to be due to *Stomiopeltis citri* Bitancourt, *Sirothyrium citri* Bitancourt being its imperfect stage. In Rhodesia, Bates also found this fungus with another unidentified fungus.[9]

Flyspeck commonly has been attributed to the same fungus as that on apple, *Leptothyrium pomi* (B. & F.) but Bates[9] found three main types on citrus in Rhodesia, probably none of which were due to the apple fungus. The flyspecks occur as black specks made of a pad of fungus hyphae on the surface. Neither smoky blotch nor flyspeck is dependent upon honeydew from insects.

A spray of 2 per cent lime sulfur solution ten weeks before picking prevents a large percentage of smoky blotch in South Africa. Smoky blotch may be bleached on picked fruits by dipping them for 30 to 45 seconds in a solution composed of 4 ounces of bleaching powder (chloride of lime) and 3 ounces of sodium bicarbonate per gallon of water. If decay is troublesome, chloride of lime and boric acid may be substituted (Bates, 1939).

Powdery Mildew

Powdery mildew, produced by *Oidium tingitaninum* Carter, is reported as common in Java, Sri Lanka, and India on leaves of various citrus species, and has been found occasionally on tangerines in California.

Powdery mildew is easily identified by white patches which, more commonly than not, occur on the upper surface of leaves. It does not spread in a perfectly circular manner, but radiates from a center of infection. The tissue between the filaments of fungus mycelium is at first a darker, watery green than normal, and later becomes yellow. Young leaves may shrivel, become dry, and adhere to the twig. No experiments are recorded

[9]G. R. Bates in a letter to H. S. Fawcett, January 29, 1942, writes: "In view of the confusion that has existed in the past in regard to the application of the term 'sooty blotch' to both pomaceous and citrus fruits blemishes, and with the further consideration that different fungi are responsible for these blemishes, I have suggested that the name 'smoky blotch' be adopted for the citrus blemish." Bates adds that *Stromiopeltis citri* Bitancourt and *Sirothyrium citri* Bitancourt have been found on citrus in Rhodesia, but that most smoky blotch there appears to be due to an unidentified fungus.

for control of mildew on citrus. Sulfur sprays or dusts may be used.

Felt

A soft, feltlike, almost leathery covering produced by the fungus *Septobasidium pseudopedicellatum* Burt or other species completely surrounds twigs. It is found in moist climates such as those of Florida, Cuba, Brazil, Argentina, Paraguay, and Taiwan. These fungi have been associated with certain scale insects, the most common of which on citrus is *Lepidosaphes beckii* (Newm.). Other species of *Septobasidium* associated with citrus scale insects in North America are *S. conidiophorum* Couch, *S. lepidosaphis* Couch, *S. pedicellatum* (Berk. & Curt.) Pat., and *S. spongium* Berk. & Curt.

The surface of the coating produced by *S. pseudopedicellatum* is smooth and compact. Beneath, it is soft and spongy. The entire enveloping cylinder is made up of minute, closely woven, mycelial threads, none of which appears to penetrate the bark. A species of scale insect is found under the coating on the surface of the bark. The fungus probably protects the insects which, in turn, make secretions favorable to the growth of the fungus. The only control usually necessary is to remove branches bearing the fungus.

Lichens

Lichens are frequently seen on twigs and branches of citrus, especially in moist situations. They are grayish green and paper-like and form small circular- to irregularly-shaped spots. They are considered harmless so far as any direct injury produced by their growth is concerned, since they obtain their own nutriment from the air or from functionless tissue on the bark surface.

The presence of lichens on the tree need not cause alarm. If the lichens increase because the tree lacks vigor, it is better to use means of bringing the tree to a virorous growing condition than to incur the expense of eliminating the lichens. They may, however, become so abundant as to be troublesome and harmful in an indirect way by shading leaves or harboring other organisms. They may be killed by spraying with a weak Bordeaux mixture or strong lime-sulfur solution.

Alga Spot

A spot produced by the partly parasitic alga, *Cephaleuros mycoidea* Karst., sometimes occurs on leaves, twigs, and fruit in southern Florida, the West Indies, and elsewhere.

The spots are slightly raised and circular-to-irregular in outline. On fruit, the surface of the colony may be covered with reddish-brown, hair-like structures. When these are absent, the surface of the algal weft is greenish-gray and velvety. The bark may be swollen and the twigs enlarged at affected parts, though only a few surface layers of cells are invaded. A severe infestation causes considerable twig dieback.

Spraying with either Bordeaux mixture or commercial lime-sulfur appears to prevent the formation of alga spots. Nonsprayed trees in areas of incidence are attacked.

Anthracnose (Including Withertip and Blossom Blight)

Anthracnose is a term used to designate effects produced on citrus by fungi such as *Gloeosporium limetticolum* Claus., *G. follicolum* Nish., and *Colletotrichum gloeosporioides* Penz.

Anthracnose of Limes.—This disease, caused by *Gloeosporium limetticolum*, causes serious damage to limes in southern Florida, Cuba, and the West Indies (fig. 1–30). The dying back and withering of young trees has suggested the term "withertip," and the frequent blighting of buds and flowers, "blossom blight." Young, rapidly growing twigs are attacked. The twigs wither and shrivel from one to several inches at the tips. Frequently the live parts distal to a lesion fall away, with formation of gum at the wound. Young leaves may die, or at least dead areas may form on the margins of tips. The petals of unopened buds turn brown and buds fall off without opening.

Young enlarging fruits subject to severe attacks can be protected with neutral, copper sprays containing 0.75 pound metallic copper in 100 gallons of water and 0.5 to 1.0 per cent oil at one- to two-week intervals. In orchards having less severe attacks, the first spray may be Bordeaux mixture with subsequent applications of lime sulfur (1 to 30 or 40). Higher, drier sites are chosen for lime planting because humid areas favor the disease.

Anthracnose of Satsumas.—This disease, caused by *Gloeosporium follicolum*, occurs in Florida and Japan (Fisher, 1970). Brown spots occur on young, actively growing trees during May and June. Fallen leaves may show watery, cloudy spots on which bright-red pustules of the fungus appear.

Fisher (1970) found *G. follicolum* causing severe damage to unsprayed Temple orange fruit in Florida. Other unsprayed varieties were also attacked. Injury to twigs and leaves, however, was found only in one tangerine orchard. The fungus causes a gray, firm, dry decay of fruit. The disease is easily controlled with a petal-fall spray of basic copper sulfate (0.75 pound per 100 gallons) followed by a December application of Zineb (1½ pounds zinc ethylenebis-dithiocarbamate per 100 gallons).

Anthracnose of Orange, Lemon, Grapefruit, and Other Citrus.—The form of anthracnose produced by certain strains of *Colletotrichum gloeosporioides* Penz. is widely distributed in citrus-growing countries. In many respects, the fungus associated with it resembles that of lime anthracnose. There seem to be forms or strains of this fungus, some of which are parasitic while others are saprophytic. Forms of this fungus are almost universally present on dead twigs or dead tissue of citrus in Florida and California. In general, it attacks only twigs, leaves, or fruit that have previously been weakened by unfavorable soil and climatic or nutritional conditions. Since other fungi, such as *Diplodia natalensis*, are often associated with this anthracnose, certain effects are probably produced by a combination of several fungi acting together.

On leaves that are nearly or quite mature, spots occur which at first are light green and later turn brown. In moist weather, dark-colored pustules may show pink spore masses over the surface of the spots. The spots are at margins or tips of leaves or, rarely, near the midribs. On branches of varieties other than limes, anthracnose is characterized by the dying back of mature twigs. The dying back is usually slow, but leaves will occasionally wither and dry up suddenly. Appresoria of the fungus are frequently found associated with a fine spotting and tear-staining of fruit. It is not safe to conclude from the mere presence of Colletotrichum fungus that it is primarily the producer of a given effect. Usually the fungus fails to attack uninjured parts, but enters as a secondary invader after the organ has been injured or killed by some other agency.

Since effective development of anthracnose of this type depends so much on lowered vitality of tree tissues, it is important to maintain the health and vitality of trees. If trees show serious symptoms of anthracnose in the twigs, pruning may be necessary to bring them back to health. Fruit uninjured by sprays and adverse weather conditions, such as cold, ice on the rind surface, hail, and wind-driven rain, apparently resist spotting and tear-staining by this fungus.

Septoria Spot

Spotting of citrus fruits and leaves by *Septoria* spp. has been found in orchards of the Mediterranean basin, South Africa, South America, Australia, India, and California. The fungi are reported to cause considerable damage in Australia by spotting fruit and defoliating lemon trees. In central California orchards, the disease is important in spotting and lowering the grade of lemons, grapefruit, and oranges (fig. 1–31).

Septoria citri Pass., *S. limonum* Pass., and *S. depressa* McAlp. are the species responsible for the disease. *S. citri* is the species commonly found in California's inland citrus orchards. The disease is of small importance in California's coastal plantings.

Symptoms.—The spots on fruit are small depressions or pits 1- to 2-mm in diameter, extending usually no deeper than the flavedo or oil-bearing tissue. Infections begin when the fruit is green and become conspicuous as the fruit turns color. The bottoms of the pits are light tan or buff with a narrow greenish margin which may eventually become reddish-brown as the fruit matures. Some of the larger, dark-brown spots are 4 to 6 mm and even as much as 10 mm in diameter, and are so deeply sunken as to extend into the albedo or white portion of the rind. Small inconspicuous Septoria spots on lemons may spread to form large brown blotches during the storage period, thus ruining the fruit for market. In the 1969 season, such blotching occurred even in orchards in Tulare County, California. Pycnidia may develop in the spots. Usually either the anthracnose fungus (*Colletotrichum gloesporioides*) or *Alternaria citri* Ellis & Pierce is found with the Septoria fungus in these spots. Combination of one or the other of the fungi with Septoria does more injury than does Septoria alone. Both *Colletotrichum* and *Septoria* may cause tear-staining which often accompanies the spotting. The rind damage lowers the grade and necessitates extensive culling.

Rain and dews in late summer, early autumn, or late spring are believed to contribute to infection from spores from pycnidia which form on dead twigs. Sprinkler irrigation, particularly the overhead type, increases the incidence of infection, as do low, rapidly fluctuating temperatures.

Fig. 1–30. Anthracnose disease. Left, anthracnose of lime leaves and fruit. Center, tear staining of lemons. Right, anthracnose spot of oranges.

Control.—In Tulare and Kern Counties, California, where the disease is important year after year on any citrus variety, a spray of 3 pounds of zinc sulfate monohydrate (or 5 pounds of zinc sulfate heptahydrate), 2 pounds of copper sulfate, and 20 pounds of hydrated lime should protect against *Septoria* spotting and brown rot, repel leafhoppers which cause rind oil spotting, and correct or protect against mottle leaf (caused by zinc deficiency) and exanthema (caused by copper deficiency). The middle of October is usually suggested for this application. However, since the leafhoppers may invade the orchard earlier some years, growers should watch for them and spray at the first indication of invasion. Where leafhoppers and mineral nutrient deficiencies are not factors, use the above spray but reduce the lime to 6 pounds per 100 gallons. When new growth develops after the first spray application and does not mature before cold weather, it is subject to cold injury and Septoria spotting. Infected leaves can then serve as a source of infection for fruit later in the season. Under these conditions, another application of 3-2-6-100 formulation should be made, if possible, in early February (Klotz and DeWolfe, 1969).

Black Spot[10]

Black spot is a fungus disease of great importance in South Africa, Australia, Taiwan, and China (Kiely, 1948, 1950; Wager, 1952; Calavan, 1960; McOnie, 1963, 1964; Kotze, 1963). It was first reported in Australia in 1895. The disease has been reported in other countries, but McOnie (1963, 1964) showed that these reports may be misleading due to the latent occurrence in citrus and other hosts of a *Guignardia* sp. which is easily confused with *Guignardia citricarpa* Kiely, the black spot pathogen.

Losses exceeding 80 per cent of the orange crop have been experienced both in Australia, where the disease has been known for 80 years, and in South Africa, where it was first recognized 54 years ago in Natal. Black spot is present but not

[10]This section revised by K. C. McOnie.

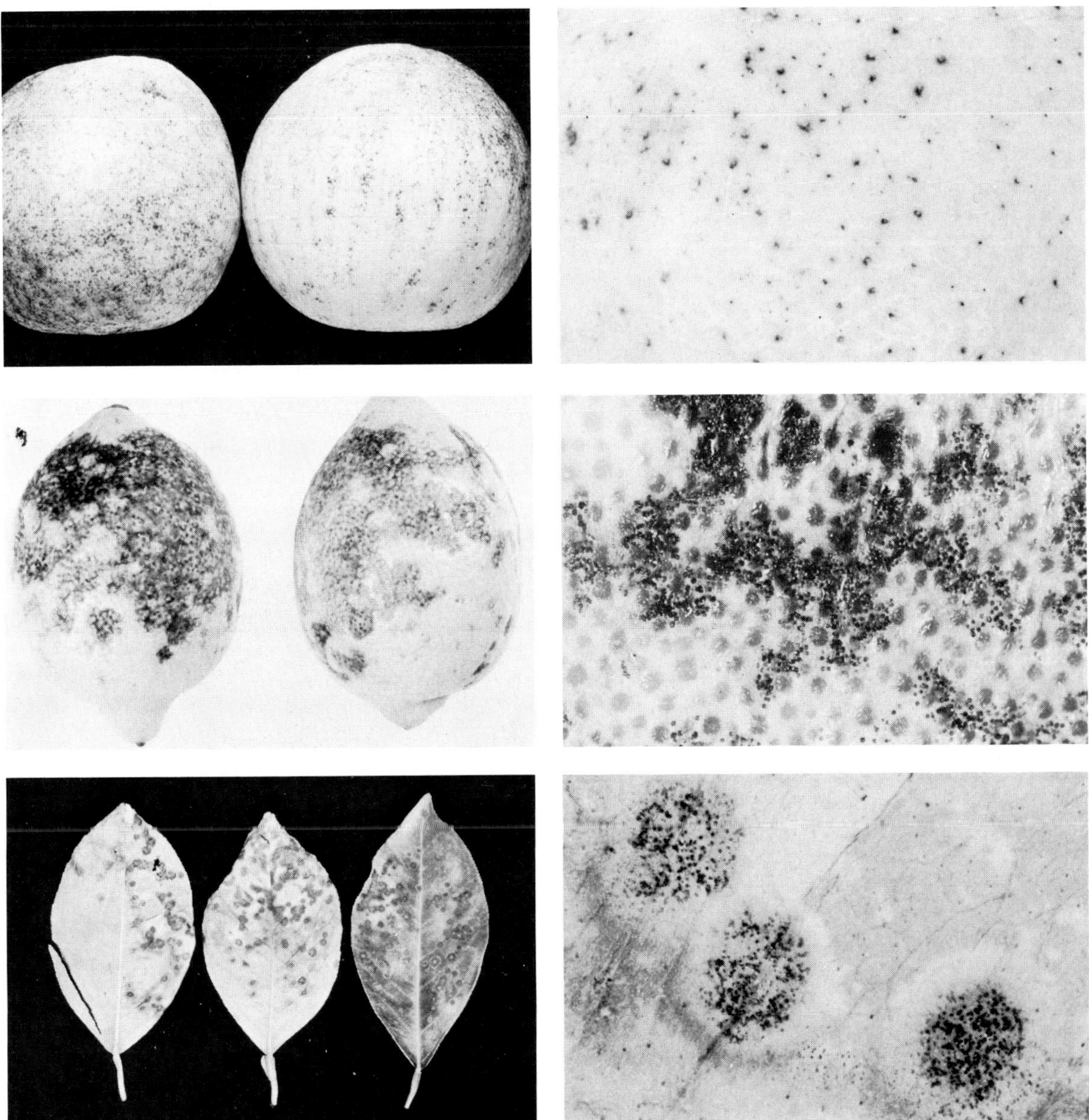

Fig. 1–31. Effects of Septoria fungus on citrus. Top left, tear staining of grapefruit. Top right, damage on Valencia orange. Center left, blotching of lemons during storage. Center right, spots on orange rind show fruiting bodies or pycnidia of causal fungus. Bottom left, damage to orange leaves. Bottom right, leaf spots enlarged (X10) to show pycnidia. (Photomicrographs by T. A. DeWolfe.)

yet serious in Swaziland and Rhodesia. According to Wager (1952): "As black spot has now occurred in so many places with marked climatic differences, there would appear to be no reason why the disease should not eventually appear in most places where citrus is grown." However, due most probably to unfavorable weather conditions in other citrus-growing areas during the period of fruit susceptibility, it has not spread to the extent expected. It has not been reported from citrus orchards of the Mediterranean basin or North America, and reports from Trinidad and South America have not been confirmed.

All commercial varieties of citrus are susceptible, particularly those such as Valencia orange and lemons which mature during warmer temperatures that favor development of symptoms. The disease is most virulent on old, weak trees. Fungus isolates closely resembling *G. citricarpa* have been found on citrus and many other plants including camellia, almond, passion fruit, and rose. McOnie isolated this fungus from fourteen different plants, including citrus, and found that although it could penetrate citrus tissues it did not cause symptoms of black spot.

Symptoms.—There are four types of fruit spots. The "speckled blotch" type may appear on immature fruit if high temperatures prevail about five to six months after blossoming. It resembles melanose superficially in that the lesions are gummy and raised. More common spots are the black-edged "hard spots" which appear on maturing oranges and relatively young lemons; the small, reddish-brown "freckle spots" which develop on mature fruit; and the "virulent spots" which develop on harvested fruit and occasionally on mature fruit on the tree during high temperatures. "Virulent spots" are not delimited and may cover much of the fruit surface. Small, gray spots with dark edges may also occur on leaves. Black, dotlike fruiting bodies (pycnidia) commonly form in various types of lesions (figs. 1–32 and 1–33).

The fungus infects only young tissues and remains dormant until temperatures reach about 70° F. For this reason, symptoms sometimes develop only after harvest, and their sudden appearance during transportation and at the retail store can cause considerable loss.

The fungus responsible for black spot is *Phoma citricarpa* McAlp., the perithecial stage of

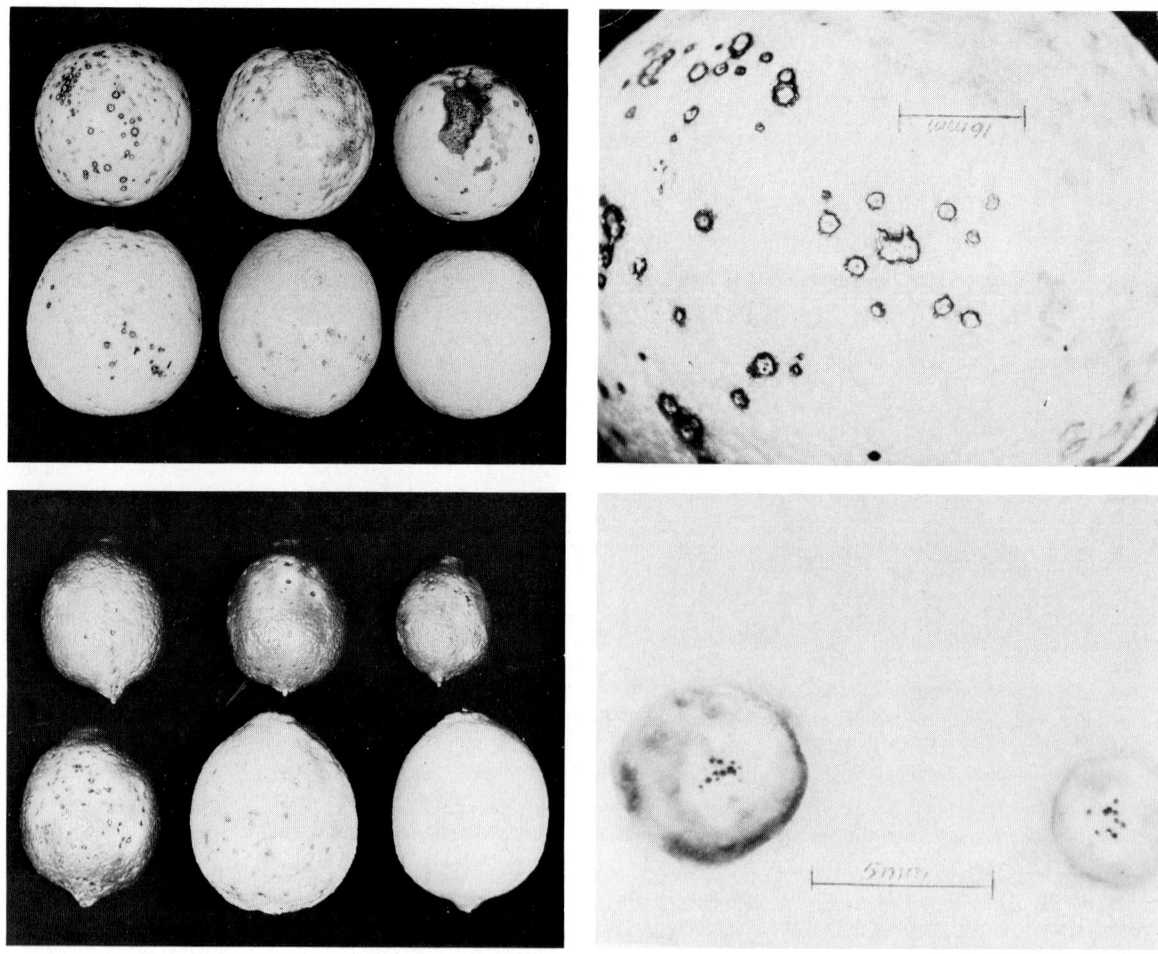

Fig. 1-32. Black spot fungus disease. Top left, lesions on orange. Top right, hard spots and freckle spots on orange. Bottom left, black spot injury to lemons. Bottom right, black spot lesions with pycnidia shown in magnification. (Photos courtesy of Dr. K. C. McOnie.)

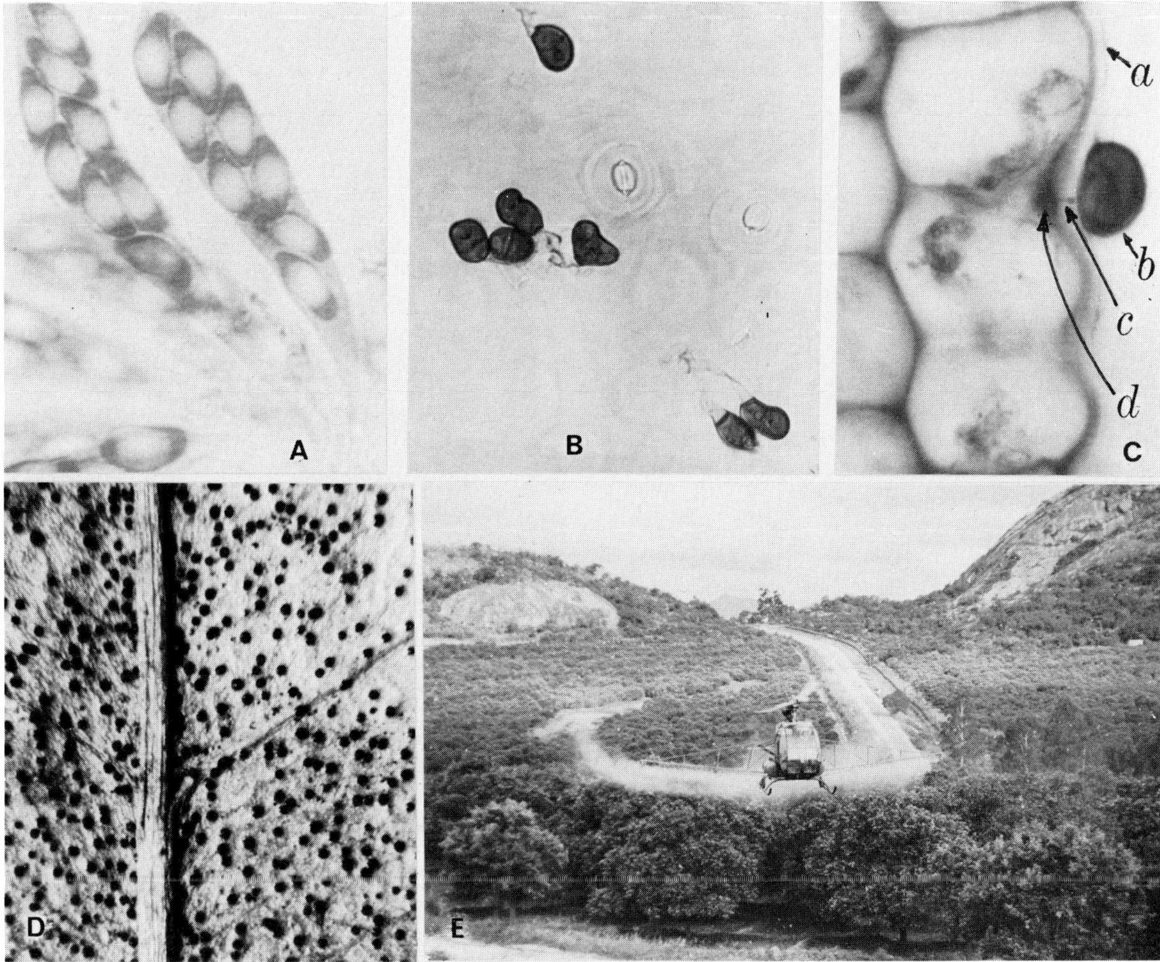

Fig. 1–33. Biology and control of black spot disease. *A*, **sexual fruiting of causal organism,** *Guignardia citricarpa*, **showing asci with mature ascospores.** *B*, **fungus infection structures (appressoria) on leaf surface.** *C*, **section through an appressorium and leaf surface (***a.* **cuticle;** *b.* **appressorium;** *c.* **infection peg; and** *d.* **dormant mycelium of latent infection producing black spot.)** *D*, **symptoms of black spot on leaf surface.** *E*, **helicopter with boom sprayer provides promising method for control of black spot. (Photos by Dr. K. C. McOnie.)**

which is *G. citricarpa* (Kiely, 1950). Pycnidia of the Phoma stage develop on fruit and leaf lesions. As many as 90 per cent of attached leaves in severely infected orchards may have latent infections. Kiely (1948) has shown that, following abscission of leaves with latent infections, alternating wet and dry warm weather favors development of vast numbers of both pycnidia and perithecia. Under such conditions, maturation of perithecia requires six to eight weeks. Mature perithecia contain asci, each with eight ascospores. The ascospores are discharged explosively into the air and distributed by air currents. The sticky pycnidiospores are distributed by rain and possibly by birds and other forms of animal life. The two spore forms cause infection of fruit, leaves, and other plant parts during moist periods when the temperature is favorable (70° F to 90° F). Chiu (1955) considers the pycnidiospores produced on fallen leaves the chief source of infection in Taiwan, but McOnie (1964) has shown that ascospores are the major infective bodies and that spores of the asexual Phoma stage are relatively unimportant in producing spots on citrus fruit. As shown by McOnie, ascospores germinating on fruit or leaf surfaces produce appressoria each of which sends in a fine infection peg through the cuticle. The appressorium expands into a small mass of mycelium between the cuticle and epidermal wall and constitutes the so-called latent infection which later produces the black spot. One to two days of continuously wet weather are necessary for infection.

Control.—The fruit is susceptible to infection for about six months after blossoming, and the duration of protection required depends on the presence of mature ascospores in the orchard during this period. In South Africa, where the spring and early summer are dry, Kotze (1963) and McOnie (1963, 1964) have shown that protection is not required for the first six to eight weeks after blossom. Wet winters and springs in Australia render protection essential from the earliest stage. In Australia, control is achieved with three sprays of 2½-1¾-100 Bordeaux mixture at six- to eight-week intervals. Kiley (1950) has recommended replacing one or more of these sprays with Zineb.† In South Africa, copper is not used, partly because of the danger of toxic accumulations in the soil, but mainly because it blemishes fruit. Control is effected by three or four sprays of Dithane M45 at 28-day intervals.

Citrus Knots, Galls, Witches'-Brooms

Sphaeropsis knot of citrus branches and twigs is not known to occur in orchards of the North American southwest. It is found in Florida, the West Indies, Egypt, Guyana, Peru, Hawaii, and the Dominican Republic (Hedges and Tenny, 1912). As indicated by artificial inoculations, all citrus varieties appear to be susceptible to the causal fungus, *Sphaeropsis tumefaciens* Hedges, but it has been found naturally only on limes and oranges. The disease can damage and even kill trees of all ages.

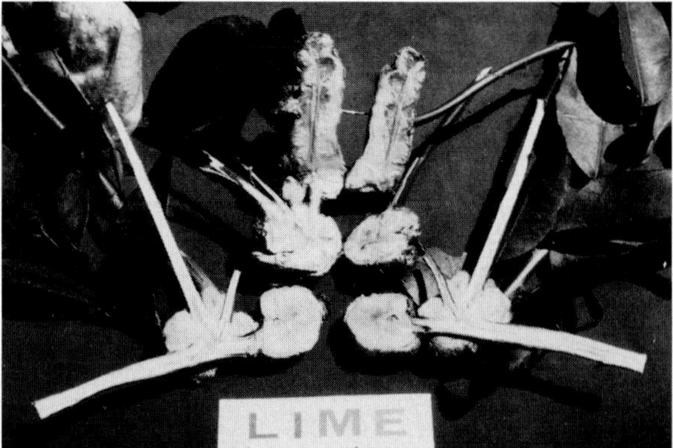

Fig. 1–34. Sphaeropsis knot caused by *S. tumefaciens* on West Indian lime (top) and Rough lemon (bottom). (Photos courtesy of Dr. Carlos H. Blazquez.)

Symptoms.—The woody growths are at first roughly spherical swellings, which have light-colored, normal-appearing bark that later darkens, fissures, and produces a large number of sprouts, giving a "witches'-broom" effect. The knots may attain a diameter of 3 inches and girdle and kill twigs and branches (fig. 1–34).

Although the fungus in artificial culture produces pycnidia and pycnidiospores, these structures have not been found on the knots. However, the fungus will live for several years in citrus tissue and, since it grows well saprophytically, probably is disseminated by pycnidiospores developed in dead tissues.

Control.—An effective means of control is to remove the affected parts several inches beyond the innermost gall, thus removing all invaded tissue.

Galls and witches'-brooms may be caused by agencies other than *S. tumefaciens*. Mutating buds sometimes give rise to structures resembling the effects produced by the fungus. The crown gall bacterium, *Agrobacterium tumefaciens* (E. F. Sm. & Town.) Conn, was found by C. O. Smith (1912) to produce galls on citrus. Woody gall of Rough lemon and *Citrus volkamericana* Ten. & Pasq. is caused by a virus (Wallace and Drake, 1960), vectors of which are the aphids *Myzus persicae* Sulz., *Toxoptera citricidus* (Kirk.), and *Aphis gossypii* Glover.

Parasitic Flowering Plants (Dodders, Mistletoes)

Symptoms.—Various vinelike species of *Cuscuta* and *Cassytha* have been found growing on

†This chemical or chemical formulation is not currently registered with or recommended for usage by the United States Environmental Protection Agency for this particular pest of citrus. Citrus producers in other countries are advised to check their country's regulations for using such treatment methods.

citrus in California, Mexico, Florida, the West Indies, and South America. *Cassytha* is greenish in color and *Cuscuta* is yellow. These dodders entwine around branches and grow so abundantly on twigs that they weaken the tree and retard growth. They can be particularly troublesome in seedbeds and nurseries. Seeds of the parasites germinate in soil, but after seedlings reach the host plant they send out rootlike extensions which penetrate the tree's bark to secure food. Connections of the parasites with the soil then disappear, and thereafter they live at the expense of the tree.

Mistletoes of the genera *Loranthus, Dedropemon,* and *Struthanthus* parasitize citrus trees. They have been reported in orchards of the Far East, South Africa, Mexico, and the West Indies. Apparently they are of no importance in countries with drier climates and cause only small damage where they attack citrus.

Control.—Control of the dodders consists of destroying them before they can spread throughout the tree, removing them from infected trees by pulling and pruning, and destroying the parasites on native plants in the vicinity of the orchard.

The mistletoes may be controlled by pruning out affected branches and eliminating native plant hosts nearby.

Leprosis

Leprosis is also known as "nail-head rust" and "scaly bark" in Florida, and as *"lepra explosiva"* in Argentina and Venezuela. It occurs also in Brazil and Paraguay, and a similar effect is found in the Orient. In Florida, it is severe only on sour oranges and on early and mid-season varieties of sweet oranges. It appears seldom on Valencias, and rarely on grapefruit. In Brazil and Argentina, leaf symptoms may occur on tangerines, lemons, limes, and citrons, as well as on sweet oranges.

The cause of leprosis is still uncertain. However, since pruning out affected parts and treatment with acaricides control the malady, it is now assumed not to be of virus origin; but Knorr (1968) has presented some data contradictory to this. In Argentina, experiments indicate that it may be transferred by means of the mite *Brevipalpus oboratus* Donnadieu. It occurs in Florida in proximity to bodies of water and also close to a species of oak, *Quercus laurifolia,* on which similar twig lesions have been found. Workers there associate the disease with the mite *Brevipalpus californicus* (Banks).

Fig. 1–35. Leprosis. (Photo by Dr. L. C. Knorr.)

The disease develops first as round or oval spots on twigs, leaves, and fruit. On twigs the spots are at first raised above the surface, and are chestnut to auburn in color; later the bark becomes glazed, hard, brittle, and cracked, tending finally to break into scales. When the spots increase in numbers, they may join, forming patches of scaly and scabby bark (fig. 1–35), with an effect resembling psorosis. However, exposing the area by removing the scales reveals a slightly convex surface in leprosis, whereas the area is slightly concave in psorosis. On fruit in Florida, the spots, 5 to 13 mm in diameter, may have a chestnut-brown center with a lemon-yellow halo which fades imperceptibly into the normal green of immature fruit. On leaves the spots resemble those on fruit, becoming brown, sometimes with slightly raised concentric rings and a yellow zone in the form of a halo.

For treatment in Florida, (1) prune out all lesions on the dead and weakened wood; (2) spray with chlorobenzilate[†] (½ pound of 25 per cent

[†]This chemical or chemical formulation is not currently registered with or recommended for usage by the United States Environmental Protection Agency for this particular pest of citrus. Citrus producers in other countries are advised to check their country's regulations for using such treatment methods.

powder in 100 gallons), or with wettable sulfur (10 pounds in 100 gallons or equivalent of lime-sulfur), or 10 ounces of dry DN (dinitro-*o*-cyclohexylphenol) in 100 gallons. In Brazil, spraying with lime-sulfur has been found effective (Knorr and Thompson, 1954).

Mesophyll Collapse

Leaves of sweet orange and grapefruit (Olson and Cooper, 1957) in the orchards of North and South America frequently show one or more dead areas of various sizes throughout the blade. There is a high incidence of the malady in coastal plantings. The surface of a spot on the lower side of the leaf is depressed, leaving veins and veinlets standing out prominently and decreasing the thickness and volume of the affected region. Internally, cells in the tissues of the spots are dead or dying; some dry out and collapse, while others enlarge. The palisade and epidermal tissues are unaffected in the early stages of the malady, but eventually die and dry following the collapse, death, and drying of the spongy mesophyll below. Fruiting bodies (acervuli) of the Colletotrichum fungus are commonly present at the surface of the spots, but have no part in originating the attack (fig. 1–36).

The cause of mesophyll collapse is as yet unexplained (Turrell, Sokoloff, and Klotz, 1943). It has been attributed to red mite injury, water deficiency, and excessive transpiration, but probably starts as physiological or nutritional imbalance. Chemical examination reveals that the ratio of potassium and sodium to calcium and magnesium is much higher in collapsed than in normal tissue, in both the aqueous and solid phases of the leaf. This suggests a relationship of cation-pectate complexes to capacity for water retention. Although potassium and sodium pectates have a greater capacity for hydration, they hold water much less tenaciously than calcium or magnesium pectate, which are normal cell constituents.

Twig Dieback

Failure of the twig terminals to secure sufficient moisture to maintain their life processes is an important cause of a twig dieback not directly due to parasitic microorganisms (Klotz *et al.*, 1962).

Symptoms.—Two types of dieback have been observed. In one type, leaves of seemingly healthy twigs die and dry up in place. Associated with this form is the appearance of gum in the wood. In the other type, gum is not evident and leaves drop before either leaves or twigs are completely dry. Large branches, even whole sections of the tree, are affected and the injury is much more serious than that caused by the first type. Factors responsible for twig dieback, resulting from failure of twigs to obtain enough water, are: soil temperatures below 55° F which retard growth and regeneration of roots and their efficiency in taking up water; inadequate root system due to injury by cultivation, excess fertilization, overwatering, and attack by fungi and insects; failure to maintain adequate soil moisture; and low humidity associated with drying winds and sunshine.

While nonparasitic factors are primary causes of these types of twig dieback, fungi and bacteria appear to extend the damage in injured twigs. Fungi, including the genera *Colletotrichum, Alternaria, Stemphylium, Coniothecium, Fusarium, Hormodendrum, Diplodia, Phomopsis, Chaetomella*, and twenty species of bacteria, have been isolated from dieback twigs. None, however, was found capable of initiating the trouble when placed in sound twigs. Moreover, many orchard spray trials with fungicides failed to show that such treatments reduced the incidence of the trouble. In fact, there was some evidence that sprays sometimes increased the incidence of dieback.

Control.—Suggestions for control or partial control of the trouble are: (1) pretreatment of tree sites with soil disinfestants to destroy fungi, nematodes, and insects parasitic on roots, enabling young trees to make an initial rapid growth and become well established with abundant roots; (2) careful or no cultivation so as not to remove roots; (3) adequate but not excessive application of fertilizer and water; and (4) withholding spray materials when plants need water, i.e., just before an irrigation or when foliage is losing water rapidly during or immediately following dry north winds or excessively hot, dry days. One of the most important orchard operations in minimizing twig dieback and resultant tree decline is to maintain an optimum content of water in the soil. This may be best accomplished by using tensiometers to supply representative readings of soil moisture at two depths throughout the orchard, and then irrigating when they indicate the necessity in order to avoid injurious deficiency of soil moisture.

June Drop of Fruitlets

The so-called 'June drop' of fruitlets is excessive when high temperature, low humidity, drying winds, and slow intake of water by roots in cold soil occur at time of setting and subsequent growth of fruit. Ability of leaves and fruit to obtain soil water fast enough to keep pace with resulting rapid transpiration can be further reduced by root injury due to over-watering, excessive chemical fertilization, infection by microorganisms (principally *Phytophthora* spp.), or nematodes.

Premature Fruit Drop

Premature fruit drop is also in part attributable to abscission induced by fungal infection of the weakened bloom and fruitlets. Species of fungi, principally including species of *Alternaria*, *Colletotrichum*, *Botrytis* (see pp. 18, 41, and 32), and severe stem-end-rotting fungi, have been isolated from the small fruit. In Belize, formerly British Honduras, the trouble, associated with an abnormal persistence of the "buttons" (floral discs with pedicils) after the fruitlets have dropped, is said to be caused by infection of floral parts by *Colletotrichum gloeosporioides* (Fagan, 1971, 1972; Reuther, 1969). C. H. Phelps isolated species of *Colletotrichum*, *Pestalotia*, *Fusarium*, and *Curvularia* (Reuther, 1969).

Spray trials by Fagan (1971, 1972) indicated that two applications of 0.2 ounce of Benlate† with 1.0 ounce of Difolatan† per gallon—the first when less than 15 per cent of blooms were at opening stage, and the second two weeks later—doubled fruit set and yield of oranges and grapefruit. Although the use of plant growth regulators suggested a promising means for increasing fruit set, investigations have thus far yielded little success (Coggins and Hield, 1968).

Fruit-Stem Dieback

Fruit-stem dieback starts near the button and extends from a few inches to as much as 3 feet up the stem. It occurs throughout California citrus orchards, mainly affecting oranges and grapefruit (Klotz and Stewart, 1948). As with June drop, the trouble is initiated during periods of water stress when dehydration of carbohydrates in the fruit stem produces gums which clog the water-conducting tracheae (Bartholomew, 1937).

Isolations from the affected fruit stems were species of *Colletotrichum*, *Alternaria*, *Diplodia*, *Phomopsis*, *Macrosporium*, and *Chaetomella*. These fungi probably play an important secondary role following the initial physiological injury.

Control consists in supplying an adequate amount of water to the root system and in spraying the trees with 2,4-dichlorophenoxyacetic acid (2,4-D). This plant growth regulator has been found to reduce mature fruit drop by delaying maturation of the abscission layer. Table 1-4 shows the effect of 2,4-D in reducing losses from fruit-stem dieback.

Water Spot of Navel Oranges

Water spot of navel oranges causes important losses in eastern Los Angeles and western San Bernardino counties of California in seasons when several days of continuously rainy weather occur during the period from January to April. Losses have also occurred in western Riverside County during very wet seasons. Water spot has also been observed as early as November (Klotz *et al.*, 1949; Klotz, 1973). Navel oranges grown in the first two mentioned areas, due to undefined factors, are particularly susceptible to this form of physiological breakdown. Orchards in this region are the only ones where the trouble is of outstanding commercial importance. It has not been reported in other countries growing navels. However, navel oranges from other areas do show similar injury when exposed to prolonged wetting, as in an experimental rain chamber. Water spot also develops in fresh wounds in Valencias, tangerines, grapefruit, and lemons. Kumquats, even in the absence of wounds, are very susceptible to the breakdown.

Symptoms.—Water spot is a nonparasitic breakdown of the rind of citrus fruits. The significant factor in its origin is the absorption of external water. The spongelike structure of the peel, together with the water-attracting properties of its cells, are important in development of the malady (fig. 1–37).

Water enters peel through places of structural weakness such as growth cracks at the navel end and fresh wounds. If wounds callous and heal

†This chemical or chemical formulation is not currently registered with or recommended for usage by the United States Environmental Protection Agency for this particular pest of citrus. Citrus producers in other countries are advised to check their country's regulations for using such treatment methods.

Fig. 1–36. Environmental disorders. Left, mesophyll collapse occurring when leaves cannot obtain enough water to keep tissues supplied. Center, windburn of leaves. Right, fruit injury caused by wind.

Table 1-4
EFFECT OF 2,4-D SPRAYS ON THE AMOUNT OF FRUIT-STEM DIEBACK

Plot	Spray Treatment	No. of Trees	Total No. of Fruit Stems Observed	Percentage of Fruit Stems With Die-Back	Percentage Reduction of Die-Back As a Result of 2,4-D Spray
Valencia oranges, I	Checks, not sprayed	12	973	38.9	
Sprayed 5-26-47	8 ppm* 2,4-D in water	12	1083	6.5	83.3
Observed 8-7-47	16 ppm 2,4-D in water	12	944	7.8	80.0
Valencia oranges, II	Checks, not sprayed	10	1072	7.7	
Sprayed 5-26-47					
Observed 8-7-47	8 ppm 2,4-D in water	10	1135	1.4	81.9
Valencia oranges, III	Checks, not sprayed	9	910	21.3	
Sprayed 10-15-46	5 ppm 2,4-D in water	7	640	10.9	49.0
Observed 8-7-47	25 ppm 2,4-D in water	7	768	15.4	18.0
Thomson navel oranges, IV	Checks, not sprayed	1	84	87.0	
Sprayed 2-28-47	Oil spray only†	1	72	87.0	
Observed 5-20-47	Oil spray + 10 ppm 2,4-D	1	73	8.0	90.8
Grapefruit, V	Checks, not sprayed	10	1023	29.8	
Sprayed 6-6-47					
Observed 7-21-47	8 ppm 2,4-D in water	10	1077	2.6	91.6

*Ppm = parts per million.
†Light medium 1⅔ per cent oil.

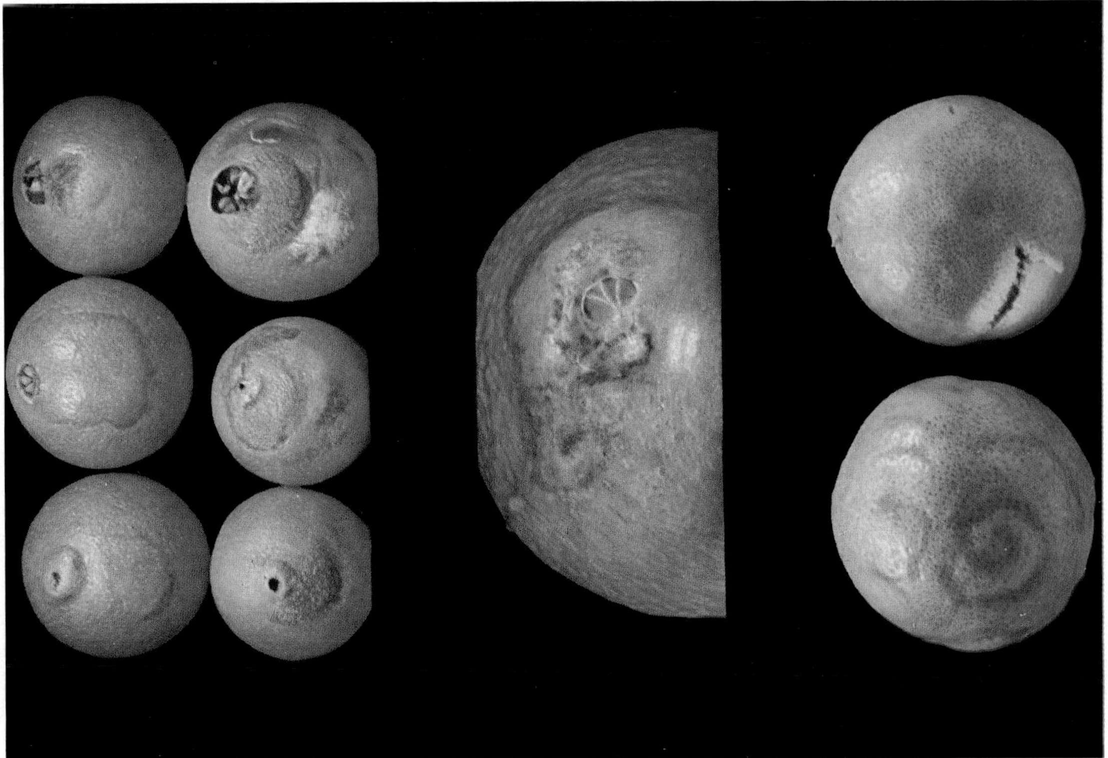

Fig. 1–37. Water spot and creasing and puffing of citrus fruits. Left and center, water spot, a nonparasitic breakdown of rind caused primarily by imbibition of external water by the albedo. Right, creasing and puffing, believed to result from the effects of climatic or soil conditions on fruit held for a long time on the tree after maturity.

before rain comes, they do not increase water spot (Klotz and Basinger, 1938). Rainy periods accompanied by winds are disastrous because mechanical injuries suffered by fruit provide entrances for water. However, wind following rains, particularly north winds and accompanying low humidity, dry off the fruit and check development of water spot. Many oranges thus become marketable if the spot has not progressed beyond the initial stages before drying. Rind injury by frost and hail also increases susceptibility to water spot. The rind of orange is naturally weak because cell division continues during maturation and new thin-walled cells are always present. These are zones of weakness in the rind where injury may occur and water may enter. The extension of the rind by cell division apparently does not keep pace with the increase in volume of the fruit as it matures during rainy periods. The absorption of water increases the volume of a fruit beyond the elasticity of the rind, thus causing minute cracks through which water enters very rapidly and, in turn, causes larger water-soaked areas with small but easily visible cracks.

Important secondary factors in the ultimate breakdown of the fruit are the freeing inside the orange of the toxic natural oil of the rind, accompanied by brown discolorations of affected areas and decay by blue and green molds.

The incidence of water spot is not correlated with density of oil glands, the amount of rind oil, or concentration of stomata in the orange rind. This is in agreement with anatomical research and observations that growth weaknesses and cracks and fresh mechanical and chemical injuries are the most efficient avenues for absorption of external water.

Water spot was first recognized as a problem in 1927, following the commercial advent in 1925 of petroleum oil sprays. These spray materials apparently so modify the rind of fruit as to increase water absorption through its surface. There is also evidence that the rind of oil-sprayed oranges is more easily injured mechanically than that of fumigated or untreated fruit.

While anatomical studies thus far have failed to show structural differences between oil-sprayed and untreated fruit, the former has been found to absorb rain water more readily than the latter. Chemical analyses have revealed differences between oil-sprayed and unsprayed or fumigated oranges. Chemical differences have also been found between oranges from the waterspot area and those from unaffected areas.

Plants grown under conditions of low light intensity, high humidity, or generous water supplies are known generally to develop a succulent or more tender growth than plants grown under more drastic conditions, such as high light intensity, low humidity, and limited water supplies. Other factors which tend to produce a more tender plant are those which accelerate plant growth, such as high nitrogen supplies and favorable soil conditions. Hardening of the plant may be brought about by exposing it occasionally to drying conditions involving all or a few of the above factors. These factors may play a part in the severity of water spot in the region where it is most acute.

Control.—Investigations seeking a control for water spot have been directed largely toward finding effective substitutes for oil spray insecticides. Although fumigation with HCN does not increase water spot incidence, the treatment is ineffective against the resistant insects of the water spot-affected, citrus-growing areas. Parathion has shown promise (Riehl and Carman, 1953). Also the possibility of delaying fruit maturity and modifying rind structure with plant-growth regulators to make it resistant to water spot has been indicated by experiments with 2,4-D (Stewart, Klotz, and Hield, 1951) and gibberellin (Riehl, Coggins, and Carman, 1965; Coggins and Hield, 1968). Where feasible, the crop could be harvested and marketed early before fruit is advanced in maturity and more susceptible to the trouble. Where heavy losses have been experienced repeatedly, trees could be topworked to Valencia or other varieties not affected. Since high nitrogen fertilization makes fruit somewhat more susceptible, care may be taken not to supply more than adequate amounts of this nutrient. The humidifying effects of dense cover crops can be reduced by mowing or eliminated by clean cultivation or oil spray control of weeds.

Creasing of Orange Fruit

Irregular grooves extending in several directions over the surface of orange fruit were formerly called creasing and puffing (fig. 1–36). The word "puffing" is now used to describe fruit with thick, loosely textured rinds. Creasing results from separations in the albedo and sinking of the overlying flavedo. The imperfection is thought to result from conditions of climate and soil modifying the physiology of over-mature fruit. Periods of dryness with slowing of growth in summer, followed by moister weather or wide fluctuations of soil moisture appear to emphasize creasing in some years. Jones *et al.* (1967) have found incidence of the disorder correlated with phosphate content of leaves; that is, creasing augmented as the phosphate content rose from a deficiency to adequacy, but still larger concentrations of phosphate were not accompanied by more creasing. Their ten years of observation on fruit from selected orange trees also suggest the possible influence of genetic factors on the variation in incidence of creasing (see chap. 2, vol. II).

Endoxerosis

Endoxerosis of lemons, also called internal decline, yellow tip, dry tip, and blossom end decline, is often confused with *Alternaria* rot, which frequently accompanies or follows it (Bartholomew, 1937). In California, it first appears about May or June, reaches maximum development in the dry summer, and extends into early autumn.

Symptoms.—Internal tissues back of the stylar end break down, dry, and become pinkish or brownish in color (fig. 1–38). Gum commonly forms in the core and either in or next to the rind. Green fruits lose luster and frequently, but not invariably, develop a yellow color in a circular area surrounding the stylar end. The cut fruit shows the gummy pinkish to brownish mass of partially dried and collapsed tissue. Gumming may even extend into the twig bearing the affected fruit. When the fruit turns yellow, the malady is more difficult to detect without cutting. However, affected fruits usually float with the stylar end upward in the washing and treating tanks (see chap. 2, vol. II).

Control.—The cause is believed to be related to water and the physiological conditions within the tree and fruit, and temperature conditions in the air and soil influencing transpiration and water stress. It is suggested, therefore, that water conditions in the soil be kept as favorable for tree health as possible by the guidance of tensiometers. Pick fruits regularly and before they become over-mature.

Peteca

Peteca is a deep pitting or sinking of the surface of lemon rind, usually sometime after the

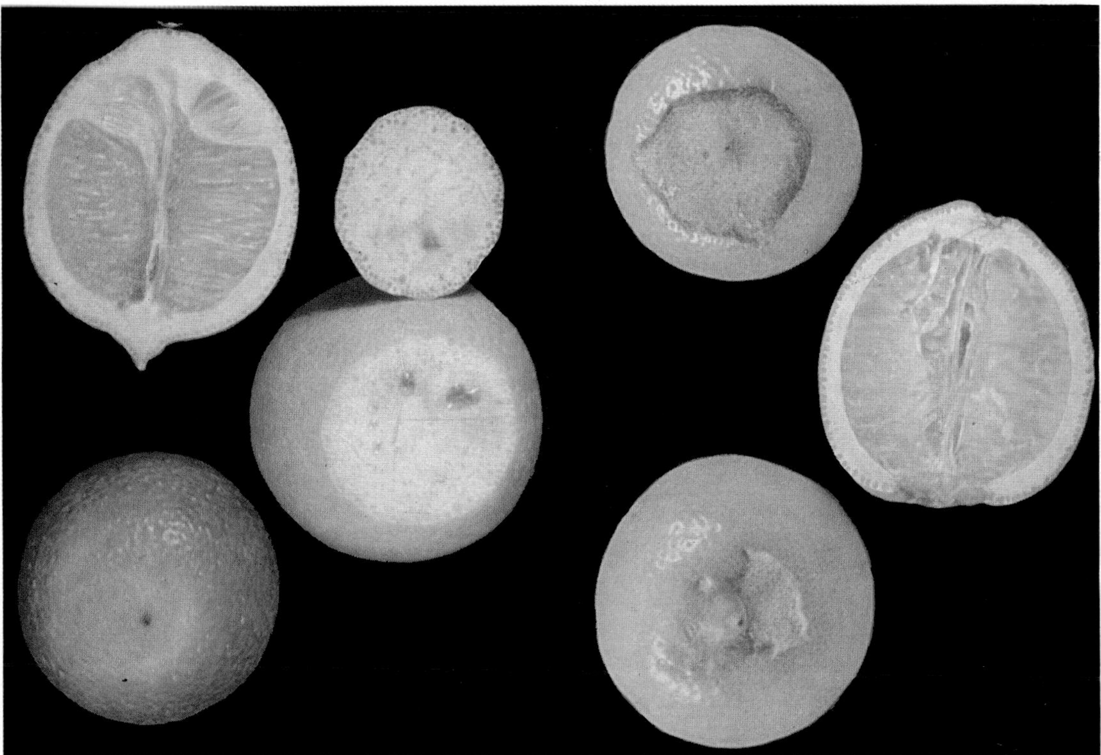

Fig. 1–38. Endoxerosis or "internal decline" of lemon fruits (left) and stylar-end rot (right), a breakdown most commonly found on Persian limes.

fruit is picked (fig. 1–39). It may appear before picking, especially following a heavy oil spray. Cells under the pits are dry and shrunken, first light, then dark in color. At first, the outer oil-bearing flavedo appears normal over the shrunken interior, but later it dries and collapses, providing an entrance for secondary organisms. Late stages of peteca resemble early stages of black pit (fig. 1–20) except that the latter always shows a surface injury through which black pit bacteria entered. No primary organism appears to be associated with peteca. It is favored by low temperatures, heavy applications of oils or wax, and forced curing. Since effects approximating peteca have been obtained by injections of the rind with small amounts of orange and lemon oils, geraniol, and methyl or ethyl alcohols, some direct product of the rind itself or some product of anaerobic respiration is suggested as a possible cause (Klotz, 1973).

Khalidy, Jamali, and Bolkan (1969) suggested from their chemical analyses that peteca results from an "accumulation and tying up" of calcium in the peel in the form of calcium oxalate and other unavailable calcium compounds.

Membranous Stain

While membranous stain (fig. 1–39) of lemon fruit has been assumed to develop in storage, it may possibly be initiated in the orchard by long continued temperatures below 55° F. The trouble appears as brown to black areas on the membranes or carpellary walls, but the central core may also become stained. Although there are no external symptoms, peteca, red blotch, or albedo browning of the rind frequently accompany membranous stain because they are favored by the same conditions. Control consists of avoiding storage temperatures below 55° F and providing adequate ventilation (Klotz, 1973).

Red Blotch

Red blotch (fig. 1–40) is an external staining of lemon fruit, suggestive of a scald. It develops only after the fruit is picked and starts as a superficial, reddish-brown discoloration on lemons in storage that were picked while somewhat immature, particularly during cold weather. It appears to be aggravated by forced curing with ethylene

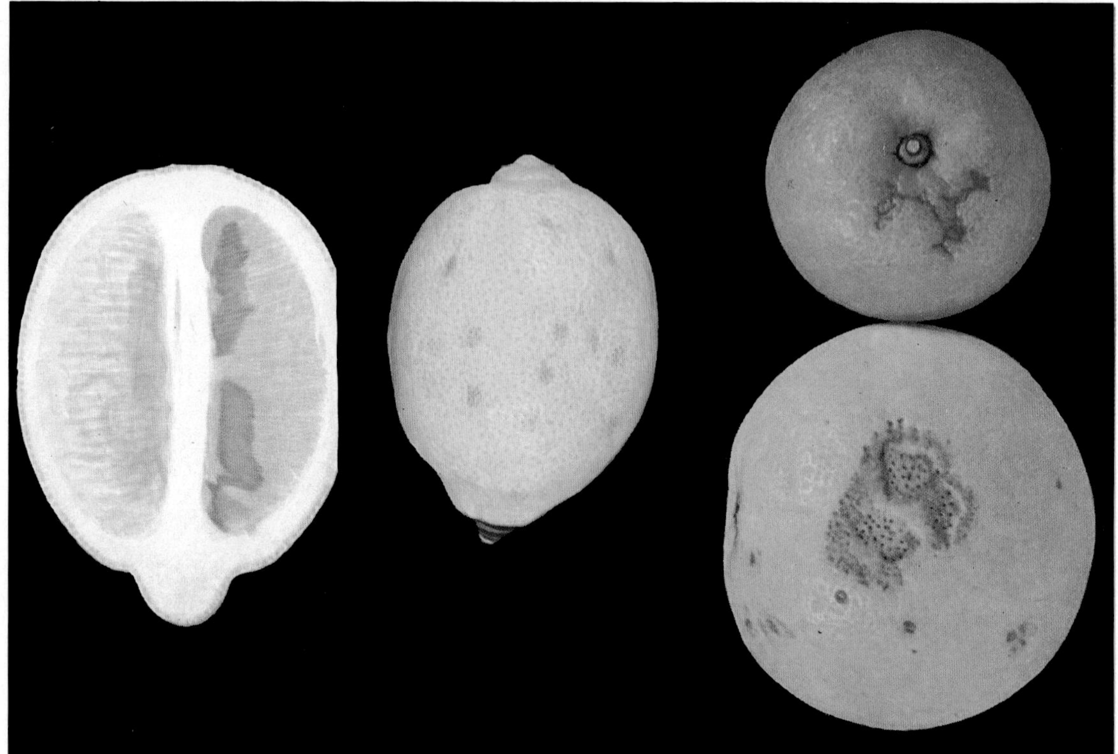

Fig. 1-39. Left, membranous stain. Center, peteca. Right, storage spot.

gas and by lack of ventilation in storage. It is thought to be due to some products of respiration, such as the alkyl esters. Similar effects have been produced experimentally by touching lemon fruit with several different esters, among them ethyl acetate. Lemons from certain groves are especially susceptible to red blotch or peteca, suggesting possible hereditary or transmissible weakness of the rind (Klotz, 1973).

Albedo Browning

Albedo browning (fig. 1–40) is a discoloration of the white, spongy portion of the peel or albedo of lemon fruit. It tends to develop on fruit in storage at too low temperatures and with poor ventilation, especially in fruit that has been stored while very dark green and immature. Forced curing seems to favor its development. Like red blotch, albedo browning seems to have a connection with abnormal respiration (Klotz, 1973).

Stylar-End Rot

Stylar-end rot is a common breakdown of Persian limes, but occasionally affects other limes and lemons. Depressed areas, which are firm or leathery and fairly dry, start as a water-soaked, whitish-to-drab, sunken patch at the base of the stylar tip and progress to involve one-quarter to one-half of the fruit. Internally, fruits resemble those affected by endoxerosis, showing dry collapsed tissue (fig. 1-38).

Although no means of prevention is known, some loss may be avoided by picking fruits before they become too mature. The malady may occur even in climates with high humidity if tree roots absorb insufficient water. Control of soil fungi and nematodes which attack fibrous roots and maintenance of as near optimum soil-moisture conditions as possible will help reduce incidence of the trouble. Stylar-end rot has been observed in California after periods of extremely high temperatures and has been induced experimentally by exposing fruits to 105° F for periods totaling 18 hours (Klotz, 1973).

Granulation and Drying

Granulation, erroneously called "crystallization," and often referred to as "dry end," most severely affects fruit picked late in the season (Bartholomew, Sinclair, and Turrell, 1941). While Valencia oranges are most frequently affected, other oranges, grapefruit, and tangerine varieties are also subject to the malady to a lesser extent.

Granulation starts while fruit is on the tree

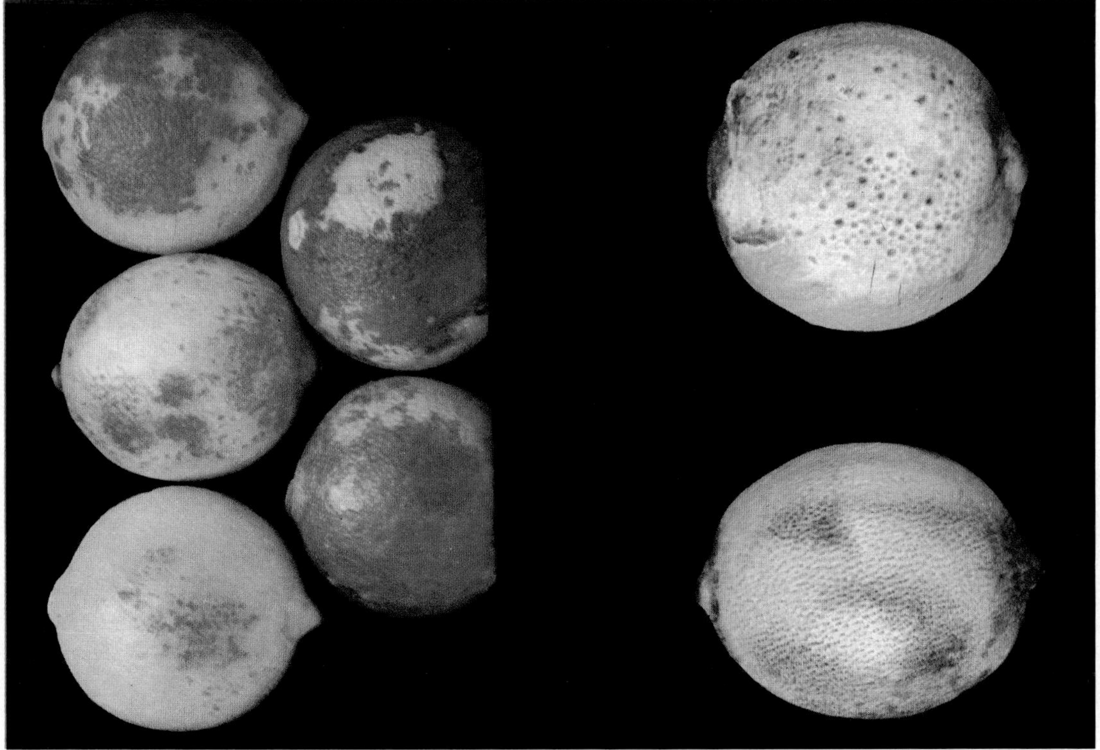

Fig. 1–40. Left, red blotch. Right, albedo browning. Both diseases appear to be connected with abnormal respiration.

and may increase rapidly during the storage (MacRill, 1940). Separation of cells in the juice sacs allows air to enter, giving the sacs a whitish appearance. Thickening and stiffening of the walls of the sacs make them hard and firm. While affected vesicles seem dry they, anomalously, have a higher water content than normal vesicles. Large and rapidly growing fruits show a greater tendency to granulation than smaller, slower growing fruits. Fruits from trees on Rough lemon and trifoliate rootstock also show a higher incidence of the trouble than those from trees on other rootstocks. Drying and collapse of juice vesicles (fig. 1–41) may accompany granulation. Early picking may avoid some loss from granulation (see also chap. 2, vol. II).

Valencia Rind Spot

Valencia rind spot develops on mature fruits in late summer or autumn if rains and high humidity occur. In California, it is found in coastal sections (Klotz, Stewart, and Baumgardner, 1947).

At first the spots are slightly sunken with little discoloration, but they later darken to shades of brown. Individual spots seem to originate from slight injuries or even from collapse of a single oil gland without any apparent mechanical injury. Later, *Colletotrichum* or *Alternaria* fungi enter the spots and start decay (fig. 1–41).

Early harvesting of the crop to avoid overmaturity will prevent excessive loss from this rind breakdown; no other practical preventive measure is presently known.

Rind Breakdown of Navel Oranges

Damage to the rind of maturing navel oranges may result from rain accompanied or closely followed by cold weather (Klotz, Coggins, and DeWolfe, 1966; Klotz, 1973). The temperature need not be low enough to freeze the pulp of fruit. Air temperatures may even be somewhat above 32° F, while a lower temperature at the fruit surface, produced by radiation to the sky, is causing injury.

Symptoms.—There may be liberation of rind oil internally and externally during exposure of water-suffused tissues, together with collapse of epidermal cells without even visible breakdown of oil glands. This results in brownish-yellow to dark-brown stains (fig. 1–41). The fungus, *Colletotrichum gloeosporioides*, can usually be found on the surface of the injuries. It is a secondary, not a primary cause of the damage.

Fig. 1–41. Three physiological disorders of fruit. Left, drying and granulation. Center, Valencia rind spot. Right, rind breakdown of navels.

Control.—The loss from rind damage and fruit drop was greatest from old, weak navel trees, apparently somewhat less from old trees that had been sprayed with 2,4-D, and still less on young trees. Damage was rare on young navels sprayed with 2,4-D. The injury could be found occasionally on Valencia fruit, but their immaturity at this time of year would seem to preclude the probability of important loss in this variety (Hield, Burns, and Coggins, 1964).

Unlike navels produced in Los Angeles, San Bernardino, and Riverside counties, fruit in Ventura County, California, is resistant to typical water spot (Riehl, Coggins, and Carman, 1965). However, it was possible to reproduce typical rind breakdown of some navels collected in Fillmore, California, in 1966, by exposing them to artificial rain followed by temperatures of 34° F to 40° F. This type of rind breakdown is not like typical water spot. Imitations of the injury have also been produced at low temperatures and high humidities by injections and external applications of orange-rind oil.

Since the important factors in the development of this type of rind injury are stage of maturity and water content of the fruit and the sequence of weather conditions, some measures can be taken to reduce loss. Bringing trees and fruit to a more cold-resistant condition by extending the period between irrigations during late fall and early winter months, and prompt and adequate protection against low temperatures will decrease loss from this and other types of rind injuries. The incidence of rind staining on fruit made injury-prone by weather conditions or other agencies may be further reduced by allowing fruit to dry slightly and using soft brushes during packinghouse processing.

Turrell, Orlando, and Austin (1964) discuss factors responsible for rind disorders of citrus fruits. For further details, see also Coggins and Eaks (1964), and Eaks and Jones (1959).

Rind Stipple of Grapefruit

Symptoms.—For many years, a pitting type of injury to the rind surface of grapefruit (Klotz *et al.*, 1968) has been ascribed to various factors, such as psorosis virus, spray burn, smog, and low temperatures accompanied by ice formation. The pattern of injury consists of small individual necrotic pits which coalesce in some areas to form larger pits (fig. 1–42). If injury takes place when fruit is green, each pit is later surrounded by a green halo which persists for a time after the fruit has acquired the yellow color of maturity. The injury differs from that occasionally caused by psorosis virus in that the latter, while showing a tendency to ring formation, is not made up of individual pits but of depressed continuous rings which later become brown and necrotic. Ice formation on the fruit surface and the other factors mentioned are apparently not necessary to the formation of rind stipple.

As yet, the blemish has not been reproduced experimentally. Observations on the time of its initiation and place of occurrence on the tree and fruit suggest a relationship to cold weather. It is oftener found on the colder north than on the warmer south side of the tree and on the area of fruit exposed to radiation to the sky. Despite lack of experimental data, the following theory about the cause seems most plausible at present.

To be susceptible, fruit must be tender and highly turgid as a result of a recent rain or irrigation, high humidity, and an overcast sky. With rapid clearing and radiation to cold sky, exposed fruit surfaces lose heat faster than they gain heat from the fruit interior. When the temperature reaches 4° C (39.2° F), water in the cell sap of the fruit rind is at maximum density and the rind epidermis has shrunken to maximum density (minimum size). Since there is no correspondingly rapid contraction of cells below the epidermis, the resulting pressure could be sufficient to cause extrusion through the stomata of some cell contents which are injurious to the rind surface.

Several factors appear to account for the concentric ring formation of the injury, which is generally (but not always) present. With dew droplets present (that is, with the dew point near 39° F), rind oil or other toxic materials of low surface tension may be taken up by the dew droplets, which spread to a film as a result of a lowering of their surface tension by the exudate. As the film slowly dries, the toxic material in it becomes more concentrated and injurious. During drying, the margin of film retreats, forming a series of fronts or concentric rings, the more rapid drying having occurred during the day and the slower during the night. The highest concentration of solute is at the film fronts. Not infrequently, the retreating film with its concentrating toxic material finally reaches a small circular necrotic area representing the center of a series of concentric necrotic rings.

Fig. 1–42. Rind stipple of grapefruit. Top, concentric rind stipple on fruit in orchard. Center, enlargement of a single set of rings. Bottom, a stoma with affected guard cells and affected surrounding auxiliary cells. (Photos by T. A. DeWolfe.)

Control.—Shading of exposed fruit and sprays of Triumph oil-lime sulfur apparently reduce the tendency of fruit to develop the injury. Because it causes fruit and leaf drop and burn under adverse weather conditions, Triumph oil-lime sulfur is seldom used now. The results of its use in this investigation, however, suggest that

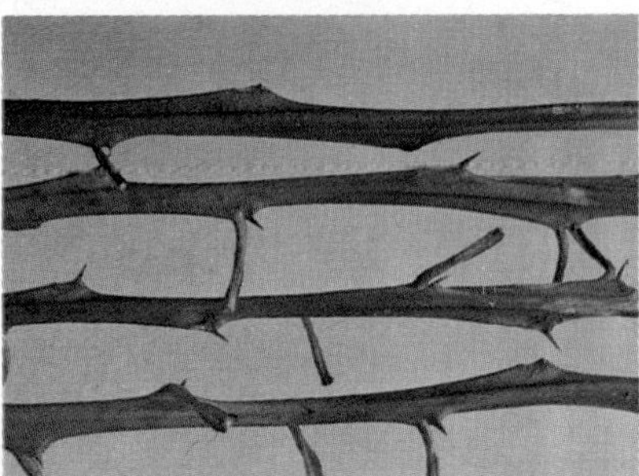

Fig. 1–43. Lightning injury to citrus. Left, sweet orange on sour orange rootstock injured by lightning. Center, green petiole bases on lightning-injured citrus. Right, damage to crown of tree caused by lightning. (Photos by J. F. L. Childs.)

materials that toughen the rind or neutralize a toxic exudate should be further investigated.

Gum Spot of Citrus Leaves

Brown spots of various sizes, impregnated with a hardened, gumlike material, appear on leaves after a slight frost followed by bright sunshine. Other factors suspected in their origin are deficiency or excess of various chemicals, cyanide fumigation, and some spray materials, but the agencies responsible and their mode of action have not been defined. The injury has not been attributed to microorganisms.

Lightning Injury

Citrus orchards in central Florida occasionally are severely damaged by lightning (Stevens, 1918; Waldron, 1923; DuCharme, 1973).

Symptoms.—Bark of twigs and young branches show greenish-yellow to yellow, glazed blotches of various shapes and sizes measuring from 6 to 100 mm in length (fig. 1–43). Later, as healing starts, the blotches become elevated, turn yellowish-brown in color, and finally break into longitudinal strips and peel off, leaving a roughened, brown scar. Thorns and leaf nodes generally do not show this effect. Although injuries are usually confined to surface layers of bark, thus permitting a renewal of bark from below the damaged surface, bark may be killed through to the wood. Several fungi, including species of *Phomopsis, Botrytis, Diplodia, Colletotrichum,* and *Alternaria,* may enter injuries and extend the damage. On striking a tree, lightning may kill a strip of bark extending to the roots. The tree is sometimes girdled at the crown where the charge passes into the soil.

Control.—Injured twigs should be pruned out and cuts disinfected. Badly injured trees should be removed. If bark is less than half destroyed at the base of the tree, injured areas should be excised, disinfected with a safe Carbolineum, and covered with thick paint or Tree Seal.

Hail and Snail Injury

While losses by downgrading of citrus fruits damaged by hailstones are infrequent in California, losses from this cause can be substantial when they occur, as in the 1968-69 season. The type of blemish caused by hail is distinguishable from similar blemishes caused by snails, slugs, and other agents (fig. 1–44). The injuries provide entrance for decay fungi, including *Penicillium* spp., *Septoria citri, Colletotrichum gloeosporioides,* and others. Losses of fruit and injury to foliage due to snails have been significant, particularly in coastal counties of California. Control measures consist of poisoning the pests with a bait of 3 per cent metaldehyde and 5 per cent calcium arsenate in bran (98 per cent), or an application of tartar emetic (2 pounds per 100 gallons) plus granulated sugar (4 pounds per 100 gallons)[11] (Lewis and LaFollette, 1941).

Damage to Leaves and Fruit by Copper Sprays

Certain citrus areas have been severely damaged by copper sprays (Klotz, Calavan, and

[11]Minimum waiting period before picking fruit is 30 days.

Fig. 1-44. Injuries caused to citrus fruits by hail (left) and snails (right).

DeWolfe, 1956). When very severe, the symptoms consist of large necrotic areas on fruit and extensive defoliation (fig. 1-45). Ordinarily, injuries are small necroses or pits which start in stomatal openings on the underside of leaves. These may burn through and show on the upper leaf surface. Partial defoliation is also the usual result.

Bordeaux and other copper sprays can cause damage in at least three ways: (1) releasing an excess of soluble copper; (2) increasing transpiration, thus causing wilting and leaf drop; and (3) lowering temperature of the tissues and increasing frost damage. Toxic amounts of copper in soils (especially in light, sandy soils) may result from spraying trees with copper fungicides and nutritional sprays (Reuther and Smith, 1954).

Dull, cool, overcast weather lessens photosynthetic activity and results in an accumulation and increased solubility of carbon dioxide; this dissolved gas causes an increase in soluble copper. Moisture from dew and fog forming on sprayed leaves and not running off promotes injury because dissolved copper remains in contact with plant surfaces, concentrates, and then becomes more corrosive as the water evaporates. Sugars in honeydew as a result of the activities of aphids and scale insects can bring copper into solution. Also, ammonia readily dissolves copper from the sprays. Considerable quantities of ammonia are lost to the air during fertilization with liquid ammonia and may contact spray deposits. Air pollution may also play an important part, since smog and sulfur oxides liberate copper ions from the sprays and also increase cell permeability. Fresh, mechanical injuries to fruit from high spray pressures and gritty material in spray and from wind and ice formation on fruit rind are darkened and made conspicuous by the presence of copper sprays.

Sprays to avoid or minimize injuries from copper are discussed on page 38.

Injury by Sulfur Fungicides-Insecticides

Figure 1-46 shows half-grown lemon leaves which have been injured by 1½ per cent lime sulfur and have become folded and distorted by subsequent growth. The very small or "feather-like" leaves—because they were not out at time of application—are apparently unaffected. Those one-fourth grown or slightly smaller have also burned at the edge, abscised, and dropped.

Fig. 1–45. Pitting of leaves and fruit by copper sprays. A portion of a pitted leaf is magnified in the inset.

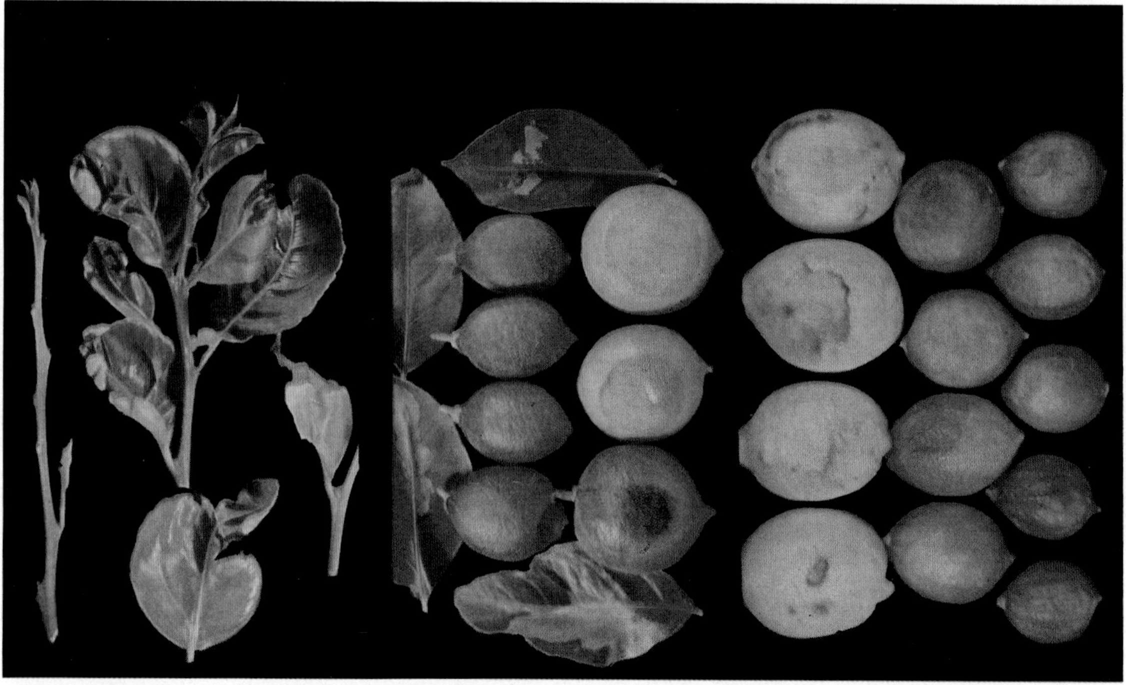

Fig. 1–46. Injuries caused by fungicides and insecticides containing sulfur and sulfur compounds. Left, leaf injury caused by lime sulfur. Center, fruit and leaf injury resulting from use of sulfur or DN dust. Right, fruit injuries caused by ammonium polysulfide.

The center panel shows typical sulfur burn on lemon fruits and leaves. The effect on oranges is similar. Wettable sulfur as a spray or some form applied as a dust followed by hot weather with slight or no air movement are important factors responsible for this serious type of injury (Turrell and Boyce, 1953). Very similar effects are produeced by DN dust (dinitro-*o*-cyclohexylphenol) under similar conditions.

The right hand panel shows injury of lemon fruits by ammonium polysulfide spray. Although necrotic areas vary somewhat in appearance from those due to injury by sulfur, it is believed that similar factors operate in both types of injuries.

Injury by Plant Growth Regulators

Proper use of chemicals that influence plant growth can result in spectacular benefits, but their use without proper precautions can cause disastrous injury to citrus trees (Coggins and Lewis, 1965; Coggins and Hield, 1968; Calavan, Dewolfe, and Klotz, 1956; Coggins *et al.*, 1965). The injury observed has been largely confined to trees under six years old, but bark of older trees can also be injured by concentrated solutions of herbicides used in weed control. Accidental applications of overly strong solutions of 2,4-D (2,4-dichlorophenoxyacetic acid) to branches have caused injury high in the trees. Also, it is best to assume that excessive amounts of herbicides reaching roots through the soil can damage the root system of any citrus tree regardless of age.

Over 5,000 young trees in southern California are known to have been ruined by 2,4-D. The most serious damage to young trees (fig. 1–47*A*, *B*) has followed application of 2,4-D herbicide sprays

Fig. 1–47. Effects of plant-growth regulators. Types of damage to roots of young citrus trees after application of 2,4-D sprays on sandy soils irrigated by sprinklers are shown in *A* and *B*. Typical symptoms of leaf curling after foliar applications of 2,4-D are shown in *C* and *D*. Among benefits achieved by careful use of plant-growth regulators are control of fruit and leaf drop and fruit-stem dieback (shown in *E*).

in orchards on sandy soils irrigated by sprinklers. Less severe damage resulted from a foliar application of the chemical for controlling leaf and fruit drop.

Symptoms.—The typical symptom of leaf curling is shown in figure 1–47 *C, D*. This can result either from direct spray application or absorption through roots. While trunk-bark injury superficially resembles brown rot gummosis, the affected bark is tan in color, has a soft, cheesy texture, and is somewhat puffed. It is usually at or below ground level, but may extend as much as two feet above ground where young trunks are covered by protectors which delay volatilization of the chemical.

Among benefits achieved by careful use of plant-growth regulators are control of fruit and leaf drop, fruit-stem dieback (fig. 1–47, *E*) (Klotz and Stewart, 1948), and Alternaria decay of oranges and stored lemons (DeWolfe, Erickson, and Branaman, 1959); increase in fruit size, delay of granulation; reduction of incidence of water spot, splitting, and black rot of navel oranges; and control of broad-leaved weeds. Hield and Erickson (1962) detailed dosages, methods of application, and precautions necessary to attain these remarkably beneficial results.

Control.—For control of fruit-stem dieback of Valencia oranges, apply 8 ppm of 2,4-D in water during May; for navels, the same concentration of 2,4-D in February; and for grapefruit, 8 ppm of 2,4-D in June.

A partial control of splitting and black rot (Alternaria rot) of oranges has been obtained by spraying with solutions of 12 to 24 ppm of 2,4-D when the fruit size range is 10 to 20 mm in diameter; higher concentrations are used for larger fruits.

To inhibit development of black buttons and Alternaria decay of lemons and prolong their storage life, include 500 ppm of 2,4-D in water-wax emulsion, applied as the last packinghouse treatment before storage.

To repeat several precautions already implied above, irrigation, particularly the sprinkler type, should be withheld as long as practicable after application of 2,4-D. The materials are more likely to damage trees on light than on heavy soils. Even dilute formulations of growth-regulating compounds should not be applied to trees under six years of age nor to trees recently topworked.

Concentrated herbicide solutions must be kept from direct contact with any part of the tree. All equipment connected with application of weed-killing concentrations of 2,4-D, including tanks, pumps, buckets, hoses, and guns should be used only for this purpose, not for foliar sprays. Spray-rigs used for foliar sprays of 2,4-D should not be used for application of any kind of spray materials to 2,4-D-sensitive crops such as cotton and grapes. When a spray application is completed, 2,4-D residues in the equipment should be reduced by several rinses with water and by allowing water from a final rinse to stand in the spray tank and hoses for several hours (Hield and Erickson, 1962).

LITERATURE CITED

ALDERTON, G. E. 1884. Treatise and handbook of orange culture in Auckland, New Zealand. Wellington, New Zealand, 76 pp.

BACH, W. J. 1929. Cotton root rot. Texas Agr. Expt. Sta. Ann. Rept. **42**:147–48.

———. 1931. Cotton root rot on Citrus. Texas Citriculture **8**(4):10.

BAINES, R., L. J. KLOTZ, T. A. DEWOLFE, and R. H. SMALL. 1962. Chemicals for control of citrus soil pests. Calif. Citrog. **47**(10):342, 359.

BARTHOLOMEW, E. T. 1937. Endoxerosis, or internal decline of lemon fruits. Univ. Calif. Agr. Expt. Sta. Bul. **605**:1–42.

BARTHOLOMEW, E. T., W. B. SINCLAIR, and F. M. TURRELL. 1941. Granulation of Valencia oranges. Univ. Calif. Agr. Expt. Sta. Bul. **647**:1–63.

BATES, G. R. 1939. Recent developments in the processing of Rhodesian oranges. Rhodesia Sci. Assoc. Proc. **37**:29–35.

BLISS, D. E. 1944. Controlling Armillaria root rot in citrus. Univ. Calif. Citrus Expt. Sta. Pap., 7 pp.

BONDAR, G. 1929. Insectos damninhos a molestias de laranjeira no Brasil. Imprensa Off. do Estado, Bahia, Brazil, 79 pp.

BRESADOLA, G. 1925. New species of fungi. Mycologia **17**:68–77.

BRIEN, R. M. 1931*a*. Pathogenicity of the bark-blotch organism. N. Zealand Jour. Agr. **43**:341–47.

———. 1931*b*. Dormancy period of the citrus bark-blotch organism. N. Zealand Jour. Agr. **43**:421.

BROADBENT, PATRICIA. 1969. Observations on the mode of infection of *Phytophthora citrophthora* in resistant and susceptible citrus roots. *In:* Chapman, H. D. (ed.). Proc. First Intern. Citrus Symp. **3**:1207–10. Univ. of Calif. Riverside, Calif.

BUGIANI, A., P. SCRIVANI, and N. LOPRIENO. 1959. Indagini sul parassitismo da *Deuterophoma tracheiphila* Petri. Montecatini Instituto di Ricerche Agr. Bul. 1959: 1–24.

CALAVAN, E. C. 1960. Black spot of citrus. Calif. Citrog. **46**:4, 18, 20–24.

———. 1961. Ferment gum disease (Rio Grande gummosis) of grapefruit. Calif. Citrog. **46**:231-32.

CALAVAN, E. C., and D. W. CHRISTIANSEN. 1958. Production of ferment gum disease in Marsh grapefruit trees by fungus inoculation. (Abstr.) Phytopathology **48**:391.

CALAVAN, E. C., T. A. DEWOLFE, and L. J. KLOTZ. 1956. Severe damage to young trees from 2,4-D. Citrus Leaves **36**(1): 8–9, 24.

CALAVAN, E. C., T. A. DEWOLFE, C. N. ROISTACHER, J. B. CARPENTER, and D. HALSEY. 1962–63. Unpublished data on file in the Dept. of Plant Pathology, University of California, Riverside.

CALAVAN, E. C., T. A. DEWOLFE, L. G. WEATHERS, L. J. KLOTZ, and D. W. CHRISTIANSEN. 1955. Treatment for the control of brown rot of citrus fruits. Citrus Leaves **35**(11):8–9.

CALAVAN, E. C., and J. M. WALLACE. 1954. *Hendersonula toruloidea* Nattrass on citrus in California. Phytopathology **44**:635–39.

CALAVAN, E. C., E. L. WAMPLER, J. R. SUFFICOOL, and H. W. ORMSBY. 1952. Gray mold infections. Citrus Leaves **32**(4):10–11.

CARPENTER, J. B., L. J. KLOTZ, T. A. DEWOLFE, and M. P. MILLER. 1959. Collapse of young citrus trees in Coachella Valley. Calif. Citrog. **45**(1):4, 19–21.

CATARA, A., M. TODARO, and G. SCARAMUZZI. 1971. Decorso del "mal secco" e comportamento di *Phoma tracheiphila* su estratti agrizzati in rapporto alle variazioni del contenuto fenolico in semenzali di arancio amaro affetti da "variegatura infettiva." Rev. Patologia Vegetale VII (Serie IV): 227–38.

CHAPMAN, H. O., and S. M. BROWN. 1942. Some fungal infections of Citrus in relation to nutrition. Soil Sci. **54**:303–12.

CHAPOT, H., and V. L. DELUCCHI. 1964. Maladies, troubles et ravageurs des agrumes au Maroc. Inst. Nat'l. de la Recherche Agronomique, Rabat, 339 pp.

CHILDS, J. F. L. 1953. An actinomycete associated with gummosis disease of grapefruit trees. Phytopathology **43**:101–03.

———. 1954. Observations on citrus blight. Proc. Fla. State Hort. Soc. **64**:33–37.

CHILDS, J. F. L., and T. C. CARLYSLE. 1974. Some scanning electron microscope aspects of blight disease of Citrus. Plant Dis. Reptr. **58**:1051–56.

CHIU, R. J. 1955. Studies on black spot of citrus. Jour. of Agr. and For. [Taiwan] **9**:1–18.

CICCARONE, A. 1957. *Elsinoe australis* Bitancourt and Jenkins agente di una 'scabbia' degli agrumi in Sicilia. Riv. Agrum. **2**(1–2):31–36.

COGGINS, C. W., Jr., and I. L. EAKS. 1964. Rind staining and other rind disorders of navel orange reduced by gibberellin. Calif. Citrog. **50**(2):47.

COGGINS, C. W., and H. Z. HIELD. 1968. Plant Growth Regulators. *In:* Reuther, W., L. D. Batchelor, and H. J. Webber (eds.). The citrus industry II: 371–89. Revised edition. Univ. Calif. Div. Agr. Sci., Berkeley.

COGGINS, C. W., Jr., H. Z. HIELD, I. L. EAKS, L. N. LEWIS, and R. M. BURNS. 1965. Gibberellin research on citrus. Calif. Citrog. **50**:457.

COGGINS, C. W., Jr., and L. N. LEWIS. 1965. Some physical properties of the navel orange rind as related to ripening and to gibberellic acid treatments. Proc. Amer. Soc. Hort. Sci. **86**:272–79.

COIT, E. 1916. Citrus blast, a new disease in California. Univ. Calif. Jour. Agr. **3**:234–35.

CUNNINGHAM, G. H. 1921. Bark blotch, *Ascochyta corticola* McAlp., a disease of lemon trees. N. Zealand Fruit Grow. **4**:134–35.

DEL ROSARIO, M. S. E. 1968. A handbook of citrus diseases in the Philippines. Univ. of Philippines Coll. Agr. Tech. Bul., 33 pp.

DEWOLFE, T. A., E. C. CALAVAN, and J. R. SUFFICOOL. 1954. *Pythium aphanidermatum*, the causal agent of damping-off in some citrus seed beds. Plant Dis. Reptr. **38**:632–33.

DEWOLFE, T. A., L. C. ERICKSON, and B. L. BRANNAMAN. 1959. Retardation of Alternaria rot in stored lemons with 2,4-D. Proc. Amer. Soc. Hort. Sci. **74**:367–71.

DEWOLFE, T. A., H. C. MEITH, A. O. PAULUS, F. SHIBUYA, L. J. KLOTZ, R. B. JETER, and M. J. GARBER. 1966. Control of citrus blast in northern California. Calif. Agr. **20**(8):12–13.

DOIDGE, E. M. 1917. A bacterial spot of citrus. Ann. Appl. Biol. **3**:53–80.

DONK, M. A. 1956. Notes on resupinate Hymenomycetes. II. The tulasnelloid fungi. Reinwardtia **3**:363–79.

DUCHARME, E. P. 1973. Lightning—A predator of citrus trees in Florida. Proc. Ann. Tall Timbers Fire Ecology Conf. 1973: 483–96.

DURBIN, R. D. 1959. The possible relationship between *Aspergillus flavus* and albinism in citrus. Plant Dis. Reptr. **43**(8):922–23.

EAKS, I. L., and W. W. JONES. 1959. Rind staining and breakdown. Calif. Citrog. **44**(12):390, 400, 402.

FAGAN, H. J. 1971. Premature fruit drop of citrus in British Honduras. Univ. West Indies Citrus Res. Bul. 18, 8 pp.

———. 1972. Control of premature fruit drop of citrus in British Honduras by aerial and ground spraying. Univ. West Indies Citrus Res. Bul. 20, 11 pp.

FAWCETT, H. S. 1936. Citrus diseases and their control. Sec. edition. McGraw-Hill Book Co., New York and London, 656 pp.

FAWCETT, H. S., and A. A. BITANCOURT. 1940. Observaciones sobre las enfermadades de los citrus en el Uruguay. Assoc. Ingen. Agron. Rev. **12**(3):3–8.

FAWCETT, H. S., and O. F. BURGER. 1911. A gum-inducing Diplodia of peach and orange. Mycologia **3**:151-53.

FAWCETT, H. S., W. T. HORNE, and A. F. CAMP. 1923. Citrus blast and black pit. Calif. Agr. Expt. Sta. Tech. Pap. **5**:1–24.

FAWCETT, H. S., and L. J. KLOTZ. 1948. Citrus diseases and their control. *In:* Batchelor, L. D., and H. J. Webber (eds.). The citrus industry. II: 495–596. Univ. Calif. Press, Berkeley and Los Angeles.

FAWCETT, H. S., and H. A. LEE. 1926. Citrus diseases and their control. McGraw-Hill Book Co., New York and London, 582 pp.

FISHER, F. E. 1961. Greasy spot and tar spot of citrus in Florida. Phytopathology **51**:297–303.

———. 1966. Tar spot of citrus and its chemical control in Florida. Plant Dis. Reptr. **50**:357–59.

———. 1970. Gloeosporium rot of citrus fruit in Florida. Plant Dis. Reptr. **54**:173–75.

GARNSEY, S. M., and R. H. YOUNG. 1975. Water flow rates and starch reserves in roots from citrus trees affected by blight and tristeza. Proc. Fla. State Hort. Soc. **88**:79-84.

GODFREY, G. H. 1946. Infectious wood necrosis and gummosis of citrus. Proc. Lower Rio Grande Val. Citrus Inst. **1**:66–70.

GRANITI, A. 1955. Morfologio di *Deuterophoma tracheiphila* Petri e considerazioni sul genere *Deuterophoma* Petri. Bol. Accad. Gioenia Sci. Nat. Catania **3**(3):1–18.

HARA, K. 1917. Small, brown round spot disease. Mycologia **9**:367–68.

HAWTHORNE, B. T., and P. H. TSAO. 1970. Effects of separation of spores from the chain and of culture age on germination of chlamydospores of *Thielaviopsis basicola*. Phytopathology **60**:891–95.

HEDGES, FLORENCE, and L. S. TENNY. 1912. A knot of citrus trees caused by *Sphaeropsis tumefaciens*. U. S. Dept.

Agr. Bur. Pl. Ind. Bul. 249, 74 pp.

HIELD, H. Z., R. M. BURNS, and C. W. COGGINS, JR. 1964. Preharvest use of 2,4-D on citrus. Calif. Agr. Expt. Sta. Circ. 528, 10 pp.

HIELD, H. Z., and L. C. ERICKSON. 1962. Plant growth regulator use on Citrus. Calif. Citrog. **47**:308, 331–34.

HODGSON, R. W. 1917. Citrus blast—a new bacterial disease. Calif. Comm. Hort. Mo. Bul. **6**:229–33.

HOLDAWAY, B. F., and P. H. TSAO. 1971. Survival of *Phytophthora parasitica* in soils. Phytopathology **61**:1321.

———. 1972. Longevity of chlamydospores of *Phytophthora parasitica* in water. Plant Dis. Reptr. **56**:971–73.

HOPKINS, J. C. F. 1933*a*. *Rhizoctonia lamellifera* Small: A distinct species of *Rhizoctonia bataticola* group of fungi. Rhodesia Sci. Assoc. Proc. **32**: 65–69.

———. 1933*b*. A list of plant diseases occurring in Southern Rhodesia. Suppl. 3. Rhodesia Agr. Dept. Bul. **896**, 4 pp.

JEPPSON, L. R. 1951. Studies on the cause and development of ridges on lime fruit. Hilgardia **21**:105–12.

JONES, W. W., T. W. EMBLETON, M. J. GARBER, and C. B. CREE. 1967. Creasing of orange fruit. Hilgardia **38**:231–44.

KHALIDY, R., A. JAMALI, and H. BOLKAN. 1969. Causes of the peteca disease of lemons as occurring in Lebanon. *In:* Chapman, H. D. (ed.) Proc. First Intern. Citrus Symp. **3**:1253–61. Univ. of Calif. Riverside, Calif.

KIELY, T. B. 1948. Preliminary studies on *Guignardia citricarpa* Kiely: The ascigerous stage of *Phoma citricarpa* and its relation to black spot of citrus. Proc. Linn. Soc. N. S. Wales **73**:249–92.

———. 1950. Control and epiphytology of black spot of citrus. N. S. Wales Dept. Agr. Sci. Bul. 71, 88 pp.

KLOTZ, L. J. 1956. Mal secco disease of citrus. Calif. State Dept. Agr. Bul. **45**:234–37.

———. 1973. Color handbook of citrus diseases. Fourth edition. Univ. Calif., Div. Agr. Sci., Berkeley, 122 pp.

KLOTZ, L. J., and A. J. BASINGER. 1938. The influence of various types of rind injury on the incidence of water spot of navel oranges. Calif. Dept. Agr. Bul. **27**:232, 241.

KLOTZ, L. J., W. P. BITTERS, T. A. DEWOLFE, and M. J. GARBER. 1967. Orchard test of citrus rootstocks for resistance to Phytophthora. Calif. Citrog. **53**:38, 55.

KLOTZ, L. J., A. M. BOYCE, H. D. CHAPMAN, G. E. CARMAN, C. CREE, W. W. JONES, W. B. SINCLAIR, E. R. PARKER, W. S. STEWART, and F. M. TURRELL. 1949. Water spot of navel oranges. Studies of the problem to 1948. Calif. Agr. Expt. Sta. Prog. Rept., 6 pp.

KLOTZ, L. J., and E. C. CALAVAN. 1969. Gum diseases of citrus in California. Second revision. Calif. Agr. Expt. Sta. Circ. 396, 26 pp.

KLOTZ, L. J., E. C. CALAVAN, and T. A. DEWOLFE. 1956. Leaf drop and copper damage to citrus. Citrus Leaves **36**(3):6–7, 26.

KLOTZ, L. J., E. C. CALAVAN, A. O. PAULUS, and T. A. DEWOLFE. 1974. Control of field diseases of Citrus. *In:* 1974-1975 Treatment Guide for California Citrus Crops. III. Plant Diseases: 46–49.

KLOTZ, L. J., E. C. CALAVAN, and G. A. ZENTMYER. 1946. The effect of Botrytis rot on lemons. Calif. Citrog. **31**:247, 262.

KLOTZ, L. J., C. W. COGGINS, Jr., and T. A. DEWOLFE. 1966. Rind breakdown of navel oranges. Calif. Citrog. **51**:174, 196.

KLOTZ, L. J., and T. A. DEWOLFE. 1969. Septoria spot of ctirus. Citrograph **54**:530–31.

KLOTZ, L. J., T. A. DEWOLFE, and R. C. BAINES. 1969. Resistance of trifoliate orange stocks to gummosis. Citrograph **54**:259–60.

KLOTZ, L. J., T. A. DEWOLFE, and P. R. DESJARDINS. 1955. Bacterial blast and black pit of citrus. Citrus Leaves **35**(1):10.

KLOTZ, L. J., T. A. DEWOLFE, L. C. ERICKSON, L. B. BRANNAMAN, and M. J. GARBER. 1962. Twig dieback of citrus trees. Calif. Citrog. **47**:74, 86–88, 90–91.

KLOTZ, L. J., T. A. DEWOLFE, and M. P. MILLER. 1967. Dry root rot may be confused with brown rot gummosis. Calif. Citrog. **52**:222–25.

———. 1969. Control of Phytophthora problems. Citrograph **54**:228, 279.

KLOTZ, L. J., T. A. DEWOLFE, D. A. NEWCOMB, and R. G. PLATT. 1966. Control of damping off of citrus seedlings. Calif. Citrog. **51**:314, 322, 324.

KLOTZ, L. J., T. A. DEWOLFE, C. N. ROISTACHER, E. M. NAUER, and J. B. CARPENTER. 1960. Heat treatments to destroy fungi in infected citrus seeds. Calif. Citrog. **46**:63–64.

KLOTZ, L. J., T. A. DEWOLFE, D. O. ROSEDALE, and M. J. GARBER. 1960. Disinfestation of some planting sites improves growth of navel orange trees on Troyer citrange rootstock. Plant Dis. Reptr. **44**:309–11.

KLOTZ, L. J., T. A. DEWOLFE, F. M. TURRELL, R. G. PLATT, and M. P. MILLER. 1968. Concentric ring stipple of grapefruit. Calif. Citrog. **53**:154–56.

KLOTZ, L. J., S. J. RICHARDS, and T. A. DEWOLFE. 1967. Irrigation effects on root rot of young citrus. Calif. Citrog. **52**:91.

KLOTZ, L. J., and W. S. STEWART. 1948. Fruit stem dieback. Calif. Agr. **2**(9):7.

KLOTZ, L. J., W. S. STEWART, and R. J. BAUMGARDNER. 1947. Rindspot and drop of Valencia oranges. Calif. Citrog. **33**:36–7.

KLOTZ, L. J., L. H. STOLZY, and T. A. DEWOLFE. 1962. A method for determining the oxygen requirement of fungi in liquid media. Plant Dis. Reptr. **46**:606–08.

———. 1963. Oxygen requirements of three root-rotting fungi in a liquid medium. Phytopathology **53**:302–05.

KLOTZ, L. J., PO-PING WONG, and T. A. DEWOLFE. 1959. Citrus irrigation water survey. Calif. Agr. **13**(11):3, 16.

KNORR, L. C. 1956. Serious diseases of citrus foreign to Florida. Fla. Dept. Agr. Bul. 5, 59 pp.

———. 1968. Studies on the etiology of leprosis in citrus. *In:* Childs, J. F. L. (ed.) Proc. 4th Conf. Intern. Organ. Citrus Virol. pp. 332–41. Univ. Fla. Press, Gainesville, Fla.

———. 1973. Citrus diseases and disorders. Univ. Fla. Press, Gainesville, Fla. 163 pp.

KNORR, L. C., R. F. SUIT, and E. P. DUCHARME. 1957. Handbook of citrus diseases in Florida. Univ. Fla. Agr. Expt. Sta. Bul. **587**, 157 pp.

KNORR, L. C., and W. L. THOMPSON. 1954. Spraying trials for control of Florida scaly bark. Plant Dis. Reptr. **38**:143–46.

KOEHLER, B., and C. M. WOODWORTH. 1938. Corn-seedling virescence caused by *Aspergillus flavus* and *A. tamarii.* Phytopathology **28**:811–23.

KOLBEZEN, M. J., D. E. MUNNECKE, W. D. WILBUR, L. H. STOLZY, F. J. ABU-EL-HAJ, and T. E. SZUSZKIEWICZ. 1974. Factors that affect deep penetration of field soils by methyl bromide. Hilgardia **42**:465–92.

KOTZE, J. M. 1963. Studies on the black spot disease of citrus caused by *Guignardia citricarpa* with particular reference to its epiphytology and control at Letaba. D. Sc.

Thesis, Univ. of Pretoria, Union of South Africa, 148 pp.

LEE, H. A. 1917. A new bacterial citrus disease. Jour. Agr. Res. **9**:1–8.

———. 1923. California scaly bark and bark rot of citrus trees in the Philippines. Philip. Agr. Rev. **16**:219–25.

LEE, H. A., and H. S. YATES. 1919. Pink disease of citrus. Philip. Jour. Sci. **14**:657–73.

LEWIS, H. C., and J. R. LAFOLLETTE. 1941. Snail control in orchards. Calif. Citrog. **26**:117, 132.

LITTAUER, F. 1947. Control of Diplodia stem-end rot and molds in Shamouti oranges with nitrogen trichloride process. Palestine Jour. Bot. [Rehovot] **6**:205–18.

LOEST, F. C. 1950. Orchard practices in relation to "collar rot" of citrus. Farming So. Africa **25**:331–33, 340

MCALPINE, D. 1899. Fungus disease of citrus trees in Australia and their treatment. Gov. Printer, Melbourne, 132 pp.

MCONIE, K. C. 1963. Annual report of the research pathologist for the year ended 31st December, 1962. So. African Cooperative Citrus Exchange, Ltd., Pretoria. No. C233/1963.

———. 1964. Speckled blotch of citrus induced by the citrus black spot pathogen, *Guignardia citricarpa*. Phytopathology **54**:1488–89,

MACRILL, J. R. 1940. Progress of granulation of Valencia oranges after picking. Calif. Citrog. **25**:386.

MARTIN, J. P., L. J. KLOTZ, T. A. DEWOLFE, and J. O. ERVIN. 1956. Influence of some common soil fungi on growth of citrus seedlings. Soil Sci. **81**(4):259–67.

MORTENSEN, E. 1947. Citrus tree decline in the Winter Garden area. Proc. Lower Rio Grande Val. Citrus Veg. Inst. **1947**:84–7.

NATTRASS, R. M. 1933. A new species of *Hendersonula (H. toruloidea)* on deciduous trees in Egypt. Brit. Mycol. Soc. Trans. **18**:189–98.

NOWELL, W. 1917. Rosellinia root diseases in the Lesser Antilles. W. Indian Bul. **16**:31–71.

———. 1923. Diseases of crop-plants in the Lesser Antilles. The West India Committee, London, 383 pp.

OLSON, E. O. 1952. Investigations of citrus rootstock diseases in Texas. Proc. Rio Grande Val. Hort. Inst. **6**:28–34.

OLSON, E. O., and W. C. COOPER. 1957. Mesophyll collapse of grapefruit leaves and defoliation following cold dry north winds in the Rio Grande Valley of Texas. Proc. Rio Grande Val. Hort. Soc. **11**:34–43.

PENZIG, O. 1887. Studi botanici sugli agrumi e sulle piante affini. Tip. Eredi Botta, Roma [Italy] Min. Agr. Indus. Com. Ann. Agr. 116, 590 pp.

PERLBERGER, J., and I. REICHERT. 1938. Experiments on albinism in citrus seedlings. Palestine Agr. Res. Sta. Bul. [Rehovot] 24, 38 pp.

PETRI, L. 1929. Sulla posizione sistemica del fungo parassita delle piante di limone affette da "mal del secco." Bol. R. Staz. Veg. (n.s.) **9**:393–96.

PRATT, R. M. 1958. Florida guide to citrus insects, diseases, and nutritional disorders in color. Univ. Fla. Agr. Expt. Sta., Gainesville, Fla. 181 pp.

QUILICO, A., C. CARDINI, F. PIOZZI, and P. SCRIVANI. 1952. I pigmenti del "Deuterophoma tracheiphila." Accad. Naz. Lincei [Roma] **12**:650-7.

RACKHAM, R. L., W. D. WILBUR, T. E. SZUSZKIEWICZ, and J. HARA. 1968. Armillaria root rot in citrus. Calif. Agr. **22**(1):16–18.

REUTHER, W. 1969. Premature fruit drop. A report on a visit to British Honduras 11–14 Nov. 1968. Univ. of West Indies. St. Augustine, Trinidad. Mimeo Rept., 9 pp.

REUTHER, W., and P. F. SMITH. 1954. Toxic effects of accumulated copper in Florida soils. Proc. Soil Sci. Soc. Fla. **14**:17–24.

RHOADS, A. S., and E. F. DEBUSK. 1931. Diseases of citrus in Florida. Univ. Fla. Agr. Expt. Sta. Bul. 229, 213 pp.

RIDGWAY, R. 1912. Color standards and color nomenclature. The Author, Washington, D.C., 44 pp.

RIEHL, L. A., and G. E. CARMAN. 1953. Water spot of navel oranges. Calif. Agr. 8(10):7–8.

RIEHL, L. A., C. W. COGGINS, JR., and G. E. CARMAN. 1965. Gibberellin to protect navel oranges from water spot. Calif. Citrog. **51**:2, 12–17.

ROGERS, D. P. 1943. The genus *Pellicularia* (Thelephoraceae). Farlowia **1**:95–118.

ROGERS, D. P., and H. S. JACKSON. 1943. Notes on the synonym of some North American *Thelephoraceae* and other resupinates. Farlowia **1**:263–336.

ROSE, D. H., C. BROOKS, C. O. BRATLEY, and J. R. WINSTON. 1943. Market diseases of fruits and vegetables: citrus and other subtropical fruits. U. S. Dept. Agr. Misc. Pubs. 498, 57 pp.

RUGGIERI, G. 1948. Fattori che condizionano o contribuiscono allo sviluppo del "mal secco," degli agrumi e metodi di lotta contro il medismo. Ann. Sper. Agr. (n.s.) **2**:1–49.

RUGGIERI, G., and G. GOIDANICH. 1953. Il "mal secco" degli agrumi. Giornale di Agricoltura **3**:1–14.

RYAN, G. F. 1958. Albinism in citrus seedlings. Calif. Agr. **12**(3):7, 12.

SAVASTANO, G., and H. S. FAWCETT. 1930. Ricerche sperimentali sul decorso patologico del mal secco nel limone. Ann. Staz. Sper. e Frutt. Agrum. Aeireale **11**:1–37.

SCARAMUZZI, G. 1965. Le malattie degli agrumi. Bologna: Officine Grofliche, Calderini, 167 pp.

SCRIVANI, P. 1954. Patogenesi, riproduzione sperimentale del mal secco da *Deuterophoma tracheiphila* Petri e ricerche sui metaboliti tossici in coltura. Phytopathol. Ztschr. **22**:83–108.

SEMANCIK, J. S., and L. G. WEATHERS. 1971. Studies on a free RNA plant virus. Seventh Conf. of Czechoslovak Plant Virol. Proc. **1971**:269–273.

SIRAG-EL-DIN, A. 1931. The citrus twig gum diseases in Egypt. Min. Agr. Egypt, Mycol. Res. Div. Bul. **109**:1–63.

———. 1934. Citrus gummosis in Egypt. Min. Agr. Egypt (Mycol. Sec.) Bul. 131, 44 pp.

SMITH, C. O. 1912. Further proof of the cause and infectiousness of crown gall. Calif. Agr. Expt. Sta. Bul. **235**:531-57.

SMITH, C. O., and L. J. KLOTZ. 1945. A more virulent black pit organism on citrus. Calif. Citrog. **30**:303.

STAHEL, G. 1940. *Corticium areolatum*, the cause of areolate leaf spot of citrus. Phytopathology **30**:119–30.

STEVENS, H. E. 1918. Lightning injury to citrus trees in Florida. Phytopathology **8**:283–85.

STEWART, W. S., L. J. KLOTZ, and H. Z. HIELD. 1951. Effects of 2,4-D and related substances on fruit drop, yield, size, and quality of Washington navel oranges. Hilgardia **21**:161–93.

STREETS, R. B., and H. E. BLOSS. 1973. Phymatotrichum root rot. Amer. Phytopath. Soc. Monograph No. 8, 38 pp.

SUIT, R. F. 1949. Parasitic diseases of citrus in Florida. Univ. Fla. Agr. Expt. Sta. Bul. 463, 112 pp.

TAGER, J. M., and S. H. CAMERON. 1957. The role of the seedcoat in chlorophyll deficiency (albinism) of citrus seedlings. Physiol. Plantarum **10**:302–05.

TAUBENHAUS, J. J., and W. N. EZEKIEL. 1936. A rating of plants with reference to their relative resistance or susceptibility to Phymatotrichum root rot. Texas Agr. Expt. Sta.

Bul. 527, 50 pp.

TSAO, P. H. 1959. Phytophthora fibrous root rot of citrus affected by soil factors. Phytopathology **49**:553.

———. 1960. A serial dilution end-point method for estimating disease potentials of citrus Phytophthora in soil. Phytopathology **50**:717–24.

———. 1962. Prevalence of *Thielaviopsis basicola* in California citrus soils. Plant Dis. Reptr. **46**:357–59.

———. 1963*a*. The relative susceptibility of certain varieties and hybrids of citrus species and relatives to *Thielaviopsis basicola*. Plant Dis. Reptr. **47**:437–39.

———. 1963*b*. Soil moisture in relation to growth reduction of sweet orange seedlings by *Thielaviopsis basicola*. Phytopathology **53**:738–39.

———. 1969. Studies on the saprophytic behavior of *Phytophthora parasitica* in soil. *In:* Chapman, H. D. (ed.) Proc. First Intern. Citrus Symp. **3**:1221–30. Univ. of Calif. Riverside, Calif.

TSAO, P. H., and J. L. BRICKER. 1966. Chlamydospores of *Thielaviopsis basicola* as surviving propagules in natural soils. Phytopathology **56**:1012–14.

TSAO, P. H., and M. J. GARBER. 1960. Methods of soil infestation, watering, and assessing degree of root infection for greenhouse in situ ecological studies with citrus Phytophthoras. Plant Dis. Reptr. **44**:710–15.

TSAO, P. H., and S. D. VAN GUNDY. 1960*a*. Pathogenicity on citrus of *Thielaviopsis basicola* and its isolation from field roots. Phytopathology **50**:86–7.

———. 1960*b*. Effect of soil temperature on pathogenesis of *Thielaviopsis basicola* on sweet orange roots. Phytopathology **50**:657.

———. 1962. *Thielaviopsis basicola* as a citrus root pathogen. Phytopathology **52**:781–86.

TURRELL, F. M., and A. M. BOYCE. 1953. Effect of quality and intensity of solar radiation on injury of lemon fruit by sulfur treatment in the field. Plant Physiol. **28**:151–76.

TURRELL, F. M., J. ORLANDO, and S. W. AUSTIN. 1964. Researchers forge a link between rind-oil spot and foggy weather. Western Fruit Grow. **18**(9):17–18.

TURRELL, F. M., V. P. SOKOLOFF, and L. J. KLOTZ. 1943. Structure and composition of citrus leaves affected with mesophyll collapse. Plant Physiol. **18**:463–75.

WAGER, V. A. 1952. The black spot disease of citrus in South Africa. Union So. Africa Dept. Agr. Sci. Bul. 303, 52 pp.

WALDRON, M. 1923. Effect of lightning on citrus. Fla. Grow. **28**(1):5.

WALLACE, J. M., and R. J. DRAKE. 1960. Woody galls on citrus associated with vein-enation virus infection. Plant Dis. Reptr. **44**:580–84.

WEATHERS, L. G. 1957. Controlling Botrytis. Calif. Citrog. **42**:216.

WEINDLING, R., and H. S. FAWCETT. 1936. Experiments in the control of *Rhizoctonia* damping-off of citrus seedlings. Hilgardia **10**:1–16.

WHITESIDE, J. O. 1970*a*. Factors contributing to the restricted occurrence of citrus brown rot in Florida. Plant Dis. Reptr. **54**:608–12.

———. 1970*b*. Etiology and epidemiology of citrus greasy spot. Phytopathology **60**:1409–14.

———. 1970*c*. Symtomatology of orange fruit infected by the citrus greasy spot fungus. Phytopathology **60**:1859–60.

———. 1971. Some factors affecting the occurrence and development of foot rot on citrus trees. Phytopathology **61**:1233–38.

———. 1972*a*. Histopathology of citrus greasy spot and identification of the causal fungus. Phytopathology **62**:260–63.

———. 1972*b*. Spray coverage requirements with benomyl for effective control of citrus greasy spot. Proc. Fla. State Hort. Soc. **85**:24–29.

———. 1973*a*. Evaluation of spray materials for the control of greasy spot of citrus. Plant Dis. Reptr. **57**:691–94.

———. 1973*b*. Phytophthora studies on citrus rootstocks. *In:* Proc. First Intern. Citrus Short Course, pp. 15–21, 176 pp.

———. 1974*a*. Environmental factors affecting infection of citrus leaves by *Mycosphaerella citri*. Phytopathology **64**:115–20.

———. 1974*b*. Zoospore-inoculation techniques for determining the relative susceptibility of citrus rootstocks to foot rot. Plant Dis.Reptr. **58**:713–17.

WILSON, E. E. 1952. Factors affecting the branch wilt disease of walnuts. Proc. Sixth Ann. Res. Conf., Cal. Fig. Inst. 1952:21–23.

ZENTMYER, G. A. 1961. Chemotaxis of zoospores for root exudates. Science **133**:1595–96.

CHAPTER 2

Virus and Viruslike Diseases

JAMES M. WALLACE

VIRUS DISEASES OF MAN and higher animals have caused great misery and often death since the earliest days of civilization. Records of viruses that affect plants are more recent; however, it is known that some plant virus diseases, although not recognized as such, existed long before the discovery of bacteria in 1683. The first published record of a plant virus disease is believed to be a description of the breaking of flower color in tulips by Carolus Clusius in 1576, a disorder now known to be due to an aphis-transmitted virus. Since Clusius, more than 400 plant viruses have been described and named; because the same virus frequently attacks several or even many different plants, diseases caused by plant viruses number far more than 400. Few kinds of economic plants are not subject to one or more virus diseases. Despite increasing study of these diseases and some outstanding successes in control, they continue to cause tremendous losses of food, fiber, and ornamental crops.

More than thirty disorders of citrus have been determined to be or suspected of being caused by viruses. These have been characterized as virus diseases largely on the bases of their infectivity, means of transmission, and the apparent absence of other disease-causing agents such as bacteria and fungi. Actually, only about seven citrus diseases have been demonstrated to be caused by viruses on the basis of electron microscopy and virus purification techniques. Furthermore, as will be brought out later in this chapter, six separately named but possibly related disorders previously assumed to be virus diseases are now known to be caused by mycoplasma or mycoplasmalike agents. Further studies may reveal that other assumed virus diseases of citrus are mycoplasma diseases. Regardless of future developments, the similarities between these kinds of diseases and those caused by viruses make it necessary to consider both in general discussions dealing with virus diseases of citrus.

Knowledge of citrus virus diseases has accumulated largely since Fawcett (1933, 1934) established the association of a specific leaf symptom with bark lesions of psorosis on sweet orange (*Citrus sinensis* [L.] Osbeck), and demonstrated that this disease is caused by a virus. Swingle and Webber (1896) first described this disorder in Florida, giving it the name *psorosis*. Later, the same disease became known as *scaly bark* in California (Smith and Butler, 1908), where it had been observed by citrus growers as early as 1891 (Fawcett, 1936).

Although the nature of *tristeza* disease was unknown at the time, it is certain that this virus disease was responsible for the failure of sweet orange trees in South Africa when attempts were made to use sour orange (*Citrus aurantium* L.) as a rootstock there during the last decade of the nineteenth century (Webber, 1943). It was not until the 1930's that tristeza was detected in citrus in the Americas, but studies of early citrus introductions to the United States by Olson and McDonald (1954), Olson and Sleeth (1954), Wallace and Drake (1955*a*), Wallace, Oberholzer, and Hofmeyer (1956), and Wallace (1957*a*) clearly showed that the tristeza virus and the seedling-yellows virus complex were present in some of the original citrus importations from China, Japan, the Philippine Islands, and Hawaii. Many of the important virus diseases now recognized in citrus appear to have originated in India and the Orient, and to have moved with citrus as it was carried to other parts of the world.

Trabut (1913) described an *infectious chlorosis* of citrus in Algeria which he reported transmissible by tissue grafts from diseased to healthy trees. No illustrations of affected plants have been found in the literature, and apparently nothing was published on this disorder after Trabut's original brief paper was presented to the Academy of Sciences in Paris. Thus, even though Trabut may have been working with a citrus virus disease, it is not possible to substantiate this fact or to identify the disease. In an English translation of Trabut's paper by Klotz (1959), it is stated that the disease described by M. Trabut may have been the disease now known as *infectious variegation*. Careful study of the description given by M. Trabut does not support this conclusion. The Algerian disease reportedly caused the death of trees within two or three years after infection. Infectious variegation does not cause trees to die. The reader of Trabut's paper will note that some of the host-plant reactions resemble tristeza effects, but other reactions differ from those of tristeza disease. Unfortunately, there is insufficient information to identify the disorder studied by M. Trabut and determine if this was the first demonstration of a transmissible virus disease in citrus.

In the decade following Fawcett's demonstration of the virus nature of psorosis in 1933, Fawcett and co-workers in California described several types of psorosis disease. Investigations disclosed that there were no important means of spread of psorosis viruses from tree to tree, and that, for the most part, diseased trees resulted from use of infected budwood. This led to the initiation in 1938 of a budwood parent-tree registration program for prevention of psorosis, supervised by the Bureau of Nursery Service, California Department of Agriculture (for details, see chapter 3.) Similar programs in the United States were later established in Texas, Florida, and Arizona, and more recently in several countries where citrus is an important industry.

Although some attention was being given to other virus or viruslike disorders of citrus in the United States and elsewhere in the world, it was not until the appearance of *tristeza* in Argentina and Brazil and *quick decline* in California that intensive research on citrus virus diseases was begun on an international level. The respective demonstrations by Fawcett and Wallace (1946) and Meneghini (1946) that quick decline in California and tristeza in Brazil were virus diseases, were followed by contributions from numerous workers which established that the two diseases were identical. In succeeding years the importance of citrus virus diseases was widely recognized, and research in this field expanded rapidly.

Increasing interest in citrus virus diseases and realization of their importance wherever citrus is grown brought delegates from eleven countries to a conference on citrus virus diseases in Riverside, California in 1957. Thirty-five papers were published in the proceedings of that conference (Wallace, 1959*a*). The International Organization of Citrus Virologists (IOCV) was established at the Riverside meeting. This organization of more than two hundred members held a second conference in 1960 in Florida, attended by ninety-five registered delegates representing sixteen countries. Forty-seven papers presented at that conference have been published (Price, 1961). A third conference was convened in 1963 in Brazil with an attendance of seventy-four registered delegates representing nineteen different countries (Price, 1965*a*). Twenty-one countries sent delegates to the fourth conference of IOCV in Italy in 1966. The published proceedings of the 1966 conference (Childs, 1968*a*) contained eighty papers of which seventy-two are reports of new research studies of citrus virus diseases. Approximately 150 delegates from 14 countries participated in the fifth conference in Japan in 1969, the proceedings of which contain 64 papers (Price, 1972). In 1972 a sixth conference of IOCV was held in Swaziland. One hundred delegates representing 18 countries attended and a total of 45 papers were read at that meeting (Weathers and Cohen, 1974). A seventh conference held in Athens, Greece in 1975 was attended by 80 participating delegates representing 25 countries. Forty-six papers presented at that conference were published in the proceedings.

Soon after IOCV was founded in 1957 (Calavan, 1976), a committee was assigned the duty of listing and abstracting all publications relating to citrus virus and viruslike diseases. Under the leadership of J. M. Bové and R. Vogel, and with the generous assistance of L'Institut Français de Récherches Fruitières Outre-Mer (I.F.A.C.), a bibliography containing brief abstracts of 945 published papers was printed (Institut Français de Récherches Fruitières Outre-Mer, 1963). Supplements to this appeared in 1966, 1969, 1972, and 1975, bringing the total number of references to more than 2500. This bibliography will be kept current by future supplements. It has already proved an invaluable aid for persons engaged in research on virus diseases of citrus.

Initiated as a project of I.O.C.V., members of this organization have cooperated with J. M. Bové and Robert Vogel who, after some years of dedicated effort and again with assistance from I.F.A.C., have compiled and printed a three volume "Description and illustration of virus and virus-like diseases of citrus." These are loose-leaf volumes with more than four-hundred removable, identifiable colored slides in plastic holders and grouped by subject to accompany the printed information for each disease or disorder. The information found in these volumes can be revised when necessary and descriptions and illustrations of newly discovered disorders can be added. Already several addenda are planned to keep this work complete and up-to-date. Nowhere else in the field of plant pathology has such a comprehensive description been prepared for the diseases that affect a single crop.

This chapter attempts to describe and discuss, somewhat in detail, most of the diseases of citrus presently considered to be caused by viruses. Included also are some disorders previously thought to be virus diseases but which are now known to be caused by mycoplasma or mycoplasmalike agents. Some space is allotted to a few disorders originally described as distinct diseases but which subsequently were shown to be caused by other known citrus viruses. Additionally, reference is made to some apparently inherited disorders of citrus.

THE PSOROSIS DISEASES

The name "psorosis" was selected by Swingle and Webber (1896) for the disease now known as psorosis A. This disease, which causes development of scaling lesions on the bark of trees of sweet orange and certain other Citrus species, had been called "scaly bark" earlier in Florida, but later came to be known as "California scaly bark" to avoid confusion with "leprosis," another bark-scaling disorder present in Florida.

Although Fawcett and Lee (1926) described "concave gum," "blind pocket,"[1] and "crinkly leaf" on citrus, they presented no information regarding causes. After his discovery of the young-leaf symptoms of psorosis in 1933, Fawcett (1936, 1939) reported that mosaic-like symptoms had been found on leaves of trees having concave gum, blind pocket, and crinkly leaf.

Fawcett and Klotz (1938) described two types of bark-scaling psorosis to which they gave the names "psorosis A" and "psorosis B." They also suggested that concave gum was closely related to psorosis. On the basis of transmission only by tissue grafts and a common symptom on young leaves, Fawcett (1939) suggested that psorosis A, psorosis B, concave gum, blind pocket, and crinkly leaf were caused by related virus strains.

Fawcett and Klotz (1939) described a psorosis-like disorder on lemons (*C. limon* [L.] Burm. f.) to which they gave the name "infectious variegation" and suggested its relationship to crinkly leaf. Other descriptions of the different psorosis types and evidence of their relationships were published by Klotz and Fawcett (1941), Fawcett and Bitancourt (1943), and Wallace (1957*b*, 1959*b*).

An active or rampant type of scaly-bark psorosis, originally described as psorosis B by Fawcett and Klotz (1938), has been determined to be a symptom type of psorosis A. Wallace (1957*b*) demonstrated that the psorosis-B reaction is induced readily on sweet orange trees inoculated by means of patch-grafts of bark taken directly from psorosis-A bark lesions. This reaction is described later in a discussion of the relationships of the different strains of psorosis virus.

Some recent studies have suggested that crinkly leaf, infectious variegation, and concave-gum disease should not be included in the psorosis group. Since this has not been definitely substantiated, and because historically these three disorders have been considered to be caused by strains of psorosis virus, they are grouped with the discussion of psorosis in this chapter.

[1]The late Mr. J. C. Perry, East Highlands Orange Company, Highland, California, first noted the "concave gum" and "blind pocket" disorders and suggested these names.

Importance and Distribution

From an economic standpoint, psorosis A has been by far the most important of the five diseases of the so-called psorosis group. Although a slow-acting disease, it has taken thousands of trees out of production. The distribution of psorosis A is more or less worldwide, but indications are that it did not spread into some countries as early or as frequently as into others. Also, it appears that this disease has become more widespread and important in regions where, by chance, infected trees of grapefruit, Washington navel, Valencia, and other sweet orange varieties have been introduced, replacing the native or local varieties to some extent. For example, there is still a relatively small amount of psorosis A in the Shamouti orange plantings in Israel, but it is fairly common there in such introduced varieties as Valencia orange and Marsh grapefruit (*C. paradisi* Macf.). Similarly, there has been very little psorosis A in the commercial citrus plantings in the Republic of South Africa. Probably one reason for this is that early introductions of sweet orange and grapefruit propagative material were not infected with this virus. A second factor in the scarcity of psorosis A in that country is an eradication program put into effect there in the early 1930's which provided for removal of all trees showing bark lesions. Although this program would not have eliminated all infected trees, it may have aided in preventing a significant buildup of the disease.

There is no record of the citrus varieties involved in the introduction of any of the psorosis viruses into the United States or the date when this occurred. Swingle and Webber (1896) studied the scaly bark form of psorosis in Florida in the 1890's, and Fawcett (1936) stated that it was observed in California at least by 1891. It is obvious that the amount of this disease in these locations increased rapidly thereafter.

Such important varieties as Washington navel, Valencia orange, and Eureka lemon were free of all of the psorosis forms when they were first introduced into the citrus industry of California. Soon, however, as a result of top-working these varieties into old, infected trees of other varieties, and subsequent use of buds from such trees, psorosis became widely distributed. When, by chance, infected trees were used as sources of budwood sent to other citrus-growing countries, these viruses were also introduced. By 1938, when the first measures were initiated in California to avoid psorosis, many thousands of citrus trees had been destroyed and other thousands of infected trees were present in orchards. In the 1940's, it was not uncommon to find old orchards where nearly all trees were in various degrees of deterioration because of psorosis A. Prior to the discovery of a means to avoid it, this disease continued to build up in Florida and Texas in the United States, and in Argentina, Brazil, Israel, Spain, and some other countries. Presently, where budwood certification programs are providing virus-free trees, the newer plantings of citrus are relatively free of psorosis A.

The other forms of psorosis have not caused serious losses. Infectious variegation is found rarely, and because infected trees usually show such striking leaf effects, propagators routinely avoid propagating from them. This is also the case to some extent with lemon trees infected with crinkly leaf virus. On some trees of lemon infected with crinkly leaf virus, fruits are small and distorted; but on other trees there seems to be very little effect on fruit production or tree longevity. Infected sweet orange varieties do not appear to be damaged significantly.

Trees infected with concave gum and/or blind pocket viruses are sometimes reduced in size, and after a few years develop bark concavities. In earlier years in California, an occasional planting of citrus contained a fairly large number of trees with these diseases, but they were never increased to the same extent as psorosis A, possibly because propagators largely avoided the abnormal or less vigorous trees as sources of budwood.

With the available knowledge of how to avoid psorosis diseases, citrus orchards free of these diseases can be established. For the most part, this is being done in countries where citrus is an important crop and production is carried out in a scientific manner.

Symptomatology

Young-leaf Symptoms.—On citrus trees infected with psorosis A (scaly-bark psorosis), young-leaf symptoms appear during the growth flushes, but the extent of symptoms varies greatly on individual trees at any given time. Also, the different species and varieties of citrus vary in symptom expression. In the case of typical flecking symptoms on young, soft leaves, small cleared spots or bands of lighter color than the rest of the leaf are present on and adjacent to veins and veinlets (fig. 2–1, *A*). The clearing and flecking may be general over the entire leaf or may occur only on portions of the leaf. At times, particularly dur ing the spring growth flush, most new leaves show symptoms; at other times, relatively few leaves display these effects.

Some of the small flecks are quite indistinct; others coalesce to form conspicuous blotchy spots, especially on leaves of lemon and lime. Symptoms are seen most readily when the leaf is shaded from direct sun and viewed against the light of the sky. The veinal clearing and banding gradually disappear as leaves mature.

On sweet orange, mandarin (*C. reticulata* Blanco), and certain other *Citrus* spp. infected with concave-gum virus, young leaves develop a zonate or "oak-leaf" pattern (fig. 2–1, *B*). Portions of the leaves outside these patterns display vein flecking or vein banding identical to the effects of psorosis-A virus. On concave-gum-infected orchard trees in California during the spring growth flush, oak-leaf pattern and leaf flecking are very common and conspicuous. These effects commonly disappear as leaves mature, but faint outlines of the pattern remain on some leaves. In summer and fall growth flushes, the predominant leaf symptom is the psorosis-A-type leaf flecking with few leaves showing the oak-leaf pattern. Trees with blind pocket develop leaf symptoms like those of psorosis A, and display no oak-leaf patterns unless there is a mixed infection with concave-gum virus. Field trees known to carry either crinkly-leaf or infectious-variegation virus commonly develop young-leaf symptoms like those of psorosis A but, as will be discussed later, indications are that most sources of these viruses studied in California also may have contained psorosis-A virus.

Fig. 2–1. Young-leaf symptoms of psorosis. *A*, typical vein flecking. *B*, Zonate or oak-leaf patterns characteristic of concave gum.

Fig. 2–2. Shock reaction of sweet orange seedlings following inoculation with psorosis virus. *A-B*, inoculated. *C*, noninoculated.

Because of the practice of inoculating small indicator seedlings to determine if budwood parent trees are carriers of psorosis virus, a third reaction should be recognized. Frequently, after inoculation and treatment of citrus seedlings as described by Wallace (1945), the early shoot growth suffers a severe shock effect (fig. 2–2). The newly developing terminal axillary shoots curve downward and small leaves show some necrosis and soon drop. Necrosis extends down the soft stems, sometimes onto older stem tissue. Usually, plants are not killed and new growth arises from points below the necrotic tissue. Leaves on this new growth may show typical vein-flecking and normally the shock reaction is not repeated. However, shock symptoms sometimes appear on plants that have been systemically infected for a long time. Shock reaction on such plants is unexplained unless it results from a delayed invasion of virus-free tissues by relatively high concentrations of virus or possibly from nonvirus causes. Normally, the shock reaction occurs on young trees infected by inoculation and not on trees propagated from virus-infected buds.

Mature-leaf Symptoms and Other Effects.—Crinkly-leaf and infectious-variegation viruses induce persistent crinkling and various degrees of leaf distortion. In the case of psorosis A, irregular blotchy or ring patterns develop. These persist on the upper surfaces of mature sweet orange leaves experimentally graft-inoculated by means of a piece of lesion bark or a bud from a lesioned twig, and the undersides of affected leaves show brownish eruptions (fig. 2–3). This effect was described originally by Fawcett and Klotz (1938) as a mature leaf symptom of psorosis B. The symptom

Fig. 2–3. Mature-leaf symptoms of psorosis A on sweet orange. The two leaves at left show patterns on upper surface. The corky eruptions which form on the under surface of affected leaves are shown on the two leaves on the right.

rarely appears under ordinary field conditions, although similar leaf effects sometimes arise from other causes.

When diagnostic leaf symptoms are not present, some of these diseases can be identified from other effects on the bark and wood of infected trees. However, the normal delay of several years in the development of bark lesions, concavities, and blind pockets on field trees, and in some instances multiple infections, add to the difficulty of identifying the various psorosis types. Additionally, the recently reported evidence by Vogel (1973) and Vogel and Bové (1974) that cristacortis virus independently causes psorosis type leaf flecking and zonate patterns like those of concave gum means that in regions where both psorosis and cristacortis disease exist, leaf symptoms alone are not sufficient for identification of the virus or viruses present.

Diseases of the Psorosis Group

Psorosis A.—Psorosis A is characterized by bark lesions which seldom develop before six years on trees propagated from infected buds. The average time for appearance of bark lesions is about twelve years. Unless tree deterioration can be delayed by treatment described later, infected trees often become worthless between ten to twenty years after lesions first appear. The Citrus species most severely affected are sweet orange, grapefruit, and mandarin. Certain other species show typical leaf symptoms when infected, but remain free of bark lesions and show no ill effects. Sour orange and lemon fall in this category.

Bark lesions usually develop first on the trunk and primary limbs of the tree. Initially, there may be a single lesion, but sometimes several lesions begin at about the same time. The lesions remain few or may continue to increase in number throughout the tree. Usually, they increase in size slowly, but on some trees lesions develop quite rapidly. Lesions commonly encircle small limbs and cause a deterioration of the parts above the affected area in a shorter time than when they occur on trunks or large primary limbs.

Psorosis-A lesions first appear as very small, pimply eruptions (fig. 2–4, *A*). Scaling of the bark in dry, irregular flakes then follows (fig. 2–4, *B*). As the lesion enlarges, gum may exude from the affected area, mostly at the margin or in advance of the bark shelling (fig. 2–4, *C*). On older, active lesions, the bark breaks away in fairly extensive sections at the margins. New bark forms within the lesion area, but usually this is somewhat impregnated with gum. There is a continuous cracking

Fig. 2–4. Bark lesions of psorosis A. *A*, **early pimple stage.** *B-C*, **later stages of lesion development.**

and sloughing of dead tissue. Soon after initiation of bark lesions, microscopic examination reveals gum layers in the xylem immediately adjacent to the cambium. These consist of a series of pockets between the medullary rays, which are filled at first with colorless, water-soluble gum. Normal wood growth proceeds for a time, followed by production of another gum layer. This process continues, with the older gum layers becoming darkly colored and more deeply buried in the wood as new bands of normal xylem develop (fig. 2–5, *A* and *B*). The gum, which is at first nonviscous and transparent, moves into the xylem vessels, accumulating at the perforation plates of the vessels, hardening, and becoming darkly colored (fig. 2–5, *C* and *D*). At later stages, other xylem tissues become impregnated with gum, and wood staining becomes apparent. At first, only small areas of stained wood are present, but staining is quite general in the wood beneath old well-advanced lesions (fig. 2–6). At this stage, the number of functioning vessels is insufficient to supply water to the parts above, and affected portions of the trees begin to deteriorate. Webber and Fawcett (1935) made a detailed study of the comparative histology of healthy and psorosis-affected tissues of sweet orange. Bitancourt, Fawcett, and Wallace (1943) explained the relation of wood alterations in psorosis to tree deterioration. Psorosis symptoms and their effects on citrus trees were later reviewed by Wallace (1957*b*, 1959*b*).

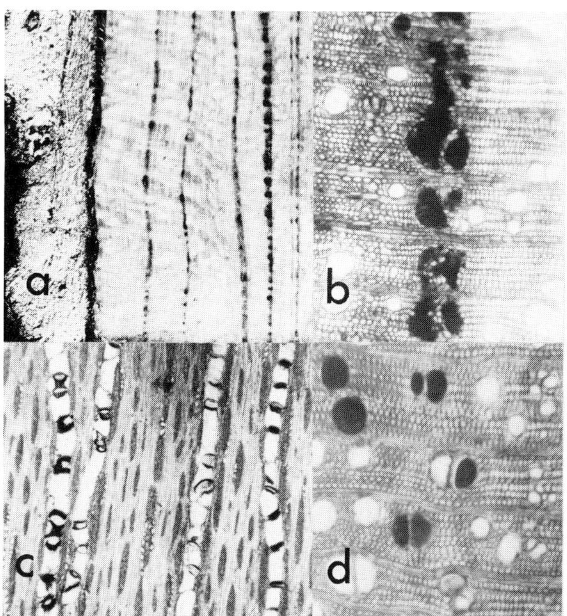

Fig. 2–5. Gum deposits in xylem tissues beneath psorosis A bark lesion on sweet orange. *A*, **series of dark-colored gum layers.** *B*, **individual layer consisting of gum pockets between medullary rays.** *C*, **tangential section showing accumulation of gum on vessel plates.** *D*, **cross-section of xylem showing gum in vessels.**

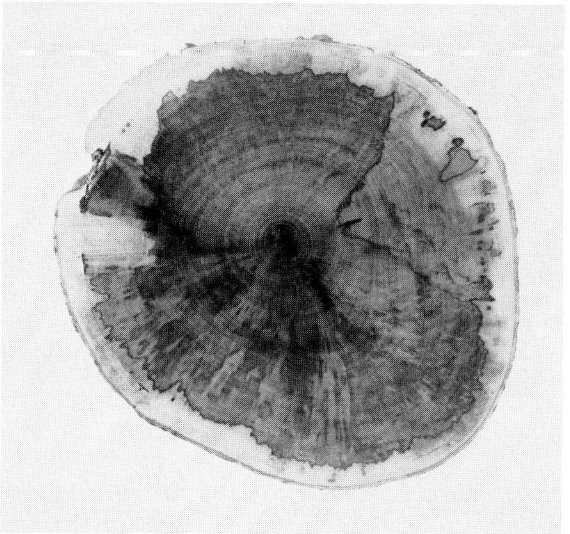

Fig. 2–6. Advanced wood-staining beneath old psorosis bark lesion.

Concave Gum.—In addition to typical young-leaf flecking and oak-leaf pattern, concave-gum virus causes the formation of concavities of various sizes and numbers, chiefly on trunks and larger limbs (fig. 2–7, *A*). The concavities remain open and eventually may involve several square inches of the wood and bark. Sometimes there is cracking of bark and slight exudation of gum in the center or around the margins of the depression. In early stages, when a concavity is being initiated, there is a rupture of bark and some exudation of gum. Wood development appears to be inhibited at these sites, which later become the centers of depressions formed as normal wood develops around these locations. Beneath a well-formed concavity, gum layers of varying frequency alternate with bands of wood and can be traced from the center to the periphery of the concavity where wood development has been normal (fig. 2–7, *B*).

Some xylem vessels in the vicinity of the concavities become plugged with gum, but not as extensively as in the case of psorosis A. No general wood staining is present. Concavities may be few or many. Injurious effects usually appear slowly and are more pronounced when concavities are numerous, but infected trees are sometimes stunted even though only a few concavities are present. This type of wood concavity has been observed chiefly on trees of sweet orange and mandarin.

Some trees that show the typical zonate leaf pattern and wood concavities also have bark lesions of the psorosis-A type. This is believed to result from a mixed infection. At the University of California Riverside, Citrus Research Center, a number of experimental inoculations from several different sources of concave gum have resulted in wood concavities, but no bark lesions, on trees infected as long as thirty years. Trees inoculated simultaneously with some of these sources of concave gum and psorosis A have developed both concavities and bark lesions during this period of time.

Blind Pocket.—The effects of blind pocket resemble those of concave gum except that blind-pocket concavities are often more numerous and usually deeper and narrower. A smaller area of wood is affected, so that as growth continues the depressions become very narrow (fig. 2–8). In the case of long-existing blind pockets, the points of origin are deep within the wood. There is usually more alteration of woody tissues at the bottom of the depression than in concave gum. Beneath the blind pockets, one may find cores of hard, gumlike tissue, ocherous salmon in color. It is not always

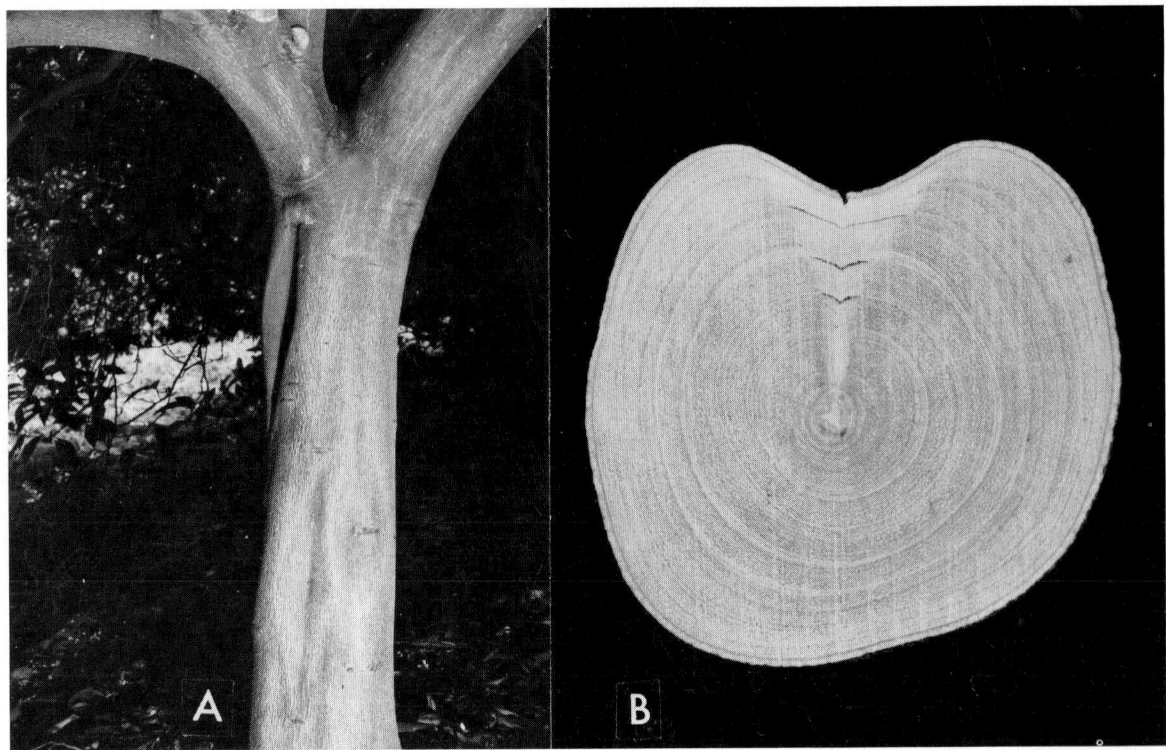

Fig. 2–7. Concave gum disease. *A*, **sweet orange tree with several large concavities.** *B*, **section through a concavity showing gum layers.**

Fig. 2–8. Blind pocket disease. Left, sweet orange tree with blind pockets on trunk. Right, section through early stage and advanced blind pockets.

possible to distinguish between the two kinds of concavities, especially during the early stage of development. However, it is evident that they are associated with two distinct virus strains because there are no oak-leaf patterns on the leaves of trees infected with blind-pocket psorosis. In California, blind pockets have been found most abundantly on trees of sweet orange and sour lemon, although some have been observed also on trees of both grapefruit and mandarin.

Although it has been generally accepted that blind-pocket psorosis does not induce bark lesions, this fact has not been clearly established. Very commonly in field trees of sweet orange that have blind-pocket concavities on the trunks and primary limbs, psorosis bark lesions are also present. Normally that situation results when a tree is infected with the viruses of blind pocket and psorosis A. However, Fawcett and Bitancourt (1943) described as "eruptive blind pocket" a form of psorosis having blind pockets and very active bark scaling. They were unable to determine if this condition resulted from blind pocket alone or a mixture of blind pocket and psorosis A. The author had an opportunity to follow the reactions of sweet orange trees inoculated in 1938 from several sources of blind pocket by H. S. Fawcett. These experimental field trees were observed for thirty years following inoculation, but their reactions did not permit final conclusions. After thirty years, some trees inoculated from blind pocket sources showed blind pockets but had no bark lesions. On others, typical psorosis A-type bark lesions were present in combination with blind pockets. Eruptive blind-pocket symptoms occasionally have developed on trees inoculated from sources not showing the eruptive scaling. On the other hand, the eruptive blind-pocket syndrome has not been reproduced consistently by inoculation from trees exhibiting these effects. Like concave gum, trees with blind-pocket disease may show no effects, but when many blind pockets are present, trees are stunted.

Crinkly Leaf.—The symptoms of crinkly-leaf psorosis were described by Fawcett (1936, 1939) and Fawcett and Bitancourt (1943) as vein-flecking of young leaves and a warped or blistered effect on old leaves (fig. 2–9). On infected lemon trees, some fruits were described as small, coarse, and bumpy. Inoculations from crinkly-leaf-infected lemon trees to sweet orange caused psorosis veinal flecking of young leaves, but crinkling of mature leaves was somewhat less than for lemon leaves. Fawcett and Bitancourt (1943) pointed out that psorosis-A bark lesions often were found on sweet orange rootstocks supporting lemon tops which showed leaf and fruit symptoms of crinkly leaf, but they emphasized that not all psorosis-A infections of lemons induced crinkly leaf. Regarding virus relationships, they suggested three possibilities: (1) crinkly leaf is a manifestation on lemon of a strain of psorosis A; (2) it is a mixture of psorosis A and some other virus; and (3) it is due to a distinct strain of psorosis. Crinkly leaf sometimes depresses growth, but in California the principal effect is distortion of lemon fruits.

Fraser (1961) described a virus disease in Australia which induces crinkling, warping, and puckering of leaves of lemon and other citrus varieties. This form of crinkly leaf is reportedly associated with circular, cleared spots on immature leaves, but causes no characteristic psorosis young-leaf flecking. The leaf spotting described by Fraser (1961) has been observed many times by the author in California, both on field trees and young trees experimentally inoculated from orchard trees. This symptom (fig. 2–10) has been recorded in California as "pinpoint spotting." Often it was found in association with psorosis young-leaf flecking, but it had not been identified with any specific psorosis type prior to the report from Australia. In California, this symptom is retained after leaves mature.

Fraser (1961) concluded that crinkly leaf is caused by a virus distinct from psorosis. She suggested that inclusion of crinkly leaf with other psorosis diseases by California workers resulted from studies on mixed infections of psorosis A which causes leaf flecking and a crinkly-leaf virus which causes leaf crinkling and spotting only. Following that suggestion, further studies were made in California by Wallace (1968). These investigations revealed that some orchard trees carrying crinkly-leaf virus also are infected with other kinds of psorosis. Further, it was demonstrated that the source of crinkly leaf maintained and studied most extensively by Fawcett and his co-workers and used by Wallace (1957*b*) in cross-protection studies was a mixture of crinkly leaf and another virus, probably psorosis A.

Subsequent studies in California were made with crinkly-leaf virus separated in two ways from contaminating virus. Among some 900 seedlings grown from a lemon tree carrying both crinkly-leaf and psorosis-A viruses, two seedlings were infected through seed transmission. These seedlings carried only the crinkly-leaf virus. The second method of separation was mechanical inoculation. Crinkly-leaf is transmitted quite easily from citrus

Fig. 2–9. Crinkly-leaf symptoms on mature leaves of Eureka lemon.

Fig. 2–10. Pinpoint spotting of crinkly leaf on leaves of Eureka lemon.

to citrus by sap-inoculation, whereas psorosis A is difficult to transmit, if it can be transmitted at all by that method. A mixed infection source was used on several occasions for mechanical inoculation, and only crinkly-leaf virus was transmitted. After separation from psorosis A, the crinkly-leaf virus caused much the same reactions as Fraser (1961) described for Australian crinkly leaf. Infected lemon plants developed pinpoint spotting and persistent crinkling of leaves. In some tests, unless a large number of seedlings were inoculated, psorosis young-leaf flecking could not be detected. On occasion, no psorosis flecking developed on sweet orange or Eureka lemon, but it appeared on one or two leaves of a single plant of sour orange or on other varieties. However, under certain conditions, the "pure" crinkly-leaf virus caused a psorosis type of young-leaf vein flecking on many leaves of several kinds of citrus. Dweet tangor (Mediterranean sweet orange X Dancy tangerine) consistently developed psorosis young-leaf symptoms when infected with uncontaminated crinkly-leaf virus.[2] Leaves from such a plant are shown in figure 2–11.

If the Australian crinkly-leaf virus is the same as that studied in California, absence of psorosis leaf flecking in Australia on experimental plants may have resulted from failure to use a sufficient range of indicator varieties under the proper environmental conditions.

Yot-Dauthy and Bové (1968) purified the California seed-transmitted isolate of crinkly-leaf virus and found it to be a polyhedral virus approximately 27 nm in diameter.

Infectious Variegation.—This disease is not of common occurrence in citrus. Because of its severe effects, infectious variegation has been easily avoided by citrus propagators, and thus has not been perpetuated to any extent in commercial plantings. In California, severe infectious variegation has been found only rarely on field trees. Experimental study in California has dealt almost exclusively with the type-strain of infectious variegation obtained from a field lemon tree in 1937. On sour orange and lemon, the virus causes various degrees of mosaic-like leaf variegation, crinkling, distortion, and "shoe-string" effect on leaves, a somewhat atypical psorosis young-leaf flecking,

[2]C. N. Roistacher, University of California Riverside Citrus Research Center, first observed that dweet tangor develops psorosis young-leaf symptoms when infected with this isolate of crinkly-leaf virus.

Fig. 2–11. Psorosis-type vein flecking on leaves of Dweet tangor infected with uncontaminated crinkly-leaf virus.

pinpoint spotting, and overall reduction of plant growth. Some of these effects are shown in figure 2–12. Fawcett and Klotz (1939), in their studies of the original source of infectious variegation, observed psorosis-like flecking on young leaves and warping and pocketing of mature leaves suggestive of crinkly leaf. These authors also reported finding a less severe strain of infectious variegation in another lemon tree in southern California.

In their original report, Fawcett and Klotz (1939) stated that in some respects California infectious variegation resembled the infectious chlorosis described on sour orange in Sicily by Petri (1931). Later, Fawcett and Klotz (1948*a*) further discussed similarities and differences between the California strain of infectious variegation and the chlorosis or *variegatura infettiva* described by Petri. They pointed out that the chief difference between the two diseases was that in Sicily no symptoms were found on lemon trees.

The illustrations of affected leaves by Petri (1931) are very similar to the symptoms of infectious variegation in California. Petri made no tissue-graft inoculations, but he speculated that the cause of the disease was a virus probably spread by a common aphid. He based this hypothesis on an apparent increase of the disease in sour oranges, indicating natural spread in nurseries. He reported that lemon seedlings in the same nurseries were not affected. Available information does not establish the identity of the disorder described by Petri. Possibly, Petri may have been studying a disorder that occurs commonly on sour orange seedlings in Sicily. This is a leaf-spotting, variegation effect which Majorana and Scaramuzzi (1963) were unable to reproduce by tissue-graft inoculation. These workers found the symptoms developed on sour orange seedlings grown outside during the winter, but not on comparable seedlings grown in glasshouses.

Grant and Smith (1960) reported the discovery of infectious variegation on two Marsh grapefruit trees in Florida. Inoculations of plants of several varieties of citrus from the infected grapefruit trees resulted in infectious-variegation symptoms identical to those produced by the original California strain, including vein banding (i.e., psorosis young-leaf flecking).

It is of interest that infectious-variegation symptoms were found in Florida on trees damaged

Fig. 2–12. Infectious variegation on Eureka lemon. ***A*****, characteristic distortion, crinkling, and chlorosis.** ***B*****, leaves with variegated or mosaic-like patterns.**

by cold. A similar occurrence of infectious variegation following freeze damage is on record in California. A ten-year-old lemon tree grown from a parent tree with slight crinkly-leaf symptoms was severely damaged by freezing in the winter of 1949–50. In the following spring, a new shoot that grew out near the margin of dead stem tissue had strong variegated patterns and leaf distortion. Inoculations from this shoot caused typical infectious variegation. These reactions and the finding of infectious variegation on frozen trees in Florida suggest that freezing or other environmental effects may possibly bring about mutations of the crinkly-leaf virus or separation of components of virus mixtures.

Using the Florida source of infectious-variegation virus, Grant and Corbett (1960, 1961) first demonstrated mechanical transmission of a citrus virus from citrus to citrus and noncitrus hosts. Majorana (1963*a*, 1963*b*) transmitted both infectious-variegation and crinkly-leaf viruses mechanically from citrus and to some herbaceous hosts and from the latter back to citrus.

Desjardins and Wallace (1962, 1966) found that cucumber (*Cucumis sativus* L.), kidney bean, (*Phaseolus vulgaris* L.), and gomphrena (*Gomphrena globosa* L.), are hosts of infectious-variegation virus and readily infected by mechanical inoculation. Desjardins and Reynolds (1963) observed symptoms on all of nineteen cucumber varieties tested, and reported that the variety "National Pickling" was the best of the group for virus assay. On cucumber, the symptoms are diffuse chlorotic rings or chlorotic spots on the inoculated cotyledons. *G. globosa* developed diffuse spots on inoculated leaves and interveinal chlorosis on systemically infected leaves. On kidney beans, variety 'Bountiful,' no symptoms developed on inoculated primary leaves, but distinct yellow vein banding appeared on systemically infected leaves seven to fourteen days after inoculation.

Dauthy and Bové (1965) infected blackeye cowpea, *Vigna sinensis* (Torner) Savi, with a California strain of crinkly leaf and a Florida strain of infectious variegation. Both viruses caused chlorotic, local lesions on inoculated leaves followed by systemic symptoms. The only difference observed was that symptoms appeared earlier on plants inoculated with infectious-variegation virus. Wallace and Majorana (1962, unpublished) found that *Crotalaria spectabilis* Roth reacted identically to crinkly-leaf and infectious-variegation viruses except that symptoms appeared first on plants inoculated with infectious-variegation virus.

Corbett and Grant (1967) purified infectious-variegation virus by density-gradient centrifugation and obtained highly infectious preparations containing polyhedral or spherical particles approximately 30 nm in diameter.

Yot-Dauthy and Bové (1968) compared purified preparations of crinkly-leaf and infectious-variegation viruses in the electron microscope and found that both contained polyhedral particles approximately 27 nm in diameter. Martelli, Majorana, and Russo (1968) described hexagonally shaped particles of about 27 nm in diameter in preparations from leaves of infectious-variegation-infected bean and cowpea. Desjardins

(1969) obtained highly purified preparations of this virus by density-gradient electrophoresis which contained icosahedral virus particles 30 nm in diameter.

Relationships of Diseases in the Psorosis Group

Fawcett (1939), Fawcett and Klotz (1938, 1939), and Fawcett and Bitancourt (1943) considered psorosis A, psorosis B, concave gum, and blind pocket to be related on the basis of a young-leaf symptom common to all. They suggested that crinkly leaf and infectious variegation also belonged in the psorosis group. Wallace (1957*b*) concluded that psorosis B is not a distinct form of psorosis after it was shown that the rampant lesion development originally described as psorosis B is merely the reaction of a healthy sweet orange to infection from bark-patch inoculum taken from a psorosis-A lesion. Young, healthy sweet orange seedlings inoculated by means of normal bark from a psorosis-A-infected tree develop young-leaf symptoms, but no bark lesions appear until after six years. These bark lesions are like those which appear in later years on orchard trees grown from psorosis-A-infected buds, beginning with light scaling in localized areas and gradually enlarging. In contrast, if infection of a healthy tree results from inoculation with a piece of lesion bark, lesions sometimes begin to develop within two months and spread quite rapidly throughout the tree. On such infected trees, some leaves remain small and chlorotic or develop a zinc-deficiency type of mottling. Other leaves attain normal size, but develop irregular, blotchy patterns with brownish eruptions on the undersurface (fig. 2–3). As the lesions extend generally over the twigs and small limbs, there is much dieback. On sweet orange plants inoculated when very young, the lesion effect is a uniform development of brownish, pimply eruptions without much scaling or flaking of the bark. On healthy old trees, lesion-bark inoculum causes early gumming above and below the site of inoculation followed by extensive bark scaling.

Sweet orange trees preinoculated from lesion-free tissue or grown from psorosis-A-infected buds from lesion-free twigs do not develop the early, severe reaction when inoculated by means of lesion bark patches. These reactions (figs. 2–13 and 2–14) constitute the cross-protection reaction described by Wallace (1957*b*), who reported a similar protection in sweet orange trees which were first inoculated separately with viruses of concave gum, blind pocket, crinkly leaf, and infectious variegation. Protection by the particular virus sources used was as good as that afforded by nonlesion psorosis-A virus except that the crinkly-leaf virus did not protect consistently. Wallace (1957*b*) concluded from these tests that the four viruses were related to psorosis A and that, as suggested earlier by Fawcett and co-workers, they should be classed as strains of psorosis.

The suggestion by Fraser (1961) that crinkly leaf is unrelated to psorosis and that sources of crinkly leaf studied in California were contaminated with psorosis A resulted in a study of these possibilities. Also, a report by Roistacher and Calavan (1965) that a number of sources of concave-gum virus did not protect against psorosis A led to a reinvestigation in California of the relationship of concave gum and psorosis A. Additionally, more study was made of protection of blind pocket virus against psorosis A. These later studies provided new information concerning the identity of some of the so-called psorosis diseases whose relation to each other was partly reported by Wallace (1968). This information was obtained largely from the use of uncontaminated viruses in cross-protection tests.

Crinkly Leaf and Psorosis A.—As mentioned in the discussion on crinkly leaf (pp. 75-77), studies in California demonstrated that not only the original source of this virus used in cross-protection studies by Wallace (1957*b*) but also some other field sources of crinkly-leaf virus were, as suggested by Fraser (1961), mixed with another psorosis strain. When the contaminating virus was eliminated either through seed or mechanical transmission, the remaining virus caused symptoms of crinkly leaf but did not protect sweet orange against psorosis-A lesion inoculum. The leaf-spotting symptom described by Fraser (1961) is a symptom of California crinkly-leaf virus. It was caused by several sources of uncontaminated virus and by the author's seed-transmitted source even after it had been partially purified by Yot-Dauthy and Bové (1968) and inoculated mechanically back to lemon.

The failure of purified crinkly-leaf virus to protect sweet orange against psorosis-A lesion inoculum is not proof that these two strains are unrelated, but merely indicates that they are not as closely related as suggested by earlier cross-protection studies. Production of a psorosis-type, young-leaf veinal flecking by uncontaminated crinkly-leaf virus on certain kinds of citrus suggests

Fig. 2–13. Reaction of healthy sweet orange to psorosis A infection from lesion and nonlesion bark patch inoculations and the protection reaction. Left to right: plant 1, infected from piece of lesion bark; plant 2, infected from nonlesion bark; plant 8, incoulated first with nonlesion bark and challenge-inoculated ten months later with two pieces of lesion bark; plant 9, a control for plant 8 which received two lesion bark patches without previous inoculation. All photographed four years after last inoculation. At that time small, slowly developing bark lesions were developing around the second inoculation sites (opposite dots) of plant 8.

that this virus is a form of psorosis. On the other hand, the ease by which it can be made to infect citrus and certain herbaceous plants by juice inoculation leaves some doubt concerning its relationship to the viruses of psorosis A, concave gum, and blind pocket.

Infectious Variegation and Psorosis A.—Wallace (1968) reported that a restudy of the infectious variegation virus source used in his earlier cross-protection tests disclosed that it consisted of infectious-variegation virus plus another psorosis virus. The mixture protected sweet orange against psorosis-A lesion inoculum. Sap inoculations with the virus mixture resulted in transmission of infectious-variegation virus only. This virus, separated from the contaminating virus, did not protect sweet orange. Thus, it appears, as in the case of crinkly leaf, that infectious-variegation virus is not as closely related to psorosis A as assumed earlier. However, as brought out in the following section, infectious-variegation is closely related to crinkly leaf. Therefore, if crinkly leaf is caused by a strain or form of psorosis virus, infectious-variegation disease properly belongs in the psorosis group.

Crinkly Leaf and Infectious Variegation.—In many respects, infectious variegation appears to be caused by an extremely virulent strain of crinkly-leaf virus, differing only in the production of severe leaf distortion. Both cause

Fig. 2–14. Psorosis-A protection reaction on sweet orange. Left, tree infected when small from psorosis-A nonlesion inoculum. This tree was systemically infected with the virus of psorosis A, but had no bark lesions when it was challenge-inoculated with lesion bark patches at the sites indicated by X's. After five years a typical slowly developing lesion was present around one inoculation site, while at the other a lesion was just beginning. Right, advanced lesion development on a control tree which was free of psorosis virus when inoculated five years earlier by means of two lesion bark patches.

pinpoint spotting and crinkling of leaves. Neither causes typical psorosis young-leaf flecking regularly on sweet orange and certain other psorosis-sensitive varieties. However, these symptoms appear occasionally on one or more leaves of some kinds of citrus and quite regularly on young leaves of Dweet tangor. Some soft leaves of Dweet tangor display veinal flecking identical with that caused by psorosis A (fig. 2–11), but others develop many very small, almost necrotic spots, possibly the pinpoint spotting reaction which tends to mask the psorosis veinal effects.

Lemon seedlings experimentally infected and displaying strong symptoms of infectious variegation sometimes produce recovered growth showing only crinkly-leaf symptoms. Juice inoculations and graft transfers from recovered growth resulted only in symptoms of crinkly leaf.

Lemon and sour orange seedlings preinoculated with virus from plants which recovered from infectious variegation or with uncontaminated crinkly-leaf virus obtained from orchard trees were not affected by inoculation with infectious-variegation virus (fig. 2–15).

On the basis of the syndrome of these two viruses and the complete protection crinkly leaf affords against infectious variegation, there seems to be no question regarding a close relationship between them. The viruses of both are readily transmitted mechanically from citrus to citrus and between certain herbaceous hosts. Similarity of symptoms on herbaceous hosts, as well as the findings by Yot-Dauthy and Bové (1968) that purified preparations of both contain polyhedral particles averaging about 27 nm in diameter, is additional evidence of relationship of the causal viruses. Majorana and Martelli (1968) made comparative studies of symptoms on herbaceous hosts and other properties of crinkly-leaf and infectious-variegation viruses and concluded they were closely related.

Blind Pocket and Psorosis A.—Information regarding protection of sweet orange by blind-pocket virus against a challenge inoculation from

Fig. 2–15. Crinkly-leaf protection against infectious variegation. ***A*****, sour orange seedling first infected with crinkly-leaf virus and then inoculated with infectious variegation virus.** ***B*****, reaction of a healthy control seedling to inoculation with infectious variegation virus.**

psorosis A lesion bark is limited. Wallace (1957*b*) reported that sweet orange seedlings first infected with blind-pocket virus were protected against psorosis A lesion inoculum. That conclusion was reached from studies of a single locally available source of blind pocket identified as F-482. Subsequently, in searching for isolates or cultures of blind-pocket virus for further study, it was found that F-482 isolate was the only one of several originally collected and established by H. S. Fawcett which had not evidenced contamination with psorosis A. Trees experimentally infected with F-482 showed psorosis young-leaf symptoms consistently and after a few years began to develop typical blind pockets. One of these trees was maintained for 33 years without showing bark lesions or symptoms of any other psorosis disease. Sweet orange seedlings preinoculated from that tree and challenged with psorosis A lesion inoculum were protected, as reported by Wallace and Drake (1969). If the protection resulted from a latent form of psorosis A virus in mixture with blind-pocket virus, it would have been expected that psorosis bark lesions would have developed on some of the infected orchard trees. In fact, trees experimentally inoculated simultaneously with blind pocket F-482 and a selected source of psorosis A developed bark lesions similar to those inoculated with the psorosis A source only.

While it is of no particular significance even in establishing a relationship between blind-pocket and psorosis A viruses, these studies suggest that blind-pocket virus may protect orange against the severe reaction that results from inoculation with psorosis A bark lesion inoculum. If that is a correct assumption, it may explain some of the inconsistent results obtained in cross-protection studies between concave-gum and psorosis A viruses as described in the following section.

Concave Gum and Psorosis A.—Typical protection was obtained by Wallace (1957*b*) in three separate trials with concave-gum source F-571 established by H. S. Fawcett in 1923. Roistacher and Calavan (1965) obtained no protection against psorosis A lesion inoculum from a source of concave gum (F-571) which, according to available records, was a transfer made in 1938 from one of five trees infected in 1923 with the original F-571 source. Wallace and Drake (1969) also obtained no protection from that source of concave gum.

However, concave gum F-850, recorded as a 1938 transfer from one of the original F-571 infected trees, provided sweet orange with protection against psorosis A. At the same time, cross-protection tests were made with three other sources of concave-gum virus established earlier by H. S. Fawcett, identified as F-481, F-416, and F-939. The five sources of concave gum listed above were inoculated to experimental sweet orange trees in 1939 and observed for periods of twenty to thirty-three years. Infected trees had shown the concave gum oak-leaf pattern regularly and developed some concavities but no bark lesions of psorosis A.

Absence of scaly-bark lesions strongly indicated that psorosis A virus was not present in any instance. When young sweet orange seedlings were preinoculated with these five concave-gum sources, those infected with F-481 and F-850 were protected against a challenge inoculation with psorosis A lesion-bark inoculum.

In seeking an explanation of protection by some sources of concave gum and none by others, it seemed that some other virus may have been present in F-481 and F-850 to provide the observed protection by these sources. For example, blind-pocket virus is difficult to detect at times when present in mixture with concave-gum virus. Except for the oak-leaf pattern of concave gum, the young leaf symptoms of the two viruses are the same. Also, it is not possible in all instances to identify the individual concavities as being those of concave gum or blind pocket. From other cross-protection studies, Wallace and Drake (1969) found that sweet orange seedlings infected with blind-pocket virus developed no symptoms of citrus ringspot when inoculated with ringspot virus. A test was made in which groups of four Madam Vinous sweet orange seedlings were first inoculated with (1) blind pocket F-482 which protects against psorosis A; (2) concave gum F-481 which protects against psorosis A; and (3) concave gum F-571 which does not protect against psorosis A. Two months later all of these trees and healthy control seedlings were inoculated with citrus ringspot virus. The interesting results were that both blind pocket F-482 and concave gum F-481 prevented development of ringspot symptoms, whereas concave gum F-571, which does not protect against psorosis A lesion inoculum, had no suppressive effect on citrus ringspot.

Results of the one experiment with ringspot as the challenging virus suggest that in instances where concave-gum virus appears to protect sweet orange against psorosis A lesion inoculum, the protection actually is due to the presence of blind-pocket virus.

Transmission and Spread

Observations over many years clearly establish that there has been no significant spread of psorosis viruses by natural means. Man himself has been largely responsible for perpetuation of these viruses and the serious losses caused by them. There is always the possibility that a vector of psorosis virus may appear among insects, mites, or nematodes; however, up to the present, transmission by such vectors has been insignificant, if it has occurred at all.

Perpetuation by Propagation from Diseased Trees.—Citrus trees infected with psorosis virus commonly show no effects on growth or reduction in yield for ten years or longer after being propagated. This explains why great numbers of infected mother trees have been used as sources of budwood. Fawcett (1934) reported that progeny trees budded in 1922 from mother trees having psorosis bark lesions began to develop bark lesions within nine years. However, prior to 1933 when Fawcett discovered the leaf symptoms of psorosis, there were no known means of avoiding use of budwood from infected trees which had not yet developed bark lesions or other obvious weaknesses brought on by infection with these viruses. Consequently, this resulted in use of budwood from infected sources and a rapid buildup of diseased trees.

Other Possible Means of Spread.—Because field observations strongly supported the conclusion that there is no significant spread of psorosis viruses by natural means from diseased to healthy citrus trees, very little study has been made of possible insect or nematode vectors. Presently, no such vectors are known. A report from Argentina by Pujol and Beñatena (1965) suggested natural spread of psorosis virus. These workers concluded that infection resulted from vector transmission rather than passage of the virus through seeds.

Over a period of years, H. S. Fawcett and J. M. Wallace made extensive tests on transmission of psorosis virus through sweet orange seeds. In approximately 20,000 seedlings grown from seeds of infected sweet orange trees, no infections were observed. In later studies by Wallace (1957*b*), two instances of transmission of crinkly-leaf virus through lemon seeds were discovered in approximately 900 seedlings. C. R. Tower, Inspector, Bureau of Nursery Service, California Department of Agriculture, reported to the author that an occasional psorosis-infected tree was found among nursery trees grown from buds from psorosis-free sources but it could not be proved that seed transmission was responsible. There is good circumstantial evidence at least that transmission of psorosis virus through seeds of such commonly used rootstock varieties as sweet orange and sour orange has not been significant. However, studies in Florida by Bridges, Youtsey, and Nixon (1965) indicated that 10 per cent or more of seedlings grown from psorosis-infected trees of Carrizo citrange (*Poncirus trifoliata* x *C. sinensis*) became infected through seed transmission of the virus. These authors diagnosed the infected seedlings on the basis of "psorosis leaf patterns," but did not identify further the type of psorosis involved. Childs and Johnson (1966) conducted studies on seedlings grown from the Carrizo citrange seed sources involved in the transmission reported by Bridges *et* *al.* (1965), and they reported from 15 to 31 per cent transmission of psorosis virus through seeds.

In Argentina, Pujol (1966) grew seedlings from a psorosis-infected Troyer citrange tree and found that seven of sixteen were infected, apparently through seed transmission. Infection was revealed by budding sweet orange to each Troyer seedling. Pujol's published illustration of symptoms on the leaves of sweet orange clearly shows the oak-leaf patterns of concave gum.

Grant and Corbett (1960, 1961), Desjardins and Wallace (1962), Desjardins and Reynolds (1963), and Majorana (1963*a*, 1963*b*) have demonstrated that infectious-variegation and crinkly-leaf viruses can be transmitted by juice inoculation from citrus to citrus and certain herbaceous hosts. Wallace and Drake (1969) have transmitted these two viruses by contaminated budding knives; however, there has been no report of infection of healthy orchard trees by pruning operations or other cultural practices.

Natural root grafting between citrus trees has been observed in both nursery rows and orchard plantings. Root grafts between diseased and healthy trees provide a means of psorosis infection. Statistical studies of distribution of psorosis-affected trees in citrus orchards by Bitancourt and Fawcett (1944) showed that in thirteen of fourteen orchards examined, there were greater numbers of diseased trees in the four tree spaces adjacent to a central diseased tree than in the spaces surrounding healthy trees. It was concluded that some natural spread of psorosis had occurred and that root grafts seemed to be the most likely means of transmission.

Weathers and Harjung (1964) obtained some transmission of psorosis virus from citrus to citrus by means of dodder, *Cuscuta subinclusa* Dur. & Hilg. Price (1965*b*) reported experimental transmission of psorosis virus by *Cuscuta compacta* Juss. In neither case was the specific kind of psorosis identified. While transmission by dodder offers possibilities for introducing the viruses into herbaceous hosts for studying the virus properties, it is not of any importance in their spread in orchards.

Control of Psorosis

Prevention.—As stated previously, the chief means by which psorosis builds up has been through use of budwood from infected mother trees for propagation of new trees. With the realization that control was largely a matter of prevention, and utilizing the information provided by the important discoveries of Fawcett (1933, 1934), a program was established in California in 1938 under the direction of the Bureau of Nursery Service, California Department of Agriculture, providing psorosis-free budwood sources for citrus nurserymen of the state (see chap. 3). Although this was a voluntary program, most leading citrus nurserymen participated in it. Since the early 1940's the majority of new citrus plantings in California have consisted of psorosis-free trees. Presently, such diseases as psorosis A, concave gum, blind pocket, crinkly leaf, and infectious variegation are rarely of importance in new plantings. Since the inception of this service, similar and more comprehensive programs designed to provide virus-free trees have been developed in California, Florida, Texas, and Arizona in the United States, and to some extent in other countries. Because this subject is treated in detail in Chapters 3 and 4 of this volume, only a brief historical account of the early California program is presented here.

Initially, freedom from psorosis in selected budwood source trees was determined entirely by visual inspection of candidate trees. This required thorough examination of young leaves at opportune times for symptom expression. Ordinarily, two seasons of field inspection were required before a tree was judged free of infection. Additionally, four trees adjacent to a candidate tree were given the same critical inspection as the candidate tree. This was done to avoid possible infection of registered mother trees by natural root grafting with an adjacent infected tree. In the California program, because the law provided for a self-supported service, a scale of fees covering application, inspection, registration, and continued inspection was established.

In the early years of the program, nurserymen were required to propagate twenty-five trees from the registered parent tree to seedlings in their nurseries, which were treated so as to provide leaf growth from both the rootstock seedling and the bud. Inspectors critically examined these trees during the first season of growth for signs of psorosis infection. Wallace (1945) developed a method of indexing candidate trees in glasshouses by grafting tissue from them to small healthy seedlings of citrus varieties which served as indicators of psorosis infection. This procedure shortened to a few weeks the time required to determine if a prospective budwood parent tree was free of psorosis. This type of indexing for psorosis and several other citrus viruses, or some variation of it, is now a standard practice in existing programs of citrus budwood certification. The discovery by workers in Florida and Argentina that psorosis virus is transmitted in significant amounts through seeds of some kinds of citrus demonstrates that trees used as rootstock seed sources should also be indexed and determined to be virus free.

Use of Nucellar Clones.—Because seed transmission of psorosis occurs infrequently in most kinds of citrus, virus-free seedlings of many citrus varieties can be obtained from infected trees. Nucellar seedling clones can be established that are free of psorosis viruses and several other citrus diseases. They remain free of the viruses (which are not spread naturally) unless they become reinfected by natural root graft to diseased trees or by man's propagative practices. Thus, if no sources of a particular citrus variety are known that are free of psorosis, nucellar seedlings of that variety usually can be obtained which will preserve the varietal characteristics and at the same time eliminate the virus. However, such nucellar seedlings should be indexed before use for psorosis to avoid any chance infection through the seed. Also, precautions should be taken to avoid infecting them with exocortis, crinkly-leaf, or infectious-variegation viruses and from contaminated budding and pruning tools.

Weathers and Calavan (1959*a*) pointed out that failure of a virus to pass through seeds of one citrus variety was not proof that it might not be seed-transmitted in other varieties. The recent discoveries in Florida and Argentina support that premise.

Elimination of Psorosis by Heat.—In studies with several plant viruses, heat treatments of various kinds have been used successfully to obtain virus-free plants or virus-free buds for increase, but up to this time there have been few reports of studies of the effect of heat treatment on psorosis virus. Grant (1957) sometimes obtained tissue free of psorosis virus from the terminal growth of infected citrus plants held for 95 days in heat chambers at constant temperatures of 95° F to 100° F. Calavan, Roistacher, and Nauer (1972) reported that the viruses of concave gum, infectious variegation, psorosis-A, tristeza, seedling yellows, and vein enation were inactivated by two to three months hot-air treatment at alternating temperatures of 40° C for 16/hr day and 30° C for 8/hr night. Tatterleaf and citrange stunt viruses were inactivated at slightly higher temperatures. In these studies it was found that preconditioning infected plants increased heat tolerance and permitted their exposure to higher treatment temperatures (Roistacher and Calavan, 1972). Thus, it is evident that thermotherapy offers a means of establishing citrus cultivars free of psorosis and certain other viruses.

Treatment of Affected Trees.—In many citrus orchards planted prior to the development of the program for providing psorosis-free trees in California, psorosis-A-infected trees were numerous. At that time, removal of the bark lesions was a common practice. The first treatment was described as "hand-scraping." It is not known who first used this treatment, but Smith and Butler (1908) recommended scraping experiments and concluded that the removal of early-stage bark

Fig. 2–16. Scraping treatment of psorosis-A infected trees. This tree had all active bark lesions scraped over a period of twelve years.

lesions was a beneficial treatment. Figure 2–16 is an interior view of a tree from which all bark lesions were scraped over a period of twelve years. There was no deterioration of this tree during that period (fig. 2–17). Untreated trees in a similar stage of disease at the beginning of the experiment showed moderate to severe decline with corresponding reductions in yields after twelve years. One of the untreated control trees is shown in figure 2–18.

Fawcett and Cochran (1944) found that activity of psorosis lesions was stopped or retarded significantly by treatment with a solution of one per cent dinitro-*o*-cyclohexylphenol in kerosene. This material, known by the trade name DN-75, created simplified lesion treatment and gave good results when applied properly before bark lesions became too far advanced. The bark-shelling resulting from DN-75 treatment is shown in figure 2–19.

In recent years, where citrus budwood has been properly selected, relatively few psorosis-infected trees have been planted. Thus, there is no longer the same need for treatment of affected trees as in earlier plantings. For this reason, and the fact that DN-75 is no longer on the market, details of hand scraping and chemical treatments of psorosis bark lesions are omitted from this chapter. Wallace (1959*b*) described and illustrated these treatments.

THE TRISTEZA-DISEASE COMPLEX

It is now well established that tristeza no longer can be considered only a disease of certain stionic combinations of citrus. The disease originally was recognized as a disorder of trees of sweet orange, mandarin, and grapefruit on sour orange and certain other rootstocks. Control or prevention was considered a somewhat simple matter of avoiding susceptible stionic combinations. From studies in different countries, it is now clear that several rather distinct diseases make up the tristeza-disease complex. Although complete agreement is lacking among investigators as to the exact relationships of these diseases, it is recognized generally that they should be treated as a disease complex.

In this discussion, four different disorders, namely tristeza, stem-pitting, seedling-yellows, and lime dieback are considered part of the tristeza-disease complex. These are treated as a

Fig. 2–17. Scraping treatment of psorosis-A bark lesions. This is an outside view of tree shown in figure 2–16 and shows its condition twelve years after treatments began.

Fig. 2–18. Psorosis A. This tree which received no treatment was in the same stage of disease as the tree shown in figure 2–17 when scraping treatments were begun on the latter.

Fig. 2–19. Removal of psorosis lesion bark by chemical treatment. Left, scaling of bark fifteen months after treatment with DN-75. Right, same tree with loose bark removed.

group in the sections dealing with history and economic importance, but are described separately in the section on symptomatology. "Tristeza" refers to the decline and/or death of budded trees of certain scion-rootstock combinations, reactions known earlier by the names "podredumbre de las raicillas" in Argentina and " quick decline" in California. Stem-pitting disease is the disorder first described on grapefruit trees in South Africa as early as 1940 by workers at the Addo Citrus Research station and subsequently studied by Hofmeyer and Oberholzer (1948) and Oberholzer, Mathews, and Stiemie (1949). This disorder occurs on budded trees of grapefruit and other citrus irrespective of the rootstock, and it also develops on seedling trees. Seedling yellows, first described by Fraser (1952), refers to the dwarfing and yellowing of lemon, sour orange, grapefruit, and other citrus. The fourth disease, lime dieback, was first described in detail by Hughes and Lister (1949, 1953), who presented experimental evidence that it was a form of tristeza.

Historical Developments

In the late 1890's, when attempts were made to use sour orange as a rootstock in South Africa, it was observed that trees of sweet orange and mandarin on this rootstock usually died or declined severely within two or three years. From an investigation by the Cape Department of Agriculture, reported by Bioletti, Gowie, and Cillie (1904), this tree failure was attributed to incompatibility between these two scion varieties and sour orange. Noting that such trees thrived in California and elsewhere, Webber (1925), after a visit to South Africa, excluded uncongeniality between scion and stock as a cause of the tree failure and expressed an opinion that it was a disease condition.

After surveying the Satsuma plantings in northern Florida and the Gulf States, W. T. Swingle (1909) advised growers that "on the sour orange, the Satsuma is a complete failure, growth being so slow and stunted that it never became more than a dwarfed bush." Although he attributed this to a "considerable degree of incompatibility," it appears likely that many of the early importations of Satsumas from Japan carried the tristeza virus, and this was the cause of the incompatibility.

Toxopeus (1937) studied what is believed to be the same disease in Java, and advanced the theory that the sweet orange top developed some substance that was lethal to sour orange root.

In Argentina, Zeman (1931) and Carrera (1933) described symptoms of a disease that had been observed there around 1930 and given the name "podredumbre de la raicilla." The first suggestion that the disease was of viral origin appears to be that of Fawcett and Bitancourt in an unpublished report of a visit to affected orchards in Argentina in 1937 (Bitancourt, 1940). After the disease became established in Brazil around 1937, Moreira (1942) apparently was the first in print to use the name "tristeza," a Portuguese word meaning "sadness or melancholy." This became the generally accepted name as the various disorders were determined to be identical or at least closely related.

The so-called quick decline disease is known to have affected some trees in California as early as 1939. Apparent spread of the disease, study of symptomatology, and observations by Halma, Smoyer, and Schwalm (1944, 1945) that the scion-rootstock relations were the same as reported in South America indicated that quick decline was the same as tristeza. Consequently, an intensive research program was quickly developed in an attempt to learn the nature of the disease and a means of control. Fawcett and Wallace (1946) reproduced the disease on healthy trees of Valencia on sour orange rootstock by graft inoculation from diseased trees and reported that the disorder was caused by a virus. Simultaneously, Meneghini (1946) in Brazil reported that tristeza was a virus disease and that the brown citrus aphid, *Toxoptera citricidus* Kirk., was a vector of the virus. In the United States this species of aphid has been found only in Hawaii, but Dickson, Flock, and Johnson (1951) demonstrated that the principal vector of quick-decline virus in California is *Aphis gossypii* Glover. Until about 1950, the lack of a short-term indicator host of tristeza virus made it necessary to use sensitive budded scion and rootstock combinations for experimental study. These kinds of test plants were unsatisfactory because of the time required to prepare them and for diagnostic symptoms to appear after inoculation. The need for a better indicator host, preferably for use as a seedling plant was recognized by all investigators of tristeza disease. Following the discovery by Hughes and Lister (1949) that an aphid-transmissible virus in diseased lime trees in the Gold Coast induced veinal flecks and stem pitting on sour lime, studies by McClean (1950) in South Africa, by Costa, Grant, and Moreira (1950) in Brazil, and by Wallace and Drake (1951) in California resulted in the development of the "lime test" for use in investigations of tristeza. It was established that seedlings of West Indian (Mexican) lime (*C. aurantifolia* [Christm.] Swing.) developed a specific kind of vein clearing and other diagnostic symptoms soon after infection with tristeza virus. This became a standard technique in subsequent studies and made it possible to show that the lime disease, stem pitting of grapefruit, tristeza, and quick decline are caused by the same virus. Tristeza vein clearing and stem pitting on Mexican lime are illustrated in figure 2–20. In addition to vein clearing and stem pitting, tristeza-infected limes sometimes develop enlarged, corky veins. In California, the effect has appeared more often on plants infected with some sources of the seedling-yellows virus complex, but this also is associated with boron deficiency in citrus.

Kitajima *et al.* (1964, 1965) found thread-like particles in the sap of a broad range of tristeza-susceptible plants and in thin sections through phloem cells of infected leaves which were not found in leaves of healthy plants. These particles also were present in plants experimently infected by the tristeza vector, *T. citricidus.* Particles measured approximately 11 x 2,000 nm. Price (1966) found the same type of flexuous rods in

Fig. 2–20. Tristeza symptoms on Mexican lime. Upper left, characteristic veinal clearing which persists as leaves harden. Upper right, abaxial surfaces of the same leaves with watersoaked appearance of the cleared parts of the veins. Bottom, twigs of infected lime seedlings with bark removed to show stem pitting.

phloem cells of lime plants with tristeza virus. Additional studies by Kitajima and Costa (1968) and Bar-Joseph, Loebenstein, and Cohen (1970) support the belief that the virus of tristeza consists of thread-like or flexuous rods such as illustrated in figure 2–21.

Economic Importance

There are no accurate statistics for an estimate of the total economic loss from tristeza throughout the citrus-producing countries of the world. Citrus plantings in South Africa and Aus-

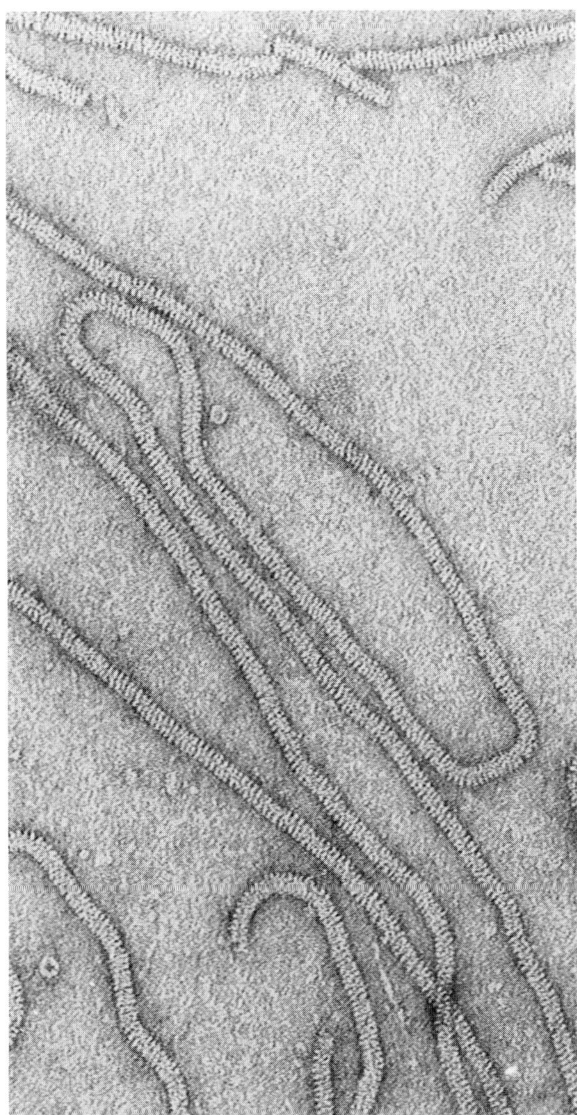

Fig. 2–21. Stringy particles of tristeza virus in partially purified preparation. (X 210,000). (Photo courtesy M. Bar-Joseph and G. Loebenstein.)

tralia have largely escaped damage from the true tristeza phase of the disease because sour orange and other susceptible rootstocks were never widely used in these countries. Since trifoliate orange (*Poncirus trifoliata* [L.] Raf.) is the principal rootstock in Japan, the disease has not caused serious losses there. With the exception of Spain, Mediterranean countries are still relatively free of damage. However, throughout the remainder of the world where citrus is grown, tristeza has caused or is causing very severe losses wherever susceptible scion-stock combinations exist.

Tristeza destroyed a large proportion of the trees of sweet orange, mandarin, and grapefruit on sour orange rootstock in Argentina. Fernandez-Valiela (1959) estimated that there were around 18 million of these trees in Argentina at the time tristeza appeared there, and by 1945 more than 10 million trees had been destroyed in the Argentine littoral. Six million or more trees in Tucuman and other provinces where tristeza made a later appearance can be added to this figure.

Bennett and Costa (1949) reported that tristeza destroyed more than 6 million trees in the state of São Paulo in Brazil within twelve years after it was found there. Burke (1958) put the loss of trees in Brazil at nearly 10 million. No statistics are available on losses in other South American countries. The disease was first observed in Peru by Bazan de Segura (1952), and since its discovery, citrus plantings on sour orange rootstock have declined to the point of unproductivity. Bertelli and Bertelli (1945) reported the presence of tristeza in Uruguay, and Ciferri (1950) described what appeared to be tristeza in Venezuela. Knorr, Malaguti, and Serpa (1960) confirmed the presence of tristeza virus in some citrus trees in Venezuela and reported at that time there had been no serious tree losses, probably because of the absence of the vector, *Toxoptera citricidus,* which has been identified there during the last two years.

It is safe to conclude that 3 million or more trees have been destroyed by tristeza in California or removed because of presence of the disease. Losses proportional to those experienced in Argentina and Brazil did not occur in California because approximately one-half of the state's citrus consisted of tristeza-tolerant stionic combinations. Furthermore, at least one important citrus area (the San Joaquin Valley) in California remained relatively free of the disease up to 1976.

Tristeza virus was detected for the first time in Florida citrus in 1951 by Grant and Schneider (1953), but no doubt it was present in some trees many years prior to actual identification. Studies by Norman *et al.* (1961), Cohen and Burnett (1961), and other workers established that tristeza is widespread in some parts of the state and that natural spread is occurring. In Florida, tree reaction to tristeza infection differs somewhat from the usual response. Although some trees develop severe decline, many infected trees show no severe symptoms. Numerous trees on sour orange rootstock have not declined even though they have been infected for from five to seven years. Also,

Cohen and Knorr (1953) and Cohen and Burnett (1961) reported that on many tristeza-infected trees in Florida the disease effect is a pronounced stunting rather than the characteristic decline and death. It was suggested that these stunted trees originated from virus-infected buds. Cohen and Burnett concluded that although some tristeza-infected trees had been found in every important citrus-growing county in Florida, the disease had made little economic impact on the citrus industry of the state up to 1961. However, Garnsey and Jackson (1975) recently reported a destructive outbreak in Central Florida.

Olson and Sleeth (1954) and Olson and McDonald (1954) found that some trees of Meyer lemon (*C. limon* x *C. sinensis*) and satsuma mandarin (*C. unshiu* Marc.) in Texas are carriers of tristeza virus. Indications are that such trees or their budwood parents were infected when they were brought into the state. There was no evidence of a detectable amount of spread from these trees to other orchard trees. Wallace and Drake (1955*a*, 1961*b*) found that most existing trees of Meyer lemon in California were carriers of the tristeza-seedling yellows virus complex. Carpenter (1956, 1957) demonstrated that many Meyer lemons in Arizona were infected with tristeza virus. Later, Allen and McDonald (1963) found some tristeza-infected Clementine mandarin trees at both the Yuma and Tempe Citrus Experiment Stations in Arizona, but there was no evidence of spread from these trees.

The discussion above refers to losses which have occurred to budded trees of susceptible scion and rootstock varieties. Other disease manifestations are also part of the tristeza-disease complex. Two of these which do not involve any scion-rootstock relationships are (1) stem pitting disease of grapefruit and (2) lime dieback, a disease of seedling lime trees. There is little published information on the occurrence of lime dieback, but Hughes and Lister (1949, 1953) reported that this disease caused serious trouble in seedling lime plantations of the African Gold Coast (Ghana). Stem pitting disease of grapefruit is known to be of considerable economic importance in the Republic of South Africa. Oberholzer (1959) stated that a majority of the grapefruit plantings there showed severe decline by their fifteenth year, even though they consisted of trees on Rough lemon (*C. jambhiri* Lush.) rootstock which do not develop typical tristeza decline. Stem pitting caused by tristeza virus is also important in Brazil, Argentina, and Australia on grapefruit and certain other citrus.

Until recently, the situation regarding tristeza and its effects in India, the Philippines, and Taiwan was not as well clarified as in the other countries mentioned. Studies by Vasudeva, Varma, and Rao (1959), Reddy and Rao (1961), Reddy (1965), and Capoor (1965) established that the tristeza-seedling yellows complex occurs in India. However, reports from India that sweet orange on Rough lemon, and sweet orange on sweet orange rootstocks were declining, and that seedlings of trifoliate orange and Rough lemon developed symptoms when inoculated with some sources of virus, suggested the presence of a pathogen other than tristeza virus.

A similar situation existed in Taiwan, where trees of Ponkan mandarin and Valencia orange on Sunki rootstock (*C. sunki* Hort. ex Tan.) declined. When these trees were indexed to lime by either tissue grafts or by means of *Toxoptera citricidus*, they commonly yielded tristeza virus. This was demonstrated by Matsumoto, Wang, and Su (1961), who also reported that seedling-yellows virus was present in some trees. These results led to the conclusion that what had been described earlier in Taiwan as "likubin disease" was the same as tristeza. Matsumoto, Su, and Chiu (1961) found what was presumed to be a strain of tristeza virus that caused severe decline of trees of Ponkan mandarin on such rootstocks as *C. sunki*, *P. trifoliata*, *C. tangerina* Hort. ex Tan. (Dancy tangerine), and *C. reshni* Hort. ex Tan. (Cleopatra mandarin); these varietal combinations are tolerant of tristeza in other countries. This source of virus caused the tristeza reaction on lime, but the possibility remained that another pathogen was responsible for the decline of trees of tristeza-tolerant stionic combinations. Some sources of tristeza virus studied in Taiwan had no effect on trees of the above combinations, and these can be assumed to be similar to the strains of tristeza virus prevailing in the United States and certain other countries.

Much the same situation occurred in the Philippines, where many thousands of citrus trees have declined since 1957. Since Bigornia and Calica (1961) and Nora (1961) identified tristeza virus in Philippine citrus, other workers have established that both tristeza and seedling yellows are widely distributed and that the efficient vector, *Toxoptera citricidus*, is present. There is good evidence that these viruses existed in the Philippines long before 1957. This probability and the fact that general decline of citrus did not occur before that date indicated that tristeza virus was not the principal cause of the tree decline that occurred after the late 1950's.

In India, seedlings of certain citrus types which have not shown tristeza-seedling yellows symptoms elsewhere have developed symptoms resembling yellows. Also in India, the Philippines, and Taiwan, stionic combinations which have been highly resistant to tristeza in other countries have declined. This suggested one of two conclusions: (1) unusually virulent strains of the tristeza virus or virus complex; or (2) an unidentified pathogen which separately, or in combination with tristeza virus, is capable of inducing disease on citrus seedlings or budded combinations that have been found resistant to tristeza and seedling-yellows in Australia, North America, South America, and South Africa. Recent investigations of the greening disease in South Africa and the decline of tristeza-tolerant trees in India, Taiwan, and the Philippines have firmly established that a psyllid-transmitted agent is the cause of much of the decline of trees of tristeza-tolerant scion-stock combinations. Details of this development are presented in later discussions of greening, citrus dieback, and leaf-mottle-yellows diseases.

In addition to countries already mentioned, the tristeza virus has been found in Chile, Egypt, Israel, Morocco, Italy, New Zealand, Japan, the Federation of Malaya, Surinam, and Guyana. Diseases which appear to be the same as tristeza have been reported from Java (Indonesia), Ceylon, and the Fiji Islands. In Chile, Egypt, and Italy it appears that there has been very little spread of the disease up to the present. Bar-Joseph, Loebenstein, and Oren (1974) demonstrated that some natural spread has occurred in Israel. In Japan, the virus is quite generally present but except for severe stem pitting effects on trees of hassaku orange has caused no damage because of the almost exclusive use of trifoliate orange and other tristeza-tolerant varieties as rootstocks. Fragmentary reports from Spain (Laurent, 1960; Beltran-Alonzo Cuevillas and Planes-Samper, 1960) disclose that tristeza is causing significant damage in some citrus areas. In other countries mentioned, no information on economic losses is available to the writer.

Symptomatology

The symptoms originally described for podredumbre de la raicilla in Argentina, tristeza in Brazil, and quick decline in California were those of affected trees of sweet orange varieties growing on sour orange rootstocks. The reaction of such trees to tristeza infection may follow one of two patterns. The most striking reaction is the sudden wilting and drying of all leaves. The leaves fall gradually, but most of the fruits remain on the tree until they become dried or mummified (fig. 2–22). In California, trees under five to six years of age commonly react in this manner. The root system of affected trees shows almost complete absence of functional feeder roots, and larger roots are found rotting back from the extremities. Undecayed roots and sometimes even the trunk up to the bud union are almost totally void of stored starch (fig. 2–23). Some trees that collapse quickly and appear to be dying make a partial recovery and remain alive indefinitely after much defoliation and some dieback of twigs and small limbs. After substantial recovery and regeneration of growth, varying amounts of stored starch reappear in the roots, and bark callus forms at the juncture of the living and decayed parts of the roots. This is followed by a weak production of new roots, but the trees never return to a normal condition.

Fig. 2–22. Collapse stage of tristeza disease. Such trees wilt suddenly and often die.

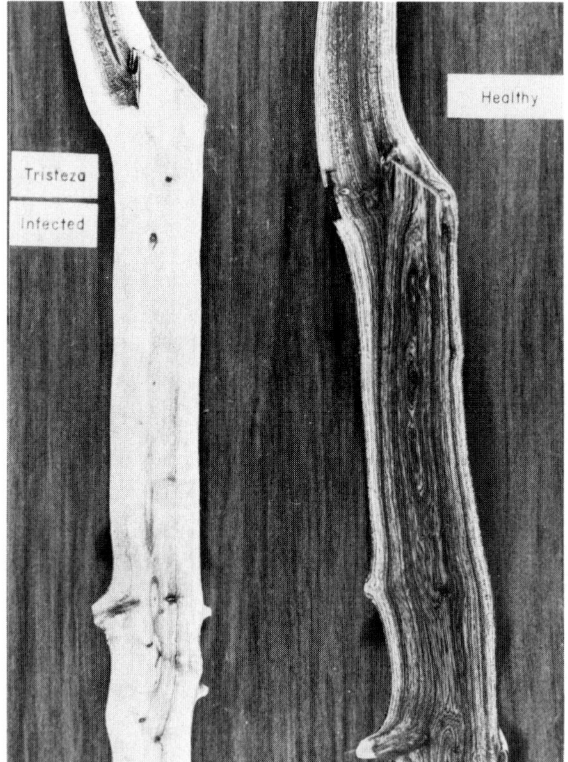

Fig. 2–23. Starch depletion in tristeza-affected trees. Left, sectioned trunk of young tree in advanced stages of tristeza stained with IKI solution to show absence of stored food in rootstock. Right, healthy tree showing normal starch both above and below bud union.

Fig. 2–24. A tristeza-infected tree making a partial recovery after having reached an advanced stage of decline. (Photo by L. J. Klotz.)

Fig. 2–25. Young orchard tree in early stages of tristeza. Frequently, an abnormally heavy crop of fruit is set and matured after infection takes place.

Older trees also sometimes collapse quickly, but usually decline gradually until they reach an equilibrium stage. Eventually, these trees may again produce some fruit, the amount depending on both the stage of decline reached initially and the extent of recovery (fig. 2–24). However, yield and fruit size never become normal, and under conditions of stress these trees may again decline or even collapse.

On mature trees of sweet orange infected with tristeza virus, the first obvious symptoms are absence of new growth, a dulling or bronzing of leaves, and premature coloring of the fruit. Often there is an abnormally heavy crop of fruit, which is smaller in size than that on unaffected trees.

On young trees, an early, conspicuous symptom is abundant flowering. This is followed by a heavy set of fruits which are held to maturity (fig. 2–25). Healthy trees of comparable age blossom much less and only rarely set and hold any fruit.

Budling trees subject to decline from tristeza reveal some microscopic symptoms before

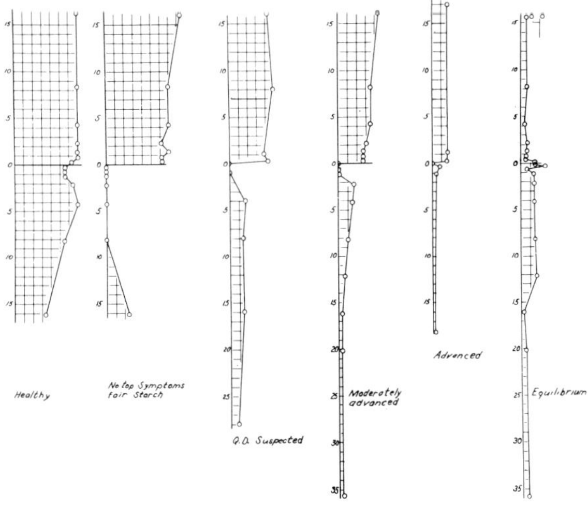

Fig. 2–26. Diagrams showing amount of functional phloem (cross-hatched areas) in bark of a healthy sweet orange tree in comparison with trees in various stages of tristeza. The bud union is at zero and the vertical line at the extreme left of each diagram represents the cambium. Circles indicate locations sampled and measured. Distance between vertical lines = 100 microns; distance between horizontal lines = 1 inch. The second and third diagrams clearly show that total loss of functional phloem may occur before trees display top symptoms. (Courtesy of H. Schneider.)

macroscopic symptoms are evident, but special techniques are required to disclose these symptoms. Schneider (1946, 1947, 1954, 1959) described sieve-tube necrosis and certain other characteristic anatomical changes in the phloem tissues of tristeza-affected trees of sweet orange on sour orange rootstock. As illustrated diagramatically in figure 2–26, after infection occurs the amount of functioning phloem is reduced to such an extent that a girdling effect results. This prevents movement of food to the root system and clearly explains the utilization of reserve starch, subsequent decay of roots, and appearance of top symptoms.

Schneider (1954) reported that the incubation period, or time between infection and appearance of top symptoms in fifteen-year-old Valencia trees, averaged twelve months, but sometimes was as long as twenty-three months. Young trees one to two years from budding may show early macroscopic symptoms within four to six months after inoculation. Using extremely small plants of very susceptible combinations, the author obtained macroscopic symptoms within two months after infection under greenhouse conditions.

Stem Pitting.—"Stem pitting" is a term used to describe depressions of different sizes and shapes in the wood of plants. Early stages of pitting are detectable only upon removal of bark. In citrus, the pits consist of depressions in the outer wood with corresponding pegs or projections on the inner face of bark. Pits of various sizes and shapes are associated with known virus infections in citrus, but it is difficult to make a specific diagnosis on the basis of wood pitting alone. It is clear that certain kinds of citrus infected with either tristeza, cristacortis, or xyloporosis commonly show pitting. The pitting of xyloporosis virus on such hosts as tangelo (*C. paradisi* x *C. reticulata*) and mandarin are perhaps sufficiently distinct for specific diagnosis if tristeza or other viruses which cause pitting are not also present. Although xyloporosis pitting varies somewhat on different citrus varieties, one usually finds the pits occurring in patches and there is evidence of gum both in the wood pits and within the bark projections. Certainly in later stages there is more disorganization of the tissues of both wood and bark from xyloporosis than when pitting is caused by other viruses.

In the case of wood pitting induced by tristeza virus, there are variations in numbers and shapes of pits dependent upon the strain of virus used and the host variety affected. In general, except in initial stages of development, tristeza pits on experimentally inoculated Mexican lime seedlings consist of longitudinal depressions of various lengths. When there are many pits, some of them coalesce to form grooves which follow the direction of stem growth and grain of the wood (see fig. 2–20, p. 90). Sometimes pitting is so extensive that the entire stem surface assumes a rugose appearance.

DuCharme and Knorr (1954) described several distinct types of pitting on a great variety of stionic combinations of citrus in Argentina. All trees studied had been exposed to infection with tristeza virus over a period of seven to eight years, and probably all of the scion buds used came from tristeza-infected trees. Other viruses such as xyloporosis, exocortis, and psorosis were no doubt present in many of the budwood sources. Thus, DuCharme and Knorr were unable to associate a particular type of pitting with a single virus.

In addition to different types of pitting in which projections from the cambial face of the bark fit into corresponding depressions in the xylem, a reverse type of pitting often is found in citrus. This form consists of small, teethlike projections, usually in great numbers, on the cambial face of the

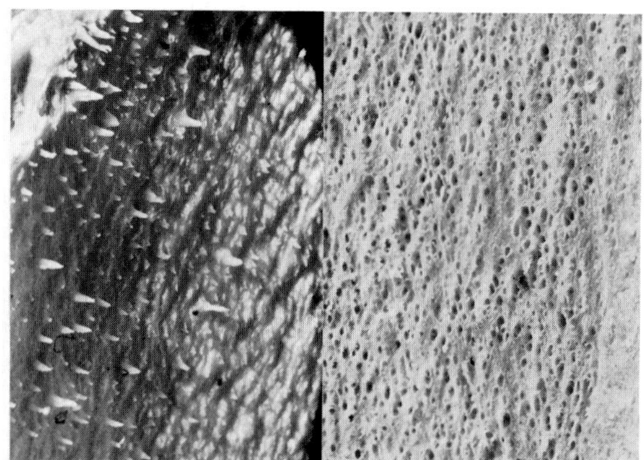

Fig. 2–27. Inverse pitting or pin-holing symptom of tristeza. Left, bark removed showing many small, sharply pointed projections extending from surface of the wood. Right, cambial face of bark with pits, each corresponding to one of the projections.

wood which fit into minute holes on the corresponding face of the bark. This reaction, illustrated in figure 2–27, was described as pin points or inverse xyloporosis by Reichert, Yoffe, and Bental (1953), who thought it to be specific for xyloporosis. Schneider (1952*a*) observed this effect in studies of sieve-tube necrosis of sour orange rootstocks under lemon tops and explained its anatomical structure. In other studies by Busby (1953), Cohen and Knorr (1954), DuCharme and Knorr (1954), and Schneider (1954), this symptom often was found to be associated with tristeza virus infection. Reviewing previous work, Reichert and Winocour (1956) concluded that this form of inverse pitting in citrus is not a specific reaction to a single virus. In support of this conclusion, Schneider (1957) observed hyperplastic ray development on trees on sour orange with a disorder he called "chronic decline." This disorder has not been shown to be an infectious disease. Additionally, Calavan (1957*a*, 1957*b*) stated that pinholing (honeycombing) is common on lemon and lime trees affected with wood pocket or lignocortosis, an apparent genetic weakness.

On some kinds of citrus, the tristeza virus complex causes extensive wood pitting which is observable externally as infected trees become older. Figure 2–28 illustrates this effect on Rabat orange inoculated with a California field source of tristeza. The stem pitting of grapefruit described in South Africa by Oberholzer *et al.* (1949), was noted earlier. These workers did not relate stem pitting of grapefruit to tristeza, but they showed that this disease was perpetuated in budwood. Numerous

Fig. 2–28. Advanced tristeza stem-pitting on field tree of Rabat orange.

workers contributed information leading to the generally accepted premise that stem-pitting symptoms are commonly associated with tristeza-virus infection. As mentioned previously, Hughes and Lister (1949, 1953) showed that trees with what was described as lime disease or lime dieback in the Gold Coast displayed vein clearing of leaves and xylem pitting and reproduced these symptoms on small lime seedlings exposed to *Toxoptera citricidus.* McClean (1950) reported that limes inoculated by means of *T. citricidus* from grapefruit trees with South African stem-pitting disease developed the same symptoms described by Hughes and Lister. In South America, Costa *et al.* (1950) showed that young grapefruit trees developed stem pitting when infected with tristeza virus and that virus from stem-pitted grapefruit trees induced vein clearing and pitting on lime seedlings like that reported from Africa. Wallace and Drake (1951) demonstrated that the virus from quick-decline-affected trees in California caused these same symptoms on lime infected either by tissue grafts or by the vector *Aphis gossypii*.

Susceptibility to tristeza stem pitting is not necessarily influenced by rootstocks, since injurious effects occur on trees of certain varieties when grown as budded trees or as seedlings. Orchard trees of grapefruit commonly develop stem pitting in South Africa, South America, and Australia, but in California this manifestation of tristeza has not been of importance on grapefruit. Most grapefruit acreage in California is in areas where tristeza has not caused significant damage to sweet orange trees. This may partly explain why stem pitting on grapefruit has not become an important disease in California. However, the author is of the opinion that the severe stem pitting of grapefruit in South Africa, South America, and Australia results from exposure of trees to seedling yellows, or strains of tristeza virus derived from seedling yellows which are spread naturally in those countries but not in California. In some experiments in California, Wallace and Drake (1955*b*) observed that seedlings of grapefruit, pummelo, and some other kinds of citrus developed strong stem pitting which began to show externally one year after inoculation with seedling yellows virus (fig. 2–29). In contrast, the same kinds of seedlings inoculated with field sources of tristeza virus developed no pitting or a slight amount which could be detected only after removal of the bark.

Observations by numerous workers, particularly Bitters, Dukeshire, and Brusca (1953), DuCharme and Knorr (1954), and Grant, Moreira, and Salibe (1960) further demonstrated that stem pitting is a common effect of tristeza virus and that under some conditions and on some varieties of citrus it becomes a serious disorder. It appears that some strains of tristeza virus induce more pitting than others. Also, as pointed out by Bitters *et al.* (1953), it seems that some rootstock varieties predispose sweet orange scion tops to pitting (fig. 2–30). It appears that the reverse may also be true; that is, the scion variety sometimes influences the degree of stem pitting shown by the rootstock.

In addition to the severe effects of stem pitting on grapefruit trees, damage now being caused on the Pera orange in Brazil demonstrates that other important citrus varieties not subject to ordinary decline when grown on certain rootstocks can still be subject to damage from the stem pitting phase of this disease. Thus, control or prevention of tristeza disease can no longer be considered a simple matter of finding stionic combinations not subject to phloem degeneration at the bud union.

Seedling Yellows.—Early observations on tristeza disease, particularly in Argentina, Brazil, and California led to the conclusion that lemon varieties such as Eureka and Lisbon were not affected by the virus even when grown on such rootstocks as sour orange. In Australia, Fraser (1952) found that many orchard trees of sweet orange and mandarin carried a virus which when inoculated by means of tissue-grafts into seedlings of Eureka lemon, Marsh grapefruit, Seville sour orange, and some citrons (*C. medica* L.), induced

Fig. 2–29. Tristeza stem-pitting on experimentally infected seedlings of *A*, ponderosa lemon; *B*, Chinese pomelo; *C*, Eureka lemon. In California, pitting has been observed only rarely on Eureka lemon.

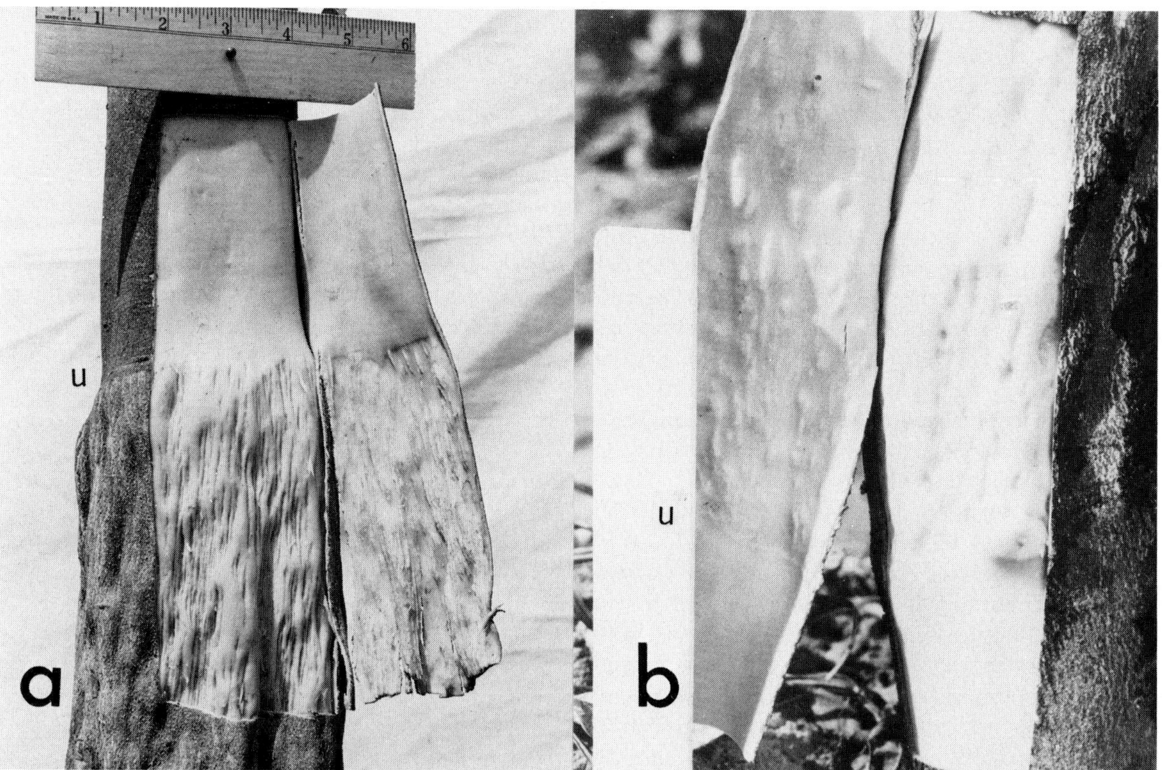

Fig. 2–30. Apparent stock-scion effect on tristeza stem-pitting. ***A*, Valencia orange scion without pitting on severely pitted Morton citrange rootstock. *B*, strong pitting on Valencia scion on Sauvage sour orange stock which is free of pitting. Bud union at "U." (Photo courtesy of W. P. Bitters.)**

a severe stunting and yellowing. This reaction was described as seedling yellows. Fraser (1952) demonstrated that seedling-yellows virus is transmissible by *Toxoptera citricidus*, but she reported that Eureka lemon seedlings inoculated by aphids were less severely affected than those inoculated by tissue-grafts. It was reported further that after a period of time, aphid-inoculated lemon seedlings resumed normal growth and no longer contained seedling-yellows virus. Fraser (1952) considered seedling-yellows virus to be distinct from tristeza but stated that it had not been found unaccompanied by tristeza virus. These conclusions were based on the fact that all sources of virus that caused seedling-yellows on Eureka lemon, for example, also caused what had been accepted as a tristeza reaction on West Indian lime (i.e., vein clearing and stem pitting).

Since the first report of Fraser (1952), investigations on seedling yellows have been made chiefly in Australia and South Africa, where this virus complex or mixture is commonly present in orchard trees of sweet orange and mandarin, and in California, where it is carried by most trees of Meyer lemon. In California, it has been found also in certain citrus introductions maintained in varietal collections, but not in orchard trees of sweet orange, lemon, grapefruit, or mandarin. In other words, there is no indication at present that seedling-yellows virus is spreading significantly by natural means (aphid vectors) in commercial citrus plantings in California. Figure 2–31 shows the effects of seedling-yellows virus on seedlings of Eureka lemon.

From the studies of Fraser (1952, 1959*a*), McClean and van der Plank (1955), McClean (1960, 1963), Wallace (1957*a*), Wallace and Drake (1961*b*, 1972*a*), Martinez and Wallace (1964), and Wallace, Martinez, and Drake (1965), it has been established that all sources of inoculum which cause symptoms of seedling yellows are accompanied by a virus that induces tristeza lime reaction but not yellows reaction. Fraser (1959*a*) concluded that her earlier belief that seedling-yellows virus is distinct from tristeza virus was incorrect, and she suggested that tristeza disease (i.e., decline of susceptible budded trees) is caused by the seedling-yellows virus and that the other accompanying virus is the stem-pitting virus. Fraser stated further that the stem-pitting virus exists in a

Fig. 2–31. Seedling yellows on lemon. *A*, **normal noninoculated Eureka lemon seedling.** *B*, **lemon seedling same age as plant** *A*, **forty-six days after inoculation with California seedling-yellows virus source No. 1.** *C*, **severely affected lemon seedling twelve months after inoculation with source 1.**

multiplicity of strains that vary widely in the amount of vein clearing and xylem pitting on West Indian lime. In support of her thesis that seedling-yellows virus is the cause of tristeza disease of budded trees, Fraser (1959*a*) reported obtaining tristeza decline of budling indicator trees with seedling-yellows virus, but not with what she described as the stem-pitting virus. Other workers, notably McClean in South Africa and Wallace and co-workers in California, have not agreed with these contentions.

McClean (1963) considered seedling yellows, stem pitting, and decline of budded trees to be reactions to a tristeza virus complex, and he stated that there is no evidence to support Fraser's contention that two distinct viruses are associated with this complex. In his studies, McClean found that all sources of tristeza virus caused stem pitting; however, some did only this, while others also caused tristeza (decline of budded trees) or both yellows and tristeza. McClean interpreted his findings as evidence that in the tristeza complex there is an association of at least two components: a stem-pitting component which alone is responsible for stem-pitting disease, and a yellows component, which either alone or combined with stem-pitting virus causes yellows and probably tristeza as well.

Results from studies in California already cited agree in general but not completely with those of McClean. Important differences are that in California, no seedling yellows has been found in trees in commercial orchard plantings, and no field sources of tristeza virus have been discovered which do not cause at least some slight disease effects on tristeza-susceptible budded trees. The virus that causes tristeza decline of budded trees in California orchards also causes stem pitting on lime and some other kinds of citrus and apparently exists as a multitude of strains. There are strains which cause either mild or severe decline on trees of sweet orange on sour orange rootstock, and weak or strong reactions on lime seedlings, but the degree of severity on budded trees is not always correlated with that on lime. It is not to be expected that the virus content of field trees in California would be the same as in South Africa and

Australia, where it is established that the seedling-yellows virus complex is spread commonly by aphid vectors. These vectors also have an opportunity to separate and spread tristeza virus directly from seedling yellows or obtain it from trees that have recovered and lost the yellows-inducing virus component. In all three locations, it has been shown that young trees of lemon, grapefruit, and sour orange experimentally infected with seedling-yellows virus frequently recover from symptoms of yellows and that the virus remaining in them will no longer cause yellows. McClean (1963) stated that field trees naturally infected with seedling-yellows virus react similarly.

In California, Wallace and Drake (1961*b*) Wallace (1965), and Wallace *et al.* (1965) found that lemon and sour orange seedlings frequently recovered from symptoms of seedling yellows (SY) and after resuming quite normal growth contained virus which caused the tristeza lime reaction but not seedling yellows (fig. 2–32). This virus was referred to as "seedling-yellows-tristeza virus" (SYT). Recovered plants usually were unaffected when challenge-inoculated with the SY source from which they recovered. Healthy lemon seedlings graft inoculated from recovered plants were provided the same degree of protection against reinfection with SY virus as had been found in the donor plants. However, the degree of protection varied, depending on the isolate of SY virus from which plants recovered and the SY isolate used for challenge inoculations.

Fig. 2–32. Growth of lemon plants after recovery from seedling yellows. ***A-B*****, cuttings from a healthy plant.** ***C-D*****, cuttings from a plant that recovered from seedling-yellows source 6.**

Martinez and Wallace (1964, 1967) demonstrated that *A. gossypii* and *T. citricidus* can transmit the SY virus complex or can selectively transmit the SYT component from SY-infected sweet orange. Subsequently, Wallace and Drake (1972*a*) found that seedlings of trifoliate orange and Troyer citrange can be infected with some sources of seedling-yellows virus and that graft transfers from these plants sometimes result in seedling yellows but in other instances only the SYT virus is transferred. Using these techniques, it was possible to establish isolates of SYT virus which had not been involved in plant recovery reactions and to study two or more aphid isolates of both SY virus complex and SYT virus derived from single stock sources of seedling yellows. Evidence was obtained that the seedling yellows-infected trees under study in California carried what can be considered to be "substrains" of both the SYT virus and the SY virus complex. This had been indicated earlier when Desjardins *et al.* (1959) separated four different seedling-yellows isolates from a single Meyer lemon plant by heat treatment.

Wallace and Drake (1972*a*) summarized studies on fourteen stock sources of SY virus obtained from different trees of Meyer lemon and other citrus grown from introductions which apparently were carriers of seedling-yellows virus when they were brought to California. Investigations dealt with: (1) differences between the individual stock sources of SY virus; (2) variations among SY isolates from individual stock sources established by aphid transfer (ASY) or citrange (CSY); (3) protection by SYT virus isolates obtained from SY stock sources through plant recovery (RSY) in comparison with SYT virus separated from SY by aphids (ASYT), or screened from SY by resistant plant hosts, e.g., citrange (CSYT); (4) studies of plants that recovered after infection with aphid-transferred SY virus (ASY) and the degree of protection by the virus (RASY) remaining in the recovered plants; and (5) comparisons among various isolates of RSY, ARSY, ASYT, and field strains of tristeza (T) virus in regard to protection of lemon seedlings against challenge inoculation with various sources or isolates of SY virus.

It is clear that the exact relationship of virus components of the SY complex is not yet understood. If the so-called seedling-yellows-tristeza (SYT) component is separated from the SY virus complex by aphid transfer, or screened out by a highly resistant host plant, it appears identical to tristeza (T) virus obtained from orchard trees in California. Like T virus, ASYT virus and that screened out by Troyer citrange (TSYT), produced the tristeza lime reaction, caused decline in varying degrees of trees of sweet orange on sour orange rootstock, and provided lemon seedlings with only a very slight protection against seedling-yellows, primarily in the form of a delayed reaction. On the other hand, it was often a different story with RSY virus derived from a recovered lemon or sour orange seedling. If the recovered plant was graft inoculated originally from a stock source of SY virus, presumably carrying multiple substrains of both the unidentified component and SYT virus, the RSY virus remaining after recovery provided the plant complete protection against the SY source from which it recovered, as well as against some other SY sources. Also, healthy lemon seedlings graft inoculated from the recovered plant were provided the same degree of protection.

If California field tristeza (T) virus is similar or identical to the SYT virus separated from SY-infected plants by aphids or by passage through resistant hosts, then it must be concluded that RSY virus remaining in yellows-recovered plants is also tristeza virus. RSY virus produces the lime reaction and depending on the isolate, causes tristeza decline of budded trees ranging from extremely mild to severe. Furthermore, because it protects plants against seedling yellows, it would appear to be related to the component of the SY complex that causes symptoms of yellows. But the severe symptoms produced on lemon seedlings by the SY virus complex and loss of the yellows-inducing component during plant recovery could be accepted as evidence of unrelatedness between the yellows-inducing component and tristeza (T) virus, because lemon trees infected with T virus from orchard trees, RSY virus from a recovered plant, or SYT virus separated from SY by aphids, retain these viruses indefinitely even though the trees remain without symptoms. On the basis of the above differences, the hypothesis could be advanced that seedling-yellows symptoms result from a combined action of tristeza virus and an unidentified virus, possibly not related to tristeza. But until the unidentified virus is isolated, its relationship to tristeza cannot be determined.

Perhaps the most puzzling reaction encountered in the studies of seedling-yellows in California is the high degree of protection RSY virus provides both recovered plants and lemon and sour-orange seedlings graft inoculated with it. This is in contrast to the almost total lack of protection by aphid-separated seedling-yellows-tristeza virus (ASYT) and tristeza (T) obtained from naturally infected orchard trees of sweet orange.

Although it would not explain all observed reactions, Wallace and Drake (1972*a*) suggested that the failure of aphid-selected SYT virus to protect plants against challenge inoculations with SY virus may result from acquisition and transfer of too few substrains of SYT virus by aphids from a given source of seedling-yellows. In other words, in the SY virus complex, the substrains of the virus that cause yellows may have corresponding substrains of SYT virus. One substrain of SYT virus may protect against one or more of the associated substrains of the yellows virus but not against all of the substrains that exist in a stock source of the SY complex. An aphid-selected SYT virus could consist of a few SYT substrains or even a single one which can protect against a limited number of substrains of the other virus component. On the other hand, after recovery of a plant that has been graft-inoculated from a stock source of SY, the recovered plant would contain the full complement of SYT substrains of that particular SY source and thus have a broader protection. Wallace and Drake (1972*a*) reported that RSY derived from a given stock source of SY protected against that SY source and some others, but gave no protection against some of the stock sources studied. Applying the above hypothesis and assuming that symptoms of seedling yellows are produced by a combined action of an unidentified virus and SYT virus, it seems that the failure of certain RSY virus isolates to protect against all stock sources may result from the existence of SY "cultures" which have no common substrains of the two virus components that make up the seedling-yellows complex.

For the record, it should be mentioned that studies in both California and South Africa are not in agreement with Fraser's suggestions (1) that the virus that causes seedling yellows is the sole cause of tristeza decline of budded trees, and (2) that the other component which always accompanies seedling-yellows virus only causes stem pitting. The author has produced typical tristeza decline on non-tolerant budded trees by infecting them with SYT virus experimentally separated from several different sources of seedling yellows. Some isolates of the accompanying virus obtained from recovered plants, which the author identifies as RSY virus, caused no symptoms on Valencia orange trees on sour-orange rootstock growing in the glasshouse. Other isolates caused mild-to-severe symptoms. When the trees with no symptoms were transferred to field plantings, many of them developed well for a period of years but all showed at least slight tristeza symptoms.

Obviously, three very different symptom manifestations are caused by viruses associated with tristeza. Regardless of the relationships of the causal viruses it is advisable to follow McClean's practice of referring to the different reactions as "stem pitting," "seedling yellows," and "tristeza," since in effect these are distinct reactions and at times must be discussed or treated as separate disorders.

Lime Dieback.—Except for the studies of Hughes and Lister (1949, 1953) and of other workers already cited, which demonstrated that lime dieback (lime disease) of sour lime in West Africa is caused by the tristeza virus, little is known of this disease as it existed there. Reportedly, it reached severe proportions as early as 1938. Hughes and Lister (1953) suggested that the same disease has been present in the West Indies for a much longer time, and they reported its presence in British-mandated Togoland. In West Africa (Ghana) where the lime industry consisted of a relatively small acreage of seedling trees, most of the trees became unproductive. It was observed that limes budded on Rough lemon rootstock yielded good crops for a few years, but a later report by Martyn (1954) stated that "attempts at rehabilitation of the lime industry by use of rough-lemon rootstock have not proved wholly successful."

On the basis of known reactions of experimentally infected Mexican lime and the performance of orchard plantings of lime under exposure to tristeza infection, it can be concluded that the lime dieback disease reported from Ghana resulted from severe stem pitting and other injury caused by certain strains of tristeza and seedling-yellows viruses. Supporting evidence for that conclusion is presented in the discussion of control of tristeza disease.

Hassaku Dwarf.—Tanaka and Yamada (1961) described a disease on hassaku orange, *Citrus hassaku* (Hort. ex. Tanaka) in Japan to which they gave the name "hassaku dwarf." It was reported that this disease had been observed for thirty years. Affected trees remained small with leaves small, pale in color, and slightly crinkled. Fruits were small with thick rinds and usually had less than normal juice. The wood of the tree trunks was pitted and grooved. Affected trees bloomed abundantly, but most of the blossoms dropped, and within fifteen to twenty years the trees became worthless.

All dwarfed hassaku trees yielded tristeza virus when indexed to Mexican lime. Tanaka, Kishi, and Yamada (1965) established that hassaku dwarf and satsuma dwarf are distinct diseases although tristeza virus always was found in trees affected by either disease. It was suggested that hassaku dwarf was caused by a severe strain of tristeza virus. Proof that tristeza virus causes hassaku dwarf has been difficult to obtain (Tanaka, Shikata, and Sasaki, 1969) because hassaku orange is monoembryonic and no virus-free true hassaku trees have been available for inoculation with tristeza virus. However, Sadai (1963) demonstrated that the causal agent of hassaku dwarf is transmitted by *Toxoptera citricidus;* subsequent studies have established that this disease is caused by tristeza virus.

Sasaki (1972) studied two sources of hassaku dwarf virus (HDV), compared with sources of virus that caused severe yellows on seedlings of Kawano natsukan (KSYV), characteristic of symptoms of citrus seedling yellows as known in other countries. Both HDV and KSYV were transmitted by *T. citricidus* and caused severe tristeza symptoms on Mexican lime. Neither virus was recovered from graft-inoculated seedlings of trifoliate orange. Sasaki reported that a virulent isolate of HDV had a protective effect against KSYV in seedlings of Kawano natsukan, whereas a mild isolate of tristeza virus obtained from a normal appearing hassaku orange tree did not protect. Sasaki (1972) suggested logically that HDV is closely related to the severe stem-pitting virus referred to by Fraser (1959*a*) in Australia. The fact that Sasaki (1972) obtained protection against seedling-yellows virus by HDV which caused hassaku dwarf, but found no protection by a source of tristeza which did not cause hassaku dwarf indicates that this disease is caused by what Wallace and Drake (1972*a*, 1972*b*) designated RSY virus, i.e., the tristezalike virus derived from the tristeza-seedling yellows virus complex through host plant recovery.

Hassaku dwarf disease is similar to stem pitting of grapefruit, Pera orange, sour lime, and some other kinds of citrus inasmuch as it is caused by a direct action of tristeza virus. Use of so-called tristeza-tolerant rootstocks, therefore, provides no control. Emphasis should be directed towards discovery and use of mild, protecting virus strains such as described elsewhere in this chapter for control of tristeza stem pitting of grapefruit and sour lime.

Natsudaidai Dwarf.—*C. natsudaidai* Hay., Daidai-mikan or Japanese summer grapefruit, is an important citrus variety in Ehime Prefecture of Japan. Nakamura (1965) described a dwarf disease of Kawano natsukan, an early variety of natsudaidai. This disorder became known as "natsudaidai dwarf." Symptoms were dwarfing of trees, stem pitting of one- to four-year-old branches, small leaves, and small hardened fruit. According to Tanaka *et al.* (1971), another disease known as natsudaidai dwarf with a different syndrome had been observed since around 1953 in Yamaguchi Prefecture. Presumably this is the same disorder described by Izawa (1966) as "withering disease of *C. unshiu.*"

Studies by Kishi (1967), H. Tanaka (1971, 1972), Tanaka, Yamada, and Kishi (1971), Tanaka and Yamada (1972), and Omori and Matsumoto (1972) have established that the disease described by Nakamura (1965), which tentatively had been named "natsudaidai dwarf 'B,' " is caused by tristeza virus and that the other, sometimes referred to as "natsudaidai dwarf 'A,' " belongs in the satsuma dwarf group.

In future references to these two diseases of *C. natsudaidai* it would be helpful if that caused by satsuma dwarf virus is identified as *"natsudaidai dwarf 'A' "* and that caused by tristeza virus as *"natsudaidai dwarf 'B.' "*

Transmission and Spread

There has been no report of successful transmission of viruses of the tristeza complex by sap-inoculation techniques. These viruses apparently are not transmitted in any significant amount through citrus seeds, although this conclusion is based largely on circumstantial evidence. The author made limited studies with seeds of Valencia orange, but obtained no seed transmission. The strongest evidence against seed transmission of tristeza virus is that in recent years many thousands of experimental lime seedlings have been grown by workers in several countries. Commonly, seed-parent trees were infected with tristeza virus, but there have been no reports of disease in noninoculated lime seedlings grown under insect-free conditions.

Weathers and Harjung (1964) confirmed earlier suggestions by Bennett and Costa (1949) that tristeza virus can be transmitted from diseased to healthy citrus plants by means of dodder *(Cuscuta subinclusa)*. This kind of transmission is of interest because it offers a possible means of separating viruses from mixtures and has other experimental uses, although it plays no part in natural spread of tristeza virus.

Bud Transmission.—The virus of tristeza is perpetuated in buds or scions from infected trees and the use of such propagative material is a means of increasing and spreading the disease under certain circumstances. The use of infected buds for propagation of new trees is practiced by necessity in countries where all orchard trees are infected. Where this situation exists, there is no alternative to use of infected buds, but they must be used only on the so-called tolerant rootstocks. For many years, this procedure seems to have been satisfactory in most respects. However, the rather serious effects of stem pitting on such citrus as lime, grapefruit, and Pera sweet orange (regardless of the kind of rootstock used) and the fact that some strains of the virus complex cause stunting of sweet orange and other varieties on all stocks, suggest that further study should be made of possible benefits from the use of budwood from mother trees known to be carrying mild strains of the virus. This is discussed later in the section dealing with control.

Transmission by Insects.—Following the original report by Meneghini (1946) that the tristeza virus is transmitted by the "brown" or "tropical" citrus aphid, *Toxoptera citricidus* Kirk. (Aphis citricidus [Kirk.]), further studies of Meneghini (1948), Bennett and Costa (1949), Grant and Costa (1951*a*), and others established that this aphid is an efficient vector and the principal agent of transmission of tristeza virus in South America, South and West Africa, Australia, and probably most countries of the Far East. This species has not been reported from the United States or from countries in the Mediterranean basin.

Dickson *et al.* (1951) demonstrated that the melon aphid, *Aphis gossypii* Glover is the vector of tristeza virus in California. Norman and Grant (1954, 1956, 1961) reported successful transmission of tristeza virus in Florida by *A. gossypii*, *A. spiraecola* Patch, and possibly *Toxoptera aurantii* Fonsc. Transmission by some other vectors has been suspected but not conclusively proved. On the basis of experimental tests, *A. gossypii* is classed as an inefficient vector in comparison with *T. citricidus*, but the extremely high populations of the former species in certain citrus areas in California have been adequate to account for the observed incidence of disease in orchard plantings. Where present, these two species usually occur in extremely high numbers, and there is little hope of preventing the spread of tristeza virus by attempting to control or reduce the aphid populations. By trapping experiments, Dickson, Flock, and Laird (1956) calculated that in one location in southern California, nearly one million aphids of five species flew into a single citrus tree in one year and that 36,000 of these were *A. gossypii*.

Both Fraser (1952) in Australia and McClean (1960) in South Africa showed that *T. citricidus*, the vector of tristeza, could also transmit the virus complex that causes seedling-yellows. In California, Martinez and Wallace (1964) demonstrated that some *A. gossypii* which fed on seedling-yellows-infected plants transmitted the entire yellows complex, but that others infected test plants with virus that caused only the lime reaction and tristeza decline of budded trees. Subsequently, Martinez and Wallace (1967) demonstrated that *T. citricidus* can transmit the entire SY complex but sometimes selectively transmits the tristeza component (SYT) from seedling-yellows-infected citrus in the Philippines. Thus, it is established that these two species of aphids are vectors of all recognized components of the tristeza-seedling yellows virus complex.

Host Range of Tristeza Virus Complex

It is evident from published reports that nearly all species and varieties of true citrus and some citrus relatives are hosts of the viruses which cause tristeza, stem pitting, and seedling yellows. However, except for slight stunting or other minor effects, some of these are symptomless carriers of the viruses when grown as seedlings, as budlings of identical scion and rootstock, or as budlings on certain other rootstocks. Outstanding exceptions to this are: (1) some acid limes are directly affected by tristeza and seedling-yellows viruses; (2) Pera sweet orange, many selections of grapefruit, and other kinds of citrus are subject to stem pitting; and (3) lemons, sour orange, grapefruit, shaddocks, and some other citrus types develop severe symptoms after infection with seedling-yellows virus when grown as seedlings or as budlings on rootstocks on which they are not seriously affected by infection with ordinary tristeza virus.

In California, it has been found that sour orange seedlings, after infection with ordinary strains of tristeza virus, fail to maintain the virus or maintain it at a low concentration. In Brazil, Costa, Grant, and Moreira (1949) reported that trifoliate orange is apparently immune to tristeza virus. In California, Wallace and Drake (1972*a*) failed to recover virus from trifoliate orange seedlings inoculated with field sources of tristeza, but found that some trifoliate orange seedlings can be infected with some strains of seedling-yellows virus.

So far, there has been no report of successful infection of noncitrus hosts with any part of the tristeza virus complex. Bennett and Costa (1949) made juice inoculations to sixty-seven species and varieties of plants, mostly annuals, but got no evidence of infection. The same workers failed to infect twelve different noncitrus hosts by means of dodder.

Control of Tristeza

Because of the high populations and wide distribution of aphid vectors of tristeza virus, control of the disease in much commercially grown citrus is largely a matter of planting trees not affected severely by the virus. Where aphid vectors and the virus are present, exposed trees cannot escape infection for very long after planting. In fact, infection is frequently quite general in citrus nurseries before trees are planted in the orchards. In regions where *A. gossypii* is the principal vector, the rate of infection is somewhat slower than where *T. citricidus* is the chief vector. In either situation, all possible procedures must be followed to prevent or lessen damage from this disease. The principal control measure is use of tolerant scion-rootstock combinations; however, rootstocks have little if any effect on scion varieties on which the virus acts directly. Examples of this are lime dieback and severe stem pitting on grapefruit, pummelos, Pera sweet orange, and some other kinds of citrus. The use of mild strains of tristeza virus to protect against virulent strains seems to offer some possibility of reducing severity of these disorders.

Rootstocks in Relation to Tristeza.—From observations on existing citrus plantings in countries where tristeza disease is present, it has been possible to determine susceptibility of trees on established rootstock varieties. It was observed early that trees of sweet orange on the widely used sour-orange rootstock are very susceptible and that trees on such well-known rootstock varieties as Rough lemon, sweet orange, and trifoliate orange are resistant. Although not recognized at the time, tristeza was responsible for the failure of sour orange as a rootstock when attempts were made to use it in South Africa in the late 1890's. Because of this, South African citrus plantings until recently have consisted of trees propagated almost exclusively on Rough lemon. Thus, South Africa did not experience such disastrous losses of trees as occurred later in South America and California when tristeza virus began to spread into the extensive acreages of trees on sour-orange rootstocks.

In addition to information obtained from earlier studies of existing commercial plantings, much experimental data have accumulated since 1945 from rootstock trials, particularly in Argentina, Brazil, and California. In this chapter, no effort is made to detail specific rootstock investigations nor to list all citrus species, varieties, and selections on which studies have been made. For the sake of brevity, available information has been pooled and certain generalizations are drawn from collective studies. The principal sources of information are a summary of rootstock studies in Brazil by Grant, Moreira, and Salibe (1961), a review of the situation in South Africa by Oberholzer (1959), California data reported by Bitters, Dukeshire, and Brusca (1953), and data supplied personally by W. P. Bitters of the University of California, Riverside.

Characterization of a particular rootstock as susceptible or resistant (tolerant) is based chiefly on whether or not trees of sweet orange or other varieties on that rootstock show significant decline when infected with tristeza virus. Although rootstock varieties are referred to as resistant and susceptible (tolerant and nontolerant) these terms actually apply to budded trees of specific scion and stock combinations. In general, mandarin and grapefruit respond much the same as sweet orange on susceptible rootstocks, but may react slower and sometimes not as severely. Also the direct effect tristeza virus has on grapefruit frequently results in the stem-pitting symptom, even though trees are growing on rootstocks that are not subject to the usual phloem necrosis near the bud union. In this discussion of rootstock relationships, we are considering only the decline and death of trees resulting from the girdling effect brought on by this type of phloem necrosis.

As groups, the sweet orange *(C. sinensis)*, and mandarin-tangerine *(C. reticulata)* varieties, when used as rootstocks for sweet orange, tangerine, and grapefruit, have been found to be resistant. That is, trees of these top-rootstock combinations are not subject to severe decline resulting from phloem necrosis in the bud-union zone. However, as previously mentioned, grapefruit and some sweet orange varieties, especially Pera orange, often develop severe stem pitting regardless of the rootstock variety, as well as when grown as seedling trees. Trifoliate orange and certain citranges *(P. trifoliata x C. sinensis)* comprise a third group of resistant rootstock varieties. The tangelos *(C. paradisi x C. reticulata)* comprise a fourth group within which there are a number of named selections that have shown a high degree of resistance when used as rootstocks. Grant *et al.* (1961) reported reactions among tangelos ranging from susceptible to resistant, suggesting a segregation of the factor for resistance as would be expected in hybrids between resistant and susceptible parents.

Stubbs (1963) reported that a selection of sour orange introduced to Australia from Israel demonstrated a high degree of tolerance to certain tristeza virus isolates when used as a rootstock for Washington navel and Valencia oranges and Ellendale mandarin. Experimentally infected test trees showed no decline up to four years. If further study demonstrates a permanent resistance in this sour orange selection to a wide range of tristeza virus strains or isolates and proves it has other desirable rootstock characteristics, it will no doubt become popular for use in many places where citrus is grown.

Information on rootstock reactions to tristeza has been obtained largely from field and experimental studies in Brazil and California where, because of natural infection, it has not been possible to compare performance of tristeza-infected trees with permanently healthy trees. Thus, observed differences in appearance, size, and fruit production of trees growing on different rootstock species or even selections within a rootstock species or hybrid group may have been due only partly to the presence of tristeza virus. It is well known that trees of a given scion variety on some rootstocks vary significantly in growth and other characteristics from trees of the same scion on certain other rootstock varieties. Thus, field tests that have been made on many stionic combinations in relation to tristeza may have revealed to some extent the combined effects of tristeza and congeniality or lack of it between respective combinations. Also, certain unfavorable environmental factors existing where trials are conducted may have influenced tree behavior.

In selecting a rootstock for use in a given region where tristeza is present, there are many factors to be considered. Briefly, these are: (1) compatibility between scion and stock varieties and other horticultural aspects; (2) existing type of soil as related to fungus root-rot, gummosis, and nematode populations; (3) resistance to fungus diseases, nematodes, and viruses other than tristeza to which the trees may be exposed; and (4) whether or not the rootstock variety is subject to severe stem pitting. Although complete information is lacking, it is known that certain kinds of citrus, which as rootstocks are not subject to the tristeza bud-union phloem necrosis, become weakened after some years as a result of tristeza stem pitting. A good example is Morton citrange. When more details of the past and current rootstock trials in California are published, further information regarding this reaction will become available. Unfortunately, some of the rootstocks which perform well under exposure to tristeza are known to be susceptible to other virus diseases such as xyloporosis and exocortis. When such rootstocks are used, it is mandatory that scion buds not carry viruses of these diseases. Mandarins, tangelos, and sweet limes are susceptible to xyloporosis (cachexia), and such popular rootstocks as Rangpur lime (*C. limonia* Osbeck), Troyer citrange, and trifoliate orange are affected by exocortis.

Some recent developments have made it evident that a rootstock that performs satisfactorily in some regions where citrus plantings are exposed to tristeza infection may not be satisfactory in all locations, or under all cultural conditions. One of the best examples of this is the decline of trees on Troyer rootstock in some parts of southern California. As has been described by Wallace and Snow (1965), Calavan *et al.* (1968), and Calavan *et al.* (1972), a significant number of trees of sweet orange on Troyer citrange rootstock are declining in California. This is occurring in some plantings located primarily within 30 miles of the Pacific ocean. Since 1961, this tree decline has increased sufficiently to be of considerable economic importance. There is no doubt that this decline is associated with tristeza infection, but it is evident that other environmental factors also play a role. This is because there are vast acreages of trees on Troyer citrange rootstock in southern California where tristeza virus is present, but where trees on this rootstock are not declining. Furthermore, the author has experimentally inoculated Troyer rootstock trees at Riverside with the most virulent sources of tristeza and seedling yellows viruses available without inducing tristeza symptoms or tree decline. At time of planting, Calavan *et al.* (1972) experimentally inoculated Valencia trees on rootstocks of Troyer and Carrizo citrange and trifoliate orange at a location in Ventura County where orchard trees on Troyer citrange were declining. It was found that trees of all three scion-stock combination declined.

Bitters and Parker (1953) established that the most tolerant scion-stock combinations showed some slight effects if the trees were experimentally inoculated soon after transfer from the nursery to the orchard. That being the case, it seems that tristeza decline of trees on Troyer citrange, trifoliate orange, and other tolerant rootstocks in some plantings in California results from tristeza infection plus other environmental factors which have not been identified. In studies by the author, virus from declining trees in Ventura County has not caused trees on Troyer citrange rootstock to decline under field conditions at the Citrus Research Center in Riverside. Thus, it seems that some other factor, probably related to tree growth, is operating in some way to combine with tristeza infection and lessen the tolerance of trees of sweet orange on Troyer citrange rootstock.

Quarantine and Eradication.—Under such situations as exist in California, where in some citrus areas there is still little or no natural spread of tristeza virus, strict quarantine should be established to prohibit the introduction of infected plants or budwood. Known symptomless carriers such as Meyer lemon should be eradicated from regions where obvious increase of tristeza is not occurring. Meyer lemon trees have been removed in several counties in California.

In countries where tristeza is not present in orchard plantings, extreme care should be taken to avoid introduction of the virus in imported budwood or plants. Also, all citrus in experimental varietal collections should be indexed for tristeza and any tree found to be infected should be destroyed.

The current absence of tristeza from some parts of the world is no guarantee that this disease will not become a problem in the future. Thus, it is advisable that the performance of known tristeza-tolerant rootstock varieties be determined as soon as possible to find rootstocks suitable for local varieties of citrus and to establish new orchards on these stocks.

Protection by Mild Virus Strains.—It has been established that tristeza virus and the tristeza-seedling yellows virus complex are comprised of strains which differ in virulence on certain citrus hosts. Grant and Costa (1951*b*) obtained virus from Barão sweet orange trees in Brazil that caused mild reactions on small trees of sweet orange on Brazilian sour-orange rootstocks and virus from other Barão trees that caused very severe symptoms. From field performance of trees of sweet orange on nontolerant rootstocks carrying mild tristeza virus, and from exposure of mildly affected experimental plants to viruliferous aphids, Grant and Costa obtained evidence that trees invaded by the mild virus were protected against the severe virus. However, it was concluded that the mild virus itself caused too much injury to permit its use as a control measure.

Oberholzer (1959) presented evidence that some grapefruit trees in South Africa are protected from severe stem-pitting injury because of the presence of avirulent strains of the causal virus.

Fraser, Long, and Cox (1968) reported on field performance of Marsh grapefruit trees propagated from orchard trees showing mild, moderately severe, or severe symptoms, and nucellar Marsh grapefruit trees experimentally inoculated with nine different mild-strain isolates. For a period of thirteen years there had been no indication that the protection by the mild virus strains was breaking down. Other field trials begun in 1959 suggested that mild virus strains in grapefruit trees growing on tristeza-tolerant rootstocks can have a protecting effect under average orchard conditions for a considerable number of years. It was stated that after the stem-pitting disease of grapefruit was first observed about 1932 in New South Wales, the greatest injury occurred in the years 1940–1950, when many trees in the eighteen to twenty-five year age group developed dieback and trunk pitting and bore very small, deformed fruit. Deterioration in later planted orchards has been less, resulting no doubt from use of budwood from vigorous, productive trees infected with mild, protecting strains of virus.

Olson (1956) reported that a strain of tristeza virus from a Meyer lemon tree which caused mild symptoms on Mexican lime, protected lime plants against a subsequent inoculation with a severe strain of virus obtained from a tree of Sueoka satsuma. From the descriptions provided, it appears that the challenging virus was seedling yellows. Apparently the mild strain from Meyer lemon was not indexed to seedling-yellows indicator varieties, but it is likely that it too was seedling yellows. This supposition can be made because all tristeza-positive Meyer lemons that have been indexed for seedling yellows in California have been found to carry the seedling yellows-tristeza complex.

In Australia, Stubbs (1964) found that an isolate from a severely stem-pitted orchard tree of grapefruit had no effect on grapefruit seedlings and provided them with a partial protection against a severe isolate of seedling yellows. He also reported that grapefruit seedlings that were healthy when planted in the field but had become infected naturally during five years of field exposure, were unaffected by inoculation with a severe isolate of seedling yellows. Stubbs (1964) found that virus isolates from Meyer lemon and Lisbon lemon differed widely in their ability to protect young trees of sweet on sour orange. Trees with the Lisbon isolate showed no effects from a challenge inoculation with severe seedling yellows during sixteen months in the glasshouse and for about two years after they were planted outside. However, after that time these trees began to show retarded growth, shoot dieback, and defoliation. This condition continued during the next three years when the trees measured 3.6 meters in height as compared to 5.9 meters for trees receiving only the mild Lisbon isolate. Healthy trees that received the same challenge inoculation were dead. Although the Lisbon isolate provided only partial protection to sweet on sour trees against experimental inoculation with a severe seedling-yellows isolate, field performance of trees experimentally inoculated with the Lisbon isolate suggests that it might provide a satisfactory permanent protection against naturally occurring virus sources to which trees would be exposed under field conditions.

Giacometti and Araújo (1965) reported that a mild strain of tristeza virus that caused no seedling yellows on Eureka lemon and sour orange, protected these species against a very severe strain of seedling yellows. In grapefruit, this isolate provided partial protection. It was reported further that plants of Gallego (Mexican) lime and grapefruit originating from buds carrying the mild tristeza virus and grown under field exposure to the severe seedling-yellows virus were "satisfactorily protected" for three to eight years.

Müller and Costa (1968) demonstrated that Gallego lime seedlings preimmunized with a number of mild isolates of tristeza virus displayed a high degree of protection against severe stem-pitting isolates. Subsequently, Müller and Costa (1972) reported that preimmunized lime trees under field exposure to tristeza developed with only a slight reduction in growth and yielded five times as much fruit as nonimmunized trees in the first three harvests.

Wallace (1973) reported on observations made on 165 acres of limes now in production at Mazoe Citrus Estates in Rhodesia under constant exposure to tristeza infection. Much of this acreage, where trees in general are performing satisfactorily, traces back to a single vigorous West Indian lime tree discovered in the early 1950's in a garden north of the city of Salisbury. It is evident that the original source tree was infected by a mild strain of tristeza virus which protected it and daughter trees propagated from it against naturally occurring virulent virus strains. Additional plantings of these limes are being made at Mazoe with careful records of budwood sources. Future performances of these plantings will establish the degree and permanence of field protection of lime trees by mild strains of tristeza virus.

Wallace and Drake (1961*b*) and Wallace *et al.* (1965) reported that strains or isolates of tristeza virus (T) from field sources gave no permanent protection to seedlings of Eureka lemon against seedling yellows. Tristeza-like virus (RSY) that remained in lemon seedlings after recovery from symptoms of seedling yellows provided good protection to the recovered plants against some isolates of seedling-yellows virus and partial or none against others. Subsequent studies by Wallace and Drake (1972*a*) demonstrated that lemon and sour orange seedlings preinoculated with certain isolates of RSY virus from seedling-yellows-recovered plants are completely protected against some sources of SY virus but have moderate or very slight protection against other sources. Of particular interest is the finding that isolates of seedling-yellows-tristeza (SYT) virus separated from a given source of SY virus by aphids (ASYT), or those separated by tissue-graft inoculations from infected resistant host plants such as trifoliate orange (TSYT), do not protect lemon seedlings to the same extent as RSY virus which remains in plants that recover from this same source of SY virus. While this would indicate that in the process of recovery from symptoms of seedling yellows, plants develop some special kind of defense that can be conferred on healthy seedlings by graft inoculation, from recovered plants, there is no experimental proof that this occurs.

Another interesting and unexplained reaction is that aphid isolates of SY virus (ASY) selected from stock sources of SY virus cause typical symptoms of seedling yellows from which lemons recover, but the virus (RASY) remaining in these recovered plants often provides lemon seedlings with no protection against SY virus, even against the ASY isolate from which the recovery virus (RASY) is derived. It is evident that recovery from seedling yellows and the resulting protection by the virus remaining after plant recovery is a complicated reaction which is not as yet understood.

The matter of protection by mild strains of tristeza virus should receive careful, well-planned study. Perhaps it cannot be expected that this kind of protection will be sufficient to permit renewed use of sour orange or other tristeza-susceptible rootstock varieties. Exhaustive trials would have to be completed before this could be considered. Certainly, it would have to be demonstrated that the mild strains being used will confer permanent protection under heavy field exposure to reinfection. But control of this kind is not needed urgently as long as productive trees can be grown on known tolerant rootstocks. Wallace and Drake (1972*b*) showed that trees of Valencia on sour orange were not affected severely by certain isolates of RSY virus obtained from seedlings of sour orange and Eureka lemon that recovered from seedling yellows. The preimmunized trees were protected against naturally occurring tristeza virus but the RSY virus itself reduced tree performance somewhat below desired levels.

Protection by mild virus strains, however, may be the only control for stem-pitting effects of tristeza and, with further developments, the above-mentioned recovery phenomenon may have some application in the control of both tristeza and seedling yellows, should this phase of the disease become important in newly planted orchards of lemon and grapefruit.

In experimental study of strain interference, all investigators should recognize that in both tristeza and seedling-yellows viruses there are a great many different strains and new strains may be arising regularly. Furthermore, in nature there may be several different virus strains or substrains in a single infected tree. Thus, single or a limited number of graft or insect transmissions will not provide complete information on the composition of a given source of virus.

EXOCORTIS

Exocortis disease was probably responsible for numerous early reports that trifoliate orange performed erratically when used as a rootstock. This resulted in an unfavorable reputation for this rootstock variety, which otherwise has many valuable attributes. In general, early references to use of trifoliate orange as a rootstock mention its dwarfing effect and that trees of certain scion varieties on this rootstock were failures. However, there were exceptions. In some instances, mandarin, satsuma, and certain sweet orange selections performed satisfactorily when grown on trifoliate orange. Some observers pointed out that the fruit produced on such trees was of exceptional quality.

The name "exocortis" is now generally used for this disease, although it has been known as "scaly butt" for many years in Australia. When this disorder was first described by Fawcett and Klotz (1948*b*), its cause was unknown, but soon thereafter Benton *et al.* (1949, 1950) presented evidence that scaly butt in Australia is caused by a virus. In California, Bitters (1952) published the first evidence of the virus nature of exocortis.

Olson (1952) gave the name "Rangpur lime disease" to a rootstock bark disorder observed on trees of some grapefruit varieties and Valencia orange on Rangpur lime and other rootstocks. It appears from the literature that Brown and Schmitz (1954) in Louisiana were the first to present evidence that Rangpur lime disease is caused by a virus and to suggest that Rangpur lime disease and exocortis had a common cause. Moreira (1955) found a similar disorder on Rangpur lime in Brazil and concluded that it was the same as exocortis. Studies by Olson and Shull (1956) in Texas, and Reitz and Knorr (1957) in Florida, supported this conclusion.

Symptomatology

The first recognized symptoms of exocortis (fig. 2–33, *A*) are those described by Fawcett and Klotz (1948*b*) on old trees of sweet orange on trifoliate orange rootstock. In advanced stages, the entire aboveground part of the stock displays bark shelling or scaling quite like the shell-bark disorder of lemon. The above authors observed stunting of trees with severe exocortis bark shelling. Benton *et al.* (1949, 1950) reported that trees with severe scaly butt in New South Wales are always stunted to a greater or lesser extent, but that occasional trees are excessively stunted without showing the bark effects on trifoliate stocks. Numerous workers have observed trees of advanced age which were moderately or severely stunted but free of bark shelling. Fraser, Levitt, and Cox (1961) reported on experimental studies of trees showing stunting only and those with both stunting and exocortis bark shelling. Although there had been insufficient time for final and conclusive results when their report was made, certain trends were evident. In studies on perpetuation of the stunting factor, detectable differences in growth rates of trees propagated from stunted and nonstunted trees usually did not appear until trees were eight to ten years old. Young trees of Bellamy navel orange, which grow vigorously on trifoliate stock, were bud-inoculated from different stunted trees and after five years there was clear evidence of transmission of a factor for stunting. The degree of stunting varied according to the source of inoculum. These workers concluded that while some cases of stunting of trees on trifoliate stock appeared to be caused by a virus, there may also be other causes for it. Norman (1965) concluded that a stunting factor that has no relation to exocortis is present in some citrus scion varieties.

It is now known that in addition to trifoliate orange and Rangpur lime, exocortis affects a wide range of citrus species and varieties. The reaction varies on different kinds of citrus, and there is considerable range in time of appearance of symptoms, degree of severity, and amount of stunting.

Weathers and Calavan (1961) reported that the first symptoms to appear on Palestine sweet lime and Dorshapo sweet lemon are vertical bark splits resembling growth cracks, which expand and fill in with new bark underneath (fig. 2–33, *B*).

The most complete descriptions of exocortis effects on trifoliate orange were provided by Benton *et al.* (1950) and Bitters (1952), who also described the reactions of such sensitive hosts as the citranges. On orchard trees of these varieties, the first scaling develops either at or below the ground line or at the bud union. Small, elongated areas of dead bark from 1/16- to 1/8-inch thick lift up in scales 1/4- to 1-inch wide and as long as 5 inches. There may be a slight amount of gum beneath the bark flakes. The rate and extent of the bark-scaling varies. Sometimes the lesions develop slowly and

Fig. 2–33. Bark-shelling and splitting caused by exocortis virus. ***A*****, restricted growth of sweet orange and advanced bark-shelling of trifoliate rootstock. (From Fawcett and Klotz, 1948.)** ***B*****, exocortis bark-splitting on Palestine sweet lime. (Photo courtesy of L. G. Weathers.)**

may be restricted to only a part of the stock for a number of years; in other instances, scaling develops quite rapidly over the entire stock. Bark-scaling extends below ground onto the roots, and frequently large roots die. Affected trees seldom die, but they may ultimately become worthless. Infected trees usually show some retardation of growth by the time first bark scaling is evident.

On orchard trees, the time required for bark scaling to show up has usually been considered to be from four to eight years. However, as more controlled studies were conducted, it was found that bark-splitting and slight scaling sometimes develop within a year and one-half after an exocortis bud is propagated on a sensitive rootstock. As described later (p. 112), sensitive indicator varieties are now known which develop diagnostic symptoms of exocortis sometimes within two months after infection. The observed variations in time of appearance of bark scaling and severity of exocortis are no doubt influenced by several factors. Fraser and Levitt (1959), Salibe (1961*a*), Calavan and Weathers (1961), and Weathers and Calavan (1961) presented evidence of the existence of strains of exocortis virus. Weathers (1960*a*) and Weathers, Harjung, and Platt (1965) found that host nutrition had an influence on the development of symptoms of exocortis on trifoliate orange. Also, Weathers, Paulus, and Harjung (1962) demonstrated that symptoms develop earliest on trees grown at a soil temperature of 35° C, which was optimum for growth of experimental citrus trees on *P. trifoliata* rootstock.

Geographic Distribution and Host Range

In most countries where use of exocortis-sensitive rootstocks has disclosed its presence or experimental search has been made, exocortis pathogen has been found in trees of many kinds of citrus. Calavan and Weathers (1959) estimated that 80 per cent of all old-clone lemon trees and nearly 100 per cent of the Eureka variety in California are infected. Salibe (1961*a*) tested 202 trees in a miscellaneous citrus variety planting at the Limeira Experimental Station in Brazil and found that 43 per cent were infected. Norman (1965) indexed 620 mature trees of twenty-seven different citrus varieties entered in the Florida Citrus Budwood Registration Program and found 55 per cent positive for exocortis.

An exception to the above findings occurs in Japan, where the principal rootstock is trifoliate orange. Yamada and Tanaka (1968) and Tanaka and Yamada (1969) reported that exocortis has been found in Japan only in citrus introduced from foreign countries and apparently has not become established in commercial plantings. This no doubt partially explains why some early reports rated trifoliate orange as an excellent rootstock for satsuma mandarin, even though it was not satisfactory when used with certain other scion varieties in some localities where exocortis was present.

Experimental studies, principally in the United States, Brazil, Argentina, and Australia, have shown that numerous kinds of citrus react to infection with exocortis. However, many of these do not develop the typical bark shelling originally described on trifoliate orange and Rangpur lime and later found to develop on some trifoliate hybrids (citranges), mandarin-limes, Persian sweet lime, and a few other kinds of citrus.

Importance of Exocortis

Exocortis is a destructive disease of citrus trees on rootstocks subject to injury by the virus. Among commonly used rootstock varieties before World War II, only trifoliate orange was known to react to exocortis infection. Later, extensive use of Rangpur lime in Brazil as a replacement for tristeza-susceptible sour orange disclosed that exocortis was commonly present in citrus there. A high incidence of the disease soon resulted in newly planted orchards where rootstocks consisted of either Rangpur lime or trifoliate orange. If these rootstocks were to be used, it was clearly established that exocortis-free scion budwood should be selected. Further studies revealed that other varieties important as rootstocks in recent years, particularly Troyer citrange, are also affected to some extent.

Numerous investigators have presented data on reductions in tree size and yield of exocortis-infected citrus trees growing on rootstocks of trifoliate orange and Rangpur lime on which exocortis symptoms were present. Sinclair and Brown (1960, and unpublished data furnished the author in 1962) reported a significant reduction in growth of exocortis-infected Washington navel orange trees on sweet orange and Cleopatra mandarin rootstocks in comparison with healthy controls, even though infected trees exhibited no exocortis bark effects. Additionally, these workers found a significant reduction in total yield of ten-year-old exocortis-infected trees on sweet orange rootstock. Calavan, Weathers, and Christiansen (1968) reported that Valencia orange trees propagated in 1955 on trifoliate orange rootstock and inoculated soon thereafter with exocortis virus yielded only 58 per cent as much fruit by weight as healthy controls in a period of five years (1962-1966). At that age, the trunk size and height of diseased trees were about half that of healthy trees.

Transmission and Spread

Until recent years, it was assumed that spread or increase of exocortis resulted largely from use of infected budwood. Calavan, Soost, and Cameron (1959) reported three infections of healthy trees growing adjacent to exocortis-infected trees in a nursery. It was suspected that these infections resulted either from root grafts or vectors. Fraser and Levitt (1959) cited an instance where one tree in a group propagated from an exocortis-free source developed symptoms of disease after it was about twenty years of age. They suggested that this infection may have resulted from a natural root graft with an infected tree in an adjacent row.

Additional evidence of lack of spread of exocortis between field trees or by transmission through seeds is found in the statement by Benton *et al.* (1950) that no noninoculated seedling tree of trifoliate orange in Australia has shown exocortis symptoms. Furthermore, Fraser and Levitt (1959) grew 1200 seedlings from exocortis-affected trees, and none showed symptoms during an observation period of eight years. On the other hand, Salibe (1961*a*) and Salibe and Moreira (1965*a*) reported that they found a mild type of exocortis by transmission in eight of eighty-nine twelve-year-old trees of nucellar Baianinha orange growing on sweet orange rootstocks. Since each nucellar Baianinha tree had been derived from a different seedling, this at least indicated natural infection of eight trees by one means or another. Other instances of apparent natural infection described by these authors were interpreted as transmission through seeds. However, in view of subsequent developments, it seems likely that infection may have taken place by some means other than seed transmission. Weathers (1965*a*, 1965*b*) successfully transmitted the exocortis pathogen by means of dodder, *Cuscuta subinclusa*, from citrus to citrus, citrus to petunia, and petunia to citrus. Once established in petunia, it was transmissible to other petunia plants by grafting and sap-inoculations.

In further studies, Weathers, Greer, and Harjung (1967) transmitted the exocortis pathogen mechanically from petunia to citron and from citron to citron. Garnsey and Jones (1967) demonstrated that it can be transmitted from infected to healthy citron plants on contaminated budding knives and pruning shears. Cohen demonstrated that propagating tools used after cutting infected Valencia orange caused infection of citron.[3]

Garnsey and Jones (1967) mentioned that infection of orchard trees through operations such as pruning and hedging may have important implications, particularly where exocortis-sensitive rootstocks are present. The high percentages of exocortis infection reported by Calavan and Weathers (1959) in California lemon orchards could have been built up through regular pruning operations if lemon trees are as easily infected as citron.

Semancik and Weathers (1968*a*, 1968*b*) partially purified the exocortis pathogen but found no evidence of typical virus particles in electron micrographs of infectious samples. From other studies, these authors suggested that the exocortis pathogen may exist in the form of free nucleic acid (i.e., it multiplies and accumulates in the host plant as free ribonucleic acid not in association with the typical virus protein coat). Other investigations have substantiated that suggestion.

Control

The once accepted conclusion that exocortis usually can be avoided by selection of noninfected budwood sources is not entirely correct. However, it is still important to practice budwood selection, and the availability of a short time indexing test now makes it easy to avoid use of infected budwood. The possibility that spread can occur between orchard trees on pruning tools makes propagation of exocortis-free trees even more essential. This is true even if neither the scion nor rootstock varieties being propagated are affected by the disease. Planting exocortis-free trees reduces the chances of further spread and buildup. The finding of Garnsey and Jones (1967) that brief exposure of contaminated tools to 70 per cent ethyl alcohol did not completely inactivate the exocortis pathogen emphasizes the need of adequate sterilization of tools when moving from one tree to another during pruning operations. It is not possible to do this when machine hedging and topping is practiced, but unless experimental study shows otherwise, equipment should be properly cleaned and sterilized before moving from one block of trees to another.

The development of the "citron-indexing test" for exocortis provided a much-needed method of avoiding infected budwood. The original test, using trees on trifoliate orange rootstock, often required several years to complete. Moreira (1961) provided an improved test for exocortis when he observed that Rangpur lime grafted on infected orchard trees or inoculated as seedlings developed yellow stem blotches, sometimes within four months (fig. 2–34). Later, affected stems developed bark splits characteristic of exocortis. Rossetti (1961) conducted similar studies and obtained stem blotching on some inoculated plants within three months.

In tests involving 116 kinds of citrus, Salibe (1961*a*) found that forty-four developed diagnostic symptoms of exocortis. Among the most sensitive varieties were Harvey lemon (*C. limon* [L.] Burm. f.) and certain selections of citron (*C. medica* L.). In Salibe's tests, healthy buds of the varieties being

[3]Personal communication to the author from M. Cohen, Univ. Fla. Agr. Res. Center, Fort Pierce, Fla., dated Sept. 11, 1969.

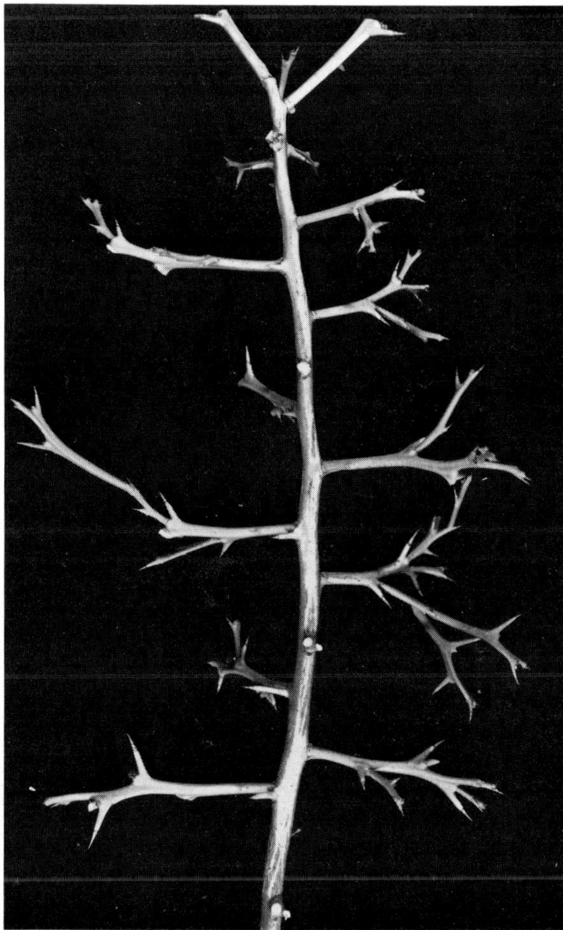

Fig. 2–34. Yellow blotching symptom of exocortis on bark of twigs of *Poncirus trifoliata.*

tested were worked onto seedlings of Caipira sweet orange inoculated previously with exocortis virus. He found that Harvey lemon developed symptoms after 110 days and that symptoms appeared on the citron after 130 to 140 days. In California, studies by Calavan *et al.* (1964) and Frolich *et al.* (1965) provided a rapid indexing test for exocortis. Two selections of citron, Etrog 60-13 and Etrog P.I. 10920, were found to be good indicators of exocortis. However, since seedlings of the two citrons did not react uniformly, these authors developed special indexing techniques using vegetative propagations of the citron indicators. This provided uniformity of indicator host plants for testing for the presence of exocortis and for studies of strains of the causal agent. Under glasshouse conditions, exocortis symptoms appeared within one to five months on Etrog citron growth (fig. 2–35). The symptoms induced on citron are present on foliage and stems and are quite easily recognized, but some sources of inocula caused much milder reactions than others. This test should become a standard part of any program aimed at selection of exocortis-free citrus budwood. For details of this method of indexing for exocortis, see Calavan *et al.* (1964) and Chapter 3.

In recent years, some efforts have been made to eliminate the exocortis pathogen from citrus by heat treatments. Rossetti, Nakadaira, and Roessing (1965) treated infected budsticks of Rangpur lime and Baianinha sweet orange for various periods of time in water at temperatures ranging from 30° C to 50° C. Their results indicated that buds surviving these treatments still carried the pathogen. Wallace and Drake (1967, unpublished) maintained exocortis-infected lemon plants at 35° C, and at different times propagated the tip portions of shoots that developed while the plants were in the heat chamber. Later, these propagations were indexed on Etrog citron to determine if the exocortis pathogen was present in these tissues. There was an indication that exocortis-free tissue may sometimes be obtained from terminal shoot growth of plants held at 35° C for two years, but in most instances that was not the case. On the other hand, Stubbs (1968) produced some exocortis-free propagations of terminal tissue from infected plants maintained at 38° C for 230 days or longer. Recently Roistacher, Navarro, and Murashige (1976) demonstrated that the exocortis pathogen could be eliminated from infected clones by shoot tip grafting.

There is still no positive evidence that the exocortis pathogen is spread by vectors, and seed transmission has not been substantiated. Nevertheless, for rootstocks, it is advisable to use seeds from trees that have indexed negatively. In all indexing to Etrog citron, the investigator should use precautions to avoid infection by contaminated budding knives. Garnsey and Jones (1967) contaminated a budding knife by drawing it through exocortis-infected Etrog citron a few times immediately before using it for propagating a bud from a healthy citron. This resulted in infection of twenty-six of thirty plants. In some limited tests, where the contaminated knife was dipped in a solution of 2 per cent NaOH plus 2 per cent of formaldehyde and rinsed with tap water, there were no infections.

Fig. 2–35. Exocortis symptoms on Etrog citron. Left, noninoculated citron. Right, citron infected with exocortis virus showing rolling of leaves and early stage of bark splitting.

Garnsey (1968) reported some transmission from Etrog citron to sweet orange and from sweet orange to sweet orange by means of a budding knife. These findings and those of Allen (1968), who similarly infected several kinds of commercial citrus and demonstrated that the exocortis pathogen remained infective for eight days on steel knife blades, suggest that pruning may be an important means of field spread. With this knowledge, it is advisable to use special precautionary measures in citrus-nursery operations. In view of the problem of frequent sterilization of budding knives and pruning tools, the simplest method of avoiding exocortis in citrus-nursery plantings is to use budwood only from sources which have been determined to be healthy. But even if that practice is followed diligently, there is always a chance of some contamination, and tools used for budding, pruning, and digging nursery trees should be disinfected at least between use on different budwood sources or tree lots.

Roistacher, Blue, and Calavan (1969) found a formaldehyde-sodium hydroxide solution effective in decontaminating budding knives and other tools, but because the solution is somewhat objectionable to use they sought other virus-inactivating treatments. They found that a readily available, inexpensive household bleach effectively inactivated exocortis pathogen on contaminated tools. Stock solution can be prepared at the rate of 1½ pints of household bleach (5.25 per cent sodium hypochlorite) per gallon of water. The solution should be stored in a cool location in capped, opaque plastic containers. For use, this solution can be poured into an open container, but it should be discarded after one day. A second solution of one part of vinegar to three parts of water plus two teaspoons of emulsifiable oil is used to neutralize the corrosive effect of the bleach solution. A one-second dip of propagating tools in the bleach solution, followed immediately by dipping in the vinegar-oil mixture, and a blotting or wiping with a clean cloth, is the recommended procedure. These same authors reported that the exocortis pathogen can also be transmitted on the hands of persons handling citrus plants, and they recommended that in removal of sprouts these be pulled off instead of rubbed as is often the practice in nursery operations.

XYLOPOROSIS (CACHEXIA)

Reichert and Perlberger (1934) described in detail a disease of sweet lime (*C. limettiodes* Tan.) in Palestine to which they gave the name *xyloporosis*. This disorder was observed as early as 1928 and had become widespread and serious by 1930. It occurred principally on commonly used sweet lime rootstocks of Shamouti sweet orange trees. Affected trees declined somewhat gradually, and became unproductive within a few years. These authors found milder symptoms on seedling trees of sweet lime, and they also observed that the disease affected mandarin but not sour lemon and grapefruit. The cause of xyloporosis was not determined by Reichert and Perlberger, who suggested that it was either a physiological disorder or a virus-induced disease.

In Brazil, Fawcett and Bitancourt (1937) observed some xyloporosis on orchard trees, and Moreira (1938) found the same disease on sweet lime rootstocks. He concluded that the disorder resulted from an incompatibility between sweet lime and Barão sweet orange.

Childs (1950, 1952) described a disease on Orlando tangelo (*C. reticulata* x *C. paradisi*) that resembled xyloporosis and to which he gave the name "cachexia." He demonstrated the virus nature of cachexia and suggested that xyloporosis and cachexia had a common identity. Later work seems to have substantiated that the two diseases are caused by the same virus, although Reichert and Bental (1961) concluded that this is not the case. If the two are the same, the question arises as to which name should be used for the virus and the disease it causes. Some workers are of the opinion that "cachexia" should be preferred because this name was used for the disease when it was shown to be caused by a transmissible virus. On the other hand, there are other investigators who believe that "xyloporosis" should have priority, since this was the name given to the disease when it was first described as a serious disorder of citrus. Actually, it seems that there can be no hard and fast rules regarding the naming of citrus virus diseases. The author favors retention of the original name assigned to a disease, particularly where usage has established it and there are no special reasons for adopting another name. When it develops that two distinct previously named diseases are caused by the same virus it will be desirable, at times, and perhaps necessary to continue to use both names to describe the disease effects. However, with respect to the causal virus, it seems advisable to assign a single name, preferably one which associates it with the first-described disease.

Geographic Distribution, Host Range, and Economic Importance

Xyloporosis virus is probably present in all citrus-growing areas of the world. It has been particularly important in Mediterranean countries and in local regions of Brazil and Argentina, where the susceptible sweet lime has been used as a rootstock. The wide distribution of xyloporosis virus in Mediterranean citrus has been established by studies and surveys of Reichert (1952, 1955, 1959), Reichert, Yoffe, and Bental (1953), Reichert and Bental (1957, 1961), Childs, Nour-Eldin, and El-Hosseiny (1956), Frezal (1957), Nour-Eldin (1959), Amizet (1959), Chapot and Cassin (1961), Vogel (1961), and Jamoussi (1961).

After the original reports of Fawcett and Bitancourt (1937) and Moreira (1938), additional studies on xyloporosis were made in Brazil by Grant, Moreira, and Costa (1957), and Salibe and Moreira (1965*b*). In Argentina, the disease has been studied by Condado (1950), Knorr and Beñatena (1952) and others. McClean and Engelbrecht (1958) demonstrated its presence in South African citrus.

Xyloporosis has been studied in Florida by Childs (1950, 1952, 1956,1959), Ducharme (1952), Childs *et al.* (1956), and Grant, Grimm, and Norman (1959). In Texas, it was investigated by Olson (1952, 1960), Olson and Shull (1956, 1962), Olson, Sleeth, and Shull (1958), and Olson, Shull, and Buffington (1961). Calavan, Carpenter, and Weathers (1958), Calavan, Christiansen, and Weathers (1961), Weathers and Calavan (1959*b*), and Calavan and Christiansen (1965) have reported on this disease in California.

The above investigations established that xyloporosis virus is widely distributed in the common citrus varieties. The sweet limes, mandarins, mandarin limes, tangelos, and alemow (*Citrus macrophylla* Wester) are the principal kinds of citrus affected by xyloporosis virus, but there are indications that not all selections within the first three groups develop symptoms. It has also been demonstrated that some acid limes, tangors, and a few miscellaneous kinds of citrus develop symptoms if infected with xyloporosis virus.

Xyloporosis remained a serious rootstock disease in Israel for many years after its discovery in 1928, primarily because sweet lime continued to be used as a rootstock. This rootstock was used to some extent in Cyprus and other countries in the Middle East, but now it has been replaced for the most part by other rootstock varieties. A common practice in Israel has been to start trees on sweet lime and inarch them to sour orange soon after they are established in orchard plantings. Reichert and Perlberger (1934) and Reichert *et al.* (1953) mentioned that the severity of xyloporosis on sweet lime rootstocks is less on trees growing in light or sandy soils. This fact seems to be well established, but does not provide a satisfactory control. Reichert and Bental (1961), who concluded that xyloporosis and cachexia are two different diseases, found severe cachexia-type symptoms on mandarins in Israel regardless of the rootstock on which they were growing. Workers in Florida, Texas, and California have encountered this same situation with some mandarin and tangelo varieties. Wallace and Martinez (1964) observed many trees of Ladu and Szinkom mandarin trees severely affected by xyloporosis in the Philippines, where the commonly used calamandarin rootstock was unaffected. Trees with advanced xyloporosis symptoms were decidedly less thrifty and productive than normal trees.

Although there are few published data on economic losses caused by xyloporosis, it is evident that this disease can cause serious decline of trees consisting of susceptible scion and/or rootstock varieties. Amizet (1959) reported that a planting of 300 trees of Wekiwa tangelo in Algeria declined so severely from xyloporosis that all were removed five years after planting.

Olson, Cohen, and Rodriguez (1956) attributed a severe dieback of tangerine trees in Mexico to xyloporosis. Reichert and Bental (1957) described moderate decline of old orchard trees of satsuma mandarin on sour orange rootstock and a severe decline when satsumas were growing on rootstocks of sweet lime. Knorr and Price (1959) gave the name "fovea" to a disorder on Murcott honey orange, which they thought was the same as xyloporosis. In plantings of that variety, which has become popular in recent years, about 15 per cent of the trees in twenty-two commercial orchards showed symptoms, and some were already in serious decline. Olson (1960) reproduced the disease on a nucellar Murcott orange by inoculating it with a known source of xyloporosis virus. Presently, there seems no reason to consider fovea distinct from xyloporosis.

Symptomatology

The reaction of citrus to xyloporosis infection results in a syndrome that ranges from simple or mild wood-pitting to advanced bark-scaling, wood disorganization, and impregnation of affected tissues with gum. It is not easy to separate some of the effects of xyloporosis from symptoms of certain other viruses. This no doubt has led to some diagnostic errors, which, in turn, can explain certain areas of disagreement among investigators of this disease, particularly regarding the susceptibility of some citrus varieties. At present, it seems advisable to diagnose on the basis of the rather well-defined symptoms. Although both the ordinary and inverse types of wood-pitting are associated with xyloporosis infection, diagnosis cannot be made on the basis of wood pitting alone.

In Reichert and Perlberger's (1931) original description of xyloporosis on sweet lime, it was stated that the first symptom to appear was a pitting of the outer face of the wood with corresponding pegs on the cambial surface of bark. The base of the pits and points of the pegs were usually brownish. These symptoms were observed sometimes within one year after the sweet lime seedlings were budded, and in early stages were confined to sweet lime tissues adjacent to the bud union. Later, pitting became more pronounced and bark was depressed in patches or bands. As trees developed, there was often an uneven overgrowth at the union which gave a knee-like shape. The wood and bark near the cambium assumed a brown color, especially the wood pits and corresponding pegs on the bark. These authors stated: "The pits in the wood are very numerous and lie so near each other that the wood seems to be perforated like a sieve." At this stage of disease, trees often were yellowed and had leaves of small size. It was reported that the trees bloomed heavily and set above-normal fruit crops.

According to Reichert and Perlberger, the third stage of the disease began with brownish discoloration of certain parts of the bark. These discolored parts, generally extending over no more than half of the stem, soon decayed. Discoloration of the bark was followed by splitting. Discolored parts of the bark became blackish, split, and peeled away in pieces. Wood near these parts dried, decayed, and became darkly discolored. When the disease reached this stage a large number of branches withered slowly until the whole tree perished. Cross-sections of the sweet lime trunk of trees in this stage showed patches or bands of discolored and somewhat disorganized tissues in outer portions of the wood (see fig. 2–36).

In his descriptions of cachexia disease, Childs (1950, 1952) included more or less the same symptoms described earlier for xyloporosis in Palestine. Additionally, he described gummy deposits and discoloration in the phloem, which appear prior to any bark splitting or scaling. Childs demonstrated that the gummy spots could be detected by shaving off the outer bark (fig. 2–36, *B*). This seems to be a reliable means of early diagnosis of infection, particularly in tangelos and mandarins. Childs (1956) and Olson *et al.* (1958) pointed out that phloem discoloration and gum impregnation in sweet lime were slight or absent. Childs (1956) reported further that among different tangelos, discoloration in the phloem was heavy, weak, or apparently absent, depending on the variety. Calavan *et al.* (1961) observed different degrees of wood-pitting between Orlando tangelo and sweet lime, and concluded that Orlando tangelo is the better indicator. They also observed inverse pitting on diseased tangelo stocks, a symptom which, although not believed to be specific for xyloporosis, had been observed on xyloporosis-affected sweet limes trees earlier by Reichert *et al.* (1953) and Reichert and Winocour (1956).

Among fifty-four citrus varieties found to be sensitive to xyloporosis virus, Calavan and Christiansen (1965) observed reactions ranging from scattered mild pitting and pegging to concentrations of large pits and pegs and patches of gummy, abnormal tissue in the cambial zone (fig. 2–37). These same authors also described the gum deposits and abnormal wood development (fig. 2–38) referred to in the early description by Reichert and Perlberger (1934).

As previously mentioned, wood pitting cannot be used alone as a specific diagnostic symptom for xyloporosis. Likewise, gum impregnation in the bark of certain kinds of citrus may result from causes other than xyloporosis. As brought out previously, Calavan (1957*a*, 1957*b*) described inverse pitting, ordinary wood pitting, as well as some gum production in lemons affected by wood pocket, an apparent genetic abnormality. However, if one is familiar with the entire range of symptom effects, diagnosis of xyloporosis on field trees of tangelos, mandarins, and sweet limes can be made with reasonable accuracy. But to identify xyloporosis as the cause of wood pitting and/or gum deposits in the bark on some kinds of citrus will require indexing to proven indicator plants including susceptible tangelos such as Orlando or Wekiwa.

Transmission and Spread

From studies in Israel, the United States, Argentina, and Brazil, it can be concluded that the virus of xyloporosis is widespread in commercial citrus. In spite of its rather common occurrence, there is as yet no established evidence of natural spread of xyloporosis virus. It can be transmitted by grafting, and there seems little doubt that the use of virus-infected buds accounts for a great proportion of the existing infected trees.

The possibility of seed transmission has been considered since the early studies of Reichert and Perlberger (1934). Numerous workers have observed wood pitting on seedling trees of sweet lime and other varieties that resembled xyloporosis pitting. This suggested infection either through seed transmission of the virus or spread by a vector of some kind. However, neither of these has been demonstrated experimentally.

Childs (1956) found wood pitting and slight phloem discoloration on twenty of thirty sweet lime seedlings which had grown in nursery rows for four years. He diagnosed these effects as mild xyloporosis and suspected that infection had come through seeds. DuCharme and Knorr (1954), Grant *et al.* (1959), and others have observed false xyloporosis-like symptoms associated with infestation of citrus scale insects. Furthermore, Carpenter and Furr (1960) described pitting and grooving in the wood, and bark pegging and furrowing as well as some gum impregnation on many kinds of unbudded citrus seedlings which had not been infested with scale insects. Various kinds of pitting are caused by the tristeza virus, and it appears that pitting sometimes develops in the absence of any known virus. Up to the present, seed transmission of xyloporosis virus has not been proved. In fact, there is more experimental evidence against than for seed transmission. Childs, Johnson, and Eichhorn (1965) obtained no evidence of seed transmission in approximately 1,700 seedlings grown from xyloporosis-infected trees of sweet lime, tangelo, sweet orange, sour orange, lemon, grapefruit, and other kinds of citrus. Olson (1965) found no xyloporosis in 113 sweet lime

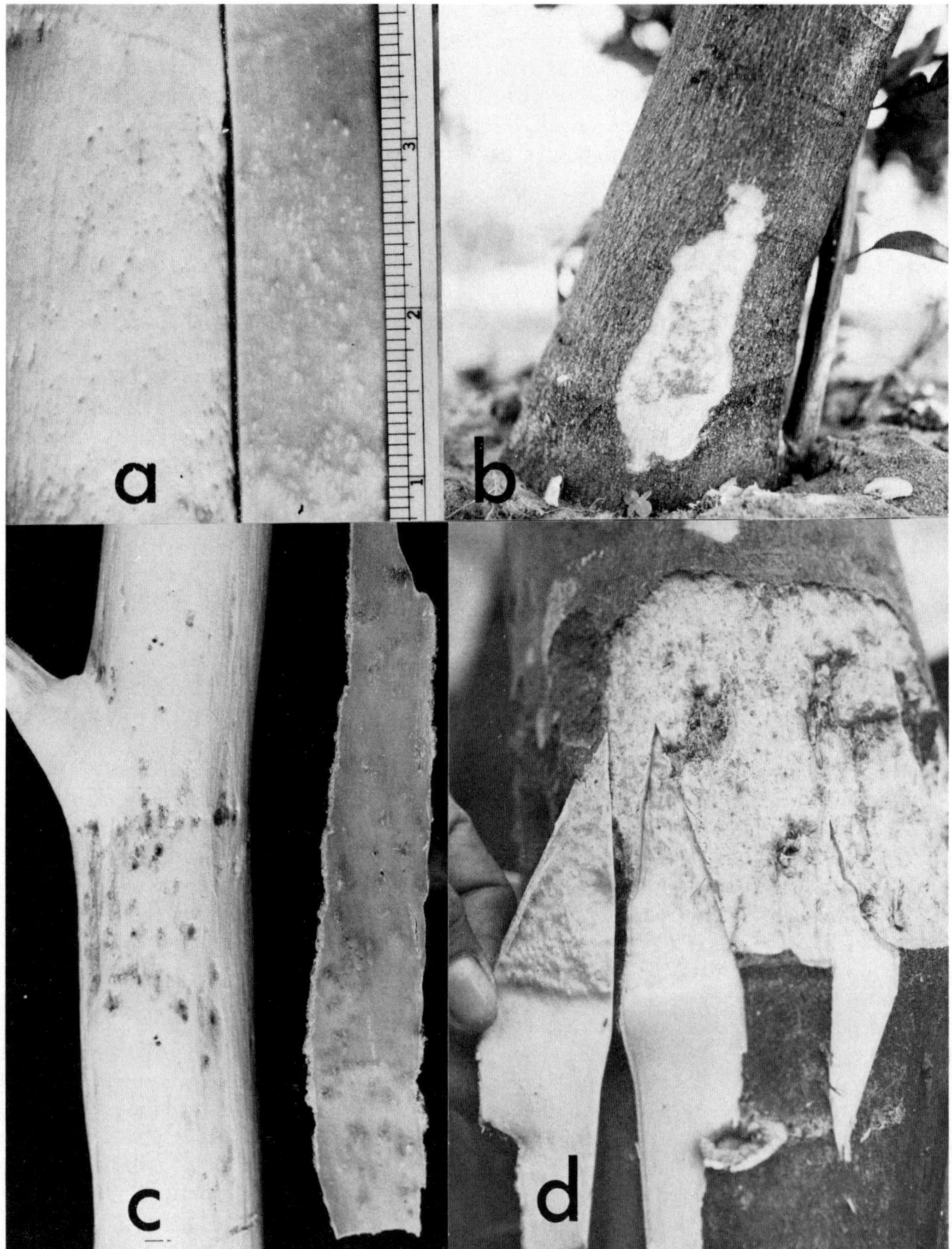

Fig. 2–36. Symptoms of xyloporosis. *A*, **mild pitting in wood and pegging of bark of Orlando tangelo rootstock of** three-year-old Marsh grapefruit tree. *B*, outer bark scraped to show gum impregnation of bark of infected Orlando tangelo. *C*, more advanced stage of disease on experimentally infected Orlando tangelo seedling. *D*, severe bark effect on Ladu mandarin which stops sharply at the union with calamandarin rootstock. (Photos *A* and *C* supplied by E. C. Calavan; *B* and *D* courtesy of J. F. L. Childs and D. Z. Rogel, respectively.)

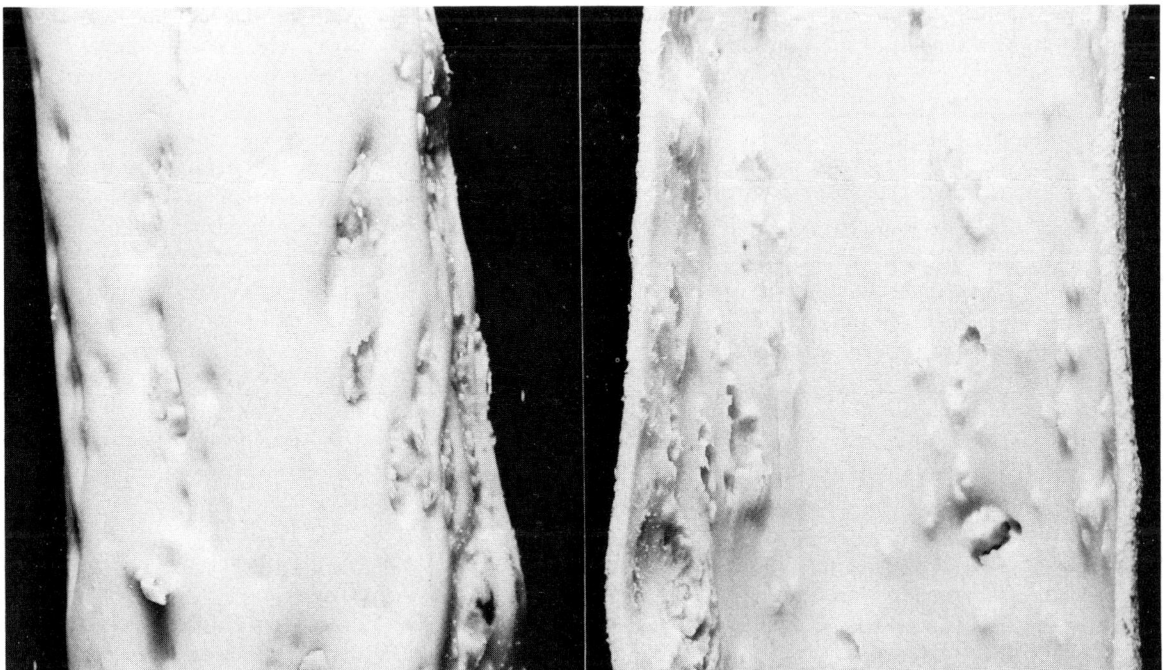

Fig. 2–37. Cambial faces of wood (left) and bark (right) of xyloporosis-infected tree of Wekiwa tangelo. (From Calavan and Christiansen, 1965.)

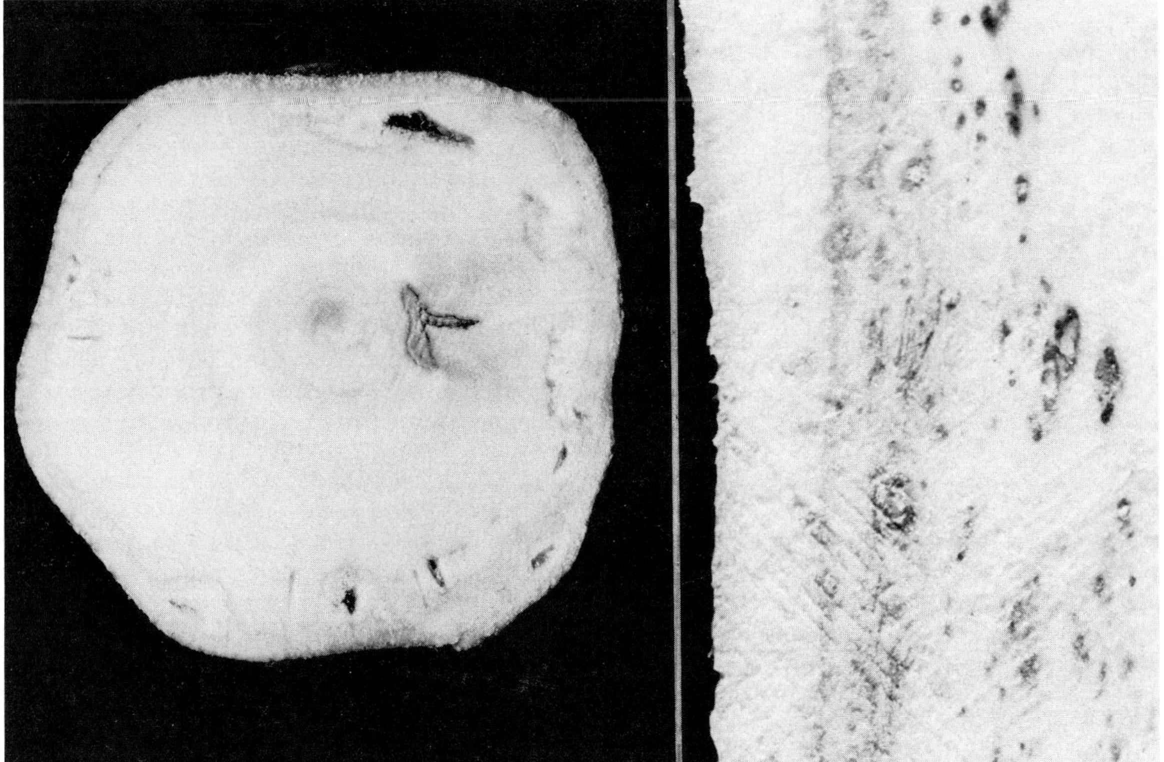

Fig. 2–38. Cross and longitudinal sections of cachexia-infected Wekiwa tangelo showing abnormal tissue and gum deposits in the wood. (From Calavan and Christiansen, 1965.)

seedlings grown from infected parent trees. These results indicate that transmission of xyloporosis virus through citrus seeds, if it takes place at all, is not of regular occurrence.

Reichert, Bental, and Yoffe (1956) reported negative results in preliminary tests for transmission of xyloporosis virus by *Toxoptera aurantii* and *Aphis gossypii*. More recently, Norman and Childs (1963) obtained no transmission in tests with three species of aphids, one leafhopper species, and cottony-cushion scale. Norman *et al.* (1959) found what appeared to be typical xyloporosis symptoms on some uninoculated Orlando tangelo seedlings grown in the field for about six years. The affected seedlings were of unknown parentage and had been obtained from a commercial nursery. If this was true xyloporosis on seedlings which had never been budded, it would represent natural infection by one means or another. There is need for more study of natural transmission of xyloporosis virus. Tests with insects have been limited to a few species, and there have been no reports of studies of nematodes as possible vectors.

Control

As indicated above, proof of natural spread of xyloporosis virus has not been established. It is well known, however, that the virus is carried by many orchard trees, and probably all trees of certain old budlines are infected. The fact that Olson *et al.* (1958) found the virus in all old-line grapefruit trees tested in Texas, but did not find it in seedling lines, suggests that the disease may be avoided by the use of nucellar lines of citrus. Although it is not absolutely necessary to use virus-free buds for propagation on rootstock varieties which are not affected, this is still a desirable practice. Certainly, if such susceptible rootstocks as sweet lime, tangelo, mandarin and *C. macrophylla* are to be used, virus-free scion bud sources should be selected. Likewise, if susceptible scion varieties are to be grown, virus-free budwood should be used. Such sources of budwood must be found by indexing procedures which require a long time to complete. Olson, Shull, and Buffington (1961), Calavan *et al.* (1961), and Childs (1968*b*) concluded that Orlando tangelo is a better indicator of xyloporosis than sweet limes.

Numerous workers have observed that citrus varieties other than those mentioned also react to xyloporosis virus. Calavan and Christiansen (1965) described a wide range of symptoms in their studies of citrus varieties and selections. The severity of symptoms varied widely on different rootstock varieties supporting tops grown from the same xyloporosis-infected tree. Also, the same rootstock sometimes gave variable responses when budded to different infected scion varieties. Similarly, individual plants within a group inoculated from the same source displayed wide differences in incubation period, or time of symptom appearance. The variations were not specifically explained, but these authors concluded that xyloporosis symptom expression may be influenced by host genetics, host physiology, environmental factors, and variations in the pathogen. In an earlier report, Olson (1954) suggested that xyloporosis symptoms may be affected by (1) uneven distribution of virus within a tree from which buds are taken; (2) differences in incubation period between varieties; (3) genetic variants among seedlings used as indicators; and (4) interference by other viruses.

Clearly, a shorter and more specific test for the xyloporosis virus has been needed. When the indexing method consists of propagation of buds from candidate tree on seedlings of xyloporosis-susceptible varieties, Calavan and Christiansen (1965) recommended using eight or more plants of at least two highly sensitive varieties and observation for a minimum of six years if none of the indicator plants develop symptoms. Many positive cases will show up earlier, but because some may be delayed it is advisable to observe all negative tests for the full six years.

Childs (1968*b*) recommended using at least three seedlings of Orlando tangelo for each candidate tree. The seedlings may be inoculated directly or inoculum buds or scions forced to form the top of the tree. The budding or grafting can be done when seedlings are 8 to 12 inches in height. Preferably, test seedlings should originate from a xyloporosis-free parent tree. Symptoms reportedly appear sooner on the test plants if they are transferred to a field planting. The first symptom is a few spots of gum in the phloem or on the cambial face of the bark. Pitting of the wood, pegging of bark, and gum impregnation of the bark develop later. If no symptoms appear on any of the Orlando test plants within five years, Childs concluded that the candidate tree can be considered free of xyloporosis (cachexia) virus.

Using a technique much like the Etrog citron test for exocortis, Salibe (1965*a*) inoculated Rangpur lime seedlings on which terminally placed buds of Orlando tangelo were forced into growth. In one experiment, xyloporosis symptoms appeared on some of the Orlando tangelo scions within ten months, and 70 per cent of the test trees showed symptoms after one year. However, only two sources of xyloporosis virus were used in these studies. It remains to be determined if this test will work equally well when a wide selection of virus strains or sources are used. This technique should be studied further because, as with the Etrog citron test for exocortis, it would eliminate the factor of seedling variation.

Roistacher *et al.* (1973) described a reaction of small trees of Parsons Special Mandarin on Rough lemon rootstock which appears to be a reliable index test for this virus. Symptoms had appeared on all of thirty test plants after one year. Two inoculum buds were put into each Rough lemon seedling which was budded at the same time with a healthy bud derived from a seedling of Parson Special mandarin. The mandarin buds were later forced to grow into a single stem. When maintained continuously in a warm greenhouse, all inoculated plants displayed gumming and discoloration at the bud union when bark was removed twelve months after the tests were started. The advanced stage of symptoms at that time clearly indicated that some of the plants would have shown this reaction in a much shorter time than one year. With further refinement of this procedure it is very likely that a reliable and reasonable short-time indexing test for xyloporosis will become available.

STUBBORN DISEASE

According to Fawcett, Perry and Johnston (1944) some nonproductive Washington navel orange trees were observed from 1915 to 1917 in California in orchards of the East Highlands Orange Company. Some of these trees were topworked in 1921 by E. R. Waite with carefully selected navel buds. The growth of scion buds was slow, and the new top exhibited the same characteristics shown by the original trees. Mr. Waite described the growth as "stubborn," a name that was adopted for the disorder by J. C. Perry, who continued to study such trees.

Reichert (1930) and Reichert and Perlberger (1931) described "little leaf" disease, first observed in citrus groves in Palestine in 1928, and thought to be caused by climatic conditions, particularly drought. In recent years, workers in Israel have recognized similarities between little leaf and stubborn and have used both names for the disorder under study there. Similarly, in Egypt, a disorder assigned the local name "safargali" is now considered to be stubborn disease. For that reason, little leaf and safargali are not treated as distinct diseases in this chapter.

In 1938, H. S. Fawcett began studies of stubborn-type Washington navel orange trees in the vicinity of Redlands, California, and of other trees on the property of the East Highlands Orange Company. Propagations from affected trees perpetuated the disorder. Fawcett, Perry, and Johnston (1944) and Fawcett (1946) reported that healthy navel buds propagated on previously inoculated sweet orange seedlings grew out with symptoms of stubborn disease. Basing diagnosis on growth characteristics and effects on fruits, Fawcett and his co-workers found stubborn-affected trees in numerous orchards in California. Further observations suggested that such symptom effects or disorders as "pink nose," "acorn fruit," and "blue albedo" on navel orange and grapefruit particularly, and the disease of grapefruit in Arizona known as "crazy top," were all related to stubborn disease.

Economic Importance

Although stubborn-affected trees have been observed in California since about 1915, their occurrence has been spotty or scattered, except in occasional orchards where high percentages of affected trees indicated that the use of diseased budwood parent sources resulted in a rather uniform infection. However, Calavan and Carpenter (1965) reported that in recent years, increasing numbers of diseased trees have been detected in nursery and young orchard plantings in California. These authors concluded that stubborn had become a major problem in all important orange- and grapefruit-producing areas in the state.

Studies by Chapot (1956, 1959, 1970), Chapot and Cassin (1961), Childs *et al.* (1956), Childs and Carpenter (1960), and Nour-Eldin (1967) established that stubborn is widely distributed in Mediterranean countries and constitutes a serious disease. The little leaf disease of citrus, first studied in Palestine by Reichert (1930) and Reichert and Perlberger (1931), was reported to have caused heavy damage when it appeared in epidemic form in young citrus groves. Patt (1964) and Pappo and Bauman (1969) consider this disease to be very similar to stubborn but the latter authors list some striking differences between the two diseases, particularly in regard to appearance of symptoms in young trees. It was reported that the disease in Israel has not been found in the nursery and symptoms are not clearly evident until 2–4 years after trees are put into orchard plantings. Pappo and Bauman (1969) state further that trees that do not show any symptoms up to 4 years in the field usually remain unaffected. On the other hand, the shortened upright shoots bearing small leaves, chlorotic mottling of mature leaves, off-season flowering, and seed abortion associated with little leaf disease are characteristic symptoms of stubborn. Certainly, the little leaf disease currently under study in Israel is very similar to stubborn and until further investigation discloses more distinct differences, it seems permissible to consider these disorders to be the same or closely related diseases. However, until the exact relationship is established or more complete knowledge for both is obtained, it should not be anticipated that the epidemiology of stubborn disease in California, for example, will necessarily parallel that of little leaf disease in Israel.

Calavan (1969) stated that the damage caused by stubborn disease in California had not been fully assessed but he estimated a total of about one million trees affected at that time. However, such an estimate provides no statistics on reduction in yield. Calavan and Christiansen (1961) and Calavan (1969) demonstrated experimentally that stubborn-affected trees react mildly or severely, apparently as a result of the existence of strains of the causal agent. Symptoms on infected orchard trees also vary from slight to strong and, as was mentioned by Fawcett and Klotz (1948*c*), the production of fruit decreases with increased severity of symptoms.

Like Pappo and Bauman (1969) in their survey for little leaf disease in Israel, many investigators in California and Morocco have observed that the percentage of stubborn-affected trees varies widely between individual orchards. Further, there are much fewer easily detected diseased trees in some districts or localities than in others. Thus, to assess the reduction in yields, extensive surveys and individual tree records must be made.

It appears now that there are more mildly- than severely-affected, non-productive orchard trees, and even though citrus production has remained reasonably good for more than fifty years in California under exposure to stubborn disease, all efforts should be expended towards its control or prevention.

Symptomatology

Calavan and Carpenter (1965) have published the most complete description of stubborn disease. They emphasized not only that symptoms are highly variable, but they may remain unnoticed or not even appear for several years on infected trees. These authors admitted that such disorders as acorn disease, blue nose, crazy top, pink nose, stylar-end greening, little leaf, and puny leaf may be symptoms of stubborn disease; but they recognized that further study may show that some of these are distinct from stubborn. The following symptom description is taken largely from Calavan and Carpenter (1965).

Effects on Trees.—Trees with stubborn disease vary widely in growth habits and other symptoms, and it is believed that some trees may be infected without showing sufficient effects to permit diagnosis with certainty. Field diagnosis can be complicated further by the fact that trees injured by freezing, heavy insect infestation, winds, improper nutrition, or certain diseases may have the appearance of stubborn-infected trees. Even those persons most familiar with stubborn disease admit that field diagnosis is sometimes difficult or impossible to make. Stubborn-infected trees with obvious symptoms have a bunchy type of growth with shortened stem internodes and smaller-than-normal leaves, which usually assume an upright position (fig. 2–39). Leaves may be abnormal in shape, sometimes mottled, and there may be excessive leaf drop. Size of mildly affected trees may be about normal, but severely affected trees are stunted and often flattened across the top. A normal and a stubborn-affected Valencia orange tree are shown in figure 2–40. Trees with stubborn disease flower irregularly and may have fruit of several sizes, although frequently most of the fruits drop while very small. Production of fruit on stubborn-infected trees varies in proportion to the severity, with few if any fruit reaching maturity on trees in advanced stages. Calavan and Carpenter (1965) reported that, in general, stubborn-affected trees of Valencia orange tend to set and mature more fruit than trees of navel orange. However, these authors pointed out that many fruits that mature on Valencia trees with stubborn disease drop soon after ripening. Figure 2–41 shows fruit production of a severely affected 7-year-old Valencia tree and that of a normal tree of the same age

Fig. 2–39. Stubborn disease. Left, three shoots from stubborn-affected tree. Right, shoot from healthy or normal tree. (From Calavan and Carpenter, 1965.)

and from the same parent bud line. The diseased tree had been experimentally inoculated with a virulent isolate of the stubborn agent before transfer from a nursery to a permanent field planting.

External Fruit Symptoms.—Fruits on stubborn-affected trees display a variety of effects. The most conspicuous of these are recurrent crops of small fruits, lopsided fruits, and acorn-shaped fruit with stem-end peel of normal thickness. In addition, the stylar end is abnormally thin and subject either to early breakdown or stylar-end greening (i.e., retention of green color in the peel on the blossom end of the fruit several weeks to months after normal color break). Another effect, blue albedo, may show externally, but sometimes is revealed only by cutting into the peel. If blue albedo is found on several fruits on an individual tree, it suggests stubborn infection. On stubborn-affected trees, some fruits begin to mummify at the time of color break or later. Some of these effects are shown in figure 2–42.

Internal Fruit Symptoms.—The principal internal fruit symptoms are imperfect development or abortion of all seeds in some fruits of normally seedy varieties, especially oranges and tangelos; peel with prominent vascular network and bluish albedo, particularly in abnormally small fruits, and sometimes externally visible; and off-shaped fruits with either insipid or bitter flavor. Calavan and Carpenter (1965) emphasized that the absence of acorn shape, blue albedo, stylar-end greening, and other fruit symptoms is not proof that trees are not infected.

In Morocco, Chapot (1959) associated both acorn-shaped and lopsided fruits with stubborn disease and observed that fruits on infected trees often failed to color uniformly. He described multiple bud development, bushy stem growth, reduced leaf size, and flowering and fruiting habits identical with those listed by Calavan and Carpenter (1965) and other workers. Chapot (1959) also mentioned that some fruits that matured on

Fig. 2–40. Stubborn disease. Left, healthy, normal, nucellar Valencia tree about seven and one-half years from budding. Right, same age tree which had been inoculated while in nursery planting. (Photo courtesy of E. C. Calavan.)

Fig. 2–41. Effect of stubborn disease on yields. Fruit in boxes in rear was from a healthy seven-year-old Valencia. Fruit in front basket was the total production of a companion tree which had been experimentally infected with a virulent source of the stubborn agent while in nursery planting. (Photo courtesy of E. C. Calavan.)

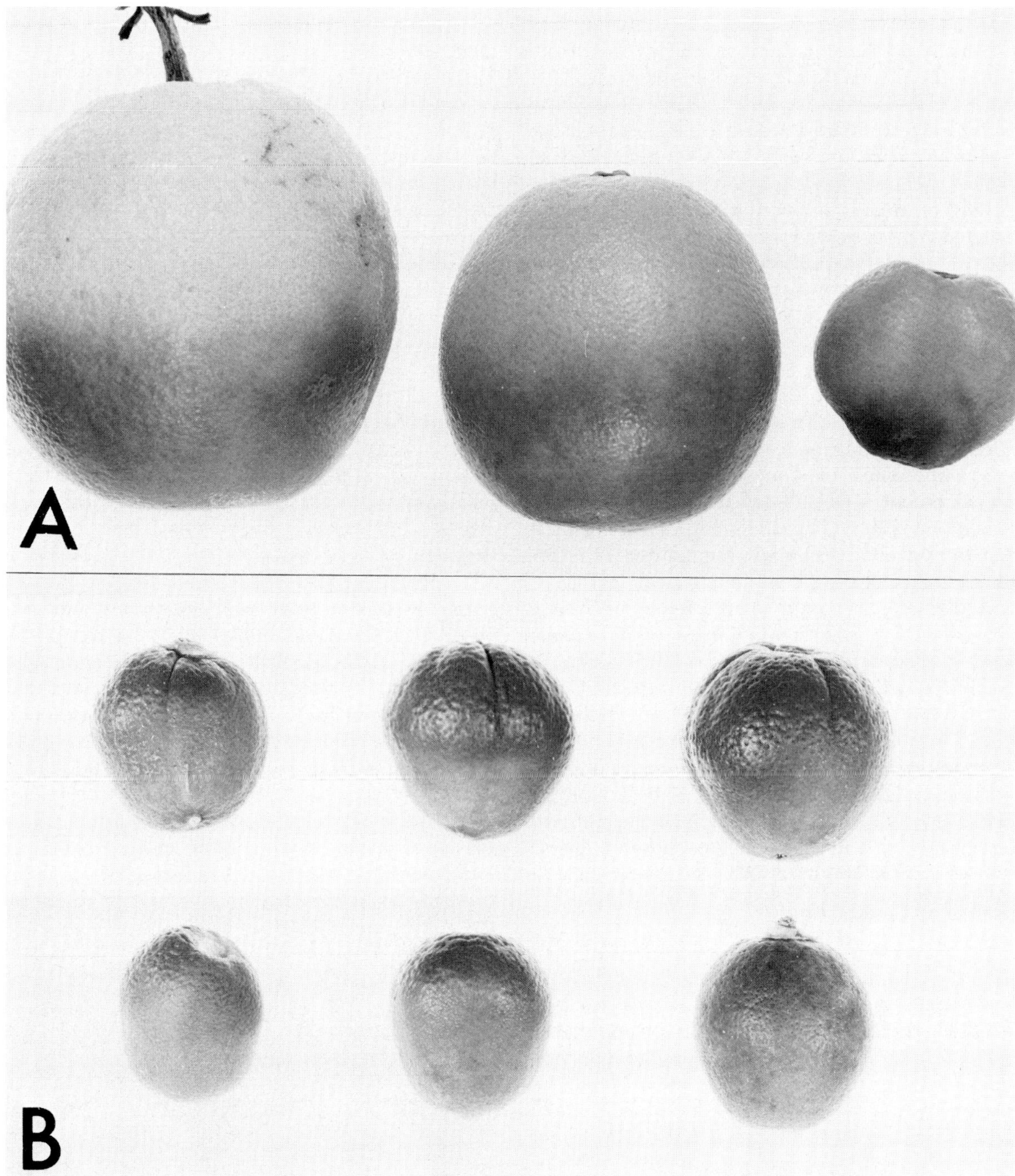

Fig. 2–42. Fruit effects associated with stubborn disease. *A*, two fruits with greening and one with early breakdown at stylar end. (Photo courtesy of E. C. Calavan.) *B*, acorn-shaped fruits from stubborn tree. (Photo by L. J. Klotz.)

affected trees often developed a secondary rot, especially on the stylar end of acorn-shaped fruits where the peel is thinner than normal.

Calavan and Carpenter (1965) reported that fruits from stubborn-infected trees contain many underdeveloped or aborted seeds (fig. 2–43). Carpenter, Calavan, and Christiansen (1965) presented details of studies of seed abortion in stubborn-affected trees of seedy varieties, and suggested that this is probably a valid symptom of stubborn disease. A similar type of seed abortion was reported by Oberholzer, Von Staden, and Basson (1965) in fruits from trees with greening disease in South Africa.

Schneider (1966) found sieve-tube necrosis in the vascular bundles of some deformed fruits on stubborn-affected trees.

Influence of Temperature on Symptom Development.—Olson and Rogers (1969) established that stubborn is a high temperature disease. Using controlled day/night temperatures, it was found that stubborn symptoms developed faster and became more severe on infected plants held at 35° C day/27° C night temperatures than on plants held at temperatures of 27° C day/23° C night. No symptoms developed on plants grown at 23° C day/ 19° C night temperatures. Bové *et al.* (1974) obtained similar results on studies of influence of temperature on symptom development of stubborn and classified the disease as heat tolerant. Saglio *et al.* (1973) demonstrated that the stubborn organism S. *citri* in culture has an optimum growth temperature of about 32° C.

Nature of Causal Agent

Fawcett *et al.* (1944) referred to the probable virus nature of stubborn disease, and Fawcett (1946) concluded that the disease was caused by a virus. This conclusion was generally accepted until the late 1960's when further investigations provided evidence that stubborn is not a true virus disease.

In Egypt, Nour-Eldin (1967) described plasmodium-like structures and spherical inclusion bodies in hypertrophied cells of tumorous growths on flowers from safargali (stubborn) trees cultured on potato dextrose agar. He suggested that the causal agent of the disease is a chytrid-like organism and not a virus. Although the structures observed by Nour-Eldin under the light microscope appeared to be associated with stubborn disease, their causal relationship was not established.

The first indication that stubborn disease might be caused by a mycoplasmalike organism was obtained in 1968 when Igwegbe (1970) discovered that an antibiotic, tetracycline, suppressed symptoms of the disease in sweet orange seedlings. Subsequent electron microscope studies of ultrathin tissue sections by Igwegbe (1970), Igwegbe and Calavan (1970), and Laflèche and Bové (1970*a*) revealed mycoplasmalike structures in sieve tubes of stubborn-infected citrus leaves which were not present in noninfected leaves. Using the same source of the stubborn pathogen (California 189), Saglio *et al.* (1971*a*) in France, and Fudl-Allah, Calavan, and Igwegbe (1971) in California, successfully cultured in liquid and on agar media, a pleomorphic organism identical with that found in sieve tubes of leaves of stubborn-infected sweet orange (fig. 2–44). Similar mycoplasmalike structures were found in Israel in trees with little leaf disease by Zelcer, Bar-Joseph, and Loebenstein (1971).

Saglio *et al.* (1973) characterized the organism associated with stubborn disease and proposed for it the name *Spiroplasma citri* (fig. 2–45). Bové *et al.* (1973) published additional data on the properties of *Spiroplasma citri*. They found that the citrus agent has certain properties in common with known representatives of the Mycoplasmatales but also has some unique properties and is similar, in some respects, to organisms belonging to the Spirochaetales. However, the stubborn organism did not have certain characteristics of

Fig. 2–43. Abnormal seeds in stubborn-affected Valencia fruits. Left, fruit and seeds of normal fruit. Right, affected fruit with darkened, shrivelled seeds. (From Calavan and Carpenter, 1965.)

spirochaetes nor did it react serologically to representatives of five different genera of spirochaetes.

Acceptance of this mycoplasmalike organism, *S. citri*, as the causal agent of stubborn disease has been based to a large extent on its regular presence in stubborn-affected trees, its absence from healthy trees, and the failure of extensive research to reveal any virus or other pathogen in diseased trees. Establishing *S. citri* as the agent of stubborn disease has had to await successful completion of the necessary rules of proof, i.e., experimental inoculation of this agent into healthy citrus by one or another means, production of the disease, and recovery of *S. citri* from the experimentally infected plants. As detailed in the following discussion, it now appears that all of these procedures have been accomplished and that it can be concluded that stubborn disease is caused by *S. citri*.

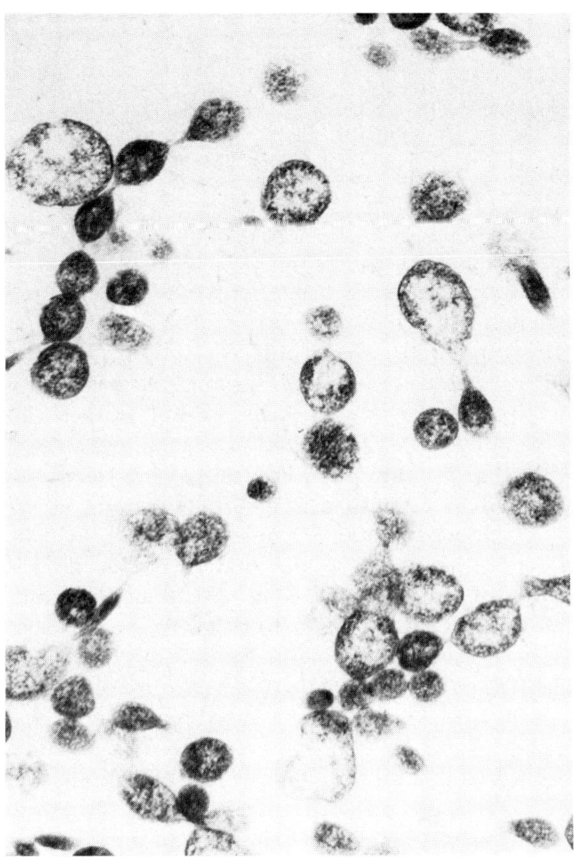

Fig. 2–44. Mycoplasma of *Spiroplasma citri* cultured on solid media from a stubborn-affected tree in Morocco. X 36,000. (Courtesy of J. M. Bové.)

Transmission and Spread

Tissue Grafting and Bud Perpetuation.—Fawcett *et al.* (1944) and Fawcett (1946) presented evidence that the stubborn disease pathogen is transmissible by tissue grafting. Calavan and Christiansen (1961) observed stunting and chlorosis within two months after tissue-graft inoculation of small seedlings of Eureka lemon, West Indian lime, and calamondin from a navel orange tree having severe stubborn symptoms. All inoculated seedlings did not develop symptoms, and severity of effects and time of appearance varied among seedlings that reacted to inoculation. Cassin (1965) in Morocco reported similar results in inoculations of Eureka lemon plants from six different stubborn-affected orchard trees.

The fact that stubborn is a bud-perpetuated disease means that many affected orchard trees originated from stubborn-infected buds. Because of symptom variability, particularly the absence of symptoms on some infected trees, propagation from diseased sources has increased the disease. Delay of symptom appearance in trees grown from infected buds and the inconsistency of symptom development within a group of trees grown from the same budwood source have contributed to a buildup of the disease. If nurserymen repeatedly propagate new trees from buds taken from nursery trees at the time they are headed or pruned for removal, the presence of a single diseased tree results in a rapid increase of diseased trees in nursery stock.

Natural Spread.—Natural spread of the stubborn agent has been suspected in both California and Morocco. Calavan and Carpenter (1965) reported instances of apparent natural infection of both orchard and nursery trees. They stated that this occurred under circumstances that strongly suggest either spread from diseased to healthy trees or infection through seed transmission, or both. In Israel, Patt (1964) made studies of the little leaf disease, which he considers to be similar to stubborn. He found some little leaf among trees of individual nucellar clones of Washington navel and Valencia orange propagated on certain rootstock varieties but not on others. Patt (1964) suggested that the disease observed in the nucellar trees may have resulted from seed transmission of the causal "virus." Calavan *et al.* (1974) stated that the stubborn pathogen is known to be present in the coats of aborted seeds from

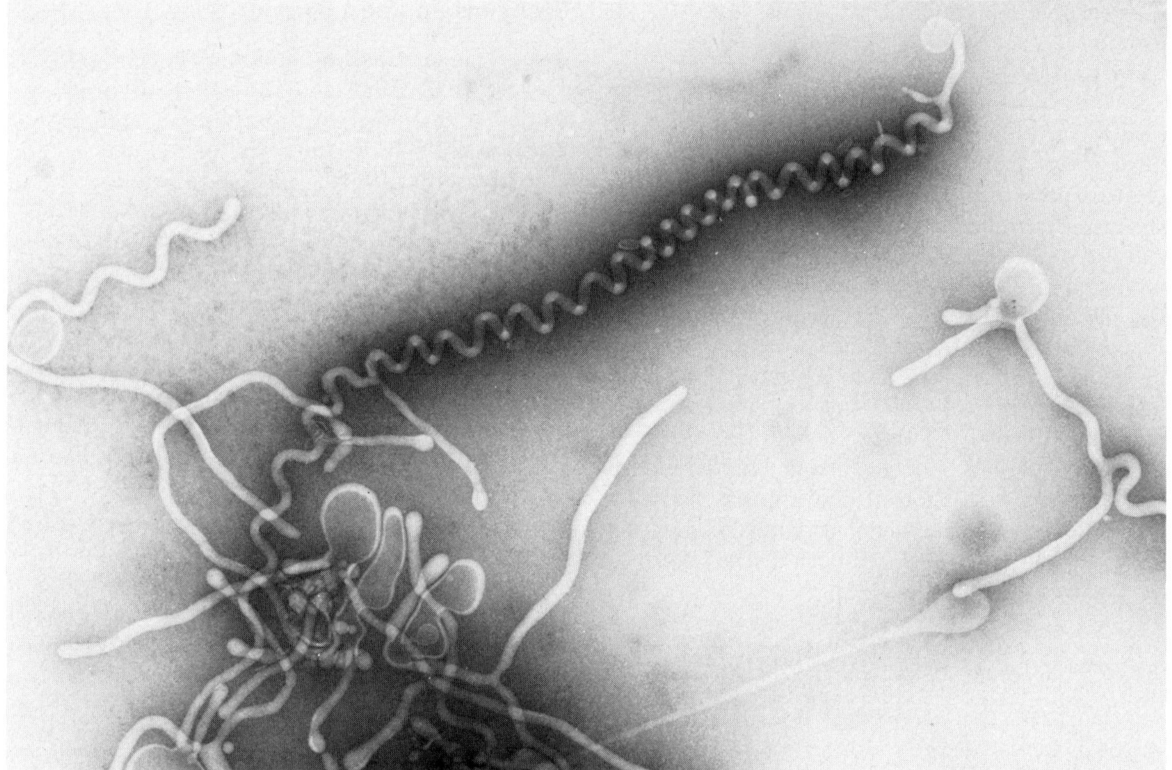

Fig. 2–45. Cells of *spiroplasma citri* showing sacklike "blebs," mycelial type strands and a spiral filament, derived from a 5-day-old culture from stubborn-diseased sweet orange shoot. X 15,000. (From Lee *et al.*, 1973.)

fruit of affected trees but that no stubborn has been found among thousands of indicator seedlings, including several hundred from moderately aborted seeds, grown indoors up to three years.

In 1968 and 1969, Calavan *et al.* (1974) made outside plantings of seedlings and budlings of Madam Vinous sweet orange and seedlings of Sexton tangelo to study natural infection. Plots were located at the University of California field stations, two in the San Joaquin Valley, one at the Moreno Ranch approximately 15 km east of Riverside, California, one at the citrus Research Center, Riverside, and the fifth planting at South Coast Field Station, near Irvine, about 20 km from the coast. A number of experimental plants developed stubborn symptoms within 18 to 24 months at all locations except the South Coast Station. During these studies, more than 400 plants were indexed either by graft transmission to indicator plants or by culturing for presence of S. *citri*. In plants which had been in the field about two years stubborn infection ranged from 0 per cent at South Coast Field Station to 48 per cent at the Moreno Ranch. Later observations and tests of plants at Moreno showed that 90 per cent had become infected within three years. Cartia and Calavan (1974) planted sweet orange seedlings at the Moreno Ranch in June, 1973; symptoms had begun to appear within 50 days. From August to November, 72 per cent of the seedlings tested from that location were infected with S. *citri* and stubborn symptoms were generally present.

Experimental Transmission by Insects.—As evidence accumulated that the causal agent of stubborn disease was being spread in the field, more efforts were made to discover its apparent vectors. Past research aimed at finding the vector had depended entirely on the procedure of feeding various insect species on diseased plants and transferring them to citrus indicator seedlings. Such studies had failed to demonstrate vector transmission. However, discovery that the suspected causal organism can be cultured in vitro provided other techniques for use in experimental insect transmission studies. First, it offered a means of determining if insects of a species under study can acquire and harbor *S. citri*. Lee *et al.* (1973) repeatedly cultured *S. citri* from beet leafhoppers, *Circulifer tenellus* (Baker), collected from sweet orange seedlings and weeds at the University of California Moreno Ranch where Calavan *et al.* (1974) had found a high incidence of stubborn in citrus seedlings. This work demonstrated that the beet leafhopper can acquire the stubborn organism naturally. Whitcomb *et al.* (1973) injected cultured *S. citri* into three other species of leafhoppers and demonstrated that it increased in the bodies of these insects. In England, Daniels *et al.* (1973) injected cultured *S. citri* into leafhoppers, *Euscelis plebejus* (Fallen), which then infected plants of white clover with *S. citri*. Spaar *et al.* (1974) transmitted *S. Citri* to chrysanthemum by means of injected *E. plebejus*.

Markham *et al.* (1974) reported transmission of *S. citri* to two of 49 citrus plants by *E. plebejus* leafhoppers following their microinjection with the organism cultured from little leaf-affected trees. In studies with the leafhopper *Scaphytopius nitridus* (DeLong), which Kaloostian and Pierce (1972) found to breed on citrus, Kaloostian *et al.* (1975) demonstrated that this species acquired *S. citri* by direct feeding on stubborn-infected sweet orange seedlings. When transferred in groups of 50 to 100 to each of ten disease-free periwinkle plants *(Vinca rosea)*, they induced disease symptoms in four plants. *S. citri* was cultured from these plants as well as others which became diseased by graft inoculation from them.

Using the membrane feeding technique, Rana *et al.* (1975) found that *C. tenellus*, *S. nitridus*, and five other homopterous insect species acquired *S. citri* when allowed to feed through membranes in contact with suspensions of cultured *S. citri* in 5 per cent sucrose. Groups of membrane-fed *C. tenellus* were caged on six Madam Vinous sweet orange seedlings and one of these became infected and developed stubborn disease. A single sweet orange seedling was exposed to membrane-fed *S. nitridus* and it developed symptoms of stubborn. *S. citri* was cultured from that seedling.

The studies just described have demonstrated that at least eleven homopterous species of insects can acquire and maintain *S. citri* by microinjection, membrane feeding, or—of primary importance—by direct feeding on stubborn-infected citrus. Infections of citrus by such insects have been successful in only a few instances but as yet only a limited number of inoculations have been made. With further experimentation it seems likely that improved techniques of direct inoculation of citrus by insect vectors of the stubborn agent will evolve which will result in higher infection percentages.

The discoveries that white clover, chrysanthemum, and periwinkle are hosts of *S. citri* and can be infected by direct inoculation by leafhopper are interesting and significant. Besides providing noncitrus hosts for experimental use, proof of the existence of such hosts probably explains the presence of *S. citri* in *C. tenellus* leafhoppers collected from areas far removed from citrus (Calavan and Gumpf, 1974).

Control or Prevention

With evidence that the causal agent of stubborn is spread by insects, control or prevention of this disease will prove more difficult than formerly thought to be. Nevertheless, certain preventive measures should be scrupulously practiced, and it is advisable to continue such procedures even in locations where there is a significant amount of natural infection in orchard plantings. For the most part, these procedures apply to nursery practices and are as follows:

1. If possible, establish citrus nurseries in locations where experimental study has shown natural spread of stubborn is not occurring.

2. Avoid stubborn-infected sources of budwood. The best means of doing this would be to establish stubborn-free mother trees in locations where it is known that natural spread of stubborn does not occur. Prior to availability of propagative material from such mother trees, budwood should be taken from selected orchard trees in stubborn-free locations. Regardless of the healthy appearance of a budwood source tree, it should be indexed for stubborn infection. Freedom from stubborn can be determined by graft inoculation to indicator seedlings or by making cultures of leaf tissue. For the inoculation method Calavan (1969) recommended the use of vigorous seedlings of sweet orange, Sexton tangelo, and grapefruit. He found Madam Vinous sweet orange to be a good indicator, but stated that some other citrus species and hybrids are also satisfactory. Many citrus nurserymen have hothouses and are sufficiently knowledgeable about stubborn disease to conduct the necessary seedling indexing. The culturing test for stubborn is somewhat easier and is probably a more reliable test, but it calls for assistance from a

research station laboratory where this type of work is being done. In states where citrus budwood certification programs are active, the culture test will probably become a routine procedure in helping to establish stubborn-free cultivars.

3. Although seed transmission has not been conclusively demonstrated, it seems advisable to use seeds from trees believed to be free of the disease and to rogue off-type seedlings from seed beds and nursery rows.

4. After propagation in the nursery, all off-type or stubborn-appearing budlings should be removed.

5. After pruning or heading back budling trees in the nursery, observe the new growth and eliminate those that develop abnormally.

6. After young trees have been planted in the orchard, those that develop abnormally during the first year or two should be replaced unless poor development is determined to be a correctable condition and not due to stubborn disease.

7. Continue to inspect trees in new plantings as they come into production and replace low-yielding trees or trees that show other evidence of stubborn disease. Top working stubborn-infected trees is a useless procedure.

8. In established orchards, some stubborn-infected trees cannot be detected with certainty by visual observation, but trees that become unproductive or produce fruits of unmarketable small sizes should be replaced.

9. In view of the recently reported evidence regarding transmission of the stubborn agent by the beet leafhopper which breeds and survives around citrus planting largely on weed hosts, clean cultivation within and around citrus plantings is recommended.

Application of other control measures must await further experimental study. Consideration must be given to whether or not the natural spread of the stubborn agent can be reduced by control of the insect vectors. With the situation such as we now understand it to be, it would seem that application of chemical sprays to citrus orchards for control of the vectors would not be an effective, economic practice. The possibility that several leafhopper species may be involved and the fact that most of these are only "visitors" to citrus trees would operate against establishing a regular spray schedule. For example, beet leafhoppers visit and feed on citrus only when they are migrating or are forced to move from beet fields at harvest time or from their weed hosts which mature or become otherwise unavailable. It would seem worthwhile, however, to grow citrus under clean cultivation and to control the growth of weeds in close proximity to orchards.

From the standpoint of producing stubborn-free nursery trees there is a possibility that heat treatment of budwood may prove to be of value. Olson and Rogers (1969) obtained no infection in 15 sweet orange seedlings, each inoculated by means of one bud derived from hot-air treated citrus budsticks which had been held for 1½ or 2 hours at 51° C and a relative humidity of 54 ± 2 per cent. Bud survival was 37.5 per cent. Roistacher and Calavan (1972) obtained no infection from buds and small stem sections treated for four hours in hot water at 50° C. The heat-treated experimental inocula came from three stubborn-infected sweet orange seedlings which had been preconditioned for 28 weeks at 38-42° C maximum and 30-31° C minimum temperatures. From two of the heat-treated preconditioned sweet orange seedlings bud survival was near 100 per cent but was low in the case of the third seedling. Roistacher and Calavan (1972) clearly demonstrated that tissue from preconditioned citrus seedlings had a much higher survival rate than that from nonpreconditioned seedlings. Such investigations should be explored further because of the possible need for and use of thermotherapy in the elimination of the stubborn agent from citrus propagative material. However, emphasis should be placed on eliminating stubborn from large quantities of budwood without preconditioning if heat treatment is to be useful to nurserymen. The desirable treatment for nurserymen who propagate large numbers of trees from field-grown parent trees or produce citrus budwood for export in large quantities must be simple, inexpensive, and reliable.

Because of the known sensitivity of S. *citri* to antibiotics, both in vivo and in vitro, additional studies should be made on the effectiveness of antibiotics in eliminating the pathogen from citrus budwood as well as suppression of disease effects by injection of the antibiotic solutions into orchard trees. Igwegbe (1970) and Igwegbe and Calavan (1973) demonstrated suppression of stubborn symptoms on the growth of infected sweet orange seedlings that developed after the seedlings had been grown 30 days in a nutrient solution containing 5 ppm achromycin. Twenty-eight of 32 treated seedlings were symptomless after eight months and it appeared that the organism had been eliminated from some seedlings.

In vitro studies of *S. citri* by Saglio *et al.* (1973), Bové *et al.* (1973), and Bowyer and Calavan (1974) demonstrated that the organism is highly sensitive to several antibiotics at concentrations of less than 1.0 μg/ml. The latter authors found it to be sensitive to six other compounds at concentrations of less than 15 μg/ml. These demonstrations of antibiotic sensitivity of *S. citri*, the apparent elimination of the greening organism (see below) from citrus budwood by immersion in antibiotic solutions, and the reported beneficial effects of injecting antibiotics into greening-affected trees are sufficient reasons for continuing and expanding such studies in connection with stubborn disease.

GREENING DISEASE

A disorder of citrus in South Africa described as "greening" or "yellow branch" was reported by Oberholzer (1947) and van der Merwe and Anderson (1947). According to Oberholzer, Von Staden, and Basson (1965), this disorder has been known in the Eastern Transvaal of South Africa since 1929. These authors reported that since 1958 this disease has caused significant losses of fruit in many orchards of both Western Transvaal and Northern Transvaal. Approximately 100,000 trees of navel and Valencia orange had become commercially unprofitable in these three citrus areas. In South Africa, greening has been primarily a disease of sweet orange, but satsuma and other mandarins, lemons, and grapefruits are also affected. Although they are treated separately in this chapter, it now seems that citrus dieback in India, likubin in Taiwan, leaf mottle (leaf mottle yellows) in the Philippines, and probably vein phloem degeneration in Indonesia are similar to greening, possibly forms of the same disease. Although reference is made to some of these disorders in this section the name greening is restricted to the disease as it is known in South Africa and nearby regions.

Symptomatology

McClean and Oberholzer (1965*a*) concluded that "greening" is not a suitable name for this disorder because it not only affects fruits but also the tree itself. They suggested "mottle-leaf" to be a more suitable name. In a very complete account of foliage, fruit, and tree symptoms, McClean and Schwarz (1970) proposed "blotchy-mottle" as an alternative name for greening disease. The following discussion of symptomatology is taken from the two publications just cited.

Severely affected trees are stunted, unthrifty, and sparsely foliated (fig. 2–46). For the most part, affected trees produce greened and worthless fruit. Root systems are poor, and the quantity of fibrous roots is reduced. There is a variety of chlorotic leaf patterns, the most distinctive being an irregular yellowing along the midrib and larger veins, spreading into adjacent tissues to produce a mottled effect (fig. 2–47). Fully mature leaves, away from the tips and on branches on the inside of trees, show the most reliable symptoms. Seasonal temperature changes have a noticeable effect on severity of symptoms. Growth from infected limbs improves in the summer with development of stronger shoots with larger leaves, giving a false impression of recovery. Symptoms usually are better defined during the cooler months.

On affected trees, new spring growth often consists of short twigs with narrow, upright yellow leaves. Some of the yellow leaves may have some dark-green spots. As the leaves mature, they turn green and the veins form a darker green network. Summer growth consists of both weak and strong branches, with leaf color at first a normal green. However, as the leaves mature, they tend to become mottled. In summer, these leaf symptoms are sometimes stronger on Valencia than on navel orange. Other effects are premature leaf drop, especially the small chlorotic growth on weak twigs, a dieback of twigs, formation of multiple buds on defoliated branches, and early flowering of these branches.

Fruits on affected trees are usually smaller than normal. The side of the fruit away from the sun tends to stay green and develops more slowly, causing the fruit to be lopsided. Fruits on the inside of the tree are described as "dirty greenish brown." Outside fruits color, but never attain a normal orange appearance. The greened fruits are of very poor quality with a bitter, unpleasant taste. Many fruits remain small and drop from the trees, and most seeds in diseased fruit are small and dark colored.

Affected trees vary widely in reaction. On some, symptoms are general, with all branches bearing abnormal leaves and fruits; on others, only an occasional branch shows symptoms, but there are all gradations between the extremes. On partially affected trees, normal parts bear normal leaves and fruits. Such trees may continue in this condition for many years without becoming generally affected. This reaction is common when older

Fig. 2–46. Greening disease in Valencia orange, Rustenburg, South Africa. *A*, **normal tree.** *B*, **tree with severe effects of greening disease from natural infection. (From McClean and Oberholzer, 1965*a*.)**

trees become infected, and explains why the disorder became known locally as "yellow branch."

McClean and Oberholzer (1965*a*) discussed symptom similarities and differences between greening and stubborn diseases. Although the two disorders differ quite strikingly in some aspects, these investigators admitted that there may be a relationship between the two diseases.

Schneider (1966) made anatomical studies of trees affected by greening disease in South Africa and found sieve-tube necrosis and excessive phloem formation in veins of yellowed leaves and severe sieve-tube necrosis in the vascular bundles of deformed fruits. In comparable studies of stubborn disease in California, he found that these effects were not consistently present nor nearly so obvious as with greening disease. From observations of greening disease in South Africa and stubborn disease in California and Morocco, Schneider (1966) concluded that the symptoms of stubborn are similar yet considerably different from those of greening disease. On the basis of overall appearance of affected trees, he classified greening as a decline disease with characteristic symptoms that are lacking on stubborn-affected trees. However, he recognized certain similarities and suggested a possible relationship between the two diseases.

Nature, Transmission, and Spread

Oberholzer and Hofmeyer (1955) obtained evidence of transmission of the causal agent of greening by tissue grafts and suggested that the disease was caused by a virus. Subsequently, work by Schwarz (1964), Oberholzer *et al.* (1965), and McClean and Oberholzer (1965*a*, 1965*b*) led to the conclusion that greening disease is caused by a graft-transmissible virus spread in the field by a citrus psyllid, *Trioza erytreae* Del Guercio. McClean and Oberholzer (1965*b*) obtained transmission with adult psyllids but not with nymphs. Seedlings of sweet orange and West Indian type lime were used as indicator plants. No symptoms of greening disease developed in transmission trials with the citrus aphid, *Toxoptera citricidus* Kirk.

McClean, Schwarz, and Oberholzer (1969) reported that the greening "virus" moves slowly in citrus trees and tends to remain confined in older trees to branches into which it is introduced. It was concluded that trees that are generally affected have received multiple inoculations by the psyllid vectors. When buds were used in propagations from greening-affected trees, less than one per cent of the progeny showed evidence of infection even when the buds were taken from fully diseased

Fig. 2–47. Leaf symptoms associated with greening disease. *A-B*, foliage from tree *B*, figure 2–46, bearing small, upright, yellow leaves; some leaves with green spots, others with interveinal chlorosis. *C*, leaf from an inoculated branch of a mature Valencia tree. *D*, leaf from a naturally infected Cape seedling. *E*, leaves of greening-affected mandarin tree showing mottling similar to that caused by zinc deficiency. (*A-D*, from McClean and Oberholzer, 1965*a*; *E*, photo supplied by R. E. Schwarz.)

trees. McClean (1970) propagated 1200 trees from either single buds, or tip grafts comprised of 2-3 cm lengths of terminal stem tissue from trees which, for the most part, showed severe and extensive symptoms of greening. Four per cent of the trees grown from buds and 64 per cent grown from tip grafts developed greening symptoms.

Laflèche and Bové (1970*a*, 1970*b*) found mycoplasma-type structures in leaves of greening-affected orange trees which were not present in healthy plants. This suggested that greening is caused by a mycoplasmalike organism. Subsequent studies by Saglio *et al.* (1971*b*) and Bové and Saglio (1974) led to the conclusion that the structures associated with greening disease differ from mycoplasma to such an extent as to exclude their classification within the Mycoplasmatales. Comparative studies of the suspected agents of South African greening and stubborn revealed very significant differences in morphology of the respective organisms, temperature requirements for symptom development in citrus infected by them, and growth of the organisms on artificial media. Fudl-Allah *et al.* (1971), and Saglio *et al.* (1971*a*) demonstrated that the stubborn organism is easily cultured on solid and in liquid media. On the other hand, Bové and Saglio (1974) reported that they had not been able to cultivate the structures associated with greening disease with the same techniques and media used for culturing the stubborn organism.

Control

In South Africa, occurrence of greening disease definitely seems to be correlated with the distribution and prevalence of the citrus psyllid. Oberholzer *et al.* (1965) stated that in the past, citrus psyllids have been important only in citrus nurseries, but since 1957 have assumed importance in many citrus orchards located at cool altitudes exceeding 3,000 feet above sea level. They suggested that psyllid buildup has been associated with continued use of parathion spray for control of red scale. They also reported that *T. erytreae* is seldom found in great numbers in hot, dry regions at low altitudes where greening is either absent or of no commercial significance. These observations suggested that environment may limit the distribution and populations of the vector and thus restrict the disease to certain citrus regions. Also, they suggested that there may be some advantage in changing the citrus pest-control program currently in use where the disease is important to a program that is less favorable to the vector.

In South Africa, efforts are being made to avoid use of budwood from localities where the disease is present and to prevent movement of nursery trees from affected to nonaffected areas. The fact that in some parts of South Africa the psyllid vector is virtually absent provides an opportunity to avoid infection of nursery stock by restricting citrus nurseries to those localities.

Schwarz (1965) demonstrated the presence of a specific fluorescent compound in the tissues of greening-affected citrus. McClean *et al.* (1969) reported that a fluorescent marker test was being used by three large citrus estates for elimination of greening-infected trees in nurseries. Subsequently, McClean (1970) made extensive tissue-graft indexing tests on nursery trees that were examined and graded infected or healthy on the basis of the presence or absence of the fluorescent marker. The results obtained from inoculations in that trial indicated that the fluorescent marker test is not always reliable. McClean had earlier found that a very low percentage of buds from diseased trees are infected and he concluded that with that situation, the time and expense of making chromatographic analysis of nursery trees was not justified. However, from later studies of use of phenolic markers for indexing citrus, Schwarz and Van Vuuren (1970) stated, "The results do not, however, give an answer to the question as to whether the presence of the marker in lemons and grapefruits is specifically correlated with greening infection, a correlation that has been firmly established with sweet orange, and with high probability also with mandarins and tangelos."

It has been shown that *D. citri* can be controlled effectively with a range of modern insecticides. Catling (1970) reported that dimethoate, in concentrations as low as 0.0025 per cent active ingredient, proved effective against eggs and nymphs of *T. erytreae*, and the same insecticide at 0.0075 per cent active ingredient gave 79 per cent kill of *D. citri* nymphs in a field test in the Philippines.

From information now available it seems that additional studies should be initiated towards development of an integrated control of the psyllid vectors of greening and related diseases. Catling (1970) recommends application of low concentrations of safe systemics such as dimethoate or demeton methyl at the first signs of a buildup of nymphs on a new growth cycle.

Schwarz and Van Vuuren (1971) introduced solutions of antibiotics by gravity flow into trunks of seven-year-old trees with greening disease. With pure preparations of tetracycline the uptake per tree ranged from 560-1500 ml. The numbers of greened fruit were recorded the year before treatment and the year following. There was 49 per cent decrease in greened fruit on five trees treated with 500 ppm tetracycline. Schwarz, Moll, and Van Vuuren (1974) presented additional information on experimental control of greening disease in field trees by injection of antibiotics.

In addition to citrus, investigations were conducted on control of mycoplasmalike diseases of other fruit trees by injection and antibiotics (Nyland and Moller, 1973). Improved methods of tree injection are being developed and this type of treatment now shows promise of partial control at least, of tree diseases caused by these antibiotic-sensitive agents. In South Africa, efforts are being made to combine systemic insecticides with antibiotics. With proper timing and schedule of tree injection, it may be possible to suppress symptoms and at the same time reduce citrus psyllid populations.

Observations on seasonal symptom development on orchard trees in South Africa by McClean and Oberholzer (1965*a*) and McClean *et al.* (1969), and experimental studies by Schwarz and Green (1972) on greening-affected trees exposed to different temperatures showed that symptoms of greening are mild or absent under hot conditions but are strong on trees growing at cool temperatures. Controlled temperature studies by Bové *et al.* (1974) showed that symptoms of South African greening develop best on plants held at 22° C/24° C, 8-hour night/16-hour-day, respectively. No symptoms developed on plants held at 27° C/32°C night/day temperatures. On the basis of these findings, the South African greening organism has been classified as heat sensitive. The correlation between temperature and symptoms clearly explains the earlier observations of Schwarz (1967) that greening symptoms are less severe in South Africa in the hot, low-lying areas than in the cool, high-lying areas. From the standpoint of control of this disease, that knowledge should be taken into consideration when the matter of replanting citrus or developing new orchards arises in South Africa.

Oberholzer *et al.* (1965) stated that the psyllid vector *T. erytreae* does not occur in any other major citrus region of the world. However, another psyllid, *Diaphorina citri* Kuway, transmits the causal agent of citrus dieback in India, likubin disease of Taiwan, and Philippine leaf mottle yellows. Catling (1970) summarized the known distribution of these two citrus psyllids. *T. erytreae* is restricted to Africa south of the Sahara, primarily in the citrus-growing countries of South Africa, Swaziland, and Rhodesia. It also has been recorded from Madagascar, Mauritius, Réunion, and Saint Helena. *D. citri* is widely distributed in the Orient and is present in Brazil. The only record of the two species existing in the same geographical region is Réunion Island, where Bové and Cassin (1968) found large numbers of *D. citri* in the hot coastal zone whereas *T. erytreae* was confined mainly to areas above 1600 feet elevation. There has been no report on transmission of the heat-sensitive greening of South Africa by *D. citri* but the author has been informed that a Poona strain of greening (Indian dieback) has been transmitted experimentally by *T. erytreae.*[4] This suggests that the heat-tolerant forms of greening could be spread in citrus in South Africa should they be introduced into regions where *T. erytreae* is present.

Catling (1972) stated that there are at least eight species of chalcidoid wasps associated with nymphs of *T. erytreae* and a fairly large number of predators which attack that psyllid species. Similarly, a number of internal parasites of *D. citri* have been identified in the Philippines, India, and West Pakistan. It is believed that these natural enemies assist in limiting vector numbers but levels of parasitism vary from season to season.

CITRUS DIEBACK DISEASE

"Citrus dieback" has been observed and studied in India at least since the 1920's (Cheema and Bhatt, 1928), but it is evident that the name "dieback" did not refer to decline from a single cause. During the past two decades, citrus plantings in India have declined in a manner suggesting that trees are suffering from a specific malady of rather recent origin. Initially, investigators of the problem tended to attribute most of the damage to tristeza virus, because it was learned that tristeza, the tristeza-seedling yellows virus complex and the efficient aphid vector, *T. citricidus*, were generally present in citrus orchards. Some workers held to this view even though extensive decline was occurring in plantings of known tristeza-tolerant trees of sweet orange and mandarin on Rough lemon rootstock. However, it was recognized that a complex situation existed in India. In addition to tristeza, other factors contributing to the decline of citrus were nutritional problems, gummosis, insect pests, twig and leaf diseases, and fungus root rots associated with waterlogging of the soil.

Nature and Symptomatology

After a three-month survey of the dieback problem in India, Fraser and Singh (1966) and Fraser (1967) concluded that the primary cause of dieback is the greening "virus." At the time of Dr. Fraser's visit, both T. K. Nariani, Indian Agricultural Research Institute, New Delhi, and S. P. Capoor, I.A.R.I., Poona, had obtained some infections with the dieback agent separate from tristeza virus and had produced symptoms on citrus varieties which do not react to tristeza virus. These results of graft-transmission were reported by Fraser *et al.* (1966).

Fraser (1967) reported that the South African vector of greening "virus," *T. erytreae* Del Guercio, had not been recorded from India, but that a native psyllid, *Diaphorina citri* Kuway, is very common in most districts. Fraser recommended that this species be studied as a possible vector. Subsequently, Capoor (1967), Nariani, Raychaudhuri, and Bhalla (1967), and Capoor, Rao, and Viswanath (1967) presented conclusive evidence that *D. citri* is a vector of the causal agent of the so-called dieback disease.

The studies of symptomatology of affected orchard trees as well as experimental trees inoculated either by tissue grafts or by citrus psyllids indicated that much dieback of citrus in India is caused by a specific disease agent, similar to that which causes greening disease in South Africa. Poor cultural practice and other diseases, particularly gummosis and root rot, are responsible for

[4]Personal communication to the author from J. M. Bové, dated June 30, 1973. Also reported by G. Massonie, M. Garnier, and J. M. Bové in a paper presented at 7th Conference I.O.C.V., Athens, Greece, October, 1975.

some loss of trees. Tristeza is important only where susceptible stionic combinations or varieties subject to stem-pitting are planted. Under field conditions, it is sometimes difficult to correctly diagnose the cause of tree decline by observation, but with the knowledge that the causal agent and its psyllid vector is present it is now a relatively simple matter to index for dieback (greening) disease and determine its distribution. Even if tristeza occurs in mixture with dieback, graft inoculation of seedlings of sweet orange, mandarins, and certain other kinds of citrus under controlled (psyllid-free) conditions will reveal the dieback agent if it is present.

Fraser *et al.* (1966) stated that the range of foliar symptoms of citrus dieback on orchard trees in India agrees in every respect with that described by McClean and Oberholzer (1965*a*) for greening disease in South Africa except that no greened fruits with bitter flavor were seen in India. It was stated that affected fruits may fall at an early stage.

Fraser (1967) found considerable variation in severity of symptoms in different districts in India and suggested symptom suppression in some localities by high temperature as reported in South Africa by McClean and Oberholzer (1965*a*). However, Fraser believed that not all variations in symptom development between districts in India can be explained satisfactorily on a climatic basis. She suggested that differences in varietal susceptibilities and the effect of associated diseases may have been responsible for some of the observed performances of a given variety in different districts.

With regard to varietal reaction, Fraser (1967) reported that all sweet orange and tangelo varieties and mandarin x sweet orange hybrids were very severely affected. Grapefruit reaction was classed as severe. Certain mandarin varieties were severely affected in some districts, but performed better in others. In one district, seedling mandarin trees were severely affected, whereas budded trees of mandarin on rootstocks of Rangpur lime and Rough lemon showed few or no symptoms. It was recognized that the rootstocks may have reduced damage caused by root-rotting fungi rather than imparting resistance to dieback or Indian greening. Whether or not some mandarin varieties are less susceptible can be determined only by careful study under conditions where other disease factors are eliminated or at least recognized and evaluated. The same applied to the question of influence of rootstock on the reaction of scion varieties to the disease.

Raychaudhuri, Nariani, and Lele (1967, 1969) found that dieback of twigs and limbs of greening-affected trees is associated with fungi such as *Colletotrichum gleosporiodes, Curvularia tuberculata, Diplodia natalensis,* and *Fusarium* spp. which enter twigs at the leaf scars after yellowed mature leaves fall from affected parts of trees. They found that these fungi inoculated into citrus seedlings were more pathogenic or caused more extensive dieback on plants previously infected with the dieback agent than on healthy plants. Thus, much twig dieback may actually be caused by fungi, but this is merely an additive affect.

Laflèche and Bové (1970*a*) found mycoplasmalike structures in sieve tubes of leaves of citrus experimentally infected from an inoculum source obtained from India. Subsequent studies by Saglio *et al.* (1971*b*) and Bové and Saglio (1974) led to the conclusion that, morphologically, the structures associated with citrus dieback in India were similar, and possibly identical to those found in greening-affected citrus in South Africa. However, Bové *et al.* (1974) reported that plants inoculated with Indian greening developed severe symptoms when held some months at low temperatures of 22-24° C as well as at higher temperatures of 27-32° C, whereas plants infected with South African greening developed severe symptoms at the lower temperatures but remained symptomless at the higher range. On the basis of present knowledge, including experimental transmission of the dieback organism by *T. erytreae*, the vector of South African greening (see above), the above authors concluded that dieback is a form of greening disease.

Control

In general, control measures for this disease are much the same as those being used or under experimental study for stubborn, greening, and other diseases of this type. Capoor and Thirumalacher (1973) reported beneficial effects of spraying severely affected trees with two tetracycline compounds and a new chemotherapeutic agent identified as B.P.-101. Injection of these materials gave better results than foliage sprays. It was reported that tetracycline-treated trees responded sooner but recovery was not as lasting as on those treated with B.P.-101.

It should be emphasized that investigations on chemotherapeutic control of plant diseases caused by antibiotic-sensitive, mycoplasma, or mycoplasmalike agents is a recent development. It has been established that certain materials inactivate the causal organisms. Some degree of field control of citrus diseases of this kind with antibiotics can be anticipated if techniques can be developed which will introduce and systemically distribute the materials throughout the trees in effective concentrations.

LEAF-MOTTLE-YELLOWS DISEASE

Although citrus has been grown for a long time in the Philippines, it became a more important economic industry as a result of the planting of new acreage following World War II. The new plantings consisted largely of mandarins, pummelos, oranges, and calamondin (*C. reticulata* var. *austera x Fortunella* sp.?). The latter, classified both a *C. mitis* Blanco and *C. madurensis* Lour. by T. Tanaka (see Vol. 1, chap. 4, p. 531), produces small acid fruits very popular in the Philippines for use with tea, fish, and salads. Calamondin is grown either as seedlings or budlings, while other varieties are grown mostly on an unidentified rootstock known locally as calamandarin.

Under tropical conditions where good cultural care is often lacking, citrus plantings in the Philippines continued to expand, but suffered from many major diseases and pests. However, even the better maintained orchards began to deteriorate quite rapidly in about 1957, with trees showing yellowing and leaf mottle followed by severe dieback. The disorder became known as "citrus yellowing," "leaf mottling," and "leaf-mottle-yellows." Initial studies on the disease by C. S. Celino, D. M. Nora, and others, which mostly remain unpublished, demonstrated that the tristeza-seedlings yellows virus complex was present in declining trees and that an efficient aphid vector of tristeza, *Toxoptera citricidus*, also was present in the Philippines. These findings led to other investigations dealing primarily with Tristeza virus as the possible cause of tree decline.

Although they were of the opinion that the decline of citrus trees in the Philippines was caused by tristeza virus, which they found in all affected trees, Nora and Baldia (1962) appear to be the first to call attention to the zinc-deficiency type of leaf mottle associated with "yellowing" disease. They also described other foliage effects and twig dieback, symptoms like those of tristeza on certain citrus hosts.

On the basis of reactions in other countries, Wallace and Martinez (1964) attributed stem-pitting of pummelo and calamondin trees in the Philippines to tristeza virus infection, but pointed out that decline of mandarin on calamandarin rootstock could not be accepted as an effect of tristeza virus until the reaction of trees of that combination could be determined by controlled experiments. Subsequent tests in California (Martinez and Wallace, 1967) demonstrated that trees of mandarin on calamandarin rootstock were not affected when inoculated with virulent strains of tristeza and seedling yellows viruses. Furthermore, Martinez and Wallace (1969) found that seedling plants of sweet orange, mandarin, and others that do not react to tristeza, developed strong symptoms when inoculated from leaf-mottle-yellows trees. These studies proved that tristeza virus was not the primary cause of tree decline in the Philippines. Supporting that conclusion is the evidence that tristeza virus had been present long before 1957 when general deterioration of citrus trees began in the Philippines. Studies by Lee (1921) reported on mottle leaf in Philippine citrus, presumably that is now known to be caused by zinc deficiency. Descriptions and illustrations were provided of normal tree growth of mandarin and Valencia orange on mandarin rootstocks, which are now known not to be affected by tristeza, and of stunted and diseased trees of these same scion varieties on pummelo rootstock, which are tristeza-susceptible combinations. Furthermore, Wallace *et al.* (1956) reported that an import of Batangas mandarin budwood from the Philippines to the United States prior to 1930 carried tristeza virus when introduced. Later, Wallace (1957*a*) found that this imported selection carried the tristeza-seedling yellows virus complex. That this virus mixture commonly is present in Philippine citrus is evident from a survey by Martinez, Nora, and Sebastian (1965), who found it in each of 638 orchard trees indexed from the Batangas and Bicol regions.

Transmission and Nature of Disease

Salibe and Cortez (1966) described in detail symptoms of this disorder in the Philippines, and referred to it as "leaf mottling disease." They reported that bud inoculations from mottled nursery trees caused no tristeza on Key lime seedlings, but caused yellow mottling and stunting on sweet orange seedlings. They noted no symptoms on test plants directly exposed to aphids *(Toxoptera citricidus)* taken from disease orchard trees or aphids permitted to feed first on experimentally infected sweet orange seedlings. They suggested in print for the first time that the leaf-mottling virus may not be tristeza and that the vector of the causal virus might be *Diaphorina citri* Kuway, in accord with facts previously established by Martinez.[5]

Martinez and Wallace (1969) concluded that this disease in the Philippines is caused by a virus distinct from tristeza and that the citrus psyllid, *Diaphorina citri,* is a vector of this virus. *D. citri* fed on orchard trees doubly infected with leaf-mottle-yellows, and tristeza-seedling yellows viruses transmitted only the agent of leaf-mottle-yellows. *T. citricidus* fed on such infected trees normally transmitted only tristeza virus or the tristeza-seedling yellows virus complex. However, in two instances, Martinez and Wallace (1968) found that tristeza-infected aphid-inoculated plants also were infected with leaf-mottle-yellows "virus." This suggested the possibility that the aphid species may sometimes transmit the latter "virus." Subsequent tests did not demonstrate that it can be transmitted by aphids, leading to the conclusion that the two plants suspected of having been infected by aphids had been exposed to infective psyllids.

Salibe and Cortez (1968) concluded that this disease in the Philippines is distinct from tristeza and that the vector of the causal "virus" is the citrus psyllid, *D. citri.* They also reported that most citrus varieties and species are affected, and pointed out similarities between the disease in the Philippines and such diseases as likubin in Taiwan, citrus chlorosis (vein-phloem degeneration) in Java, and greening in South Africa.

Martinez and Wallace (1969) concluded that leaf-mottle-yellows disease in the Philippines is the same as dieback in India. They suggested that inasmuch as dieback disease in India is now referred to as "greening disease," the disease in the Philippines should also be given the name "greening."

Martinez, Nora, and Armedilla (1970) and Martinez, Nora, and Price (1971) reported that the causal agent of leaf-mottle-yellows was inactivated in buds of budsticks immersed 25 minutes in a 1,000 ppm solution of tetracycline hydrochloride. It also was found that foliage sprays (100 ppm) applied at 3-day intervals for ten weeks improved growth and overall appearance of severely affected plants. This suggestion that leaf mottle yellows is a mycoplasma type disease was supported by simultaneous investigations by Laflèche and Bové (1970*a*) which showed that mycoplasmalike organisms are associated with South African greening, stubborn, and Indian dieback diseases. Subsequently, as noted by Bové and Saglio (1974), sieve tubes of citrus leaves of plants infected with Philippine leaf-mottle disease were found to contain structures morphologically similar to those previously found associated with South African greening and Indian dieback. In studies of influence of temperature on symptom expression by Bové *et al.* (1974), plants infected with Philippine leaf-mottle disease, like those with Indian decline (dieback), developed symptoms faster when held at temperatures of 27°-32° C, a range at which plants infected with South African greening developed no symptoms. This, and the fact that the Indian and Philippine diseases have the same vector, indicate that these diseases are identical.

Host Range

Martinez and Wallace (1969) inoculated fifty different citrus species and varieties with Philippine leaf-mottle-yellows and found that all commonly grown mandarin and sweet orange selections developed severe symptoms. Grapefruit, sour orange, Rough lemon, Eureka lemon, Rangpur lime, and Palestine sweet lime were slightly less affected. Calamondin, alemow *(C. macrophylla),* and *Severinia buxifolia* were mildly affected. Troyer and Carrizo citrange, trifoliate orange, *Aeglopsis chevalieri* Swing., and *Triphasia trifolia* (Burm. f.) P. Wils. were symptomless hosts. Trees of mandarin and sweet orange varieties on rootstocks of the citranges and trifoliate orange reacted as severely to inoculation as when inoculated as seedling plants. There was no evidence that the symptomless host rootstocks conferred resistance to the scion varieties. Previous infection of plants with the viruses of tristeza, seedling yellows, exocortis, psorosis, and xyloporosis gave no protection against leaf-mottle-yellows. In fact, plants doubly inoculated with tristeza-seedling yellows and leaf-mottle-yellows reacted more severely than those infected with only leaf-mottle-yellows.

In South Africa, Schwarz[6] observed that greening-affected citrus trees on Rough lemon and

[5]Personal communications with detailed progress reports and substantiating photographs submitted to the author by A. L. Martinez, dated August 12, 1965, and May 24, 1966.

[6]Personal communication to the author from R. E. Schwarz, dated January 20, 1968.

trifoliate orange naturally infected in the orchard, developed better and produced more normal fruits than equally infected trees on sweet orange rootstock. He attributed this difference to extreme sensitivity of sweet orange to the causal agent of greening. Fraser (1967) cited an instance in India of severe decline of greening-affected mandarin on its own root at a location where trees on Rough lemon were still productive. However, subsequent developments in countries where these diseases are present indicate that rootstocks confer no significant resistance to the scion varieties and there is very slight chance that commercial fruit varieties can be found with sufficient resistance to provide control.

Control

Leaf-mottle-yellows disease has virtually eliminated citrus as a commercial crop in the Philippines, particularly in the provinces of Batangas, Laguna, and Quezon and threatens to destroy the plantings in other parts of the country. Production of citrus in the future will depend on whether or not control of the disease can be accomplished by application of antibiotics to affected trees and control of the psyllid vector such as now being investigated on a field basis against greening disease in South Africa. If successful treatments are developed for control of greening it would be expected that these would control leaf-mottle-yellows disease also.

LIKUBIN DISEASE

The name "likubin" originally referred to decline and death of trees of mandarin and sweet orange on Sunki mandarin rootstock in Taiwan. Matsumoto *et al.* (1961) reported on investigations of this disorder in mimeographed monthly reports. Matsumoto *et al.* (1961) described symptoms and presented some information on host range. Because tristeza virus and the tristeza-seedling yellows virus complex was often present in the diseased trees under study, it was concluded that likubin disease was a form of tristeza. However, it was observed that some sources of inocula caused severe decline of scion-rootstock combinations which were known to be tristeza-tolerant in other countries. For example, trees of mandarin or sweet orange on trifoliate orange, Troyer citrange, and Cleopatra mandarin graft-inoculated from some diseased orchard trees resulted in severe decine or death. Furthermore, some orchard trees on Sunki mandarin rootstock were reacting severely after becoming infected naturally, presumably by vectors.

Wallace (1963) observed similarities between likubin and tristeza symptoms on budded orchard trees but emphasized that certain stionic combinations that declined in Taiwan did not suffer from tristeza in other countries. It also was pointed out that tristeza and/or seedling yellows infection caused no symptoms on seedling plants of sweet orange and mandarin, both of which reacted severely when infected from some sources of inocula in Taiwan. Wallace (1963) recommended further study to identify the cause of likubin disease.

Matsumoto and Su (1966) presented additional information on symptomatology, varietal reaction, strains of the causal agent, and transmission by both grafting and *Toxoptera citricidus*. They recognized certain differences between likubin and tristeza but retained the belief that the two diseases were closely related. Matsumoto, Su, and Lo (1968) suggested the presence of a virus component that is common for tristeza and likubin plus some additional component in likubin-affected citrus. Su and Matsumoto (1972) demonstrated that tristeza or the seedling yellows virus complex was not the cause of likubin. Other studies by Chen, Miyakawa, and Matsui (1972, 1973), Su and Leu (1972), and Tanaka and Doi (1974) established that mycoplasmalike organisms are associated with likubin disease in Taiwan and that these organisms are transmitted by the psyllid, *D. citri*. Tanaka and Doi (1974) did not find these organisms in chlorotic leaves of Ponkan mandarin nor in the alimentary canal of citrus psylla *(D. citri)* collected in Kyushu, Japan.

Morphological studies of Su and Leu (1972) and Tanaka and Doi (1974) indicate that the pleomorphic bodies associated with likubin disease are identical with those believed to be the causal agents of the Asian form of greening disease. Su and Leu (1972) reported that the likubin agent was inactivated in small scion sticks by immersion for fifteen hours in a 100 ppm solution of tetracycline hydrochloride (achromycin). Also, they reported that hot water treatment at 50° C for ten minutes inactivated the agent of likubin while having no effect on tristeza or the seedling-yellows virus complex.

If successful control measures become available for use against any of the diseases belonging to the citrus greening group they also should be useful in controlling likubin disease.

CITRUS VEIN-PHLOEM DEGENERATION

Tirtawidjaja, Hadiwidjaja, and Lasheen (1965) gave the name "citrus vein-phloem degeneration" to a graft-transmissible disorder of citrus in Java. It was considered to be a virus disease, and was reported to have caused a loss of hundreds of thousands of trees in Java. A conspicuous symptom on affected trees was a type of chlorosis resembling deficiency symptoms of such elements as nitrogen, zinc, manganese, and iron. Although tristeza virus was apparently widely distributed in Java, Tirtawidjaja *et al.* (1965) concluded that tristeza virus was not the cause of this particular chlorosis and decline. They reported that chlorosis of foliage was accompanied by vein-phloem collapse and accumulation of starch. Graft transfers from chlorotic trees to seedlings of West Indian lime resulted in tristeza-like vein clearing, chlorosis, vein-phloem collapse, and starch accumulation. From declining trees not showing the characteristic chlorosis, inoculations to West Indian lime were said to result in tristeza-like vein clearing, without chlorosis or phloem collapse.

Tirtawidjaja *et al.* (1965) suggested that a virus other than tristeza was the cause of the tree decline in Java because (1) aphid-transmitted tristeza virus from chlorotic trees caused vein clearing on West Indian lime, but did not cause vein-phloem degeneration on seedlings of lime, Rough lemon, and other varieties; and (2) seedlings of trifoliate orange, which had been reported not to be a host of tristeza virus in Brazil, proved to be a symptomless carrier of the vein degeneration virus when inoculated by tissue grafts. Failure to reproduce the disease with aphid-transmitted tristeza virus is the best evidence that another agent causes the disease.

Tirtawidjaja *et al.* (1965) pointed out that this citrus disease in Java has certain similarities to the likubin disease in Taiwan, but they concluded that more information is needed before it can be accepted that the two are the same. Salibe and Cortez (1966) suggested that vein-phloem degeneration disease may be the same as the leaf-mottle disease in the Philippines. With further study, it seems likely that it will be proved to belong to the greening group of diseases. In that case, any successful control measures developed for that type of citrus disease would be expected to be effective in controlling vein-phloem degeneration disease.

VEIN ENATION AND WOODY GALL

Wallace and Drake (1953, 1959, 1960) described citrus vein enation and demonstrated that it is caused by a virus transmitted in California by the green peach aphid, *Myzus persicae* (Sulz.). In South Africa, McClean (1954) reported on studies of vein enation demonstrating that the causal virus is transmitted by *T. citricidus.* In California, Laird and Weathers (1961) corroborated transmission by *Myzus persicae,* and also obtained transmission by *Aphis gossypii.* Fraser (1958) reported that veinenation virus appeared to be widespread in Australia.

Fraser (1958, 1959*b*) described a bud-transmissible disorder on Rough lemon which she named "woody gall." Following her suggestion[7] that there might be a relation between vein enation and woody gall, Wallace and Drake (1960) demonstrated that woody gall is caused by the vein-enation virus. In addition to observation in Australia, naturally occurring woody galls have been observed in California, South Africa, and Peru on Rough lemon seedlings and Rough lemon rootstocks of budded trees. Vein-enation symptoms also have been found on Daidai orange in Japan, where Tanaka and Yamada (1961) demonstrated that the virus is carried also by some trees of satsuma mandarin, Washington navel orange, and Eureka lemon.

The discovery and naming of the vein-enation virus, with the subsequent disclosure that this virus causes the more important gall effects, creates a problem of nomenclature which is not easily resolved. The name "vein enation" has priority. However, because the so-called galls that result from the virus are more important from a disease aspect than leaf symptoms, the name "woody-gall virus" is sometimes used. There seems to be no means of avoiding the use of two names for this virus which causes two such distinctive diseases. Hooper (1968) and Hooper and Schneider (1969) described in detail the anatomy and cytology of the so-called galls associated with this virus. Their conclusions were that the outgrowths which develop on leaves, as well as on thorns, are not enations and that the woody structures on stems and roots are not true galls. They described all of these as "tumors" and suggested that more suitable names would be "citrus tumor virus" and "citrus tumor disease." This appears to

[7]Personal communication to the author from L. R. Fraser, dated December 16, 1957.

be a valid observation, but with the established usage of the terms "vein enation" and "woody gall" for this citrus disease, the substitution of another name for the disease and its causal virus would create considerable confusion.

Symptomatology and Host Range

Vein Enation.—The conspicuous leaf symptoms of citrus vein enation are projections or papillae on the lateral veins and veinlets of the underside of leaves, with corresponding depressions on the upper surface (fig. 2–48). These vary in size from only slight swellings to peglike structures extending as much as one mm from the leaf surface. To the touch, these swellings usually seem to be sharply pointed, but under magnification some of them are seen to be either knobshaped or cupped. The enations may be few or many on an individual leaf. A single plant may have some of them on many leaves or only on some leaves. Although less developed, the same kind of structures appear on the large thorns. Some kinds of citrus are symptomless hosts of the virus. On others the enations are very small and can be detected infrequently. In California, the enations have developed more conspicuously on Mexican lime and sour orange than on Rough lemon, sweet orange, mandarin, Eureka lemon, and grapefruit. Under field conditions, only sour orange and Mexican lime develop strong

Fig. 2–48. Citrus vein enation. ***A*****, enations on veins of sour lime.** ***B*****, indentations on upper surface of leaf corresponding to enations.**

leaf enations. In citrus varieties that develop only the leaf enations, the presence of the virus seems to have no injurious effects. In some citrus-growing areas of California, the virus is common in both orange and lemon trees, but in other localities it has not been found.

Woody Gall.—From field observations and limited experimental studies, it appeared until recently that among commercially used citrus varieties, only Rough lemon and sour lime were subject to extensive gall development. A Rangpur-lime "type" developed some galls in California, but in one test true Rangpur lime did not. However, Bazan de Segura and Ferrand (1969) reported that galls developed on Rangpur lime rootstocks under natural exposure in Peru. In some earlier greenhouse tests in California, an unidentified lime from India and *C. volkameriana* Pasq. proved to be very susceptible. The latter species has received some attention as a rootstock in recent years. Bitters (1968) reported that in trials at the South Coast Field Station in southern California, all trees were infected with vein-enation virus and galls were developing on *C. volkameriana* rootstocks. Bazan de Segura and Ferrand (1969) reported that this variety develops woody galls in Peru.

In California, old trees of Rough lemon and Mexican lime have been found with woody galls on the trunks and limbs, but all study of gall initiation and development has been made on young experimental seedlings or budlings of these varieties. On seedling trees of Rough lemon and lime, it is possible to detect visually very early stages of gall development. The first signs are slight swellings, often adjacent to a thorn or at the base of small twigs. However, galls sometimes arise at points distant from these locations. If the swellings are true woody galls, the bark covering them assumes a light or grayish color. Later, the surface of the bark over the small gall begins to roughen. True galls enlarge slowly and assume a somewhat irregular shape. Early stage galls are shown in figure 2–49, *A*. With further development (fig. 2–49, *B*), the galls present the "cauliflower-like" appearance described by Fraser (1958). Individual galls sometimes grow together to form what appears to be a single gall covering as much as one-third to one-half of the circumference of the affected tree.

Galls also develop on roots of affected lime and Rough lemon trees. On trees growing in soil or in sand cultures, the numbers of galls were less than on trees grown in liquid nutrient solution. In

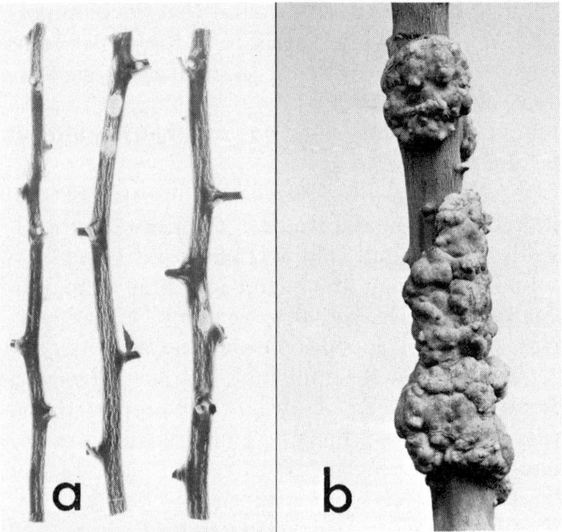

Fig. 2–49. Woody gall. ***A*****, early-stage galls on sour lime.** ***B*****, advanced galls on Rough lemon.**

the solution, great numbers of galls giving the appearance of nematode galls developed even on very small rootlets (fig. 2–50).

Influence of Tissue Wounding on Gall Development

Studies by Wallace and Drake (1961*a*) demonstrated that citrus woody galls commonly develop as a result of wounding of tissues of plants infected with the vein-enation virus. This was first observed on plants of Rough lemon experimentally infected with vein-enation virus by tissue-graft inoculation. On such plants, galls often developed at the site where buds or scions were inserted for inoculation. Later, it was demonstrated that galls could be stimulated to form when small stems of infected plants were punctured by needles or other sharp-pointed instruments (fig. 2–51).

It has not been determined if galls can develop in the absence of wounds. Many galls develop on infected lime and Rough lemon plants which have received no known artificial wounding, but it may be that natural growth wounds lead to production of such galls. On Rough lemon and Mexican lime woody galls commonly develop at one or both sides of thorns (fig. 2–52). This suggests that the emergence and development of thorns, or their presence as the stems enlarge, cause tissue ruptures and thus provide the proper conditions for galls to be initiated. Other studies have revealed that virus-free Rough lemon plants commonly have slight swellings on one or both sides of the thorns which resemble early stages of gall formation. Removal of the bark shows that these are not true woody galls, but instead appear to be undeveloped thorns (fig. 2–53). Since true galls develop so often at these sites on plants infected with vein-enation virus, it appears that development of these structures creates tissue wounds and thus initiates galls. Because such structures on healthy plants so closely resemble early-stage gall development and because other kinds of galls sometimes develop on citrus, some of the bark must be removed to make the correct diagnosis. If the swelling has resulted from the initiation of a true woody gall, the exposed wood surface has a roughened or pitted appearance because of the presence of many adventitious buds. The normal swellings on opposite sides of thorns are nearly always associated with a short, woody projection or spear, somewhat in a folded position parallel to the cambial surface. Other noninfectious galls, apparently of genetic origin, do not develop the cauliflower appearance, and the face of the wood remains smooth.

Fig. 2–50. Woody-gall development on roots of sour lime infected with vein-enation virus.

Fig. 2–51. Stimulation of woody-gall development by wounding Rough lemon infected with vein-enation virus. Left, gall development three and one-half months after young stem was punctured in six places. Right, same stem four years after wounding. The six wound-induced galls have coalesced and joined other galls that developed where twigs were removed at top.

Fig. 2–52. Citrus woody gall on Rough lemon seedling. These virus-induced galls commonly develop near the base of a thorn, sometimes in pairs.

Importance of Woody Gall

There is as yet insufficient experience with woody gall phase of this disease to establish its potentialities or importance. In Florida and Arizona, where Rough lemon is an important rootstock, there have been no reports of the presence of affected trees or of vein-enation virus. In spite of the presence of the virus in South Africa, where much of the citrus acreage consists of trees on Rough lemon rootstock, the disease apparently has not assumed any importance. In California areas where vein-enation virus is widespread, Rough lemon is not used as a rootstock. At the University of California Citrus Research Center in Riverside, thirty- to forty-year-old trees on Rough lemon stocks show some gall development, but do not appear to have been affected to any noticeable degree. It may be that these trees were well-established before becoming infected, and thus have not suffered from infection with this virus.

Among the few old sour lime trees at the Citrus Research Center, some have numerous galls on their trunks and limbs. Injury, if any, is very slight; but, in this instance also, there is no information as to the age and size of the trees when they became infected.

The situation in Peru differs from that elsewhere. After tristeza became important in that country, Rough lemon was adopted as the principal rootstock for new citrus plantings. In some locations, almost all trees in plantings eight to ten years of age show advanced woody-gall development on the Rough lemon rootstocks. Indications are that these trees were infected when quite small. Up to the present, yields in general have not been reduced, but the trunk caliper is less on trees with advanced gall development. This effect may eventually cause some reduction in yields.

A more alarming aspect in some localities of Peru is that infection occurs in the nursery. Very probably some Rough lemon seedlings are infected before they are budded; when this occurs, a collar of gall tissue forms at the bud union which reduces tree growth. In 1964, the author visited a citrus nursery in the Cañete Valley of Peru where a low percentage of the trees showing this condition were being discarded. The author has produced this reaction experimentally by budding previously inoculated Rough lemon seedlings to navel orange and Eureka lemon (fig. 2–54). Bazan de Segura and Ferrand (1969) described severe gall development, stunting, and decline on young orchard trees in

Fig. 2–53. Normal swellings on Rough lemon seedlings. *A*, **swellings at sides of thorns resemble early-stage woody gall.** *B*, **with bark removed to show thorn-like structure.**

Peru which apparently became infected in the nursery.

Rough lemon *(C. volkameriana)* and possibly Rangpur lime seem to be the only commonly used rootstock varieties subject to woody gall disease. Although Fraser (1959*b*) reported finding two trees of sour orange and one Eureka lemon with symptoms of woody gall, the author has been unsuccessful in stimulating gall development on Palestine sweet lime, Marsh grapefruit, sour orange, sweet orange, Ponkan mandarin, and Eureka lemon by artificial wounding of infected trees. In other experiments, when bark chips of Rough lemon containing a small gall were grafted to some of these varieties, the galls continued to develop slightly, but only from the Rough lemon tissue. On rare occasions, galls of one kind or another have been observed on field trees of lemon, sweet orange, and mandarin in California, but these have not proved to be true woody gall.

Transmission of Causal Virus

Studies of McClean (1954), Wallace and Drake (1953), and Laird and Weathers (1961) established that three species of aphids, *T. citricidus*, *Myzus persicae*, and *Aphis gossypii*, are vectors of vein-enation virus. The virus is also easily transmitted by tissue grafting, but 100 per cent infection is not always obtained in this manner from field trees, because the virus is not uniformly distributed throughout some trees.

Control

Except where susceptible rootstock varieties such as Rough lemon and *C. volkameriana* are being used, there actually may be little need for trying to avoid this disease. Although not proven by experience at this time, indications are that where trees on Rough lemon stock become infected early and develop extensive galls, it would be wise to use other rootstock varieties. There is no

Fig. 2–54. Woody galls on Rough lemon rootstock of young navel orange tree. Healthy navel scion tip-grafted on previously infected Rough lemon seedling. Photographed two and one-half years after propagation.

information regarding direct damage to trees of sour lime. Where the virus is present and transmitted by aphids, it would be of little value to attempt to propagate from uninfected lime trees. It is advisable, however, to avoid use of infected budwood for propagation of trees to be planted in locations where the virus is not present. There always remains the possibility that other untested varieties can be affected adversely by this virus. Furthermore, it is wise to avoid the increase and spread of any citrus virus, particularly into places where it does not exist. The vein-enation virus has been shown by Weathers (1960*b*, 1961) to react synergistically with the unrelated citrus yellow-vein virus, causing a much more severe disease effect than results from separate infections with these two viruses.

SATSUMA DWARF

According to Yamada and Sawamura (1952), the disease now known as "satsuma dwarf" was first observed in Shizuoka Prefecture of Japan in 1937. These same authors (1950) reported reproduction of the disease in healthy citrus plants graft-inoculated from diseased trees. They concluded that a virus was responsible for this disorder, which they named "dwarf disease of satsuma orange." The name was later shortened to "satsuma dwarf." Yoshi and Omori (1951, 1952) also studied the disease, likewise concluding that it was caused by a virus.

Tanaka and Yamada (1961) stated that the disease is widespread in Japan, where it causes severe damage in some orchards and less damage or none in others. They cited instances of small plantings of satsuma orange trees where all trees were so severely affected there was no production of fruit. Japanese workers speculate that this disease is spreading within orchards and to previously unaffected plantings. It has not been reported in other citrus-producing countries.

Symptomatology

In describing satsuma dwarf, Yamada and Sawamura (1952, 1953) stated that growth inhibition of new twigs and abnormally shaped leaves are the most noticeable characteristics of affected trees. These effects are exhibited chiefly on growth developing during the spring season. Instead of normal terminal growth of single stems, there is a tendency towards multiple stem development with shortened internodes, resulting in a bushy appearance. Leaves on affected shoots are sometimes small and curled upwards into a spoon shape, but the most striking symptom is boat-shaped leaves. Young leaves roll downward at the tips, and as they enlarge, their sides curl in the same direction. Affected terminal shoots are shown in fig. 2–55. Mature, hardened, boat-shaped leaves are also evident on the shoots illustrated.

Symptoms often appear localized on one part of a tree, but the number of affected branches increases each year until the entire tree may be affected. Trees become weaker and less productive with time, but seldom are killed by the disease. The clusters of newly formed leaves of affected branches are chlorotic, but if trees are well nourished the leaves assume a normal color as they mature. It has been reported that severity of symptoms is less on vigorous, well-fertilized trees, although this has not been established conclusively. Satsuma-dwarf virus may be the direct cause of

Fig. 2–55. Satsuma-dwarf foliage symptoms. The spring growth on affected satsuma mandarin trees consists of multiple terminal branches with small, narrow, chlorotic leaves. Older leaves curl downwards and inwards from the margins to form a "boat-shape." (Photo courtesy of S. Yamada.)

reduced vigor, and variations in degree of vigor may result from the existence of different strains of the virus.

Transmission and Spread

Yamada and Sawamura (1953) reported on studies of transmission by grafting, juice inoculations, insect vectors, and through soil. They reported that the disease was reproduced on healthy plants graft-inoculated with tissue from diseased plants, even when no permanent tissue connections were established. On one-year-old satsuma trees graft-inoculated in the greenhouse, symptoms developed within one year. Juice inoculations from citrus to citrus gave no infections. Plants grown for three years in soil from the vicinity of diseased trees remained healthy. Yamada and Sawamura (1953) also investigated the matter of insect transmission and concluded that a fulgorid, *Geisha distinctisima* (Walker) is a vector of satsuma-dwarf virus. They also suspected that the black citrus aphid, *Toxoptera aurantii*, might be a vector. However, there now seems to be some doubt that *Geisha distinctisima* is a vector of this virus. Yamada has informed the writer that he has been unable to confirm the earlier conclusion that this insect transmits satsuma-dwarf virus and that it is not a vector.[8]

Tanaka and Kishi (1963), Kishi and Tanaka (1964), and Tanaka *et al.* (1965) demonstrated that numerous herbaceous plants develop disease symptoms after mechanical inoculation with expressed sap of affected satsuma trees. Symptoms were produced on nine of thirty-one species of leguminous plants. Among the leguminous plants, blackeye cowpea and kidney bean var. 'Satisfaction,' appeared to be the best indicators of the virus transferred from satsuma-dwarf affected trees. Inoculation of non-leguminous plants revealed that only one of twenty-seven species tested, namely sesame (*Sesamum indicum* L.), developed symptoms.

Symptoms on sesame were local, necrotic lesions on inoculated leaves followed by systemic infection. The systemically infected leaves first showed vein clearing, followed by vein necrosis, and production of mottled, stunted, malformed leaves. Field sources of satsuma dwarf were always contaminated with tristeza and/or the seedling-yellows virus complex, but by graft inoculation of seedlings of trifoliate orange, Japanese workers were sometimes successful in screening out the tristeza virus and demonstrating that it is not responsible for the symptoms on herbaceous plants. Kishi (1968) injected citrus with sap from infected herbaceous plants and reproduced symptoms of satsuma dwarf. S. Tanaka (1972) reported more than 50 per cent infection of satsuma seedlings approach-grafted to infected plants of sesame and *Crotalaria spectabilis* Roth. Tanaka, Saito, and Kishi (1968) isolated satsuma-dwarf virus from sap-inoculated kidney bean plants. They obtained a highly infectious preparation containing spherical particles 26 nm in diameter.

In studies of "withering disease" of natsudaidai, now considered to be a form of satsuma dwarf, Izawa (1966) observed what he interpreted to be transmission from tree to tree through soil. Tanaka *et al.* (1971) found evidence of similar spread of this same disorder in Yamaguchi Prefecture but it was not determined how this takes place.

Kishi (1967) failed to transmit satsuma-dwarf virus in trials with three species of aphids, and *Geisha distinctisima* which earlier had been suspected to be a vector. Kishi reported transmis-

[8]Personal communication to the author from S. Yamada, dated October 12, 1965.

sion through seeds of kidney bean but not through seeds of sesame and citrus.

Varietal Reaction to Satsuma Dwarf

Studies on the susceptibility of citrus to satsuma-dwarf virus have included, for the most part, species grown in Japan or available for testing there. Among varieties found to be susceptible by Tanaka *et al.* (1965), satsuma mandarin is the most important commercially. No information has been presented regarding the reaction of other mandarin varieties. The above workers reported that Washington navel orange, Eureka lemon, and Duncan grapefruit developed no symptoms when inoculated. Subsequent studies by Miyakawa (1969, 1972), H. Tanaka (1971, 1972), and Tanaka and Yamada (1972) showed that numerous citrus species and varieties became infected with satsuma-dwarf virus when graft-inoculated. None developed the severe symptoms that occur on satsuma but some displayed nonpersistent symptoms ranging from slight leaf mottling to chlorotic blotching, with leaf distortion on some varieties.

Tanaka and Yamada (1961) reported that nearly all orchard trees in Japan are infected with tristeza virus. Tanaka (1971) found that many symptomless orchard trees of satsuma and sweet orange (on trifoliate orange rootstock) and trees with symptoms of satsuma dwarf were carriers of the seedling-yellows virus complex. Eliminating tristeza and seedling yellows from sources of satsuma-dwarf virus by screening through trifoliate orange, as described by Tanaka, Yamada, and Nakanishi (1971), Kishi (1972) compared the reaction of satsuma seedlings to satsuma-dwarf virus and to a mixture of satsuma-dwarf and seedling-yellows viruses. It was demonstrated that the presence of seedling-yellows virus strongly accentuates symptoms of satsuma-dwarf disease. It was concluded that the severe reaction of satsuma trees results from a synergistic reaction between the two viruses.

Control

Although the means of spread of satsuma-dwarf virus is not clearly understood, there seems to be no doubt regarding the increase of the disease in plantings of satsuma mandarin in Japan. Until more is known of the role of insect vectors, it is not possible to evaluate measures for control or prevention. Presently, it is advisable to avoid use of infected trees as sources of budwood in the propagation of new trees. Severely affected trees should be removed as an economic measure, even though it is not known if removal of such trees will have an influence on spread of the disease within an orchard. At least, it would appear to be a wise precaution to remove affected trees when they show up in orchards that have been free of the disease previously. Yamada and Sawamura (1953) made studies of the citrus host range of satsuma dwarf by topworking scions of different kinds of citrus onto affected satsuma trees. Twenty-one varieties showed no symptoms after two years. Thus, it appears that topworking affected trees to varieties that remain symptomless may offer a means of converting affected satsuma trees into productive trees. As yet, there have been no reports that this has been done on a commercial basis. Even if such a practice proved successful it would do nothing towards continued production of the valuable satsuma mandarin.

CITRUS TATTER LEAF

"Citrus tatter leaf" was first described by Wallace and Drake (1962). The name "tatter leaf" is descriptive of the marginal irregularity of leaves of affected plants, particularly of *C. excelsa* Wester. More than 500 individual citrus trees of various kinds, both domestic and foreign, have been indexed on *C. excelsa* in a varietal improvement program of the University of California Citrus Research Center, but the virus has been found only in Meyer lemon.

Symptomatology and Varieties Affected

After Wallace and Drake (1962) described tatter-leaf symptoms on *C. excelsa* and Mexican lime, these same authors (1963) found that Troyer citrange and citremon (*Poncirus trifoliata* x *C. limon*) developed strong leaf mottle, stem pitting, and other effects when inoculated directly from Meyer lemon or from *C. excelsa* previously inoculated from Meyer lemon. These reactions on citrange and citremon were described as tatter leaf. Garnsey (1964) found that seedlings of Rusk citrange reacted similarly to inoculations from Meyer lemon, and assumed that the tatter-leaf virus was responsible. However, subsequent studies by Wallace and Drake (1968) and Càtara and Wallace

(1970) demonstrated that the symptoms produced on citranges and citremons are not caused by tatter-leaf virus, but are symptoms of another virus which is present in mixture with tatter-leaf virus in Meyer lemon and can be separated from it.

Wallace and Drake (1968) proposed the name "citrange stunt" for the disease caused by the virus which has no effect on *C. excelsa* when separated from tatter-leaf virus. Additional information on citrange-stunt virus and its effects on citrus is presented separately (see below). From the later studies, evidence was obtained that leaf blotching and veinal effects on Mexican lime originally described as being caused by tatter-leaf virus apparently are effects of that virus, but these symptoms develop inconsistently on lime. Of the citrus varieties tested, only *C. excelsa* has developed the characteristic ragged or malformed leaves. Tatter-leaf virus has never been obtained separate from the virus of citrange stunt. In studies in California, all Meyer lemons found to carry tatter-leaf virus also were infected with citrange-stunt virus.

Sour orange, Eureka lemon, sweet orange, and Rough lemon are symptomless hosts of tatter-leaf virus. Often it was not recovered from inoculated plants of Mexican lime and was never obtained from trifoliate orange.

The most reliable diagnostic effects now attributed to this virus are those originally described on *C. excelsa*, namely, leaf blotching and the ragged or misshapened leaves (fig. 2–56). After infected *C. excelsa* plants developed clusters of affected leaves, subsequent growth often was symptomless, and after three months or more, inoculations from these plants to healthy *C. excelsa* gave no symptoms. The virus is commonly found in clonally propagated Meyer lemon plants which trace back to the original introduction of this citrus selection. These Meyer lemon plants frequently also carry the citrange-stunt virus and the tristeza-seedling-yellows virus complex. Some Meyer lemon sources of seedling yellows cause such severe effects on *C. excelsa* that symptoms of tatter leaf are masked or fail to develop.

Citrange-stunt virus not mixed with tatter-leaf, tristeza, and seedling-yellows viruses has been obtained by passing virus from a tristeza-free Meyer lemon through *C. excelsa*. Citrange-stunt

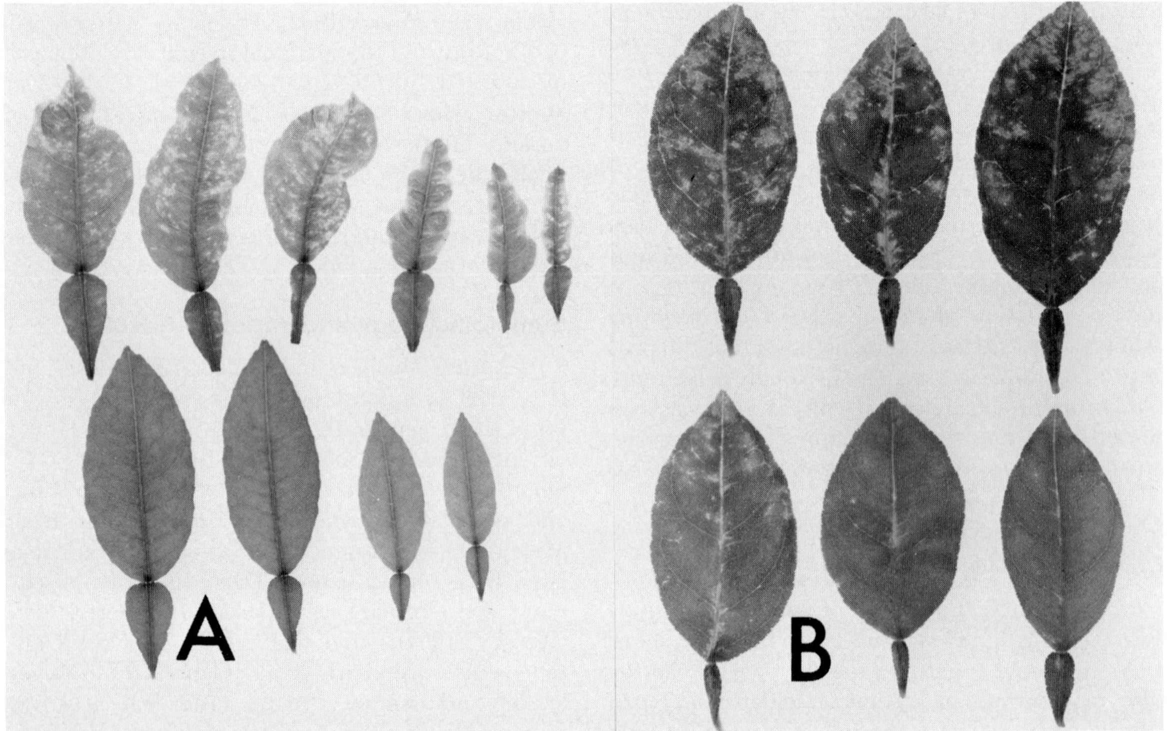

Fig. 2–56. Tatter-leaf symptoms. *A*, blotched and ragged leaves of *Citrus excelsa* and normal leaves. *B*, blotching and vein-banding of affected West Indian lime.

virus alone causes no symptoms on *C. excelsa*, but this citrus species is a host of the virus. Presently, tatter-leaf virus seems to be of no economic importance, but as with all citrus viruses it is advisable to avoid its increase and distribution.

It is now evident that in recent studies of mechanical transmission and virus purification, presumably concerned with tatter leaf, investigators were actually working with the citrange-stunt virus component of the tatter leaf-citrange stunt mixture. This is explained in the separate discussion of citrange stunt.

CITRANGE STUNT

Wallace and Drake (1968) reported that further studies of citrus tatter-leaf infections obtained from Meyer lemon demonstrated that the reactions of Troyer citrange and citremon, originally considered to be tatter-leaf symptoms, are caused by another virus present in mixture with tatter-leaf virus in Meyer lemon. Because of the severe effects on growth of the citranges, the name "citrange stunt" was proposed for this disease. Like tatter-leaf virus, citrange-stunt virus has been found only in Meyer lemon. Whether or not it ever occurs in Meyer lemon in the absence of tatter-leaf virus has not been determined. On occasion, *C. excelsa* plants inoculated directly from Meyer lemon failed to show symptoms of tatter leaf, but were found to have been infected with citrange-stunt virus. Since this sometimes happened when *C. excelsa* was inoculated from a Meyer lemon source known to carry tatter-leaf virus, failure of tatter-leaf symptoms to develop could not be taken as evidence that the inoculum source did not contain the tatter-leaf virus.

Separation and Identification of Citrange-Stunt Virus

Troyer and numerous other citranges, citremon, and other hybrids of trifoliate orange react severely to infection with citrange-stunt virus. Although Troyer citrange and citremon 1448 have been used for the most part, in studies in California, Garnsey (1964) found that Rusk citrange is an excellent indicator for citrange stunt.

Even though plants of *C. excelsa* develop tatter-leaf symptoms rather regularly after inoculation from Meyer lemon, they do not maintain tatter-leaf virus. No special efforts have been made to determine how long after infection tatter-leaf virus can be obtained from *C. excelsa*. Transfers from plants known to have been infected were usually made four months or longer after they were inoculated. Inoculations from such plants gave symptoms of citrange stunt on Troyer citrange or citremon, but did not give tatter-leaf symptoms on *C. excelsa*. Usually, after one passage through *C. excelsa*, the remaining virus causes citrange stunt on the citranges, but back-inoculations from these to *C. excelsa* result in no symptoms. On the other hand, Troyer citrange infected directly from Meyer lemon develops citrange-stunt symptoms, and back transfers from these citrange plants to *C. excelsa* result in symptoms of tatter leaf. After some months, however, these *C. excelsa* plants, like those infected directly from Meyer lemon, can be shown to contain citrange-stunt virus, but are free of tatter-leaf virus.

Symptomatology

Infected seedlings of some of the citranges and other trifoliate-orange hybrids develop bright yellowish mottle and sometimes distinct ringspots. Affected leaves become twisted or curved and slightly distorted. Where large chlorotic spots extend from the leaf edge to the midrib, normal expansion of tissues does not occur, causing irregular margins and an abrupt bending of leaves (fig. 2–57, *A*).

The overall effect of citrange stunt seems to vary among individual seedlings. Most seedlings of Troyer and Rusk citrange or citremon 1448 develop strong leaf symptoms following inoculation, but some continue growing with much less stunting than others. Some seedlings that are infected when small are permanently stunted. They make very little growth and develop few if any leaves. Some shoots remain without leaves or terminal growth, with the lateral buds becoming swollen or multiple. Other infected seedlings continue to enlarge, but show leaf symptoms and irregular or zig-zag stems. Superficial lesions arise on one side of soft, growing stems which retard elongation at that site. Continued growth of the opposite side of the lesioned stem causes it to bend, sometimes at a 90-degree angle. This may be repeated so that the stem assumes a zig-zag condition. An example of twig lesions and abnormal stem growth is shown in figure 2–57, *B*.

Fig. 2–57. Tatter-leaf symptoms. *A*, healthy (left) and three affected leaves of citremon. *B*, stem lesions and zig-zag growth of Troyer citrange.

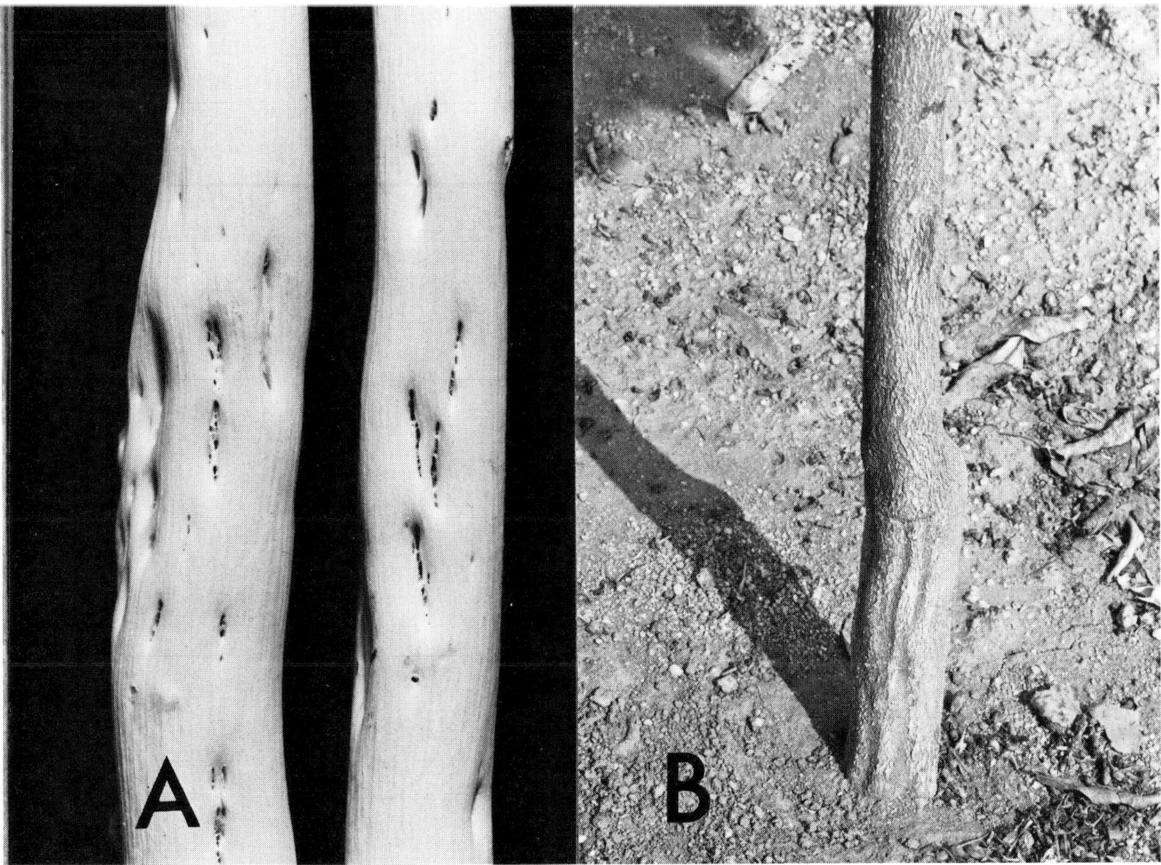

Fig. 2–58. Stem-pitting effects of tatter-leaf virus. *A*, **xylem pitting on young citremon seedling.** *B*, **grooving or fluting of Troyer citrange rootstock under tatter-leaf infected navel orange.**

As infected seedlings of citremon and citrange become older, deep pits develop in the wood. These are often in vertical alignment. As they enlarge, some of them merge so as to form longitudinal grooves which at later stages give the tree trunks a fluted appearance. Pitting in the wood of citremon seedlings is shown in figure 2–58, *A*. Figure 2–58, *B* illustrates fluting of the rootstock of a young budling of navel on Troyer rootstock.

Transmission and Spread

Citrange-stunt virus is readily graft-transmissible from citremon, citranges, and some symptomless citrus hosts to susceptible citrus indicator varieties. Additionally, it is mechanically transmissible from citrus to citrus to some herbaceous hosts. Semancik and Weathers (1965) infected seventeen different herbaceous hosts by juice inoculation. Some of these developed no symptoms, but were shown to be infected by inoculation from them to cowpea, *Vigna sinensis* (Torner) Savi, which develops necrotic local lesions and systemic mottle.

Semancik and Weathers (1965) reproduced citrange-stunt symptoms on Troyer citrange by mechanical inoculation from *C. excelsa*. Lime became infected but was symptomless. At that time, information on the presence of citrange-stunt virus in mixture with tatter-leaf virus had not been obtained. These investigators assumed that mechanical transmission from *C. excelsa* to Troyer citrange involved tatter-leaf virus. However, they recognized that until it was demonstrated that the virus in mechanically inoculated herbaceous plants would cause symptoms in citrus there was a possibility that this might be another virus associated with tatter-leaf infection.

Yarwood (1963) reported mechanical transmission of a virus from Meyer lemon to several kinds of herbaceous plants, but did not identify the virus. Fulton (1966) compared Yarwood's virus culture with one obtained from Weathers on tobacco (*Nicotiana clevelandii* Gray), cowpea, and *Chenopodium quinoa* Willd., and observed no difference. Some mechanically inoculated citrus plants, although showing no symptoms, were demonstrated to be infected by assaying for virus on cowpea. Graft inoculations were made from several citrus seedlings (West Indian lime and Rough lemon) to citrange and citremon seedlings. These developed the symptoms originally described as tatter leaf by Wallace and Drake (1963), but which later were considered by them to be symptoms of citrange stunt. Càtara and Wallace (1970) demonstrated that it was the virus of citrange stunt that was transmitted mechanically in the above studies.

Importance

Citrange-stunt virus has been found only in Meyer lemon, which is unaffected by it; thus, up to now, citrange stunt is only an experimentally induced disease. However, should this virus find a means of natural spread, it appears to have the potential to assume importance wherever citranges, citremons, or other sensitive hybrids of *Poncirus trifoliata* are in use as rootstocks.

Calavan, Christiansen, and Roistacher (1963) described a severe reaction of two trees of satsuma mandarin on Troyer citrange rootstock, which had been inoculated from a Meyer lemon. Once it became known that the source of inoculum included tatter-leaf virus and because other noncontaminated sources of seedling-yellows virus had no effect on similar trees, it was concluded that the diseased condition of the two trees resulted from tatter-leaf virus or from a combination of tatter-leaf and another virus.

Working with virus from a Meyer lemon not infected with seedling-yellows, Wallace and Drake (1968) demonstrated that young budded trees of navel on rootstocks of citremon and Troyer citrange inoculated at an early age are severely stunted by the virus carried by Meyer lemon. Figure 2–59 shows stunting of a three-year-old

Fig. 2–59. Citrange stunt. Left, three-year-old tree of navel on Troyer citrange inoculated with citrange-stunt virus three months after propagation. Right, noninoculated control tree.

navel on Troyer citrange inoculated soon after it was propagated. After five years, such inoculated trees were about one-half the size of healthy controls. Inasmuch as these same effects have been produced experimentally with inocula that do not contain tatter-leaf virus or other known viruses, it is concluded that they result from infection with citrange-stunt virus.

As long as citrange-stunt virus remains without a means of natural spread, it can cause no great damage. However, it is advisable as a precautionary measure to include one of the satisfactory indicators in all citrus budwood virus-indexing programs. There is the possibility that on occasion infected Meyer lemon may be worked onto and infect trees of popular commercial scion varieties from which, by chance, propagative budwood may be taken. Trees resulting from propagation of infected buds on rootstocks other than the *P. trifoliata* hybrids would remain symptomless, and could serve towards a further buildup and distribution of the virus. An extra precaution which should be considered in important citrus-producing areas is the eradication of all old-clone Meyer lemon trees.

IMPIETRATURA

Ruggieri (1955) described a disorder of citrus in Sicily to which he gave the name "impietratura" (from Italian *pietra*, stone). Later, Ruggieri (1960, 1961) reported that the disease was reproduced on other citrus by tissue-graft inoculation and suggested that it was a virus disease. Papasolomontos (1961) observed impietratura on grapefruit in Cyprus. Chapot (1961) observed symptoms of this disease in Morocco, Lebanon, Turkey, and Greece. He concluded that it had been present for many years in some of these countries. Papasolomontos (1965) reported that by 1961 the disorder was present in all grapefruit-producing areas of Cyprus.

Papasolomontos (1969) stated that this disorder was first described by Reichert and Hellinger (1930) and Yedidyah (1937) in Israel. The latter author suggested that it was caused by a virus or viruslike organism. The disease has been found in Israel, Italy, Cyprus, Greece, Turkey, Lebanon, Sardinia, Corsica, Spain, Algeria, and Morocco.

According to Papasolomontos (1969), there is commonly a reduction in numbers of mature fruit on affected trees, because a number of the fruit drop off before they attain much size. Additional loss results because affected fruits are not suitable for the commercial export market. Sometimes as much as 80 per cent of the fruit that matures on affected trees is unmarketable as fresh fruit.

Symptomatology and Varieties Affected

According to Ruggieri (1961), impietratura can be easily found by an examination of trees which are bearing more-than-normal quantities of small-sized fruits. If such trees are infected, the small fruits—even when green—are hard and inelastic on some areas of the peel. The corresponding albedo is brown and hard. Small fruits always show the internal symptoms, whereas normal-sized fruits have milder or sometimes no symptoms. Hard, brown, gummy deposits are present in the albedo at the stem-end of the fruit, and gum is found in the vessels of the stem several centimeters away from the fruit. On severely affected fruits, there are brownish spots on the surface which are sometimes depressed or appear as bumps or protuberances. Beneath the surface spots, there are pockets of gum, either liquified or hardened. These fruit symptoms are shown in figure 2–60.

The gumming in and around the fruit stem is apparently responsible for the heavy fruit drop during the summer months. Because most of the affected fruits drop before maturity, it is advisable to examine trees when the green fruits are about one and a half inches in diameter. However, even the abnormally small fruits may show no external symptoms. For this reason, it is necessary at times to section the fruits to detect internal symptoms in the albedo.

Papasolomontos (1965) stated that, apart from the fruit symptoms, diseased trees appear to be normal in all respects. This seems to set this disease apart from both copper and boron deficiency disorders.

On the basis of studies of impietratura in several countries of the Mediterranean basin, it appears that sweet oranges and grapefruit are affected more severely than other kinds of citrus. Ruggieri (1961) reported that Clementine mandarin fruits are affected, but to a lesser degree than oranges. The symptoms of impietratura had not been found in the field on lemon nor was it reproduced experimentally on lemons by Ruggieri

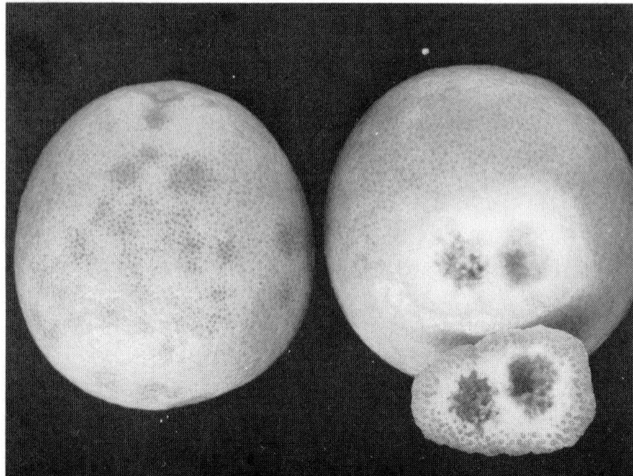

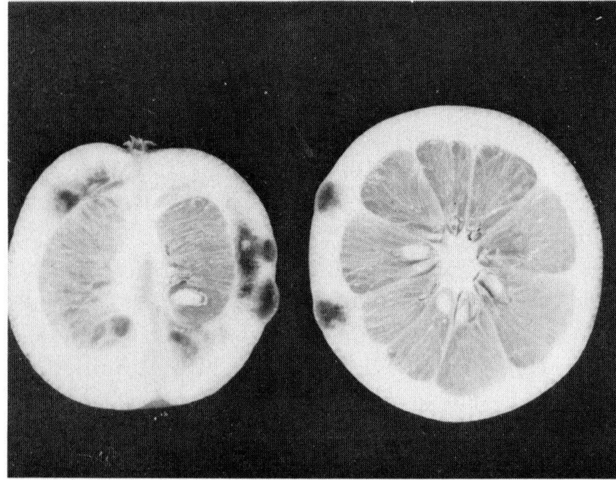

Fig. 2–60. Symptoms of impietratura on fruit. Top, surface spotting and gum pockets in albedo of Royal grapefruit. Bottom, sectioned fruit with gum pockets in albedo. (Photo courtesy of H. Chapot.)

(1961) in inoculation trials. However, Papasolomontos (1969) included lemon as one of the kinds of citrus affected, and also reported that tangelo and Rough lemon are subject to the disease. Scaramuzzi, Càtara, and Cartia (1968) also list lemon as susceptible. These authors observed psorosis leaf symptoms on some of the orchard trees from which they obtained impietratura inocula, and indexing of trees that were being inoculated in the orchard revealed that some were infected by an unidentified form of psorosis.

Bar-Joseph and Loebenstein (1970) indexed sixty-four orchard trees showing fruit symptoms of impietratura and in every instance observed characteristic leaf flecking of psorosis. Inoculation from two grapefruit trees resulted in oakleaf patterns like those of concave gum. Symptoms in the remaining tests were those of psorosis-A leaf flecking. Inasmuch as the impietratura-affected orchard trees displayed no psorosis-A bark lesions, nor leaf symptoms of crinkly leaf or infectious variegation, Bar-Joseph and Loebenstein (1970) suggested that the symptoms on index seedlings were caused by either concave gum or blind pocket virus which accompanies impietratura or that impietratura itself is a constituent of the psorosis complex. On the other hand, in his review of impietratura, Papasolomontos (1969) made no mention of leaf symptoms associated with the disease. Earlier he had informed the author that in greenhouse indexing tests of impietratura-affected trees, no specific leaf symptoms were observed.[9]

Further studies are needed to determine if the leaf symptoms found by Bar-Joseph and Loebenstein associated with impietratura are symptoms of that disease or if they resulted from the presence of another virus.

Transmission and Spread

Both Ruggieri in Sicily and Papasolomontos in Cyprus reported that symptoms developed on healthy trees inoculated from diseased trees by means of tissue-grafts. Both authors found that some grapefruit trees developed fruit symptoms within a few months after inoculation.

Ruggieri (1965) stated that grapefruit trees on sour orange rootstock are the best known indicators of this disease. On the basis of certain field observations, he suggested that grapefruit on Rough lemon may not develop symptoms. On the other hand, Papasolomontos and Economides (1967) found that Rough lemon rootstock did not reduce fruit symptoms but, conversely, seemed to increase the amount of affected fruit over that found on trees on other rootstocks. Terranova and Scuderi (1968) also reported that Rough lemon as a rootstock does not suppress symptoms of impietratura.

There is no experimental proof of spread of impietratura virus other than by grafting or bud perpetuation. Its widespread occurrence in grapefruit plantings suggests that there is natural spread by some means. Papasolomontos (1965) reported that in a planting of 204 Marsh seedless grapefruit trees in Cyprus, the disease was found on 80 trees

[9]Verbal communication with the author, 1966.

in 1961 and on 125 trees in 1964. He also stated that the diseased trees occurred in groups and suggested possible spread by root-grafting. However, a similar spread could result from transmission by certain types of insect vectors or by nematodes, but there have been no reports of investigations of spread by vectors.

Papasolomontos (1969) pointed out that studies in Cyprus, Italy, and Israel indicate that the number of diseased trees has been increasing from year to year. This increase has occurred in younger plantings. In Israel, Bental and Yoffe (1968) examined trees originally inoculated in 1937 by Yedidyah, and after many years found no evidence of spread to adjacent noninoculated trees. In Sicily, Cartia and Càtara (1974) selected an orchard of 20-year-old-trees and studied the development of impietratura over a period of nine years. During the first three years there was an increase in the number of trees showing symptoms, but in the last six years no additional affected trees were found. Pappo and Oren (1974), in Israel, observed healthy trees growing adjacent to impietratura-affected trees for eight years and found no evidence of transmission. Although this does not prove that natural spread may not occur under some conditions, it at least suggests that the increased numbers of diseased trees found in Cyprus (Papasolomontos, 1969), in Israel (Pappo, Bauman, and Oren, 1967) and in Sicily (Terranova and Scuderi, 1968; Scaramuzzi, Càtara, and Cartia,1968) may have resulted from the use of budwood from old infected trees not exhibiting conspicuous symptoms. Several of the investigators cited above have observed that diseased trees often tend to produce fewer affected fruits as they become older, and that more fruits from normal bloom develop symptoms than fruits from late bloom.

Control

In view of the lack of information regarding natural spread of impietratura, it cannot be concluded that the planting of healthy trees will prevent the disease completely. However, it is advisable to avoid propagation of new trees from infected sources. Until a completely reliable method of diagnosis or detection of infected trees is available, avoidance of infected budwood sources must rely chiefly on careful inspection of mother trees. Efforts should be made to find plantings of young trees which have shown no affected fruits during at least three years of fruit production and to use such trees as sources of budwood. Although nothing is known regarding seed transmission, seeds for the production of rootstocks should be selected from trees which show no evidence of impietratura. Both budwood and rootstock source trees can be indexed for impietratura if some impietratura-free young grapefruit trees of bearing age are available. Normally, such trees would be available only under field conditions where natural infection, if it exists, would make the tests unreliable.

In indexing for impietratura, Terranova and Scuderi (1968) recommended placing buds or bark patches from the citrus tree being tested into flowering twigs of nucellar grapefruit trees of bearing age. The inoculum should be inserted not more than 10 to 15 cm back of flower buds, and inoculations should be made during the regular blooming period. These authors state that symptoms usually appear on the adjacent fruits within three to four months and that fruit on noninoculated twigs serve as controls.

Unless a simpler indexing procedure can be found for the impietratura virus, which can be carried out under controlled conditions and which does not require the use of fruiting trees, the avoidance of infected propagative material will remain difficult. Until such a technique is available, the establishment of healthy propagative sources must be accomplished largely by careful inspection and trial plantings of selected material. There is an urgent need for expansion of research on diagnosis and indexing, as well as on the matter of natural spread of impietratura virus.

CITRUS RING SPOT

In California, Wallace and Drake (1968) reported on studies of a previously undescribed virus symptom on citrus to which they gave the name "citrus ring spot."

In 1944, C. R. Tower, Bureau of Nursery Service, California Department of Agriculture, found a psorosis-like bark lesion on a 3-inch limb of a sixty-year-old Lisbon tree near Corona, California, but he was unable to find any leaf symptoms. At that time, inoculations of sweet orange seedlings by means of bark patches from the lesion area gave negative results. In 1949, Mr. Tower supplied more material from the same source which was used for tissue-graft inoculation of seedlings of sweet and sour orange, Eureka and Lisbon lemon, and Brazilian sweet lime. These seedlings developed psorosis leaf flecking, but later there appeared some brilliant, yellowish spots, some in the form of small ring spots. By cutting out sections of leaves showing these spots and using them for leaf-patch inoculations, infections resulted in which the ring-spot effect was the dominant symptom. Because the ring spots were associated with leaf flecking of psorosis which could not be eliminated, no further study was made of that source of virus. Subsequently, in miscellaneous indexing of orchard trees, some of which were infected with psorosis virus, ring-spot symptoms were encountered on rare occasions, usually occurring as a few spots on only one or two leaves of some test plants. On one occasion, symptoms of ring spot appeared in plants which did not show any psorosis leaf flecking. This source of virus was maintained for further study.

Symptomatology

Eureka lemon, grapefruit, sour orange, sweet orange, Mexican lime, citremon, *C. excelsa*, and some other kinds of citrus develop strong symptoms of ring spot, but most experimental studies of this virus have been made with Eureka lemon, sweet orange, and grapefruit as hosts.

After infection from tissue grafts, the soft, newly developed leaves show faint, chlorotic spots, and some parts of the veins may be cleared or chlorotic. In the first stages, the leaf effects are somewhat like the chlorotic spotting and vein-flecking of psorosis, but later these become bright yellow spots or distinct circular or irregular rings. The ring effects sometimes extend along the veins. These symptoms are shown in figure 2–61. At times, the first symptom to appear (especially on sour orange) is a distinct vein clearing resembling that of tristeza (fig. 2–62, *B*). On leaves of sweet orange, there may be a variety of effects, one of which resembles the mature-leaf symptom of psorosis A, except that the undersides of the leaves do not become roughened or corky (fig. 2–62, *D*).

On occasion, necrotic lesions develop on soft stems of affected plants. These remain somewhat localized or may completely encircle the stem, causing the parts above the lesion to die (fig. 2–63). Although this reaction has been observed only on experimentally infected plants under greenhouse conditions, it is of interest because, as already mentioned, ring spot was first encountered in plants inoculated from an orchard lemon tree which showed a small bark lesion. Experimentally infected sweet orange trees growing in the field at Riverside, California, have shown very slight leaf symptoms but no bark lesions or other effects during seven years of observation.

Transmission and Spread

The ring-spot virus is easily transmitted by tissue grafting. In numerous trials, there was no transmission from citrus to citrus by mechanical inoculation techniques. Desjardins, Drake, and French (1969) transmitted the virus by dodder *(Cuscuta subinclusa)* from citrus to citrus and to petunia and periwinkle and back to citrus. These two herbaceous species are symptomless hosts of citrus ringspot virus.

No studies have been made of possible vector transmission, and there is no information regarding spread from tree to tree.

Distribution and Importance

Very little is known of the distribution of citrus ring-spot virus. As mentioned earlier, it has been encountered several times in California in miscellaneous indexing, but no orchard trees have been found with symptoms. Specimen leaves showing ring-spot symptoms have been received by the author from Florida and Central America. In 1966, the author saw two orchard trees in Spain which appeared to have mild ring-spot symptoms, and he was shown fresh leaf specimens from an orchard tree in Sicily that had typical, strong symptoms. Only faint leaf symptoms have appeared on three experimentally infected sweet orange trees planted in the field at Riverside, California. Possibly symptoms are masked under the prevailing environmental conditions. At present, citrus ring spot does not appear to be an important disease of citrus. No specific control measures are required, but known infected trees should not be used as propagative sources.

CITRUS YELLOW VEIN

Weathers (1957) assigned the name "citrus yellow vein" to a disease found in 1956 in Eustis limequat (*C. aurantifolia* x *Fortunella japonica*) trees in California. He demonstrated that the causal agent was transmitted readily by grafts from affected to healthy trees of several citrus varieties.

Fig. 2–61. Symptoms of citrus ring spot. Left to right, leaves of Eureka lemon, sour orange, and sweet orange with bright spots and rings.

Additional studies demonstrated that yellow vein is caused by a virus apparently unrelated to other known citrus viruses. This virus was found in four Eustis limequat trees and, although investigations showed that it had a wide host range within the citrus family, there was no evidence of natural spread in the field.

Citrus yellow-vein virus is of interest primarily because of the synergistic reactions between it and other citrus viruses. The interactions of yellow vein and other citrus viruses have been studied and described by Weathers (1960*b*, 1961).

Symptomatology

Weathers (1960*b*) stated that symptoms of citrus yellow vein are similar on different citrus species and varieties. He described them on experimentally infected West Indian lime as follows:

". . . the first symptoms begin to appear in the developing leaves of the infected plants and consist of yellowing of the main veins. The yellowing is usually continuous along the petiole, midrib, and main vein. The petioles and veins of the leaves sometimes appear swollen. At times the yellowing extends down the petioles into the young twigs for a distance of several inches. In some cases the yellowing extends into the tissue adjacent to the veins, giving them the appearance of being greatly enlarged. Smaller veins may not be uniformly affected, and frequently there are yellowed areas separated by areas appearing normal. The discoloration is sometimes more pronounced on one half of the leaf than on the other, and it appears on both upper and under surfaces of the leaf. Affected plants are not dwarfed." Leaves of several kinds of citrus affected by yellow-vein virus are shown in figure 2–64. Limited studies have indicated that nearly all *Citrus* species are susceptible to the virus. Species on which symptoms have been pro-

Fig. 2–62. Other leaf symptoms of citrus ring spot. *A*, **normal leaf of sour orange.** *B*, **leaf with tristeza-like vein-clearing which later disappears or develops into rings or blotches.** *C-D*, **leaves illustrate the strong blotchy patterns sometimes occurring on sweet orange.**

duced by inoculation are Florida Rough lemon, calamondin, sweet orange, sour orange, grapefruit, Rangpur lime, lemon, mandarin, tangelo, citrange, and kumquat. Symptoms observed in citrange, grapefruit, lemon, sour orange, sweet orange, and tangelo were relatively mild, sometimes appearing only on an occasional leaf. Many plants with mild symptoms recovered and showed no symptoms thereafter. Transmissions from some recovered plants failed to reproduce yellow vein. Trifoliate orange seemed to be immune.

Transmission

Transmission from diseased to healthy plants was successful only by means of living tissue grafts. Attempts failed to transmit yellow-vein virus from citrus to citrus by means of dodder (*Cuscuta subinclusa* Dur. & Hilg.). Likewise, no transmission resulted in several attempts to transmit the virus to citrus and to some herbaceous hosts by various mechanical methods.

Interactions of Yellow Vein with Other Citrus Viruses

Weathers (1960*b*) reported that in lime plants infected with both yellow-vein and psorosis viruses, the symptoms of yellow vein were greatly suppressed, but the psorosis symptoms were stronger than shown by plants infected only with psorosis virus. Even more striking synergistic effects were noted in plants of lime, sweet orange, lemon, and Rough lemon doubly infected with yellow-vein and vein-enation viruses. On plants of these species inoculated only with yellow-vein virus, an occasional young leaf showed mild vein yellowing with no symptoms on subsequent growth. The vein-enation virus alone in these hosts caused the production of varying numbers of enations on the under surface of the leaves. With neither virus was there evidence of an effect on growth. Plants inoculated with both viruses, regardless of the sequence of introduction of the two, produced severe vein-yellowing symptoms

Fig. 2–63. Citrus ring spot. Twigs from infected sweet orange showing ringspots on leaves and dieback of stems above sites where necrotic lesions developed.

throughout the entire plants. Leaves of Mexican lime infected with yellow-vein virus alone are compared to leaves from plants infected with both yellow-vein and vein-enation viruses in figure 2–65. When both viruses were present the vein enations became brilliant yellow and appeared enlarged. Subsequent growth of the plants was restricted, and leaves remained small. On many leaves, yellowing extended into all of the veinlets, so that almost the entire leaf became yellow. After eight months, doubly-infected plants were about one-third normal size and some of the plants died.

Weathers (1963) used this synergistic reaction to demonstrate that the two sources of yellow-vein virus studied by him consist of two different strains. It was not possible to distinguish between the two sources on the basis of their separate effects on the citrus hosts. However, when each was combined with vein-enation virus, one combination caused much more yellowing and dwarfing than the second. In this way, the existence of strains of yellow-vein virus was clearly established.

Importance

Nothing is known of the origin of the yellow-vein virus or whether it has ever existed in field-grown citrus other than the four Eustis limequat trees found infected in California. The virus

Fig. 2–64. Citrus yellow-vein symptoms. Left to right, Orlando tangelo, limequat, Troyer citrange, calamondin, and West Indian lime. (Photo courtesy of L. G. Weathers.)

Fig. 2–65. Synergistic reaction of yellow-vein and vein-enation viruses. Top, three leaves of West Indian lime with yellow vein alone. Bottom, three leaves from a lime plant doubly infected with the viruses of yellow vein and vein enation. (Photo courtesy of L. G. Weathers.)

itself is interesting because of its interaction with other citrus viruses. The studies of this virus have contributed the knowledge that in citrus, as with some other plants, some viruses which by themselves have little effect on host plants can produce severe disease effects if some other virus is present. For this reason, it is advisable to eradicate any known infected field tree and to avoid introducing the yellow-vein virus experimentally into trees growing in the open from which it might possibly be moved to other trees by vectors.

It is not known if there are vectors capable of spreading yellow-vein virus, but because this possibility exists the known infected trees of Eustis limequat in California have been destroyed. This precaution reduces the chances of the virus being spread to other citrus trees where, if combined with vein-enation virus, it might cause damage.

LEAF CURL

"Leaf curl disease" was described by Salibe (1959, 1965*b*) in Brazil, where it had been found on only two orchard trees. It was first observed on a Pera orange tree at the Limeira Citrus Experiment Station. Among a group of old trees which were severely pruned, one tree responded by the production of new growth on which nearly all leaves were curled in a manner similar to the effects of heavy aphid infestation. This was followed by a dieback of branches, which according to Salibe (1959) gave the tree an appearance similar to that described in Florida for citrus blight. The tree flowered abundantly, but developed only a few fruits of small size. Shoots were weak and broke off easily under slight pressure. Some gum was present in the xylem vessels, and the surface of the wood of the main branches and trunk had some channeling suggestive of pitting. Later, a twelve-year-old Hamlin sweet orange with similar symptoms was found in Araras.

Transmission and Spread

Salibe (1959, 1965*b*) was unable to reproduce leaf-curl disease by sap-inoculation, but demonstrated that the disease is perpetuated in propagations and that graft-inoculations from the two affected orchard trees reproduced the disease in seedling trees of Caipira sweet orange. The source of infection in the two known infected trees has not been explained. The apparent absence of spread from these trees, as well as from experimentally infected trees in nursery plantings, suggests that natural spread is extremely rare, if it occurs at all.

Within two months after buds from diseased trees were placed in seedlings of Caipira sweet orange, old leaves became yellow and subsequently dropped. New shoots then developed on which the leaves were severely curled. Some seedlings of Caipira sweet orange and sour orange died within one year after inoculation. Experimentally infected seedling trees are shown in figure 2–66. Without further evidence to the contrary, it can be concluded that citrus leaf curl is a virus disease.

Varietal Reaction

Experimental inoculations by Salibe (1959, 1965*b*) resulted in the production of leaf curl symptoms on Eureka and Sicilian lemons, Hamlin, Pera, Baianinha, and Caipira sweet oranges, Dancy and Willowleaf mandarin, Marsh grapefruit, citrons, shaddock, Mexican lime, and sweet lime. In these tests, Rangpur lime, trifoliate

Fig. 2–66. Symptoms of citrus leaf-curl disease on Caipira sweet orange. Left, seedling tree with normal leaves and clusters of curled leaves. Right, seedling with all leaves severely curled. (Photo courtesy of A. A. Salibe.)

orange, and Cleopatra mandarin did not develop symptoms. It was determined that the susceptibility of different varieties was not affected by rootstock.

Possible Relation to Other Citrus Viruses

Salibe's studies seem to have eliminated other known viruses as possible causes of leaf curl. On the basis of present knowledge, it appears that this disorder is caused by a virus distinct from other citrus viruses. From published photographs of young, experimentally infected citrus trees, the general effects seem to resemble those of the satsuma-dwarf disease in Japan. However, as brought out by Salibe (1959), sweet orange inoculated with satsuma-dwarf virus in Japan did not develop typical leaf curl symptoms.

Importance

Because of its rare occurrence, citrus leaf-curl disease presently is of no economic importance. It is of interest, however, because it has the potential of becoming a very serious disease should it begin to spread in the orchards. It is evident from observations in Brazil that affected trees become almost completely unproductive. Until there is evidence of natural spread and increase of this disease, no control measures are necessary other than to avoid propagation from any tree showing symptoms of this virus-induced disease. As a precaution, all infected orchard trees should be destroyed upon discovery.

CRISTACORTIS

Vogel and Bové (1964) described a severe stem-pitting disorder on sour orange and Tarocco orange in Corsica. Symptoms were reproduced by tissue-graft inoculations from affected Tarocco trees to Orlando tangelo, and it was concluded that the effects on the variety did not resemble the symptoms of xyloporosis. Although the individual pits resembled early concavities of concave-gum and blind-pocket psorosis, there was good evidence that the stem-pitting of sour orange was not caused by the virus of either of these citrus diseases. Vogel and Bové (1964) concluded that the

Fig. 2–67. Symptoms of cristacortis. *A*, **stem pitting on trunk of Orlando tangelo four years after inoculation.** *B*, **cross section of affected branch of Orland tangelo. (Photos courtesy of R. Vogel.)**

disorder was caused by a new virus, a new strain of a known virus, or a virus complex.

Since the original description of this disease, other studies by Vogel and Bové (1967, 1968), Zanardi, Anedda, and Follesa (1968), Servazzi, Marras, and Foddai (1968), Scaramuzzi and Càtara (1968), and Vogel (1973) have demonstrated that it is quite generally present in many varieties of citrus in Corsica, Sardinia, Sicily, and North Africa. To identify and separate this transmissible form of stem pitting on citrus from other kinds of pitting of known or unknown causes, Vogel and Bové (1968) proposed the name "cristacortis" (*crista*, crest; *cortis*, cortex bark) for this disorder.

Symptomatology

The most conspicuous symptom of cristacortis is the extensive pitting of trunk and main branches (fig. 2–67, *A*). The pits consist of narrow longitudinal depressions, indistinguishable from those associated with blind pocket disease in California. The internal symptoms, shown in figure 2–67, *B*, also are very similar to the effects of blind pocket but, as observed by Vogel and Bové (1974), differ widely from concave gum. From limited observations of cristacortis-affected trees in Corsica and Italy, and from study of photographs such as that shown in figure 2–67, *B*, the author is of the opinion that without additional information such as varietal susceptibility, distribution of the respective diseeases, etc., it may be difficult sometimes to determine if such trees are affected by cristacortis, blind pocket, tristeza, or citrange stunt. Certainly, the pitting effects associated with these four diseases are very similar during some stages of development. It perhaps is of value to point out that cristacortis trees normally develop pits much sooner after being infected and in much greater numbers than blind pocket trees. An apparent difference between the pitting of cristacortis as compared to that of tristeza and citrange stunt is that the pits of the latter two diseases often merge or enlarge to form conspicuous grooves. However, cristacortis pitting (fig. 2–68) sometimes is identical to that associated with both tristeza and citrange stunt.

Although Vogel and Bové (1964) first observed cristacortis on sour and Tarocco orange, and subsequent studies in Corsica, Sicily, and Sardinia have shown that high percentages of Tarocco orange are affected, cristacortis appears to be quite different from the disorder described as "Tarocco pit" by Russo and Klotz (1963).

Vogel and Bové (1964) mentioned the weak appearance of severely pitted branches which bend towards the ground. De Martino, Scuderi, and Terranova (1972) studied tree size, yields, and fruit quality of diseased and healthy 11-year-old Tarocco sweet orange on sour orange rootstock and found significant reductions in trunk circumference, number of fruits, and total soluble solids/acid ratio in trees with symptoms of cristacortis. The average size of fruits actually was larger on diseased trees but fruits were much fewer in number.

Vogel and Bové (1972) stated that all Corsican sources of cristacortis virus also contain a strain of psorosis virus which they concluded to be concave gum, and that most sources also contain exocortis virus. Their investigations established that cristacortis virus is not related to tristeza, cachexia, or exocortis viruses and further, that cristacortis disease is not a synergistic response to infection with a combination of cachexia, exocortis, and concave gum viruses. Vogel and Bové (1974) reported that psorosis young-leaf symptoms, presumably leaf flecking and oak-leaf patterns, developed on indicator citrus seedlings inoculated from cristacortis sources which were apparently free of concave-gum virus. These authors considered the possibility that psorosis type young-leaf effects may be a symptom of cristacortis, placing this disease within the so-called psorosis group. Vogel and Bové (1972) stated that because psorosis A, concave gum, blind pocket, crinkly leaf, infectious variegation, and possibly cristacortis induce similar young-leaf effects, these cannot be used to diagnose a specific disease. From the standpoint of the so-called group of five psorosis diseases, this has been recognized since H. S. Fawcett's early discoveries, with only concave gum being specifically diagnosed on the basis of the characteristic oak-leaf patterns.

Fig. 2–68. Cristacortis stem pitting on three-year-old Tarocco orange. (Photo courtesy R. Vogel.)

In a comprehensive report on studies by Vogel (1973) in Corsica, it was concluded that cristacortis is caused by a virus which is different from, and apparently not related to, any other known virus that affects citrus plants. It was concluded further that all sources of cristacortis produce vein-flecking and oak-leaf patterns on citrus leaves similar to those associated with scaly bark psorosis and concave gum. Evidence is presented to indicate that these symptoms are not the result of the presence of the viruses of these latter diseases in the cristacortis-infected trees. Vogel (1973) emphasized that the usual seedling indexing procedures will not distinguish between psorosis and cristacortis infection in the regions where both diseases are present. Thus, specific diagnosis of cristacortis infection will require the use of indicator varieties which develop extensive pitting if infected with cristacortis virus and the test plants must be observed over the period of time required for characteristic pitting to develop.

Host Range and Importance

From the studies made in Corsica, Sicily, and Sardinia, it appears that most of the commonly grown sweet orange varieties, including Washington navel, many mandarin varieties, grapefruit, shaddock, sour orange, some varieties of lemons and tangelos, and trifoliate orange are susceptible and develop the characteristic pitting.

In Sicily, Scaramuzzi and Càtara (1968) found the disease in twenty-six of thirty-six orchards surveyed. More than 2,000 trees were examined and 22.7 per cent were affected. In Sardinia, Servazzi, Marras, and Foddai (1968) and Zanardi, Anneda, and Follesa (1968) found that 10 to 25 per cent of the trees were affected in most orchards. Affected trees in different plantings of Tarocco orange ranged from 26 to 65 per cent. In some orchards of Moro sweet and Avana mandarin, affected trees reached 50 per cent or higher.

Until further information is available on the effects of cristacortis on trees propagated from infected buds or infected in another manner while quite young, no conclusions can be made regarding the economic importance of this disease. However, on the basis of the known effects of tristeza stem-pitting on grapefruit, Mexican lime, and Pera sweet orange, cristacortis disease seems to have the potential of causing reduced yields of many of the commercial citrus varieties.

Transmission and Control

The causal agent of cristacortis, now considered to be a virus, is transmissible by means of tissue grafts. Vogel and Bové (1972) found no evidence of seed transmission in trials with sour orange and obtained no transmission in preliminary tests with *Aphis spiraecola* and *Toxoptera aurantii*. If it can be determined that the virus is not spread by natural means, there is hope that selection of virus-free propagative material will provide satisfactory control. Vogel and Bové (1968) reported that graft-inocluated seedlings of Orlando tangelo showed cristacortis pitting in less than one year. If it is established that all sources of cristacortis virus cause the psorosis-like leaf effects, this will provide a simple and faster means of selecting noninfected trees for use as budwood sources. In the meantime, additional efforts should be made to learn if the virus is spread by vectors or through citrus seeds.

GUM-POCKET OF PONCIRUS TRIFOLIATA

This disease was described in South Africa by Schwarz and McClean (1969). It resembles disorders reported from Argentina by Fernandez-Valiela, Fortugno, and Corizzi (1965) and Foquet and Oste (1968). Its symptoms appear on trifoliate orange rootstock and in South Africa it is found almost exclusively on trees grown from a single source of Palmer Navel and one source of Olinda Valencia oranges. Association of gum-pocket with some sources of Palmer navel and Olinda Valencia but not with others is good evidence that it is caused by an infectious agent. Furthermore, Schwarz (1971) obtained evidence of graft transmission of an infectious agent to Orlando tangelo from gum-pocket-affected trees which were not carriers of exocortis or xyloporosis.

Symptomatology

Symptoms of gum-pocket appear on trifoliate orange rootstock within two to three years after budding and affected trees may show severe stunting and decline within five years. The primary lesions are gum pockets in the bark and wood of the trifoliate stock (fig. 2–69). Eventually these lesions may extend from the bud union to the soil level but do not appear on the roots. Initially, the lesions contain soft brownish gum and can be located by paring away the outer bark. Later, the gum hardens and the affected tissue becomes necrotic. The necrosis extends into the outer layers of wood, occasionally appearing as deep fissures. The affected parts of the bark and wood die, causing uneven growth and distortion, at some stages resembling advanced stem-pitting such as caused by tristeza or citrange-stunt viruses. After the disease becomes advanced, much of the bark of the trifoliate stock dies and decays. Upon examination of affected trees at the Crocodile Valley Estates near Nelspruit, it appeared to the author that the lesions had developed first on the northwest side of the stock. Commonly, the death of bark and wood was well advanced on that part, whereas the remainder of the stock showed the pitted effect, uneven growth, and pox-like bark lesions. In old advanced stages, however, almost all bark of the stock was dead. Bark above the bud union was normal and a cross-section of the sweet orange scion close to the union revealed no wood decay. Cross sections of affected trifoliate stock sometimes showed that new wood layers had formed over old lesions, causing them to become buried and somewhat isolated.

Distribution

In the same plantings, some trees, presumably grown from the same source of budwood, are normal. These provide a sharp contrast to the small, poorly developing trees which show gum pocket effects on the rootstock. Schwarz and McClean (1969) examined more than 3,000 trees of Palmer navel and Olinda Valencia on three trifoliate orange selections and found that 76 per cent were diseased. On the other hand, they reported the total absence of gum pocket disease in other plantings of sweet orange, including Palmer navel and old clone Valencia on trifoliate stock.

Possible Origin of the Disease

With exception of two Eureka lemon trees and one old clone Valencia tree, all of the gum-pocket trees were found to consist of scions of Palmer navel and Olinda Valencia, both nucellar

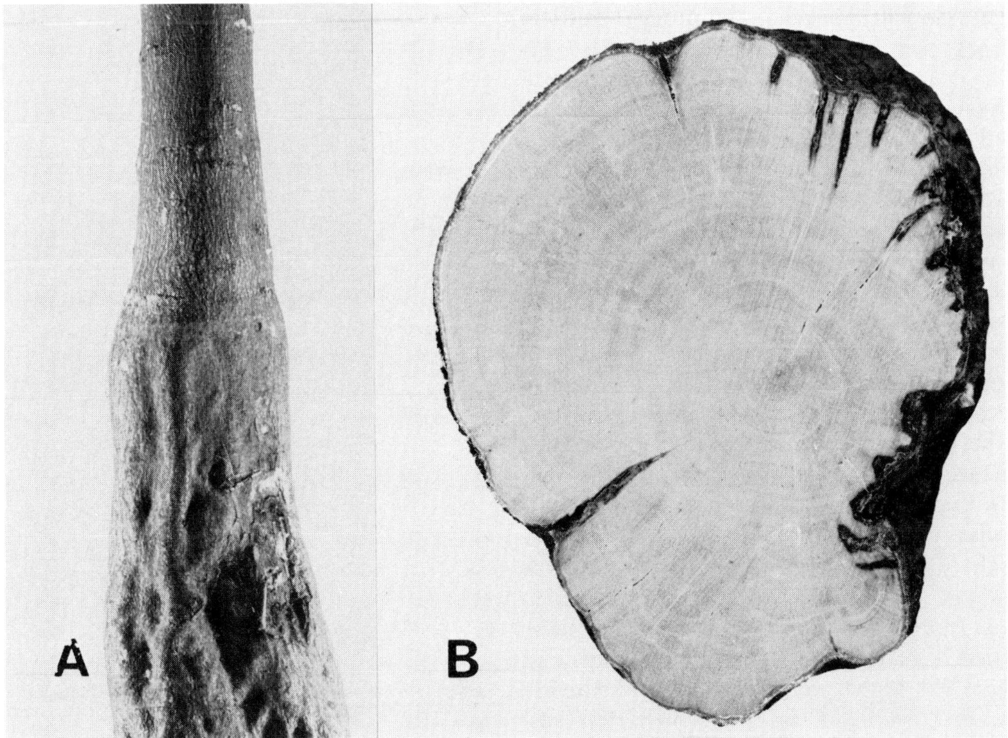

Fig. 2–69. Gum pocket disease of trifoliate orange. *A*, external appearance of tree of Palmer navel on trifoliate orange with gum pocket affecting the rootstock only. (Photos courtesy of R. E. Schwarz.)

lines. Schwarz and McClean (1969) stated that in the early experimental plantings of Palmer navel and Olinda Valencia, some trees were inoculated from a Cecily grapefruit in an attempt to introduce a mild protecting strain of tristeza (stem-pitting) virus. It is now suspected that the Cecily grapefruit tree contained a second virus that was transmitted along with tristeza virus and that this second virus is the cause of gum pocket. This explanation seems logical because trees of Palmer navel and Olinda Valencia on trifoliate orange stock have developed normally in some plantings in South Africa. Budwood for these normal trees no doubt came from clones of these varieties which had not been graft-inoculated from Cecily grapefruit.

Control

There is no evidence of natural spread of the causal agent of gum-pocket disease; therefore, control is a matter of prevention. Future propagations of Palmer navel and Olinda Valencia should be made from sources known not to carry the agent of gum-pocket. This should be done even when rootstocks other than trifoliate orange are used because it is advisable not to increase these infected clones. In presently existing plantings, all gum-pocket trees as well as normal appearing trees in the same planting should be removed because the normal trees may be latent carriers of gum-pocket. Their removal will eliminate further propagation from them.

Schwarz (1971) is of the opinion that Orlando tangelo can be used as an indicator of the gum-pocket agent. Further studies need to be made to corroborate that and to develop the best methods of conducting the necessary indexing.

MULTIPLE SPROUTING DISEASE

Searle (1969) described off-type sweet orange trees in Rhodesia. Schwarz (1970) described similarly affected trees in South Africa to which he gave the name "multiple sprouting disease." Majorana and Schwarz (1972) mechanically transmitted an agent, presumably a virus, from multiple sprouting trees to *Chenopodium quinoa* Willd., *Chenopodium auranticolor* Coste and Reyn., *Nicotiana glutinosa* L., and several varieties of cowpea, *Vigna sinensis* (L.) Endl., all of which developed viruslike symptoms, and to *Celosia argentea* L. and *Gomphrena globosa* L., which became infected without showing symptoms. Examination of partially purified preparations and ultrathin sections of leaves from affected trees under an electron miscroscope revealed no virus-like particles. Majorana and Schwarz (1972) concluded that there was insufficient evidence to decide whether the agent that infected the herbaceous hosts was the cause of citrus multiple sprouting or was merely associated with it. Schwarz (1970) reported that retransmission from *C. quinoa* and cowpea infected by mechanical inoculation from citrus was not successful. However, other studies indicated that multiple sprouting is a distinct infectious disease and until evidence to the contrary is obtained, it seems advisable to classify it as such.

The disease has been recorded from three different locations in South Africa and at one site in Rhodesia. In the Central Transvaal, Schwarz (1970) found groups of three-to-seven affected trees in seven-year-old Joppa and three-year-old Hamlin oranges. At Zebediela Estates in Northern Transvaal, 5 per cent of the trees in an orchard of six-year-old Valencia orange and 25 per cent of the trees in an adjacent block of twelve-year-old Navel orange showed symptoms of multiple sprouting. At Mazoe Estates in Rhodesia, Searle (1969) found infection ranging from 0.43 to 32.4 per cent in different blocks of Premier sweet orange.

Fig. 2–70. Tree of sweet orange on Rough lemon showing bushy growth on one side extending to the ground. Arrow points to overgrowth at bud union or "pinched stock" which is often found on trees with multiple sprouting. (Photo courtesy of C. M. Searle.)

Symptomatology

Mildly affected trees have symptoms or growth effects resembling those caused by copper deficiency, bud mite (*Aceria sheldoni* Ewing), or genetic factors, but none of these are known to cause the extremely abnormal condition displayed by the severely affected trees. Searle (1969) described two types of affected trees. Type 1 trees are larger than surrounding normal trees of the same age, bushy and willowy, often lopsided with brittle branches growing to the ground and with multiple branching throughout the tree (fig. 2–70). The Rough lemon rootstock of such trees has a smaller diameter than the sweet orange trunk, a condition that has been described in South Africa as "pinched stock." On normal trees of Valencia on Rough lemon, the rootstock is equal size or larger than the sweet orange trunk immediately above the bud union. On trees with multiple sprouting disease many shoots develop from a single bud, giving the branches a witches'-broom appearance (fig. 2–71). The extra weight causes the lower limbs to bend to the ground and sometimes limbs higher up on the trees snap off. Searle (1969) described type 2 trees as bushy and vigorous but without constricted bud unions (pinched stock). Trees of Premier sweet orange were observed to lose their upright growth habits, but affected Valencia trees became larger than normal. The author had an opportunity to examine trees with this disorder at the Mazoe Estates in 1972 and observed the growth effects previously described by Searle (1969) and Schwarz (1970). Additionally, it was noted that affected trees could be spotted easily throughout the plantings because of their lighter color.

Experimental Transmission

The author was informed that topworking affected trees with buds from normal-appearing

Fig. 2–71. Multiple sprouting disease. Busy, witches'-broom effect on a lateral branch which had grown normally for some period of time before multiple sprouting began. (Photo courtesy of A. P. D. McClean.)

Valencia trees resulted in symptoms of multiple sprouting on the newly formed top growth. Schwarz (1970) graft-inoculated seedlings of sweet orange, sour orange, lemon, grapefruit, West Indian lime, Rough lemon, and trifoliate orange. Although the inocula used carried seedling-yellows virus, some of the above, particularly sour orange, grapefruit, and lemon, developed internode stunting, leaf abscission, and dieback of developing side shoots, disease effects clearly distinguishable from those caused by seedling-yellows virus. Inoculated seedlings of Rough lemon and trifoliate orange showed no symptoms. Schwarz (1970) had no explanation for the fact that graft-inoculated sweet orange seedlings developed very mild symptoms and that the severe effects on sour orange, lemon, and grapefruit consisted chiefly in internode shortening. It was suggested that absence of bud mites from the experimental trees may have lessened symptom severity. Further study needs to be made on that possibility. It would also seem advisable to investigate the role of the tristeza-seedling-yellows virus complex since presumably it is present in all trees showing symptoms of multiple sprouting. If by chance that virus complex reacts synergistically with the mechanically transmissible virus to cause multiple sprouting disease, the reaction of orchard trees might differ from that of experimentally inoculated seedling trees maintained in a glasshouse.

Field Spread

Observations on the occurrence of multiple sprouting in both South Africa and Rhodesia indicate that natural spread is occurring but means of spread is not known. Schwarz (1970) stated that bud mites can be ruled out as the primary cause of the disorder. The author learned[10] that some studies have been underway in Rhodesia on the bud mite as a vector of a causal agent.

Control

Until more information is available, no specific control measures can be recommended other than, as proposed by Schwarz (1970), removal of affected trees. After having seen severely affected orchard trees, the author supports that recommendation. It is clear that the diseased trees become unproductive and should not be left to provide a possible source of infection for other trees. This disorder has the potential of causing significant tree losses. It should be studied

[10]Verbal communication with C. M. Searle, September, 1972.

thoroughly to determine its exact nature, means of spread, and possible control and/or eradication.

TAROCCO PIT

Russo and Klotz (1963) reported that many Tarocco orange trees in the Lentini district of Sicily were affected by a disorder which they described as "an unusual form of concave-gum disease." They gave the disorder the name "Tarocco pit." Symptoms consist of numerous depressions or concavities on the trunk and limbs with the severest effects appearing near the bud union. In the centers of the concavities, there are round holes from 1 mm to 2 cm in diameter from which a material like ground cork extrudes. Upon removal of unruptured bark, many circular holes may be found in the wood. Apparently, these are in an early stage of development and filled with soft, whitish, meristematic tissue, which darkens as it becomes infiltrated with gum. Still later, the infection breaks through to the outer bark surface and produces the ground cork-like material.

Affected trees were reported to be about a third smaller than normal trees or those showing ordinary symptoms of concave gum. Affected trees bore greater numbers of fruit than healthy trees, but fruits were smaller. The diseased trees displayed typical oak-leaf patterns and leaf flecking of concave gum.

Evidence was obtained that the disorder is bud-perpetuated. Sweet orange seedlings inoculated from diseased Tarocco trees developed psorosis leaf flecking and oak-leaf pattern, but there has been no report of reproduction of the pitting effect. It was evident that concave-gum virus was present in the affected Tarocco trees. Whether another virus was present in combination with that of concave gum has not been determined. If these severe effects were due solely to concave-gum virus, it would seem that these trees were infected with a more virulent strain of this virus and one which causes a different symptom than has been encountered previously. Further study of this disorder is needed before its nature can be established.

FAILURE OF RANGPUR LIME ON SWEET ORANGE

In the course of propagating some selections of Rangpur lime, Frolich (1958) found that one selection, designated C 26–1, grew normally on sour orange rootstock. When propagated on sweet orange, however, growth ceased during the second year. In a preliminary transmission test, results indicated that the failure of selection C 26–1 on sweet orange was due to a graft-transmissible agent, presumably a virus. Frolich and Hodgson (1961) presented additional information on this disease, and reported finding the same infectious agent in a plant of Diamante citron (*C. medica* L.). A Rangpur lime (D 4–24) free from this agent was used in inoculation experiments for demonstration of transmission and reproduction of the disease. Inoculations sometimes failed, particularly when tissue from terminal shoots was used as inoculum. Also, an occasional bud from clone C 26–1 developed into a normal tree. These reactions indicated uneven distribution of the agent in infected plants.

Graft inoculations caused severe dwarfing, chlorosis, and sparse foliage of trees of Rangpur lime on sweet orange rootstock (fig. 2–72). On experimentally infected trees, the diameter of the sweet orange rootstock became much less than that of the Rangpur lime scion (fig. 2–73). Reciprocal grafts of sweet orange on Rangpur lime were not affected. Seedlings of sweet orange and Rangpur lime were unaffected when inoculated.

Other studies on nucellar seedlings from the infected old clone Rangpur lime C 26–1 indicated that the causal agent is sometimes transmit-

Fig. 2–72. Failure of Rangpur lime on sweet-orange rootstock. Left, three-year-old tree grown from diseased Rangpur lime bud on sweet orange. Right, same age tree grown from healthy bud. (Photo courtesy of E. F. Frolich.)

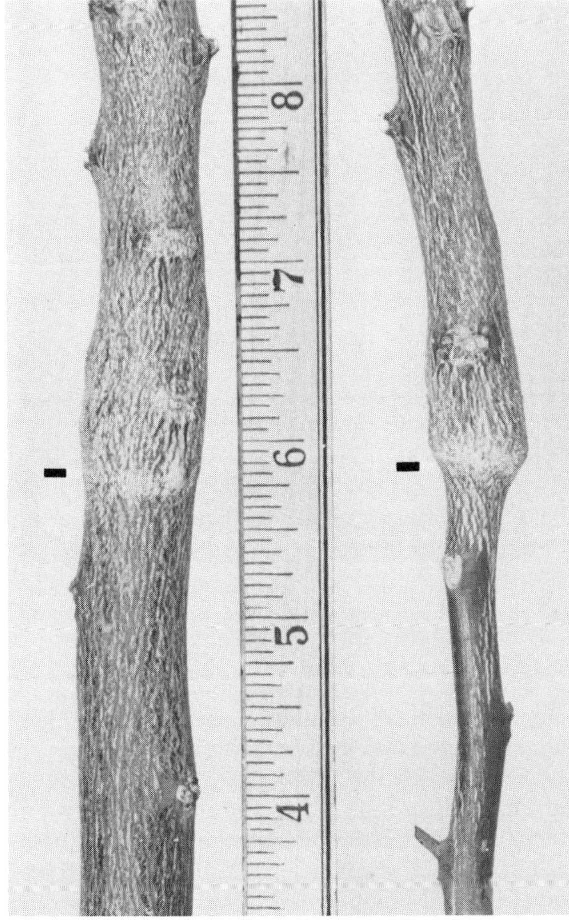

Fig. 2–73. Failure of Rangpur lime on sweet orange. Left, tip-graft union of healthy Rangpur lime on sweet orange. Right, union of diseased Rangpur lime on sweet orange. Bud unions are at 6 on scale. Note underdeveloped sweet orange stock of diseased tree. (Photo courtesy of E. F. Frolich.)

ted either through seeds or by a vector. Frolich has since observed that several healthy control trees developed symptoms after growing normally in the field for five years.[11] This suggests transmission by a vector rather than through seeds. The fact that in similarly spaced trees there was no evidence of transmission of exocortis virus between infected and healthy trees suggests that root-grafting was not common. There was no evidence that any of the known citrus viruses were responsible for this disorder. Therefore, it appears that Frolich and Hodgson (1961) are correct in assuming that a new or previously undescribed virus or viruslike agent is the cause of this tree failure.

Little is known of the economic importance or potentialities of this agent other than its serious effects on trees of Rangpur lime and Diamante citron on sweet orange rootstock. It has been demonstrated that it has no effect on trees of sweet orange on Rangpur lime rootstock. Other studies by Frolich showed that trees of Eureka lemon and some varieties of mandarin on sweet orange rootstock were not affected by inoculation.[12]

The disorder is of interest because it represents an example of a tree failure similar to a number of the so-called bud union disorders or "incompatibilities" which have not been attributed to viruses or other infectious agents. On the other hand, this tree failure is similar to the tristeza reaction of trees of sweet orange on sour orange rootstock in that it develops on trees of one combination of scion and rootstock, but not on the reverse combination of the same two varieties. Also, like tristeza, graft-inoculated seedling trees of the respective varieties are not affected.

GUMMY BARK OF SWEET ORANGE

A disorder of trees of sweet orange on sour orange rootstock in Egypt was described by Nour-Eldin (1956, 1959) as "phloem discoloration of sweet orange." Because further study by Nour-Eldin (1968) showed that the gummy deposits are largely in the outer bark tissues, the name was changed to "gummy bark of sweet orange." Affected orchard trees are usually stunted and suffer severe leaf drop in the winter. When the bark is scraped into the discolored region, circumferential, reddish-brown, gum-impregnated streaks are visible. On some trees, apparently in early stages of the disorder, the discoloration is near the bud union. In later stages, it extends upwards for 24 inches or more (fig. 2–74, *A*) but is not evident in bark of the sour orange rootstock. Often the wood of the sweet orange has a channel or groove type of pitting (fig. 2–74, *B*) or there may be individual pits in the xylem with corresponding pegs on the cambial face of the bark (fig. 2–74, *C*). On trees with heavy pitting in the sweet orange, there may be slight pitting in the sour orange rootstock.

Nour-Eldin (1968) reproduced this disease by graft inoculation to healthy sweet orange on sour orange trees. Inoculated trees developed a reddish-brown circumferential line at the bud

[11]Personal communication to the author from E. F. Frolich, dated August 7, 1962.
[12]Personal communication to the author from E. F. Frolich, dated July 8, 1965.

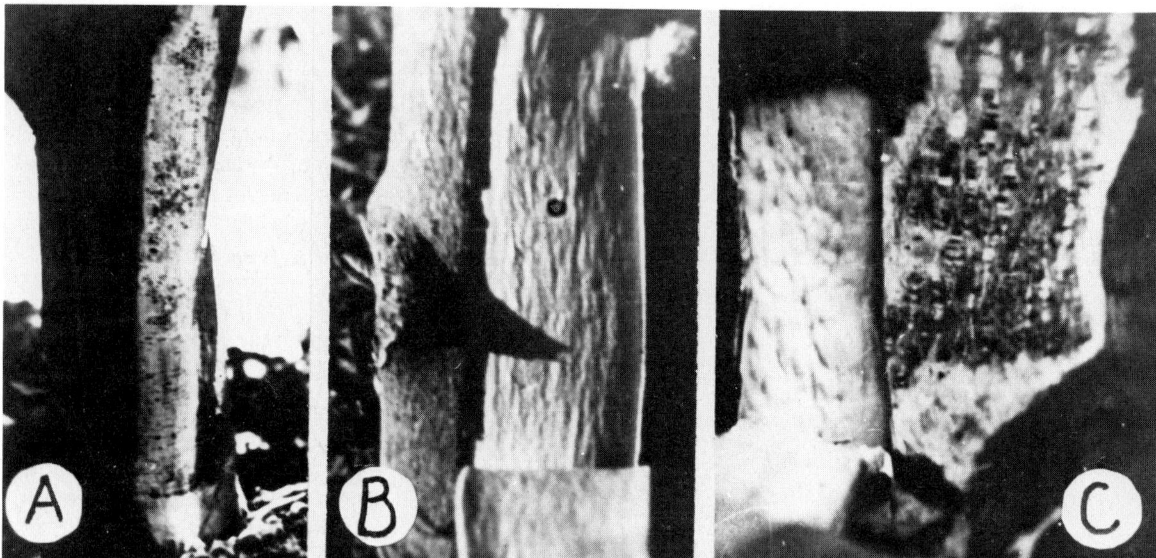

Fig. 2–74. Gummy bark of sweet orange on sour orange rootstock. *A*, **bark scraped to show gum deposits in bark of sweet orange, but not extending into rootstock.** *B*, **bark peeled showing grooved type of pitting in sweet orange.** *C*, **scraped area with gum in bark and peeled area showing a different kind of wood pitting. (Photo courtesy of F. Nour-Eldin.)**

union after about five years. With additional time, other gummy streaks appeared in the bark, and there was slight pitting in the wood. Although affected trees often carried viruses of psorosis, xyloporosis, and exocortis, experimental study seemed to eliminate these as causes of gummy bark. Fifty per cent of the trees examined in some plantings in Egypt showed gummy bark. The same disorder has been observed in Saudi Arabia and in the Sudan.

Except where sour orange rootstock continues to be used as a rootstock, gummy bark disease of sweet orange is unlikely to assume importance unless trees on other rootstocks also become affected, or if the apparent causal virus induces other kinds of disease. Nour-Eldin (1968) concluded that the gummy-bark virus is the cause of one type of bud-union constriction of trees of sweet orange on Rough lemon rootstock. This is discussed in the following section.

BUD-UNION CREASE

Since the practice of propagating citrus of one species on rootstocks of a different species first began, many bud-union abnormalities have been observed. Their effects range from slight injury to complete failure. Some of these abnormalities definitely result from genetic incompatibility; some are caused by viruses such as tristeza; others remain unexplained although virus infection has been suspected as a cause.

Some of the most frequently observed bud-union disorders are those of trees of sweet orange on Rough lemon rootstock. These comprise a range of macroscopic effects, but the most common are "bud-union crease," an intermittent or continuous depression in the wood immediately at the bud union, with corresponding projections from the inner face of the bark. In some instances, the outer bark appears normal, but often there are narrow or quite broad necrotic bands of bark at the bud union, with only a thin layer of living tissue adjacent to the cambium. A bud union of this type is illustrated in figure 2–75.

Bud-union disorders of trees of sweet orange on Rough lemon rootstock have been studied by numerous investigators, including Grant, Moreira, and Costa (1957) and Salibe (1961*b*) in Brazil, Fernandez-Valiela (1961) in Argentina, McClean and Engelbrecht (1958) in South Africa, and Grimm, Grant, and Childs (1955) and Bridges and Youtsey (1968) in Florida. Studies made so far have not correlated this disorder specifically with any of the commonly known citrus viruses, although such viruses as xyloporosis, exocortis, psorosis, and tristeza are often present in affected trees.

Frequently some clones of a particular sweet orange variety or selection growing on

Figure 2–75. Bud union crease of tree of Shamouti orange on Rough-lemon rootstock. In addition to the crease in the wood there is a band of necrotic bark at the bud union.

Rough lemon rootstock develop a bud-union disorder, whereas other clones of the same variety grow normally. Recent studies by Bridges and Youtsey (1968) clearly demonstrated that nucellar clones of Pineapple, Hamlin, and Valencia sweet orange on Rough lemon stock developed no bud-union crease in Florida, whereas some but not all old clones of these commonly produced trees with bud-union crease. The authors determined that the viruses of tristeza, xyloporosis, exocortis, psorosis, and vein enation were not associated with the disorder. They concluded that a virus or a genetic factor is the cause.

From the description provided, it appears that Bridges and Youtsey (1968) studied a bud-union abnormality very similar to that referred to by Nour-Eldin (1968), which he concluded was caused by the sweet orange gummy-bark virus. Nour-Eldin (1968) reported that trees indexed positively for gummy bark also indexed positively for bud-union constriction. Nour-Eldin found no bud union effect up to eight years on trees of nucellar sweet orange on Rough lemon, but the same kind of trees developed bud-union constriction within four years after inoculation from gummy-bark trees.[13] This is acceptable evidence that the bud union effect is caused by a virus or viruslike agent, but it does not establish positively that it is the gummy-bark pathogen. If the two disorders—sweet orange gummy bark and Rough lemon rootstock bud-union crease—have a single cause in Egypt, it seems that gummy-bark disease would have been observed in other countries where Rough lemon rootstock trees commonly show bud-union crease, but where trees of sweet orange on sour orange stock have not developed gummy bark.

Regardless of the cause of bud-union disorders in citrus, efforts should be made to avoid them by selecting scion budwood, when possible, from sources known from prior use to develop normally on the rootstock to be used. In the case of bud-union failures demonstrated to be caused by virus infection, the selection of virus-free scion budwood for use on healthy rootstock seedlings should provide normal trees unless the causal virus is being spread naturally from tree to tree in the orchards. In that case, as with tristeza disease, it will be necessary to abandon the use of susceptible stionic combinations.

SOME APPARENTLY INHERITED DISORDERS OF CITRUS

There are numerous disorders of plants which are not infectious and others which have not been studied sufficiently to classify them regarding infectiousness. Schneider *et al.* (1961) suggested that among these disorders, which may resemble certain virus effects, some are apparently inherited and should be so designated. These authors classified as inherited such citrus disorders as "lemon sieve-tube necrosis," which is associated with lemon decline, and "woodpocket" or "lignocortosis," a destructive, noninfectious disorder of some selections of Lisbon lemon and Tahiti lime. These two disease conditions develop independently of any rootstock-scion interaction. It was suggested that other disorders probably belonging in this category of inherited diseases are crinkle-scurf of Valencia orange (Knorr, 1953), chimeric breakdown of Tahiti lime fruits (Knorr and Childs, 1957), and a seed-perpetuated exocortis-like disorder of trifoliate orange (Calavan *et al.*, 1959).

[13]Personal communication to the author from F. Nour-Eldin, dated March 26, 1969.

Disorders depending upon some rootstock-scion relationship but considered by Schneider *et al.* (1961) to be inherited include certain of the so-called incompatibilities. Examples of these are the cyclic decline of Eureka and certain Lisbon lemon clones on sour orange rootstocks which Schneider (1952*a*, 1952*b*, 1956) named "sour-orange-rootstock necrosis," decline of Eureka lemon on trifoliate orange rootstock, and decline of Eureka lemon, certain tangelo selections, and other hybrids on rootstocks of Troyer citrange. Probably numerous other so-called bud-union disorders are also inherited weaknesses. Among these, for example, may be the disorder described by Weathers and Calavan (1959*c*) on calamondin trees on several different rootstocks and the decline of certain kinds of citrus growing on calamondin rootstock described by Cooper and Olson (1956) and Olson (1954, 1958).

There are other disorders, which no doubt are of genetic nature but some of these have not been investigated sufficiently to establish that viruses are not involved as causal factors. Many workers have observed, for example, that trees of certain sweet orange selections on Rough lemon rootstock regularly develop bud-union weaknesses. In some instances, there is an indentation of the wood at the union corresponding to an inner-bark projection. In others, there are rings of corky or necrotic bark encircling the trunk at the bud union with various kinds of creasing or overgrowths of the wood beneath. Another bud-union weakness shows up as a pronounced overgrowth of the scion at the union. Presently, this weakness occurs quite regularly in California plantings of lemon trees on various rootstocks.

Because many of the bud-union abnormalities have a serious effect on the growth and longevity of citrus trees, it is important to search for causes and means of avoiding them. Some of the effects closely resemble the reaction to infection with known viruses, but it is clear that viruses are not responsible for a number of these disorders. With others, although the exact cause is not understood, evidence based on the present methods of detecting the presence of viruses favors the exclusion of viruses as causal factors. Reichert, Bental, and Ginsburg (1965) described a bud-union constriction on declining trees of Marsh grapefruit on sour orange rootstock in Israel. They demonstrated that the trees were not infected with tristeza virus. Incompatibility was ruled out because trees of Marsh grapefruit on sour orange normally show no bud-union constriction. Because of the presence of inverse pitting on the sour orange stock and certain anatomical aspects of the bud-union tissues, it was suggested that the bud-union disorder may have been caused by xyloporosis virus. However, further experimental evidence is needed before this conclusion can be made.

In addition to the bud-union abnormalities of citrus, other viruslike effects are encountered which apparently are also inherited. Various types of bark disorders, including roughness or scaling and splitting and such effects as gumming, wood pitting, abnormal foliage and some kinds of galls, are observed on citrus which can be perpetuated but not transmitted and reproduced on normal plants. Still other noninfectious abnormalities arise on citrus as a result of bud mutations. Although some of these closely resemble symptoms of certain virus diseases, it can be readily established that they are genetic in nature.

Because some of the abnormalities mentioned above have assumed considerable economic importance, the author agrees with the suggestion of Schneider *et al.* (1961) that the apparently inherited disorders should be recognized as a distinct group of diseases as is done for the so-called nutritional diseases of plants. The anatomical studies of Schneider (1952*a*, 1952*b*, 1956, 1957) provide a means of identifying and distinguishing between certain disorders. Furthermore, they show that some of the slowly developing diseases can be detected many years before they affect the health of the tree. These anatomical studies also suggested a method for selection of scion and rootstock varieties which are less subject to certain of these weaknesses. Further investigations possibly could provide other techniques useful in preventing losses from apparently inherited diseases.

FUTURE OUTLOOK

Since Fawcett (1933) demonstrated that citrus psorosis disease is caused by a virus—the first proof that citrus trees are subject to this kind of disease agent—investigations have disclosed that numerous other diseases of citrus are caused by viruses. In recent years it has been established that stubborn is not a virus disease, as it was thought to be for many years, but is caused by a newly discovered type of pathogen, a mycoplasma. Through extensive research, it has been learned also that several serious disorders which are now considered to belong to the "greening" group of citrus diseases are caused by agents which resemble mycoplasma but differ sufficiently from true mycoplasma to suggest that another, previously unknown pathogenic agent causes these diseases.

Diseases such as tristeza, exocortis, and xyloporosis have made it necessary to abandon or restrict the use of some long-used rootstock varieties and to find others not subject to these diseases. Control of the virus and viruslike diseases may depend on discovery of resistance in previously untried scion varieties or hybrid selections. With a change to new citrus types for both scion and rootstock use, new disease problems can be expected. Some of these will be susceptibility to known pathogens or to newly identified viral or mycoplasmalike agents. Thus, it is clearly evident that citrus virologists will continue to play an important part in maintaining a successful and profitable citrus industry throughout the world.

LITERATURE CITED

ALLEN, R. M. 1968. Survival time of exocortis virus of citrus on contaminated knife blades. Plant Dis. Reptr. **52**:935–39.

ALLEN, R. M., and H. H. MCDONALD. 1963. Tristeza discovered in tangerines in Arizona. Prog. Agr. (Arizona) **15**(2):8–9.

AMIZET, L. 1959. Contribution to the study of xyloporosis in Algeria. *In:* Wallace, J. M. (ed.). Citrus virus diseases. Pp. 125–28. Univ. Calif. Div. Agr. Sci., Berkeley, Calif.

BAR-JOSEPH, M., and G. LOEBENSTEIN. 1970. Leaf flecking on indicator seedlings associated with citrus impietratura in Israel: a possible indexing method. Plant Dis. Reptr. **54**:643–45.

BAR-JOSEPH, M., G. LOEBENSTEIN, and J. COHEN. 1970. Partial purification of viruslike particles associated with the citrus tristeza disease. Phytopathology **60**:75–78.

BAR-JOSEPH, M., G. LOEBENSTEIN, and Y. OREN. 1974. Use of electron miscroscopy in eradication of tristeza sources recently found in Israel. *In:* Weathers, L. G., and M. Cohen (eds.). Proc. 6th Conf. Intern. Organ. Citrus Virol. Pp. 83–85. Univ. Calif. Div. Agr. Sci., Richmond, Calif.

BAZAN DE SEGURA, C. 1952. La "tristeza" de los citricos en el Peru. Min. Agr. Direc. Gen. Agr. (Lima) Informe **77**: 14 pp.

BAZAN DE SEGURA, C., and A. FERRAND. 1969. Woody gall: its distribution and importance in new and old citrus plantings in Peru. *In:* Chapman, H. D. (ed.). Proc. First Intern. Citrus Symp. **3**:1449–51. Univ. Calif., Riverside, Calif.

BELTRAN-ALONZO CUEVILLAS, D. J. L., and D. S. PLANES-SAMPER. 1960. La tristeza. Informacion Técnica Boletin, Depto. Tecnico de Industria Quimicas Serpiol: 18 pp.

BENNETT, C. W., and A. S. COSTA. 1949. Tristeza disease of citrus. Jour. Agr. Res. **78**:207–37.

BENTAL, A., and I. YOFFE. 1968. The impietratura disease of citrus fruits. FAO Plant Protect. Bul. **16**:64–65.

BENTON, R. J., F. T. BOWMAN, L. FRASER, and R. G. KEBBY. 1949. Selection of citrus budwood to control scaly butt in trifoliata rootstock. Agr. Gaz. N. S. Wales **60**:31–34.

———. 1950. Stunting and scaly butt of citrus associated with *Poncirus trifoliata* rootstock. N. S. Wales Dept. Agr. Sci. Bul. **70**: 20 pp.

BERTELLI, J. C., and L. K. DE BERTELLI. 1945. Estudio etiológico de la "podredumbre de los raicillas" o tristeza de los citros. Asoc. Ing. Agron. Rev. **17**:15–32.

BIGORNIA, A. E., and C. A. CALICA. 1961. Tristeza in the Philippines. *In:* Price, W. C. (ed.). Proc. 2nd Conf. Intern. Organ. Citrus Virol. Pp. 101–06. Univ. Fla. Press, Gainesville, Fla.

BIOLETTI, F. T., W. GOWRIE, and P. J. CILLIE. 1904. Citrus culture in Cape Colony. Report of Commission of Inquiry into the causes of the failure of citrus trees in Cape Colony. Cape Colony Agr. Jour., Cape of Good Hope **21**:1–20.

BITANCOURT, A. A. 1940. A podridão das radicelas dos citrus na provincia de Corrientes, Argentina. O. Biologico **6**:285–88, 356–64.

BITANCOURT, A. A., and H. S. FAWCETT. 1944. Statistical studies of distribution of psorosis–affected trees in citrus orchards. Phytopathology **34**:358–75.

BITANCOURT, A. A., H. S. FAWCETT, and J. M. WALLACE. 1943. The relations of wood alterations in psorosis of citrus to tree deterioration. Phytopathology **33**:865–83.

BITTERS, W. P. 1952. Exocortis on trifoliate. Citrus Leaves **32**(9):14–16, 34.

———. 1968. Valencia orange rootstock trial at South Coast Field Station. Calif. Citrog. **53**:163, 173–74.

BITTERS, W. P., N. W. DUKESHIRE, and J. A. BRUSCA. 1953. Stem pitting and quick decline symptoms as related to rootstock combinations. Citrus Leaves **33**(2):8–9, 38.

BITTERS, W. P., and E. R. PARKER. 1953. Quick decline of citrus as influenced by top-root relationships. Calif. Agr. Expt. Sta. Bul. **733**: 35 pp.

BOVÉ, J. M., E. C. CALAVAN, S. P. CAPOOR, R. E. CORTEZ, and R. E. SCHWARTZ. 1974. Influence of temperature on symptom expression of California stubborn, South Africa greening, India citrus decline, and Philippines leaf mottling diseases. *In:* Weathers, L. G., and M. Cohen (eds.). Proc. 6th Conf. Intern. Organ. Citrus Virol. Pp. 12–15. Univ. Calif. Div. Agr. Sci., Berkeley, Calif.

BOVÉ, J. M., and J. CASSIN. 1968. Problems of agriculture. A report on survey in Reunion. IFAC-CNRA, Versailles. (Mimeographed.)

BOVÉ, J. M., and P. SAGLIO. 1974. Stubborn and greening: a review, 1969-1972. *In:* Weathers, L. G., and M. Cohen (eds.). Proc. 6th Conf. Intern. Organ. Citrus Virol. Pp. 1–11. Univ. Calif. Div. Agr. Sci., Berkeley, Calif.

BOVÉ, J. M., P. SAGLIO, J. G. TULLY, A. E. FRUENDT, Z. LUND, J. PILLOT, and D. TAYLOR-ROBINSON. 1973. Characterization of the mycoplasma-like organism associated with "stubborn" disease of citrus. Ann. N. Y. Acad. Sci. **225**:462–70.

BOWYER, J. W., and E. C. CALAVAN. 1974. Antibiotic sensitivity in vitro of the mycoplasmalike organism associated with citrus stubborn disease. Phytopathology **64**:346–49.

BRIDGES, G. D., and C. O. YOUTSEY. 1968. Further studies of the bud union abnormality of rough lemon rootstocks with sweet orange scions. *In:* Childs, J. F. L. (ed.). Proc. 4th Conf. Intern. Organ. Citrus Virol. Pp. 236–39. Univ. Fla. Press, Gainesville, Fla.

BRIDGES, G. D., C. O. YOUTSEY, and R. R. NIXON. 1965. Observations indicating psorosis transmission by seed of Carrizo citrange. Proc. Fla. State Hort. Soc. **78**:48–50.

BROWN, R. T., and F. B. SCHMITZ. 1954. Exocortis transmission studies. Louisiana State Univ. Agr. Expt. Sta. Ann. Rept. 1952–53:184–85.

BURKE, J. HENRY. 1958. Citrus industry of Brazil. U. S. Dept. Agr., For. Agr. Serv., For. Agr. Rept. **109**: 24 pp.

BUSBY, J. N. 1953. Tristeza in Florida. Citrus Indus. **34**(8):5–7.

CALAVAN, E. C. 1957*a*. Wood pocket disease of lemons and seedless limes. Calif. Citrog. **42**:265–68.

———. 1957*b*. Wood pocket disease of lemons and seedless limes. II. Perpetuation and transmission studies. Calif. Citrog. **42**:300-04.

———. 1969. Investigations of stubborn disease in California: Indexing, effects on growth and production, and evidence of virus strains. *In:* Chapman, H. D. (ed.). Proc. First Intern. Citrus Symp. **3**:1403–12. Univ. Calif., Riverside, Calif.

CALAVAN, E. C., and J. B. CARPENTER. 1965. Stubborn disease of citrus trees retards growth, impairs quality, and decreases yields. Calif. Citrog. **50**:86–87, 96, 98–99.

CALAVAN, E. C., J. B. CARPENTER, and L. G. WEATHERS. 1958. Observations on distribution of cachexia of citrus in California and Arizona. Plant Dis. Reptr. **42**:1054–56.

CALAVAN, E. C., and D. W. CHRISTIANSEN. 1961. Stunting and chlorosis induced in young-line citrus plants by inoculations from navel orange trees having symptoms of stubborn disease. *In:* Price, W. C. (ed.). Proc. 2nd Conf. Intern. Organ. Citrus Virol. Pp. 69–76. Univ. Fla. Press, Gainesville, Fla.

———. 1965. Variability of cachexia reactions among varieties of rootstocks and within clonal propagations of citrus. *In:* Price, W. C. (ed.). Proc. 3rd Conf. Intern. Organ. Citrus Virol. Pp. 76–85. Univ. Fla. Press, Gainesville, Fla.

CALAVAN, E. C., D. W. CHRISTIANSEN, and C. N. ROISTACHER. 1963. Symptoms associated with tatter-leaf virus infection of Troyer citrange rootstocks. Plant Dis. Reptr. **47**:971–75.

CALAVAN, E. C., D. W. CHRISTIANSEN, and L. G. WEATHERS. 1961. Comparative reactions of Orlando tangelo and Palestine sweet lime to cachexia and xyloporosis. *In:* Price, W. C. (ed.). Proc. 2nd Conf. Intern. Organ. Citrus Virol. Pp. 150–58. Univ. Fla. Press, Gainesville, Fla.

CALAVAN, E. C., E. F. FROLICH, J. B. CARPENTER, C. N. ROISTACHER, and D. W. CHRISTIANSEN. 1964. Rapid indexing for exocortis of citrus. Phytopathology **54**:1359–62.

CALAVAN, E. C., and D. J. GUMPF. 1974. Studies on citrus stubborn disease and its agent. Coll. Inst. Nat. Sante Rech. Med. **33**:181–86.

CALAVAN, E. C., M. K. HARJUNG, A. E.-S. A. FUDL-ALLAH, and J. W. BOWYER. 1974. Natural incidence of stubborn in field-grown citrus seedlings and budlings. *In:* Weathers, L. G., and M. Cohen (eds.). Proc. 6th Conf. Intern. Organ. Citrus Virol. Pp. 16–19. Univ. Calif. Div. Agr. Sci., Richmond, Calif.

CALAVAN, E. C., R. M. PRATT, B. W. LEE, and J. P. HILL. 1968. Tristeza related to decline of trees on citrange rootstock. Calif. Citrog. **53**:75, 84–88.

CALAVAN, E. C., R. M. PRATT, B. W. LEE, J. P. HILL, and R. L. BLUE. 1972. Tristeza susceptibility of sweet orange on Troyer citrange rootstock. *In:* Price, W. C. (ed.). Proc. 5th Conf. Intern. Organ. Citrus Virol. Pp. 146–53. Univ. Fla. Press, Gainesville, Fla.

CALAVAN, E. C., C. N. ROISTACHER, and E. M. NAUER. 1972. Thermotherapy of citrus for inactivation of certain viruses. Plant Dis. Reptr. **56**:976–80.

CALAVAN, E. C., R. K. SOOST, and J. W. CAMERON. 1959. Exocortis-like symptoms on unbudded seedlings and rootstocks of *Poncirus trifoliata* with seedling line tops and probable spread of exocortis in a nursery. Plant Dis. Reptr. **43**:374–79.

CALAVAN, E. C., and L. G. WEATHERS. 1959. The distribution of exocortis virus in California citrus. *In:* Wallace, J. M. (ed.). Citrus virus diseases. Pp. 151–54. Univ. Calif. Div. Agr. Sci., Berkeley, Calif.

———. 1961. Evidence for strain differences and stunting with exocortis virus. *In:* Price, W. C. (ed.). Proc. 2nd Conf. Intern. Organ. Citrus Virol. Pp. 26-33. Univ. Fla. Press, Gainesville, Fla.

CALAVAN, E. C., L. G. WEATHERS, and D. W. CHRISTIANSEN. 1968. Effect of exocortis on production and growth of Valencia orange trees on trifoliate orange rootstocks. *In:* Childs, J. F. L. (ed.). Proc. 4th Conf. Intern. Organ. Citrus Virol. Pp. 101–04. Univ. Fla. Press, Gainesville, Fla.

CAPOOR, S. P. 1965. Presence of seedling yellows complex in the citrus of South India. *In:* Price, W. C. (ed.). Proc. 3rd Conf. Intern. Organ. Citrus Virol. Pp. 30–35. Univ. Fla. Press, Gainesville, Fla.

———. 1967. Virus diseases of fruits. Indian Hort. **11**(4):64–69.

CAPOOR, S. P., D. G. RAO, and S. M. VISWANATH. 1967. A vector of the greening disease of citrus in India. Indian Jour. Agr. Sci. **37**:572–76.

CAPOOR, S. P., and M. J. THIRUMALACHAR. 1973. Cure of greening affected citrus plants by chemotherapeutic agents. Plant Dis. Reptr. **57**:160–63.

CARPENTER, J. B. 1956. Identification of tristeza in Meyer lemon in Arizona. Plant Dis. Reptr. **40**:8.

———. 1957. Further studies on tristeza in Meyer lemon in Arizona. Plant Dis. Reptr. **41**:1014–15.

CARPENTER, J. B., E. C. CALAVAN, and D. W. CHRISTIANSEN. 1965. Occurrence of excessive seed abortion in citrus fruits affected with stubborn disease. Plant Dis. Reptr. **49**:668–72.

CARPENTER, J. B., and J. R. FURR. 1960. Wood pitting of undetermined cause in unbudded citrus seedlings. Plant Dis. Reptr. **44**:916–18.

CARRERA, C. 1933. Informe preliminar sobre una enfermedad nueva comprobada en los citros de Bella Vista (Corrientes). Argentina Min. Agr. Bol. Mens. **34**:275–80.

CARTIA, G., and E. C. CALAVAN. 1974. Further evidence of natural spread of citrus stubborn disease. Rivista di Pathol. Vegetale (Serie 4) **10**:219–24.

CARTIA, G., and A. CATARA. 1974. Studies on impietratura disease. *In:* Weathers, L. G., and M. Cohen (eds.). Proc. 6th Conf. Intern. Organ. Citrus Virol. Pp. 123–26. Univ. Calif. Div. Agr. Sci., Richmond, Calif.

CASSIN, J. 1965. Research on stubborn disease in Morocco. *In:* Price, W. C. (ed.). Proc. 3rd Conf. Intern. Organ. Citrus Virol. Pp. 204–06. Univ. Fla. Press, Gainesville, Fla.

CATARA, A., and J. M. WALLACE. 1970. Identification of citrange stunt as the mechanically transmissible virus from Meyer lemons doubly infected with citrange stunt and tatter leaf viruses. Phytopathology **60**:737–38.

CATLING, H. D. 1970. Distribution of the psyllid vectors of citrus greening disease, with notes on the biology and bionomics of *Diaphorina citri*. FAO Plant Protect. Bul. **18**:8–15.

———. 1972. Factors regulating populations of psyllid vectors of greening. *In:* Price, W. C. (ed.). Proc. 5th Conf. Intern. Organ. Citrus Virol. Pp. 51–57. Univ. Fla. Press, Gainesville, Fla.

CHAPOT, H. 1956. Une nouvelle maladie à virus des agrumes dans le Moyen-Orient. Soc. Sci. Nat. Phys. Maroc, Compt. Rend. Séances Mensuelles **22**(6):99–105.

———. 1959. First studies on the stubborn disease of citrus in some Mediterranean countries. *In:* Wallace, J. M. (ed.). Citrus virus diseases. Pp. 109–18. Univ. Calif. Div. Agr. Sci., Berkeley, Calif.

———. 1961. Impietratura in Mediterranean countries. *In:* Price, W. C. (ed.). Proc. 2nd Conf. Intern. Organ. Citrus Virol. Pp. 177-81. Univ. Fla. Press, Gainesville, Fla.

———. 1970. Citrus production problems in the Near East and North Africa. United Nations Devel. Program, FAO Report TA **2870:** 95 pp.

CHAPOT, H., and J. CASSIN. 1961. Maladies et troubles divers affectant les citrus au Maroc. Al Awamia [Rabat] **1**:107–42.

CHEEMA, G. S., and S. S. BHATT. 1928. The dieback disease of citrus trees and its relation to the soils of western India. Dept. Agr. Bot. **155**:1–48.

CHEN, M., T. MIYAKAWA, and C. MATSUI. 1972. Simultaneous infections of citrus leaves with tristeza virus and mycoplasmalike organism. Phytopathology **62**:663–66.

———. 1973. Citrus likubin pathogens in salivary glands of *Diaphorina citri*. Phytopathology **63**:194–95.

CHILDS, J. F. L. 1950. The cachexia disease of Orlando tangelo. Plant Dis. Reptr. **34**:295–98.

———. 1952. Cachexia disease, its bud transmission and relation to xyloporosis and tristeza. Phytopathology **42**:265–68.

———. 1956. Transmission experiments and xyloporosis-—cachexia relations in Florida. Plant Dis. Reptr. **40:** 143–45.

———. 1959. Xyloporosis and cachexia—their status as citrus virus diseases. *In:* Wallace, J. M. (ed.). Citrus virus diseases. Pp. 119-24. Univ. Calif. Div. Agr. Sci., Berkeley, Calif.

——— (ed.). 1968*a*. Proc. 4th Conf. Intern. Organ. Citrus Virol. Univ. Fla. Press, Gainesville, Fla. 404 pp.

———. 1968*b*. Cachexia (xyloporosis). *In:* Indexing procedures for 15 virus diseases of citrus trees. U. S. Dept. Agr. Handbook **333**:16–19.

CHILDS, J. F. L., and J. B. CARPENTER. 1960. Observations on stubborn and other diseases of citrus in Morocco in 1959. Plant Dis. Reptr. **44**:920–27.

CHILDS, J. F. L., G. R. GRIMM, T. J. GRANT, L. C. KNORR, and G. NORMAN. 1956. The incidence of xyloporosis (cachexia) in certain Florida citrus varieties. Citrus Indus. **37**(4):5–8.

CHILDS, J. F. L., and R. E. JOHNSON. 1966. Preliminary report of seed transmission of psorosis virus. Plant Dis. Reptr. **50**:81–83.

CHILDS, J. F. L., R. E. JOHNSON, and J. L. EICHHORN. 1965. The question of seed transmission of cachexia-xyloporosis. *In:* Price, W. C. (ed.). Proc. 3rd Conf. Intern. Organ. Citrus Virol. Pp. 90-94. Univ. Fla. Press, Gainesville, Fla.

CHILDS, J. F. L., F. NOUR-ELDIN, and N. EL-HOSSEINY. 1956. Observations on Egyptian citrus diseases. Citrus Indus. **37**(10):11–16.

CIFERRI, R. 1950. A decline of citrus plants in Venezuela. Nature **165**:32.

COHEN, M., and H. C. BURNETT. 1961. Tristeza in Florida. *In:* Price, W. C. (ed.). Proc. 2nd Conf. Intern. Organ. Citrus Virol. Pp. 107–12. Univ. Fla. Press, Gainesville, Fla.

COHEN, M., and L. C. KNORR. 1953. Present status of tristeza in Florida. Proc. Fla. State Hort. Soc. **66**:20–22.

———. 1954. Honeycombing—a macroscopic symptom of tristeza in Florida. Abstr. Phytopathology **44**:85.

CONDADO, C. 1950. Xyloporosis in Bella Vista, Corrientes. IDIA **3**(33–34):47–50.

COOPER, W. C., and E. O. OLSON. 1956. Review of studies on adaptibility of citrus varieties as rootstocks for grapefruit in Texas. Jour. Rio Grande Valley Hort. Soc. **10**:6–9.

CORBETT, M. K., and T. J. GRANT. 1967. Purification of citrus variegation virus. Phytopathology **57**:137–43.

COSTA, A. S., T. J. GRANT, and S. MOREIRA. 1949. Investigacões sobre a tristeza dos citros. Bragântia **9**:59–80.

———. 1950. A possible relationship between tristeza and stem-pitting disease of grapefruit in Africa. Calif. Citrog. **35**:504, 526–28.

DANIELS, M. J., P. G. MARKHAM, B. M. MEDDINS, A. K. PLASKITT, R. TOWNSEND, and M. BAR-JOSEPH. 1973. Axenic culture of a plant pathogenic spiroplasma. Nature **244**:523–24.

DAUTHY, D., and J. M. BOVÉ. 1965. Experiments on mechanical transmission of citrus viruses. *In:* Price, W. C. (ed.). Proc. 3rd Conf. Intern. Organ. Citrus Virol. Pp. 250–53. Univ. Fla. Press, Gainesville, Fla.

DE MARTINO, E., A. SCUDERI, and G. TERRANOVA. 1972. Effect of cristacortis on growth and productivity of Tarocco sweet orange. *In:* Price, W. C. (ed.). Proc. 5th Conf. Intern. Organ. Citrus Virol. Pp. 176–77. Univ. Fla. Press, Gainesville, Fla.

DESJARDINS, P. R. 1969. Purification, electron microscopy, and serology of citrus viruses—a review. *In:* Chapman, H. D. (ed.). Proc. First Intern. Citrus Symp. **3**:1481–88. Univ. Calif., Riverside, Calif.

DESJARDINS, P. R., R. J. DRAKE, and J. V. FRENCH. 1969. Transmission of citrus ringspot virus to citrus and non-citrus hosts by dodder (*Cuscuta subinclusa* Dur. and Hilg.). Plant Dis. Reptr. **53**:947–48.

DESJARDINS, P. R., and D. A. REYNOLDS. 1963. Varietal reaction in cucumber to the infectious variegation virus of citrus. Plant Dis. Reptr. **47**:1071–73.

DESJARDINS, P. R., and J. M. WALLACE. 1962. Cucumber, an additional herbaceous host of the infectious variegation strain of citrus psorosis virus. Plant Dis. Reptr. **46**:414–16.

———. 1966. Host reactions to citrus infectious variegation virus indicating wide diversity of virus strains. Phytopathology **56**:575.

DESJARDINS. P. R., J. M. WALLACE, E. S. H. WOLLMAN, and R. J. DRAKE. 1959. A separation of virus strains from a tristeza-seedling yellows complex by heat treatment of infected lime seedlings. *In:* Wallace, J. M. (ed.). Citrus virus diseases. Pp. 91–95. Univ. Calif. Div. Agr. Sci., Berkeley, Calif.

DICKSON, R. C., R. A. FLOCK, and M. M. JOHNSON. 1951. Insect transmission of citrus quick decline. Jour. Econ. Ent. **44**:172–76.

DICKSON, R. C., R. A. FLOCK, and E. F. LAIRD, JR. 1956. Citrus aphids and the spread of tristeza, or quick decline. Citrus Leaves **36**(8):10, 31.

DUCHARME, E. P. 1952. Xyloporosis of citrus. Citrus Mag. [Florida] **14**(5):25–27.

DUCHARME, E. P., and L. C. KNORR. 1954. Vascular pits and pegs associated with disease in citrus. Plant Dis. Reptr.

38:127–42.

FAWCETT, H. S. 1925. Bark diseases of citrus trees in California. Univ. Calif. Agr. Expt. Sta. Bul. **395:** 61 pp.

———. 1929. Citrus psorosis (scaly bark). Calif. Citrog. **14:**235, 238.

———. 1933. New symptoms of psorosis, indicating a virus disease of citrus. Phytopathology **23:**930.

———. 1934. Is psorosis of citrus a virus disease? Phytopathology **24:**659–67.

———. 1936. Citrus diseases and their control. 2nd edition. McGraw-Hill Book Co., Inc., New York and London. 656 pp.

———. 1939. Psorosis in relation to other virus-like effects on citrus. Abstr. Phytopathology **29:**6.

———. 1946. Stubborn disease of citrus, a virosis. Phytopathology **36:**675–77.

FAWCETT, H. S., and A. A. BITANCOURT. 1937. Relatorio sôbre as doenças dos citrus nos estados de Pernambuco, Bahia, São Paulo e Rio Grande do Sul. Rodriguesia **3:**213–36.

———. 1943. Comparative symptomatology of psorosis varieties on citrus in California. Phytopathology **33:**837–64.

FAWCETT, H. S., and L. C. COCHRAN. 1944. A method of inducing bark-shelling for treatment of certain tree diseases. Phytopathology **34:**240–44.

FAWCETT, H. S., and L. J. KLOTZ. 1938. Types and symptoms of psorosis and psorosis-like diseases of citrus. Phytopathology **28:**670.

———. 1939. Infectious variegation of citrus. Phytopathology **29:**911–12.

———. 1948*a*. Citrus diseases and their control. *In:* Batchelor, L. D., and H. J. Webber (eds.). The Citrus Industry. **II:**495–596. Univ. Calif. Press, Berkeley and Los Angeles.

———. 1948*b*. Exocortis of trifoliate orange. Citrus Leaves **28**(4):8.

———. 1948*c*. Stubborn disease, one cause of nonbearing in Navels. Citrus Leaves **28**(3):8–9.

FAWCETT, H. S., and H. A. LEE. 1926. Citrus diseases and their control. McGraw-Hill, New York and London. 582 pp.

FAWCETT, H. S., J. C. PERRY, and J. C. JOHNSTON. 1944. The stubborn disease of citrus. Calif. Citrog. **29:**146–47.

FAWCETT, H. S., and J. M. WALLACE. 1946. Evidence of virus nature of citrus quick decline. Calif. Citrog. **32:**88–89.

FERNANDEZ-VALIELA, M. V. 1959. The present state of tristeza in Argentina. *In:* Wallace, J. M. (ed.). Citrus virus diseases. Pp. 85–89. Univ. Calif. Div. Agr. Sci., Berkeley, Calif.

———. 1961. Citrus virus diseases in Argentina. *In:* Price, W. C. (ed.). Proc. 2nd Conf. Intern. Organ. Citrus Virol. Pp. 231–37. Univ. Fla. Press, Gainesville, Fla.

FERNANDEZ-VALIELA, M. V., C. FORTUGNO, and F. CORIZZI. 1965. Incidence of bud-union crease in citrus trees grafted on *Trifoliate* rootstock in the Delta del Paraná and San Pedro areas of Argentina. *In:* Price, W. C. (ed.). Proc. 3rd Conf. Intern. Organ. Citrus Virol. Pp. 182–86. Univ. Fla. Press, Gainesville, Fla.

FOGUET, J. L., and C. A. OSTE. 1968. Disorders of trifoliate orange rootstock in Tucumán, Argentina. *In:* Childs, J. F. L. (ed.). Proc. 4th Conf. Intern. Organ. Citrus Virol. Pp. 183–89. Univ. Fla. Press, Gainesville, Fla.

FRASER, LILIAN. 1952. Seedling yellows, an unreported virus disease of citrus. Agr. Gaz. N. S. Wales **63:**125-31.

———. 1958. Virus diseases in Australia. Proc. Linn. Soc. N. S. Wales **83**(1):9–19.

———. 1959*a*. The relation of seedling yellows to tristeza. *In:* Wallace, J. M. (ed.). Citrus virus diseases. Pp. 57–62. Univ. Calif. Div. Agr. Sci., Berkeley, Calif.

———. 1959*b*. Woody gall, a suspected virus disease of rough lemon and other citrus varieties. Proc. Linn. Soc. N. S. Wales **84**(3):332–34.

———. 1961. Lemon crinkly leaf virus. *In:* Price, W. C. (ed.). Proc. 2nd Conf. Intern. Organ. Citrus Virol. Pp. 205–10. Univ. Fla. Press, Gainesville, Fla.

———. 1967. Citrus die-back in India. Rept. to Dept. External Affairs, Canberra, Australia. 95 pp.

FRASER, L., and E. C. LEVITT. 1959. Recent advances in the study of exocortis (scaly butt) in Australia. *In:* Wallace, J. M. (ed.). Citrus virus diseases. Pp. 129–33. Univ. Calif. Div. Agr. Sci., Berkeley, Calif.

FRASER, L., E. C. LEVITT, and J. COX. 1961. Relationship between exocortis and stunting of citrus varieties on *Poncirus trifoliata* rootstock. *In:* Price, W. C. (ed.). Proc. 2nd Conf. Intern. Organ. Citrus Virol. Pp. 34–39. Univ. Fla. Press, Gainesville, Fla.

FRASER, L. R., K. LONG, and J. COX. 1968. Stem pitting of grapefruit—field protection by use of mild virus strains. *In:* Childs, J. F. L. (ed.). Proc. 4th Conf. Intern. Organ. Citrus Virol. Pp. 27–31. Univ. Fla. Press, Gainesville, Fla.

FRASER, L. R., and D. SINGH. 1966. Greening virus: a new threat to citrus industry. Punjab Hort. Jour. **6:**104-07.

FRASER, L. R., D. SINGH, S. P. CAPOOR, and T. K. NARIANI. 1966. Greening virus, the likely cause of citrus dieback in India. FAO Plant Prot. Bul. **14:**127–30.

FREZAL, P. 1957. Sur la présence en Algérie de la tristeza et de la xyloporose des citrus. Extr. du procès-verbal de la séance du 20 Mars. Acad. d'Agr. de France. 4 pp.

FROLICH, E. F. 1958. A disorder of Rangpur lime on sweet orange rootstock. Plant Dis. Reptr. **42:**500–01.

FROLICH, E. F., E. C. CALAVAN, J. B. CARPENTER, D. W. CHRISTIANSEN, and C. N. ROISTACHER. 1965. Differences in response of citron selections to exocortis virus infection. *In:* Price, W. C. (ed.). Proc. 3rd Conf. Intern. Organ. Citrus Virol. Pp. 113–18. Univ. Fla. Press, Gainesville, Fla.

FROLICH, E. F., and R. W. HODGSON. 1961. A disorder of Rangpur lime and citron on sweet orange. *In:* Price, W. C. (ed.). Proc. 2nd Conf. Intern. Organ. Citrus Virol. Pp. 166–71. Univ. Fla. Press, Gainesville, Fla.

FUDL-ALLAH, A., E. C. CALAVAN, and E. C. K. IGWEGBE. 1971. Culture of a mycoplasmalike organism associated with stubborn disease of citrus. Abstr. Phytopathology **61:**1321.

FULTON, R. W. 1966. Mechanical transmission of tatter leaf virus from cowpea to citrus. Phytopathology **56:**575.

GARNSEY, S. M. 1964. Detection of tatter leaf virus of citrus in Florida. Proc. Fla. State Hort. Soc. **77:**106–09.

———. 1968. Exocortis virus of citrus can be spread by contaminated tools. Citrus Indus. **49:**13–16.

GARNSEY, S. M., and J. W. JONES. 1967. Mechanical transmission of exocortis virus with contaminated budding tools. Plant Dis. Reptr. **51:**410–13.

GARNSEY, S. M., and J. L. JACKSON, JR. 1975. A destructive outbreak of tristeza in Central Florida. Proc. Fla. State Hort. Soc. **88:**65–69.

GIACOMETTI, D. C., and C. M. ARAUJO. 1965. Cross protection from tristeza in different species of citrus. *In:* Price, W. C. (ed.). Proc. 3rd Conf. Intern. Organ. Citrus Virol. Pp. 14–17. Univ. Fla. Press, Gainesville, Fla.

GRANT, T. J. 1957. Effect of heat treatments on tristeza and psorosis viruses in citrus. Plant Dis. Reptr. **41:**232-34.

GRANT, T. J., and M. K. CORBETT. 1960. Mechanical transmission of the infectious variegation virus of citrus. Nature **188:**519–20.

———. 1961. Mechanical transmission of infectious variegation virus in citrus and noncitrus hosts. *In:* Price, W. C. (ed.). Proc. 2nd Conf. Intern. Organ. Citrus Virol. Pp. 197–204. Univ. Fla. Press, Gainesville, Fla.

GRANT, T. J., and A. S. COSTA. 1951*a*. Studies on transmission of the tristeza virus by the vector, *Aphis citricidus*. Phytopathology **41**:105–13.

———. 1951*b*. A mild strain of the tristeza virus of citrus. Phytopathology **41**:114–22.

GRANT, T. J., G. R. GRIMM, and P. NORMAN. 1959. Symptoms of cachexia in Orlando tangelo, none in sweet lime, and false symptoms associated with purple scale infestations. Plant Dis. Reptr. **43**:1277–79.

GRANT, T. J., S. MOREIRA, and A. S. COSTA. 1957. Observations on abnormal citrus rootstock reactions in Brazil. Plant Dis. Reptr. **41**:743–48.

GRANT, T. J., S. MOREIRA, and A. A. SALIBE. 1960. Report on general aspect of tristeza and stem pitting in citrus varieties in São Paulo, Brazil. Proc. Fla. State Hort. Soc. **73**:12–16.

———. 1961. Citrus variety reaction to tristeza virus in Brazil when used in various rootstock and scion combinations. Plant Dis. Reptr. **45**:416–21.

GRANT, T. J., and H. SCHNEIDER. 1953. Initial evidence of the presence of tristeza or quick decline of citrus in Florida. Phytopathology **43**:51–52.

GRANT, T. J., and P. F. SMITH. 1960. Infectious variegation of citrus found in Florida. Plant Dis. Reptr. **44**:426–29.

GRIMM, G. R., T. J. GRANT, and J. F. L. CHILDS. 1955. A bud union abnormality of rough lemon rootstock with sweet orange scions. Plant Dis. Reptr. **39**:810–11.

HALMA, F. F., K. M. SMOYER, and H. W. SCHWALM. 1944. Quick decline associated with sour rootstocks. Calif. Citrog. **29**:245.

———. 1945. Rootstock in relation to quick decline of citrus. Calif. Citrog. **30**:150–51.

HOFMEYER, J. D. J., and P. C. J. OBERHOLZER. 1948. Genetic aspects associated with the propagation of citrus. Farming So. Africa **23**:201–08.

HOOPER, G. R. 1968. Unpublished Ph.D. thesis on file in the Dept. of Plant Pathology, University of California, Riverside, Calif.

HOOPER, G. R., and H. SCHNEIDER. 1969. The anatomy of tumors induced on citrus by citrus vein-enation virus. Amer. Jour. Bot. **56**:238–47.

HUGHES, W. A., and C. A. LISTER. 1949. Lime disease in the Gold Coast. Nature **164**:880.

———. 1953. Lime dieback in the Gold Coast, a virus disease of the lime, *Citrus aurantifolia* (Christm.) Swingle. Jour. Hort. Sci. **28**:131–40.

IGWEGBE, E. C. K. 1970. Studies on the nature and transmission of the causal agent of stubborn of citrus: Association of a mycoplasmalike organism with the disease. Ph.D. thesis on file at the Dept. of Plant Pathology, University of California, Riverside, Calif.

IGWEGBE, E. C. K., and E. C. CALAVAN. 1970. Occurrence of mycoplasmalike bodies in phloem of stubborn-infected citrus seedlings. Phytopathology **60**:1525–26.

———. 1973. Effect of tetracycline antibiotics on symptom development of stubborn disease and infectious variegation of citrus seedlings. Phytopathology **63**:1044–48.

INSTITUT FRANÇAIS DE RÉCHERCHES FRUITIÈRES OUTRE-MER. 1963. Maladies à virus des Agrumes: Analyses des publications de 1926 a 1962. Paris 16e. 155 pp.

IZAWA, H. 1966. Investigations on withering disease of *Citrus unshiu* Marcov. in Gamagori District, Aichi Prefecture. Bul. Aichi Hort. Expt. Sta. **5**:1–9.

JAMOUSSI, B. 1961. Citrus virus diseases in Tunisia. *In:* Price, W. C. (ed.). Proc. 2nd Conf. Intern. Organ. Citrus Virol. Pp. 253–55. Univ. Fla. Press, Gainesville, Fla.

KALOOSTIAN, G. H., G. N. OLDFIELD, H. D. PIERCE, E. C. CALAVAN, A. L. GRANETT, G. L. RANA, and D. J. GUMPF. 1975. Leafhopper may be a natural vector of citrus stubborn disease. Calif. Agr. **29**(2):14–15.

KALOOSTIAN, G. H., and H. D. PIERCE. 1972. Note on *Scaphytopius nitridus* in California. Jour. Econ. Entomol. **65**:880.

KISHI, K. 1967. Studies on indicator plants for citrus viruses. IV. On the properties of the sap-transmissible virus associated with satsuma dwarf and some other virus-like diseases. Bul. Hort. Res. Sta. Japan., (Series A) **6**:115–31.

———. 1968. Studies on the indicator plants for citrus viruses. V. Retransmission of the causal virus of satsuma dwarf from herbaceous host to citrus. Ann. Phytopathol. Soc. Japan **34**:224–30.

———. 1972. Accentuation of satsuma dwarf symptoms by seedling-yellows virus. *In:* Price, W. C. (ed.). Proc. 5th Conf. Intern. Organ. Citrus Virol. Pp. 82–84. Univ. Fla. Press, Gainesville, Fla.

KISHI, K., and S. TANAKA. 1964. Studies on indicator plants for citrus viruses. II. Mechanical transmission of the virus causing satsuma dwarf to sesame (*Sesamum indicum* L.). Ann. Phytopath. Soc. Japan **29**:142–48.

KITAJIMA, E. W., and A. S. COSTA. 1968. Electron microscopy of the tristeza virus in citrus leaf tissues. *In:* Childs, J. F. L. (ed.). Proc. 4th Conf. Intern. Organ. Citrus Virol. Pp. 59–64. Univ. Fla. Press, Gainesville, Fla.

KITAJIMA, E. W., D. M. SILVA, A. R. OLIVEIRA, G. W. MÜLLER, and A. S. COSTA. 1964. Thread-like particles associated with tristeza disease of citrus. Nature **201**:1011–12.

———. 1965. Electron microscopical investigations on tristeza. *In:* Price, W. C. (ed.). Proc. 3rd Conf. Intern. Organ. Citrus Virol. Pp. 1–9. Univ. Fla. Press, Gainesville, Fla.

KLOTZ, L. J. 1959. On infectious chlorosis of citrus [English translation of note by M. Trabut in Compt. Rend. Acad. Sci., Paris 156:243–44, 1913] Calif. Dept. Agr. Bul. **48**:195–96.

KLOTZ, L. J., and H. S. FAWCETT. 1941. Color handbook of citrus diseases. Univ. Calif. Press, Berkeley and Los Angeles. 90 pp.

KNORR, L. C. 1953. Transmission trials with crinkle-scurf of citrus. Plant Dis. Reptr. **37**:503–07.

KNORR, L. C., and H. N. BEÑATENA. 1952. Xyloporosis en mandarino común de Concordia. IDIA [Buenos Aires] **5**(57):19–20.

KNORR, L. C., and J. F. L. CHILDS. 1957. Occurrence of woodpocket (blotch), chimeric breakdown, and endoxerosis in Florida, with particular reference to Tahiti lime. Proc. Fla. State Hort. Soc. **70**:75–81.

KNORR, L. C., G. MALAGUTI, and D. SERPA. 1960. Descubrimiento de la "tristeza" de las citricas en Venezuela. Agron. Trop. [Maracay, Venezuela] **10**(1):3–12.

KNORR, L. C., and W. C. PRICE. 1959. Fovea—a disease of the Murcott. Citrus Mag. **22**(1):16–19, 26.

LAFLÈCHE, D., and J. M. BOVÉ. 1970*a*. Mycoplasmes dans les agrumes attients de "greening," de "stubborn," ou de maladies similaires. Fruits **25**:455–65.

———. 1970*b*. Structures de type mycoplasme dans les feuilles d'orangers attients de la maladie du "greening." Compt. Rend. Acad. Sci. **270**:1915–17.

LAIRD, E. F., and L. G. WEATHERS. 1961. *Aphis gossypii*, a vector of citrus vein-enation virus. Plant Dis. Reptr. **45**:877.

LAURENT, R. 1960. Intéressantes communications de M. Chapot sur l'impietratura" au Maroc et sur la "Tristeza" en Espagne et ses conséquences. Fruits Primeurs **30**:246–49.

LEE, H. A. 1921. The relation of stocks to mottled leaf of citrus trees. Philipp. Jour. Sci. **18**:85–95.

LEE, I. M., G. CARTIA, E. C. CALAVAN, and G. H. KALOOSTIAN. 1973. Citrus stubborn disease organism cultured from beet leafhopper. Calif. Agr. **27**(11):14–15.

MCCLEAN, A. P. D. 1950. Possible identity of three citrus diseases. Nature **165**:767–68.

———. 1954. Citrus vein-enation virus. So. African Jour. Sci. **50**:147–51.

———. 1960. Seedling yellows in South African citrus trees. So. African Jour. Agr. Sci. **3**:259–79.

———. 1963. The tristeza virus complex: its variability in field-grown citrus in South Africa. So. African Jour. Agr. Sci. **6**:303–32.

———. 1970. Greening disease of sweet orange: its transmission in propagative parts and distribution in partially diseased trees. Phytophylactica **2**:263–68.

MCCLEAN, A. P. D., and A. H. ENGELBRECHT. 1958. Xyloporosis, cachexia, and abnormal bud unions in South Africa citrus trees. So. African Jour. Agr. Sci. **1**:349–414.

MCCLEAN, A. P. D., and P. C. J. OBERHOLZER. 1965*a*. Greening disease of the sweet orange: evidence that it is caused by a transmissible virus. So. African Jour. Agr. Sci. **8**:253–76.

———. 1965*b*. Citrus psylla, a vector of the greening disease of sweet orange. So. African Jour. Agr. Sci. **8**:297–98.

MCCLEAN, A. P. D., and R. E. SCHWARZ. 1970. Greening or "blotchy-mottle" disease of citrus. Phytophylactica **2**:177–94.

MCCLEAN, A. P. D., R. E. SCHWARZ, and P. C. J. OBERHOLZER. 1969. Greening disease of citrus in South Africa. *In:* Chapman, H. D. (ed.). Proc. First Intern. Citrus Symp. **3**:1421–25. Univ. Calif., Riverside, Calif.

MCCLEAN, A. P. D., and J. E. VAN DER PLANK. 1955. The role of seedling yellows and stem pitting in tristeza of citrus. Phytopathology **45**:222–24.

MAJORANA, G. 1963*a*. Transmissione sperimentale della "psorosi a foglia bollosa" e della "variegatura infettiva" su diverse specie e cultivar di agrumi. Riv. Patol. Veg., Serie III, **3**:225–32.

———. 1963*b*. Richerche sulla "psorosi a foglia bollosa" e sulla "variegatura infettiva" degli agrumi. Riv. Patol. Veg., Serie III, **3**:251–70.

MAJORANA, G., and G. P. MARTELLI. 1968. Comparison of citrus infectious variegation and citrus crinkly-leaf virus isolates from Italy and California. *In:* Childs, J. F. L. (ed.). Proc. 4th Conf. Intern. Organ. Citrus Virol. Pp. 273–80. Univ. Fla. Press, Gainesville, Fla.

MAJORANA, G., and G. SCARAMUZZI. 1963. Studies on Petri's variegation of sour orange leaves. *In:* Price, W. C. (ed.). Proc. 3rd Conf. Intern. Organ. Citrus Virol. Pp. 254–59. Univ. Fla. Press, Gainesville, Fla.

MAJORANA, G., and R. E. SCHWARZ. 1972. Studies on two mechanically transmissible citrus viruses. *In:* Price, W. C. (ed.). Proc. 5th Conf. Intern. Organ. Citrus Virol. Pp. 188–92. Univ. Fla. Press, Gainesville, Fla.

MARKHAM, P. G., R. TOWNSEND, M. BAR-JOSEPH, M. J. DANIELS, A. PLASKITT, and B. M. MEDDINS. 1974. Spiroplasmas are the causal agents of citrus little-leaf disease. Ann. Appl. Biol. **78**:49–57.

MARTELLI, G. P., G. MAJORANA, and M. RUSSO. 1968. Investigations on the purification of citrus variegation virus. *In:* Childs, J. F. L. (ed.). Proc. 4th Conf. Intern. Organ. Citrus Virol. Pp. 267–72. Univ. Fla. Press, Gainesville, Fla.

MARTINEZ, A. L., D. M. NORA, and A. L. ARMEDILLA. 1970. Suppression of symptoms of citrus greening disease in the Philippines by treatment with tetracycline antibiotics. Plant Dis. Reptr. **54**:1007–09.

MARTINEZ, A. L., D. M. NORA, and W. C. PRICE. 1971. Observations on greening in the Philippines. Animal Husbandry and Agr. Jour. (Philippines) **6**:21–22.

MARTINEZ, A. L., D. M. NORA, and N. M. SEBASTIAN. 1965. The prevalence of seedling yellows virus disease of citrus in the Philippines as detected by indexing procedures. Abstr. Jour. Philipp. Phytopathology **1**:36.

MARTINEZ, A. L., and J. M. WALLACE. 1964. Studies on transmission of the virus components of citrus seedling yellows by *Aphis gossypii*. Plant Dis. Reptr. **48**:131–33.

———. 1967. Citrus leaf-mottle-yellows disease in the Philippines and transmission of the causal virus by a psyllid, *Diaphorina citri*. Plant Dis. Reptr. **51**:692–95.

———. 1968. Studies on leaf-mottle-yellows disease of citrus in the Philippines. *In:* Childs, J. F. L. (ed.). Proc. 4th Conf. Intern. Organ. Citrus Virol. Pp. 167–76. Univ. Fla. Press, Gainesville, Fla.

———. 1969. Citrus greening disease in the Philippines. *In:* Chapman, H. D. (ed.). Proc. First Intern. Citrus Symp. **3**:1427–31. Univ. Calif., Riverside, Calif.

MARTYN, E. B. 1954. Virus dieback disease of limes and other citrus in the Gold Coast. Rept. Commonwealth Mycol. Conf. **5**:144–45.

MATSUMOTO, T., and H. J. SU. 1966. Likubin or Huanglungpin, citrus virus disease closely related to tristeza. Jour. Agr. Assoc. China (Taiwan), New Series No. **56**:76–86.

MATSUMOTO, T., H. J. SU, and K. Y. CHIU. 1961. Studies on the so-called "likubin" or decline of citrus trees. Monthly reports Nos. 34 and 38. National Taiwan University Phytopathological Laboratory.

MATSUMOTO, T., H. J. SU, and T. T. LO. 1968. Likubin. *In:* Childs, J. F. L. (ed.). Indexing procedures for 15 virus diseases of citrus. U. S. Dept. Agr. Handbook **333**:63–67.

MATSUMOTO, T., M. C. WANG, and H. J. SU. 1961. Studies on likubin. *In:* Price, W. C. (ed.). Proc. 2nd Conf. Intern. Organ. Citrus Virol. Pp. 121–25. Univ. Fla. Press, Gainesville, Fla.

MENEGHINI, M. 1946. Sôbre a natureza e transmissibilidade do doencia "tristeza" dos citrus. O. Biologico **12**:285–87.

———. 1948. Experiências de transmissão da doenca "tristeza" dos citros pelo poulgão preto da laranjeira. O. Biologico **15**:115–18.

MIYAKAWA, T. 1969. Susceptibility of citrus spp. and other related plants to the satsuma dwarf virus. Ann. Phytopathological Soc. Japan **35**:224–33.

———. 1972. Reaction of some citrus and herbaceous plants to satsuma dwarf virus strains. *In:* Price, W. C. (ed.). Proc. 5th Conf. Intern. Organ. Citrus Virol. Pp. 65–71. Univ. Fla. Press, Gainesville, Fla.

MOREIRA, S. 1938. Xyloporosis. Hadar [Tel-Aviv] **11**:234–37.

———. 1942. Observações sôbre a "tristeza" dos citrus ou "podridão das radicelas." O. Biologico **8**:269–72.

———. 1955. A moléstia "exocortis" e o cavalo de limoeiro cravo. Rev. Agr. [Piracicaba] **30**:99–112.

———. 1961. A quick field test for exocortis. *In:* Price, W. C. (ed.). Proc. 2nd Conf. Intern. Organ. Citrus Virol. Pp. 40–42. Univ. Fla. Press, Gainesville, Fla.

MÜELLER G. W., and A. S. COSTA. Further evidence on protective interference in citrus tristeza. *In:* Childs, J. F.

L. (ed.). Proc. 4th Conf. Intern. Organ. Citrus Virol. Pp. 71–82. Univ. Fla. Press, Gainesville, Fla.

———. 1972. Reduction in yield of Galego lime avoided by preimmunization with mild strains of tristeza virus. *In:* Price, W. C. (ed.). Proc. 5th Conf. Intern. Organ. Citrus Virol. Pp. 171–75. Univ. Fla. Press, Gainesville, Fla.

NAKAMURA, S. 1965. On the dwarf of Kawanonatsukan. Kaiu Engei. **18:**38–40.

NARIANI, T. K., S. P. RAYCHAUDHURI, and R. B. BHALLA. 1967. Greening virus of citrus in India. Indian Phytopath. **20:**146–50.

NORA, D. N. 1961. Initial evidence of the presence of tisteza disease of citrus in the Philippines. Rept. to Philipp. Bur. Plant Indus. Seminar, Manila. 11 pp. (Mimeographed.)

NORA, D. M., and J. G. BALDIA. 1962. Progress studies on tristeza of citrus in Batangas. Paper read at First Science Congress, Bur. Plant Industry, Lamao Expt. Sta. Philippines. 12 pp. (Mimeographed.)

NORMAN, G. G. 1965. The incidence of exocortis virus in Florida citrus. *In:* Price, W. C. (ed.) Proc. 3rd Conf. Intern. Organ. Citrus Virol. Pp. 124–27. Univ. Fla. Press, Gainesville, Fla.

NORMAN, G. G., R. R. NIXON, JR., L. HORNE, and J. T. GRANTHAM. 1959. Symptoms indicating xyloporosis in uninoculated Orlando tangelo seedlings. Plant Dis. Reptr. **43:**1120–21.

NORMAN, G., W. C. PRICE, T. J. GRANT, and H. BURNETT. 1961. Ten years of tristeza in Florida. Proc. Fla. State Hort. Soc. **74:**107–11.

NORMAN, P. A., and J. F. L. CHILDS. 1963. Attempted transmission of xyloporosis of citrus with insects. Proc. Fla. State Hort. Soc. **76:**48–50.

NORMAN, P. A., and T. J. GRANT. 1954. Preliminary studies of aphid transmission of tristeza virus in Florida. Proc. Fla. State Hort. Soc. **66:**89–92.

———. 1956. Transmission of tristeza virus by aphids in Florida. Proc. Fla. State Hort. Soc. **69:**38–42.

———. 1961. Variations in aphid transmission of tristeza virus. *In:* Price, W. C. (ed.). Proc. 2nd Conf. Intern. Organ. Citrus Virol. Pp. 126–31. Univ. Fla. Press, Gainesville, Fla.

NOUR-ELDIN, F. 1956. Phloem discoloration of sweet orange. Phytopathology **46:**238–39.

———. 1959. Citrus virus disease research in Egypt. *In:* Wallace, J. M. (ed.). Citrus virus diseases. Pp. 219–27. Univ. Calif. Div. Agr. Sci., Berkeley, Calif.

———. 1967. A tumor-inducing agent associated with citrus trees infected with safargali (stubborn) disease in the United Arab Republic. Phytopathology **57:**108–13.

———. 1968. Gummy bark of sweet orange. *In:* Childs, J. F. L. (ed.). Indexing procedures for 15 virus diseases of citrus trees. U. S. Dept. Agr. Handbook **333:**50-53.

NYLAND, G., and W. J. MOLLER. 1973. Control of pear decline with a tetracycline. Plant Dis. Reptr. **57:**634–37.

OBERHOLZER, P. C. J. 1947. The present status of citrus nutrition in South Africa. So. Africa Dept. Agr. Citrus Nutr. Bul. **271:** 14 pp.

———. 1959. Host reactions of citrus to tristeza virus in South Africa. *In:* Wallace, J. M. (ed.). Citrus virus diseases. Pp. 35–43. Univ. Calif. Div. Agr. Sci., Berkeley, Calif.

OBERHOLZER, P. C. J., and J. D. J. HOFMEYER. 1955. The nature and control of clonal senility in commercial varieties of citrus in South Africa. Bul. Faculty Agr., Univ. Pretoria, Pretoria, South Africa. 46 pp.

OBERHOLZER, P. C. J., I. MATHEWS, and S. F. STIEMIE. 1949. The decline of grapefruit trees in South Africa: a preliminary report on so-called "stem pitting." So. Africa Dept. Agr. Sci. Bul. 297.

OBERHOLZER, P. C. J., D. F. A. VON STADEN, and W. J. BASSON. 1965. Greening disease of sweet orange in South Africa. *In:* Price, W. C. (ed.). Proc. 3rd Conf. Intern. Organ. Citrus Virol. Pp. 213–19. Univ. Fla. Press, Gainesville, Fla.

OLSON, E. O. 1952. Investigations of citrus rootstock diseases in Texas. Proc. Rio Grande Valley Hort. Inst. **6:**28–34.

———. 1954. Some bark and bud-union disorders of mandarin and mandarin-hybrid rootstocks in Texas citrus plantings. Proc. Amer. Soc. Hort. Sci. **63:**131–36.

———. 1956. Mild and severe strains of tristeza virus in Texas. Phytopathology **46:**336–41.

———. 1958. Bud-union crease, a citrus disorder associated with some kumquat-hybrid rootstocks and scions. Jour. Rio Grande Valley Hort. Soc. **12:**27–34.

———. 1960. Xyloporosis (cachexia or fovea) disease of Murcott honey "orange" in Texas. Jour. Rio Grande Valley Hort. Soc. **14:**26–28.

———. 1965. Evidence that xyloporosis does not pass through seeds of Palestine sweet lime. *In:* Price, W. C. (ed.). Proc. 3rd Conf. Intern. Organ. Citrus Virol. Pp. 86–89. Univ. Fla. Press, Gainesville, Fla.

OLSON, E. O., M. COHEN, and T. RODRIGUEZ. 1956. Tangerine decline in the state of Nuevo Leon, Mexico. Jour. Rio Grande Valley Hort. Soc. **10:**34–37.

OLSON, E. O., and J. R. MCDONALD. 1954. Tristeza in satsuma varieties in Texas. Plant Dis. Reptr. **38:**439–41.

OLSON, E. O., and B. ROGERS. 1969. Effects of temperature on expression and transmission of stubborn disease of citrus. Plant Dis. Reptr. **53:**45–49.

OLSON, E. O., and A. V. SHULL. 1956. Exocortis and xyloporosis: bud-transmission virus diseases of Rangpur and other mandarin-lime rootstocks. Plant Dis. Reptr. **40:**939–46.

———. 1962. Size and yield of 12 year-old Valencia orange trees on various rootstocks in presence or absence of exocortis and xyloporosis viruses. Jour. Rio Grande Valley Hort. Soc. **16:**40–43.

OLSON, E. O., A. SHULL, and G. BUFFINGTON. 1961. Evaluation of indicators for xyloporosis and exocortis in Texas. *In:* Price, W. C. (ed.). Proc. 2nd Conf. Intern. Organ. Citrus Virol. Pp. 159–65. Univ. Fla. Press, Gainesville, Fla.

OLSON, E. O., and B. SLEETH. 1954. Tristeza virus carried by some Meyer lemon trees in Texas. Proc. Rio Grande Valley Hort. Inst. **8:**84–88.

OLSON, E. O., B. SLEETH, and A. V. SHULL. 1958. Prevalence of viruses causing xyloporosis (cachexia) and exocortis (Rangpur lime disease) in apparently healthy citrus trees in Texas. Jour. Rio Grande Valley Hort. Soc. **12:**35–43.

OMORI, H., and H. MATSUMOTO. 1972. The cause of stem pitting and small fruit in Natsudaidai trees. *In:* Price, W. C. (ed.). Proc. 5th Conf. Intern. Organ. Citrus Virol. Pp. 143–46. Univ. Fla. Press, Gainesville, Fla.

PAPASOLOMONTOS, A. 1961. Preliminary report on a new disorder of grapefruit. Countryman [Nicosia]. Nov.-Dec. Pp. 15–16.

———. 1965. The present status of impietratura, a citrus disease in Cyprus. Plant Dis. Reptr. **49:**111–13.

———. 1969. A report on impietratura disease of citrus, its distribution and importance. *In:* Chapman, H. D. (ed.). Proc. First Intern. Citrus Symp. **3:**1457–62. Univ. Calif., Riverside, Calif.

PAPASOLOMONTOS, A., and C. V. ECONOMIDES. 1967. Effect of rootstock on the incidence of impietratura diseased grapefruit fruits. Plant Dis. Reptr. **51**:684–86.

PAPPO, S., and I. BAUMAN. 1969. A survey of the present status of little-leaf (stubborn) disease in Israel. *In:* Chapman, H. D. (ed.). Proc. First Intern. Citrus Symp. **3**:1439–44. Univ. Calif., Riverside, Calif.

PAPPO, S., I. BAUMAN, and Y. OREN. 1967. Impietratura of citrus fruits. Alom Hamotea **10**:508–15.

PAPPO, S., and Y. OREN. 1974. Observations on impietratura of grapefruit and Shamouti in Israel. *In:* Weathers, L. G., and M. Cohen (eds.). Proc. 6th Conf. Intern. Organ. Citrus Virol. Pp. 127–30. Univ. Calif. Div. Agr. Sci., Richmond, Calif.

PATT, J. 1964. Observations on the appearance of the "little leaf" (stubborn) disease of citrus. Plant Dis. Reptr. **48**:761–62.

PETRI, L. 1931. Variegatura infettiva delle foglie di "citrus vulgaris" Risso. Boll. R. Staz. Patol. Veg. **11**:105–14.

PRICE, W. C. (ed.). 1961. Proc. 2nd Conf. Intern. Organ. Citrus Virol. Univ. Fla. Press, Gainesville, Fla. 265 pp.

——— (ed.). 1965*a*. Proc. 3rd Conf. Intern. Organ. Citrus Virol. Univ. Fla. Press, Gainesville, Fla. 319 pp.

———. 1965*b*. Transmission of psorosis virus by dodder. *In:* Price, W. C. (ed.). Proc. 3rd Conf. Intern. Organ. Citrus Virol. Pp. 162–66. Univ. Fla. Press, Gainesville, Fla.

———. 1966. Flexuous rods in phloem cells of lime plants infected with citrus tristeza virus. Virology **29**:285–94.

PUJOL, A. R. 1966. Transmission de psorosis a traves de la semilla de citrange Troyer. INTA, Estacion Exp. Agropecuaria Concordia Serie Technica No. 10. 4 pp.

PUJOL, A. R., and H. N. BEÑATENA. 1965. The study of psorsis in Concordia, Argentina. *In:* Price, W. C. (ed.). Proc. 3rd Conf. Intern. Organ. Citrus Virol. Pp. 170–74. Univ. Fla. Press, Gainesville, Fla.

RANA, G. L., G. H. KALOOSTIAN, G. N. OLDFIELD, A. L. GRANETT, E. C. CALAVAN, H. D. PIERCE, I. M. LEE, and D. J. GUMPF. 1975. Acquisition of *Spiroplasma citri* through membranes by homopterous insects. Phytopathology **65**:1143–45.

RAYCHAUDHURI, S. P., T. K. NARIANI, and V. C. LELE. 1967. Citrus dieback complex: a serious threat to citrus industry in India. Abstracts Intern. Symp. Subtrop. and Trop. Hort. Pp. 54–55. I.A.R.I., New Delhi.

———. 1969. Citrus die-back problem in India. *In:* Chapman, H. D. (ed.). Proc. First Intern. Citrus Symp. **3**:1433–37. Univ. Calif., Riverside, Calif.

REDDY, G. S. 1965. Citrus decline in India with special reference to virus infection in different stionic combinations. *In:* Price, W. C. (ed.). Proc. 3rd Conf. Intern. Organ. Citrus Virol. P. 225. Univ. Fla. Press, Gainesville, Fla.

REDDY, G. S., and P. GOVINDA RAO. 1961. Is there tristeza in Andhra Pradesh, India? *In:* Price, W. C. (ed.). Proc. 2nd Conf. Intern. Organ. Citrus Virol. Pp. 132–35. Univ. Fla. Press, Gainesville, Fla.

REICHERT, I. 1930. Diseases new to citrus, found in Palestine. Phytopathology **20**:999–1002.

———. 1952. Xyloporosis in citrus. Proc. 13th Intern. Hort. Congr. [London] **2**:1275–80.

———. 1955. New light on xyloporosis and tristeza. Proc. 14th Intern. Hort. Congr. [Netherlands] **3**:1413–22.

———. 1959. A collection of reports on the results of EPPO mission on citrus viruses carried out in seven Mediterranean countries. Rehovot, Israel, July 1959. 110 pp. (Mimeographed.)

REICHERT, I., and A. BENTAL. 1957. Decline of satsuma mandarin oranges in Israel. FAO Plant Prot. Bul. **5**:156–58.

———. 1961. On the problem of xyloporosis and cachexia diseases of mandarin. Plant Dis. Reptr. **45**:356–61.

REICHERT, I., A. BENTAL, and O. GINSBURG. 1965. Bud-union constriction disorder of grapefruit on sour orange in Israel. *In:* Price, W. C. (ed.). Proc. 3rd Conf. Intern. Organ. Citrus Virol. Pp. 192–98. Univ. Fla. Press, Gainesville, Fla.

REICHERT, I., A. BENTAL, and I. YOFFE. 1956. Transmission experiments on the tristeza and xyloporosis diseases of citrus. Ktavim [Israel] **6**:69–75.

REICHERT, I., and E. HELLINGER. 1930. Internal decline physiological disease of citrus fruits new to Palestine. Hadar [Tel-Aviv] **3**:220–24.

REICHERT, I., and J. PERLBERGER. 1931. Little leaf disease of citrus trees and its causes. Hadar [Tel-Aviv] **4**(8):3–8.

———. 1934. Xyloporosis, the new citrus disease. Jewish Agency for Palestine Agr. Exp. Sta. [Rehovot] Bul. **12**:1–50.

REICHERT, I., and E. WINOCOUR. 1956. Inverse pitting in xyloporosis and tristeza. Phytopathology **46**:527–29.

REICHERT, I., I. YOFFE, and A. BENTAL. 1953. Shamouti orange on various rootstocks and its relation to xyloporosis. Palestine Jour. Bot. [Rehovot] **8**:163–84.

REITZ, H. J., and L. C. KNORR. 1957. Occurrence of Rangpur lime disease in Florida and its concurrence with exocortis. Plant Dis. Reptr. **41**:235–40.

ROISTACHER, C. N., R. L. BLUE, and E. C. CALAVAN. 1969. Preventing transmission of exocortis virus. Calif. Citrog. **54**:91, 100, 102.

———. 1973. A new test for citrus cachexia. Citrograph. **58**:261–62.

ROISTACHER, C. N., and E. C. CALAVAN. 1965. Cross-protection studies with strains of concave gum and psorosis viruses. *In:* Price, W. C. (ed.). Proc. 3rd Conf. Intern. Organ. Citrus Virol. Pp. 154–61. Univ. Fla. Press, Gainesville, Fla.

———. 1972. Heat tolerance of preconditioned citrus budwood for virus inactivation. *In:* Price, W. C. (ed.). Proc. 5th Conf. Intern. Organ. Citrus Virol. Pp. 256–61. Univ. Fla. Press, Gainesville, Fla.

ROISTACHER, C. N., L. NAVARRO, and T. MURASHIGE. 1976. Recovery of citrus selections free of several viruses by shoot tip grafting *in vitro*. *In:* Calavan, E. C. (ed.). Proc. 7th Conf. Intern. Organ. Citrus Virol. Pp. 186–193. Dept. Plant Path. Univ. of Cal., Riverside, Calif.

ROSSETTI, VICTORIA. 1961. Testing for exocortis. *In:* Price, W. C. (ed.). Proc. 2nd Conf. Intern. Organ. Citrus Virol. Pp. 43–49. Univ. Fla. Press, Gainesville, Fla.

ROSSETTI, VICTORIA, J. T. NAKADAIRA, and C. ROESSING. 1965. Experiments on heating budwood to eliminate exocortis virus. *In:* Price, W. C. (ed.). Proc. 3rd Conf. Intern. Organ. Citrus Virol. Pp. 268–71. Univ. Fla. Press, Gainesville, Fla.

RUGGIERI, G. 1955. Le arance impietrate. Rivista Agrumicoltura **1**(2):65–69.

———. 1960. Present position of citrus virus diseases in Italy. Rept. of Intern. Conf. Virus Diseases of Citrus. Acireale, Sicily, Sept., 1959. E.P.P.O., Paris.

———. 1961. Observations and research on impietratura. *In:* Price, W. C. (ed.). Proc. 2nd Conf. Intern. Organ. Citrus Virol. Pp. 182–86. Univ. Fla. Press, Gainesville, Fla.

———. 1965. On the impietratura of grapefruit. *In:* Price, W. C. (ed.). Proc. 3rd Conf. Intern. Organ. Citrus Virol. Pp. 179–81. Univ. Fla. Press, Gainesville, Fla.

RUSSO, F., and L. J. KLOTZ. 1963. Tarocco pit. Calif. Citrog. **49**:221–22.

SADAI, K. 1963. Studies on the insect vector of Hassaku dwarf. Chyugoku Nogyo Kenkyu **27**:76–77.

SAGLIO, P., D. LAFLÈCHE, C. BONISSOL, and J. M. BOVÉ. 1971a. Isolement et culture in vitro des mycoplasmes associes au 'stubborn' des agrumes et leur observation au microscope electronique. Compt. Rend. Acad. Sci. Paris, Serie D **272**:1387–90.

———. 1971b. Isolement, culture et observation au microscope electronique des structure de type mycoplasme associes à la maladie du Stubborn des agrumes et leur comparaison avec le structures observees dans le cas de la maladie du Greening des agrumes. Physiol. Veg. **9**:569–82.

SAGLIO, P., M. L'HOSPITAL, D. LAFLÈCHE, G. DUPONT, J. M. BOVÉ, J. G. TULLY, and E. A. FREUNDT. 1973. *Spiroplasma citri* gen. and sp. n.: A mycoplasma-like organism associated with "stubborn" disease of citrus. Intern. Jour. Syst. Bacteriol. **23**:191–04.

SALIBE, A. A. 1959. Leaf curl—a transmissible virus disease of citrus. Plant Dis. Reptr. **43**:1081–83.

———. 1961a. Contribuição ao estudo da doenca exocorte dos citros. Thesis for Doctor of Agronomy on file at School of Agricultura da Universidade de São Paulo.

———. 1961b. Scion-rootstock incompatibilities in Brazil. *In:* Price, W. C. (ed.). Proc. 2nd Conf. Intern. Organ. Citrus Virol. Pp. 172–76. Univ. Fla. Press, Gainesville, Fla.

———. 1965a. A quick test for xyloporosis virus. *In:* Price, W. C. (ed.). Proc. 3rd Conf. Intern. Organ. Citrus Virol. Pp. 95–98. Univ. Fla. Press, Gainesville, Fla.

———. 1965b. Susceptibility of citrus varieties to leaf-curl virus. *In:* Price, W. C. (ed.). Proc. 3rd Conf. Intern. Organ. Citrus Virol. Pp. 175–78. Univ. Fla. Press, Gainesville, Fla.

SALIBE, A., and R. E. CORTEZ. 1966. Studies on the leaf mottling disease of citrus in the Philippines. FAO Plant Prot. Bul. **14**:141–44.

———. 1968. Leaf mottling—a transmissible disease of citrus. *In:* Childs, J. F. L. (ed.). Proc. 4th Conf. Intern. Organ. Citrus Virol. Pp. 131–36. Univ. Fla. Press, Gainesville, Fla.

SALIBE, A. A., and S. MOREIRA. 1965a. Seed transmission of exocortis virus. *In:* Price, W. C. (ed.). Proc. 3rd Conf. Intern. Organ. Citrus Virol. Pp. 139–42. Univ. Fla. Press, Gainesville, Fla.

———. 1965b. Reaction of types of citrus as scion and rootstock to xyloporosis virus. *In:* Price, W. C. (ed.). Proc. 3rd Conf. Intern. Organ. Citrus Virol. Pp. 70–75. Univ. Fla. Press, Gainesville, Fla.

SASAKI, A. 1972. Comparison of hassaku dwarf and seedling yellows viruses. *In:* Price, W. C. (ed.). Proc. 5th Conf. Intern. Organ. Citrus Virol. Pp. 162–66. Univ. Fla. Press, Gainesville, Fla.

SCARAMUZZI, G., and A. CATARA. 1968. Studies on sour orange stem-pitting in Sicily. *In:* Childs, J. F. L. (ed.). Proc. 4th Conf. Intern. Organ. Citrus Virol. Pp. 201–05. Univ. Fla. Press, Gainesville, Fla.

SCARAMUZZI, G., A. CATARA, and G. CARTIA. 1968. Investigations on impietratura. *In:* Childs, J. F. L. (ed.). Proc. 4th Conf. Intern. Organ. Citrus Virol. Pp. 197–200. Univ. Fla. Press, Gainesville, Fla.

SCHNEIDER, H. 1946. A progress report on quick decline studies: histological studies (Part III). Calif. Citrog. **31**:198–99.

———. 1947. Quick decline and tristeza similarities. Citrus Leaves **27**(8):10–11.

———. 1952a. Necrosis of sieve tubes below bud-union of lemon trees on sour orange rootstock. Citrus Leaves **32**(3):10–11, 35, 37.

———. 1952b. Bud-union problems of lemon trees on sour orange rootstock. Calif. Citrog. **37**:208–12.

———. 1954. Anatomy of bark of bud-union, trunk, and roots of quick-decline-affected sweet orange trees on sour orange rootstock. Hilgardia **22**:567–601.

———. 1956. Decline of lemon trees on sour orange rootstock. Calif. Citrog. **41**:117–20.

———. 1957. Chronic decline, a tristeza-like bud-union disorder of orange trees. Phytopathology **47**:279–84.

———. 1959. The anatomy of tristeza-virus-infected citrus. *In:* Wallace, J. M. (ed.). Citrus virus diseases. Pp. 73–84. Univ. Calif. Div. Agr. Sci., Berkeley, Calif.

———. 1966. South Africa's greening disease and Morocco's stubborn disease. Calif. Citrog. **51**:299–305.

SCHNEIDER, H., J. W. CAMERON, R. K. SOOST, and E. C. CALAVAN. 1961. Classifying certain diseases as inherited. *In:* Price, W. C. (ed.). Proc. 2nd Conf. Intern. Organ. Citrus Virol. Pp. 15–21. Univ. Fla. Press, Gainesville, Fla.

SCHWARZ, R. E. 1964. An insect-transmissible virus trapped on sweet orange seedlings in orchards where greening disease is common. So. Africa Jour. Agr. Sci. **7**:885–90.

———. 1965. A fluorescent substance present in tissues of greening-affected sweet oranges. So. Africa Jour. Agr. Sci. **8**:1177–80.

———. 1967. Results of a greening survey on sweet orange in the major citrus growing areas of the Republic of South Africa. So. Africa Jour. Agr. Sci. **10**:471–76.

———. 1970. A multiple sprouting disease of citrus. Plant Dis. Reptr. **54**:1003–07.

———. 1971. The value of Orlando tangelo as an indicator for the graft-transmissible gum-pocket disease of *Poncirus trifoliata*. Phytophylactica **3**:151–54.

SCHWARZ, R. E., and G. C. GREEN. 1972. Heat requirements for symptom suppression and inactivation of the greening pathogen. *In:* Price, W. C. (ed.). Proc. 5th Conf. Intern. Organ. Citrus Virol. Pp. 44–51. Univ. Fla. Press, Gainesville, Fla.

SCHWARZ, R. E., and A. P. D. MCCLEAN. 1969. Gum-pocket, a new virus-like disease of *Poncirus trifoliata*. Plant Dis. Reptr. **53**:336–38.

SCHWARZ, R. E., J. N. MOLL, and S. P. VAN VUUREN. 1974. The control of citrus greening disease and its psylla vector by trunk injection of tetracyclines and insecticides. *In:* Weathers, L. G., and M. Cohen (eds.). Proc. 6th Conf. Intern. Organ. Citrus Virol. Pp. 26–29. Univ. Calif. Div. Agr. Sci., Richmond, Calif.

SCHWARZ, R. E., and S. P. VAN VUUREN. 1970. Centrifugal extraction of phenolic markers for indexing citrus greening and avocado sun-blotch diseases. Phytophylactica **2**:65–68.

———. 1971. Decrease in fruit greening of sweet orange by trunk injection of tetracyclines. Plant Dis. Reptr. **55**:747–50.

SEARLE, C. M. 1969. A preliminary report on off-type trees. Mazoe Citrus Estates (Rhodesia). 15 pp.

SEMANCIK, J. S., and L. G. WEATHERS. 1965. Partial purification of a mechanically transmissible virus associated with tatter leaf of citrus. Phytopathology **55**:1354–58.

———. 1968a. Characterization of infectious nucleic acid associated with infection by exocortis virus of citrus. Phytopathology **58**:1067.

———. 1968b. Exocortis virus of citrus: association of infectivity with nucleic acid preparations. Virology **36**:326–28.

SERVAZZI, O., F. MARRAS, and A. FODDAI. 1968. Investigations on citrus cristacortis in Sardinia. *In:* Childs, J. F. L. (ed.). Proc. 4th Conf. Intern. Organ. Citrus Virol. Pp.

229–31. Univ. Fla. Press, Gainesville, Fla.

SINCLAIR, J. B., and R. T. BROWN. 1960. Effect of exocortis disease on four citrus rootstocks. Plant Dis. Reptr. **44**:180–83.

SMITH, R. E., and O. BUTLER. 1908. Gum diseases of citrus trees in California. Calif. Agr. Expt. Sta. Bul. **200**:235–70.

SPAAR, D., H. KLEINHEMPEL, H. M. MULLER, A. STANARIUS, and D. SCHIMMEL. 1974. Culturing mycoplasmas from plants. Coll. Inst. Nat. Sante Rech. Med. **33**:207–13.

STUBBS, L. L. 1963. Tristeza-tolerant strains of sour orange. FAO Plant Prot. Bul. **11**:8–10.

———. 1964. Transmission and protective inoculation studies with viruses of the citrus tristeza complex. Austral. Jour. Agr. Res. **15**:752–70.

———. 1968. Apparent elimination of exocortis and yellowing viruses in lemon by heat therapy and shoot-tip propagation. *In:* Childs, J. F. L. (ed.). Proc. 4th Conf. Intern. Organ. Citrus Virol. Pp. 96–99. Univ. Fla. Press, Gainesville, Fla.

SU, H. J., and S. C. LEU. 1972. Study on the pathogen complex causing likubin of citrus in Taiwan. I. Nature of mycoplasma-like organism associated with the disease. Proc. Nat. Sci. Council **5**:109–25.

SU, H. J., and T. MATSUMOTO. 1972. Further studies on the complex causing likubin of citrus in Taiwan. *In:* Price, W. C. (ed.). Proc. 5th Conf. Intern. Organ. Citrus Virol. Pp. 28–34. Univ. Fla. Press, Gainesville, Fla.

SWINGLE, W. T. 1909. The limitation of the satsuma-orange to trifoliate-orange stock. U. S. Dept. Agr. Bur. Plant Indus. Circ. **46**:10 pp.

SWINGLE, W. T., and H. J. WEBBER. 1896. The principle diseases of citrus fruits in Florida. U. S. Dept. Agr. Div. Veg. Phys. Path. Bul. **8**: 42 pp.

TANAKA, H. 1971. Present status of investigations on citrus virus diseases in Japan. Rev. Plant Protect. Res. (Japan) **4**:81–85.

———. 1972. Mechanical transmission of viruses of Satsuma dwarf and Natsudaidai dwarf from citrus to citrus. Ann. Phytopath. Soc. Japan **38**:156–60.

TANAKA, H., and S. YAMADA. 1969. Indexing for exocortis and its damage on citrus trees in Japan. Bul. Hort. Res. Sta. Japan, Series **B**, **9**:181–95.

———. 1972. Evidence for a relationship among the viruses of satsuma dwarf, citrus mosaic, navel infectious mottling, natsudaidai dwarf, citrus variegation and citrus crinkly leaf. *In:* Price, W. C. (ed.). Proc. 5th Conf. Intern. Organ. Citrus Virol. Pp. 71–75. Univ. Fla. Press, Gainesville, Fla.

TANAKA, H., S. YAMADA, and K. KISHI. 1971. Symptoms and occurrence of navel orange infectious mottling and natsudaidai dwarf. Bul. Hort. Res. Sta. Japan, Series **B**, **8**:141–47.

TANAKA, H., S. YAMADA, and J. NAKANISHI. 1971. Approach to eliminating tristeza virus from citrus by using trifoliate orange seedings. Bul. Hort. Res. Sta. Japan, Series **B**, **11**:151–65.

TANAKA, S. 1972. Transmission of satsuma dwarf virus from herbaceous plants to citrus by approach grafts. *In:* Price, W. C. (ed.). Proc. 5th Conf. Intern. Organ. Citrus Virol. Pp. 80–82. Univ. Fla. Press, Gainesville, Fla.

TANAKA, S., and Y. DOI. 1974. Studies on mycoplasmalike organisms suspected cause of citrus likubin and leaf mottling. Tamagawa Faculty of Agr. Bul. **14**:64–70.

TANAKA, S., and K. KISHI. 1963. Studies on indicator plants for citrus viruses. I. Mechanical inoculation on leguminous plants with sap from satsuma dwarf tree. Ann. Phytopath. Soc. Japan **28**:262-69.

TANAKA, S., K. KISHI, and S. YAMADA. 1965. Researches on the indicator plants of satsuma dwarf and Hassaku dwarf viruses. *In:* Price, W. C. (ed.). Proc. 3rd Conf. Intern. Organ. Citrus Virol. Pp. 260–67. Univ. Fla. Press, Gainesville, Fla.

TANAKA, S., Y. SAITO, and K. KISHI. 1968. Purification of satsuma dwarf virus. *In:* Childs, J. F. L. (ed.). Proc. 4th Conf. Intern. Organ. Citrus Virol. Pp. 267–88. Univ. Fla. Press, Gainesville, Fla.

TANAKA, S., E. SHIKATA, and A. SASAKI. 1969. Studies on Hassaku-dwarf virus. *In:* Chapman, H. D. (ed.). Proc. First Intern. Citrus Symp. **3**:1445–48. Univ. Calif., Riverside, Calif.

TANAKA, S., and S. YAMADA. 1961. Citrus virus diseases in Japan. *In:* Price, W. C. (ed.). Proc. 2nd Conf. Intern. Organ. Citrus Virol. Pp. 247–52. Univ. Fla. Press, Gainesville, Fla.

TERRANOVA, G., and A. SCUDERI. 1968. Further research on the impietratura disease of citrus. *In:* Childs, J. F. L. (ed.). Proc. 4th Conf. Intern. Organ. Citrus Virol. Pp. 242–47. Univ. Fla. Press, Gainesville, Fla.

TIRTAWIDJAJA, S., T. HADIWIDJAJA, and A. M. LASHEEN. 1965. Citrus vein-phloem degeneration virus, a possible cause of citrus chlorosis in Java. Jour. Amer. Soc. Hort. Sci. **86**:235–43.

TOXOPEUS, H. J. 1937. Stock-scion incompatibility in citrus and its cause. Jour. Pom. Hort. Sci. **14**:360–64.

TRABUT, L. 1913. Chlorose infectieuse des citrus. Compt. Rend. Acad. Sci., Paris **156**:243–44.

VAN DER MERWE, A. J., and F. G. ANDERSON. 1947. Chromium and manganese toxicity. Farming So. Africa **12**:439–40.

VASUDEVA, R. S., P. M. VARMA, and D. G. RAO. 1959. Transmission of citrus decline by *Toxoptera citricidus* Kirk. in India. Curr. Sci. [India] **28**:418–19.

VOGEL, R. 1961. Citrus virus diseases in Corsica. *In:* Price, W. C. (ed.). Proc. 2nd Conf. Intern. Organ. Citrus Virol. Pp. 242–44. Univ. Fla. Press, Gainesville, Fla.

———. 1973. Le cristacortis: une nouvelle maladie à virus des agrumes. Thèse présente à L'Université de Bordeaux II pour obtenir le grade de Docteur ès Sciences Naturelles. 153 pp.

VOGEL, R., and J. M. BOVÉ. 1964. Stem pitting sur bigaradier et sur oranger 'tarocco' en Corse: une maladie à virus. Fruits **19**:269–74.

———. 1967. Le "stem-pitting" du bigaradier et de l'oranger 'tarocco'. Fruits **22**:235–38.

———. 1968. Cristacortis, a virus disease inducing stem pitting on sour orange and other citrus species. *In:* Childs, J. F. L. (ed.). Proc. 4th Conf. Intern. Organ. Citrus Virol. Pp. 221–28. Univ. Fla. Press, Gainesville, Fla.

———. 1972. Relation of cristacortis virus to other citrus viruses. *In:* Price, W. C. (ed.). Proc. 5th Conf. Intern. Organ. Citrus Virol. Pp. 178–84. Univ. Fla. Press, Gainesville, Fla.

———. 1974. Studies on the cause of leaf symptoms associated with cristacortis disease of citrus. *In:* Weathers, L. G., and M. Cohen (eds.). Proc. 6th Conf. Intern. Organ. Citrus Virol. Pp. 131–34. Univ. Calif. Div. Agr. Sci., Richmond, Calif.

WALLACE, J. M. 1945. Technique for hastening foliage symptoms of psorosis of citrus. Phytopathology **35**:535–41.

———. 1957*a*. Tristeza and seedling yellows of citrus. Plant Dis. Reptr. **41**:394–97.

———. 1957*b*. Virus-strain interference in relation to symptoms of psorosis disease of citrus. Hilgardia **27**:223–46.

——— (ed). 1959*a*. Citrus virus diseases. Proc. Intern. Conf. Citrus Virus Diseases. Univ. Calif. Div. Agr. Sci., Ber-

keley. 243 pp.
———. 1959*b*. A half century of research on psorosis. *In:* Wallace, J. M. (ed.). Citrus virus diseases. Pp. 5–28. Univ. Calif. Div. Agr. Sci., Berkeley, Calif.
———. 1963. Comments on citrus virus diseases and a report of the role of these diseases in Taiwan. Proc. Symp. on Present Agr. Improv. and Reconstruct. Prog. 16. College of Agr. Natl. Taiwan University. 14 pp. (Reprint.)
———. 1965. Protection in citrus after recovery from seedling yellows and loss of the yellows-inducing virus. Phytopathology **55:**1081.
———. 1968. Recent developments in the citrus psorosis diseases. *In:* Childs, J. F. L. (ed.). Proc. 4th Conf. Intern. Organ. Citrus Virol. Pp. 1–9. Univ. Fla. Press, Gainesville, Fla.
———. 1977. Strain interference reactions among citrus viruses with reference to their use for disease control. Proc. First Intern. Citrus Cong., **2:**569-73. Murcia, Spain.
WALLACE, J. M., and R. J. DRAKE. 1951. Recent developments in studies of quick decline and related diseases. Phytopathology **41:**785–93.
———. 1953. A virus-induced vein enation in citrus. Citrus Leaves **33:**22–23.
———. 1955*a*. The tristeza virus in Meyer lemon. Citrus Leaves **35**(1):8–9.
———. 1955*b*. Unpublished data on file in the Department of Plant Pathology, University of California, Riverside.
———. 1959. Citrus vein enation. *In:* Wallace, J. M. (ed.). Citrus virus diseases. Pp. 163–65. Univ. Calif. Div. Agr. Sci., Berkeley, Calif.
———. 1960. Woody galls on citrus associated with vein-enation virus infection. Plant Dis. Reptr. **44:**580–84.
———. 1961*a*. Induction of woody galls by wounding of citrus infected with vein-enation virus. Plant Dis. Reptr. **45:**682–86.
———. 1961*b*. Seedling yellows in California. *In:* Price, W. C. (ed.). Proc. 2nd Conf. Intern. Organ. Citrus Virol. Pp. 141–49. Univ. Fla. Press, Gainesville, Fla.
———. 1962. Tatter leaf, a previously undescribed virus effect on citrus. Plant Dis. Reptr. **46:**211–12.
———. 1963. New information on symptom effects and host range of citrus tatter-leaf virus. Plant Dis. Reptr. **47:**352–53.
———. 1967. Unpublished data on file at Department of Plant Pathology, University of California, Riverside.
———. 1968. Citrange stunt and ringspot, two previously undescribed virus diseases of citrus. *In:* Childs, J. F. L. (ed.). Proc. 4th Conf. Intern. Organ. Citrus Virol. Pp. 177–83. Univ. Fla. Press, Gainesville, Fla.
———. 1969. Unpublished data on file at Department of Plant Pathology, University of California, Riverside.
———. 1972*a*. Studies on recovery of citrus plants from seedling yellows and the resulting protection against reinfection. *In:* Price, W. C. (ed.). Proc. 5th Conf. Intern. Organ. Citrus Virol. Pp. 127–36. Univ. Fla. Press, Gainesville, Fla.
———. 1972*b*. Use of seedling-yellows recovery and protection phenomena in producing tristeza-tolerant, susceptible scion-rootstock combinations. *In:* Price, W. C. (ed.). Proc. 5th Conf. Intern. Organ. Citrus Virol. Pp. 137–43. Univ. Fla. Press, Gainesville, Fla.
———. 1974. Field performance of tristeza-susceptible citrus trees carrying virus derived from plants that recovered from seedling yellows. *In:* Weathers, L. G., and M. Cohen (eds.). Proc. 6th Conf. Intern. Organ. Citrus Virol. Pp. 67–74. Univ. Calif. Div. Agr. Sci., Richmond, Calif.
WALLACE, J. M., and G. MAJORANA. 1962. Unpublished data on file at Department of Plant Pathology, University of California, Riverside.
WALLACE, J. M., and A. L. MARTINEZ. 1964. Observations on citrus diseases in the Philippines. FAO Plant Protect. Bul. **12:**1–5.
WALLACE, J. M., A. L. MARTINEZ, and R. J. DRAKE. 1965. Further studies on citrus seedling yellows. *In:* Price, W. C. (ed.). Proc. 3rd Conf. Intern. Organ. Citrus Virol. Pp. 36–39. Univ. Fla. Press, Gainesville, Fla.
WALLACE, J. M., P. C. J. OBERHOLZER, and J. D. J. HOFMEYER. 1956. Distribution of viruses of tristeza and other diseases of citrus in propagative material. Plant Dis. Reptr. **40:**3–10.
WALLACE, J. M., and G. F. SNOW. 1965. Report on decline of orange trees on Troyer citrange rootstock. Calif. Citrog. **50:**369, 378–79, 382–83.
WEATHERS, L. G. 1957. A vein-yellowing disease of citrus caused by a graft-transmissible virus. Plant Dis. Reptr. **41:**741–42.
———. 1960*a*. The effect of host nutrition on the development of exocortis in *Poncirus trifoliata*. Phytopathology **50:**87.
———. 1960*b*. Yellow-vein disease of citrus and studies of interactions between yellow-vein and other viruses of citrus. Virology **11:**753–64.
———. 1961. Responses of citrus to concurrent infection with two or more unrelated viruses. *In:* Price, W. C. (ed.). Proc. 2nd Conf. Intern. Organ. Citrus Virol. Pp. 187–96. Univ. Fla. Press, Gainesville, Fla.
———. 1963. Use of synergy in the identification of strains of citrus yellow vein virus. Nature **200:**812–13.
———. 1965*a*. Transmission of exocortis virus of citrus by *Cuscuta subinclusa*. Plant Dis. Reptr. **49:**189–90.
———. 1965*b*. Petunia, an herbaceous host of exocortis virus of citrus. Phytopathology **55:**1081.
———. 1969. Mechanical transmission of viruses from citrus to citrus and herbaceous plants. *In:* Chapman, H. D. (ed.). Proc. First Intern. Citrus Symp. **3:**1473–79. Univ. Calif., Riverside, Calif.
WEATHERS, L. G., and E. C. CALAVAN. 1959*a*. Nucellar embryony—a means of freeing citrus clones of viruses. *In:* Wallace, J. M. (ed.). Citrus virus diseases. Pp. 197–202. Univ. Calif. Div. Agr. Sci., Berkeley, Calif.
———. 1959*b*. The occurrence of cachexia and xyloporosis in California lemon varieties, with particular reference to the old-line Eureka lemon. Plant Dis. Reptr. **43:**528–33.
———. 1959*c*. A bud-union disorder of calamondin trees in California. *In:* Wallace, J. M. (ed.). Citrus virus diseases. Pp. 179–84. Univ. Calif. Div. Agr. Sci., Berkeley, Calif.
———. 1961. Additional indicator plants for exocortis and evidence for strain differences in the virus. Phytopathology **51:**262–64.
WEATHERS, L. G., F. C. GREER, JR., and M. K. HARJUNG. 1967. Transmission of exocortis virus of citrus to herbaceous plants. Plant Dis. Reptr. **51:**868–71.
WEATHERS, L. G., and M. K. HARJUNG. 1964. Transmission of citrus viruses by dodder, *Cuscuta subinclusa*. Plant Dis. Reptr. **48:**102–03.
WEATHERS, L. G., M. K. HARJUNG, and R. G. PLATT. 1965. Some effects of host nutrition on symptoms of exocortis. *In:* Price, W. C. (ed.). Proc. 3rd Conf. Intern. Organ. Citrus Virol. Pp. 102–07. Univ. Fla. Press, Gainesville, Fla.
WEATHERS, L. G., A. O. PAULUS, and M. K. HARJUNG. 1962. Effect of soil temperature on the development of exocortis in *Poncirus trifoliata*. Phytopathology **52:**32.
WEBBER, H. J. 1925. A comparative study of the citrus industry

of South Africa. So. Africa Dept. Agr. Bul. **6:** 106 pp.

———. 1943. The "tristeza" disease of sour-orange rootstock. Proc. Amer. Soc. Hort. Sci. **43:**160–68.

WEBBER, IRMA E., and H. S. FAWCETT. 1935. Comparative histology of healthy and psorosis-affected tissues of *Citrus sinensis*. Hilgardia **9:**71–109.

WHITCOMB, R. F., J. G. TULLY, J. M. BOVÉ, and P. SAGLIO. 1973. Spiroplasmas and Acholeplasmas: multiplication in insects. Science **182:**1251–53.

YAMADA, S., and K. SAWAMURA. 1950. Satsuma dwarf. Abstr. General meeting of Japanese Hort. Soc., Aichi Prefecture. [In Japanese.]

———. 1952. Studies on the dwarf disease of satsuma orange, *Citrus unshiu* Marcovitch. Preliminary report. Hort. Div., Tokai-Kinki Agr. Expt. Sta. Bul. **1:**61–71.

———. 1953. The dwarf disease of satsuma orange and future problems. Plant Prot. [Japan] **7:**267–72. [In Japanese.]

YAMADA, S., and H. TANAKA. 1968. Virus diseases of citrus and researches conducted on them in Japan. Japan Agr. Res. Quarterly **3:**10–14.

YARWOOD, C. E. 1963. Mechanical transmission of a latent lemon virus. Abstr. Phytopathology **53:**1145.

YEDIDYAH, S. 1937. Citrus growing. Hassadeh Publ. Co., Tel-Aviv. 478 pp [In Hebrew.]

YOSHI, K., and S. OMORI. 1951. Studies on satsuma dwarf disease. Jour. Fruit Trees and Hort. **4**(4):1–10. [In Japanese.]

———. 1952. Satsuma dwarf disease. Plant Prot. [Japan] **6**(3):20–21. [In Japanese.]

YOT-DAUTHY, D., and J. M. BOVÉ. 1968. Purification of citrus crinkly-leaf virus. *In:* Childs, J. F. L. (ed.). Proc. 4th Conf. Intern. Organ. Citrus Virol. Pp. 255–63. Univ. Fla. Press, Gainesville, Fla.

ZANARDI, D., G. ANEDDA, and B. FOLLESA. 1968. A special form of stem pitting in Sardinian citrus trees. *In:* Childs, J. F. L. (ed.). Proc. 4th Conf. Intern. Organ. Citrus Virol. Pp. 240–41. Univ. Fla. Press, Gainesville, Fla.

ZEMAN, V. 1931. Una enfermadad nueva en los naranjales de Corrientes. Physis **19:**410–11.

ZELCER, A., M. BAR-JOSEPH, and G. LOEBENSTEIN. 1971. Mycoplasma-like bodies associated with little-leaf disease of citrus. Israel Jour. Agr. Res. **21:**137–42.

CHAPTER 3

Registration, Certification, and Indexing of Citrus Trees

E. CLAIR CALAVAN, STANLEY M. MATHER, and E. H. McEACHERN

REGISTRATION AND CERTIFICATION programs for citrus serve primarily to provide propagative materials and nursery stock true-to-name and as free as possible from important pests and pathogens. Any such program should consider the nature of the disease and pest problems involved, geographic factors, the size and nature of the industry involved, the legal authority and restrictions under which the program will operate, and the probability of cooperation by industry leaders.

Excessive losses caused by virus diseases of citrus (see chap. 2) can be most effectively and economically controlled or avoided by an integrated protection program including the use of clean certified stock, tolerant selections of stionic combinations, and appropriate quarantine, detection, and suppression measures.

In susceptible varieties or combinations, the control of certain virus diseases, including psorosis, tatter leaf, citrange stunt, and cachexia-xyloporosis, depends almost entirely on the use of clean parent material because these viruses are normally spread only by the movement of infected propagative material and nursery stock. Clean stock is useful also in limiting or preventing damage from vector-transmitted diseases such as tristeza, stubborn, and greening in areas where natural spread is slow or nonexistent.

The background, organization, indexing procedures, and other technical features of citrus registration and certification programs for the production of clean, true-to-name, high quality stock are presented in this chapter, with special emphasis on the California situation.

CALIFORNIA REGISTRATION AND CERTIFICATION PROGRAMS

History

The development of citrus registration and certification programs was greatly influenced by outbreaks of disease caused by bud graft-transmissible virus and mycoplasma pathogens of citrus trees. The widespread occurrence of psorosis early in this century was overshadowed by tristeza (quick decline) from the 1940's to the 1960's. Exocortis became common with the increased use of citrange and trifoliate orange rootstocks in the 1950's. Stubborn disease, caused by *Spiroplasma citri* (Saglio *et al.*) spread rapidly since about 1940 and greatly influenced citrus registration and certification in California. Additional details of the relationships between programs and diseases are given later in this chapter.

The seedling citrus trees grown in California during the early years of the citrus industry are presumed to have been practically virus-free. However, many of these trees had undesirable features such as low production, thorniness, excessive seediness, inferior flavor, and poor keeping qualities. Consequently, several of the better citrus selections were established in commercial orchards before the existence of citrus viruses was known. These were collected by travelers and plant explorers from various parts of the world and introduced into California prior to the enactment of plant quarantine regulations. We are now aware that one or more viruses were carried by most of the citrus selections imported as budwood or trees and that most of these viruses have, by one means or another, spread to other trees.

The need for choosing and maintaining superior trees as scion parents has been known a long time, possibly for centuries. The Fruit Growers Supply Company in Los Angeles, California, recognizing the importance of obtaining the best budwood to provide good high yielding trees "for the success of the orchardist and the future of the industry," established a Bud Selection Department in 1917 to procure and distribute budwood from superior trees. Eligibility of each tree was determined largely by records of superior yields over a period of at least three years and by generally satisfactory fruit quality and appearance of the tree (Mortensen, 1917). A. D. Shamel of the United States Department of Agriculture and others served as advisors and consultants to the Bud Selection Department (Hutchens, 1925). By 1933, the department had kept yield records on a total of 57,796 trees and had used about ten per cent of these as sources of more than five million buds provided to growers (Barnes, 1933). For several years the annual supply of buds was about 500,000, but by 1932 it had dropped to 116,000.

In the absence of knowledge of techniques for the detection of viruses and certain inheritable weaknesses that destroy or reduce the productive capacity of citrus trees, it was inevitable that relatively young precocious trees with heavy crops were frequently chosen as budwood sources. Unfortunately, such trees and their progeny often had a short productive life. The reasons for the premature decline of these trees, determined later, included inheritable tendencies to sieve-tube necrosis of lemons, wood pocket of lemons, and abnormal bud unions with certain rootstocks. Moreover, precocious trees often were infected by viruses such as exocortis, psorosis, and cachexia-xyloporosis.

Several citrus viruses and the stubborn pathogen were very widely distributed in California and elsewhere by the inadvertent use of budwood from infected trees. The Fruit Growers Supply Company Budwood Department was powerless to avoid widespread distribution of stubborn and the viruses of psorosis, exocortis, and cachexia from many infected symptomless or mildly affected trees. Therefore, notwithstanding the distribution of several million buds from apparently superior trees, grower dissatisfaction with many inexplicably inferior trees grown from buds obtained from the Budwood Department, together with economic problems in the 1930's, led to abandonment of the program.

The Psorosis (Interim) Program (1937-1973)

A new means for improving the quality of citrus nursery stock was provided in 1933. During that year, Dr. H. S. Fawcett of the Citrus Experiment Station at Riverside discovered that psorosis is caused by a virus and that characteristic symptoms (fig. 2–1) are present in some young leaves of infected plants. This discovery led to the establishment by the California Department of Agriculture in 1937 of a voluntary program for official registration of citrus trees found free from psorosis symptoms. This program, operated by the Nursery Service with some assistance from plant pathologists, was based primarily on periodic inspection for bark and leaf symptoms of psorosis in the candidate trees themselves, with supplemental inspection of nursery stock. This inspection was conducted especially during the spring flush of growth. Later, an efficient indexing technique was developed (see p. 201) and used by Dr. J. M. Wallace for precise evaluations of certain candidate trees (Wallace, 1945). This psorosis freedom program, in effect in modified form until 1974, is discussed in detail below.

In 1936, Dr. Fawcett outlined the biological conditions for registration:

1) The trees should be 15 years old or older, or should be provably derived from trees which are older than 15 years and available for inspection;

2) A careful examination of the bark should reveal no "least sign" of psorosis;

3) Examination of at least 15 rapidly growing young shoots, distributed throughout the tree, should not show mosaic-like or leaf-flecking symptoms.

The Southern California Citrus Nurserymen's Association then passed a resolution requesting the California Department of Agriculture to organize a service for inspection for psorosis in trees selected by nurserymen, from which trees they would take buds for propagation of citrus trees in nurseries. Accordingly, on March 1, 1937, the Bureau of Nursery Service announced such a service, stipulating that insepction and report would be made, but that there would be no certification of buds. The field work was placed in the hands of a senior nursery inspector, Mr. C. R. Tower, who received instructions from Dr. Fawcett. Thus, the first official registration program for citrus tree nursery stock was brought about.

From 1937 to 1961, the registration of trees was based on field inspection for leaf and bark symptoms of psorosis as outlined by Dr. Fawcett. Reliable propagating sources were made available to nurserymen and citrus fruit growers through this program.

The discovery, in 1939, of quick decline (tristeza) in California attracted much public attention by 1944. By that time, there were more than 600 citrus trees on the registry. The number of registered trees increased to a peak of 1,315 in 1948. Following the outbreak of tristeza virus in southern California and rapid post-war urbanization, the number of registered trees under the terms of the program was gradually reduced to 135.

In 1961, the threat of the spread of tristeza through nursery stock into newly established citrus areas outside the quick decline quarantine area became apparent. At the request of citrus nurserymen, the psorosis program was amended to include indexing for tristeza and vein enation, as well as for the psorosis virus. By 1962, 284 trees were registered under the terms of this revised program. In 1963, applications for registration were filed with the Department of Agriculture for the registration of more than 2,600 trees. By 1973, registrations had declined to 1,098 trees, including trees registered in the long-range program described later in this chapter.

The amended psorosis program permitted a selected tree to be registered if it was not less than five years of age providing the following conditions had been met: (1) the inspection and indexing for tristeza on Mexican lime and a suitable indicator host for psorosis were complete; and (2) the tree was found in good vigor, free from apparent mutations or disorders which might obscure disease symptoms or make the tree undesirable as a propagating source.

Registration was for a period of three years and trees could be re-registered by repeating the inspection and indexing. Further refinements in the indexing for exocortis virus were included as a part of the program in 1965. Two buds from each candidate tree were placed in each of four Mexican lime seedlings, two buds in each of two citron selections on Rough lemon rootstock, and two buds in each of two Pineapple sweet orange seedlings. These tests were made in the greenhouse and observed through several successive flushes of growth for a six-month period. The psorosis program was active until 1974 when it was replaced by a new Regulation for the Registration and Certification of Citrus Trees.

Meanwhile psorosis proved to be less dangerous and more easily preventable in California than at least two other citrus diseases, stubborn and tristeza (quick decline). Stubborn disease, present in California citrus orchards since about 1915 (Calavan, 1969), was found in 1944 to be graft-transmissible and erroneously assumed to be of viral nature. Stubborn is now known to be caused by a mycoplasmalike organism (Igwegbe and Calavan, 1970; Markham *et al.*, 1974; Rana *et al.*, 1975) which has been characterized as *Spiroplasma citri* (Saglio *et al.*, 1973). Drs. Fawcett and Wallace reported in 1946 that quick decline is caused by a graft-transmissible virus (Fawcett and Wallace, 1946). The same year, Meneghini (1946) confirmed the viral nature of tristeza in Brazil and proved the virus can be spread by an aphid vector, *Toxoptera citricidus*, not found in California. However, another less efficient aphid vector of tristeza, *Aphis gossypii*, was identified in California (Dickson, Flock, and Johnson, 1951).

By 1962, tristeza virus had been spread by vectors and transported in buds or nursery stock to most commercial citrus areas in the Los Angeles basin. In addition, most of the trees once registered by the Nursery Service for psorosis freedom were dead or were located within the tristeza-quarantined area. Some of the few remaining registered trees were lemons or trees not imminently threatened by tristeza, but growing in areas from which the movement of budwood was restricted.

Other factors contributing to the diminishing use of the psorosis registration program from 1944 to 1962 were the voluntary nature of the program, the knowledge that it contained no special provisions for avoiding registration of trees infected by viruses other than those of the psorosis group, and the increasingly extensive use of nucellar seedling selections that were generally presumed to be virus free. By the mid-1950's, stubborn and several citrus viruses including tristeza, seedling-yellows tristeza, vein enation, cachexia, and exocortis, had been widely distributed in California, and had caused extensive damage to commercial citrus orchards in some areas. Stubborn, tristeza, psorosis, and exocortis had destroyed, damaged, or were threatening large segments of the industry. Citrus production losses from these diseases were estimated to be about 20 per cent (Calavan, 1958), notwithstanding the extensive use of nucellar selections. Many trees of nucellar budlines were found infected by tristeza, psorosis, exocortis, and vein enation viruses. Exocortis disease was frequently seen in young trees on trifoliate orange and Troyer citrange rootstocks used to replace the highly tristeza-sensitive sour orange rootstocks which were not visibly affected by exocortis. A more comprehensive program than the psorosis registration program was needed.

The Long-range Program (1962-1973)

By 1955, research workers and many growers recognized that citrus is highly vulnerable to several diseases spread by insects or other vectors, and to certain other diseases spread mostly by tissue grafts (as in propagation) and possibly by unknown methods. Inasmuch as index methods (see p. 201) had been developed for all the important citrus virus and viruslike diseases in California except stubborn, it was apparent that most of the inadvertent distribution of viruses in infected stock could be avoided by careful periodic indexing of budwood parent trees and by other precautionary measures.

Accordingly, following a series of discussions in 1955 and 1956, the Citrus Research Advisory Committee asked the University of California to assume responsibility for the development and maintenance of "variety foundation plantings" to serve as standard sources of true-to-name scion and rootstock varieties of citrus (Reuther, 1959; Reuther *et al.*, 1968; Nauer *et al.*, 1967). The University accepted and the Citrus Variety Improvement Program (CVIP)† was inaugurated in 1957 and greatly expanded the following year. The expectation was that 10 years or more would be required to make true-to-name, thoroughly tested material available for commercial use. In 1961, some CVIP selections on which short-term indexing requirements had been completed were established in the foundation planting and in long-term indexing plots at what is now the University of California Lindcove Field Station, east of Visalia. The University and the California Department of Agriculture then formalized a set of procedures governing the maintenance and use of propagative material produced by the CVIP.

Several important developments related to citrus virus and mycoplasmalike diseases made it unwise for the citrus industry to depend only on the original version of the voluntary program for psorosis freedom and on nonindexed nucellar selections while awaiting clean stock from the long-range program. Among these developments were: (1) tristeza infestations involving thousands of trees were detected in the San Joaquin Valley in 1961 (Calavan, 1963); (2) many trees propagated from nucellar budlines were found to be virus-infected and unsuitable for commercial use; (3) short-term indexing methods were devised for exocortis (Calavan *et al.*, 1964), stubborn (Calavan and Christiansen, 1965), and cachexia (Roistacher, Blue, and Calavan, 1973); (4) exocortis virus proved to be easily transmissible on knives and other tools (Garnsey and Jones, 1967); (5) stubborn disease was found to be widespread in Valencia and several other important commercial varieties formerly considered to be tolerant or immune, and had obviously been spread by some natural or cultural means other than grafting (Calavan *et al.*, 1974); (6) stubborn often was exceptionally difficult to detect, presumably because of the absence or low concentration of the pathogen, *S. citri*, in much of the infected tree; and (7) the beet leafhopper, *Circulifer tenellus* (Baker) (Lee *et al.*, 1973; Oldfield *et al.*, 1976), and *Scaphytopius nitridus* (DeLong) (Kaloostian *et al.*, 1975) were found to be carriers and vectors of *S. citri*.

Strong efforts have been made to prevent or restrict the spread of citrus virus diseases, particularly since 1955. Meyer lemon-free districts were formed in central California in 1955 for the purpose of eliminating Meyer lemon trees, known to be generally infected with tristeza-seedling yellows virus, from all locations near and within commercial citrus areas. Another Meyer lemon-free district was set up in the Coachella Valley. The California Department of Food and Agriculture, in cooperation with County Departments of Agriculture, continues to operate a program of tristeza detection and eradication. Since the districts were established, many Meyer lemon trees, numerous infected mandarins, and many infected sweet orange trees found in the San Joaquin or Coachella Valleys have been removed.

The threat of tristeza in the San Joaquin Valley in 1961 changed the outlook for the prevention and control of citrus virus diseases in areas still

†This program has been renamed (1977) The Citrus Clonal Protection Program (CCPP).

relatively tristeza free. Plant pathologists recommended that until an adequate amount of clean, tested propagative materials could be provided, great care should be exercised—including indexing for tristeza—not only in selecting material for propagation in the areas not already heavily infested with tristeza, but also in registering psorosis-free trees.

Regulations were made that all citrus propagative material (except seeds) scheduled to be grown, grafted, or planted in a Meyer lemon-free district must be obtained only from trees found to be tristeza free, to the satisfaction of the Director of Agriculture. These regulations were put into effect as soon as practicable. Permits are required for movement of plants, buds, cuttings or scions of citrus into these districts. In 1968, the regulations were applied also to extensive tristeza-suppressive areas outside the Meyer lemon-free districts.

Thus, tristeza, which caused the loss or disuse of most registered citrus trees from 1944-1961, became the major reason for the unprecedentedly heavy use of buds and grafts from registered citrus trees from 1961-1973. The Psorosis Registration Program held back and reduced the tristeza threat in Meyer lemon-free districts and in some suppressive districts. This program was capably supplemented by integrated tristeza-detection and suppression programs operated by growers' organizations (especially the Central California Tristeza Control Agency), by the California Department of Food and Agriculture and the various counties, with active participation from the University of California and the U.S. Department of Agriculture. The incidence of psorosis and exocortis in new plantings was also greatly reduced by extensive use of the expanded Psorosis Registration Program which operated simultaneous with the Long-range Program.

New regulations for the Long-range Registration and Certification Program for citrus became effective on August 8, 1962 and culminated several years of intensive cooperative investigations and research work by representatives of the citrus industry, the University of California, the U.S. Department of Agriculture, and the California Department of Food and Agriculture. The details of the regulations, effective until 1974, were developed cooperatively by staff members of the University of California Citrus Research Center and Agricultural Experiment Station (CRC-AES) at Riverside, members of the Citrus Variety Subcommittee of the California Citrus Research Advisory Committee, the California Citrus Nurserymen's Society, citrus growers, and the California Department of Food and Agriculture.

The Long-range Program was based upon selections placed in the CVIP by horticulturists and plant pathologists of the University of California. CVIP trees cleared by short-term indexing for psorosis, tristeza, and vein-enation viruses were established in a foundation planting at the Lindcove field station, Tulare County. Required testing for other pathogens included exocortis, cachexia-xyloporosis, and stubborn indexing. Following the fruiting of the trees and upon completion of indexing, individual trees in the foundation block were registered by the Department to serve as sources of scion wood for the propagation of mother block trees, used mainly for propagating nursery-increase blocks and sometimes for propagating certified nursery stock.

Nurserymen who had qualified by raising rootstocks in seed beds fumigated in accordance with the regulation propagated trees which eventually were registered after they were established in a mother-block planting.

The regulations required that a candidate (mother block) tree must be grown in soil treated in an approved manner for soil-borne pests in each stage of its production beginning with preparation of the seed bed. The mother block location also was required to be fumigated to avoid contamination from possible soil-borne virus diseases and other pests which might debilitate the young trees. Short-term indexing was continued on mother-block trees by annual indexing on Mexican lime plants for tristeza; psorosis indexing was done every third year. At least one visual inspection was made each year. Registrations of foundation trees and candidate trees in a mother block were not made until the trees had produced sufficient fruit to give acceptable evidence that they were not off-type. The regulations also provided safeguards against the registration of candidate trees from mutant scions. The minimum number of trees planted in a mother block was no less than four of any one selection; no less than two trees of any one selection were on the same rootstock variety; and no more than two candidate trees propagated from a single budstick were permitted in a single motherblock. These restrictions made possible the prompt detection of any tree that was not true to type.

As candidate trees became eligible for registration, nurserymen could propagate young citrus trees in nursery row plantings eligible for certification. Provision was made for nursery-increase blocks for use as additional sources of scion wood. Trees in a nursery-increase block less than eighteen months old from budding could, under close supervision, be used as sources of scions for propagating certified nursery stock. This provision was considered necessary to prevent drastic stripping of registered trees.

Several special precautions were required for the registration and certification of citrus trees. A mother block, nursery-increase block, certified block, or planting of nursery stock being grown for planting in a mother block was required to be not less than 50 feet distant from any established citrus tree not similarly entered in the program. Each planting location was subject to approval of the Department and had to be in an area having minimal risks for spread of infectious pests by drainage, flooding, irrigation, or other means. Plantings entered in the program had to be kept in a thrifty growing condition and pests had to be effectively controlled. Suitable precautions were taken in cultivation, irrigation, movement, use of equipment, and other farming practices to guard against spread of soil-borne pests into plantings in the long-range program. Any plants found off-type or virus-infected were required to be removed immediately. The regulations prescribed a high degree of supervision in the handling of the registered trees and propagation of nursery stock.

The cost of producing registered or certified stock was higher than for stock not subject to the voluntary regulations of the Long-range Program. In addition to the required fees, the conditions of isolation and special handling of registered trees and certified nursery stock imposed on the nurserymen hidden costs that often were far in excess of the fees paid. Education of agricultural groups and consumers is essential to the conduct of such programs. Without support of the agricultural groups, nurserymen frequently find it impossible to compete where purchasers are apathetic or unaware of the benefits to be gained from purchasing stocks produced under the terms of the formal program.

Nurserymen who participated in the growing of certified stock also shared in the benefits. Many participants noted increased yield, vigor, and uniformity of nursery stock grown from clean propagative sources. The availability of such conveniently located sources simplified the collection of scion wood or cuttings at less cost than when obtained from numerous plantings of conjectural value at widely separated locations.

The Long-range Citrus Registration and Certification Program remained effective through 1973. The first certified nursery trees produced under the Long-range Program were dug and planted on October 25, 1968 (Platt, 1969). Unfortunately, stubborn disease incidence in mother blocks and elsewhere soared to new highs in the 1960's. The Psorosis Program contained no provision other than occasional tree inspection for the detection of stubborn, which is often difficult to diagnose. Despite the elimination of many obviously stubborn-infected trees by nurserymen and growers, the ominous threat from stubborn continued and extensive changes had to be made to combine the Long-range Registration and Certification Program with the Psorosis Program and eliminate the mother-block provision of the former.

The Combined Program (1974-present)

The current citrus registration and certification program in California is designed to include the best features of both earlier programs and to minimize their weaknesses. Natural spread of stubborn disease, especially in mother blocks and nurseries, weakened the Long-range Program. It was, therefore, decided to eliminate the mother-block provision while retaining provisions for registration of superior privately owned and foundation-block trees. Budwood from registered trees may be used directly for production of certified nursery stock or for the production of nursery-increase blocks. Budwood may be cut from nursery-increase blocks for eighteen months after the original budding.

The new regulations for the registration and certification of citrus trees were drawn up in 1973 by the California Department of Food and Agriculture Nursery and Seed Services with advice from citrus nurserymen, the U.S. Department of Agriculture, and the University of California; they became effective in January, 1974. These new regulations provide for registration, on a voluntary basis, of citrus rootstock and scion sources for the propagation of certified nursery stock. The regulations limit registration and certification to the varieties or clones considered to be the best available from a pest cleanliness standpoint. They also outline the procedures for inspection and indexing. A schematic diagram of the combined program is shown in figure 3–1. This program has been previously discussed by Calavan (1974).

For purposes of clarity, the definitions used in the new regulations, their general provisions, and the required inspection and testing procedures are quoted below from the text of the regulations (Anon., 1974).

"Citrus trees, for which provisions have been included in this article, may be registered for the purpose of providing rootstock and scion sources for the propagation of certified nursery stock when inspected and tested for virus or graft-transmissible diseases and other pests by procedures outlined in this article. Registration and certification are limited to varieties or clones that are considered to be the best available in the industry from a pest cleanliness standpoint.

3000. *Definitions:* Words defined in the General Provision and Sections 5001–5008 of the Food and Agricultural Code of California have the same meanings in this article and in addition:

(a) *'Virus-infected'* means infected by a serious virus or other graft-transmissible disease or manifesting symptoms or behavior characteristic of a serious virus or other graft-transmissible disease.

(b) *'Index'* means testing a plant for infection by grafting with tissue from it to an indicator plant or by other approved means.

(c) *'Virus-free'* means plants produced under terms of this regulation and free of serious virus or other graft-transmissible disease as determined by index testing and inspection procedures outlined in this article.

(d) *'Off-type'* means different from the variety, strain, or selection listed on the application for registration or certification.

(e) *'Selected tree'* means a tree for which registration is intended when inspection and testing are completed.

(f) *'Tested tree'* means a tree tested for virus infection and found to be in compliance with specific quarantine requirements but not eligible for registration under the terms of this regulation.

(g) *'Registered'* means a registration number has been assigned by the Department to a tree that has been inspected and tested in accor-

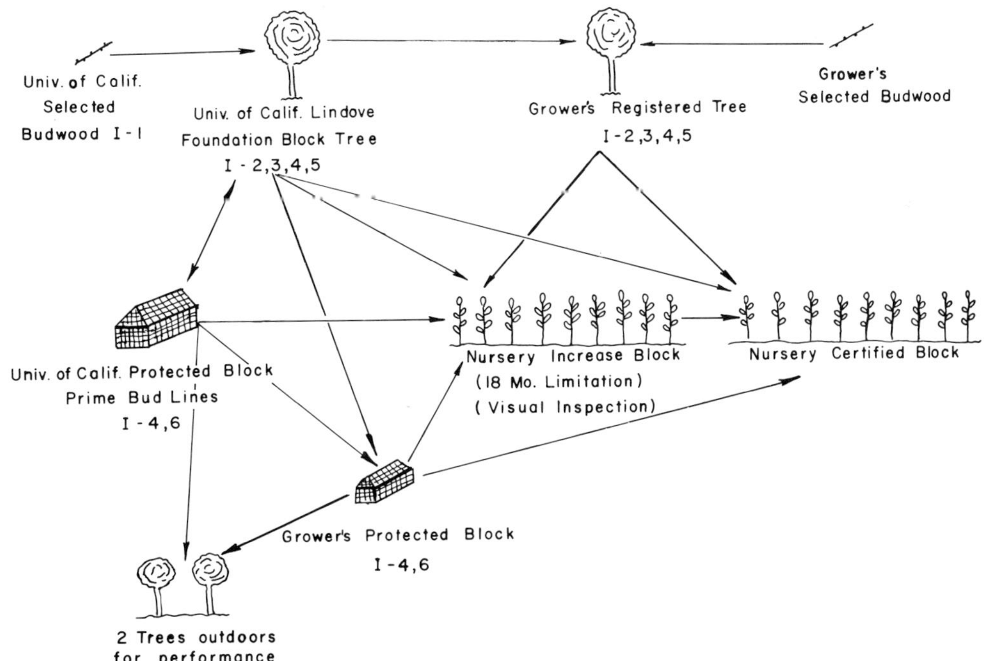

Fig. 3–1. Sketch of the combined citrus registration and certification programs for California (seed trees and Meyer lemon trees excepted).

- **I-1** Indexed for tristeza, seedling yellows-tristeza, psorosis, concave gum, exocortis, vein enation, yellow vein, dweet mottle, crinkly leaf-infectious variegation, and cachexia.
- **I-2** Indexed for tristeza, psorosis, vein enation and exocortis prior to registration.
- **I-3** Re-index for exocortis every 3 years and psorosis every 6 years.
- **I-4** Visual inspection each year and prior to budwood collection.
- **I-5** Indexed for tristeza within one year prior to budwood collection.
- **I-6** Indexed for exocortis every 3 years and tristeza every 6 years.

dance with the provisions of this article to serve as a source of propagating material for certified nursery stock.

(h) *'Foundation block'* means an outdoor planting, maintained by state or federal agencies, in which trees may be registered to serve as a primary source of propagating material.

(i) *'Protected foundation block'* means an indoor planting, maintained by state or federal agencies, in which trees may be registered to serve as a primary source of propagating material.

(j) *'Protected block'* means an indoor planting of trees in an approved glasshouse or screenhouse, propagated and grown there with foundation stock scions, which are to be registered and maintained by an applicant as a source for growing nursery increase trees or certified nursery stock.

(k) *'Nursery increase block'* means a planting of citrus nursery stock, propagated directly from registered trees. Trees in a nursery increase block which are 18 months old or less from budding or grafting may be used as a supplementary source of scions for growing certified nursery stock.

(l) *'Certified block'* means a planting of citrus nursery stock for the production of certified nursery stock.

(m) *'Foundation stock'* means propagating material produced from a registered tree in any foundation block or from properly indexed material propagated and grown in an approved state, federal, or university glasshouse or screenhouse.

(n) *'Registered stock'* means propagating material from a registered tree.

(o) *'Registered increase stock'* means propagating material from a nursery increase block.

(p) *'Certified citrus nursery stock'* means trees propagated by using scions from registered stock, and certified in accordance with the provisions of this article.

(q) *'Registered protected stock'* means propagating material from a registered protected tree.

3001. *General Provisions:* Participation in this program shall be voluntary and may be withdrawn at the option of the applicant. Registration or certification shall not imply any warranty on the part of the Department or of any employee thereof. Registration, certification, approvals, and supervision mentioned herein shall be conducted by the Department.

(a) *Responsibility of applicant:* The applicant shall be responsible for the:

(1) Selection of the tree for testing.

(2) Selection of the location and of the proper maintenance of any plants being grown under the provision of this article.

(3) Application for the registry or reregistry of plants being grown under the provision of this article.

(4) Identity of all plants entered in this program.

(b) *Location of plantings:* Each planting location shall be subject to approval and shall be in an area having minimal risks for spread of infectious pests by drainage, flooding, irrigation, or by other means.

A protected block, nursery increase block, and certified block shall be located not less than 50 feet distant from any established citrus tree. Each nursery increase block and certified block shall be a separate planting sufficiently apart from any other planting to maintain its identity.

Selected trees for registration, other than those grown in a protected block, may be selected from any location with the approval of the Department.

(c) *Maintenance of plants:* All plants entered in this program shall be kept in a thrifty growing condition and pests shall be effectively controlled. Suitable precautions shall be taken in cultivation, irrigation, movement, and use of equipment, and in other farming and nursery practices to guard against spread of pests to plants entered in this program.

To assure that the inspections required herein may be made properly and to provide close working knowledge of field operations, the applicant shall notify the Department in advance of any planting, propagating, or pruning operation or removal of nursery stock or trees in any planting entered in this program.

All pruning shears, saws, or other implements shall be disinfected in an approved manner prior to any fruit picking or cutting on any selected or registered tree, or any clonal selection within an increase block or certified block.

Any plant found to be off-type, showing symptoms characteristic of stubborn disease, or infected with a virus, may be required to be removed immediately from any planting. Approval may be given to remove off-type parts of a registered tree without revoking registration of the tree.

Labeling of each selected or registered tree and of nursery stock growing in plantings entered in the program to identify it as to rootstock and as to its scion source shall be done in an approved manner.

(d) *Eligibility and planting requirements:*

(1) *Rootstock propagation:* The rootstock of any plant entered in the program may be grown from seed or it may be vegetatively propagated providing the propagating wood meets the same requirements as the scion to be used for the plant.

(2) *Foundation block:* A selected tree may be planted in a foundation block when propagated with a scion from a registered tree in a foundation block or when propagated from a greenhouse- or screenhouse-grown scion that has passed the short-term inspection and testing procedures required in section 3002 of this article and has completed or is under the cachexia-xyloporosis index. The tree may be registered when inspection and testing procedures prescribed in section 3002 have been completed with satisfactory results and when the tree has produced sufficient fruit to give acceptable evidence that it is not off-type. A selected tree found to be ineligible for registration shall be removed from a foundation block.

(3) *Protected block:* Trees in a protected block shall be grown in an approved manner and the rootstock for each tree shall be horticulturally suited to the scion variety.

At least two trees propagated from the same budstick of each protected block tree shall be planted outdoors in a climate suitable for the variety, for inspections for growth habits, trueness to variety, and disease symptoms.

A protected block tree may be registered when it is at least 9 months old and has shown good normal growth free of disease symptoms. A tree shall be removed from a protected block when it is found to be ineligible for registration. Registration of a protected block tree may be cancelled if the duplicate outdoor tree produces an excessive amount of off-type fruit and off-type growth.

(4) *Registered outdoor trees:* Any tree registered under the terms of the Regulation for Registration of Citrus Trees Found Free From Psorosis Symptoms, amended effective January 10, 1968, and/or the Regulation for Registration and Certification of Citrus Trees, amended effective July 17, 1971, is eligible for inspection and indexing for registration under the terms of this regulation.

(5) *Selected outdoor trees:* Any individual orchard, yard, or container tree may be selected for inspection and indexing for registration under the terms of this regulation.

(6) *Nursery increase block:* Scions used to propagate the nursery stock therein shall be from registered trees. Within 18 months of propagation, scions may be taken from the block for use in growing certified nursery stock. Trees in a nursery increase block also may be certified.

(7) *Certified block:* Scions used to propagate the nursery stock therein for certification shall be from registered trees or from a nursery increase block."

3002. *Inspection and Testing Procedures:* Inspection and indexing procedures prescribed in this article may be made by the University of California, the United States Department of Agriculture, or the [California] Department [of Agriculture] and shall be conducted in an approved manner at times determined as suitable by the Department. In the indexing procedures required in this section, the Department may approve the substitution of other indicator plants, if equally suitable, or may approve indexing on a fewer number of indicator plants, or may approve other procedures for testing for virus infection if determined equally suitable.

Additional inspections or indexing other than provided in this section may be required by the Department if seasonal conditions or other factors tend to obscure virus symptoms or make adequate inspection impossible, or when virus infection is suspected, or when virus symptoms may be masked in a particular variety.

The Department shall assign a number to a selected tree pending registration.

(a) *Trees in a foundation block:* The scion parent of any tree planted in a foundation block shall have been indexed for and not found to be infected with the viruses of citrange stunt, concave gum, exocortis, psorosis, tatter-leaf, seedling-yellows tristeza, tristeza, vein enation and yellow vein by short-term indexing on *Citrus excelsa*,

Dweet tangor, Etrog citron, Mexican lime, sour orange, sweet orange, and Troyer citrange plants. The scion parent or the selected tree must be indexed for cachexia-xyloporosis virus in Parson's Special mandarin plants in a warm glasshouse and these indicator plants must remain free of cachexia symptoms for at least one year before the selected tree may be registered. Only the tristeza and exocortis indexes shall be required if the scion parent of the selected tree is a registered tree in a foundation block. Trees to be planted in a foundation block must be grown in an approved glasshouse or screenhouse.

Following planting in a foundation block, a tree shall be indexed on Mexican lime for tristeza and vein enation viruses and on suitable indicators for psorosis and exocortis viruses within the 12-month period before registration. In subsequent years after registration, tristeza indexing shall be repeated within one year prior to budwood collection from a registered tree. Each registered tree shall be reindexed for exocortis virus every third year and for psorosis virus every sixth year. Each foundation block tree shall receive one or more visual inspections each year. The fruit of bearing trees, except lemons, shall also be inspected each year after color break.

(b) *Trees in a protected block:* Each tree in a protected block shall be indexed for exocortis every third year and for tristeza every sixth year. In addition, annual visual inspection is required for each tree.

(c) *Non-protected, selected trees of participants:* A selected tree and trees adjacent to it shall be given at least one visual inspection prior to registration. The selected tree also shall be indexed on Mexican lime and Etrog citron and a suitable indicator host for psorosis prior to the initial registration. Such selected trees shall be of good vigor and free from apparent mutations, or disorders which may obscure disease symptoms or make the tree undesirable as a propagating source.

Indexing for tristeza virus is required for a registered outdoor tree each year in which approval for cutting budwood is requested; for exocortis indexing is required every third year, and for psorosis every sixth year.

Each tree shall be given one visual inspection each year. For fruiting trees outdoors, inspection shall be during the period that mature fruits are on the tree after color break.

(d) *Order of indexing:* Indexing shall be made in the order in which applications are received and as indicator host plants are available.

(e) *Three year registration period:* Registration shall be for a period of three years from June 30 in the calendar year in which indexing is commenced.

(f) *Registration may be continuous:* Registration may be continuous provided application for inspection and testing is filed with the Department prior to the expiration date of registration.

(g) *Nursery increase block, certified block:* One visual inspection shall be made each year of plants in a certified block or in a nursery increase block before buds are cut.

(h) *Refusal or cancellation of registration or certification:* Registration or certification may be refused or cancelled for any plants in part or all of the planting if:

(1) The requirements of this article have not been met.

(2) A selected or registered plant is found to be off-type or virus-infected. At the discretion of the Department, a plant growing outdoors, determined to be infected with vein enation virus or tristeza, may be registered or certified when it is growing in an area where such virus is known to be prevalent.

(3) A tree is found to be within the range of possible root graft of another tree found to be virus-infected.

(4) The pest cleanliness requirements for nursery stock in the nursery inspection regulations of the California Administrative Code have not been met.

(5) For any reason the identity of a plant becomes uncertain or has not been properly maintained.

(6) A registration number is misused or misrepresented.

(7) An accumulated percentage of more than one-half percent of the trees of the same variety on the same kind of rootstock are found virus-infected in a nursery increase block or more than two percent virus-infected or stubborn affected trees in a certified block. Either visual inspections or the results of indexing or both may be used as a basis for calculating the number of trees that may be infected."

The combined program has been used by several citrus nurserymen and should do much to reduce the distribution of virus-infected or stubborn-infected material in California. The University of Calfornia made budwood from the CVIP Lindcove foundation block and from its protected blocks in the quarantine facility at Riverside available for sale to qualified nurserymen. Some 50,000 buds were sold from the foundation blocks during the first two and one-half years. Few buds have been sold from the protected block. Inasmuch as the program provides only for voluntary compliance, there is some question as to the extent to which it will be used. A compulsory regulation should be more effective. Nevertheless, the California programs, directly and indirectly, have substantially improved the average quality of citrus nursery stock in California.

Citrus Seed Tree Program

A program providing for the registration of citrus seed trees was adopted in California in 1972, primarily to avoid citrus virus transmission from parent to seedling, which occurs occasionally with certain psorosis viruses, but also to help insure trueness to type.

The applicant is responsible for the selection of seed trees and may submit trees five years of age or older for registration, provided they are of good vigor and free of apparent mutations, disorders, or diseases.

The Department of Food and Agriculture Nursery and Seed Services inspects each candidate tree at least once and indexes it for psorosis prior to registration. Registration is for six years and may be continuous providing application for re-registration is filed before the expiration date.

Registration may be canceled if virus infection is found in the candidate tree within the possible range of root graft. However, at the discretion of the Department, a candidate tree determined to be or likely to be infected with a virus other than psorosis may be registered when it is in an area where such virus is known to be prevalent and is not being subjected to eradication or control.

Improved Meyer Lemon Program

In October, 1975, new California regulations for the registration of virus-free improved Meyer lemon trees became effective (Anon., 1975). A clone of virus-free Meyer lemon, CVIP No. 319, was released by the University of California to the citrus nursery industry (Roistacher, Calavan, and Nauer, 1972). In 1976, the California Department of Food and Agriculture ruled that propagation of old-clone Meyer lemons (most of which carry seedling-yellows tristeza and tatter leaf viruses) must be stopped, and that only virus-free improved Meyer lemon trees should be propagated after 1976. This action was taken to limit the distribution of seedling-yellows tristeza virus in California.

Coordination and Development of California Programs

The successful development of certification and registration in California citrus has been due to the close working relationship among the University of California, the United States Department of Agriculture, and the California Department of Food and Agriculture, and the cooperation and support of growers and nurserymen. In this cooperative effort the responsibilities of each agency and the industry were clearly defined.

University of California and U.S. Department of Agriculture research workers contributed heavily in their development of clean propagating materials and methods used in identifying and excluding virus diseases from plants selected for their horticultural qualities. Methods were devised to maintain pest cleanliness of the stocks. The information developed was drafted into regulations that established procedures to be followed by the nurserymen, the Department of Food and Agriculture, and the University in the identification, maintenance, inspection, and testing of stocks grown for registration or certification.

The development of indexing and other technical advances made it possible to detect and eliminate many detrimental virus diseases and other plant pests that have infiltrated citrus plantings. Before 1960, efforts towards reducing or restricting the incidence of virus diseases were based on quarantine restrictions and visual inspection of plants. Many insect, weed, and plant pathogen pests were excluded by these well-directed efforts, but experience has shown that certain viruses and the mycoplasmalike organism, *Spiroplasma citri*, were sometimes present without being detected. The procedures of indexing, together with inspection of plant propagating sources, have greatly reduced the incidence of virus diseases in nursery stock.

The Quick Decline Interior Quarantine established in 1947 delimited the area of southern California where tristeza virus is known to be readily spread by *Aphis gossypii*. The quarantine was revised to require permits for the movement of citrus nursery stock from any source into or within several major centers of commercial citrus lying outside the quarantined area but in which the natural spread of tristeza was slow or not apparent. These areas are now termed "suppressive" areas and "Meyer lemon-free" districts. Only citrus nursery stock propagated from sources which have been tested and found free from tristeza virus are eligible for the permits.

In 1962, it became apparent that tristeza virus was present outside the quarantined area but had spread very slowly or not at all in the San Joaquin Valley. The California Citrus Nurserymen's Society then requested that the Department initiate the indexing, for tristeza, on all registered trees. The regulations for registration of citrus trees found free from psorosis symptoms were modified accordingly, as previously noted.

Simultaneously the citrus pest district control act was amended providing for the formation of local districts for the control and eradication of citrus pests, collection of taxes, manner of operation, and reimbursement for trees removed. This work was legally extended to the detection of tristeza virus in established groves by indexing.

Revision of the Quick Decline Interior Quarantine became effective May 15, 1963, making the indexing of parent citrus trees mandatory for tristeza virus in Meyer lemon-free districts and resulting in a sudden increase in participation in the registration program. In the ensuing three-year period, a total of 5,174 trees were tested and more than 4,000 were on the registry. During the past few years, the decrease in new citrus plantings has been accompanied by a decrease in tree registrations.

Legal Authority and Significance of California Program

Registration and certification in California are formalized programs authorized by the California Agricultural Code (Murphy, 1969). The law requires that the operation of such programs be self supporting through fees collected for the inspecting, testing, and supervising work done by the California Department of Food and Agriculture. The section of law is an enabling act permitting the Director of Food and Agriculture to establish rules and regulations governing the inspection of plants and premises for the purpose of registration or certification.

Regulations are adopted as part of the California Administrative Code after a public hearing at which the proposals are thoroughly discussed and explained.

Guidelines established in the regulations are determined not only from basic facts that must be considered but also from the practical problems that confront nurserymen in the production and maintenance of stock.

The formalized regulations establish the guidelines which must be followed by both participants and governmental agencies involved in the program. Conservation procedures are employed to lend stability to the programs and eliminate short-cuts which may lead to the recontamination or loss of identity of the stock so produced.

The registrations or certifications made by the Department attest to the authenticity of procedures, inspection, and testing techniques as described in the formalized regulations. Certifications indicate that the stock has been produced under careful supervision of field men of the California Department of Food and Agriculture and the County Agricultural Commissioners and that the procedures required by the regulations have been met.

The programs provide no warranty that registered or certified nursery stock is "pathogen free." Such terms are relative rather than absolute. If it were possible to obtain an established stock of such purity, its maintenance in the pure condition might be impossible or at least not commercially feasible. It follows, then, that at least some pathogens which are of minor importance or of general distribution must be tolerated to some degree. The principal effort is needed against the more serious and important pathogens for which control, suppression, or eradication is needed.

First consideration is given the plant pests to be excluded. Pests considered to be worthwhile subjects for a particular program are those that do not lend themselves to reasonable or practical control measures once they become established in a commercial planting, or those not readily detected by ordinary inspection. Viruses causing systemic diseases and soil-borne pathogens, including nematodes, are examples of such pests. Protection against many pests commonly associated with nursery stock in California is given thorough enforcement by County Agricultural Commissioners of mandatory nursery inspection laws that regulate the sale and handling of nursery stock within the State.

The meaning of certified nursery stock is

becoming known to many agriculturists as being associated with the best stock available to the industry from a pest cleanliness standpoint. The use of the words "registered" or "certified" as applied to nursery stock is protected by provision of the Agricultural Code of California. It is unlawful to sell or transport to the purchaser any nursery stock represented to be registered or certified nursery stock unless it has been produced and labeled in accordance with the procedures and in compliance with the rules and regulations of an official agency.

The terms "registration" and "certification" have separate meanings as applied to nursery stock being grown under the terms of the various regulations. Until 1974, the regulations of the interim program provided only for registration of established plants that might be used as sources of citrus propagating stock, but did not extend official certification to nursery stock propagated from them. Both the Long-range Program for the registration and certification of citrus trees adopted in 1962 and the combined program started in 1974 provided for certification of nursery stock propagated from a registered tree. In these programs, provision was made for identifying nursery stock meeting all the requirements for the regulation when harvested, and the issuance of official tags was made in evidence of the certification. Certified stock is considered as the end product sold for the production of commercial crops. Stock of this kind, stored or shipped, is identified by a blue tag. Official seals are also used to assure the continued identity of the stocks when shipped to other locations for resale.

Financing of California Programs

Financing of indexing as well as the registration and certification work is important. During its first few years, the CVIP was financed primarily through the general fund for plant pathological and horticultural research at the University of California. Shortages of public funds threatened the continued existence of the work, making it apparent that funds from the citrus industry itself would be needed if the work were to progress. It also became apparent that the cost of the program could not be borne solely by the nurserymen participating in the registration and certification programs of the Department. As previously mentioned, the official registration and certification work of the Department of Food and Agriculture is required to be self supporting through fees collected from the participants. Because of the high cost of indexing, fees for the registration were increased to $35 per tree in 1974.

It has been estimated that the University of California invested $600,000 in CVIP from its inception up to July 1, 1967. Continuing annual costs of the program are estimated to be $60,000 or more, only a small portion of which is recovered from budwood sales. A special committee of the CVIP determined that it would be desirable to find a means to finance and assure continuation of the program. Work of this kind is necessarily a long-term project. As old selections are discarded because of disease or for other reasons, new ones need to be developed. Several years are required to develop fruiting trees in foundation blocks in order to assure fruit true to type. The temporary cessation of work for even a short interval of time would cause irreparable damage to the program.

As a result of committee and growers' efforts, the California-Arizona Citrus League contributed $30,000 to assure the immediate continuation of the program in 1967. Then a research marketing order for the citrus industry in California was created. Such orders are authorized by the Agricultural Code and are administered by an advisory board under the supervision of the Director of Food and Agriculture. The California Citrus Improvement Program administered by the Citrus Advisory Board became effective on October 24, 1968 following a favorable referendum covering all citrus growers in the State of California.

Through the marketing order, the Citrus Advisory Board during the 1968-69 year supported research projects totaling more than $321,000. About $35,000 annually is provided the CVIP and another $7,500 was, for several years, provided for the citrus registration and certification work of the Department. The latter amount was used to defray the fixed cost of greenhouses required for indexing. This financial support has made it possible to continue indexing, registration, and certification of citrus trees at a cost within the reach of nurserymen.

THE FLORIDA PROGRAM

The Citrus Budwood Certification Program at Winter Haven, Florida is operated by the Citrus Budwood Registration Bureau, Division of Plant Industry, Florida Department of Agriculture and Consumer Services. Within ten years of its inauguration in 1952, it developed into the world's largest operation for the registration of citrus. This program is voluntary and its purpose "is to assist nurserymen and growers to grow citrus trees free from virus diseases" (Norman, 1959). At least 20 million trees were produced from registered trees in the 1960's (Bridges, 1970), and since 1968, 86 per cent of the citrus nursery stock produced in Florida has been registered or validated. In addition, many thousands of trees in company-owned nurseries have been propagated from registered bud sources (Bridges, 1974). A policy revision of the Florida program was made in 1969 (Anon., 1969). Registered parent trees must be vigorous, productive, true to type, and free of certain diseases. In recent years more emphasis has been placed on horticultural factors. In common with most registration programs of this type, the policy statement contains a disclaimer stating that registration shall not imply any warranty on the part of any employee of the program. The policy statement further provides that all inspections and investigations incidental to registration will be done by duly appointed employees or agents of the State Plant Board (later incorporated into the Florida Department of Agriculture and Consumer Services as the Division of Plant Industry).

The Florida program has dealt extensively with nucellar bud-line trees (Bridges, 1974; Bridges and Youtsey, 1974). Some of the nucellar bud-line trees outyielded comparable old-line selections. Exocortis-free budwood from 13 commercial citrus varieties was obtained from the program's work with nucellar seedlings and budlines (Bridges, 1974).

Preregistration Procedures

In order to participate in the Florida program, a grower or nurseryman may apply to the Citrus Budwood Registration Bureau, agree to comply with all regulations of the program, and pay an application fee of $25.00, entitling him to examination of not more than 40 trees of all varieties. The trees proposed for registration must be at least ten years old, vigorous, productive, and apparently true to type.

Trees selected by the applicant, and the four trees surrounding each tree, are examined by an inspector when flushes of growth are present in order to determine whether or not the candidate tree is free of Florida gummosis, blight, decline, leprosis, bud mutations, and also free of symptoms of stubborn disease, tristeza, cachexia-xyloporosis, and any kind of psorosis or other recognizable bud-transmissible disease. The four surrounding trees are inspected visually for symptoms of bud-transmissible disease.

If a candidate tree and the four trees around it pass the preliminary inspection, they are reinspected over a period covering two spring growth flushes, including the preliminary inspection. Preliminary inspection must be done while mature fruit is on the candidate tree.

Indexing tests for exocortis, psorosis, tristeza, and cachexia-xyloporosis must also be completed with buds taken from the candidate trees before the trees are registered as free of these diseases. A candidate tree is eligible for registration as psorosis-free if it and its sweet orange and tangelo index trees are symptomless through two successive spring growth flushes. A candidate registered as psorosis-free may be registered as cachexia-xyloporosis-free after four years of symptomless indexing on Orlando tangelo seedling rootstocks and may be registered as exocortis-free after six years of satisfactory performance on trifoliate orange seedling rootstocks and 12 months of negative indexing on citron. Most indexing, except for tristeza and some for exocortis, is done in nursery-type index plots. Tristeza indexing and the citron test for exocortis are done in a glasshouse with four seedlings being used for each candidate tree tested for tristeza and 10 Etrog citron cuttings for each tree tested for exocortis. Some exocortis indexing on citron is done indoors and, because of increasingly common severe reactions from tristeza virus in the citron indicator plants, a knife transfer from bud-inoculated citron tissue to healthy citron cuttings under glass is being implemented. Additional details of indexing are available from the Citrus Budwood Registration Office in Winter Haven, Fla.

Registration Procedures

Candidate trees are registered as parent trees, with indication of their apparent freedom from those diseases (psorosis, cachexia-xyloporosis, and exocortis) indicated by the results from the full period of indexing, as listed above. A registration fee of $10.00 per tree is payable when results are made available.

Scion-grove Trees

Scion-grove trees may be grown and registered, in accordance with the regulation, from budwood of a registered parent tree or budwood foundation grove tree. Scion-grove trees are limited to 350 trees of any one variety per applicant. In addition to the $25.00 application fee, a charge of $1.00 per scion-grove tree is made.

Propagation of Nursery Stock from Registered Trees

Nurserymen are required to keep their stocks of trees budded from registered parents in rows separate from non-registered stock and labeled so that all plants can always be identified. Copies of Growers' Registered Nursery Plants are provided for the Citrus Budwood Registration Bureau.

Trees from registered nursery plots may qualify to be sold as premium quality citrus nursery stock if production practices included a series of additional requirements designed to provide a high degree of control for seed- and soil-borne pathogens (Bridges, 1970).

Budwood Foundation Grove

A planting of selected nucellar and old-line citrus has been maintained by the Budwood Registration Bureau but, due to the high incidence of tristeza, many trees could not be kept free of tristeza virus.

In 1974, relocation of the budwood foundation grove to a new location near Dundee was begun (Bridges, 1974). Many sweet orange, mandarin, and tangelo trees in the original foundation block had become infected by tristeza virus (Bridges and Youtsey, 1972).

Validation

A new feature, validation (Bridges, 1965), has been added to the Florida program. Validation is a cooperative system for assuring correct identification, timely indexing, and authentic plantings of new scion and rootstock varieties released by state and federal research agencies. Nurserymen receiving authorized budwood may bud it only on previously unbudded rootstocks in separate rows and supply a nursery plat within 30 days. A fee of $25.00 is required from each cooperator in the validation program.

Psorosis virus has been under mandatory control in Florida since January, 1961. In 1973, the supply of budwood free of psorosis, xyloporosis, and exocortis viruses was adequate for all standard varieties except Temple tangor and Thompson grapefruit which seem to be totally contaminated with exocortis virus.

Seed-source Trees

The Florida program contains provisions for registration and validation of seed-source trees. Approval of seed fruit by Citrus Budwood Registration Program personnel prior to harvest is required. The trend to careful seed selection in Florida is expected to continue (Bridges, 1974).

THE TEXAS PROGRAM

A voluntary program for citrus budwood certification in Texas began in 1948 as a cooperative effort by the Texas Agricultural Experiment Station, the Crops Research Division of the U.S. Department of Agriculture, and the Rio Grande Valley Nurserymen's Association at Weslaco (Sleeth, 1959; Sleeth and Olson, 1961). The more important features of the initial program in Texas were essentially those outlined by Fawcett (1948) when he visited the Rio Grande Valley. Briefly summarized from Sleeth (1959), these procedures were:

"1) Selection of promising, apparently healthy trees by nurserymen or growers.

2) Preliminary inspection by the Psorosis Inspector and entry of the tree as a candidate if no obvious diseases are found in it or in adjacent trees within 35 feet.

3) Propagation of candidate buds on sour orange, Cleopatra mandarin, and Mexican lime, followed by inspection of leaves of scion and stock during spring growth flushes for at least two years.

4) Registration of candidate tree, provided it and its progeny remain free of psorosis symptoms during the entire test period.

5) Increase of budwood supply by establishment of scion groves by planting progeny from registered trees.

6) Certification of nursery stock grown under strict supervision of the Psorosis Inspector from budwood cut from registered trees."

By 1957, there were 595 trees registered as psorosis-free: 376 grapefruit, 214 orange, 3 tangelo, and 2 tangerine. Nineteen scion groves with 3,619 trees averaging five years of age had been established. During the period 1951-1957, seven million nursery trees were propagated from registered trees but only about 200,000 of these were tagged and sold as certified trees. Despite the small amount of certified nursery stock produced, the extensive use of buds from registered trees and trees adjacent to registered trees resulted in an overall improvement in the quality of citrus nursery stock. By 1960, at least 90 per cent of citrus stock grown in Texas was propagated from registered psorosis-free trees, from their progeny in scion groves, or from apparently healthy trees adjacent to registered trees (Sleeth, 1961).

The work of Olson (1952) and Olson and Shull (1956) led to a reevaluation and suggestions for modification of the Texas Citrus Budwood Certification Program. It was proposed that the program include indexing for exocortis, cachexia-xyloporosis, and tristeza, in addition to psorosis. The proposed improvements were never formally adopted and the Texas program has been inactive since about 1962 (Timmer, 1974).

Old-budline grapefruit trees in Texas were found to be consistently infected with cachexia, exocortis, or both; nearly all old-budline trees of other species also were infected, but young budlines were not infected with cachexia or exocortis (Sleeth, 1961). By 1960, of 227 psorosis- and tristeza-free trees under test, 143 had been found infected with cachexia, exocortis, or both. A foundation plot established by the Experiment Station from progeny of trees in which no virus was found still exists.

THE BRAZILIAN PROGRAMS

Following the loss of most of its citrus trees to tristeza in the 1940's and 1950's, Brazil rebuilt and expanded its citrus industry, largely by planting trees of nucellar budlines on tristeza-tolerant (especially Rangpur lime) rootstocks.

The Brazilian situation provided an excellent opportunity for propagating large numbers of trees from carefully indexed parent trees, largely nucellar, on tristeza-tolerant rootstocks. This was done in budwood programs, two of which have been especially important: the federal program for the Rio area and the São Paulo state program.

The Rio Program

Indexing for psorosis, cachexia-xyloporosis, and exocortis was done on trees before registration of selections that often were chosen for their relative freedom from, or mild symptoms of, tristeza stem pitting. Selections were made on various ranches (Giacometti and Leite, 1961) for propagation by nurserymen and/or establishment in a varietal planting. This program has apparently been less extensively used than the São Paulo program, but is has contributed some useful selections for the Rio citrus area.

São Paulo Program

In the State of São Paulo, the Budwood Certification Service has for more than 15 years operated an inspection, indexing, and registration service (Anon., 1960, 1961, 1962). The number of nucellar trees produced in the state increased from 232,000 in 1961 to 3,961,000 in 1969.[1] Thus, this program has been one of the most productive in the world. The principal varieties in the São Paulo program are Valencia and Navel sweet orange, but more than a million nucellar budline trees of other varieties were produced in 1969.

The São Paulo program was established after a very extensive survey established the occurrence of exocortis, cachexia-xyloporosis, and psorosis in high percentages throughout the citrus areas of the state (Rossetti and Salibe, 1961). Indexing in the São Paulo program has been conducted on Rangpur lime for exocortis, on Orlando tangelo for cachexia-xyloporosis, and on Caipira sweet orange for psorosis. Registrations have been made for periods of five years and the regulation contains provisions for the registration of old-budline as well as nucellar budline trees of some varieties.

All trees in the Brazilian programs are assumed to be tristeza-infected, but some effort has been made to avoid tristeza virus strains causing severe pitting of the candidate selection.

OTHER PROGRAMS

Several states and countries besides those already mentioned operate registration and certification programs or have operated them in past years. Arizona (Allen, McDonald, and Rodney, 1974) has an active program similar to those of Florida and California but on a smaller scale. There are also programs in Colombia (Giacometti and Rios-Castaño, 1967), Sicily (Scaramuzzi, Càtara, and Cartia, 1968), France, Morocco, Israel, Spain, Turkey, South Africa, Australia (Broadbent and Fraser, 1976; Turpin, 1970; Levitt, 1961), and several other countries. Spain has a new and modern program which includes provision for obtaining virus-free selections from nucellar seedlings and from shoot-tip grafting *in vitro* from infected old-budline selections (Navarro *et al.*, 1976). Most programs use a number of features described

---

[1]Letter from Dr. V. Rossetti, Instituto Biologico, São Paulo, dated May 4, 1970.

herein for the California programs, but few are nearly as complete with respect to inspection and indexing.

Probably the greatest numbers of registrations have been made in Florida and São Paulo State in Brazil. These programs have been responsible for millions of trees (Anon., 1960, 1961, 1962; Bridges, 1974) but could not avoid tristeza infection of young trees.

In the Mediterranean region, only Spain is known to have large numbers of tristeza-infected trees. Some countries have produced their own nucellar budlines (Scaramuzzi *et al.*, 1968) and some have imported nucellar material from other counties.

INDEXING

The identification of citrus viruses is based mainly on diagnostic symptoms in trees or on indexing, which is the testing of a plant for the presence of a virus or other pathogen. Indexing procedures have been described for nearly all citrus diseases known or presumed to be caused by viruses or mycoplasmalike organisms. The procedures normally depend on specific and sometimes general reactions by inoculated citrus or other host plants that are especially sensitive to the pathogen involved. Some citrus varieties are said to be self-indexing for certain viruses; that is, under normal conditions the plant reacts specifically to the presence of the virus. Plants of many citrus varieties, however, react vaguely and slowly, if at all, to most citrus viruses. Pathogens in symptomless plants can be readily detected only by inoculating them into other plants, usually vigorous young seedlings or budlings of highly sensitive varieties, called indicators. This is tissue-graft indexing. Chemical tests, serology, culturing, and electron microscopy may also be used for indexing for certain pathogens.

Chemical Indexing

Pathogens affect the physiology of diseased plants; the detection of pathogen-induced changes in host physiology is called chemical indexing. The procedures for chemical indexing are usually fast. Paper or thin layer chromatography may be used to separate certain compounds which indicate infection by specific pathogens (Feldman and Hanks, 1969; Feldman *et al.*, 1971; Feldman, Hanks, and Garnsey, 1972). Probably the most commonly used of all chemical indexing methods is that described by Schwarz (1968*a*, 1968*b*) for greening. Gentisoyl glucoside is present in the tissues of trees infected with greening or stubborn but is more abundant in greening-infected trees (Feldman and Hanks, 1969, Schwarz, 1968*a*). Schwarz (1968*b*) detected greening disease by placing cut fruit directly under a fluorescent lamp.

The presence of exocortis virus can be detected by the presence of scopoletin and umbelliferone in the tissues (Feldman *et al.*, 1971). Coumarins can be detected in exocortis-infected Etrog citron plants (Càtara and Cartia, 1971; Feldman *et al.*, 1972; Fudl-Allah, Sims, and Calavan, 1974).

Chemical indexing is considered to be generally less reliable than tissue-graft indexing for identifying specific pathogens but has been extensively used in South Africa to detect greening in citrus nursery trees (Schwarz, 1968*b*). Sometimes chemical changes in the host plant are not specifically related to a single pathogen or the changes may occur only in one or a few species (Feldman and Hanks, 1969; Feldman *et al.*, 1972). Chemical indexing measures only certain effects of the pathogen on the host; it does not directly detect the pathogen. The use of appropriate healthy and diseased controls is necessary.

Serology

Serological indexing for pathogen identification is rapid and provides a direct, specific measure of the pathogen; however, serological techniques have rarely been used to detect citrus pathogens. Desjardins (1969) reviewed the status of the serology of citrus viruses. More recently, other reports have appeared on the use of serology for detecting certain citrus viruses (Garnsey and Purcifull, 1969; Primo *et al.*, 1971). Garnsey and Purcifull (1969) made practical use of serology for identifying one citrus virus. Purification or partial purification of more citrus viruses may lead to wider use of serology for detecting the viruses in infected plants.

Culturing

The stubborn disease pathogen, *Spiroplasma citri* (Saglio *et al.*, 1973) is often readily culturable from infected citrus tissues or from carrier insects (Fudl-Allah, Calavan, and Igwegbe, 1972; Daniels *et al.*, 1973; Saglio *et al.*, 1971; Lee *et al.*, 1973). Young leaves and stem tips are finely chopped and placed in the special media described below. Then they are filtered through a 0.45 micron filter and incubated at 32° C. *S. citri* grows well on a special medium containing 2.1 gm Difco PPLO broth, 1.0 gm sucrose, 0.1 gm fructose, 0.1 gm glucose, 0.1 gm tryptone, 20 ml horse serum, 0.1 gm dry yeast extract, 3 ml 25 per cent fresh yeast extract, 1.0 ml phenol red solution (0.1 g/100 ml), 70 ml water, and 5.0 gm sorbitol (sucrose may be substituted for sorbitol). Addition of 2.1 ml penicillin (0.1 g/100 ml) is desirable but not essential. The ingredients—excepting horse serum, fresh yeast extract, and penicillin which are filtered through a 0.2 micron filter—are adjusted to pH 7.5-7.8 and autoclaved at 121° C (15 psi) for 20 minutes. The organism is identified by dark-field microscopy which reveals tiny spinning spirals (fig. 3–2) or by electron microscopy of pellets from liquid media (fig. 2–45) (Fudl-Allah, *et al.*, 1972). Growth of *S. citri* changes the red broth to amber and creates slight turbidity in the cultures in one to four weeks.

Sweet orange, grapefruit, tangelo, and tangerine are self indicators for stubborn disease and under hot conditions can often be diagnosed in the field. However, culturing is useful for confirming doubtful cases. It has been noted that culturing is more successful during warm or hot periods than during cool ones.

Citrus viruses are not culturable, except in suitable living host tissues. The greening organism (mycoplasmalike or bacterialike) of South Africa has not been cultured and will not grow on the medium used for *S. citri.*[2] An organism has been cultured from greening-affected citrus trees in India (Ghosh *et al.*, 1971).

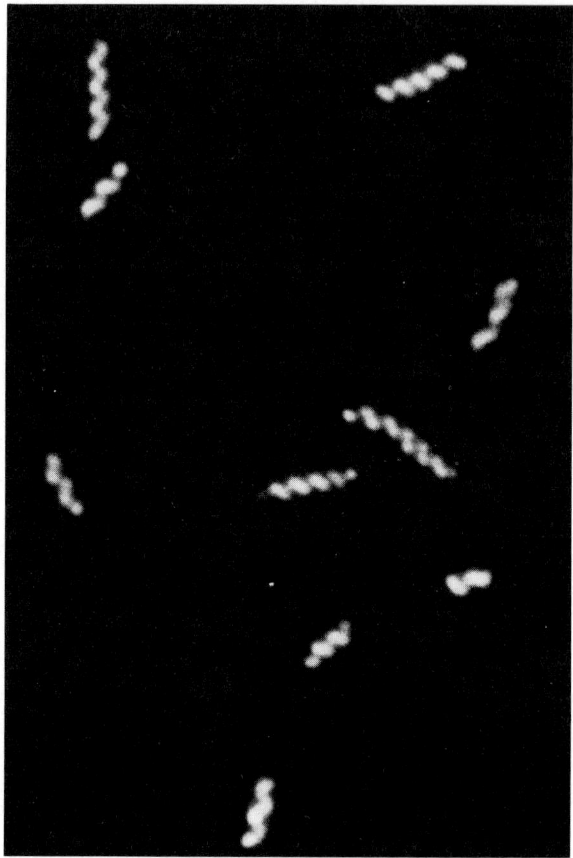

Fig. 3–2. ***Spiroplasma citri*, the stubborn pathogen, from a fast-growing young broth culture; photographed through a dark-field microscope. (Photo courtesy of I. M. Lee.)**

Electron Microscopy

The electron microscope has been useful in diagnosing greening and stubborn diseases (Igwegbe and Calavan, 1970; Laflèche and Bové, 1970) and tristeza (Bar-Joseph and Loebenstein, 1970*a*). The organisms associated with greening and stubborn were readily observed by electron microscopy and were sufficiently different in ultrathin sections to permit diagnosis of these diseases. Strong differences between membranes of the stubborn and likubin (greening) organisms have been illustrated by Garnier, Latrille, and Bové (1976). Bar-Joseph and Loebenstein (1970*a*), using a partially purified virus suspension from 25 gm of bark of diseased trees, were able to observe the threadlike particles of tristeza virus and thereby diagnose tristeza whether or not symptoms were present.

Kitajima *et al.*, (1964, 1965) first observed the long flexuous rods associated with tristeza infection in dips and exudates from tristeza-infected citrus leaves. Price (1966) later observed the rods in place in infected lime tissue. Purified and partially purified preparations of some other citrus viruses have been observed by electron microscopy (Desjardins, 1969) but have been of very limited value in diagnosis. Most of the observations were made on citrus variegation and crinkly leaf viruses. Semancik and Weathers (1965) reported partial purification of the virus now called citrange stunt. Tanaka, Saito, and Kishi (1968) reported purification of the Satsuma-dwarf virus from infected sesame plants.

Although several citrus viruses and myco-

[2]P. Saglio and J. M. Bové. Station de Physiologie et de Biochimie Végétales, Centre de Récherches de Bordeaux, Institut National de la Récherche Agronomique, Port-de-la-Maye, France.

plasmalike pathogens can be identified by electron microscopy, the electron microscope has been little used for diagnosis except for tristeza (Bar-Joseph and Loebenstein, 1970*a*), where it was used primarily because it permitted rapid detection of diseased trees in connection with an eradication program.

Tissue-Graft Indexing

Successful and reliable tissue-graft indexing requires that the indicator plants be carefully inoculated and well tended in an environment favorable to the development of good symptoms and protected from accidental infections. Detection of citrus viruses by graft transmission has been reviewed by Roistacher (1976).

Soil and Environment.—The soil or mix in which indicator plants are grown preferably should be sterilized, or at least free of organisms such as citrus nematode *(Tylenchulus semipenetrans)*, *Phytophthora* spp., and *Pythium* spp. that attack citrus. Symptoms of virus infection may be strong or may fail to appear in plants weakened or damaged by insects, mites, poor nutrition, improper watering, cold or heat.

Appropriate fertilization and a suitably standardized soil or potting mix free of harmful pest organisms are essential to the satisfactory performance of indicator plants. Experimental work begun at Riverside, California in 1957 indicated that citrus seedlings grown in the U. C. soil mixes described by Baker *et al.* (1957) develop severe micronutrient deficiencies (Nauer *et al.*, 1967). Studies of the effects of initial soil-mix composition, fertilization, and pH on citrus seedlings showed certain soil mixes and liquid fertilizer programs satisfactory for growing superior index plants. Prolonged use of ammonium nitrate lowers the pH of any of the U. C. mixes (Labanauskas, Nauer, and Roistacher, 1967; Nauer *et al.*, 1967). Citrus plants kept in U. C.-type mix in containers for an extended period should receive calcium nitrate or some other non-acidifying nitrogen fertilizer (Nauer *et al.*, 1967). The following method (Nauer, Roistacher, and Labanauskas, 1968) is being used for the production of high quality citrus seedling indicator and rootstock plants for the CVIP.

Equal parts of fine sand (particle size $^1/_{50}$ to $^1/_{500}$ inch in diameter), peat moss, and redwood shavings are thoroughly mixed with macro- and micro-nutrients in a large cement-type mixer and steam-sterilized. The redwood shavings are not essential. Macronutrients used per cubic yard of mix are 2.5 pounds of single superphosphate, 3.75 pounds of dolomitic lime, and 1.25 pounds of calcium carbonate lime. Micronutrients used per cubic yard of mix are 2.25 ounces of copper sulfate, 0.75 ounce zinc sulfate, 0.75 ounce manganese sulfate, 1.25 ounces ferrous sulfate, 0.02 ounce boric acid, and 0.01 ounce ammonium molybdate. The micronutrients are dissolved in water to facilitate mixing.

Liquid fertilizer containing 4½ pounds of ammonium nitrate and 2 pounds of muriate of potash per 1,000 gallons is applied from a siphoning device once a week (more frequently if needed) in amounts sufficient to provide for leaching through drain holes at the bottom of the containers. The pH of the medium is controlled between 5.0 and 6.5 insofar as possible. After about a year of continual fertilization with ammonium nitrate, the pH of U. C.-type mixtures at Riverside may drop to pH 4.0 or below in one-gallon cans, necessitating repotting in a new soil mix or the use of other means for raising the pH.

The above method has been used satisfactorily in greenhouses in several areas in California, but may require some modification in situations with widely different environments and water quality.

Insects and mites are more easily controlled in carefully screened houses having air-lock entrances than in ordinary glasshouses. Great care must be exercised to avoid introduction of insect and mite pests on equipment, clothing, and workers, as well as on budwood and other plant materials. Appropriate pesticides should be used when necessary to control infestations. Weekly fumigations may be necessary in some facilities and, if they can be done successfully without injury to the plants, are preferable to sprays that result in undesirable and sometimes confusing deposits and injuries. The choice of pesticides depends on which pests have to be controlled, their stages of development, the sensitivity of the plants, safety factors, and availability.

Phytophthora and pythium infections can be avoided or minimized by sanitary procedures including treating all seed at 125° F for 10 minutes in agitated hot water (Klotz and Calavan, 1969), avoiding the use of any seedlings grown in infested or unsterilized soil, keeping muddy or dirty feet and shoes off greenhouse benches, using only clean equipment and tools, and treating wooden benches annually or semiannually with a solution of copper naphthenate (Roistacher and Baker, 1954). Bench tops should be slotted or otherwise well-ventilated and drained to prevent the spread of zoospores in water running across the bench top. Splashing should be avoided insofar as possible. The floor of the greenhouse should be well-drained and should be liberally dusted with Bordeaux mixture or other copper fungicide. Dirt floors should be covered with a layer of fine gravel about 3 inches deep.

If any plants develop symptoms of phytophthora or pythium infections, they and their containers should be removed and sterilized at once and the surrounding area of the benches or beds involved should be given additional treatment with copper naphthenate or Bordeaux mixture. Phytophthora infestations, once common in greenhouses almost everywhere, were eliminated more than a decade ago from the facilities of the CVIP and have been kept under control there and in many other operations by the sanitary precautions listed above. Healthy indicator plants may be produced under various temperature conditions. Many varieties grow best between 75° and 95° F, so growth may be slowed, when desired, by holding them at cool temperatures.

Following inoculation, plants should be kept in well-lighted situations and at temperatures considered favorable to symptom development. Information regarding the effect of temperature on symptom development is sketchy at best but, in general, it is recommended that plants be held at moderate temperatures (65° to 80° F) for about two weeks. Following this brief period of incubation they should be subjected to temperatures ranging up to 90° or 95° F for exocortis (Calavan, unpublished information) and to 95° F for stubborn indexing (Olson and Rogers, 1969). Schwarz (1968*c*) recommended temperatures of 70° to 73° F for development of greening symptoms. Recommended temperatures for indexing various diseases are given in table 3–1.

Index plants should be carefully examined (read) at regular intervals beginning about two or three weeks after inoculation for most indexing and six months or more after inoculation for cachexia and impietratura indexing. Readings should coincide with appropriate stages of new leaf and shoot growth.

Healthy, uninoculated indicator plants should be used in all indexing work for purposes of comparison because markings or patterns that may easily be confused with symptoms of viral infection may be due to injuries, malnutrition, temperature extremes, chemical, and inheritable disorders. Also, accidental infections may result from seed, vector, and mechanical transmission of certain viruses.

When possible, the use of positive controls, e.g., indicator plants inoculated with the appropriate virus or viruses, should be used to assist in the timing of examinations and in confirming the reliability of the index.

The essential features of any indexing program depend on its purpose and the circumstances under which it is operated. For example, an indexing program in a region where tristeza virus is rare and can be suppressed may be directed specifically toward the detection of tristeza virus, as in the tristeza detection and suppression programs conducted by the Central California Tristeza Control Agency and the California Department of Food and Agriculture. These programs are carried out by qualified personnel using Mexican lime indicator plants in greenhouses having some degree of temperature control. When a program has as its primary purpose the provision of propagative material free of certain pathogens, it must utilize indicator plants sensitive to these pathogens and grow them in a situation highly favorable to symptom development. Sometimes it is necessary to avoid confusing the symptoms of one disease with those of another by using indicator plants that react strongly to a specific virus but which show little or no reaction to another. Thus, Orlando tangelo is preferable to sweet lime as a long-term index variety for xyloporosis because Orlando reacts strongly to cachexia and usually very weakly or not at all to tristeza. Similarly, the vein-clearing symptoms caused by some strains of psorosis virus in Mexican lime may be confused with those caused by tristeza. In this case, the occurrence of stem pitting several months after inoculation reveals the presence of tristeza virus, whereas plants infected only by psorosis virus are not pitted.

Comprehensive indexing programs are used in several countries. The most extensive of these operations are in California, Israel, Florida, and Brazil. The CVIP in California includes indexing on indicator plants for all the known virus or other graft-transmissible diseases of citrus.

The principal indexing procedures for citrus virus diseases were compiled for publication by the Committee on Indexing Procedures, Diagnosis, and Nomenclature of the International Organization of Citrus Virologists (Childs *et al.*, 1968). Most of the indexing procedures described in the follow-

TABLE 3–1
INDICATOR PLANTS AND SYMPTOMS PRODUCED ON THEM BY THE PRINCIPAL VIRUS AND MYCOPLASMALIKE AGENTS

Disease	Indicator Plants	Symptoms on Indicator Plants	Optimal Temperature (°F)	Incubation Period
Blind Pocket (see also psorosis)	Mandarin, sweet orange, lemon	Leaf flecking and/or vein clearing.	65–78	4–8 weeks
Cachexia-Xyloporosis		Gum in Parsons Special near union and point of cutback; pits in wood and gum in bark of long-term indicators.	80–95	1 year on Parsons Special; 2 years or more on others.
Citrange Stunt (see also tatter leaf)	Troyer, Carrizo, or Rusk citrange	Distortion and blotching of young leaves and twigs. Later symptoms are zigzag growth of branches and wood pitting.	65–78	4–8 weeks
Concave Gum	Dweet tangor, mandarin, sweet orange	Oak-leaf pattern and flecks in young leaves.	65–78	5–10 weeks
Crinkly Leaf (see also infectious variegation)	Citron, mandarin; sweet orange, sour orange, lemon	Crinkling of leaves, leaf flecking.	65–78	3–8 weeks
Cristacortis	Orlando tangelo, sour orange, sweet orange	Concave gum or psorosis-like leaf symptoms may appear but are not diagnostic. Pitting and gumming of stems of Orlando and sour orange in later stages.	moderate	10 months or more; leaf symptoms sooner
Dweet Mottle	Dweet tangor	Psorosis-like mottle on leaves.	65–78	6–9 weeks
Exocortis	Etrog citron (Arizona 861; USDCS 60–13; some others)	Leaf and stem epinasty: cracking of midvein; browning of underside of veins; stunting, blotching and cracking of stem; wrinkling and browning of petiole; browning of petiole; browning of leaf tip.	80–95	3–16 weeks
Greening	Sweet orange, tangelo	Stunting, leaf blotching and chlorosis.	cool type 65–75 warm type 70–95	4–12 weeks

TABLE 3–1 (CONTINUED)

Disease	Indicator Plants	Symptoms on Indicator Plants	Optimal Temperature (°F)	Incubation Period
Hassaku Dwarf (see also tristeza)	*Citrus obovoidea* and Mexican lime	Small upfolded leaves, vein clearing.	— —	
Impietratura	Grapefruit, sweet orange	Hard, gummy deposits in rind and core of fruit; psorosis-like leaf symptoms may occur but are insufficient for diagnosis.	— —	Leaf symptoms may appear in a few months; one year or more for fruit symptoms.
Infectious Variegation (see also crinkly leaf)	Citron, mandarin, sweet orange, sour orange, and lemon	Leaf flecking, speckling, crinkling, variegation, and distortion.	65–75	3–8 weeks
Leaf Curl	Caipira sweet orange	Extreme curling of leaves, stunting.	— —	
Psorosis	Sweet orange, mandarin, Mexican lime. Dweet tangor, citron	Clear flecks along veinlets; sometimes ring-like patterns on mature leaves; rapid dieback of new growth (shock) usually followed by recovery.	65–78	4–8 weeks
Ring spot	Lemon, Rough lemon, sour orange, sweet orange	Yellowish rings with green islands on some leaves; sometimes vein clearing and stem lesions.	65–80	4–12 weeks
Satsuma Dwarf	White sesame, Satisfaction kidney bean, and Blackeye cowpea by sap inoculation. Satsuma for long-term test	Necrotic spots and streaks from sap inoculation (see text); leaves bent downward, boat-shaped or spoon-	Cool to moderate	— —

[illegible]	...can lime, *C. excelsa*	grapefruit, *C. excelsa*, and lemon; stem pitting of Mexican lime; corky veins may develop late on Mexican lime.		
Stem Pitting (see also tristeza)	Mexican lime and grapefruit; long-term test on grapefruit needed for stem pitting diagnosis.	Pitting of the stem (delayed in grapefruit), vein clearing of leaves of Mexican lime.	65–80	8–16 weeks; 2 years or longer in grapefruit
Stubborn	Sweet orange, tangelo	Stunting and leaf mottle, leaves smaller than normal, shortened leaf internodes.	80–92	4–12 weeks
Tatter Leaf (see also citrange stunt)	*Citrus excelsa*	Blotching, vein chlorosis and distortion of leaves, ragged edges on some leaves.	65–78	4–8 weeks
Tristeza	Mexican lime; *Citrus macrophylla*, *C. excelsa*.	Veinlet clearing in young leaves; stem pitting.	65–78	3–24 weeks
Vein Enation, Woody Gall	Mexican lime, *C. volkameriana*, Rough lemon, sour orange, and Rangpur lime	Enations on underside of veinlets of Mexican lime and sour orange; galls on trunks of *C. volkameriana*, Rough lemon, Rangpur lime, and Mexican lime.	65–85	4–12 weeks for vein enations; often longer for woody galls
Yellow Vein	Mexican lime, Rough lemon, Etrog citron, *C. macrophylla*	Bright yellow veins in leaves; yellow blotches on stems.	65–80	2–8 weeks

ing pages are based largely on the above report. Significant recent modifications have been included for several of the procedures and it is expected that more improvements will be made in indexing procedures for several of the diseases.

Table 3–1 lists the principal virus diseases or presumed virus diseases for which indexing procedures are known, the principal varieties of indicator plants, the usual symptoms, suitable temperatures for symptom development, and the usual incubation periods. It is worth noting that some plants such as Mexican lime, sweet orange, and Orlando tangelo are useful for indexing several pathogens. Additional details are included in the text on pages 209–19. A comprehensive indexing program can be conducted by using Mexican lime, sweet orange, Etrog citron, Parsons Special mandarin, Dweet tangor, and Troyer citrange indicator plants.

Grafting Techniques.—Most indexing for citrus viruses and mycoplasmalike pathogens is still done by graft inoculation of citrus indicator plants, despite the increasing use of chromatography, serology, and electron microscopy. For details of some of the conventional methods such as chip budding, T-budding, side grafting, or top grafting, refer to USDA Agricultural Handbook 333 or to a horticultural textbook (also see chap. 1, vol. III). Leaf-piece grafts may also be used, require only small amounts of inoculum, and may be used on very small plants. A new leaf-disc method (Blue *et al.*, 1976) utilizes round leaf pieces cut with a paper punch and taped with nontoxic transparent tape into holes punched in leaves of the indicator plants (fig. 3–3). By punching across the midveins of the leaves, the midveins of the inoculum pieces may be aligned with the midveins of the indicator plants. Results obtained for tristeza indexing in very small indicator plants are excellent; those for psorosis are inferior to results from bud grafting.

Leaf tissue may also be grafted into cuts in stems of indicator plants. For stubborn indexing this method is highly successful if the cut end of midvein phloem is placed in contact with the cut end of the indicator phloem. A double-bladed knife is useful for rectangular leaf-piece grafts.

Fruit grafts are useful in diagnosing stubborn disease. Partially grown fruits develop symptoms of stubborn when grafted onto stubborn-affected plants (Olson, 1969).

A wide variety of grafting techniques can be used successfully for indexing graft-transmissible citrus pathogens. Healthy, well-maintained indicator plants, including positive and negative controls, are the principal requirements. Vinyl plastic tape about 3.5 mils thick or other budding tape can be used to hold grafts in place and protect them from desiccation. Plastic bags may be inverted over large grafts to reduce desiccation if necessary.

Indexing Procedures

The following indexing procedures have been abstracted largely from USDA Agricultural Handbook 333 (Childs *et al.*, 1968), but include

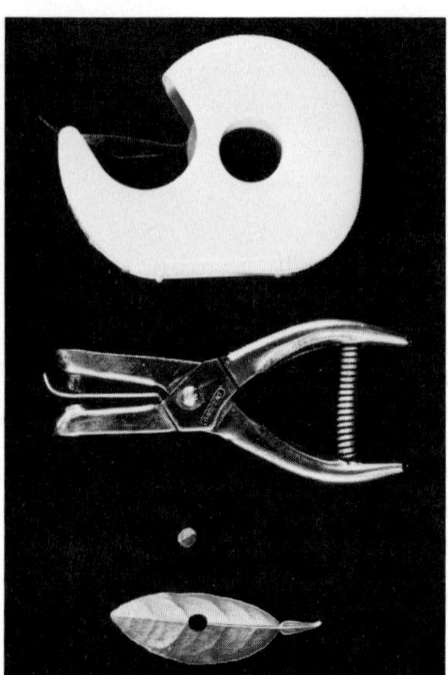

Fig. 3–3. Punched leaf disc grafting of small citrus seedlings. This method is useful for tristeza indexing.

updating for certain diseases.

Cachexia-xyloporosis.—There are two principal methods of indexing for cachexia virus: a short-term and a long-term index. The short-term index requires about a year to complete (Roistacher *et al.*, 1973) and the long-term requires two to eight years. Four plants should be used to index each candidate tree.

For the short-term index, buds of Parsons Special mandarin seedlings are grafted onto Rough lemon seedlings which are simultaneously inoculated with two or more buds from the plant being tested. The plants are then placed in a very warm glasshouse, preferably between 80° and 95° F, where the Parsons Special scions are forced into rapid growth. After about four months, the Parsons Special shoots are cut back to 7 inches above the union and forced to grow out again. After another four months the scions are again cut back to 10 inches above the union. One year after inoculation the indicator plants are examined for gumming by peeling the scion bark at the bud unions and branch junctions. Positive symptoms include gum and darkening of the tissues in these regions (fig. 3-5). It is important to include positive and negative control plants for comparison. If the glasshouse is too cool, symptoms will be delayed or absent.

Long-term indexing for cachexia virus can be done in the field with several species of indicator plants, including Orlando tangelo, Parsons Special mandarin, Palestine sweet lime, and Rangpur lime; the first two are the better indicators. Palestine sweet lime is easily pitted by tristeza so is of little use as a cachexia indicator when tristeza virus is present. Rangpur lime is usually less sensitive to cachexia and more sensitive to exocortis virus than Orlando tangelo and Parsons Special mandarin.

Indicator varieties may be used in the field as seedlings or as scions. Seedlings can be grafted, when they are 20 to 50 cm high, with buds from the candidate trees. Indicator scions can be grown on inoculated rootstocks such as Rough lemon to obtain a very rapid growth which will sometimes develop symptoms within about a year, but which usually requires two years or more. The first symptoms are pits in the wood and small spots of gum in the phloem or on the cambial face of the wood near the bud union (figs. 2–36 and 2–37). Pinholing of the affected bark may occur. Inoculated indicator seedlings develop similar symptoms in the older portions of the plants. Rectangular or lens-shaped 'windows' of bark may be removed periodically for inspection which usually begins about two years after inoculation.

Early development of symptoms is favored by a hot environment and symptoms may be delayed several years in cool areas. Evaluation of results is greatly facilitated by including positive and negative control indicator plants. Negative controls reveal reactions to tristeza virus and positive controls show when the reaction to cachexia should occur. Symptomless long-term indicators should be retained at least six years (eight years under cool conditions) before being considered cachexia virus-free.

Cristacortis.—Cristacortis may be indexed in Orlando tangelo and sour orange seedlings by grafting buds or leaf pieces from the candidate tree. About four indicator plants should be used. Stem symptoms may appear within ten months on inoculated Orlando seedlings or may require somewhat longer to appear (Vogel, 1973). Symptoms are deep, elongated pits in the wood and pronounced crested pegs which extend from the bark and are impregnated with gum near the crests (figs. 2-68 and 3-4). Gum is also deposited in the wood extending radially inward from each crest (fig. 3-4) (Vogel, 1973). The large pits are visible from the outside as enlongated or lens-shaped depressions (fig. 3-4).

Vogel (1973) noted that a leaf symptom resembling that of psorosis is consistently associated with cristacortis but does not differentiate cristacortis from psorosis. Plants lacking leaf symptoms may be assumed to be cristacortis-free. Cristacortis-infected indicator plants develop leaf symptoms within a year and normally show pitting symptoms within three years.

Exocortis.—Citrus exocortis viroid (CEV) can be detected in from about three weeks to six months on two or more Etrog citron seedlings or scions (Calavan *et al.*, 1964). The seedlings or scions must be from a clone known to be sensitive to CEV infection, such as Arizona 861 or USDCS 60–13. Citron seedlings have been shown to be satisfactory for exocortis indexing (Garnsey and Whidden, 1973). Recently Roistacher *et al.* (1977) found an extremely sensitive citron (861–S–1). Exocortis viroid does not appear to be seed transmitted.

Two or more buds, pieces of bark, or leaf patches from the candidate trees are grafted into each indicator plant. If citron scions are used, the citron buds may be grafted simultaneously and

Fig. 3–4. Symptoms of cristacortis and concave gum. Top left, cristacortis pitting in trunk of four-year-old Orlando tangelo seedling. Bottom left, crests of cristacortis on the cambial face of the bark of sour orange. Top right, concave gum (upper) and cristacortis (lower) symptoms in cross-section of Orlando tangelo trunks. Note gum layers in concave gum-infected trunks. Bottom right, concave gum and cristacortis symptoms in cross-section of an Orlando tangelo trunk. (All photos courtesy of R. Vogel.)

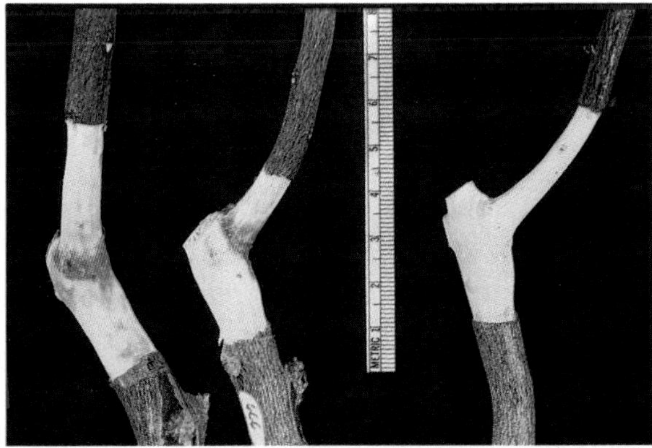

Fig. 3–5. Cachexia symptoms in Parsons Special mandarin on Rough lemon rootstock. Plants at left and middle show gum deposits beneath and in the bark near the bud union. Plant at right is a healthy control. (Photo courtesy of C. N. Roistacher.)

forced to grow as soon as possible. When this is done, citron growth may be severely stunted and may fail to flush; thus, some workers prefer to use citron seedlings or established healthy citron scions on a vigorous rootstock such as Rough lemon. The candidate buds are not permitted to develop into shoots. Positive and negative control indicator plants should be used for evaluation of the indexing.

Great care must be exercised to avoid contaminating indicator plants and scions because CEV is easily moved on knife blades and fingers (Garnsey and Jones, 1967; Roistacher, Calavan, and Blue, 1969), and can survive on blades for a long time (Allen, 1968; Roistacher and Calavan, 1974). Exocortis viroid can be quickly inactivated on tools by a 1 per cent solution of sodium hypochlorite (a 1:4 dilution of commercial household bleach) as recommended by Roistacher *et al.* (1969).

Indicator plants should be examined for symptoms of CEV infection soon after the first new flush of citron growth appears and each two or three weeks thereafter for about six months. Symptoms to look for are: epinasty of the leaves (figs. 2–35 and 3–6), cracking of the lower side of the midveins of leaves, browning of the underside of

Fig. 3–6. Exocortis symptoms on indicator plants. Top left, leaf epinasty on Etrog citron. Top right, browning of veins on underside of Etrog leaf. Lower left, wrinkling of Etrog petiole. Lower right, yellow blotches on stems of Rangpur lime. (All photos except lower right courtesy of C. N. Roistacher.)

the veins (fig. 3–6), and twisting or horizontal wrinkling of the petioles (fig. 3–6). Other symptoms may include dwarfing, stem epinasty, yellow blotching of the stem (fig. 3–6), and small corky lesions or vertical cracking of the stem. Roistacher *et al.* (1977) have described and illustrated symptoms of mild CEV on citron 861–S–1.

Exocortis viroid can be detected by other methods which usually require more time and space than the citron method. Another method deserves mention although it was abandoned in California because it was only about 50 per cent effective. This is the Rangpur lime index. Rangpur lime is used as the scion of an inoculated seedling or is grown as an inoculated seedling. The appearance of yellow blotches on the Rangpur lime shoots from four months to more than a year after inoculation indicates the presence of CEV (fig. 3–6). The blotches are usually located near thorns on shoots that have grown rapidly. Inoculated trifoliate orange plants often react in a similar way (fig. 2–34).

In addition to graft indexing, chemical methods may sometimes be of limited use in diagnosing exocortis. Childs, Norman, and Eichhorn (1958) devised a phloroglucinol test for CEV in trifoliate orange. Feldman *et al.* (1971) and Fudl-Allah *et al.* (1974) described chromatographic methods of indexing for CEV under certain conditions.

Several noncitrus hosts of CEV are known. Weathers (1965) reported that petunia is a host and can be inoculated mechanically. Later, Weathers, Greer, and Harjung (1967) found other solanaceous hosts and Weathers and Greer (1972) transmitted exocortis viroid mechanically to gynura. Gynura is a good indicator of moderate or severe CEV isolates but may not react to mild isolates (Kapur, Weathers, and Calavan, 1974).

Greening Disease.—Sweet orange or tangelo seedlings are used for indexing greening in South Africa (Schwarz, 1968*c*). Valencia and midseason orange varieties and Orlando, Minneola, and Seminole tangelo varieties are satisfactory indicators. In the Orient, mandarin seedlings such as Ponkan are suitable. Regardless of the indicator plants used, the nutrition must be good because some minor element deficiencies cause symptoms resembling those of greening. During the index period, plants inoculated with South African greening should be kept at temperatures below 75° F most of the time while those with oriental greening (sometimes called likubin or leaf mottling) may be held at temperatures up to 85° F or higher (Bové *et al.*, 1974).

Graft sticks from shoots having leaves with symptoms should be used for inoculation. Ten to 20 indicator plants are suggested for each index because the pathogen seems to be unevenly distributed in the host and the percentage of transmission often is low.

Citrus species such as grapefruit and lemon are susceptible to greening but are affected by some strains of tristeza virus, especially seedling yellows, so it is inadvisable to use them in some situations. All greening indicator varieties are susceptible to stubborn. Kagzi lime has been used as an indicator of greening in India (Capoor, 1965). Under most conditions citrus is self-indicating for greening; indexing is used largely for verification of what is already apparent.

Typical blotchy-mottle leaf symptoms appear on infected indicator plants two to four months after inoculation (fig. 2–47). The range of symptoms found on orchard trees usually occurs on infected plants in a cool greenhouse or, in the case of oriental greening, under cool or warm conditions.

Chromatographic indexing has been used extensively in South Africa to detect greening (Schwarz, 1968*b*) but may be less accurate than tissue-graft indexing. The albedo of sweet orange fruits from infected trees fluoresces in ultraviolet light with a wavelength of 365 mμ. Gentisoyl glucoside can be extracted from the albedo or bark of many infected trees and identified by chromatographic methods (Feldman and Hanks, 1969; Schwarz, 1968*a*). This substance also occurs in stubborn-diseased trees (Feldman and Hanks, 1969).

Examination of ultrathin sections of the midveins of leaves of stubborn-infected or greening-infected trees reveals mycoplasmalike bodies in the sieve tubes (Laflèche and Bové, 1970; Igwegbe and Calavan, 1970). The envelope enclosing the greening organism is about twice the thickness of the membrane surrounding the stubborn organism (Saglio *et al.*, 1971; Garnier *et al.*, 1976).

Gummy Bark.—The identification of this disease is based on the development of gum deposits in the bark of sweet orange trees on sour orange rootstock (Nour-Eldin, 1968). Indexing requires four years or more, so an alternative combination such as sweet orange on Rough lemon rootstock must be used as an indicator plant in areas where tristeza is present and spreading.

Young grafted plants large enough to set in the field may be used as indicators. Buds from candidate trees are grafted into indicator plants which are then planted in a field and grown for about four years before examination. Symptoms are stunting and gum-impregnated bark (fig. 2–74). When the bark is scraped carefully, streaks of reddish brown gummy tissue appear, especially near the bud union. Sometimes streaks of gummy bark extend two feet or more above the union. Pitting of the wood is also common at the union and in the sweet orange bark. Nour-Eldin (1968) reported two types of pitting. One type gives a grooved appearance to the cambial face of the wood; the other type, more common, is a round conoid pitting (fig. 2–74). Pegs projecting from the bark into the wood are impregnated with gum. Severe gumminess of the bark may or may not be accompanied by severe wood pitting.

Impietratura.—Impietratura can be indexed on young bearing two- or three-year-old grapefruit or sweet orange trees (Ruggieri, 1968). Inoculations can be made in the fall, as bud or side grafts, and symptoms should appear in the spring more than a year later. Diseased fruits are characterized by skin hardening and albedo gumming (Papasolomontos, 1969) (fig. 2–60). Sometimes the disease can be detected externally by feeling the fruits for hard spots in the peel. The peel hardening sometimes is followed by small protuberances or by a halo of yellow around the hardened area. Green spots may appear on the fruits over gum pockets and fail to color normally during ripening (fig. 2–60). Hard, gum-beaded areas may occur in the albedo near the stem end and gum may extend several centimeters into the stem.

Indexing may be safely done outdoors because there is apparently no natural spread of impietratura (Cartia and Càtara, 1974).

A psorosis-like leaf symptom has been detected associated with impietratura (Bar-Joseph and Loebenstein, 1970*b*). This leaf symptom reveals the presence of a pathogen but is of little diagnostic value.

Psorosis, Blind Pocket, Concave Gum, Crinkly Leaf, and Infectious Variegation.—For indexing purposes all of these diseases may be considered as a group because they have certain common or overlapping features. For registration and certification purposes it is not essential to determine which of these diseases is present. The same can be said of impietratura and cristacortis which also may cause psorosis-like symptoms on indicator seedlings (Bar-Joseph and Loebenstein, 1970*b*; Vogel, 1973).

Indicator plants for this group of viruses are sweet orange, lemon, and mandarin. Various sweet orange varieties are satisfactory; among the best known are Bessie, Indian River, Koethen, Madam Vinous, Parson Brown, and Pineapple. Eureka and Lisbon lemon seedlings are useful, especially for crinkly leaf and infectious variegation, but other lemons should serve as well. Sour orange seedlings also are good indicators for these two viruses. Mandarin or mandarin hybrid varieties should be included as psorosis indicators because they react well to some mild psorosis-like viruses (Wallace, 1968*c*; Roistacher and Blue, 1968). Dweet mottle virus causes symptoms only on Dweet tangor, a very sensitive indicator (Roistacher and Blue, 1968).

Kara, King, and Dancy mandarins are good indicators for most psorosis and psorosis-like viruses, but Dweet tangor is more sensitive. During the winter several hours of supplemental artificial lighting daily favor symptom development. Temperatures in the range of 65° to 78° F are favorable for psorosis symptoms; high temperatures may suppress symptoms.

Indexing is done by grafting buds or leaf patches into the stems of pencil-sized, or smaller, seedling indicators, which are then cut back to force new shoot growth from several points near the sites of the grafts. About four indicators with two-to-four grafts per candidate should be used. New growth on indicator plants should be examined at least twice a week for symptoms because symptoms are often ephemeral and intermittent in their occurrence. Periodic examination should be continued for at least eight weeks.

Vein flecking (pale translucent flecks along the veinlets) of young leaves has been assumed to be a common symptom of the psorosis diseases. Other symptoms that occur with some psorosis virus infections are shock and oak-leaf patterns (figs. 2–1, 2–2, and 3–7). Vein flecking (figs. 2–1 and 3–7) is a highly variable form of vein banding, sometimes occurring as only a few flecks and at other times as hundreds of flecks per leaf. Oak-leaf patterns may show as zonate zigzag lines extending lengthwise of the leaf on each side of the midvein (figs. 2–1 and 3–7). The clearings from psorosis vein flecking are normally less distinct and less restricted to the veins than those caused by tristeza, but it is sometimes difficult to distinguish between these viruses on indicators such as Mexi-

Fig. 3–7. Leaf and shoot symptoms of psorosis and concave gum. Upper left, psorosis shock symptoms with dieback on sweet orange seedling. Upper right, oak-leaf pattern of concave gum on sweet orange leaf. Lower left, the middle and right Dweet tangor leaves show flecking and spotting from common psorosis. Lower right, Dweet tangor leaves with psorosis vein flecking. (All photos courtesy of C. N. Roistacher.)

can lime, which are sensitive to both viruses. Flecks caused by psorosis virus may coalesce so that part of the leaf has an abnormally pale color. Psorosis sometimes causes small circular spots or irregularly shaped chlorotic areas on lemon plants. Practically all leaf symptoms disappear as citrus leaves mature except in plants infected by relatively uncommon strains that cause mature leaf symptoms, usually consisting of yellowish circular rings about ⅛- to ½- inch in diameter but sometimes showing conspicuous yellow to dark green line patterns (fig. 2–3).

Oak-leaf patterns have generally been assumed to be associated with concave gum and often are, but many concave gum-infected leaves show no oak-leaf pattern. It is possible that this symptom is not restricted to plants infected with concave gum virus. Concave gum virus causes rings of gum to be deposited in the wood of infected trees (fig. 3-4).

The first visible evidence of some strains of psorosis virus is a shock reaction. First symptoms are twisting and bending of young shoots. Then the young leaves drop off and all shoots formed after decapitation and inoculation die back (figs. 2–2 and 3–7). For a time, new leaves may fall off before they can develop the vein flecking symptom.

Crinkly leaf and concave gum viruses do not appear to cause a shock reaction. Common psorosis, blind pocket, and infectious variegation viruses often do cause a severe shock effect in the first growth after infection.

The crinkly leaf virus causes only slight or no symptoms on young leaves; later the crinkling develops in some leaves as they expand. Crinkly leaf causes pinpoint spotting on lemon leaves (fig. 2–10). Infectious variegation virus causes shock, then blotching and distortion of leaves, and finally variegation and distortion (fig. 2–12).

There are several psorosis-like effects that are not caused by psorosis (Wallace, 1968*c*) but which may be easily mistaken for it. Seedling Eureka lemon plants may develop leaf spotting symptoms, possibly from air pollution damage. Genetic abnormalities sometimes imitate psorosis symptoms and a form of variegation sometimes occurs, especially in lemons, following freeze damage or other injury. A common cause of leaf-flecking outdoors is aphids, or other sucking insects, which damage the young leaves. Much confusion can be avoided by always including positive and negative controls with the index plants for candidate trees.

Ring spot.—Citrus ring spot virus can be indexed on lemon, Rough lemon, sour orange, sweet orange, and several other indicator plants. Buds, side grafts, or leaf-patch grafts may be used as inoculum on plants having a stem diameter of ⅛ to ¼ inch. About a month or more after inoculation the young leaves of infected indicator plants show faint chlorotic spots and develop clearing or chlorosis on some portions of the veins. Later, the spots and chlorotic parts of the veins on the upper surface of the leaves turn yellow and green islands appear so that small yellow rings with green centers are formed (fig. 2–61). As the leaves mature, the yellow rings and spots become more conspicuous, especially when they coalesce to form large yellowish blotches (fig. 2–62) (Wallace and Drake, 1968; Càtara and Grasso, 1968). Spots, blotches, rings, and vein clearing sometimes appear on the undersides of leaves, but have less yellow color there.

Leaves of inoculated sweet orange plants sometimes develop large ring patterns or blotches resembling mature leaf symptoms of psorosis. On some varieties of citrus, ring spot causes a shock effect characterized by dropping of young leaves and death of tender stems and sometimes by lesions on the stems.

Satsuma Dwarf.—Satsuma dwarf may be indexed on healthy young Satsuma scions or on several species of plants, especially white sesame (*Sesamum indicum* L.), Blackeye cowpea (*Vigna sinensis* [Tomer] Sani), and Satisfaction kidney bean (*Phaseolus vulgaris* L.) or other suitable indicators (Tanaka, 1968).

To index on Satsuma scions, inoculate outdoors in the spring or summer, using adequate positive and negative controls. Examine the plants the following spring for the characteristic downward (abaxially) curved leaves. Two types of leaf symptoms may appear: narrow boat-shaped and dwarfed spoon-shaped (fig. 2–55) (Tanaka, 1968).

The following procedures were suggested by Tanaka (1968) for indexing on herbaceous plants: White sesame, Blackeye cowpea, or Satisfaction kidney bean are grown in small containers in the glasshouse. Sesame seedlings are inoculated with sap on the first and second true leaves; cowpea or kidney bean are inoculated in pairs of primary leaves. The sap is prepared from young shoots or fruit rind by grinding with anywhere from an equal to twice the volume of 0.05 to 0.10 molar solution of potassium acid phosphate or phosphate buffer of pH 7.0. Plants are inoculated by rubbing with sap and carborundum. Inoculated plants are kept at about 82° F for sesame and 77° F for the legumes.

Several days after inoculation, infected sesame plants develop chlorotic spots which later become necrotic spots with a yellowish halo. Systemically infected leaves show vein clearing, then malformation and curling and finally vein necrosis which spreads, causing death of whole leaves. Infected cowpeas develop necrotic streaks on the petioles and stems and infected kidney beans show vein clearing and mosaic.

Stubborn.—Stubborn is usually self-indicating on all commercial varieties of citrus, but for diagnosis or confirmation in doubtful cases, it may be indexed on several especially sensitive indicator varieties. Stubborn indexing is of value principally in cool areas where symptoms are somewhat masked or in trees with mild symptoms. Sweet orange (especially the Madam Vinous variety), Cuban shaddock, Sexton tangelo, and Parsons Special mandarin are good indicators for the stubborn pathogen.

A mycoplasmalike organism, *Spiroplasma citri*—not a virus—is the cause of stubborn (figs. 2–44, 2–45, and 3–2). Graft indexing of stubborn requires one to six months in a warm glasshouse (daytime temperatures 80° to 95° F). A total of 20 or more pieces of tissue (buds, side grafts, or young leaf grafts) should be put into ten or more seedlings for each candidate indexed. Vigorous indicator plants with a stem diameter of 3/16 to 5/16 inch are suitable and should be cut back to a height of about 1 foot at the time of inoculation. Retain as many leaves as possible to help start vigorous new growth and place the inoculum below and directly in line with one or more remaining buds. Each indicator plant should be trained to grow a single shoot. Inspection for leaf and shoot symptoms should be made twice each month. Positive and negative control plants should be included for comparison.

Positive reactions to stubborn disease infection in indicator plants include general stunting, short leaf internodes, and small rigid, often upright, cupped, and mottled leaves (fig. 3–8) (Calavan, 1968). The leaves may show a variety of pale green or yellow banding and streaking along the veins. The patterns often resemble those caused by nutritional imbalance and are not diagnostic unless absent in the negative control plants. Diagnosis of stubborn is considered to be definite when inoculated indicators develop a pale green mottle only near the pinched-in distal end of the leaf (fig. 3–8). On some infected leaves, both the marginal and interveinal areas near the tips are pale green.

Young infected leaves provide excellent inoculum for grafting indicator plants. Cut small rectangular pieces, 0.2 x 0.4 inch, across the midvein, insert them under bark flaps on the indicator plant, and wrap them with plastic tape. The top horizontal cut edge of the leaf pieces should be in contact with the horizontal cut at the top of the bark flap so that sieve-tube cells of the leaf piece and indicator plant can readily unite.

For culture indexing of stubborn by isolation of *S. citri*, see the section under "Culturing."

Tatter Leaf and Citrange Stunt.—Tatter leaf was described by Wallace and Drake (1962) and has been found in the United States naturally occurring only in Meyer lemon. Citrange stunt was described as another disease, apparently caused by another virus (Wallace and Drake, 1968). Both viruses are found naturally occurring in Meyer lemon and both are mechanically transmissible (Càtara and Wallace, 1970; Garnsey, 1974) so it seems possible that they are strains of the same virus. The tatter leaf virus or strain can be indexed on *Citrus excelsa* but apparently can be lost from many citrus hosts, including citranges and citremons, which are good indicator plants for citrange stunt virus. Citrange stunt reportedly causes no visible reaction on *C. excelsa* plants (Càtara and Wallace, 1970). Tatter leaf virus causes blotchy spotting, somewhat resembling the effects of psorosis on lemons or limes, when it is tissue-graft inoculated into *C. excelsa* (fig. 2–56). Some of the newly developing leaves have tattered, irregular margins. In some plants, abnormal leaves continue to appear for weeks or months but normal growth recurs later. In other plants production of symptomless leaves is soon resumed. Symptoms of tatter leaf usually appear within one to two months after inoculation. Inoculations may be made by bud, bark, or leaf-patch graft.

Citrange stunt virus apparently has a wider host range than tatter leaf virus and, by definition, does not cause tatter leaf of *C. excelsa*. However, it does cause yellowish mottling, vein banding, and failure of one side of the leaflet to develop on Troyer, Carrizo, and Rusk citranges and on citremons. This virus also causes stunting and wood pitting in these hosts, with the individual pits somewhat vertically aligned, and with zigzag growth of the stems and branches. Sometimes corky lesions appear on the stems.

The natural occurrence of tatter leaf and citrange stunt viruses in the United States appears to be restricted to Meyer lemon but in Japan a virus associated with the "Dai-Make" bud-union disorder occurs in Satsuma and seems to be identical to citrange stunt virus (Miyakawa and Matsui, 1976). It is worthy to note that one or more serial passages of citrange stunt and tatter leaf viruses through *C. excelsa* and various other varieties often results in loss of the isolate or isolates that cause tatter leaf symptoms in *C. excelsa*. Therefore, because tatter leaf is not known to occur in the absence of citrange stunt virus, the preferred index plants for the mixtures are citrange and citremon.

Tristeza and Seedling-yellows Tristeza.—Tristeza can often be diagnosed by histological examination of tissues at the bud union of intolerant combinations of top and rootstock. However, indexing on sensitive indicator plants is necessary to determine the presence of the virus in tolerant combinations and to detect mild strains of tristeza virus in any combination. The lime test is commonly used to detect ordinary tristeza virus. In order to identify the seedling yellows strain, indicator varieties that will show a seedling yellows reaction must be used; these are lemon, sour orange, and grapefruit. Mexican lime will react to seedling yellows tristeza in a manner similar or identical to the common tristeza reactions.

The Mexican lime has been adopted as the best overall indicator plant for tristeza and reacts very well at cool to to-moderate temperatures (65° F to 78° F). Symptoms are likely to be masked in sustained temperatures of 85° F, or higher. The Mexican lime is also known as West Indian lime, baladi lime, and Key lime. The Galego lime of Brazil and the Kagzi lime of India are similar or identical.

Lime plants should be grown to a height of 4 to 6 inches and transplanted 3 or 4 to a one-gallon container. Care should be taken to discard all off-type and slow-growing plants. Plants are ready for use when the stems reach a diameter of approximately 3/16 inch. Use of the leaf-disc graft technique (fig. 3–3) permits the use of much smaller plants (Blue *et al.*, 1976).

Inoculations can be made with bark or leaf patches, buds, shields without buds, or side grafts. It is advisable to use 3 or 4 plants for each candidate. Indicator plants should be cut back at the time of inoculation to leave two or more buds of the indicator above the grafts. Growth from these buds should develop symptoms of tristeza during the first or second flush. Growth from the grafts should be eliminated. Grafts should be examined in about two weeks to determine survival.

The first symptoms of tristeza or seedling yellows on infected lime plants usually are chlorosis and cupping of the terminal leaves of the young shoots that develop after inoculation, often within 3 to 4 weeks (Wallace, 1968*a*). With very mild strains of tristeza virus the chlorosis and cupping may not occur. Vein clearing may appear about four weeks after inoculation or may be delayed somewhat longer. By transmitted light the vein clearing usually appears as narrow translucent flecks or lines of varying lengths but generally not involving the entire vein (figs. 2–20 and 3–8). There is considerable variation in the amount and distribution of the vein-clearing symptom, presumably due to virus strain and host differences. The underside of a leaf with vein clearing shows watersoaked areas matching the vein areas that appear cleared when viewed by transmitted light (fig. 2–20). If indicator plants are kept more than three months, they should be pruned to stimulate new growth.

Infected lime indicator plants develop stem pitting (fig. 2–20) within a few months after inoculation. Sometimes five to six months are required for stem pitting to develop. Pits are revealed by stripping the bark from the stems. If enough growth has occurred, pits may appear on the main stem but sometimes, especially in infected plants that have grown slowly, pits may be confined to small hardened shoots that developed after inoculation. If neither leaves nor stems show symptoms at suitable temperatures in six months, the test should be considered negative.

The seedling yellows tristeza virus usually causes early and severe symptoms in Mexican lime but some strains of common tristeza virus may cause equally severe reactions. Seedling yellows often causes prominent corky veins in lime and this may help to identify it (fig. 3–8). However, the best indicators for seedling yellows are Eureka or Lisbon lemon seedlings which develop chlorotic foliage and become noticeably stunted when infected with seedling yellows virus (fig. 2–31). Stubborn disease can cause similar symptoms on lemon but causes no vein clearing of Mexican lime.

The strains of tristeza virus that cause stem pitting of grapefruit (or Hassaku dwarf) may be indexed on Mexican lime for the detection of tristeza virus. To differentiate these strains from common tristeza, they must be indexed on grapefruit seedlings or scions for several years. In areas where grapefruit stem-pitting tristeza virus spreads naturally, the indexing must be done indoors. All tristeza indexing should be done indoors to avoid naturally spread tristeza virus or, in tristeza-free areas, the possible spread of the virus to nearby healthy plants.

Vein Enation and Woody Gall.—Mexican lime, Rough lemon, and sour orange are excellent indicator plants. Inoculations should be by bud or side graft and symptoms usually begin to appear as vein swelling on the lower surface of leaves in about a month. Leaf symptoms range from mild swelling to conspicuous pointed or ridged projections on the under surface of the leaves (fig. 2–48). Corresponding shallow depressions occur on the upper surface.

The woody gall symptom is not essential for diagnosis but may first appear on small green twigs about two months after inoculation (Wallace,

Fig. 3-8. Symptoms of stubborn disease and tristeza on indicator plants. Upper left, comparison of healthy (left) and stubborn-infected Madam Vinous sweet orange seedlings. Note small leaves, stunting, and short internodal space of the stubborn plant. Upper right, comparison of normal (top) and stubborn-infected sweet orange leaves. Note pale mottle near tips of infected leaves. Lower left, vein clearing of tristeza-infected Mexican lime leaf. Lower right, vein corking on lower side of seedling yellows tristeza-infected leaves of Mexican lime.(All photos courtesy of C. N. Roistacher.)

1968*b*). Galls often develop near thorns or at injury sites. At first the galls appear as slight gray swellings on green twigs. Growing galls become irregular and the bark covering the tissue roughens and becomes lighter colored than normal (fig. 2–49). The gall tissue itself is very hard and the cambial face of the wood of galls is lightly pitted from numerous undeveloped buds and light green from chlorophyll. Shoots sometimes grow from old galls.

Yellow Vein.—Mexican lime, Rough lemon, and Etrog citron are among the best indicator plants for yellow vein (Weathers, 1968), a rare virus disease of citrus reported only from California. When yellow vein occurs alone or in combination with psorosis, its behavior is so erratic that identification is difficult. Yellow vein virus can be most reliably diagnosed in the presence of vein enation virus (Weathers, 1960, 1968). The suggested procedure is: inoculate young indicator plants with a pure culture of vein enation virus, usually by grafting, then after vein enation symptoms are well-developed graft-inoculate the plants with candidate tissues. Examine the plants weekly for symptoms on developing leaves. If yellow vein virus is present, symptoms should appear at moderate temperatures in 2 to 8 weeks.

The first symptom to appear is yellowing of the main veins; then some of the smaller veins are regularly affected (figs. 2–64 and 2–65). Yellow areas may be separated by normal green areas and one half of the leaf may be more affected than the other. Symptoms appear on both sides of the leaf.

LITERATURE CITED

ALLEN, R. M. 1968. Survival time of exocortis virus of citrus on contaminated knife blades. Plant Dis. Reptr. **52**:935–39.

ALLEN, R. M., H. H. MCDONALD, and D. R. RODNEY. 1974. Progress report and citrus foundation budwood release 1974 through the Arizona Cooperative Citrus Registration-Certification Program. Ariz. Agr. Expt. Sta. Rept. 272 (Mimeo). 16 pp.

ANONYMOUS. 1960. Registro de matrizes sadias de citros. O Biologico **26**:190.

ANONYMOUS. 1961. Registro de plantas matrizes de citros. O Biologico **27**:61–62.

ANONYMOUS. 1962. Registro de mudas di citros para produzir-pomares sadios. O Biologico **28**:113–14.

ANONYMOUS. 1969. [Florida]. Citrus Budwood Registration Program. Statement of policy. Florida Dept. Agr., Citrus Budwood Registration, Winter Haven, Fla. 10 pp. (Mimeographed).

ANONYMOUS. 1974. [California]. Regulation for registration and certification of citrus trees. Calif. Dept. Food and Agr., Sacramento. (Mimeo.)

ANONYMOUS. 1975. [California]. Regulations for registration and certification of Improved Meyer lemon trees. Calif. Dept. Food and Agr., Sacramento. 6 pp. (Mimeo.)

BAKER, K. F., P. A. CHANDLER, R. D. DURBIN, J. FERGUSON, J. W. HUFFMAN, O. A. MATKIN, D. E. MUNNECKE, C. N. ROISTACHER, W. R. SCHOONOVER, and R. H. SCIARONI. 1957. The U. C. system for producing healthy container-grown plants. Univ. Calif. Manual 23, 332 pp.

BAR-JOSEPH, M., and G. LOEBENSTEIN. 1970*a*. Rapid diagnosis of the citrus tristeza disease by electron microscopy of partially purified preparations. Phytopathology **60**:1510–12.

———. 1970*b*. Leaf flecking on indicator seedlings, associated with citrus impietratura in Israel: a possible indexing method. Plant Dis. Reptr. **54**:643–45.

BARNES, A. E. 1933. [California]. Fruit Growers Supply Company Annual Report of the General Manager for the year ended December 31, 1932. 15 pp.

BLUE, R. L., C. N. ROISTACHER, G. CARTIA, and E. C. CALAVAN. 1976. Leaf-disc grafting—a rapid indexing method for detection of some citrus viruses. *In:* Calavan, E. C. (ed.). Proc. 7th Conf. Intern. Organ. Citrus Virol. pp. 207–12. IOCV, Riverside.

BRIDGES, G. D. 1965. Validation of scion and rootstock varieties. Citrus Indus. **46**(11):27–28.

———. 1970. Certification of premium quality citrus nursery stock. Citrus Indus. **51**(9):7–8.

———. 1974. The Florida Citrus Budwood Program. *In:* Jackson, L. K., A. H. Krezdorn, and J. Soule, (eds.). Proc. 1st Intern. Citrus Short Course—Citrus rootstocks. pp. 131–36. Florida Coop. Ext. Service, Inst. Food and Agr. Sci., Univ. Fla., Gainesville, Fla.

BRIDGES, G. D., and C. O. YOUTSEY. 1972. Natural tristeza infection of citrus species, relatives and hybrids at one Florida location from 1961–1971. Proc. Fla. State Hort. Soc. **85**:44–47.

———. 1974. Yield variations among citrus nucellar seedling clones at the Florida State Budwood Foundation Grove. Proc. Fla. State Hort. Soc. **87**:85–87.

BROADBENT, P., and L. R. FRASER. 1976. The Australian Citrus Improvement Programme. *In:* Calavan, E. C. (ed.). Proc. 7th Conf. Intern. Organ. Citrus Virol. pp. 204–06. IOCV, Riverside.

CALAVAN, E. C. 1958. Importance of virus diseases. Calif. Citrog. **43**:230.

———. 1963. New threat from tristeza. Calif. Citrog. **48**:267, 282.

———. 1968. Stubborn. *In:* Childs, J.F.L. (ed.). Indexing procedures for 15 virus diseases of citrus trees. Pp. 35–43. U.S. Dept. Agr., Agr. Res. Serv., Agr. Handbook 333, Washington, D.C.

———. 1969. Investigations of stubborn disease in California: indexing, effects on growth and production, and evidence for virus strains. *In:* Chapman, H. D. (ed.). Proc. First Intern. Citrus Symp. **3**:1403–12. Univ. of Calif. Riverside, Calif.

———. 1974. Registration and certification of citrus propagative materials in California. *In:* Jackson, L. K., A. H. Krezdorn, and J. Soule (eds.). Proc. 1st Intern. Citrus Short Course—Citrus rootstocks. Pp. 137–45. Fla. Coop. Ext. Serv., Inst. Food and Agr. Sci., Univ. Florida, Gainesville, Fla.

CALAVAN, E. C., and D. W. CHRISTIANSEN. 1965. Rapid indexing for stubborn disease of citrus. Phytopathology **55**:1053. (Abstract).

CALAVAN, E. C., E. F. FROLICH, J. B. CARPENTER, C. N. ROISTACHER, and D. W. CHRISTIANSEN. 1964. Rapid indexing for exocortis of citrus. Phytopathology **54**:1359–62.

CALAVAN, E. C., M. K. HARJUNG, A.E.A. FUDL-ALLAH, and J. W. BOWYER. 1974. Natural incidence of stubborn in field-grown seedlings and budlings. *In:* Weathers, L. G., and M. Cohen (eds.). Proc. 6th Conf. Intern. Organ. Citrus Virol. Pp. 16–19. Univ. Calif. Div. Agr. Sci., Berkeley.

CAPOOR, S. P. 1965. Presence of seedling yellows complex in the citrus of South India. *In:* Price, W. C. (ed.). Proc. 3rd Conf. Intern. Organ. Citrus Virol. Pp. 30–35. Univ. Fla. Press, Gainesville, Fla.

CARTIA, G., and A. CÀTARA. 1974. Studies on impietratura disease. *In:* Weathers, L. G., and M. Cohen (eds.). Proc. 6th Conf. Intern. Organ. Citrus Virol. Pp. 123–26. Univ. Calif. Div. Agr. Sci., Berkeley.

CÀTARA, A., and G. CARTIA. 1971. Possibilita d'impiego di un metodo chromatografico per la diagnosi dell infezioni di <<exocortite>> degli agrumi in materiale siciliano. Riv. Patol. Veg. S. 4, **7**:173–80.

CÀTARA, A., and S. GRASSO. 1968. Una nuova virosi degli agrumi per L'Italia: "La maculatura anulare" ("Ring Spot"). Riv. Patol. Veg. S. 4, **4**:261–66.

CÀTARA, A., and J. M. WALLACE. 1970. Identification of citrange stunt as the mechanically transmissible virus from Meyer lemons doubly infected with citrange stunt and tatter leaf viruses. Phytopathology **60**:737–38.

CHILDS, J.F.L., J. BOVÉ, E. C. CALAVAN, L. R. FRASER, L. C. KNORR, F. NOUR-ELDIN, A. A. SALIBE, S. TANAKA, and L. G. WEATHERS (eds.). 1968. Indexing procedures for 15 virus diseases of citrus trees. U.S. Dept. Agr., Agr. Res. Serv., Agr. Handbook 333, Washington, D.C. 96pp.

CHILDS, J.F.L., G. NORMAN, and J. L. EICHHORN. 1958. A color test for exocortis infection in *Poncirus trifoliata*. Phytopathology **48**:426–32.

DANIELS, M. J., P. G. MARKHAM, B. M. MEDDINS, A. K. PLASKITT, R. TOWNSEND, and M. BAR-JOSEPH. 1973. Axenic culture of a plant pathogenic Spiroplasma. Nature **244**:523–24.

DESJARDINS, P. R. 1969. Purification, electron microscopy and serology of citrus viruses—a review. *In:* Chapman, H. D. (ed.). Proc. First Intern. Citrus Symp. **3**:1481–88. Univ. Calif., Riverside, Calif.

DICKSON, R. C., R. A. FLOCK, and METTA MCD. JOHNSON. 1951. An insect vector of the citrus quick decline disease. Calif. Citrog. **36**:135, 169–70.

FAWCETT, H. S. 1948. Citrus diseases in the Lower Rio Grande Valley. Calif. Citrog. **33**:362–63.

FAWCETT, H. S., and J. M. WALLACE. 1946. Evidence of the virus nature of citrus quick decline. Calif. Citrog. **32**:50, 88–89.

FELDMAN, A. W., G. D. BRIDGES, R. W. HANKS, and H. C. BURNETT. 1971. Effectiveness of the chromatographic method for detecting exocortis virus infection in *Poncirus trifoliata*. Phytopathology **61**:1338–41.

FELDMAN, A. W., and R. W. HANKS. 1969. The occurrence of a gentisic glucoside in the bark and albedo of virus-infected citrus trees. Phytopathology **59**:603–06.

FELDMAN, A. W., R. W. HANKS, and S. M. GARNSEY. 1972. Localization and detection of coumarins in exocortis-virus-infected citron. *In:* Price, W. C. (ed.). Proc. 5th Conf. Intern. Organ. Citrus Virol. Pp. 239–44. Univ. Fla. Press, Gainesville, Fla.

FUDL-ALLAH, A.E.-S.A., E. C. CALAVAN, and E.C.K. IGWEGBE. 1972. Culture of a mycoplasmalike organism associated with stubborn disease of citrus. Phytopathology **62**:729–31.

FUDL-ALLAH, A.E.-S.A., J. J. SIMS, and E. C. CALAVAN. 1974. Indexing of exocortis virus-infected citron by using thin-layer chromatography. Plant Dis. Reptr. **58**:82–85.

GARNIER, M., J. LATRILLE, and J. M. BOVÉ. 1976. *Spiroplasma citri* and the organism associated with likubin: comparison of their envelope systems. *In:* Calavan, E. C. (ed.). Proc. 7th Conf. Intern. Organ. Citrus Virol. Pp. 13–17. IOCV, Riverside, Calif.

GARNSEY, S. M. 1974. Mechanical transmission of a virus that produces tatter leaf symptoms in *Citrus excelsa*. *In:* Weathers, L. G., and M. Cohen (eds.). Proc. 6th Conf. Intern. Organ. Citrus Virol. Pp. 137–40. Univ. Calif. Div. Agr. Sci., Berkeley.

GARNSEY, S. M., and J. W. JONES. 1967. Mechanical transmission of exocortis virus with contaminated budding tools. Plant Dis. Reptr. **51**:410–13.

GARNSEY, S. M., and D. E. PURCIFULL. 1969. Serological detection of a citrus virus in leaf extracts from field trees. Proc. Fla. State Hort. Soc. **81**:56–60.

GARNSEY, S. M., and R. WHIDDEN. 1973. Severe, uniform response by monoembryonic seedlings of the Arizona 861 selection of 'Etrog' citron *(Citrus medica)* to citrus exocortis virus (CEV). Plant Dis. Reptr. **57**:1010–12.

GHOSH, S. K., S. P. RAYCHAUDHURI, A. VARMA, and T. K. NARIANI. 1971. Isolation and culture of mycoplasma with citrus greening disease. Curr. Sci. **40**:299–300.

GIACOMETTI, D. C., and N. LEITE. 1961. The budwood registration program for the Rio citrus area. *In:* Price, W. C. (ed.). Proc. 2nd Conf. Intern. Organ. Citrus Virol. Pp. 216–19. Univ. Fla. Press, Gainesville, Fla.

GIACOMETTI, D. C., and D. RIOS-CASTAÑA. 1967. Programa de certificacion de yemas para la propagacion de citricos en Colombia. Rev. Agr. Tropical **23**:277–87.

HUTCHENS, F. B. 1925. Annual report of the general manager of fruit growers supply company for the year ended December 31, 1924. Los Angeles, Calif. 14 pp.

IGWEGBE, E. C. K., and E. C. CALAVAN. 1970. Occurrence of mycoplasmalike bodies in phloem of stubborn-infected citrus seedlings. Phytopathology **60**:1525–26.

KALOOSTIAN, G. H., G. N. OLDFIELD, H. D. PIERCE, E. C. CALAVAN, A. L. GRANETT, G. L. RANA, and D. J. GUMPF. 1975. Leafhopper—natural vector of citrus stubborn disease? Calif. Agr. 29(2):14–15.

KAPUR, S. P., L. G. WEATHERS, and E. C. CALAVAN. 1974. Studies on strains of exocortis virus in citron and *Gynura aurantiaca*. *In:* Weathers, L. G., and M. Cohen (eds.). Proc 6th Conf. Intern. Organ. Citrus Virol. Pp. 105–09. Univ. Calif. Div. Agr. Sci., Berkeley.

KITAJIMA, E. W., D. M. SILVA, A. R. OLIVEIRA, G. W. MÜLLER, and A. S. COSTA. 1964. Thread-like particles associated with tristeza disease of citrus. Nature **201**:1011–12.

———. 1965. Electron microscopical investigations on tristeza. *In:* Price, W. C. (ed.). Proc. 3rd Conf. Intern. Organ. Citrus Virol. Pp. 1–9. Univ. Fla. Press, Gainesville, Fla.

KLOTZ, L. J., and E. C. CALAVAN. 1969. Gum diseases of citrus in California. Calif. Agr. Expt. Sta. Circ. No. 396. 26 pp.

LABANAUSKAS, C. K., E. M. NAUER, and C. N. ROISTACHER. 1967. Initial soil-mix and postplanting liquid fertilization effects on nutrient concentrations in Valencia orange seedling leaves. Hilgardia **38:**569–77.

LAFLÈCHE, DOMINIQUE, and J. M. BOVÉ. 1970. Cytopathologia Végétale.—Structures de type mycoplasme dans les feuilles d'orangers atteints de la maladie du greening. Compt. Rend. Acad. Sci., Paris **270:**1915–17.

LEE, I. M., G. CARTIA, E. C. CALAVAN, and G. H. KALOOSTIAN. 1973. Citrus stubborn disease organism cultured from beet leafhopper. Calif. Agr. **27**(11):14–15.

LEVITT, E. C. 1961. NSW Co-operative Bud Selection Society's system of parent tree registration and virus screening. The Citrus News **67:**86.

MARKHAM, P. G., R. TOWNSEND, M. BAR-JOSEPH, M. J. DANIELS, A. PLASKITT, and B. M. MEDDINS. 1974. Spiroplasmas are the causal agents of citrus little-leaf disease. Ann. Appl. Biol. **78:**49–57.

MENEGHINI, M 1946. Sôbre a natureza e transmissibilidade da doenca "tristeza" dos citrus. O Biologico **12:**285–87.

MIYAKAWA, T., and C. MATSUI. 1976. A bud-union abnormality of Satsuma mandarin on *Poncirus trifoliata* rootstock in Japan. *In:* Calavan, E. C. (ed.). Proc. 7th Conf. Intern. Organ. Citrus Virol. Pp. 125–31. IOCV, Riverside, Calif.

MORTENSEN, A. M. 1917. Report by the manager of the fruit growers supply company, Los Angeles, Calif. 8 pp.

MURPHY, G. H. (ed.) 1969. Agricultural Code. State of California, Department of General Services. Sacramento. 1003 pp.

NAUER, E. M., E. C. CALAVAN, C. N. ROISTACHER, R. L. BLUE, and J. H. GOODALE. 1967. The Citrus Variety Improvement Program in California. Calif. Citrog. **52:**133, 142, 144, 146, 148, 151, 152.

NAUER, E. M., C. N. ROISTACHER, and C. K. LABANAUSKAS. 1967. Effects of mix composition, fertilization, and pH on citrus grown in U.C.-type potting mixtures under greenhouse conditions. Hilgardia **38:**557–67.

———. 1968. Growing citrus in modified UC potting mixtures. Calif. Citrog. **53:**456, 458, 460–61.

NAVARRO, L. 1976. The Citrus Variety Improvement Program in Spain. *In:* Calavan, E. C. (ed.). Proc. 7th Conf. Intern. Organ. Citrus Virol. Pp. 198–203. IOCV, Riverside, Calif.

NORMAN, G. G. 1959. Ability to produce increasing with each passing year. Citrus Indus. **40**(7):8–9, 11.

NOUR-ELDIN, F. 1968. Gummy bark of sweet orange. *In:* Childs, J. F. L. *et al.* (eds.). Indexing procedures for 15 virus diseases of citrus trees. Pp. 50–53. U.S. Dept. Agr., Agr. Res. Serv. Agr. Handbook 333, Washington, D.C. 96 pp.

OLDFIELD, G. N., G. H. KALOOSTIAN, H. D. PIERCE, E. C. CALAVAN, A. L. GRANETT, and R. L. BLUE. 1976. Beet leafhopper transmits citrus stubborn disease. Calif. Agr. **30**(6):15.

OLSON, E. O. 1952. Investigations of citrus rootstock disease in Texas. Proc. Rio Grande Valley Hort. Inst. **6:**28–34.

———. 1969. Symptoms of stubborn disease in Citrus and Poncirus fruit grafted onto virus-infected seedlings. Phytopathology **59:**168–72.

OLSON, E. O., and B. ROGERS. 1969. Effects of temperature on expression and transmission of stubborn disease of citrus. Plant Dis. Reptr. **53:**45–49.

OLSON, E. O., and A. V. SHULL. 1956. Exocortis and xyloporosis; bud-transmission virus diseases of Rangpur and other mandarin-lime rootstocks. Plant Dis. Reptr. **40:**939–46.

PAPASOLOMONTOS, A. 1969. A report on impietratura disease of citrus; its distribution and importance. *In:* Chapman, H. D. (ed.). Proc. First Intern. Citrus Symp. **3:**1457–62. Univ. of Calif., Riverside, Calif.

PLATT, R. G. 1969. First certified trees dug and planted at California Citrus Nurserymen's Society annual meeting. Calif. Citrus Nursery Soc. Yearbook **8:**10–12.

PRICE, W. C. 1966. Flexuous rods in phloem cells of lime plants infected with citrus tristeza virus. Virology **29:**285–94.

PRIMO, E., E. HERNANDEZ, M. MARTINEZ, P. CUNAT, and R. VILA. 1971. Diagnostico precoz de la tristeza del naranjo. I. Separacion y reacciones serologicas de particulas nucleoproteicas. Reprinted from Revista de Agroquimica y Technologia de Alimentos 11, No. 2. 7 pp.

RANA, G. L., G. H. KALOOSTIAN, G. N. OLDFIELD, A. L. GRANETT, E. C. CALAVAN, H. D. PIERCE, I. M. LEE, and D. J. GUMPF. 1975. Acquisition of *Spiroplasma citri* through membranes by homopterous insects. Phytopathology **65:**1143–45.

REUTHER, W. 1959. A program for establishing and maintaining virus-free citrus stock. *In:* Wallace, J. M. (ed.). Citrus virus diseases. Pp. 215–17. Univ. Calif. Div. Agr. Sci., Berkeley.

REUTHER, W., E. C. CALAVAN, E. M. NAUER, and C. N. ROISTACHER. 1968. Citrus Variety Improvement Program provides wide benefits. Calif. Citrog. **53:**205, 222–24, 226, 228, 275–78, 280.

ROISTACHER, C. N. 1976. Detection of citrus viruses by graft transmission: a review. *In:* Calavan, E. C. (ed.). Proc. 7th Conf. Intern. Organ. Citrus Virol. Pp. 175–84. IOCV, Riverside, Calif.

ROISTACHER, C. N., and K. F. BAKER. 1954. Disinfesting action of wood preservatives on plant containers. Phytopathology **44:**65–69.

ROISTACHER, C. N., and R. L. BLUE. 1968. A psorosis-like virus causing symptoms only on Dweet tangor. *In:* Childs, J.F.L. (ed.). Proc. 4th Conf. Intern. Organ. Citrus Virol. Pp. 13–18. Univ. Fla. Press, Gainesville, Fla.

ROISTACHER, C. N., R. L. BLUE, and E. C. CALAVAN. 1973. A new test for citrus cachexia. Citrograph **58:**261–62.

ROISTACHER, C. N., and E. C. CALAVAN. 1974. Survival of exocortis virus on contaminated blades. Citrograph **59:**250, 252.

ROISTACHER, C. N., E. C. CALAVAN, and R. L. BLUE. 1969. Citrus exocortis virus—chemical inactivation on tools, tolerance to heat and separation of isolates. Plant Dis. Reptr. **53:**333–36.

ROISTACHER, C. N., E. C. CALAVAN, R. L. BLUE, L. NAVARRO, and R. GONZALES. 1977. A new more sensitive citron indicator for detection of mild isolates of citrus exocortis viroid (CEV). Plant Dis. Reptr. **61:**135-39.

ROISTACHER, C. N., E. C. CALAVAN, and E. M. NAUER. 1972. Virus-free Meyer lemon trees. Citrograph **57:**270–71.

ROSSETTI, V., and A. A. SALIBE. 1961. Occurrence of citrus virus diseases in the State of São Paulo. *In:* Price, W. C. (ed.). Proc. 2nd Conf. Intern. Organ. Citrus Virol. Pp. 238–41. Univ. Fla. Press, Gainesville, Fla.

RUGGIERI, G. 1968. Impietratura. *In:* Childs, J.F.L. (ed.). Indexing procedures for 15 virus diseases of citrus trees. Pp. 60–62. U.S.D.A. A.R.S. Agr. Handbook 333. Washington, D.C.

SAGLIO, P., DOMINIQUE LAFLÈCHE, CHRISTIANE BONISOL, and J. M. BOVÉ. 1971. Isolement, culture et observation au microscope électronique des structures de type mycoplasme associées a la maladie du stubborn des agrumes et leur comparaison avec les structures observées dans le cas de la maladie du greening des agrumes. Physiol. Veg. **9**:569–82.

SAGLIO, P., M. LHOSPITAL, D. LAFLECHE, G. DUPONT, J. M. BOVÉ, J. G. TULLY, and E. A. FREUNDT. 1973. Spiroplasma citri gen. and sp. n.: a mycoplasmalike organism associated with "stubborn" disease of citrus. Intern. Jour. Syst. Bact. **23**:191–204.

SCARAMUZZI, G., A. CÀTARA, and G. CARTIA. 1968. La selezione sanitaria degli agrumi per le virosi e risultati sperimentali conseguiti in Sicilia. Riv. Pat. Veg. Ser. IV. **4**:213–46.

SCHWARZ, R. E. 1968*a*. Thin layer chromatographical studies on phenolic markers of the greening virus in various citrus species. So. Afr. Jour. Agr. Sci. **11**:797–802.

———1968*b*. Indexing of greening and exocortis through fluorescent marker substances. *In:* Childs, J.F.L. (ed.). Proc. 4th Conf. Intern. Organ. Citrus Virol. Pp. 118–24. Univ. Fla. Press, Gainesville, Fla.

———. 1968*c*. Greening disease. *In:* Childs, J.F.L. (ed.). Indexing procedures for 15 virus diseases of citrus trees. Pp. 87–90. U.S. Dept. Agr., Agr. Res. Serv., Agr. Handbook 333. Washington, D.C.

SEMANCIK, J. S., and L. G. WEATHERS. 1965. Partial purification of a mechanically transmissible virus associated with tatter leaf of citrus. Phytopathology **55**:1354–58.

SLEETH, B. 1959. The Citrus Budwood Certification Program in Texas. *In:* Wallace, J. M. (ed.). Citrus Virus Diseases. Pp. 233–35. Univ. Calif. Div. Agr. Sci., Berkeley.

———. 1961. Indexing citrus for viruses in Texas. *In:* Price, W. C. (ed.). Proc. 2nd Conf. Intern. Organ. Citrus Virol. Pp. 226–30. Univ. Fla. Press, Gainesville, Fla.

SLEETH, B., and E. O. OLSON. 1961. Release of Texas virus-indexed citrus budwood. Jour. Rio Grande Valley Hort. Soc. **15**:19–24.

TANAKA, S. 1968. Satsuma dwarf. *In:* Childs, J.F.L. (ed.). Indexing procedures for 15 virus diseases of citrus trees. Pp. 56–59, U.S. Dept. Agr., Agr. Res. Serv., Agr. Handbook 333. Washington, D.C.

TANAKA, S., Y. SAITO, and K. KISHI. 1968. Purification of Satsuma dwarf virus. *In:* Childs, J.F.L. (ed.). Proc. 4th Conf. Intern. Organ. Citrus Virol. Pp. 287–88. Univ. Fla. Press, Gainesville, Fla.

TIMMER, L. W. 1974. The Texas Budwood Certification Program—An Autopsy. *In:* Jackson, L. K., A. H. Krezdorn, and J. Soule (eds.). Proc. 1st Intern. Citrus Short Course—Citrus rootstocks. Pp. 146–49. Fla. Coop. Ext. Service, Inst. Food and Agr. Sci., Univ. Florida. Gainesville, Fla.

TURPIN, J. W. 1970. Citrus improvement in New South Wales, Australia (Mimeo) 6 pp.

VOGEL, R. 1973. Le cristacortis: une nouvelle maladie a virus des agrumes. D. Sc. thesis, L'Université de Bordeaux II. 153 pp.

WALLACE, J. M. 1945. Technique for hastening foliage symptoms of psorosis of citrus. Phytopathology **35**:535–41.

———. 1968*a*. Tristeza and seedling yellows. *In:* Childs, J.F.L. (ed.). Indexing procedures for 15 virus diseases of citrus trees. Pp. 20–27. U.S. Dept. Agr., Agr. Res. Serv., Agr. Handbook 333. Washington, D.C.

———. 1968*b*. Vein enation and woody gall. *In:* Childs, J.F.L. (ed.). Indexing procedures for 15 virus diseases of citrus trees. Pp. 44–49. U.S. Dept. Agr., Agr. Res. Serv., Agr. Handbook 333, Washington, D.C.

———. 1968*c*. Psorosis A, blind pocket, concave gum, crinkly leaf, and infectious variegation. *In:* Childs, J.F.L. (ed.). Indexing procedures for 15 virus diseases of citrus trees. Pp. 5–15. U.S. Dept. Agr., Agr. Res. Serv., Agr. Handbook 333. Washington, D.C.

WALLACE, J. M., and R. J. DRAKE. 1962. Tatter leaf, a previously undescribed virus effect on citrus. Plant Dis. Reptr. **46**:211.

———. 1968. Citrange stunt and ringspot, two previously undescribed virus diseases of citrus. *In:* Childs, J.F.L. (ed.). Proc. 4th Conf. Intern. Organ. Citrus Virol. Pp. 177–83. Univ. Fla. Press, Gainesville, Fla.

WEATHERS, L. G. 1960. Yellow-vein disease of citrus and studies of interactions between yellow-vein and other viruses of citrus. Virology **11**:753–64.

———. 1965. Petunia, an herbaceous host of exocortis virus of citrus. Phytopathology **55**:1081 (Abstract).

———. 1968. Yellow vein. *In:* Childs, J.F.L. (ed.). Indexing procedures for 15 virus diseases of citrus trees. Pp. 54–55, U.S. Dept. Agr., Agr. Res. Serv. Agr. Handbook 333. Washington, D.C.

WEATHERS, L. G., and F. C. GREER, JR. 1972. Gynura as a host for exocortis virus of citrus. *In:* Price, W. C. (ed.). Proc. 5th Conf. Intern. Organ. Citrus Virol. Pp. 95–98. Univ. Fla. Press, Gainesville, Fla.

WEATHERS, L. G., F. C. GREER, JR., and M. K. HARJUNG. 1967. Transmission of exocortis virus to citrus and herbaceous plants. Plant Dis. Reptr. **51**:868–71.

CHAPTER 4

Regulatory Measures for Pest and Disease Control

DAN Y. ROSENBERG, ELEY H. McEACHERN
F. LOUIS BLANC, DANIEL W. ROBINSON, AND H. LEN FOOTE

QUARANTINE

MANY INSECT PESTS AND plant diseases are more or less specific in their action; that is, they attack only certain groups of related host plants within the limits of specific climatic conditions. Therefore, when a cultivated plant is introduced into a country where no related plants occur, it is likely to be fairly free from attack by serious pests and diseases endemic to the area. This is because the native insects and plant diseases are largely unable to adapt quickly to such hosts. This desirable condition has not, as a rule, been maintained for any significant length of time in any particular locale since extensive movement of nursery stock and other commodities on which pests and diseases may be carried has resulted in the introduction and establishment of many of them.

In the most important citrus-producing areas of the world, interest in better varieties or stocks of the genus *Citrus* is itself a stimulus to introduction. Thus, the major pests and diseases (here includes insects, mites, mollusks, vertebrates, nematodes, plant diseases, parasitic plants, and weeds) of *Citrus* spp. are common to many of the major production areas as a result of their dissemination through early plant introductions and other types of human transport. Several species occur rather generally in the important citrus areas, although some of them are free from one or another of these pests (Ryan *et al.*, 1969). Some major insect pests widely distributed include: the California red scale, *Aonidiella aurantii* Mask.; the Florida red scale, *Chrysomphalus aonidum* L.; the purple scale, *Lepidosaphes beckii* Newm.; the citrus mealybug, *Pseudococcus citri* Risso; the Spanish red scale, *C. dictyospermi* Morg.; the citrus whitefly, *Dialeurodes citri* Riley & Howard; and the Mediterranean fruit fly, *Ceratitis capitata* Wied. Among diseases widely distributed are: brown rot gummosis, *Phytophthora* spp.; melanose (*Diaporthe citri* Fawcett); psorosis, a virus; tristeza, a virus; and exocortis, a viroid. The citrus nematode, *Tylenchulus semipenetrans* Cobb, is widely distributed in the citrus areas of the world. Quarantine procedures clearly benefit citrus growers by preventing the introduction and establishment of pests (or by greatly reducing such a likelihood) in citrus-producing areas still free of them. This is especially true in regions like California which has topographical and ecological features favoring isolation of growing areas (Ryan *et al.*, 1969).

It may reasonably be assumed that under primitive conditions (i.e., before the advent of agriculture and commerce), all forms of life had reached stability as far as geographical distribution is concerned (Ryan *et al.*, 1969). A method of natural dissemination has always existed for every organism: it has either been provided with some means of locomotion (such as the ability to swim, crawl, or fly), or it has been transmitted by an agency (such as animals, or air and water currents) which moves it from place to place.

The agencies of natural distribution are not universally operative and often are nullified by barriers which counteract natural dispersal. These barriers are of various types, but may be classified into three general categories: (1) topographical, (2) climatological, and (3) biological. A topographical barrier may be an ocean, a high mountain range, or a desert which an organism cannot traverse. A climatic barrier may be a zone which an organism cannot cross because of unfavorable meteorological conditions such as heat, cold, humidity, or aridity. A biological barrier may be a zone which an organism is unable to cross because its food plant or host is not present there.

In addition, certain environmental requirements must be met by a given locality before pest organisms can exist and reproduce. For instance, most plants require certain soil, water, and climatic conditions. In their geographic distribution, animals are limited to areas where their particular kind of food exists. Thus, we have three factors which determine the natural distribution of organisms: the host distribution, barriers to movement, and the ecological conditions on which the existence of the particular species depends. Effectiveness of the natural means of movement varies greatly among species. Because of the long periods of time during which it has had an opportunity to act, however, a species has always been able to distribute itself from its point of origin to all localities where the environment and host occurrence are suitable for its existence, except where extensive natural barriers have intervened.

The Purpose of Plant Quarantine

There are many areas where a given pest species could thrive if it were introduced; however, very often it does not exist because its natural means of dispersion has not been adequate to surmount effective natural barriers. Man, with his development of fast methods of transportation, especially of agricultural products, has inadvertently provided more effective means of crossing these natural barriers. Unless preventive measures are taken, the ultimate effect of man's increasing mobility will be that all pest species will occupy all areas on Earth which environmentally favor them and their hosts. The development of plant quarantine is an attempt to delay or prevent these consequences so far as pests and diseases of crop plants are concerned (Ryan *et al.*, 1969).

The sole purpose of plant quarantine, then, is to protect, as far as possible, agricultural areas from infestation by pests and diseases of crop plants which might establish themselves rather easily. This is done by establishing regulations designed to restrict human activities which tend to breach or circumvent the natural barriers to pest movement.

Principles and Limitations of Plant Quarantine

The establishment of a quarantine should rest on certain fundamental prerequisites:

1. The pest concerned should be an actual or expected threat to substantial interests.

2. The proposed quarantine must represent a necessary or desirable measure for which no effective substitute is available involving less interference with normal activities.

3. The success of the quarantine, either for preventing introduction or for limiting spread, must be reasonably assured.

4. The economic gain expected from a proposed quarantine must outweigh both the cost of administration and the interference with normal activities.

5. A quarantine must have a valid biological basis for its establishment. Any regulation whose objective is other than that indicated or defined by the terminology of the regulation—i.e., political or economic gain—is open to and worthy of serious criticism, *even though the actual objective may itself be desirable.*

6. The extent of restrictions imposed by quarantine should be only such as are believed necessary to accomplish the desired end; on the other hand, the objective of a quarantine should not be jeopardized by omission of feasible and necessary restrictions.

Dispersal

Since the efficacy of quarantine measures is influenced so much by the nature of dispersal, the methods by which pests and diseases may gain access to areas previously free from them is of great interest and importance. As far as quarantine is concerned, dispersal may be somewhat arbitrarily divided into two categories: local and long distance.

Local dispersal is brought about largely, but not entirely, by distribution methods which are not new to man's activities. These include natural movement by flight, crawling, and the effect of wind not only on flying and some wingless insect forms, but also on fungus spores and bacteria. Other means of dispersal are transport of young insects and pathogenic organisms by birds (on their feet or in nesting material), carriage by other forms of life, and by running water. Local dispersal is also brought about by man's influence through the local movement of animals, by farm implements, the exchange of plants, and through ignorance or deliberate evasion of quarantine rules which are in effect.

Long distance dispersal takes place entirely as a result of man's activities, mainly through the transportation of commodities such as seed, nursery stock, fruits, vegetables, and other plants or plant parts. Many pests such as beetles may be transported in vehicles or in commodities with which they have no biological relation, but into which they have found their way accidentally. The short distance spread of pests cannot ordinarily be prevented or even appreciably retarded by quarantine action, since man has little or no control over the agencies which make natural dissemination possible. Quarantines designed to prevent natural spread over short distances may be justified to support eradication programs with the objective of eliminating the pest from an infested area. Primarily, regulations designed to prevent the purely local movement of commodities and appliances deemed to be pest carriers are difficult to justify when it is recognized that natural spread not subject to control will, in all likelihood, distribute the pest over the same area in about the same time, irrespective of the regulation.

Relation of Shipping to Dispersal.—Records of the Federal Government and of states which impose plant quarantines to prevent the introduction or spread of agricultural pests reveal that the hazard of pest introduction is directly related to the number of shipments of plant material from one place to another and the number of people in transit between any two places. The improved interstate highway system and the speed of transportation by, for example, jet aircraft, have a significant bearing on dispersal. In fact, the overall trend toward the increased transportation of agricultural material and people has a direct bearing on the introduction of agricultural pests. With the increasing demand for the movement of plants and plant materials, the need for keeping abreast of this trend—with appropriate plant protection—is essential.

In placing a quarantine in effect, consideration must be given to accomplishing reasonable protection to agriculture with minimum inconvenience to the public. In general, living plants or plant parts form the most dangerous carriers of insect pests and plant diseases; but when only certain plant parts are attacked, other parts may be transported safely in commerce. For example, the citrus whitefly is not transported on the fruit but only the leaves; therefore, fruit from an infested area may safely be admitted to an area free from this pest. The Mediterranean fruit fly attacks only the fruit; as a result, citrus budwood from an infested area can be admitted safely into an uninfested area, but not with soil or roots since this insect pupates in soil. It is obvious, then, that an intimate knowledge of the biology of the pest is fundamental to devising quarantine measures to prevent its spread.

Conditions Necessary for Pest Species Establishment

Several requirements must be fulfilled if an introduction is to result in establishment of a pest species. Special conditions for the infection or infestation of the host plants such as wounds or abrasions must sometimes exist. Occasionally, the organism must be introduced at particular times of the year. The introduction must also occur in the immediate vicinity of the host plant. Pest species which require alternate host plants, such as white pine blister rust fungus, must be introduced into a locality where both host species occur. With few exceptions, the insect pests brought in must be fertilized females or both sexes must be admitted simultaneously if reproduction is to occur. The organism must be introduced in sufficient numbers to insure that at least a few will persist even after unfavorable climatic conditions, host resistance, and attack by natural predators or other forms of attrition have taken their toll. In general, then, it will be seen that the chances are usually against successful establishment by the introduction of a very few scattered insect or plant disease organisms. This fact has been well demonstrated experimentally where the introduction of plant-feeding insects is attempted for the purpose of controlling certain weeds (for example, the introduction of insects into northern California to control the Klamath weed).

The establishment of a pest or disease in a locality previously free from it does not guarantee its economic importance there. Climatic conditions such as the amount and seasonal distribution of rainfall, humidity, and fog, temperature ranges and extremes, as well as soil conditions, have a great deal to do with the abundance of pests and the virulence of plant diseases. An insect pest or plant disease which is of major importance to citrus in some parts of the world may be introduced in other areas where citrus is also an important crop and be of no economic importance whatever. For example, Citrus melanose *(Diaporthe citri)* is a disease of economic importance in humid citrus regions, but is of almost no economic significance in California, where the climate is semiarid to arid.

That introductions so often fail to establish pests and diseases permanently in new habitats is of fundamental importance to plant quarantines. It is impossible to prevent every introduction by legal restrictions, but if introductions happen frequently enough or on a sufficiently large scale, sooner or later the right combination of conditions will occur and establishment will result. Plant quarantine aims to make these introductions so infrequent, so scattered, or so infinitely small that establishment would be either long deferred or altogether prevented.

Adherence to Quarantine Regulations

If a quarantine program is to be successful, its restrictions must be fully maintained, and all persons affected by it must adhere to its requirements. To achieve this end, the quarantine administrations should seek the intelligent cooperation of the public affected, rather than depend exclusively on police power, imposition of penalties, or the use of court action.

The authority that exercises the right to establish the quarantine should utilize the means for biological research in order both that the quarantine may be made more efficient and that restrictions may be lessened wherever possible. The need for research, however, should not delay establishing a quarantine believed by authorities (i.e., in an emergency) to be desirable, thereby jeopardizing the objective that might otherwise have been reached.

As conditions change or as more facts become available, the quarantine should be promptly modified either by inclusion of restrictions necessary to its success or by removal of requirements found to be unnecessary. The need to modify the quarantine as conditions change is a continuing one and, thus, demands continuing attention. If the quarantine has attained its objective, or if events clearly prove that the desired end is not possible because of the adopted restrictions, the measure should be promptly reconsidered, with a view either to repeal it or to substitute other means.

Because of the tremendous increase in both human and agricultural traffic, the hazard of pest or disease introduction has become greater in recent years. Since quarantines are not perfect in preventing introduction, it is recognized that there will be increased introduction of pests or diseases escaping quarantine detection. For this reason, it is essential that quarantine programs be supplemented with detection programs and plans for eradication or control of outbreaks as they are discovered.

Methods of Enforcing Plant Quarantines

Inspection at Destination.—This was probably the first method used to prevent the spread of pests and diseases and it is still used in many places. It consisted of inspection at a delivery point of imported materials thought to be possible carriers, and rejection of any materials showing possible signs of infestation or infection. However, experience has demonstrated repeatedly the impossibility of preventing the introduction of most insect pests and diseases simply by this type of inspection. Not only is it physically impossible to examine any great amount of such material with the necessary care, but is is often impossible to detect the presence of disease even with the most minute examination. Most plant-feeding insects likely to be transported on nursery stock or fruit have certain stages which are inconspicuous or hidden and, therefore, not easily detected. With respect to many insect and nematode pests, inspection of every plant part, perhaps even making tissue examinations with a microscope, would be required to positively establish its freedom from infestation. Relatively few insects are conspicuous enough on nursery stock to make the necessarily cursory inspection of commerical shipments a reliable safeguard against infestation. As for plant diseases, in some cases a considerable time (sometimes two or three years) must elapse before conspicuous symptoms appear on the host. The pathogenic organism may be present and the infection be well underway without external evidence of its presence, especially in the case of viruses which cause symptomless latent infection in many hosts. Thus, it is impossible to detect such diseases by plant inspection.

It is not maintained, however, that such inspection is entirely ineffective. Certain conspicuous pests and diseases could be excluded by this means. Perhaps careful inspection of all incoming material or rejection of the entire lot at the first indication of infestation or infection might delay the entry of pests somewhat. Inspection might perhaps be justified as a protection against minor pests and diseases. It may be argued that inspection yields valuable information on geographical distribution of insect pests and diseases upon which quarantines may be based. A sound quarantine program will not ordinarily permit host plants or fruits which originate in the infested area to pass into a clean area merely on the condition that inspection fails to reveal infestation or infection. Instead, quarantine should prohibit the passage across quarantine lines of all hosts of a prohibited pest unless the shipment is accompanied by evidence of a treatment that eliminates the pest.

It should be pointed out that this conclusion does not lessen the necessity of inspection service. In addition, inspections are essential to prevent the entry of contraband or restricted material.

Use of Embargoes.—An alternative to the inspection system is the embargo, i.e., the absolute exclusion of certain material from the area to be protected. While embargoes, in conjunction with natural barriers, would effectively prevent the entry of dangerous insect pests and diseases, a serious objection to this method is its interference with trade. General use of embargoes would result in a condition of economic isolation which would be more detrimental to both producers and consumers than any major pest. It is necessary, therefore, to seek a compromise method which possesses most of the safety features of exclusion and yet permits the conduct of interarea and interstate commerce. This requirement can be most satisfactorily met by the adoption of a system of controlled introduction of agricultural commodities under regulation.

Inspection at Point of Origin.—Another system utilized to some degree is the inspection of shipments and their certification at point of origin. Under such a system, which can be justified only when natural dispersal into the protected area is prevented by barriers, a general control is set up over all incoming plant material. Plants and plant parts including fruits and vegetables are permitted entry if one of the following requirements is met: (1) they originate in an area where such insect pests or disease are believed not to occur; (2) they have been produced and packed under conditions that preclude danger of infestation or infection; (3) they have been or may be subjected to treatment which will destroy live infestation or infection.

For example, Unshu oranges (satsumas) from Japan are now permitted into Alaska, British Columbia, Hawaii, and several northwestern states subject to origin certification for freedom from citrus canker. The fruit is not permitted, however, to be reshipped out of these areas. Origin certification for freedom from burrowing nematode causing spreading decline of citrus is required on all plants sent to California from Florida and other areas known to be infested with this pest.

Certification at point of origin indicating compliance with these requirements is sound provided the organization issuing the certificate is reliable and has facilities for obtaining dependable data or otherwise carrying out the requirements.

Many diseases and pests have more than one host; therefore, a knowledge of host relations is essential if quarantine action is to be sound. It is futile to quarantine some and permit the entry of other carriers of the same pest or disease originating in the infested area(s).

The system of controlled introduction under restriction is applicable only to pests and diseases of known economic importance. It must be recognized, however, that many major insects and diseases have been relatively rare and unimportant until transported out of their natural habitat. Undoubtedly, there are insects, diseases, and other pests in many parts of the world which would have serious economic consequences if they became established in a new habitat. There is no way of knowing what these are or where they may occur. Protection against them is possible only if the political unit (country, state, principality) is willing to make itself independent of commerce in plants and plant products with other political units.

Current Quarantines Protecting the U.S. Citrus Industry

Many quarantine regulations have been written and are being enforced to protect the citrus industry from new and serious pests and diseases. Some regulations protect individual states and some protect the entire country.

To provide insurance against the entry of soil-borne nematodes, diseases, and insects, soil from all foreign countries (except Canada) is prohibited entry into the United States. The threat of citrus canker's becoming established in the United States is greatly lessened by two federal foreign quarantines prohibiting the entry of citrus plants, plant parts, and fruit from countries in which citrus is infested with this disease.

Importation of citrus fruits and peel is prohibited from South American countries known to be infested with sweet orange scab or "Cancrosis B." Fruits and plants that are known carriers of Mediterranean fruit fly, oriental fruit fly, and citrus black fly may not be imported from foreign infested countries unless they have been properly treated to eliminate these pests. Hosts of mal secco disease are prohibited from importation into citrus-producing states from countries with known infestations.

To prevent the introduction of citrus canker, tristeza, and other citrus pathogens, Florida restricts the introduction of citrus plants and plant parts into their state. A special permit is required to import citrus nursery stock, budwood, and seed into Texas from Florida. Arizona, a relatively pest-free state, lists twenty-one citrus pests in its quarantine regulation and requires that a permit be issued before citrus nusery stock can be shipped there.

At various times, citrus fruits sent to California or Arizona from Florida were required to be fumigated for Mediterranean or Caribbean fruit fly. The U. S. Department of Agriculture currently (1977) requires treatment of citrus fruit for the Mexican fruit fly from Texas when sent to other citrus-producing states. California prohibits the entry of citrus nursery stock, cuttings, etc., from all states except Arizona.

NURSERY INSPECTION

Importance and Purpose of Nursery Inspection

Nursery stock is a primary means by which new or harmful citrus pests and diseases may be introduced or spread within any given locality. Such an introduction may well serve as a focal point from which an organism may spread to become an economic threat to citrus production or to nurserymen who may be holding nursery stock for later distribution to growers.

The benefits and returns from production of nursery trees are far greater than the original value of the nursery stock produced. For example, the annual return in California from food crops grown from nursery stock is in excess of $1 billion. California citrus fruits alone accounted for more than $291 million in 1975 (Anon., 1976). The net return from the production of any crop may be greatly affected by the pest and disease condition, vigor, and trueness-to-variety of nursery stock planted.

The detrimental effects of insects, bacteria, fungi, viruses, nematodes, weeds, and other pests are well understood (see chaps. 1, 2, 3, 5, 6, and vol. III, chap. 3) particularly by nurserymen and by plant regulatory officials. Between 1972 and 1976, tremendous strides have been made in California to produce high-quality nursery stock relatively free of many plant pests and diseases which may adversely affect both agricultural and ornamental plantings (see chap. 3).

Principles of Nursery Inspection

A plant pest or disease undetected by inspection of host plants at the point of destination has an inherent advantage in its ability to survive, even though it is introduced into a new ecological situation not necessarily favorable to its development. The pest or disease may be dormant or persist at an undetectable level until conditions are proper for its development. The development itself may be initiated by climatic changes or by further transport to areas where more favorable conditions exist. The perishable nature of nursery stock makes rapid transport and handling a matter of priority. In turn, this further enhances the opportunity for survival of pests or diseases which may be carried by nursery stock.

Research has provided many techniques and procedures which may be considered tools for use in safeguarding valuable nursery stock or crop land. There are few, if any, agricultural crops so valuable as nursery stock. The value of citrus nursery stock from one acre in California in the mid 1970's was estimated to be above $30,000, depending upon quality and condition at time of sale. The higher the value, however, the higher the risk. Therefore, it is important for any nurseryman or regulatory official at point of origin to insure against infestation or infection of this important crop. The degree of protection "purchased" in this manner by nurserymen should be commensurate with the value of the crop. The cost of inspection and supervision by tax-supported officials is equally justified by the protection offered to valuable crop and ornamental plantings represented in the nursery growing ground.

Methods of Nursery Inspection

The hazards of introducing or maintaining serious pests or diseases which may accompany nursery stock are obvious. Effective origin inspection provides a means to eliminate or greatly reduce the hazards of transporting pests. The success of a regulatory program at origin requires several inspections to be made in any twelve-month period. Frequency of inspection should be based on the pest or disease potential in any area where nursery stock is grown or maintained. For example, citrus nursery stock grown adjacent to established citrus plantings infested with red scale would require more supervision than an isolated planting. The presence of yellow nut grass *(Cyperus esculentus)* is frequently an obvious pest hazard which is often overlooked. Such weed pests may not be detectable at time of digging and particularly after completion of the balling of citrus nursery stock.

Surveying the nursery location.—Close familiarity with local pest problems and an intimate knowledge of a nursery growing ground's pest history, its environs, and its sources of plant propagative materials, are needed to judge the frequency and type of inspection needed to assure a desirable degree of freedom from pests and diseases. Times of inspection are geared to the knowledge of symptom expression and life histories of the pests and diseases likely to infest the growing nursery crop. The "annual inspection" of a nursery is no longer enough in light of present knowledge and technical proficiency in detection, control, eradication, and exclusion of plant pests and diseases. With these considerations in mind, experienced personnel can successfully detect limited or incipient infestations which may become troublesome in the future if they go undetected.

The concept of a modern nursery inspection program must go further than the simple acts of actual survey, detection, or suppression. Possible pest or disease conditions or risks should be weighed carefully by nurserymen, landowners, and regulatory personnel in selecting a site for growing nursery stock. All known procedures should be considered to exclude or prevent the introduction of harmful plant pests which may or may not be of general distribution in the area of a prospective growing ground.

The growing of nursery stock may introduce soil-borne pathogens or other pests to a property through rooted or seedling plants used as root stocks. Citrus rootstocks transplanted to the nursery row may carry the citrus nematode which, later, may affect the production of citrus or grapes. *Phytophthora cinnamomi*, the causal pathogen of avocado root rot, is another example of a pest which may be introduced through transplants or even by seed. The risk of infection by serious viruses known to spread in nature is another consideration of prime importance. Conversely, the nursery crop may become infested or infected when planted on land previously cropped or adjacent to established host plants which may have harbored harmful plant pests.

Manpower and Inspection

Considerable manpower is needed to provide the degree of inspection and supervision required to enforce laws which regulate the sale and handling of nursery stock. To satisfy this need in California, the California Food and Agricultural Code names County Agricultural Commissioners as co-enforcing officers with the Department of Food and Agriculture. California is unique among the various states in its regulatory organization. The Agricultural Commissioner, under local administration, enforces state law at the county level. Nursery regulations and policies are developed by the Department of Food and Agriculture and County Agricultural Commissioners working cooperatively with representative nurserymen and other members of the agricultural industry.

The Department coordinates and supervises the enforcement work by County Agricultural Commissioners of the nursery inspection and nursery stock grades and standards laws. This cooperative work is designed to establish and maintain uniformity in the general statewide program of nursery inspection activity.

Protective Methods

Procedures and plant protection techniques available to nurserymen and regulatory officials are numerous, providing that proper and adequate equipment and facilities can be made available.

Nematode Protection.—The development of laboratory methods for the detection of nematodes has provided a valuable tool for excluding harmful nematodes from nursery growing grounds. This may be accomplished prior to planting nursery crops by sampling roots of established plants or by obtaining soil samples from the selected site. Laboratory examination of root or soil samples may reveal the presence of serious nematode pests; however, failure to detect nematodes upon such examination does not assure the absence of nematodes. Lining-out stock to be used in the propagation of nursery stock may be sampled and inspected using laboratory methods prior to planting in the nursery row. Lots found infested with harmful nematodes should be discarded.

Fumigation using recommended nematocides applied under competent supervision may also be employed. Dosages of such materials must be sufficiently high to give control to a point approaching eradication. Pretreatment, treatment, and post-treatment handling procedures have proven effective in excluding or preventing nematode infestations of field-grown nursery stock destined for orchard planting. Treatments applied in areas where the contamination risk is low may be sufficient to provide a degree of assurance that the nursery stock produced will be relatively free from nematode pests.

Virus Protection.—Index testing of propagating sources is another tool helpful in excluding known virus diseases. Short term tests for tristeza, psorosis, and exocortis viruses have been developed and are now in practice. In California, an optional program for the registration and certification of citrus trees found free from virus or graft-transmissible diseases and other pests is in effect (see chap. 3). This and similar programs for other kinds of nursery stock are designed to exclude important viruses, graft-transmissible diseases, fungi, and nematodes which cannot be detected by ordinary means of inspection. From a pest-cleanliness standpoint, participants are providing the best available nursery stock for commerical plantings. Although participation is voluntary, nursery stock registration and certification are further refinements of nursery stock regulatory procedures already followed in California.

Insect Protection.—The use of methyl bromide gas as a fumigant for ridding nursery stock of citrus red scale and other surface pests has proven effective. Well-timed cleanup or preventive spray programs carried out with proper equipment can minimize, if not exclude, many of the more common insect pests or diseases from the confines of a nursery growing ground. For example, citrus red scale has been excluded successfully from host plants growing adjacent to infested citrus orchards. Propagative sources should be carefully scrutinized for presence of red scale and other important insect pests.

Weed Protection.—Nursery growing grounds should be examined for noxious weeds prior to establishment of field-grown nursery stock. Methyl bromide fumigation, similar to that applied for the exclusion of plant parasitic nematodes (see chap. 7), also is effective in greatly reducing the noxious weed problem. Selective herbicides may also be used to good advantage (see chap. 3, vol. III).

PEST AND DISEASE DETECTION

Purpose and Goals of Pest and Disease Detection

Pest and disease detection is the search for a pest in a geographical area where it had not previously been known to occur. It is sometimes classed along with population density surveys and delimitation surveys as one of many types of pest survey.

The major purpose of detection is to discover a newly established alien pest or disease infestation in its incipiency and to eradicate it—if that is necessary—with minimal difficulty, cost, and environmental contamination. The ultimate cost of eradication is usually directly related to the length of time between its initial establishment and its discovery.

Serious plant pests and diseases have plagued and challenged man in his agricultural endeavors throughout history. Man's increasing mobility and technological advances in transportion have resulted in introducing plant pests and diseases whose dispersal had previously been limited by natural barriers. Examples of such introductions are: (1) citrus canker and Mediterranean fruit fly into Florida; (2) Mediterranean, melon, and oriental fruit fly into Hawaii; (3) citrus blackfly into Mexico; (4) Mexican bean beetle into California; (5) khapra beetle into the southwestern United States and northwestern Mexico; and (6) white-fringed beetle into Alabama.

The detection of alien crop pests and diseases is usually a governmental function and may be administered at the national, state, or local (i.e., county) level. In California, a cooperative combination of federal, state, and county departments of agriculture administers detection.

Pest detection is usually a central link in the total chain of "pest and disease prevention." First, quarantines should be established to exclude or delay the introduction of foreign plant pests and diseases. Second, a sound detection system should be maintained to insure early discovery of new pest or disease establishments. Third, as soon as an important foreign pest has been detected and its area of infestation delimited, the regulatory agency and other interested parties must decide whether or not eradication is feasible. Fourth, if eradication is not attempted, or if it fails, means of managing the new pest must be instigated to minimize losses. These management techniques may involve biological control, confinement by local quarantines, chemical control, host-free periods, host-free areas, or a combination of several of these methods.

California has been one of the pioneer states in identifying the need for quickly detecting alien pests and diseases and developing a program of action. In 1946, a study by a Joint Legislative Interim Committee led to a recommendation made to the California State Legislature in 1947 which resulted in legislation and funds for a permanent staff of detection plant pathologists and entomologists. Since then, the program has expanded to include weed and vertebrate biologists, nematologists, and a remote sensing specialist.

The U. S. federal government initiated a nationwide cooperative insect pest "survey" program in 1952 under the leadership of Avery S. Hoyt, Chief of the Bureau of Entomology and Plant Quarantine, U. S. Department of Agriculture. The purposes of this survey were to "(1) assist farmers and others to more adequately protect their crops from insect attack, (2) assure more prompt detection of newly introduced insect pests, (3) lead to the development of a workable insect pest forecasting service, (4) aid manufacturers and suppliers of insecticides and control equipment to determine areas of urgent need, and (5) in case of necessity, provide a countrywide skeleton structure, to be expanded as needed, to combat any attempts at biological warfare."

Because of the broad base of this program, not all entomologists agreed with it. Some states preferred to stress the measurement of insect population densities and seasonal fluctuations. Other states, including California, placed greater emphasis on detection of newly introduced pests.

The consequences of insufficient detection are exemplified in the disastrous introduction and spread of Mediterranean fruit fly in Florida in 1929 and 1930. Since detection tools and programming in those days were in their infancy, the fly invaded most of the citrus groves in an area encompassing twenty counties. Eradication was long and difficult, and was accomplished at the cost of $7 million.

Methods Used in Citrus Pest and Disease Detection

Some of the more common means and tools used for detecting alien pests and diseases are listed below.

Visual Search.—At ground level, this is the most widely used detection method. Examples include the search for insects (e.g., citrus blackfly), alien fruit-eating birds, crop-depredating mammals, and plant diseases (e.g., citrus canker).

Aerial Photography and Aerial Search.—These are generally classed under the heading of "remote sensing." This group of techniques is becoming increasingly important due to recent scientific advances that make newly established pests and diseases discernible from aircraft or remote sensing satellites like the Earth Resources Technology Satellite (ERTS) orbited at high altitudes. Examples include the search for spreading decline and tristeza disease in Florida and for stubborn disease in California.

Trapping with Attractants.—This is exemplified by the use of ammonium carbonate used in Frick traps and by methyl eugenol and Trimedlure in Steiner traps for detecting oriental fruit fly and Mediterranean fruit fly.

Mechanical Devices.—There are numerous mechanical detection devices, but two of the more common ones are sweep nets and vacuum collectors for collecting flying or plant surface insects, such as homopterous vectors of stubborn disease of citrus.

Soil Sampling.—This is the most common method for detecting soil pests of citrus including the burrowing nematode and the citrus nematode.

Planning For and Evaluating Detection

In planning pest detection coverage for any geographical or political area (e.g., a country, state, county, or valley), the entire land area can be divided into the program types listed below.

High Hazard Points.—This includes extra high risk pest introduction locations such as air terminals, seaports, and military bases. These should be inspected visually every year. This detection should include citrus plants in the peripheral blocks of residential properties.

Urban Areas.—This includes residential

and metropolitan areas where citrus pest and disease host plants occur. Detection can best be covered by a systematic (grid) type sampling wherein a certain number of residential properties are inspected in each square mile.

Croplands.—All areas planted to citrus crops can be covered on a systematic sampling plan such as selecting one section in each group of four each year, and inspecting one planting of citrus in the selected sections.

Nonvulnerable.—This is where there are no citrus pest or disease host plants or where there is practically no hazard of alien pest or disease introduction. These areas can be eliminated from the detection program.

Evaluation of Detection

The real proof of an adequate detection program is in having discovered each newly introduced and established pest while the infestation is still in a very small area. Since the frequency of new finds may not be great enough to provide a base for judgment, a periodic evaluation should be made of the quantity and quality of all phases of the detection work to provide an effectiveness measurement.

The Future of Detection

It appears that the need for detection will increase with the passage of time. Practically all alien pest and disease introductions are related to the movement of man and the commodities he has grown or manufactured. New trade relationships are developing with distant countries that had little or no communication in the past. Relative to pest detection, this means that pest and disease organisms will now be carried that, in the past, had no chance of being transported to new geographical areas.

On the bright side, man is discovering new and better methods and technology for detecting newly established alien plant pests and diseases. In the field of remote sensing, the evaluation of various combinations of energy wavelengths reflected from plants to aircraft or earth satellites is approaching the point of pest species recognition. Pheromones of many of the most destructive insect pests have now been chemically identified and synthesized, providing pest detection forces with strong attractants that enable early discovery of these pests by an adequate trapping program. Exchange of plant pest and disease descriptions, specimens, photographs, and biologies among laymen and scientists from various countries (especially among those of similar latitudes) will improve the training of field detection staffs and result in increased effectiveness.

Citrus growers throughout the world have much to gain by developing and maintaining a system of watchfulness for newly introduced pests and diseases. Even though the genus *Citrus* is believed to have been native to the subtropical and tropical regions of Asia and the Malay Archipelago, many of the known major citrus pests and diseases are native to other parts of the world and some originated on noncitrus host plants. Prominent examples are:

- Mediterranean fruit fly, *Ceritítis capitata* (Wied.), native to Africa, but not yet known to occur in the origin countries of *Citrus.*
- Mal secco, caused by *Phoma tracheiphila* Petri, a fungus disease known only in the Mediterranean region and the Middle East.

Thus, even the "citrus-origin" countries of Asia need to be protected from devastating citrus pests of other parts of the world.

Among the most destructive citrus pests and diseases are the following which, if not already present in a citrus-growing region, should be subjects of active detection:

- Citrus blackfly, *Aleurocanthus woglumi* (Ashb.)
- Mediterranean fruit fly, *Ceratitis capitata* (Wied.)
- Mexican fruit fly, *Anastrepha ludens* (Loew)
- Oriental fruit fly, *Dacus dorsalis* (Hend.)
- California red scale, *Aonidiella aurantii* (Mask.)
- Citrus canker, *Xanthomonas citri* (Haase) Dowson
- Burrowing nematode, *Radopholus similis* (Cobb) Thorne
- Greening disease (vector-transmitted organism similar to stubborn, not fully described as yet)
- Stubborn, *Spiroplasma citri,* graft- and vector-transmitted
- Mal secco, *Deuterophoma tracheiphila* (Petri)
- Tristeza, a graft- and vector-transmissible virus
- Young tree decline or blight (cause unknown) (see chap. 2)
- Black spot, *Guignardia citricarpa* (Kiely)

ERADICATION OF INTRODUCED PESTS AND DISEASES

Purpose and Goals of Eradication

Eradication can be defined as an action to eliminate an established pest or disease from a specified area. Eradication actions are usually publicly sponsored phases of a program to prevent widespread or permanent establishment of pests newly introduced into an area where they could cause serious losses. Legal authorities for the conduct of eradication actions in the United States are provided in various state and federal codes.

Eradication, thus, is the preferred means to prevent permanent establishment of pests and diseases that "leak" through exclusion efforts. To be economically justifiable and technically feasible, eradication generally depends upon early detection and adequate technology. While eradication actions may involve suppression or control efforts, the final goal is the total extermination of the offending organism. Often, where new pests are involved, eradication technology is not available and retardation of spread of the pest through suppression and other efforts is necessary to allow time for research and development of new technologies.

Principles and Limitations of Eradication

Following the entry of an immigrant pest or disease into a new area, some basic steps are necessary to achieve eradication. Variations in the nature of different pest and disease types result in wide differences in the suitability and confidence of the operational actions taken to reach these objectives. These steps and operations are discussed in detail in the following sections.

Confirming Presence of the Pest.—Detection and identification of alien pests and diseases in the United States are generally considered to be the responsibilities of federal and state agricultural agencies. Major citrus-growing states such as Arizona, California, and Florida have detection and identification programs. These provide trained personnel to detect and collect field samples and to make laboratory determinations of identity. Detection efforts are limited to visual observations in most instances, but the development and use of aids such as traps have greatly improved the confidence that early detection of some insect pests can be achieved. It is important to confirm that an actual infestation exists. Traps can reveal the presence of adult fruit flies, for example, before eggs or larvae are produced in the new area.

Evaluating the Situation.—Evaluation requires consideration of all factors which affect the scope, feasibility, and advisability of an eradication action commitment.

Delimiting the Area Affected.—Delimitation is the action taken to determine the extent of infestation. A variety of survey tools are utilized to make this determination as rapidly and accurately as possible. Visual inspections to observe symptoms or actual organisms are a common mode of operation; but they can be very expensive, and sometimes are unreliable or even impossible. Traps utilizing general attractants such as ammonium carbonate or fermenting liquids for fruit flies, and others using specific attractants such as pheromones for California red scale, Comstock mealybug, and other insects reduce costs and improve effectiveness of surveys. Use of indexing to disclose tristeza disease when surveying symptomless carriers is effective but remains costly and ponderous as an operational procedure.

Determining Density of the Population.—The number of areas or per cent of an area affected by the pest is a major factor determining the cost of an action. This is often a dynamic factor and may be complicated by seasonal variations in numbers or by migrations or alternations between different host plants.

Determining Local Host Range.—One of the most important and influential factors that can affect the success of an eradicative action and the degree of support such an action receives is the number, type, and value of plants or products affected. The inclusion of citrus among the host plants of the Mediterranean fruit fly undoubtedly swayed the decision toward eradicative action against this pest in Florida. Pests and diseases, when transported to a new area, may adapt to previously unknown hosts. The existence of a virus or mycoplasmalike disease in symptomless host species or varieties may make eradicative efforts very difficult or even impossible.

Evaluating Location and Habitat.—Eradicative action is affected by the site of pest establishment. A citrus pest or disease in a grove poses a different problem than the same pest or disease on trees in a residential area. To the same extent, an infected tree in a city park would require a different approach than a similar tree in a forest. The differences affect not only choice of pesticide but also several other decisions.

Analyzing Expected Method and Rate of Spread.—This factor determines the type and scope of regulatory action as well as the time frame for emergency actions to prevent escape of the pest or disease to new areas. Mobile forms which walk or fly or are wind- or water-borne present one type of problem. Forms which occur in or on readily moved plant parts, soil, or implements present another problem. The stage of development of the organism likely to be spread—spores, seeds, eggs, larvae, adults, or colonies—to some extent determines the risk of new establishment. The anticipated rate of spread determines the area or zone beyond known infestation that must be included in the action. In the case of diseases caused by viruses or mycoplasmalike organisms, the important factor may be the distance an insect vector can fly or be carried by wind.

Determining Means to Prevent Spread or Re-entry.—This factor may be essential when there is no confident eradicative technology for a given pest. Simply preventing the spread of a given pest or disease allows time to initiate research and to develop more permanent eradicative or control measures. Prevention of both spread and re-entry are needed to give confidence that long-term prevention of pest establishment is possible. Principal actions taken are quarantines of individual properties or affected areas, suppression at origin, public information, and other deterrents against pest and disease movement.

Evaluating Eradicative Capability.—It must be determined if there is a technology, strategy, or a vulnerability of the pest or disease which might lead to confidence that eradication could be achieved if it were attempted.

Weighing Cost/Benefit and Environmental Impact.—The benefits of eradication must be weighed in comparison with costs and any adverse impacts on the environment. This is the factor that deals with short-term effects and expenditures and long-term freedom from problems. Differences between available alternative actions and their cost/benefit ratios must also be considered.

Obtaining a Commitment to Eradicate.—A commitment to eradicate a pest or disease infestation means, at the very least, providing (1) the legal authority, (2) the funds with which to operate, (3) an agreement regarding who will be responsible for certain actions, and (4) a plan and schedule detailing when and how the actions are to be pursued.

Intercepting the Life Cycle.—The key element in pest and disease eradication appears to be the utilization of one or more kinds of technology which will preclude reproduction until all members of the population are dead or all sources of infection eliminated. Many technologies have been successfully utilized, including some that are unique. These include the following.

Direct killing of all organisms in the pest or disease population may be accomplished by fumigating, dusting, or spraying with a chemical; by changing the environment with heat, cold, moisture, or dryness; by physical destruction such as hoeing of weeds, eradication of alternate hosts, or removal and destruction of infected plants.

Indirect killing may be achieved by removing essential plants or parts of plants required as food; by applying chemicals that change morphological development, act as anti-feeding or anti-metabolite agents, or as barriers to normal life needs in other ways.

Interruption of successful breeding activity may be brought about by release of laboratory-reared and -sterilized populations; by trapping to remove all of one sex from a population; by disrupting the normal communication needed to bring male and female together; by removing fruiting portions of weeds; or by chemosterilization of one or both sexes.

These and other technologies may be used in combination to produce desired results. To choose the optimum strategy requires knowledge of weak points in the organism's life cycle and continuing evaluation and modification of the approach as needed.

Confirming That Eradication Has Been Achieved.—Confirming that the goal of eradication has been met can pose difficult problems. Searching for pests or diseases when numbers are very low is, in some circles, considered wasted effort. From this feeling comes the expression that "the spray gun is the best inspector." A general rule of thumb that has proven successful for eradication programs conducted in California has been to treat until no pests or diseases can be found, treat another three years, then survey yet another three years before declaring eradication complete. As a modification of this plan, there have been plans indicating three generations of the pest or disease rather than three years in the formula. The latter has been employed in fruit fly eradication programs in California.

CITRUS DISEASE ERADICATION PROGRAMS

Plant disease and pest eradication is directed at eliminating an organism from a given area. More specifically, eradication is restricted to organisms having a significant impact on major crops. Complete eradication requires detecting all infected hosts and destroying the organism, usually by destroying the host. Complete detection of all infections can be difficult and results obtained may indicate an excellent level of control with incidence suppressed below .01 per cent. This was accomplished with peach yellow leaf roll in certain areas of California (Nichols, 1967). Eradication attempts are certainly warranted in citrus where exploiting resistance is complicated by many virus diseases of varying importance on different varieties and rootstocks. Eradication programs have been conducted for citrus canker, *Xanthomonas citri* (Haase) Dowson; burrowing nematode, *Radopholus similis* (Cobb) Thorne; tristeza; and Mediterranean fruit fly, *Ceratitis capitata* (Wied.).

Citrus canker was eradicated in Florida, South Africa, and Australia (Klotz, 1973) where trees were sprayed with a mixture of kerosene and petroleum oil and then burned. Precautions were taken to disinfect workmen's tools and clothing to prevent workers from becoming an avenue of spread. Eradication of citrus canker in the United States from Florida, Alabama, Louisiana, Mississippi, and eastern Texas represents one of the broadest applications of the eradication concept to date. Between 1914–1931, a total of 257,745 grove trees and 3,093,110 nursery trees were destroyed in Florida (Rhoads and DeBusk, 1931).

The Mediterranean fruit fly (*C. capitata*, Wied.) was discovered in the heart of Florida's large citrus-growing area in 1929. A massive eradication program was mounted which involved ground spraying of all citrus and other host plants one or more times in a twenty-county area. The eradication was successful, but required eighteen months and the expenditure of about $8 million. This pest was again detected in the Miami area in 1956, and it spread to twenty-eight counties before it was brought under control. It was eradicated by the spraying of vast areas with improved bait sprays, applied largely by aircraft. This second campaign required sixteen months and cost about $10 million (Ebeling, 1959).

Tristeza eradication projects were operative in the mid 1970's in California and Israel. Tristeza eradication in California's San Joaquin Valley (Pratt, Calavan, and Hill, 1969) resulted in the removal of 17,000 infected grove trees since 1963. This project operates in 161,000 acres of citrus. This broad application of the eradication concept is made possible by an extremely low rate of spread by the vector *Aphis gossypii* (Glover). Efforts in southern California's Coachella Valley have resulted in the destruction of 446 infected grove trees; natural spread is unknown in this desert area of 18,000 acres.

Tristeza eradication efforts in Israel resulted in the removal of more than 230 trees in the Sharon Plain as of June, 1973 (Bar-Joseph and Loebenstein, 1973). Israeli workers are supplementing Mexican Lime indexing with electron microscopy of partially purified preparations (Bar-Joseph, Loebenstein, and Oren, 1973). *Aphis gossypii* (Glover) is reported to be a semipersistent vector in Israel. Efforts to control aphids as a means of preventing virus spread are generally ineffective.

Meyer lemons are a symptomless carrier of seedling yellows tristiza virus (Wallace and Drake, 1955), and approximately 5,000 trees have been destroyed in California tristeza eradication districts. Subsequently, this prized ornamental was found to contain two additional viruses, tatterleaf and citrange stunt (Wallace and Drake, 1963, 1968). These viruses have been eradicated from two Meyer lemon selections by heat treatment (Roistacher *et al.*, 1972). Regulations were adopted permitting the dissemination of a virus-free Meyer lemon in all of California beginning in 1975.

Efforts to eradicate burrowing nematode in Florida originally concentrated on pull-and-treat methods. The infested portions of orchards were bulldozed, trees stacked and burned, and the area fumigated with D-D. Eradication of *Radopholus similis* (Cobb) Thorne was not successful and efforts were redirected at preventing spread. Barriers 32 feet wide were fumigated around infested orchards at six-month intervals and kept free of weeds with diuron (DuCharme, 1972). Currently, responsibility for establishing chemical barriers is being transferred from governmental agencies to growers. Also resistance has been found in Milam and Carrizo rootstocks (Ford and Feder, 1969).

Salibe (1973) reported that a serious deterioration of trees of unknown etiology was found in citrus trees in a localized area in Brazil. The trees involved were destroyed and there has been no reoccurrence. This application of the eradication concept in Brazil exemplifies the value of detecting and eradicating incipient infections.

Considering the citrus-producing areas still free of tristeza, greening, stubborn, young tree or sand hill decline, cachexia, cristacortis, citrus canker, burrowing nematode, and other diseases, eradication of incipient infections may play an important part in preventing establishment of these and other diseases.

Eradication efforts are subject to failure due to many factors. Initial information developed under the pressure of time and budget may not fully reflect the magnitude of the problem. Detection may rely on recognition of a rather imprecise set of visual symptoms, and symptomless carriers may not be detected. Indexing methods or laboratory techniques may not be sufficiently sensitive to detect all symptomless carriers or pick up early or latent infections.

Growers may be unwilling to permit destruction of symptomless carriers. The resources in manpower and equipment may be insufficient to the task. Nevertheless, successful eradication programs have been instituted. Considering the difficulties, successful suppression programs that reduce diseases having major economic impact below economic threshold levels are justified and warrant the expenditure.

Successful disease eradication or suppression is based on a fundamental knowledge of the disease. During the course of an eradication project, efforts should be directed towards applying diagnostic methods to disease detection. Quarantines should be adopted to prevent reintroduction. Although regulations and laws form a legal base for eradication, they do not substitute for grower cooperation.

LITERATURE CITED

ANONYMOUS. 1960. Plant pest detection. U.S. Dept. Agr. Agr. Res. Service. ARS 22–63. 8 pp.

ANONYMOUS. 1974. Plant pest detection manual. Exclusion and Detection Unit. Calif. Dept. Food and Agr. Sacramento, Calif.

ARMITAGE, H. M. 1948. Permanent surveys for insect pests. Bul. Calif. Dept. Agr. **37**:29–32.

———. 1953. State surveys in relation to national insect problems. Jour. Econ. Ent. **46**:1123–25.

BAR-JOSEPH, M., and G. LOEBENSTEIN. 1973. Effects of strain, source plant, and temperature on the transmissibility of citrus tristeza virus by the melon aphid. Phytopathology **63**:716–720.

BAR-JOSEPH, M., G. LOEBENSTEIN, and Y. OREN. 1974. Use of electron microscopy in an eradication program of tristeza sources recently found in Israel. *In:* Weathers, L. G., and M. Cohen (eds.). Proc. 6th Conf. Intern. Organ. Citrus Virol. Pp. 83–85. Univ. Calif. Div. Agr. Sci. Richmond, Calif.

BLANC, F. L. 1973. Detection for alien fruit flies in California through use of trapping device. Pest Control Circ. No. 428. Sunkist Growers Inc., Van Nuys, Calif.

DUCHARME, E. P. 1972. *Kallstroemia maxima*, a new host of *Radopholus similis*. Plant Dis. Reptr. **56**:85.

EBELING, WALTER. 1950. Subtropical Entomology. Lithotype Process Co. San Francisco, Calif. 747 pp.

———. 1959. Subtropical Fruit Pests. Univ. Calif. Div. Agr. Sci., Berkeley, Calif. 436 pp.

FORD, H. W., and W. A. FEDER. 1969. Development and use of citrus rootstocks resistant to the burrowing nematode. *In:* Chapman, H. D. (ed.). Proc. First Intern. Citrus Symp. **2**:941–48. Univ. of Calif., Riverside, Calif.

NICHOLS, C. W. 1967. Bureau of plant pathology. Calif. Bur. Plant Path. spec. pub. Bul. Calif. Dept. Agr. **56**:82–87.

PRATT, R. M., E. C. CALAVAN, and J. P. HILL. 1972. The tristeza suppression and eradication program in California. *In:* Price. W. C. (ed). Proc. 5th Conf. Intern. Organ. Citrus Virol. Pp. 158–61. Univ. Fla. Press, Gainesville, Fla.

QUAYLE, H. J. 1938. Insects of Citrus and Other Subtropical Fruits. Comstock Publishing Co., Ithaca, N. Y. 583 pp.

RHOADS, A. S., and E. F. DEBUSK. 1931. Diseases of citrus in Florida. Fla. Agr. Expt. Sta. Bul. No. **229**. 213 pp.

ROISTACHER, C. N., E. C. CALAVAN, E. M. NAUER, and W. REUTHER. 1972. Virus-free Meyer lemon trees. Citrograph **57**:250, 270–71.

RYAN, H. J. 1969. Plant Quarantines in California. Univ. Calif. Div. Agr. Sci. Berkeley, Calif. 251 pp.

SALIBE, A. 1973. The Brazilian citrus industry. Proc. 1st Intern. Citrus Rootstock Shortcourse. Fla. Coop. Extension Serv. IFAS. Univ. Fla., Gainesville, Fla. Mimeograph. 173 pp.

WALLACE, J. M., and R. J. DRAKE. 1955. The tristeza virus in Meyer lemon. Citrus Leaves **35**(1):8–9, 23.

———. 1962. Tatter leaf, a previously undescribed virus effect on citrus. Plant Dis. Reptr. **46**:211–12.

———. 1968. Citrange stunt and ringspot, two previously undescribed virus diseases on citrus. *In:* Childs, J. F. L. (ed.). Proc. 4th Conf. Intern. Organ. Citrus Virol. Pp. 177–83. Univ. Fla. Press, Gainesville, Fla.

CHAPTER 5

Vertebrate Pests of Citrus

MAYNARD W. CUMMINGS and REX E. MARSH

A VERTEBRATE PEST IS ANY native or introduced, wild or feral, non-human vertebrate animal. Vertebrates, simply stated, have a jointed spinal column (vertebrae) and include fishes, amphibians (frogs and salamanders), reptiles (turtles, lizards, and snakes), birds, and mammals. Throughout the citrus-growing regions of the world, birds and mammals represent the major classes of vertebrate pests. In the United States, rodents and lagomorphs (rabbits and hares) represent the two most important orders of vertebrate pests that cause substantial economic losses of citrus.

This chapter places the greatest emphasis on the biology, damage, and control of the most important pest species, largely using California situations as examples of control or management methodology. Vertebrate pests of either minor or only potential importance are discussed near the end of the chapter in much less detail, or are merely mentioned. The authors recognize that different groups of vertebrate pest animals may be implicated in varying degrees of damage in other citrus-growing regions of the world—particularly in the more tropical countries. Various bird species in some regions, such as parrots in Belize (British Honduras) and parrots and blue birds in Argentina (Burke, 1967), may cause as much or more damage than, for example, the rodents of that area. Fortunately, economic losses attributed to birds in the United States are relatively low.

Those citrus regions of the world that sustain heavy losses to birds are at a distinct disadvantage because of the general lack of practical and highly effective bird control techniques. Even though all citrus-growing regions have developed methods for reducing damage by vertebrate pests, the sophistication of the methodology cannot come close to that used in insect control. This can be attributed to a number of factors, probably the most important of which is that damage resulting from vertebrate pests is not so widespread as that caused by insects or certain plant diseases. Therefore, much less research has been devoted to resolving vertebrate pest problems than has been devoted to solving disease or entomological problems. Considering the limited monetary resources available to those involved in research and other aspects of alleviating vertebrate pest damage, the advancements in methodology have been significant, notably the development of the mechanical pocket gopher baiter. Other new approaches to some vertebrate problems are being pursued rather intensely, as exemplified by current research with rodent chemosterilants.

Growers suffering from depredations by vertebrate pest species are interested in reducing the extent of damage the pest presently causes or may cause in the future. While the words "control" and "management" are both used often, and sometimes interchangeably in relation to vertebrate pests, their meaning varies depending on the species, its numbers, the magnitude of the losses, and the particular area's total ecology. In the instance of rodents, control may be accomplished directly by reducing the numbers of animals in the population until a tolerable level is reached. With some species, such as deer, the tolerable level is zero in a young citrus grove; without killing the deer, however, fencing is the only way protection can be achieved. With birds, complete protection is impossible with control technology.

The term "eradication" has an entirely different connotation: it means the total elimination of a pest species from a rather sizable region, such as a valley or island, that has somewhat natural boundaries. Present concepts in vertebrate pest management do not advocate the eradication of any native species from its natural range of distribution except for local areas. The eradication of an introduced (non-indigenous) species which either is a pest or has the potential for becoming one, may be biologically sound and highly desirable.

Some vertebrate pest specialists think that much greater attention should be directed towards preventing the unwanted introduction of new vertebrate species by more rigid importation laws and regulations, with greater emphasis placed on limiting the introduction of exotic birds and mammals offered for sale as pets. Efforts should also be increased in educating children and the general public on environmental hazards of introducing exotic vertebrates. California and a few other states have regulations more rigid than those of the federal government for prohibiting the importation or introduction of species considered potential pests, either from an economic or public health viewpoint. As far as we know, California—under the auspices of the California Department of Food and Agriculture, and with the cooperation of county departments of agriculture and other state agencies—is the only state that has a highly organized and extensive program operated by trained biologists specifically to detect the presence of unwanted introduced vertebrates. The concept is based on the adage that an ounce of prevention is worth a pound of cure. By locating incipient infestations of introduced pests, such as the monk parakeet *(Myiopsitta monachus)*, it is economically and ecologically more feasible to instigate programs either of containment or eradication. The program also provides the necessary lead time for researchers to develop controls or management programs to keep damage minimal should other efforts fail.

CONTROL OF VERTEBRATES

Control of vertebrate pest damage may be grouped in three general categories: (1) habitat manipulation (environmental management); (2) behavioral manipulation; and (3) population reduction (reductional control).

Habitat Manipulation

Habitat manipulation or modification is a well-established management tool for many vertebrate pests. Vertebrates whose attributes make them capable of becoming pests may increase in number through man's alteration of their natural environment. For example, grazing of annual grassland by livestock will increase ground squirrels (*Spermophilus* spp.) but decrease meadow mouse (*Microtus* spp.) populations. Growing alfalfa will favor meadow mice and pocket gophers. The cultural practices used for a particular crop will also influence the pest status of a species; for example, weed-free levees in rice fields will decrease the number of Norway rats *(Rattus norvegicus)*. Failing to burn the stubble of a grain field in regions of northern California provides harborage and food for a large population of meadow mice which otherwise would have perished during the cold winter, leaving a much-reduced breeding population for the coming spring.

Cultural practices used in citrus can influence certain pest species. California citrus nurserymen slip paper, foil, or plastic tubes over the seedlings as they are lined out in the nurseries to prevent sucker growth; this practice undoubtedly reduces damage by jack rabbits *(Lepus californicus)* which may get into the nursery. The possible harborage of insect pests was listed as a disadvantage of establishing windbreaks (Platt, 1973). In California, there is little doubt that in some situations windbreaks and the vegetation beneath contribute to the presence of vertebrate pests such as ground squirrels and meadow mice.

Intercrops of lima or garbanzo beans planted between rows of young citrus trees, as is sometimes done in California, may increase the attractiveness of the grove to such species as jack rabbits and deer *(Odocoileus hemionus)* by providing desirable food items and additional cover for rodents and rabbits. Conversely, it has been observed that the intercrop plantings may seasonally serve as a convenient alternate food for the vertebrate pest. If the preference for the annual crop is greater than that for citrus, the citrus may be spared of damage; however, this approach to the problem is not sufficiently reliable to be put into practice as a wildlife management technique.

It is important to remember that citrus cultural practices, including the type of irrigation, tillage, and the kind of trunk wraps used to prevent sunburn or frost damage, may all have a direct bearing on vertebrate pest numbers and/or damage. Cover crops, intercrops, orchard border sanitation, and the maintenance of weed-free groves will favorably or unfavorably influence the suitability of the area for a particular pest species. When new cultural practices are in the planning stage, adequate consideration must be given to undesirable side effects involving vertebrate pests and weighed accordingly. It is often advisable to discuss in advance the new or proposed changes in cultural practices with those knowledgeable in economic zoology so that potential problems may be anticipated and appropriate corrective measures taken.

Methods of excluding vertebrate pests from citrus groves by fencing, as well as rodent- or bird-proofing of citrus packing, processing, or storage buildings, can logically be included under either habitat or behavioral manipulation

Behavioral Manipulation

Behavioral manipulation involves techniques capable of altering or modifying some behavior of a pest species to eliminate or reduce the degree of economic damage caused. Good examples of techniques for manipulating behavior are repellents, which can rather broadly be defined as physical (mechanical) or chemical materials which cause predictable reactions resulting from stimuli such as sight, smell, touch, taste, and hearing, or a combination of two or more of these. Physical repellents could include sound- or noise-producing devices such as acetylene or carbide exploders or revolving or flashing lights. Chemical repellents generally influence behavior through taste, smell, or sometimes touch (e.g., the tacky or sticky substances placed on limbs and trunks of trees to discourage the work of a woodpecker or sapsucker).

Population Reduction

Population reduction can be divided into two functional categories: direct (artificially-induced mortality) or indirect (lowering population through implementation of some agent or mechanism). Direct population reduction makes use of toxic baits or gases (chemical methods) or means such as trapping or shooting (physical methods).

In the United States and throughout most of the world, reductional control of rodents and lagomorphs is most often accomplished with toxic baits, for these are generally the quickest, cheapest, and most effective means of reducing pest populations.

Indirect reduction control generally involves techniques that are slower in action and, thus, of a subtle nature, such as chemosterilant use, genetic manipulation, and various methods of biological control.

Chemosterilants.—Chemosterilants have been studied with considerable intensity in the past few years, particularly for the control of rats *(Rattus)*, and to a lesser extent for the control of other pest rodent species (Marsh and Howard, 1973). The value of chemical compounds in reducing reproduction in vertebrate pest populations has been proven biologically sound and, hopefully, will play an important future role in reducing damage caused by some of the major rodent pests to agricultural crops. Presently, no rodent chemosterilant has been studied sufficiently to be registered in the United States, although one is available for feral pigeon *(Columba livia)* control. Data presently being collected on several experimental compounds is advancing this approach significantly. Birth control should not be viewed as a panacea for all vertebrate pests nor for all situations, for all such biologically active compounds have their limitations.

The application of chemosterilants in integrated control programs offers the greatest hope. The use of chemosterilants as a follow-up to toxic baits or other conventional methods of direct reductional control will provide maximum benefits by slowing the potential for population recovery. Many of our most serious vertebrate pests, particularly rodents and lagomorphs, have a very steep population growth curve: to artificially push them off the plateau of that curve by any means onto the precipitous slope of the classical sigmoid curve is of no avail unless additional pressures are applied. This is where chemosterilants can play a key role (Howard, 1967).

Genetic Manipulation.—There is no question that more innovative investigations are needed in the areas of rodent control, and natural lethal or sterile genetic syndromes appear to hold some promise (Marsh and Howard, 1973). Investigations are under way to evaluate an unusual genetically sterile syndrome by introducing it into a wild population of Norway rats, in order to set in motion a continuing negative effect on fertility (Stanley and Gumbreck, 1964). The most recent reports continue to be encouraging (Glass, 1974), but genetic manipulation in solving vertebrate pest problems remains in the early stages of development. One great advantage of genetic control is that it will be highly selective, affecting a single species; within that species, it will affect only the population whose genetic makeup has been altered.

Biological Control.—Biological control can be viewed as indirect population reduction for it involves such tactics as the deliberate introduction of fatal or debilitating pathogens or exotic predators. While biological control has been quite effective for the control of certain insects and weed pests, it has met with little success in vertebrate pest control. Predators and, to a lesser extent, known disease organisms with the potential for adequately reducing populations of vertebrate pests to very low levels are not host-specific. This is one reason for the present lack of suitable biological control methods. Once a disease or predator has been released into an ecosystem which satisfies its requirements for survival and reproduction, man has little if any control over its future effect on the biota.

Numerous examples exist of predators being introduced to control vertebrate pests and, with few exceptions, not resolving the original pest problem but almost always becoming pests themselves by preying on desirable vertebrates (Howard, 1967). One of the classic examples is the mongoose *(Herpestes auropunctatus)* introduced to control rats, and now considered to be a factor in the decline of the rare nene or Hawaiian goose *(Branta sandvicensis)*. The mongoose may be largely responsible also for the extermination of the Manx shearwater *(Puffinus puffinus)* in the Hawaiian Islands (Wodzicki, 1973). Too often it is forgotten that most of our major pest vertebrates are very successful animals, having very high reproductive rates, wide environmental tolerances, and high adaptability. These are part of the makeup contributing to their pest status; but, more important, these same characteristics make their control by biological means known today of questionable value. In support of wildlife conservationists, it is fortunate that those experts in managing vertebrate pests have long recognized the associated hazards inherent in using natural organisms to control higher animals. Many of the most cherished wildlife species are few in number, or restricted in distribution, and many are rare and endangered. Introduced predators which are not host-specific might severely affect these populations, with little if any detrimental effect on pest species. In fact, predators of many pest species have been found to benefit the pest population as a whole, increasing its reproductive potential. Howard (1974) suggests that predation on some pest species may actually contribute to maintaining overall higher densities than might exist in the absence of some predators.

Since vertebrate pests are higher animals, man himself may fall victim to any introduced diseases intended for vertebrate pest control. When *Salmonella* bacteria were used to control rats, rodent droppings carrying the bacteria then contaminated human food, resulting in food poisoning and human death (Storer, 1958). One example frequently cited as evidence of the value of biological control with the use of pathogens is the introduction of myxoma virus to control European rabbits *(Oryctolagus cuniculus)*. Myxomatosis was brought to Australia in 1950 for the control of the introduced and devastating European rabbit. This virus was originally obtained from naturally occurring infections in wild rabbits in South America. Once the disease took hold, some rather remarkable reductions in rabbit numbers occurred in the initial years; however, due to the development of resistance by the host, this did not last (Cherrett *et al.*, 1971). The current decrease in the efficacy of myxomatosis is due to the development of less virulent strains of the virus. Some 672 strains of myxoma virus have now been recovered from the field in Australia, demonstrating the change from a predominance of highly virulent strains in the initial epizootics to a mixture of strains varying from high (rare) to very low virulence (Marshall and Fenner, 1960).

The significance of less virulent strains is believed by some to be overemphasized, and where this does occur, a highly virulent strain can be reintroduced relatively easily into the rabbit population.[1] Myxomatosis was introduced (accidentally or otherwise) into Britain and initially

[1]Personal communication from G. W. Douglas, Chairman, Vermin and Noxious Weeds Destruction Board, Melbourne, Australia.

reduced the rabbit population substantially; but it is interesting to note that this method of control is now considered to be inhumane and has been declared illegal in Britain (Cherrett *et al.*, 1971).

The introduction of diseases or predators is often suggested by the uninformed as the best and most natural approach to reducing the density of vertebrate pest species; past history and present knowledge indicate that the biological implications and potential environmental catastrophes associated with these approaches are far-reaching and generally irreversible once initiated. No use of rodenticides or avicides in vertebrate pest control has been as devastating to such a wide variety of non-target species as has been the deliberate introduction of certain exotic predators. Any use of biological control of vertebrate pests should be studied in great depth and reviewed most critically before implementation.

MAMMAL PESTS IN THE UNITED STATES

The most economically important species of vertebrate pests that damage citrus in the United States are rodents (pocket gophers, mice, etc.) and lagomorphs (hares and rabbits).

Rodents are members of the order Rodentia and, since they are herbivorous (although many are considered omnivorous), it is not surprising that they conflict with man's interest in cultivated crops. The order Rodentia is characterized by an upper and lower pair of sharp, chisel-like incisor teeth which are used for gnawing.

Hares *(Lepus)* and rabbits *(Sylvilagus)* are not rodents, although they often are thought of as such because of their general size and feeding habits. They belong to the order Lagomorpha, which is characterized by two rows of upper incisor teeth, making a total of four upper incisors instead of two as in the Rodentia.

Rodents and lagomorphs are major pests of citrus and their gnawing and feeding habits kill, stunt, or weaken trees. Trees that have been damaged by these mammals are more susceptible to diseases and other physiological stresses. Even minor damage to roots or trunks may permit pathogenic organisms such as brown rot gummosis to gain entry into a plant. The yield of severely damaged trees may be greatly decreased for a number of years. Deer, though they represent a totally different group of animals, also can cause severe damage to newly planted trees. Their browsing may drastically stunt or weaken a tree, retarding its growth for several years. Fortunately, damage to fruit may involve only the immediate crop.

Some citrus groves have constant problems with certain vertebrate pests unless the animals can be excluded. In other groves the problem is localized and sporadic, correlated with seasonal changes, fluctuations in pest population density, or other factors that influence the number or behavior of the pests. Because of such fluctuations and sporadic damage, growers sometimes become lax in their control or prevention programs, permitting rodent populations to get temporarily out of hand or to go undetected until after serious losses have occurred. A continuous surveillance for vertebrate pests should be carried out, just as it is for insect pests. The most effective solution to the vertebrate pest issue is never to permit the problem to reach a level where serious economic losses occur.

Rodent, lagomorph, and deer problems are nearly always most severe in young groves, particularly those planted adjacent to undeveloped or uncultivated land. As an orchard increases in age and/or where adjoining lands are modified so that they no longer support pest populations, serious damage from some species may eventually subside or disappear. Once certain pests such as meadow mice and ground squirrels are eliminated from an orchard, they may never become a problem again if cultural practices do not favor them. With other pests which have been reduced in number by poisoning or trapping, it may be possible to keep them at a low population density through periodic control efforts or other preventive measures, thus keeping economic losses minimal.

Pocket Gophers

Biology.—There are three genera of pocket gophers in the United States, all belonging to the family Geomyidae. The genus *(Thomomys)*, represented by eight species, occurs over most of western North America. Seven species of *Geomys* are found on the plains and prairies and in the eastern Gulf States. The yellow-faced pocket gopher *(Pappogeomys)* (Jones, Carter, and Genoways, 1973) occurs from southeastern Colorado through eastern New Mexico and western Oklahoma, and south through western Texas into Mexico. Pocket gophers are not found in the northeastern United States.

The pocket gopher offers an excellent example of why it is so important to properly identify a pest species by its acceptable vernacular or scientific name rather than by local names. In Florida pocket gophers are commonly called "salamanders" and the land tortoise *(Testudo polyphemus)* often is called a "gopher." To complicate the situation even more, in the midwest, ground squirrels *(Spermophilus)* are sometimes locally called "gophers." The use of the term "gopher" rather than the vernacular name pocket gopher could obviously lead to considerable confusion, especially in a widely circulated publication concerned with control techniques.

Pocket gophers are stout-bodied, short-legged rodents having two pairs of prominent incisor teeth (fig. 5–1). External fur-lined cheek pouches open outside the lips on each side of the mouth and are used for carrying food. The head is blunt with visible ears, although both the ears and eyes are quite small. The head and body measure about six to eight inches in length and the tail is less than half the body length and scantily haired (fig. 5–2).

Fig. 5–1. Pocket gopher *(Thomomys).* The front feet, long claws, and prominent incisor teeth that are exposed even when the mouth is closed make this animal well suited for digging in soil and gnawing.

Pocket gophers are fossorial and seldom travel on the surface. They dig complex burrow systems that may extend over several hundred square feet, with enlarged chambers serving as storage areas for food or as nests for rearing young.

The pocket gopher burrows found in the citrus-growing areas of California are about 2 inches in diameter and usually located from 6 to 14 inches below the ground surface. Excavated soil is pushed to the surface by the use of the forefeet, forming characteristic crescent-shaped mounds 8 inches or more across. An active pocket gopher may create several mounds in one day. Mounds (fig. 5–3) are pushed up from the ends of short lateral runs which branch off the main runways. The surface openings of the burrows are usually left plugged with soil. Fresh surface mounds may not appear when the soil moisture content is low. Ordinarily, each burrow system is occupied by a single pocket gopher, except during the breeding season or when the female is rearing young.

Fortunately, pocket gophers are less prolific than many other rodents. Normally one litter a year is produced; however, some evidence exists indicating that in a favorable habitat as many as two or possibly even three litters may be raised. The average litter contains five or six young.

Fig. 5–2. The pocket gopher *(Thomomys bottae),* a capable digger, is shown removing soil from its burrow beneath a young orange tree.

Damage.—The pocket gopher's food consists mainly of the underground parts of plants, chiefly roots, bulbs, and tubers. Green stalks and leaves of herbaceous plants, which can be cut and

Fig. 5–3. Frequent inspections should be made to detect the first signs of pocket gopher activity so that control measures can be instigated immediately. Weed-free groves make the burrowing activities of pocket gophers readily visible.

pulled into the burrow, are also consumed in large amounts. Damage to citrus trees results when pocket gophers cut small roots or gnaw bark from either roots or the base of trees. It is not uncommon to find trees completely girdled a few inches below the soil line (fig. 5–4). Pocket gophers can cause substantial economic loss in citrus nurseries and newly planted orchards by girdling numerous trees in a relatively short period (Cummings, 1962*a*). Pocket gopher burrows contribute to irrigation water diversion and sometimes to extensive soil erosion (fig. 5–5).

The magnitude of pocket gopher damage to citrus in the early 1920's prompted R. W. Hodgson (1923) to write a nineteen-page circular titled "Saving the Gophered Citrus Tree," which dealt with bridge-grafting and inarching methods for saving gopher-damaged trees. Today, because of better surveillance and improved control measures, there is rarely a need for such grafting techniques for repairing rodent damage.

Since pocket gopher damage is below ground and not visible, it often goes undetected until a tree exhibits outward physiological stresses (Moore, 1955; Moore, Skou, and Nauer, 1956). By this time, however, the tree may be beyond help. Stress symptoms may resemble those caused by drought, nutrient deficiencies, certain diseases, and even previous insect damage. Trees exhibiting

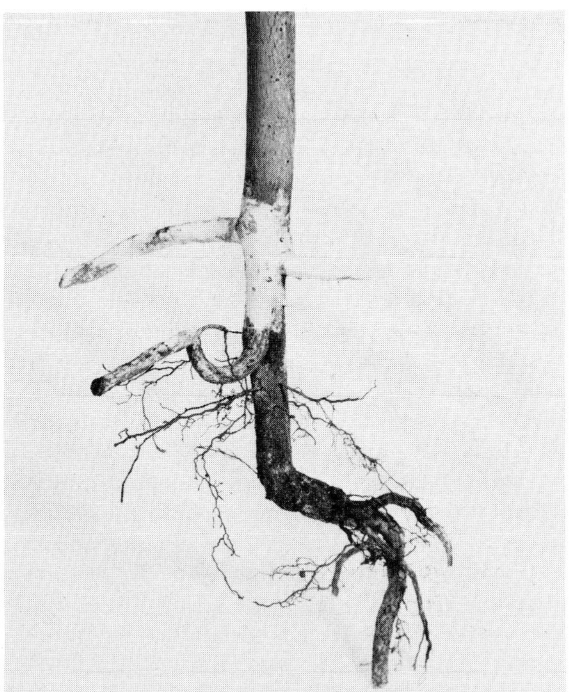

Fig. 5–4. Pocket gopher damage to a young orange tree only recently planted.

Fig. 5–5. In contoured or terraced citrus groves, pocket gophers definitely cause damage to the trees but may also cause considerable loss of irrigation water through diversion by the burrow system. The associated soil erosion may ultimately cause terrace breakdown.

chlorosis or withering, particularly when symptoms are confined only to certain branches or to one side of a tree, should thus be checked for rootgirdling before more involved examination for disease or chemical deficiencies is undertaken. If damage is discovered early, even completely girdled productive trees sometimes can be saved by inarching seedlings into healthy tissue above the girdled area. Bridge-grafting also has been used to span a girdled region. Bridge-grafting and inarching are not always successful in saving trees; fortunately, these methods are needed much less often today than in the past. Although the unchecked pocket gopher still remains a serious threat to citrus, recent improvements in control methodology and habitat modification by total or strip weed control prevent gophers from becoming as numerous as in the past.

Hose-pull or drag line sprinkler and drip irrigation systems which use plastic water lines either below or at the soil surface are highly vulnerable to animal damage (fig. 5–6). Pocket gophers, meadow mice, rats, hares, rabbits, and even coyotes *(Canis latrans)* have been responsible for gnawing or chewing the plastic lines. Any of the rodent or rabbit species that occur in the citrus groves may be involved. The species causing the damage can many times be identified by incisor impressions left in the plastic or by characteristic types of damage known to be caused by certain species (fig. 5–7).

Repairing damaged plastic lines can be time-consuming and expensive. In most instances, serious damage to the system cannot be neglected for long because of both water loss and the potential for soil erosion. All types of plastics seem to be attacked, but the severity may differ depending on the diameter of the lines, their hardness, etc. No known suitable repellent has proven effective to date, but the manufacturers of the components of these systems are keenly interested in developing plastic lines less tempting to rodents.

Control.—Pocket gophers may be controlled effectively and even eliminated from sizable citrus orchards. Elimination is not accomplished without persistent effort, however, and reinvading animals must be eliminated promptly.

Large pocket gopher populations are controlled most economically with poison baits. Until recently, baits were dropped by hand into their underground runways. The development of a tractor-drawn bait applicator (fig. 5–8) has greatly simplified and economized pocket gopher control

Fig. 5–6. The drag-line type of sprinkler system used in this citrus grove is often subjected to gnawing damage from rodents and rabbits.

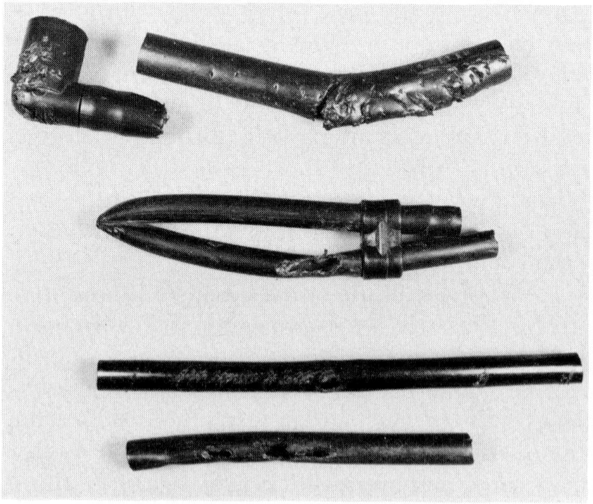

Fig. 5–7. Examples of mammal damage to plastic drip or drag hose irrigation lines lying on the soil surface. Pocket gophers are frequently responsible for damage where the plastic pipe is buried beneath the soil, but are less apt to be involved with surface lines. The top two examples represent damage caused by coyotes. The damage to the kink at the end of the line is believed to be caused by meadow mice, while the sample next to the bottom showing a series of incisor marks is characteristic of jack rabbits. The last sample could be pocket gopher, but the width of the teeth marks is more indicative of smaller species such as meadow mice or deer mice.

Fig. 5–8. The mechanical gopher-bait applicator offers a quick inexpensive way of controlling pocket gophers. Before new citrus groves are planted, the land should be completely rid of pocket gophers. The machine illustrated is a three-point hitch model manufactured by Blackwelder Manufacturing Company. (Photo courtesy of Blackwelder Mfg. Co.)

(Kepner *et al.*, 1962), offering a rapid, inexpensive means of eliminating a high percentage of the population in infested fields with a once-over operation.

The mechanical bait-applicator, sometimes called a burrow builder, constructs an artificial burrow beneath the soil and deposits preset quantities of toxic grain bait at fixed intervals. The artificial burrow formed intercepts most of the burrow systems of pocket gophers one or more times. Pocket gophers readily explore the artificial tunnels and consume bait found within (Rosedale and Cummings, 1962). This machine has been a major contribution to control methodology and has revolutionized pocket gopher control by virtually replacing the former trapping and handbaiting operations which were time-consuming, costly, and often inadequate (Marsh and Cummings, 1976).

The bait-applicator consists of four basic components in addition to the supporting frame: (1) a depth-adjustable, burrow-forming shank; (2) a rolling coulter to cut surface trash and shallow roots ahead of the shank; (3) a bait-metering device; and (4) a presswheel to drive the metering unit and close the knifelike slit (fig. 5–9) made in the ground by the upper portions of the shank. The bait is dropped into the artificial burrow through a tube built or cast into the rear portion of the burrow-forming shank.

For satisfactory results, the soil should be reasonably firm below the top three or four inches and be moist enough so that smooth, clean burrows are formed. Well-formed burrows are important in achieving a high degree of pocket gopher control, but even poorly formed burrows will frequently provide acceptable control. In general, soil moisture should be near the upper limit of the range for good plowing or cultivating. In California, the depth of the artificial burrow should average 8 to 10 inches. However, in some groves with light soil

Fig. 5–9. The narrow slit in the sod between the citrus rows is the only evidence indicating the grove has been baited mechanically for pocket gophers.

and bermudagrass *(Cynodon dactylon)* or other sod cover, a shallower burrow just under the sod may provide excellent results. Artificial burrows are made between each row of trees.

Infestations of pest species should be controlled as part of the site preparation before a new citrus grove is planted. On open land, artificial burrows are formed in parallel rows spaced at 20- to 25-foot intervals between rows. Seriously infested sites may require two treatments with a mechanical gopher-bait applicator for maximum control. In land preparation, the entire acreage should be treated; if a second treatment is necessary, the artificial burrows should be constructed at a 90° angle to those in the first treatment, assuming the land is reasonably level. Too often, vertebrate pests and their potential for damaging young trees are not adequately considered when planning new groves. With a little forethought, potentially serious problems can be avoided at a fraction of the expense that may be required after planting. Where previous control has nearly eliminated the pest from established citrus groves, only the isolated infested portions of the orchard or the perimeter need to be retreated to prevent pocket gophers from reinvading from surrounding fields.

Grain baits prepared with strychnine alkaloid* are extensively used for pocket gopher control. A relatively new rodenticide called Gophacide®[2] *(0,0*-bis (*p*-chlorophenyl) acetimidoyl phosphoramidothioate), an organophosphate, has been proven highly effective for pocket gophers. Baits prepared at 0.1 or 0.2 per cent level are effective, with the higher concentration most frequently used in the mechanical bait applicator. Unfortunately, the distributing firm may discontinue marketing this rodenticide in the United States. For the proper bait and application rate, citrus growers should consult their local county agent or agricultural authority.

The manufacturer's instructions provided with the bait should be followed explicitly. Hand-baiting with bait prepared with strychnine is done on small acreages or where an infestation has been reduced to a few animals. The use of strychnine-treated fresh baits of carrots, sweet potatoes, or parsnips achieves good control with hand-baiting, but cannot be used in most commercially available burrow builders. Vegetable baits are cut in convenient sizes—approximately 1½ by ½ by ½ inches —and then washed and drained. Bait is prepared by dusting one-quarter ounce of powdered strychnine alkaloid over 4 quarts of the dampened bait. For uniform distribution of the poison, the bait should be shaken or rolled in a lidded container until evenly coated. For best results, fresh baits should be prepared daily and old unused bait should be disposed of by burying. Control is achieved by inserting several baits in each main gopher runway through a small opening made with a pointed probe. Each burrow system should be baited in at least two locations. Combination grain and dried-fruit (raisins or chopped prunes) baits containing strychnine (0.25–0.6 per cent) are also used for hand-baiting.

Trapping is an effective means for supplementing or maintaining control after baiting where only a few invading pocket gophers are involved. Success depends upon the proper use of traps and the perseverance of the trapper. The two most commonly used traps are the Macabee, a two-pronged snap type, and a choker type called the California 44 box trap (fig. 5–10) (Anon., 1958). The box trap is most commonly used in southern California, being a particular favorite in many citrus orchards (Cummings, 1962*b*).

Traps are most effective when set in main runways which, soil texture permitting, can be located with a pointed probe in the same manner

[2]Gophacide is a registered trade name of Chemagro Corporation.

*In California a permit is required from the county Agricultural Commissioner when this material is used for field rodent or other pest vertebrate control.

used in hand-baiting. The runways are dug open with a shovel or garden trowel, and the traps are inserted well into the burrows. It is best to set two traps in order to intercept the gopher from either direction. Openings made for setting the traps should be covered with sod or soil so that little or no light reaches the traps (fig. 5–11).

Other methods of controlling gophers include gassing or burrow fumigation and protecting trees with wire netting (hardware cloth), but neither of these is notably effective; hence, they are seldom used today as control methods in commercial citrus groves. Barriers have also been placed around citrus groves (fig. 5–12) to fence them out. These may also reduce meadow mouse infestations. Where basin or flooding types of irrigation are practiced, this periodic flooding may discourage pocket gophers and meadow mice to some degree. Many gophers can be killed by an alert irrigator with the aid of a dog when the pests are driven out of their burrows by the water. This practice alone, however, is not adequate to relieve all gopher damage and should be supplemented with poisoning or trapping.

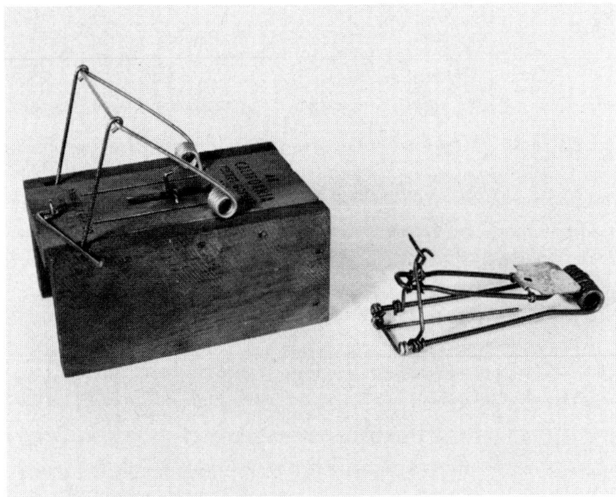

Fig. 5–10. Left, California 44 pocket gopher box trap; right, Macabee gopher trap.

Meadow Mice

Biology.—Meadow mice (*Microtus* spp.), also called voles and field mice, are blunt-nosed, short-eared, chunky little rodents with small eyes and short legs (fig. 5–13). These mice have relatively coarse fur which is usually dark or grayish brown in color. When full-grown they are larger than house mice and smaller than rats and have rather short tails. The genus *Microtus* is represented by a number of species having a combined range covering most of the United States, including the citrus-growing areas. Pine mice *Microtus (Pitymys) pinetorum*, a closely related

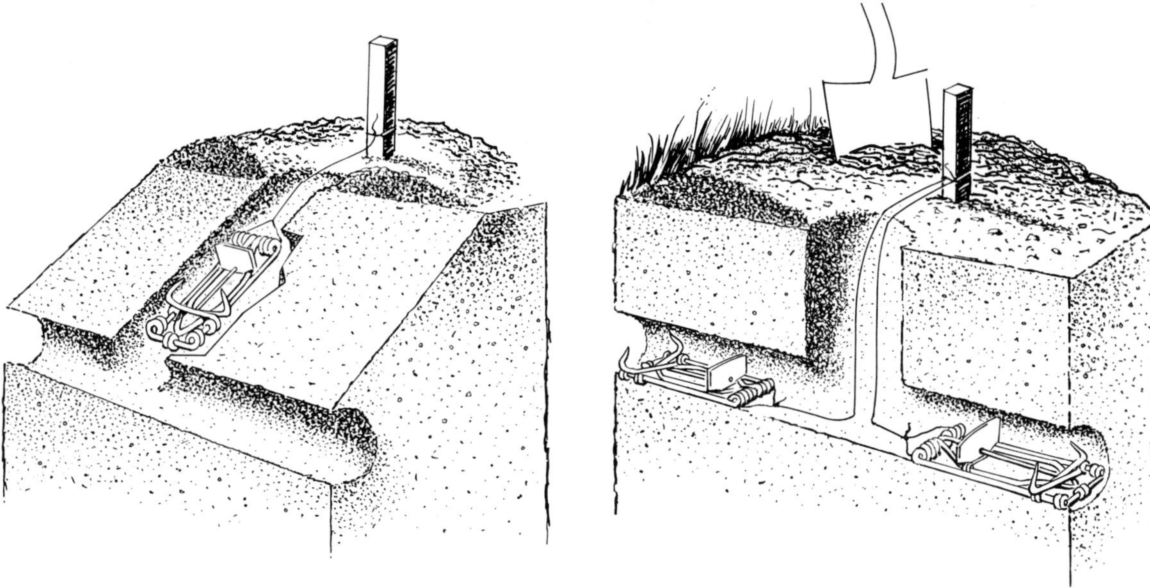

Fig. 5–11. Trap placement for pocket gophers. A single Macabee trap can be placed in each lateral tunnel. It is usually more effective to locate and open a main tunnel, and set traps in each direction of the burrow. Traps should be set well back into the burrow from the opening made by shovel or trowel. A shovel full of soil is used to close the opening to prevent light from entering.

Fig. 5–12. To prevent pocket gophers from invading the citrus groves from uncultivated areas, growers in some areas have resorted to burying ½ by ½ inch hardware cloth about 24 to 30 inches in the soil with about 6 inches of the wire bent outward at the bottom at a 90° angle. A 12- to 18-inch extension is left above ground to deter rodents moving on the soil surface.

Fig. 5–13. The meadow mouse *(Microtus californicus)* is a chunky little rodent with a blunt nose and relatively small ears.

group, have been reported to gnaw the bark from the base of young citrus trees in Florida. They will be discussed briefly later.

Meadow mice are active throughout the year and are normally found in habitats supporting dense ground cover. They sometimes prefer moist areas where ample herbaceous vegetation exists. When populations are high, they make a complex network of well-used surface trails or runways. They construct short, shallow burrows with underground nesting chambers. Burrow openings are numerous (fig. 5–14). The potential breeding rate of meadow mice is high and under favorable conditions they may, during certain years, multiply to enormous populations, reaching "plague" proportions. The amount of freshly cut vegetation and

Fig. 5–14. Meadow mice are active during the day and, when numerous, may be seen or heard moving about. This young orange tree has been completely girdled as far up on the trunk as could be reached, and some of the major roots have been severed. Such severe damage is the result of an extremely dense mouse population.

fresh droppings found in the runways indicates the number of mice present. Cotton rats (*Sigmodon* spp.), prevalent in some citrus areas, leave similar signs, but their trails and feces are somewhat larger (Ludeman, 1962).

Damage.—Meadow mice feed on almost any vegetative plant part, including stems, roots, bark, and seeds of a variety of plants. They have been responsible for serious damage to range forage, alfalfa, cereals, and root crops, in addition to most varieties of fruit trees. The mice damage or kill citrus trees by gnawing through the bark to the cambium layer. Complete or partial girdling of the trunk from just below the soil line up to as far as they can reach on the trunk frequently occurs where mice are left uncontrolled (figs. 5–15 and 5–16). As in the case of pocket gopher damage, tree injuries can sometimes be repaired by bridge-grafting or inarching (figs. 5–17 and 5–18). Trees which have had their trunks or roots damaged by meadow mice or other rodents respond favorably to heavy pruning. Such treatment helps the balance between root and top (Johnston and Moore, 1953). Where low hanging branches touch the ground, mice may feed on all the vegetative parts accessible, including fruit. With suitable habitat, the extent and severity of damage may vary from year to year, for meadow mouse populations are cyclic and in years of high density, damage to infested groves may be extensive throughout an entire citrus-growing region.

Fig. 5–15. A young orange tree girdled nearly up to the budded stock by meadow mice. Mouse burrows extend right up to the base of the tree.

Fig. 5–17. An excellent example of inarching used to save trees girdled by meadow mice. Damage had occurred three years earlier in August and the tree was inarched in November of the same year.

Fig. 5–16. An orange tree partially girdled by meadow mice at Citrus Research Center and Agricultural Experiment Station, Riverside, California. (Photo by the late H. J. Quayle.)

Fig. 5–18. Inarching and bridge grafting are sometimes used on the same tree in an attempt to save severely girdled trees. The damage resulted from neglect and weed growth which favored the development of a dense population of meadow mice. The expense of saving this particular grove was substantial because over 50 per cent of the trees required either inarching, bridge-grafting, or both.

Control.—Preventive measures such as habitat modification are most effective, but cultural practices which produce favorable mouse habitat should be avoided where possible. Cover crops and weed growth encourage meadow mice by providing food and cover, as do thick mulches beneath trees (figs. 5–19 and 5–20). Mulches and vegetation should be kept cleared away from the tree trunk for a radius of at least three feet. In orchards where nontillage soil management practices are carried on without cover crops or the addition of organic mulches, problems with meadow mice and gophers are generally greatly diminished (Johnston, 1953; Storer, 1948). The elimination of weeds from an entire grove with herbicides effectively removes suitable habitat for both the meadow mouse and the pocket gopher.

In California, however, serious meadow mouse infestations are known to develop in weed-free nontilled groves, particularly in years of high mouse populations. Groves especially prone to these infestations are those which have a long history of meadow mouse problems prior to adoption of current cultural practices or those where ideal mouse habitat is located in the immediate vicinity, thus providing a continuing source of reinfestation (fig. 5–21). From outward appearances such groves would not be considered suitable for supporting mice, since they lack dense vegetative cover and a thick mulch. Under these conditions, however, a high meadow mouse population in surrounding habitats may cause rapid and extremely serious damage to the trees. This is partially because there is little else in the way of food available. This illustrates how some rodent species, when under the pressure of a rapidly increasing population or when their normal habitat has been modified, can adapt to the new environment.

In these situations, direct reductional control with toxic baits is the only practical way to eliminate the meadow mouse threat. Frequent inspections are necessary with repeat treatments with toxicants conducted as required.

Grain baits treated with zinc phosphide* (1.0–2.0 per cent) are commonly used for meadow mouse baiting. They are formulated at the rate of 1 pound of zinc phosphide powder to 100 pounds of steam-crushed whole oats or crimped oat groats with mineral or vegetable oil used as an adherent. Coarse-cracked corn is sometimes used, but is not generally recommended because it is more readily accepted by birds. For broadcast application, the concentration of zinc phosphide is doubled to approximately 2.0 per cent. Strychnine*-poisoned grain (0.3–0.5 per cent) is sometimes used as an alternate toxicant for hand-baiting of runways or burrow entrances. Baits containing strychnine alkaloid are not recommended for broadcast application, however, because strychnine is a fast-acting poison and may produce unpleasant warning symptoms, causing the mice to cease feeding before a lethal amount is found and consumed.

Bait of freshly-diced or cubed apple, sweet potato, or carrot is sometimes used for hand-baiting meadow mice (Weinburgh, 1964), although

Fig. 5–19. Bermudagrass beneath young citrus offers ideal habitat for meadow mice and pocket gophers.

Fig. 5–20. Weeds or undisced cover crops beneath citrus trees provide habitat conducive to both meadow mice and pocket gophers.

Fig. 5–21. Grassy field in foreground was heavily infested with meadow mice which eventually moved into the weed-free adjacent orange grove, causing severe girdling damage to some trees.

apple is generally preferred most. Fresh bait is dusted lightly with zinc phosphide* powder. At certain times of the year, bait of freshly cut apples is accepted much better than grain, but it is more expensive to prepare and does not lend itself to mechanical broadcast baiting.

Hand-baiting with grain or fresh apple gives the most effective control. A spoonful of grain or several cubes of apple are placed directly in an active runway, burrow entrance, or at several spots around the trunk of a tree. Where large acreages are involved, hand-baiting of runways may be too expensive and machine broadcasting of grain baits may be the most economical approach, since more acres can be treated in less time. Various types of broadcasters have been used and many tractor- or tailgate-mounted, whirling-disc type seeders or fertilizer spreaders work well. The application rate varies, depending on the mouse population and thoroughness of coverage, but generally it is below 10 pounds per acre. Hand-cranked, cyclone-type seeders are also valuable for disseminating grain bait.

Broadcasting of bait does have its limitations: where low-hanging branches provide dense foliage nearly to the ground, the broadcast bait may not penetrate in amounts sufficient to reduce the mice in the vicinity of the tree trunks. This can be partially overcome if the broadcaster is mounted so it throws the bait beneath the foliage skirt. Aircraft can be effectively used in very young orchards since the foliage canopy is too sparse to deflect the bait from the trunk region. The choice of methods of baiting will depend on the situation and circumstances.

Because of their increased safeness to non-target species, anticoagulant baits (i.e., Fumarin®, Pival®, warfarin, diphacinone, and chlorophacinone) have occasionally been used where acute rodenticides such as zinc phosphide* and strychnine* were considered too hazardous. Because anticoagulant rodenticides are accumulative toxicants and must be consumed over several days, ample bait must be provided continuously until the population is controlled. Small bait boxes have been used to expose anticoagulant baits. Tube-like expendable bait stations containing an amount equivalent to about ½ cup of bait placed near a tree trunk may be sufficient. With dense populations, more than one treatment may be necessary to provide all mice with lethal doses.

Anticoagulant baits have been explored experimentally for controlling meadow mice and other mice of similar size (Libby and Abrams, 1966; Marsh, Cole, and Howard., 1967). Bait blocks made of anticoagulant-treated grain baits embedded in paraffin have also been found effective in some situations (Marsh and Plesse, 1960).

Control of meadow mice by spraying the ground cover or cover crop with an insecticide (endrin) has been employed in some regions, especially in deciduous fruit orchards. But the increasing concern about the effects of using persistent chlorinated hydrocarbons such as endrin has stimulated research to develop the anticoagulant chlorophacinone as an alternative for ground cover spraying to control meadow and pine mice. Ground cover spraying of endrin has not been either recommended or used in California for such purposes because of both the high rates required to kill mice and the potential hazards to non-target animal species.

Young citrus trees can be protected from meadow mice by cylindrical wire guards placed around the tree trunk. These are made of ¼-inch or ½-inch mesh hardware cloth, 24 inches wide and with a diameter sufficient to allow at least several years' growth without cutting into the tree. Guards must extend about 6 inches below the soil surface. Such protection of young trees can serve a double purpose. If the wire guard is 36 inches high, it will exclude jack rabbits (fig. 5–22).

*In California a permit is required from the county Agricultural Commissioner when this material is used for field rodent or other pest vertebrate control.

Fig. 5–22. Hardware cloth cylinder provides protection from jack rabbits and, if buried several inches into the ground, offers some protection against meadow mice. Such cylinders should not be relied on entirely for protection against meadow mice, however, since mice occasionally dig under the wire.

Meadow mice rarely climb, so they present no problem of going over a guard; when numerous, however, they may dig beneath the wire. Materials other than hardware cloth are sold for tree guards, but although some may be less expensive and more convenient to use, few give protection equivalent to hardware cloth. Plastic, cardboard, and other trunk guards made of fiber materials are advantageous for preventing sun-scald and frost damage.

Several commercial animal repellents are available for painting or spraying on tree trunks, but their value in providing adequate protection against this rodent is very limited because damage may occur at, or just beneath, the soil level. Trapping is of little use in commercial groves and fumigation (gassing) is ineffective because of the nature of the burrow system.

Fig. 5–23. The California ground squirrel *(S. beecheyi)* frequently constructs its burrow systems among rock outcroppings, along fences, or beneath trees.

Ground Squirrels

Biology.—Ground squirrels are members of the family Sciuridae with *Spermophilus* leading the list of genera of greatest economic importance. Distribution in the United States places most ground squirrel species west of the Mississippi River; however, the *S. tridecemlineatus* does extend as far east as Ohio. In California, *S. beecheyi* (fig. 5–23) is the species responsible for extensive agricultural damage to range forage and cereal crops; to a lesser degree, it also damages a wide variety of both vegetable and fruit crops, including some damage to citrus.

The California or Beechey ground squirrel is active during the day and, although similar in size to the tree squirrel, can be distinguished from it by its flecked or mottled fur. Unlike tree squirrels (*Sciurus* spp.), ground squirrels usually live in colonies and their underground burrows often form extensive connecting systems. When frightened, they seek cover in their burrows, unlike tree squirrels which generally climb trees to escape. An adult may weigh from 1 to 2½ pounds. Females produce one litter each year, averaging six to eight offspring (Dana, 1962).

Damage.—When California ground squirrels take up residence in citrus groves, their burrow systems, dug in the root zone of trees, may expose roots to drying or divert irrigation water, eventually leading to weakened trees and erosion. Burrows in the banks of irrigation canals may also contribute to breakthroughs. Terraced groves are particularly vulnerable to damage by the burrowing of squirrels. Capable climbers, ground squirrels cut off and eat appreciable amounts of citrus fruit and will consume an entire orange, including rind, pulp, and seeds. Squirrels may travel some distance (200–1,000 feet) from colonies in adjacent rangeland or other uncultivated land to feed on oranges, and often they are seen carrying partially eaten fruits back to their burrows. Because of their size, relatively few squirrels can cause an unbelievable amount of fruit loss. Ground squirrel damage to orange plantings in California probably dates back to the Spanish missionary period; early mission records frequently mention the damage caused by ground squirrels to their mission gardens. Grinnel and Dixon (1918) reported the damage to citrus by ground squirrels and Henderson and Craig (1932) mention the damage to citrus and other fruits by squirrels in their book on *Economic Mammalogy*. Ground squirrel populations have been greatly reduced in a large portion of major citrus-growing areas of California; hence, their importance to citrus culture seems to have diminished significantly since the early part of the century.

Control.—Ground squirrels are not repelled by any chemical or physical means known today. It is almost impossible to exclude ground squirrels by fencing, and no known feasible type of habitat modification has any appreciable influence on reducing damage below an acceptable economic level. Thus, reductional control through the use of toxic fumigants, poison baits, traps, or shooting is the only effective control measure available.

Fumigants such as carbon bisulfide[3] are volatile materials used for gassing ground squirrels in their burrows. Carbon bisulfide can be applied by saturating a wad of jute, cotton waste, or other absorbent material with about 2 ounces (60 ml) of the liquid and placing it deep within the burrow entrance. The opening is then plugged with a shovel of soil. Carbon bisulfide is highly flammable and explosive. Methyl bromide,[4] although more toxic to all animals, is not flammable and is gaining in popularity as a fumigant. It can be applied to burrows from small pressurized containers with rather inexpensive equipment. The treated holes must then be sealed to prevent the gas from escaping. Fumigants such as these work best when the soil is moist, since much gas escapes from dry soil.

Trees may be severely injured or killed with the use of either of these two phytotoxic fumigants if burrows occur among the roots. It is recommended that these toxic fumigants be used by trained personnel and only where the material will not injure trees. Because of its potential toxicity to humans, the use of methyl bromide is regulated by law in California.

There also are commercial gas cartridges available which release substantial amounts of toxic gases when ignited by a fuse. The lit cartridge is inserted into the burrow system and then all entrances are closed with soil. Gasses produced by these cartridges are generally not considered phytotoxic and may be used in burrows beneath trees, but they should be used in accordance with manufacturer's instructions.

In California, lethal baits are the primary means of suppressing large squirrel populations. Strychnine-alkaloid*-treated grain baits are used quite commonly for the subspecies *S. b douglasii* in the citrus-growing area of Butte and Tehama Counties, because this subspecies is highly susceptible to strychnine and readily accepts it in baits. Strychnine is less effective on other subspecies of *S. beecheyi* and, therefore, its use is limited to the fall when squirrels are pouching grain. The strychnine is absorbed while the grain is in their cheek pouches.

Zinc phosphide* is probably the most commonly used acute rodenticide for controlling squirrels in citrus-growing areas. An effective zinc phosphide formula for ground squirrels, meadow mice, and rats is as follows: oat groats (crimped or semirolled), 100 pounds; lecithin-mineral oil combination, 22 ounces; and zinc phosphide (90 per cent), 16 ounces.

---

[3]In California, certain fumigants such as carbon bisulfide and calcium cyanide, when used in rodent or other vertebrate control, require a use permit regardless of where they are applied.

[4]In California, no permit is required to use the fumigant methyl bromide for rodent or other vertebrate control, providing the material is packaged in containers holding 1½ pounds or less.

*In California a permit is required from the county Agricultural Commissioner when this material is used for field rodent or other pest vertebrate control.

The zinc phosphide powder is mixed with the lecithin-mineral oil; an even suspension is obtained more quickly if the liquid is heated slightly. The toxic suspension is then poured over the grain and thoroughly mixed. For field use, the bait is scattered in small amounts near the burrow entrances. One pound of treated grain will treat approximately 60 burrows.

Sodium fluoroacetate (1080) is the most effective rodenticide for ground squirrels; like strychnine, however, it is highly toxic. It also has the undesirable characteristic of causing secondary poisoning, particularly in canines that consume the dead squirrels. In California, the use of sodium fluoroacetate is strictly regulated by law, and its use for field rodent control is limited to governmental agencies. Sodium fluoroacetate (1080) should be used in citrus groves only when no other toxicant will achieve the desired control and where the hazard to non-target species is absent or minimal.

Where a ground squirrel infestation is localized, anticoagulant rodenticides are useful, and because of their safety they are gaining in popularity. The treated grain baits are offered to squirrels in covered bait boxes or other types of bait stations placed in the immediate vicinity of a squirrel colony. Ample bait must be provided at each station to assure continuous feeding until control is achieved. For citrus areas that have a high human population, anticoagulants are probably the safest rodenticides that can be used.

Small populations of troublesome squirrels can be removed with wire live-catch traps. Modified wooden pocket gopher traps (figs. 5–24 and 5–25) baited with grain, walnuts, or citrus have been employed successfully (Becker, 1940). They are much more effective than live-catch traps and with some effort can be used to control relatively sizable infestations, although the cost of labor will be much greater than with the use of toxic baits. The lack of hazards to children and pets may more than justify the additional cost of this technique.

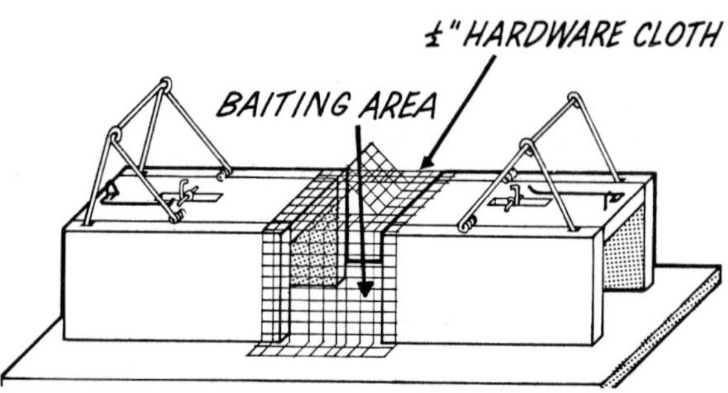

Fig. 5–24. Two California 44 pocket gopher traps modified and secured to base board. Such traps are effective for both ground and tree squirrels.

Jack Rabbits

Biology.—Jack rabbits belong to the genus *Lepus*, the family Leporidae (which include rabbits and hares), and the order Lagomorpha. They should more accurately be called hares for they are not true rabbits, as are cottontails of the genus *Sylvilagus* and domestic rabbits (*Oryctolagus cuniculus*). When the term "rabbit" is mentioned in relation to agricultural depredations in the western United States, however, it invariably means jack rabbits.

Lepus californicus is the black-tailed jack rabbit (fig. 5–26). It ranges throughout the southwest and is the species responsible for citrus damage in California, Arizona, and Texas. The black-tailed jack rabbit is about as large as a house cat, has long ears, short front legs, and long hind legs, and when frightened, can outrun most breeds of dogs. This species does not build nests, but does make depressions (forms) in the soil beneath a bush or some other vegetation for seclusion. The peak breeding season occurs during the spring months, but jack rabbits may produce as many as three litters a year with three to eight young per litter. When born, the young are fully haired with eyes open, and within a few days can move about quite rapidly.

Damage.—Their food includes a wide variety of plants including grain, alfalfa, various vegetables, field crops, and fruit trees. Jack rabbit dam-

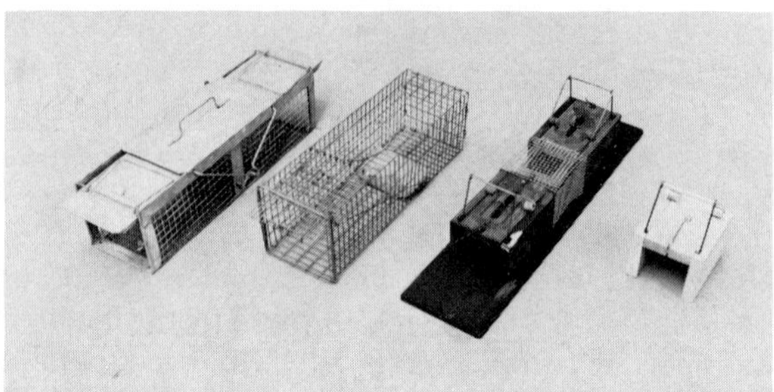

Fig. 5–25. Four traps that can be used to remove ground squirrels from citrus groves. Left to right: Havahart live trap; Tomahawk (National) live trap; two California 44 gopher traps combined and modified to capture squirrels; and a custom-designed, oversized pocket gopher type trap with a strong spring and some trigger modifications, used in the Los Angeles, California, area for trapping squirrels.

Fig. 5–26. The large ears are characteristic of black-tailed jack rabbit. This animal becomes active at dusk and, hence, its damage will not be evident until the following morning. (Photo courtesy of Jack K. Clark.)

age is one of the most common complaints growers have in California when establishing new vineyards and orchards that adjoin land inhabited by this species. Young citrus plantings are no exception. In California, Texas, and Arizona, jack rabbits attack young citrus groves, especially those adjacent to undeveloped or uncultivated open areas, gnawing the bark from trunks and clipping whatever small branches are within reach.

They are particularly destructive to young nursery trees. Jack rabbits also have been reported to eat citrus fruit on low-hanging limbs and fruit which has fallen to the ground.

Control.—Where jack rabbits are a constant threat to young groves, exclusion from the grove may be the best means of control. Galvanized poultry netting of 1-inch mesh and at least 48 inches high supported with appropriate posts makes a satisfactory rabbit-proof fence. The bottom 6 inches of wire should be bent outward at right angles and buried 6 inches to prevent rabbits from digging beneath the fence. Fencing is useful for small acreages, but its expense makes it less practical for large orchards. When deer-proof fences are constructed to protect an orchard, the additional expense of making the enclosure rabbit-tight may be worthwhile.

Besides a rabbit-proof enclosure, tree guards offer the most protection. Tree wraps or protectors may be a solid sheet, net, or mesh of a variety of materials including metal, plastic, paper, cardboard, or other fibrous material. Cylinders of wire mesh around each tree provide positive protection from debarking and can be made of 1-inch mesh poultry netting formed around the tree with joined ends. They should be large in diameter and tall enough so that the trunk and young branches are screened from the rabbits. Stakes or wooden spreaders may be used to keep the wire cylinder in position. If ¼- or ½-inch hardware cloth is used for the cylinders (fig. 5–22), the trees also can be protected in part from meadow mice *(Microtus)*, provided they are anchored at a depth several inches into the soil. Jack rabbits sometimes stand on their hind legs to reach over the trunk guards and eat foliage and clip young limbs. Severe stunting may result if rabbit damage is repeated for several years.

Chemical repellents also are marketed as a means of reducing or preventing rabbit damage to trees. Of the various repellents available, ziram (zinc dimethyl dithiocarbamate-cychlohexylamine complex) and those containing thiram (tetra-methylthiuram disulfide) are the ones most often used. When these repellents are sprayed or painted on trunks or foliage, the trees are temporarily protected from jack rabbit damage. All repellents should be used in accordance with manufacturer's recommendations. These generally suggest repeated applications, particularly where new growth occurs. Repeat applications may also be necessary if repellency has been diluted by rain or sprinkler irrigation. The effectiveness of repellents diminishes when other types of rabbit foods become scarce.

Some situations warrant the use of poison bait to reduce jack rabbit numbers, but since state game laws differ, local game officials should be consulted to ascertain the legality of a poisoning program. Some states classify hares and rabbits as game animals. Rolled barley treated with strychnine* at the rate of 5 ounces of strychnine alkaloid per 100 pounds of grain is a common bait mixture (Johnson, 1964). Fresh chopped alfalfa and apples are sometimes used as bait. Before the actual poisoning, nontoxic prebait (bait material without poison) should be offered to get the animals used to feeding at the site and to make certain

*In California a permit is required from the county Agricultural Commissioner when this material is used for field rodent or other pest vertebrate control.

the poison bait material will be taken when provided later. Where strychnine or other acute toxicants are used for control, prebaiting is essential to achieve effective control.

Jack rabbits do not accept thinly scattered grain bait. Both prebait and toxic grain bait should be applied in amounts of about ¼ cup, placed either in small piles or scattered over a very small area. The baited spots should be spaced every 20–40 feet in rabbit trails, particularly where well-defined trails intersect. Jack rabbits have a tendency to follow furrows and this has on occasion been put to practical use by artificially producing a furrow with some implement and baiting directly in the furrow. In freshly worked soil, the depressions a vehicle's wheels make are excellent baiting sites.

An important note of caution is that rabbit bait should never be placed where deer or livestock will be exposed to it in lethal amounts. Special fenced baiting sites are sometimes employed to exclude deer and livestock (Wetherbee, 1967). Considerable information is available on how to control jack rabbits with toxic baits, but the techniques vary with the situation. Even if poisoning programs are conducted in accordance with the best available information, they still frequently do not suppress jack rabbit populations sufficiently to prevent some damage from occurring.

Anticoagulant baits have been used on jack rabbits experimentally and with encouraging results. Bait must be exposed in amounts sufficient to provide multiple feedings for the entire rabbit population. Chicken or turkey feeders have worked quite well for exposing anticoagulant baits; they should be maintained continuously in a grove as long as rabbits remain a problem. This practice is gaining wide acceptance in California, particularly in Fresno and its adjacent counties.

While removal of cover crops and weeds in a grove modifies the habitat, making it less suitable for such species such as pocket gophers and meadow mice, it will not have the same influence on jack rabbits. For example, jack rabbits remain quite numerous in some groves in Tulare County, California, where weeds are controlled chemically under a nontillage soil-management practice. In this case, the cultural practices may actually favor the jack rabbits. It appears that in these instances, the rabbits use the citrus grove primarily as a sanctuary or resting area, at least in the daytime, venturing from older groves at dusk to feed on other vegetation in adjacent fields. In contrast to the amount of damage done to newly planted trees, jack rabbits do little damage to mature trees, or it goes undetected even where the animals are fairly numerous.

The value of shooting or the use of dogs such as whippets should not be overlooked as an effective means of eliminating small numbers of rabbits. Best results are achieved in early morning or evening when rabbits are most active. Rabbit drives have been used in the past, but they are not sufficiently effective to justify the expense.

Cottontails

Biology and Damage.—Cottontails belong to the genus *Sylvilagus,* which are true rabbits, and are members of the order Lagomorpha. The genus is found in practically all parts of the United States. In California, the desert cottontail *(S. audubonii)* is the species probably most often responsible for occasional damage to citrus (fig. 5–27). The range of this species encompasses most of the citrus-growing areas of the southwest. Cottontails

Fig. 5–27. The cottontail rabbits, *Sylvilagus,* are sometimes responsible for gnawing on both young citrus trees and plastic irrigation lines. (Photo courtesy of Michael E. R. Godfrey.)

are smaller than jack rabbits and have shorter ears. Their young differ from those of jack rabbits in that they are naked, blind, helpless, and remain for several weeks in a protective nest lined with fur. They generally inhabit areas of dense cover such as rock piles, thickets, brushy areas, or sparsely wooded sites with underbrush. They subsist mostly on tender herbaceous plants, but on occasion they will move into a citrus grove and feed on bark of young trees or low hanging limbs of mature trees.

Control.—This genus can be excluded by fencing or by protection with the same type of tree guards used for jack rabbits. Repellents used for jack rabbits can also be used for cottontails. Cottontails are classed as a game animal; therefore, local game officials should be consulted if reductional control becomes necessary. In California, there are special provisions for reductional control of cottontails if they are causing agricultural damage.

Tree Squirrels

Biology.—Tree squirrels include two genera of rodents: *Sciurus* and *Tamiasciurus*. *Sciurus* is the most important from the viewpoint of economic damage. The absence of dorsal stripes, spots, or flecks, and the lack of internal cheek pouches distinguishes the tree squirrels from the ground squirrels. Chiefly arboreal, tree squirrels have longer and bushier tails than ground squirrels. Tree squirrels range over all of the United States, but only two species seem to be implicated in citrus damage. The fox squirrel *(Sciurus niger)* is the largest of the North American tree squirrels, and is distributed throughout much of the eastern half of the country except for the northeastern states. It has been introduced into California, unfortunately, and is well established over relatively large areas in a number of locations within the state. The fox squirrel should not be confused with the native western gray squirrel *(S. griseus)*, which has not been reported as a citrus pest. *S. carolinensis*, another gray squirrel, ranges throughout the eastern half of the country and has been reported a pest to citrus in Florida. It, too, has been introduced into several areas of California; however, it remains in rather localized areas at this time. In California, perhaps this species should be eradicated; at least attempts should be made to prevent its spread and to keep it from competing with the native western gray squirrel.

Damage.—The fox squirrel is a typical tree squirrel that inhabits wooded areas and spends much of its time in trees. In California, where these squirrels become numerous, they eat or destroy fruit, and the damage to citrus and nut crops can reach economic proportions. In cities, where the fox squirrel may be plentiful, it is not uncommon for them to feed on the fruit of backyard citrus trees. The eastern gray squirrel *(S. carolinensis)* has been reported to eat fruit and also to gnaw the bark of young trees in Florida.

Control.—Tree squirrels are virtually impossible to exclude from an orchard. Habitat manipulation to discourage this species also is impossible, and effective repellents to protect citrus from tree squirrels do not presently exist. The only effective way to resolve the problem is through reductional control. Since tree squirrels are considered game animals in most states, consultation with local game officials is necessary before undertaking reductional control measures. In California, game regulations under certain conditions provide for reducing depredating tree squirrels.

Where there is a season on tree squirrels, increased hunting pressure may help keep them in check. They provide excellent hunting and are considered good eating.

Ordinarily, trapping is an effective control method. Modified wooden box-type gopher traps have proven very effective and are more economical than live-catch traps. The gopher traps are modified by removing the wooden back. The trigger slot is lengthened with a pocket knife to permit the trigger to swing freely in both directions, making it possible for the animal to pass beneath the trigger loop of the unset trap. A piece of ½- or ¼-inch hardware cloth is used to extend and close the back end of the trap (fig. 5–24.) This provides a baiting area and forces the animal to enter only from the front. The trap is secured to a base board and nailed on top of a horizontal limb in a tree where fruit losses are occurring. A handful of nut meats placed well behind the trigger mechanism will attract the squirrels. For best results, baited traps are left unset for several days until squirrels become accustomed to entering the trap for bait. After squirrels have become familiar with the traps, they are rebaited and the triggers are set. A considerable number of tree squirrels can be taken with relatively few traps if they are kept in continuous operation while damage is occurring.

Rarely is the problem of tree squirrels serious enough to warrant the use of toxic baits, even if game regulations permit such control.

Cotton Rats

Biology.—Cotton rats belong to the genus *Sigmodon* and the hispid cotton rat *(S. hispidus)* is the most widely distributed species of this genus in the United States. They are small animals about half the size of Norway rats, with a chunky body, narrow head, and short, rounded ears largely hidden by fur. Their coarse hair is grizzled gray in color, and the scantily-furred tail is about half as long as the body (fig. 5–28). Their range in the United States is throughout the southern states, into some north central states, and west into southern California. Originally in California they were found only along the Colorado River, but in recent years cotton rats have extended their range into more of southern California (Clark, 1972).

They inhabit a variety of places including roadside ditches, waste borders of cultivated lands, moist meadows, and salt marshes (Weinburgh, 1964). Cotton rats occasionally reach very high cyclic population levels as do meadow mice *(Microtus)*.

Damage.—In California, the hispid cotton rat does some damage to citrus. Clark (1972) reported on a 13-acre Valencia orange grove located in the Imperial Valley which sustained heavy damage from cotton rats. Tree trunks were girdled and a high percentage of trees were either severely set back or killed. Fallen fruit were completely hollowed out. Cotton rats are known to feed on a wide variety of field crops and the extension of the cotton rat's range within California may make this species economically more important in the future. Cotton rats have also been reported to cause damage to citrus in Texas (Storer, 1948).

Control.—Strychnine*-treated crushed oats, milo, and barley are used as bait to control cotton rats. Milo is the least desirable bait because it is more readily accepted by birds. Bait is placed in runways in teaspoonful quantities. Cubed carrots, sweet and common potatoes, and grain prepared at the ratio of 1½ pounds of zinc phosphide* to 100 pounds of bait material are also used for controlling cotton rats (Ludeman, 1962). In general, control methods for cotton rats closely parallel those used for meadow mice.

As with meadow mice, the threat of cotton rats can be reduced by habitat manipulation. The elimination of heavy grass and weed growth makes an area less desirable to these animals.

Fig. 5–28. Cotton rats *(Sigmodon hispidus)* sometimes cause damage to citrus. The damage resembles that of meadow mice, so it is important to properly identify the offending species so appropriate corrective measures can be taken. (Photo courtesy of Dell O. Clark.)

Woodrats

Biology.—The woodrat of the genus *Neotoma* is locally called the pack rat or trade rat. It is a native rodent similar in size to introduced rats of the genus *Rattus*, but differentiated from them by having hairy or bushy tails. Its color ranges from a light buff to gray. The hair is longer and softer than that of a Norway rat, the ears are much more conspicuous, and the eyes are larger.

Woodrats inhabit brushy or wooded areas and usually build prominent dome-shaped houses (dens) 2 to 4 feet in height on the ground. More spherical-shaped nests are sometimes built up in trees.

Damage.—In California, citrus groves planted adjacent to uncultivated areas with suitable habitat for woodrats *(N. fuscipes)* sometimes are damaged by this species (fig. 5–29). Skillful in climbing, they venture into the trees and cut small twigs for nest building, gnaw the bark from limbs, or sever stems of fruit, dropping it to the ground. Fruit is eaten or gnawed upon sufficiently to make it insalable. Damage is usually confined to those trees located close to the woodrats' natural habitat. Woodrats rarely construct nests in or beneath citrus trees.

Control.—Population reduction, when necessary, is most often accomplished by trapping or by using toxic baits. Once a nest or den is located, ordinary snap-type rat traps are effective in taking these rats if they are baited with a section of citrus or apple tied securely to the trigger.

*In California a permit is required from the county Agricultural Commissioner when this material is used for field rodent or other pest vertebrate control.

Fig. 5–29. Woodrat *(Neotoma fuscipes)*. **Superficially, woodrats resemble the introduced rats** *(Rattus)*, **but the fur is softer and the tail has considerably more hair. (Photo courtesy of Jerry P. Clark.)**

Walnuts, dried prunes, and raisins have also proven to be acceptable baits. Traps should be placed at the entrance of ground nests or across runways leading from the nest. Wire live-catch traps are also effective in capturing rats. The fact is that woodrats are relatively easy animals to trap.

Where sizeable woodrat populations are causing damage, toxic baits usually offer the quickest and most economical control method. Rolled or hulled barley, steam-rolled or lightly crushed oats, and steel-cut or crimped oat groats have all proven to be acceptable grain baits. Grain intended to be used for control should be field-tested for acceptance prior to treatment.

Bait of steam-rolled or crimped oat groats treated with zinc phosphide* (1.0 per cent) is effective for woodrats just as it is for meadow mice and ground squirrels. Five grams (approximately 1/5 ounce) of this bait scattered in trails or runways near the entrance of a den can be expected to produce desired control. Anticoagulant grain baits have been used in bait stations, and grain baits embedded in paraffin have also been used (Marsh, 1962). Raisins, dried prunes, dried apricots, and walnut meats have proven effective bait material when dusted with zinc phosphide. In certain instances, freshly cubed apples and sectioned citrus baits dusted with zinc phosphide have also worked well.

To alleviate damage through preventive measures such as habitat modification would involve the removal of all favorable woodrat habitat next to the grove. This is not desirable, practical, or economically feasible in most situations.

Pine Mice

Pine mice *(Microtus pinetorum)*, were formerly placed in the genus *Pitymys*, but now are included with their close relatives, *Microtus* spp. Pine mice are close relatives of the genus *Microtus*, are absent from the western half of the country and, therefore, are not a problem in California, Arizona, or Texas citrus groves. They occur over much of the area east of the Mississippi River but extend only into the northern portion of Florida. On at least one occasion, pine mice caused damage to a citrus grove involving about 200 acres in the northern portion of Florida's citrus belt.[5] This mouse is differentiated from other meadow mice by its shorter tail and shorter and denser fur; in addition, it is more subterranean in its habits. It gnaws bark and girdles the trunks and roots of citrus trees. Because they are more subterranean, pine mice are usually more difficult to control than other meadow mice, although they are susceptible to the same toxicants. Special artificial burrow builders which have been constructed for control of pine mice in apple orchards could presumably be used in citrus groves as well. Except for minor modifications, these machines are similar to the burrow builder used for pocket gopher control. If the range of the pine mouse ever expands to include more of the citrus-growing area of Florida, it might become a pest of greater concern.

Roof Rats

Biology.—The roof rat *(Rattus rattus)*, sometimes called the black rat or Alexandrine rat, is a member of the family Muridae. It was introduced when this country was first settled, probably escaping from rat-infested sailing ships (fig. 5–30). This rat is found primarily along the coastal regions of the southeast, the southern states bordering the Gulf of Mexico, and the western states bordering the Pacific Ocean. It also extends inland for some distance in some areas. Not only does this species occur in the most important citrus-growing areas of California and Florida, but damage in citrus groves has been reported in both states.

The adult rats weigh about ½-pound and are about 15 inches long, including the tail. Their noses are more pointed and their ears and eyes are

*In California a permit is required from the county Agricultural Commissioner when this material is used for field rodent or other pest vertebrate control.

[5]Personal communications from F. P. Lawrence, Citrus Extension Specialist (retired), Univ. of Florida, Gainesville, Fla.

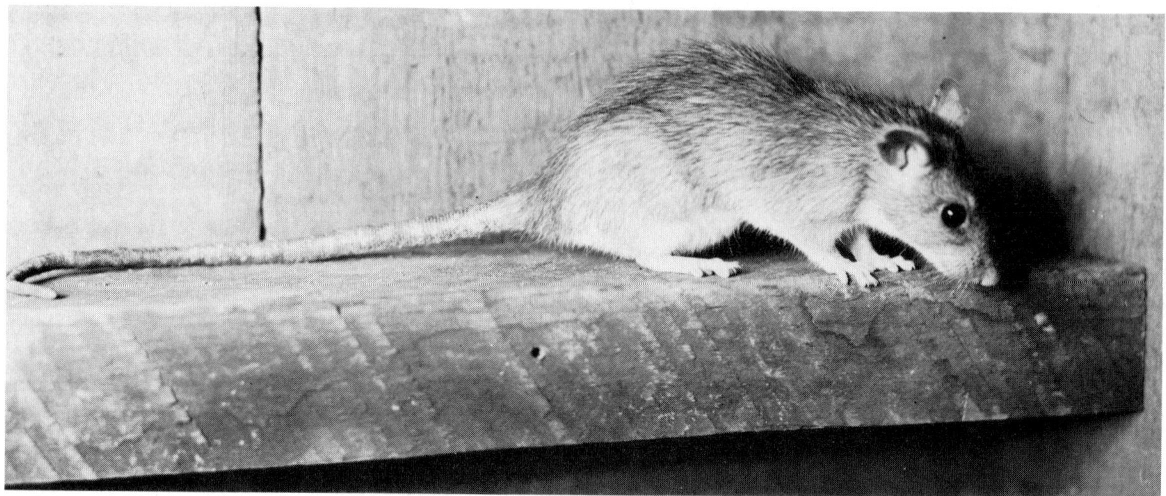

Fig. 5–30. Roof rat *(Rattus rattus).* **Its tail is longer than its body, its snout is pointed, and its ears and eyes are larger than those of the Norway rat.**

larger than those of their close relative, the Norway rat *(R. norvegicus).* Roof rats have high reproductive rates, averaging about 6 young per litter; they may breed several times per year.

Damage.—Roof rats are excellent climbers and out-of-doors may nest in palms, citrus, and other trees with dense foliage. In back yards they may nest in thick ornamental shrubs or in dense vines, but almost always above the ground. They seem to prefer fruit and nuts as food. Roof rats have on occasion been troublesome in citrus orchards in parts of California and Florida, where they gnaw into mature fruits and eat the seed and pulp (Worth, 1950). Both oranges and lemons have been damaged. Where rats are numerous, bark may be gnawed on the scaffold limbs. This frequently occurs on the underside of the limb, at the point where it branches and gives the rat a footing from which to feed.

Control.—Where rats cause damage in citrus groves, the use of poisons is the most practical means of control. Control can be achieved with baits containing either an acute rodenticide such as zinc phosphide*, or with a chronic type anticoagulant rodenticide as mentioned below in the "Control" subsection of "Commensal Rats and House Mice." Particular attention should be given to controlling the rats around the perimeter of the grove to prevent reinfestation. Bait boxes are convenient for exposing anticoagulant baits; they conserve and protect the bait material as well as restrict feeding to the target species. Paraffin type bait blocks containing anticoagulants are very effective and can be secured to limbs six feet or more above the ground.

Where only a few rats are involved, trapping may be effective. Ordinarily rat snap traps can be secured to limbs in the trees and baited with citrus, raisins, prunes, or nut meats. The traps should be baited and left unset until the bait is being readily consumed. Once traps are being visited regularly they can then be set.

As with woodrats and tree squirrels, habitat modification is of little value with this species and repellents are also ineffective because of the type of damage occurring.

Commensal Rats and House Mice

Biology and Damage.—Introduced old world rats of the genus *Rattus* are represented by the Norway rat *(R. norvegicus)* (fig. 5–31), and the roof rat *(R. rattus).* The roof rat *(R. rattus)* has been discussed previously because it is a pest of citrus groves. Roof rats and Norway rats can also become problems in citrus packinghouses and storage facilities. The amount of fruit they consume is usually minute compared to that which they destroy or contaminate. When numerous, they may ruin an appreciable number of packing cartons by their gnawing. House mice *(Mus musculus)* (fig. 5–32) belonging to the same rodent family (Muridae) may be responsible for damaging pack-

*In California a permit is required from the county Agricultural Commissioner when this material is used for field rodent or other pest vertebrate control.

Fig. 5–31. The Norway rat *(Rattus norvegicus)* **has a blunt nose, slightly haired ears, small eyes, and a tail which does not exceed the combined length of the head and body. (Photo courtesy of Jerry P. Clark.)**

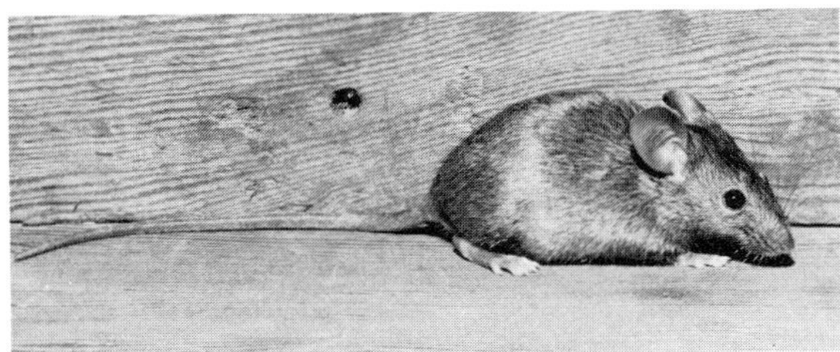

Fig. 5–32. House mouse *(Mus musculus).* **The eyes are small and the tail scantily haired. (Photo courtesy of Jerry P. Clark.)**

ing containers beyond use. They are not considered pests of citrus groves. Norway rats and house mice are found almost everywhere in the United States and are responsible for substantial losses to all types of stored food commodities.

Control.—Control by exclusion or rodent-proofing is the most permanent solution to preventing rodents from infesting buildings; however, complete exclusion from buildings is sometimes difficult to attain, especially with house mice. Reinvasion of the building from outside sources is a constant problem. Much can be done to alleviate a rat menace by eliminating rat harborage both inside and outside infested buildings. Reduced amounts of harborage (e.g., lumber piles, boxes, weeds, etc.) result in fewer rats, and thus help limit the problem. Sanitation within processing and packing plants has eliminated or greatly reduced problems with rats. New citrus-packing and storage facilities are generally quite rat-proof.

Much has been written about control of commensal rodents in food storage processing plants. Space permits only the briefest coverage of the subject here. For this reason, techniques used infrequently in structural pest control have been omitted. In the United States there are rigid laws and regulations concerning sanitation in food-packing, -processing, and -storage facilities. The rodenticides permissible and methods of use are frequently changed to take advantage of newer developments or to eliminate materials no longer considered appropriate. Latest information on the control of commensal rodents in citrus-packing, -processing, and -storage facilities may be obtained from state or federal sanitation inspectors.

Trapping may be the simplest way of removing a few rats or house mice from a building. The ordinary spring snap trap is the best and cheapest. Traps should be baited with bread crumbs, nut meats, peanut butter, bacon, or other preferred foods.

Although trapping with snap traps can eliminate small infestations, poisoning—where permissible—is relied upon as the most efficient means of controlling a large population of rodents. Heavy infestations of rats and mice may be controlled with the use of single-dose rodenticides like zinc phosphide and a new rodenticide (Peardon, 1974) called Vacor® (N–3–pyridylmethyl N'–p–nitrophenyl urea).

Two acute rodenticides, ANTU (alpha-naphthylthiourea) and red squill, are reasonably effective against Norway rats but are not against roof rats or house mice. Strychnine* is not effective against rats but is against house mice. Prepared on canary grass seed or cereal baits, strychnine on occasion is used as an acute toxicant to control house mice (Marsh and Howard, 1977).

The anticoagulant rodenticides such as warfarin, Pival®, Fumarin®, diphacinone, and chlorophacinone, presently are extensively used in structural rat and mouse control. Anticoagulants are cumulative rodenticides requiring ingestion over a period of several days to two weeks before death occurs. The longer durations of feeding are essential for the more resistant house mouse. Many ready-to-use rat and mouse baits are commercially available, and most, if used in accordance with directions, will give satisfactory control. Water baits can be prepared with soluble salts of anticoagulants. Such treated solutions give good

*In California a permit is required from the county Agricultural Commissioner when this material is used for field rodent or other pest vertebrate control.

control where other water sources are limited or may be temporarily restricted to the rats while control is in progress, (Howard and Marsh, 1976).

Often it is more prudent and convenient for a packinghouse manager to hire a licensed structural pest control operator (PCO) to carry on rat and mouse control or preventive control measures, since the PCO will be abreast of the latest methods, laws, and regulations governing such control programs.

Raccoons

The raccoon *(Procyon lotor)*, belonging to the family Procynoidae, is present in the citrus-growing areas of the United States and occasionally is responsible for eating oranges (Worth, 1950). Once it establishes a particular feeding habit, it may be necessary to remove offending animals by shooting or by using live-catch or leg-hold traps. These ringtailed, black-masked animals are considered of very minor economic importance to the citriculture in this country.

Opossums

Like the raccoon, the opossum *(Didelphis virginiana)* is nocturnal and omnivorous and will, on occasion, develop a taste for citrus fruits in groves (Worth, 1950) and home yards in some areas of California where the animal is numerous. Presumably, this occurs in other parts of the country where citrus is within the distribution range of the opossum. This grayish, long-haired, pointed-nosed animal has a prehensile, rat-like tail, and belongs to the primitive marsupial order of mammals. It is native to eastern and southeastern portions of the United States. It was deliberately introduced into several areas of California for hunting purposes many years ago and has extended its range since then to include nearly all of the citrus-growing areas of the state. Apparently, the opossum also is suspected of causing some damage to citrus in Trinidad (Greenhall, 1966).

Opossums are easily caught in box traps, or with a number 2 leg-hold trap, either with baits or trail sets in locations where they have caused damage. A wide variety of baits may be used, although fish and canned dog or cat food work well. Since opossums are considered game in some states, game officials should be consulted prior to hunting them. Hunting at night is also an effective means of ridding a grove of a few animals which have become pests.

Armadillos

The nine-banded armadillo *(Dasypus novemcinctus)* is a rather unusual mammal with the body, head, tail, and legs covered with hard armor-like plates. The armadillo has extended its range northward and eastward from Texas, and now is also found in much of the southeast. In Florida, where it was introduced, it has spread throughout most of the state. Its burrowing activities create problems by filling in ditches with soil and weakening dikes, resulting in erosion and water losses (Neill, 1952; Fitch, Goodrum, and Newman, 1952). Burrows may be 7 to 8 inches in diameter and from 10 to 15 feet in length depending on the soil type (Kalmbach, 1943). Reports from Florida indicate that the burrows dug beneath citrus trees may damage the root system not only by permitting entrance of disease organisms but also by causing excessive aeration of the root system.

Where control is necessary, live-catch or leg-hold traps (No. 1 or 1½) can be effective using over-ripe apples as bait (Miller, 1970). Fumigants such as calcium cyanide or carbon bisulfide are effective, although these were not registered (as of 1977) by the Environmental Protection Agency for such use on this species. Carbon bisulfide is toxic to trees and is not recommended for use in burrows extending beneath trees or other desirable vegetation. Efforts should be made to prevent the introduction of the armadillo into areas where it does not now occur.

Tortoises

The land tortoise *(Testudo polyphemus)* is covered in this section for convenience, although it is not a mammal but rather a reptile. In Florida, land tortoises have been reported to frequent citrus groves where their large burrows are not only a nuisance, but also may contribute to tree death (Storer, 1948) when they are dug beneath young trees. In many respects, the type of damage attributed to this animal is similar to, but less severe than, that of the armadillo (see above). At times, the grower may resort to using a long pole with a hook on the end to reach in and pull the animal out for removal (Lawrence, 1965). Calcium cyanide dust placed well into the burrow was used in past efforts at control. This tortoise is called a "gopher" by Floridians.

Deer Mice

Mice of the genus *Peromyscus* are distinguished from other mice by tail length and by their large, nearly naked ears. In California, the most widely distributed member of this genus is *P. maniculatus*, commonly called the deer mouse because of its large thin ears and large eyes (fig. 5–33).

These small rodents are very abundant in logged over forest land and frequently prevent forest regeneration through their seed-eating activities. They seldom cause problems in agricultural crops, although they have been implicated in digging up and eating melon and several other types of seeds planted in areas where they are found in relatively high numbers. Deer mice can be found in many grassland areas of California. In one particular instance, deer mice were found to have been responsible for severe damage to a young lemon grove in Tulare County. The mice crawled up inside the trunk wrappers and gnawed the bark from young trees. Some damaged trees were completely girdled and had to be replaced (fig. 5–34). Rodent-damaged trees and gnawed drip-irrigation lines in this particular grove indicate the types of problems which might be expected where former cattle rangeland is planted to citrus (fig. 5–35). Constant inspections for evidence of rodent or rabbit damage must be conducted in this type of planting so that corrective measures can be applied as soon as a problem is identified.

Deer mouse damage of this type has never been observed previously by the authors in a commercial citrus grove. Since deer mice are very susceptible to anticoagulant rodenticides, treated grain bait was used to reduce the deer mouse population and alleviate damage. Poisoned bait

Fig. 5–34. A young lemon tree with the trunk wrapper partially removed to expose girdling damage caused by deer mice.

Fig. 5–33. Deer mouse *(Peromyscus maniculatus)*. A small mouse with relatively large eyes and ears. (Photo courtesy of Jerry P. Clark.)

Fig. 5–35. The planting of former grassland or rangeland to citrus can frequently lead to a variety of rodent and rabbit problems, particularly when the grove is young.

would be the recommended method of control when the problem does arise.

Moles

Moles, part of the family Talpidae, are fossorial animals, as are pocket gophers. They do not belong to the order Rodentia, but to the order Insectivora. Most members of this group of mammals feed primarily on insects or other invertebrates. Their presence in citrus groves is of concern because of the water which may be diverted by their burrow systems (fig. 5–36); this, in turn, may create erosion problems. The broadfooted mole *(Scapanus latimanus)* is the species encountered in California citrus-growing regions.

When control is necessary, traps designed specifically for moles are effective, but time consuming. Rarely are moles numerous enough in citrus to warrant a poison program.

Fig. 5–36. Moles traveling just beneath the soil surface, and feeding primarily on insects, leave a characteristic trail of heaved soil.

Bats

Greenhall (1966) reported incidences where Valencia organges were fed upon by the greater spear-nosed bat *(Phyllostomus hastatus hastatus)* in Trinidad. In that same article, Greenhall cited a reference to flying foxes *(Pteropus)* feeding on mandarins in Australia. Reports of citrus damage by bats are very rare and no such reports have occurred in the United States. Fortunately, the introduction and release of exotic fruit-eating bats is prohibited in this country.

Deer

Biology.—Deer, the most important big game species in this country, are found in suitable habitat throughout the United States. They are even-toed ungulates belonging to the order Artiodactyla, as do our domestic cattle, sheep, and goats. In the United States, deer of the family Cervidae have branched or multipronged antlers that normally are worn by males and shed annually.

Damage.—Deer are the largest of our citrus pests and can be a serious problem, particularly where young citrus groves are planted next to uncultivated land inhabited by these animals (fig. 5–37). A very typical example of deer depredation occurred on about 200 acres of young lemon trees planted in San Luis Obispo County, California. Since this planting was quite removed from any other citrus and adjacent to open rangeland, the extensive damage was predictable. Deer can nearly completely strip young trees of foliage. In California, where mule deer *(Odocileus hemionus)* populations may be high and the summers are always dry, the lush foliage of citrus under irrigation is highly attractive to deer. Damage may be sufficiently extensive that the small limbs are eaten or broken causing severe stunting and distortion of the development of a good framework of scaffold branches. Deer are also problems to citrus in other states, with some rather substantial damage occurring in Florida involving white-tailed deer *(O. virginianus)* (Beckwith and Stith, 1968). In planting new groves, consideration should be given to potential deer problems.

Control.—A deer problem can be resolved for the most part by complete fencing of a citrus orchard. Although there are many designs of deer-proof fences, a woven mesh wire (4 x 4 inches) fence 6 feet high is usually adequate for upright fences on level ground (Longhurst *et al.*, 1962). In California, deer normally will not jump a 6-foot fence; but, if pressed by dogs or humans, they are capable of clearing an 8-foot fence. In some areas 7-foot fences are erected for added protection against deer invading a grove. Adequate gates or deer guards permit entry into the grove and yet exclude the deer.

Fig. 5–37. Citrus groves surrounded by uncultivated land frequently have the most severe rodent, rabbit, and deer problems.

Sometimes drift fences are constructed just along the side of the grove adjacent to the uncultivated (wild) land with the other sides of the grove left unfenced. This approach to the problem, although less expensive, is rarely satisfactory with high value crops such as citrus because if the deer are hungry enough, they will go around the ends of drift fences to enter the grove.

An important factor to remember is that deer fences must be checked regularly. Damaged wire, broken gates, and soil washouts beneath fences, for example, which permit deer access, must be repaired.

In California, permits can be obtained to kill deer that are involved in crop depredation. While this is not to be considered a long-term approach, it does offer some temporary and immediate relief at critical times when deer are extremely numerous or when natural deer browse is in short supply. Shooting an animal may be the only practical way of removing a deer which has managed to negotiate a deer fence and is trapped within the fenced grove.

Feral burros *(Equus asinus)* along the Colorado River in southern California have been known to feed on orange fruit and foliage. Although these burros are rare in occurrence, a deer-proof fence will eliminate them as well as other problems concerning escaped and stray domestic livestock.

Pilfering of citrus fruit from the trees by man may be the most serious animal problem faced by the citrus growers in the United States and the other world citrus-growing areas. However, our original definition of vertebrate pests at the beginning of the chapter excluded man. The subject is mentioned here because deer-proof fences or 6-foot cyclone type fences do help reduce the loss of citrus to these non-paying consumers. In some locations, such losses of citrus fruit undoubtedly exceed by far losses from other vertebrates. Posting of the property with signs, fencing, and patrols may all be helpful in reducing this problem.

AVIAN PESTS IN CITRUS

Bird species, constituting the class Aves, are important pests of citrus culture in some parts of the world. Fortunately, birds presently are not considered significant citrus pests in either California or the other citrus-growing areas in the United States. This may change if the introduced species known to attack citrus increase in numbers or expand their range, or if additonal introductions take place which are left unchecked.

Parrots

Belonging to the order Psittaciformes, parrots (including parakeets, macaws, cockatoos, lories, and others) are readily distinguished from other birds by their short, blunt, rounded bill with the curved upper mandible fitting neatly over the lower one. Most are brilliantly colored.

Today there remain some 332 species of parrots distributed mainly in the Southern Hemisphere; most are prevalent in the tropical regions. Their fondness for fruits and cereals puts many members of this order in direct conflict with man's interest. Crop damage has been reported from many countries where parrots are native, but few objective studies have been conducted on the severity and magnitude of the problem. In regions where subsistence farms come under attack from parrots, the problem could take on substantial significance and crops might have to be protected (Forshaw, 1973). Parrots as a group probably cause more damage to world citrus production than any other order of birds.

For the most part, we have listed only those species of the diversified order of parrots which have a liking or potential liking for citrus fruit. There are undoubtedly many other parrot species involved in citrus damage, at least to a minor degree, in their native regions. A number of the parrots mentioned have been introduced into the United States and several are established as feral populations in the wild.

According to Bull (1973), some 11 exotic species of parrots have been observed in the wild in the New York City area alone, but nearly all have failed to establish themselves. The notable exception is the monk parakeet *(Myiopsitta monachus)*. Although the psittacine birds have been implicated as carriers of several diseases (e.g., parrot fever and Newcastle's disease), they remain favorites of aviculturists, and thousands are sold by the pet industry annually. The threat of escaped or released members of the parrot group becoming established in the United States is of considerable concern to agriculturists and naturalists alike (Bull, 1973; Bull and Ricciuti, 1974; Courtenay and Robins, 1975; Hardy, 1973; Owre, 1973; Shields, Grubb, Jr., and Telis, 1974).

The red-capped parrot *(Purpureicephalus spurius)* has been reported to attack citrus fruits in southwestern Australia. The eastern rosella parrot *(Platycercus eximius)*, native of southeastern Australia and introduced into New Zealand, is already causing damage to citrus crops (Rostron, 1969).

A parrot of South America which can cause considerable damage in orange groves is the maroon-bellied conure, *Pyrrhura frontalis* (Wetmore, 1926). Citron fruit *(Citrus medica)* is one of the preferred foods of the purple-bellied parrot *(Triclaria malachitacea)*, which occurs in southeastern Brazil (Sick, 1968).

The red-lored Amazon *(Amazona autumnalis)*, which is found in Central America from eastern Mexico south to the Amazon Basin and western Ecuador, is a common and widely distributed resident of most parts of Belize, formerly British Honduras, though possibly less numerous in the extreme south (Forshaw, 1973). There are reports of parrots raiding ripening citrus in Belize (Russel, 1964). This noisy bird can be seen in flocks from a few pair up to a hundred individuals.

This same species has been observed in the wild in the southern California city of San Bernardino (Hardy, 1973). It if becomes well established, it could definitely be a threat to the citrus industry there.

Another parrot, related to the red-lored Amazon which attacks cultivated fruits including oranges and mangoes, is the orange-winged Amazon, *Amazona amazonica* (Poonai, 1969). This parrot is widely distributed in South America and is known to congregate in the thousands at roosts. A flock of eight orange-winged Amazons has been observed in the wild in Coral Gables, Florida, and if this species becomes well established, the citrus of that region may suffer economic damage.

The white-fronted Amazon *(Amazona albifrons)* is now present in Florida and believed to be breeding there (Owre, 1973). Although its potential for damaging citrus is unknown, it should be suspect.

On the Isle of Pines, Cuba, flocks of the Cuban Amazon parrot (*Amazona leucocephala*) were observed in grapefruit orchards twisting the stems of the unripe fruit until they dropped to the ground (Walkinshaw and Baker, 1946).

Several yellow-headed Amazons *(Amazona ochrocephala)* have been observed in the wild in the New York City area, and although they are tropical South American parrots, at least two escapees survived the northern winter by feeding on crabapples (Bull, 1973).

The yellow-headed Amazon has also been reported fairly common in parts of southern California. Flocks of up to 30 have been observed, although it has not definitely been determined whether they are breeding and reproducing in the wild; circumstantial evidence suggests that they probably are. The fondness of these parrots for tangerines in backyard trees and for eating oranges (Hardy, 1973) suggests that this introduced parrot could become a pest of the citrus industry in southern California.

The red-crowned Amazon *(Amazona viridigenalis)* has been observed in the wild in the southern California city of Pasadena (Hardy, 1973). Sightings are rare, however, and they are not believed to be established to date as a breeding species. Native to Mexico, this species is the most abundant of the feral Amazons now established in southeastern Florida (Owre, 1973). Its potential for damaging citrus is unknown to the authors.

The rose-ringed parakeet *(Psittacula krameri)*, budgie *(Melopsittacus undulatus)*, black-hooded parakeet or nanday conure *(Nandayus nenday)*, and canary-winged parakeet *(Brotogeris versicolorus)* all have been reported in the wild in southern California. Only the latter species, which seems well established as a feral population, has been observed feeding on citrus, and this was on the buds of orange trees. There seems little doubt that both the canary-winged parakeet and black-hooded parakeet are potential threats to citrus. The canary-winged parakeet has also become established in southern Florida and is found locally there in fairly large numbers (Owre, 1973).

The state of Florida has the dubious honor of having a number of other exotic members of the parrot group reported in the wild, including rose-ringed parakeet, budgie, the orange-fronted parakeet *(Aratinga canicularis)*, the brown-throated parakeet *(Aratinga pertinax)*, and the orange-chinned parakeet, *Brotogeris jugularis*, (Owre, 1973). Some of these will not be pests of citrus and the role of others as pests of cultivated crops remains to be seen.

Monk Parakeets.—One parrot species which is of the most immediate concern in California is the monk parakeet *(Myiopsitta monachus)*, a gregarious bird originally ranging from central Bolivia and southern Brazil south to central Argentina, but now introduced and established in Puerto Rico and the United States.

Although not numerous, monk parakeets have been reported from scattered and isolated areas encompassing a wide geographic region of the continental United States (e.g., New Jersey, New York, Ohio, California, and Florida) (Davis, 1974). Its adaptability to a variety of climatic conditions and habitats in the United States has been adequately documented; hence, we can conclude that it can survive very well in this country. Present populations are believed to have resulted from pet birds being turned loose, escapes from aviaries, or inadvertent releases through handling mishaps at airports or shipping docks.

Small flocks of feral monk parakeets have been sighted in San Diego and Orange Counties in southern California. From one to three monk parakeets also have been sighted in the wild in Fresno, San Bernardino, San Joaquin, Santa Barbara, Sonoma, and Ventura Counties in California. The parakeets have constructed nests in Orange County and presumably have bred successfully (Davis, 1974). Monk parakeets have been breeding in the Miami, Florida area since at least 1969 (Owre, 1973), about 3 years prior to the first sighting in California.

The monk parakeet has been described as a colorful bird, about 11½ inches from head to tail. The dorsal feathers are a greenish-grey color with yellower under parts; wings are green with blue secondaries and flight feathers; forehead, face, throat and breast are grey; tail is bluish-green, long, and pointed. Sexes are alike in coloration, but the female tends to be somewhat more robust with a longer and stronger beak (Davis, 1974).

Where numerous, the monk parakeet constructs large communal nests with separate compartments which are quite conspicuous and unlike those of any of our native species.

In its native area, the monk parakeet is a highly gregarious bird and associates in flocks of from ten to more than a hundred. In addition to damaging citrus, flocks also damage ripening cereal crops (Bull, 1973). Crop losses in its native area range from 2 to 15 per cent, with some as high as 45 per cent annually (Davis, 1974). Bump (1971) describes the monk parakeet as one of the worst pests of agriculture in Argentina.

Davis (1974) mentions that oranges are among the preferred fruits of the monk parakeet in California and that if it becomes well established throughout the state's citrus-growing areas, it could cause an estimated loss to the citrus industry amounting to $291,143 annually. The losses are calculated on the basis of 0.1 per cent loss of the total value of the citrus crop compiled by crop statistics for 1974–75 and published by the California Crop and Livestock Reporting Service.

Various methods directed toward control of this species are discussed by Dana *et al.* (1974). Since relatively few birds exist in California, eradication of the monk parakeet is being attempted by shooting. Presently, the importation, transportation, and possession of the monk parakeet is prohibited by law in California.

Destruction of communal nests in some areas of their native range is accomplished by setting them afire with petrol-soaked rags attached to long poles. This approach is largely unsuccessful because it is not based on a sound knowledge of the biology of the species (Forshaw, 1973). Truly effective and environmentally acceptable controls for protecting citrus from this species in their native countries do not presently exist.

Red-Whiskered Bulbuls

The red-whiskered bulbul *(Pycnonotus jocosus)* is an introduced bird belonging to the order Passeriformes and the family Pycnonotidae. It is native to India, China, Burma, Malaysia, Java, Sumatra, Cambodia, and North and South Vietnam (Roberson, 1972).

This species is a popular cage bird, which has resulted in deliberately released or escaped birds being observed or becoming established in the wild in Melbourne and Sydney, Australia, in Miami, Florida, and Los Angeles and San Diego, California (Roberson, 1972). As of January, 1972, forty-seven feral specimens had been taken in southern California by the Los Angeles County Department of Agriculture (Hardy, 1973).

This species is about 7- to 8-inches long, dull brown above, white below, with a crested black head and an oval white cheek patch narrowly rimmed with black. A black patch, like the start of a collar, marks either side of the chest. A small scarlet fan of whiskers springs from the lower posterior corner of the brown eye. The whiskers can be raised and lowered like the crest (Anon., 1971).

The population growth and habits of the red-whiskered bulbul in Florida have been well documented by Carleton and Owre (1975). Although this species eats some insects, its main diet consists of fleshy, soft, sweet tropical fruits. Citrus fruits are known to be hollowed out by bulbuls in Florida, but Carleton and Owre (1975) have suggested that such behavior by bulbuls may be only an enlarging of a previous puncture in the rind. Possibly woodpeckers or some other species cause the initial damage and bulbuls are involved only secondarily. This is supported by the fact that caged bulbuls ignore intact oranges left in their cages for 24 hours with no other food available, although slices of oranges are readily accepted by captive birds (Carleton and Owre, 1975).

Whether the red-whiskered bulbul will be a serious threat to the citrus industry in this country is questionable, but there is enough evidence that it will damage other types of cultivated fruits and berries sufficiently to warrant its eradication whenever and wherever feasible.

Recorded calls of the red-whiskered bulbul have been played over loudspeakers to lure the feral birds within shooting range in southern California. Thanks to the persistent efforts of the California Department of Food and Agriculture and the diligent work of the local county agricultural commissioners, this species may be eliminated from the state. The bulbul, like the monk parakeet, is prohibited by law and cannot be legally imported or possessed as a pet in California.

Woodpeckers

In an early bulletin of the United States Department of Agriculture on the food of the woodpeckers of the United States (Beal, 1911), there were several extensive accounts of the damage to oranges in Florida by the red-bellied woodpecker *(Centurus carolinus)* which occurred in the late nineteenth century. This woodpecker was then apparently abundant and was locally called by such names as the "orange sapsucker" and "orange borer," for it not only ate the pulp of the mature fruit, but damaged the trees by boring holes in them. Weed and Dearborn (1916) make only brief mention of woodpeckers damaging oranges. Recent accounts of such damage in Florida have been mentioned (Carleton and Owre, 1975). Occasional incidents often may go undetected or unreported.

Woodpeckers belong to the order Piciformes and are not considered a pest of any consequence to citrus. If corrective measures were needed over a rather large area, frightening devices would be one recommendation. Occasionally sapsuckers have been reported making rows of holes circling the trunks or limbs of citrus in

Fresno County, California. Growers resorted to treating the damaged areas with silver paint with an asphalt base and this has successfully repelled the birds in most instances. In other kinds of tree crops, the sticky paste types of non-toxic bird repellents are painted or applied to limbs where woodpeckers or sapsuckers are making holes. This may discourage the birds completely or drive them to other trees or to untreated limbs.

Crows

Crows *(Corvus brachyrynchos)*, which belong to the family Corvidae, were reported to have stripped the bark from a number of very young citrus trees a number of years ago on at least one occasion in Orange County, California. More recently, in August 1972, instances of crow damage in a young orange grove near the city of Gavilan, in Riverside County, California was brought to our attention. Crows were pecking small holes in the bark and stripping bark from the tree trunks. In both of these instances the damage occurred after the cardboard trunk guards had been removed. In another locality, crows have been involved in tearing the trunk wraps from young trees. The reason for this particular behavior is not clear, but the bark damage was similar to that reported elsewhere in young apple orchards that was attributed to ravens *(Corvus corax)*. Crow damage can be halted by using almost any type of wire protective trunk guard, but the damage must be detected early before it becomes extensive. In one instance, methiocarb (Mesurol®) [4–(methylthio)–3, 5–xylyl N–methylcarbamate], a broad-spectrum avian repellent, was experimentally applied to tree trunks and reported to be effective. Methiocarb is not registered for this use, however, and thus cannot be recommended. Temporary relief may be achieved with the use of carbide exploders, assuming the orchards are some distance from populated areas where objections to the noise would not prohibit their use.

The extent of the damage does not justify reductional control; however, if this is a lasting, learned behavior in crows, greater damage may be experienced in the future.

Miscellaneous Birds

In California, some bird species have been reported to present problems because of their droppings. Blackbirds of the genera *Euphagus* and *Agelaius*, doves *(Zenardura macroura)*, quail *(Lophortyx californica)* and, to a lesser extent, the introduced starling *(Sturnus vulgaris)* and other native species are sometimes involved. Quail seem to be the most serious offender in Tulare County, California.

Bird droppings contaminating fruit are of concern because fouled fruit requires cleaning or is more frequently culled out and not packed for market at all. It is fortunate that contamination by droppings is generally confined to an occasional fruit, and is not considered severe except in isolated or localized situations. Bird species which are gregarious or have communal roosts in citrus groves obviously have greater potential for contamination than the nongregarious species. Birds nesting in citrus may also be responsible for contamination of the fruit beneath or near the nest.

Disbudding by birds and bird-pecked fruit are both relatively rare in California; however, this may change in the future because of introduced potential pest birds.

Sound frightening or scaring devices, such as automatic exploders, discussed under "Bird Control Methodology" (below) may be the best method for discouraging birds from utilizing citrus groves as roosts, although this may be impractical in all but the most severe situations. In order to be effective, frightening devices must be employed as soon as there is the slightest indication that birds may be starting to use a grove as a roosting site and before a communal roost is well established. Once the birds become established at a particular roost site it may be difficult, if not impossible, to break this habit. Birds having seasonal communal roosts will frequently return to the same site year after year.

In the past, there has been no need (at least in California) for any of our native bird species to be reduced in numbers through shooting, trapping, or poisoning programs in order to protect citrus.

BIRD CONTROL METHODOLOGY

Scaring of birds from crops as a method of preventing depredation is almost as old as agriculture itself. Hand clapping, striking two sticks or other items together, and throwing various objects were used many years ago, and in some localities are still employed. The list of scaring or frightening devices has grown to include the following devices: man-like scarecrows; hawks and owls (both live and artificial mockups); shiny or colorful, wind-moved, twirling or reflecting objects; patrols with rifles, shotguns, or firecrackers; roman candles, flares, and other pyrotechnics. Flashing and revolving lights, projectile bombs, and delayed double-action shotgun shells are improvements over earlier methods. Carbide exploders, air horns and, more recently, amplified distress or alarm calls of birds, and finally even low-flying aircraft have been used to frighten birds from crops (Williams and Neff, 1966).

The ingenuity used in devising frightening methods for birds has challenged the imagination of many agriculturists throughout the world, as is evidenced by the development of hundreds of variations on the above methods. Biologists today still rely on this basic fright concept but, because of technological advances and a better understanding of biological principles, the equipment being used is much more sophisticated.

Although frightening methods are relied upon to a major extent for bird control, they have some shortcomings. Like chemical repellents involving taste, odor, or touch, frightening methods tend to discourage feeding or roosting at one site, but may drive the birds to an adjacent orchard where damage will continue. In some instances, the birds may be dispersed over a great enough area so that damage may go unnoticed or economic losses will be shared by enough growers so that no one grower is seriously affected.

Automatic carbide exploders have been used for a number of years to frighten birds from various crops. In the United States, they are probably currently being used more than any other frightening device. These devices have a chamber into which an explosive gas such as acetylene is released, and then automatically ignited by a spark, resulting in a loud explosive "bang." The loud report is made directional by a megaphone type horn placed over the explosion chamber outlet. Most of these devices can be adjusted to go off at various time intervals.

The most recent and successful application of sound for bird control is the use of animal communication signals. Essentially this involves the recording of specific types of acoustical signals produced by the pest species, which will stimulate desirable and predictable behavior when heard by that species. For example, distress calls have been put to practical use for frightening starlings and other birds, and feeding calls have been used to attract crows to a hunter. Modern technology permits making highly accurate recordings of these acoustical communication signals that can be played back at the appropriate time and place so as to be of practical value in altering bird behavior.

Loud noises or sounds are disturbing to man and some domestic animals. On the other hand, these reproduced communication signals —because they represent meaningful language to birds at relatively low intensities—can be much more practical (Frings, 1965). Distress calls and other useful bio-acoustical signals are often quite specific in action, affecting a single bird species without disturbing another.

Apparently, shooting and poisoning are used often in some parts of the world to temporarily relieve local damage by parrots (Forshaw, 1973). It has been suggested that alternate food be provided to entice parrots away from crops (Forshaw, 1973), but it is doubtful that this is a practical answer to problems occurring in commercial citrus groves.

The red-whiskered bulbul and, more recently, the monk parakeet, both of which have been observed in the wild in southern California, have brought about efforts by the California Department of Food and Agriculture and the applicable county departments of agriculture to ascertain the distribution of these species within the state. The present policy, which is a wise one, is to eradicate them whenever located. Shooting has been the method employed to date. Hopefully, this approach will prevent them from becoming permanently established in California, or at least forestall their becoming established, as inevitable as that may be.

If the extermination of introduced pest birds is feasible, it may be justified to protect citrus and other susceptible crops. It is unfortunate that positive remedial actions were not taken against the monk parakeet in the eastern states before it became well established.

Bird problems in agricultural crops are almost always difficult to resolve satisfactorily with present methodology, but there is some hope of new developments in repellents that can be applied directly to fruit to prevent depredation. Chemosterilants and chemicals which produce a fright response have been effective on some pest birds, but have not been used in protecting citrus.

As stated previously, we are fortunate in the United States that birds currently are a very minor threat to the citrus industry.

SAFETY PRECAUTIONS

Certain general safety precautions should be adhered to besides those which appear on labels of chemical products for vertebrate pest control.

1. Lethal agents such as rodenticides and avicides should be considered dangerous enough to cause death.

2. Toxic baits should be placed where the target species has good access to them, but where they provide minimal exposure to nontarget wildlife.

3. Only responsible individuals should be permitted to handle technical or concentrated rodenticides or avicides. Those who formulate mammalian or avian baits for their own use should exercise extreme care in handling the toxic concentrates. When necessary or applicable, these people should wear rubber gloves, aprons, and/or proper respiration equipment.

4. When personnel work near bait-mixing machines or simply handle baits, they should not smoke, eat, drink, or place their hands near their mouths. Exhaust fans or wind currents should be designed to draw toxic dust particles away from workers.

5. After preparing or handling baits, personnel should wash hands and face completely, using soap, a good brush, and plenty of water.

6. All bait-mixing utensils should be cleaned thoroughly, and should be used solely for bait preparation.

7. We recommend using prepared or ready-to-use baits wherever possible. Commercial formulators are governed by various regulations which generally require that their operations be relatively safe for employees.

8. Where feasible after a poisoning program, dead carcasses should be picked up immediately. Rodent and rabbit carcasses should be handled with rubber gloves or tongs, and should either be burned (unless prohibited by law) or buried deep enough so they will not be dug up by cats, dogs, or other carnivores. This will help avoid contracting certain diseases.

9. All bait containers, bait stations, unused baits, and rodenticide and avicide concentrates should be labeled with appropriate warnings. This means that bait must be stored away from children, preferably in locked and labeled cabinets. Access to all materials should be restricted to authorized, responsible individuals.

10. Employers and/or supervisors of vertebrate control programs must be certain that employees/subordinates are fully informed of the hazards involved and of necessary safety precautions. All instructions for use provided by manufacturers should be carefully read and followed. Great care must be exercised to avoid accidents which might either poison or harm people, pets, livestock, or other nontarget species. One of the most important safety undertakings is the attempt to anticipate and take precautions against all situations or conditions that make accidents likely. Toxic materials should never be employed where significant hazards are likely.

ACKNOWLEDGMENTS

This chapter is for the most part original, but some information was derived from Chapter XVI by T. Storer in Volume II of the 1948 edition of *The Citrus Industry*.

The authors are indebted to many California Agricultural Extension Service Farm Advisors, with special thanks to Karl Opitz, Donald Rosedale, Robert Platt, John Pehrson, and Marvin Miller, who provided us with useful information.

The completeness of coverage would not have been possible without assistance and comments from members of the California Department of Food and Agriculture and from the various county departments of agriculture, with special reference to Ralph Bare, Dell Clark, Richard Dana, Charles Siebe, Michael Keffer, Jon Shelgren, William Clark, Si Dudley, and Conrad Schilling.

Fred Lawrence, Morris Baily, Jr., and W. T. Mendenhall were kind enough to provide information on vertebrate pests from other citrus-growing regions in the country, which is most appreciated.

We are also grateful to our colleague Dr. Walter E. Howard for his technical and editorial comments.

LITERATURE CITED

ANONYMOUS. 1958. Gopher control. Western Citrus Grower **4**(1):C12–C13.

ANONYMOUS. 1971. Plant pest detection manual. Calif. Dept. Agr. Looseleaf volume.

BEAL, F. E. L. 1911. Food of the woodpeckers of the United States. U.S. Dept. Agr., Biol. Survey, Bul. **37**:64 pp.

BECKER, E. M. 1940. An effective ground squirrel trap. Calif. Dept. Agr. Bul. **29**(3):152.

BECKWITH, S. L., and L. G. STITH. 1968. Deer damage to citrus groves in south Florida. Proc. 21st Ann. Conf. SE Assoc. Game and Fish Comms. **1968**:32–38.

BULL, J. 1973. Exotic birds in the New York City area. The Wilson Bul. **85**(4):501–505.

BULL, J., and E. R. RICCIUTI. 1974. Polly want an apple? Audubon **76**(3):48–54.

BUMP, G. 1971. The South American monk, quaker, or grey-headed parakeet. Wildlife Leaflet *496*. U. S. Dept. Interior, Fish and Wildlife Service, Bureau of Sport, Fisheries and Wildlife. 4 pp.

BURKE, J. H. 1967. The commercial citrus regions of the world. *In:* Reuther, W., H. J. Webber and L. D. Batchelor (eds.). The citrus industry **1**:40–189. Univ. Calif. Press, Berkeley and Los Angeles.

CARLETON, A. R., and O. T. OWRE. 1975. The red-whiskered bulbul in Florida: 1960–71. The Auk **92**(1):40–57.

CHERRETT, J. M., J. B. FORD, I. V. HERBERT, and A. J. PROBERT. 1971. The control of injurious animals. St. Martin's Press. New York. 210 pp.

CLARK, D. O. 1972. The extending of cotton rat in California—their life history and control. Proc. Fifth Vertebrate Pest Contr. Conf. [Fresno, Calif.] **1972**:7–14.

CUMMINGS, M. W. 1962*a*. Pocket gopher control. Calif. Citrog. **47**(7):250–252, 254.

———. 1962*b*. Control of pocket gophers. Proc. First Vertebrate Pest Contr. Conf. [Sacramento, Calif.] **1962**:113–125.

COURTENAY, W. R., and C. R. ROBINS. 1975. Exotic organisms: an unsolved, complex problem. BioScience **25**:306–313.

DANA, R. H. 1962. Ground squirrel control in California. Calif. Dept. Agr. Bul. **51**(3):141–146.

DANA, R., R. THOMPSON, A. BISCHOFF, D. CLARK, L. DAVIS, and M. KEFFER. 1974. Monk parakeet pest evaluation report. Calif. Dept. Food Agr. 23 pp.

DAVIS, L. R. 1974. The monk parakeet: a potential threat to agriculture. Proc. Sixth Vertebrate Pest Contr. Conf. [Anaheim, Calif.] **1974**:253–257.

FITCH, H. S., P. GOODRUM, and C. NEWMAN. 1952. The armadillo in the southeastern United States. Jour. Mammalogy **33**(1):21–37.

FORSHAW, J. M. 1973. Parrots of the world. Doubleday and Company, Inc. Garden City, New York. 584 pp.

FRINGS, H. 1965. Sound in vertebrate pest control. *In:* Proc. Second Vertebrate Pest Contr. Conf. [Anaheim, Calif.] March 4 & 5, **1964**:50–56.

GLASS, B. P. 1974. The potential value of genetically sterile Norway rats in regulating wild populations. Proc. Sixth Vertebrate Pest Contr. Conf. [Anaheim, Calif.] **1974**:49–54.

GREENHALL, A. M. 1966. Oranges eaten by spear-nosed bats. Jour. Mammalogy **47**(1):125.

GRINNEL, J., and J. DIXON. 1918. Natural history of the ground squirrels of California. Calif. State Comm. Hort. Month. Bul. **7**:597–708.

HARDY, J. W. 1973. Feral exotic birds in southern California. Wilson Bul. **85**(4):506–512.

HENDERSON, J., and E. L. CRAIG. 1932. Economic mammalogy. Charles C. Thomas. Springfield, Illinois. 397 pp.

HODGSON, R. W. 1923. Saving the gophered citrus tree. Univ. Calif. Agr. Expt. Sta. Circ. **273**:19 pp.

HOWARD, W. E. 1967. Biocontrol and chemosterilants. *In:* Kilgore, W. W. and R. L. Doutt (eds.). Pest control: biological, physical and selected chemical methods. Pp. 343–386. Academic Press, New York, N.Y.

———. 1974. The biology of predator control. Addison-Wesley Module in Biology, No. 11. Addison-Wesley Publ. Co. Reading, Mass. 48 pp.

HOWARD, W. E., and R. E. MARSH. 1976. The rat: its biology and control. Univ. Calif. Agr. Ext. Serv. Leaflet **2896**:1-22.

JOHNSON, W. V. 1964. Rabbit control. Proc. Second Vertebrate Pest Contr. Conf. [Anaheim, Calif.] **1964**:90–96.

JOHNSTON, J. C. 1953. Citrus soil management. Univ. Calif. Agr. Expt. Sta. Leaflet **19**:8 pp.

JOHNSTON, J. C., and P. W. MOORE. 1953. Pruning citrus trees. Univ. Calif. Agr. Expt. Sta. Leaflet **18**:8 pp.

JONES, J. K., JR., D. C. CARTER, and H. H. GENOWAYS. 1973. Checklist of North American mammals north of Mexico. Occas. Papers Mus. Texas Tech. Univ. No. **12**:1–14.

KALMBACH, E. R. 1943. The armadillo: its relation to agriculture and game. Texas Game, Fish and Oyster Comm. and U. S. Fish and Wildlife Serv. 61 pp.

KEPNER, R. A., W. E. HOWARD, M. W. CUMMINGS, and E. M. BROCK. 1962. U. C. mechanical gopher-bait applicator construction and use. Univ. Calif. Agr. Ext. Serv. Pub. **AXT–32** (rev.):12 pp.

LIBBY, J. L., and J. ABRAMS. 1966. Anticoagulant rodenticide in paper tubes for control of meadow mice. Jour. Wildlife Manage. **30**:512–518.

LONGHURST, W. M., M. B. JONES, R. R. PARKS, L. W. NEUBAUER, and M. W. CUMMINGS. 1962. Fences for controlling deer damage. Univ. Calif. Agr. Expt. Sta. Circ. **514**:19 pp.

LUDEMAN, J. A. 1962. Control of meadow mice, kangaroo rats, prairie dogs, and cotton rats. Proc. First Vertebrate Pest Contr. Conf. [Sacramento, Calif.] **1962**:144–163.

MARSH, R. E. 1962. Wood rats. Calif. Dept. Agr. Bul. **51**(3):147–148.

MARSH, R. E., R. E. COLE, and W. E. HOWARD. 1967. Laboratory tests on the effectiveness of prolin mouse tubes. Jour. Wildlife Manage. **31**:342–344.

MARSH, R. E., and M. W. CUMMINGS. 1976. Pocket gopher control with mechanical bait applicator. Univ. Calif. Agr. Ext. Serv. Leaflet **2699**:1-7.

MARSH, R. E., and W. E. HOWARD. 1973. Prospects of chemosterilant and genetic control of rodents. Bul. Wld. Health Organ. **48**:309–316.

———. 1977. The house mouse: its biology and control. Univ. Calif. Agr. Ext. Serv. Leaflet **2945**:1-28.

MARSH, R. E., and L. F. PLESSE. 1960. Semipermanent anticoagulant baits. Calif. Dept. Agr. Bul. **49**:195–197.

MARSHALL, I. D., and F. FENNER. 1960. Studies in the epidemiology of infectious myxomatosis of rabbits. Jour. Hygiene Camb. **58**:485–488.

MILLER, J. E. 1970. Armadillo control Agr. Ext. Serv. Leaflet **466**:7 pp.

MOORE, P. W. 1955. Underground problems brought to surface. Calif. Citrog. **40**:251–252.

MOORE, P., S. SKOU, and E. NAUER. 1956. The gopher menace. Calif. Citrog. **41**:273–275.

NEILL, WILFRED T. 1952. The spread of the armadillo in

Florida. Ecology **33**:282–284.

OWRE, O. T. 1973. A consideration of the exotic avifauna of southeastern Florida. Wilson Bul. **85**:491–500.

PEARDON, D. L. 1974. A new series of selective rodenticides. Proc. Sixth Vertebrate Pest Conf. [Anaheim, Calif.] **1974**:58–62.

PLATT, R. G. 1973. Planning and planting the citrus orchard. *In:* Reuther, W. (ed.). The citrus industry **3**:48–79. Univ. Calif. Press, Berkeley and Los Angeles.

POONAI, N. O. 1969. Nature conservation in tropical South America, Part III. Bird and man in the tropics. Fla. Nat. **42**:128–130, 142.

ROBERSON, R. C. 1972. Potential bird pests of California fruit and grain crops. Nat. Pest Control Operators News. **32**(5):14–15.

ROSEDALE, D. O., and M. W. CUMMINGS. 1962. Mechanical bait applicator controls gophers in citrus. Calif. Agr. **16**(9):14.

ROSTRON, A. 1969. Rosella parrots: New Zealand's most beautiful pest. N.Z. Agri. Jour. p. 40.

RUSSEL, S. M. 1964. A distributional study of the birds of British Honduras. Am. Arn. Un. Arn. Monogr. No. **1**:1–95.

SHIELDS, W. M., T. C. GRUBB, JR., and A. TELIS. 1974. Use of native plants by monk parakeets in New York. Wilson Bul. **86**:172–173.

SICK, H. 1968. Vogelwanderungen im kontinentalen Südamerika. Vogelwart **24**:217–243.

STANLEY, A. J., and L. G. GUMBRECK. 1964. New genetic factors that affect fertility in the male rat. **In:** Proc. Fifth Intern. Cong. Animal Reprod. Artificial Insemination. [Trento, Italy] 6–13 Sept. **1964**:3 pp.

STORER, T. I. 1948. Injury by rodents and its control. *In:* Batchelor, L. D. and H. J. Webber (eds.). The citrus industry **2**:331–346. Univ. Calif. Press, Berkeley and Los Angeles.

STORER, T. I. 1958. Controlling field rodents in California. Univ. Calif. Agr. Expt. Sta. Circ. (rev.) **434**:50 pp.

WALKINSHAW, L. H., and B. W. BAKER. 1946. Notes on the birds of the Isle of Pines, Cuba. Wilson Bul. **58**:133–142.

WEED, C. M., and N. DEARBORN. 1916. Birds in their relations to man. J. B. Lippincott Company, Philadelphia. 390 pp.

WEINBURGH, H. B. 1964. Field rodents, rabbits, and hares: public health importance, biology, survey, and control. U. S. Dept. Health, Education & Welfare, Publ. Health Serv., CDC. 87 pp. (Mimeo.).

WETHERBEE, F. A. 1967. A method of controlling jack rabbits on a range rehabilitation project in California. Proc. Third Vertebrate Pest Conf. [San Francisco, Calif.] **1967**:111–117.

WETMORE, A. 1926. Observations on the birds of Argentina, Paraguay, Uruguay, and Chile. Bul. U. S. Nat. Mus. No. **133**:448 pp.

WILLIAMS, C. S., and J. A. NEFF. 1966. Scaring makes a difference. *In:* Stefferud, A. (ed.). Birds in our lives. U.S. Govt. Printing Office, Washington. 561 pp.

WODZICKI, K. 1973. Prospects for biological control of rodent populations. Bul. Wld. Hlth. Organ. **48**:461–467.

WORTH, C. B. 1950. Field and laboratory observations on roof rats, *Rattus rattus* (Linnaeus), in Florida. Jour. Mammalogy **31**(3):293–304.

IN MEMORIAM
CURTIS PAUL CLAUSEN
1893-1976

Curtis Paul Clausen was born in Randall, Iowa, on March 28, 1893. His long and highly productive life encompassed the diverse professions of scientist, explorer, author, sports enthusiast, and *bon vivant*. Curtis grew to manhood in a typically American environment. In 1901, his parents—Danish immigrants—established themselves and their five children on a farm in Oklahoma. In 1910, the family moved to Ontario, California.

In 1914, Curtis graduated from the University of California, Berkeley, with a B.S. degree and honors in Entomology. In 1920, he received the M.S. degree from U.C. Berkeley in the same subject. After a brief assistantship in Entomology under H. J. Quayle at the U.C. Citrus Experiment Station (1914–1915), he accepted a position at the State Insectary in Sacramento as assistant to the superintendent, H. S. Smith. From 1916 to 1918, Clausen explored Japan, China, and the Philippines for natural enemies of citrus scale insect pests, and sent them live to the State Insectary for propagation and ultimate field evaluation.

After service in the U.S. Army Coast Artillery, he joined the U.S. Department of Agriculture in 1920 as Specialist in the Bureau of Entomology. He spent 13 years studying pest insects and their predators and parasites in the Far East. Later, he explored extensively in Mexico, Central and South America, and Europe, investigating the strange behavior of newly discovered insect species, such as the natural enemies of the Japanese beetle and the citrus blackfly.

His full devotion to the pursuit of knowledge in this fascinating field was interrupted incidentally by such pastimes as angling, golf, and billiards, all accompanied by an extraordinary passion for tobacco, pipe, and cigar. Although not a gregarious person, his quiet conversations and references to his many humorous and interesting experiences made him an extremely pleasant companion.

By 1931, when he was stationed in Washington, D.C., Clausen had worked up a card catalogue of about 6,000 references to the life histories and behavior patterns of insect predators and parasites. This was the beginning of his monumental book, *Entomophagous Insects* (1940), which was reprinted by the Hafner Publishing Company in 1972. Subsequent explorers for insects to control agricultural pests have found this book an invaluable source.

He authored the following widely acclaimed publications: "Biological Control of Insect Pests," in *New Crops for the World* (Macmillan, 1954); "Parasites and Predators," in the *1952 USDA Yearbook;* and *USDA Technical Bulletin No. 1139, Biological Control of Insect Pests in the Continental United States* (1956). After retirement from the University of California, he edited *Agricultural Handbook No. 480*, published in 1976 by the Agricultural Research Service of the USDA. Its title was *Introduced Parasites and Predators of Arthropod Pests and Weeds: A World Review*. In addition to these publications, Clausen reported his research findings in over 60 papers during his lifetime. His last paper, "Phoresy Among Entomophagous Insects," appeared in the *Annual Review of Entomology* on the day of his death; he died February 28, 1976, in Oklahoma City.

From 1934 to 1951, Clausen was in charge of the Division of Foreign Parasite Introductions and also of the Division of Control Investigations from 1942 to 1951. In the U.S. Department of Agriculture and, later, at the University of California, he was administratively responsible for research in the developing fields of insect pathology, i.e., use of bacteria, fungi, and viruses in insect and mite control, and in the use of insects for weed control. He retired from the USDA in 1951; however, after a few months of fishing and golfing in Florida, he was persuaded to accept appointment as Professor of Biological Control and Chairman of the Statewide Department of Biological Control at the University of California. In 1959, he was given Emeritus status, and in 1966 the University awarded the honorary LLD degree in recognition of his outstanding accomplishments in Entomology, particularly in the field of Biological Control.

Clausen was a Fellow of the American Association for the Advancement of Science, a member of Alpha Zeta, Sigma XI, the Washington Academy of Sciences, the Washington Entomological Society, and the Hawaiian Entomological Society. He was a corresponding member of Sociedad Arthropologia Argentina and Sociedad Agricola Colombia, a Fellow of the Entomological Society of America, Vice-President (1949) and President (1950) of the American Association of Economic Entomologists, and an Honorary Member (elected in 1960) of the Entomological Society of Japan, an honor which he was the first foreigner to receive.

The many friends, colleagues, and acquaintances of Curtis Paul Clausen in this country and abroad regarded him as a truly fine gentleman and scholar. Declining health, especially during his last year, interfered greatly with his writing and permitted contact with only a few of his friends. His very distinguished career in Biological Control added immeasurably to the stature of Entomology throughout the world, and continues to stimulate students to specialize in that increasingly important discipline.

Professor Clausen died February 28, 1976 following a prolonged and incapacitating illness. This chapter, revised by the author in 1967, is being published without the benefit of an updating revision. It represents a memorial contribution from a pioneering and truly distinguished and knowledgeable expert whose entire professional career was concerned with the biological control of insects and mites on citrus crops. While reviewers have noted the significant changes of direction and emphasis in biological control endeavors that have been gaining definition and support during the intervening decade, they have also acknowledged the wholly substantive and useful content of the revised chapter as a basic documentation of the essential background of information relevant to the biological control of citrus pests throughout the world. For this reason the editors have deemed it desirable and useful to publish the revised chapter as originally submitted by Professor Clausen.

It should be noted here that two chemical formulations discussed by Professor Clausen are either no longer available (Schradan) or banned for use (DDT) in the United States.

—Ed.

CHAPTER 6

Biological Control of Citrus Insects

C. P. CLAUSEN

BIOLOGICAL CONTROL OF INSECT pests has been properly defined by H. S. Smith (1948) as *the suppression of a pest by means of the introduction, propagation, and dissemination of the predators, the parasites, and the diseases by which it is attacked.* Practically all insects are, in nature, subject to some degree of control by various enemies, and their influence, when not promoted by man, is designated as *natural control* to differentiate it from biological control. The great majority of native plant-feeding insects is under effective control at a non-economic level, and consequently presents no need for biological control efforts.

In nature, every insect, or for that matter every living organism, is subjected to a variety of influences that tend to limit or restrain its increase. These include climatic conditions, food supply, host resistance, parasitic and predaceous enemies and disease organisms, and cultural practices, to mention only a few. Collectively, these make up what is generally termed *environmental resistance.* When these restraining influences are inadequate the insect is able to increase to the point at which it brings about economic injury to the plant host. The introduction of new natural enemies into the environment adds to the sum total of this resistance and economic control may thereby be achieved.

In most instances, it may be assumed that attack by one or more natural enemies upon a pest species has some value in reducing the intensity of the infestations, but this is not always the case. If the pest population is the maximum that the plant host can support, elimination of a considerable portion of the population by parasitization or predation may merely replace other mortality factors such as starvation and overcrowding, and the infestation therefore may remain at the maximum.

Most biological control projects are undertaken only after the pest species has attained its maximum population and is at equilibrium, though at an injurious level, over at least a portion of its geographic range. This being so, the relative capacity for increase of the pest and its natural enemies loses its significance. Many natural enemies employed effectively in biological control have a lower reproductive potential than their hosts, while others have a much higher potential. The latter may be the result of a higher reproductive capacity, as measured by the number of eggs laid, or of the production of several generations to each one of the host. It has often been asserted that this factor has a direct bearing on the time required to achieve economic control, a subject that is discussed in a later section of this chapter (p. 315).

BIOTIC CONTROL AGENTS

The biotic, or living, organisms utilized in the biological control of insect pests comprise a wide range of parasitic and predaceous insects, as well as the disease-producing organisms, represented by the fungi, bacteria, viruses, protozoa, and nematodes.

The parasitic insects are those in which development of the individual from egg to maturity is at the expense of a single host individual. The parasites may be solitary in habit, a single one developing in and destroying a host individual, or, at the other extreme, several thousand may reach maturity in a single host. The latter is known to occur among several hymenopterous parasites of lepidopterous caterpillars. The parasite may develop internally in the body of the host, as is the case with most of those attacking scale insects, mealybugs, and whiteflies, or externally, in which case the developing larva sucks the blood of the host and may finally consume the entire body contents. The species having the latter habit usually attack hosts living in sheltered places, such as leaf mines and burrows in twigs.

The parasitic species that attack the pest insect directly and cause its death are known as primary parasites, but unfortunately there are many others, designated as hyperparasites, that subsist not upon the pest insect but upon the immature stages of the primary parasites, and are therefore harmful. The wasps (Hymenoptera) comprise the great bulk of parasitic species utilized in the biological control of citrus pests.

The predaceous insects are usually highly mobile in both the adult and larval stages and differ in habit from the parasites in that several, and in many instances a large number of host insects, are consumed by each individual in the course of its development. The adults of the predaceous species often feed upon the same insect stages as provide food for their larvae, thus enhancing the value of such species. The most common and best known of the predaceous insects are the coccinellid beetles or ladybugs, that are seen everywhere feeding on aphids, scale insects, mealybugs, etc., and the lacewings, hover flies, and others. In general, the predators feed upon a wider range of insects than do the parasites, yet there are conspicuous exceptions, as a number of them are highly specialized for attack upon a specific host.

Vertebrate predators, such as birds and certain rodents, are often highly important factors in the natural control of insect pests, especially the Lepidoptera and Coleoptera, but few of them have been intentionally transported from one country to another for pest control. A conspicuous exception is the giant toad *Bufo marinus* (L.) of the West Indies, first transported from Barbados to Jamaica in 1884, which has been generally distributed over the tropics, though for control of pests other than those attacking citrus.

The disease-producing microorganisms are often highly effective in reducing pest insect outbreaks but have not been utilized in biological control to the same extent as have the parasitic and predaceous insects. Many of them are highly dependent on favorable climatic conditions, being effective mainly during periods of high humidity and rainfall.

THE HISTORICAL BACKGROUND OF BIOLOGICAL CONTROL

Knowledge of the parasitic habits of some insects dates back to at least the fifteenth century and the actual utilization of predaceous insects for pest control is far from being a modern development. It is recorded that, about 200 years ago, the Arabs of Yemen in the Middle East brought colonies of predaceous ants from the mountains and placed them in the date palm trees for control of another ant species that was destructive to these trees. In South China, the use of predaceous ants for pest control may even antedate the practice in Yemen. It is recorded by Groff and Howard (1924) that the citrus growers of South China purchase and place colonies of the red tree ant *Oecophylla smaragdina* F. in their trees, and even provide them with bamboo runways from tree to tree, for protection from insect pests. This ant binds a cluster of leaves together to form its compact nest in the trees, and the adults are very aggressive in driving off other insects. The chief value of the ant is said to be against the stink bugs and boring beetles, and in the destruction of caterpillars. The real economic value of the above practice has not been determined experimentally. On the debit side, the ants unquestionably foster scale insects, mealybugs, etc. Regardless of any value these large and ferocious ants may have, their presence in a modern citrus orchard would not be tolerated.

While several earlier efforts have been made in the introduction of natural enemies of insects from one country to another, the real beginning of sustained work in the biological control of these pests dates back only to 1888, when the United States Department of Agriculture undertook the importation from Australia of natural enemies for control of the cottony-cushion scale, a highly destructive pest of citrus in California. Concurrently with this work, and in the years immediately thereafter, was the importation of a large number of predators, mainly coccinellid beetles, for control of other citrus pests, such as the black scale, California red scale, and others. The spectacular success attained in control of the cottony-cushion scale led to continuation of efforts for similar control of a wide range of other pests of citrus, and the work in California has progressed at an accelerated pace to the present time. While the early work in 1888–89 was by the U.S. Department of Agriculture, that of the following years, during 1981–92, was on a cooperative basis between that organization and the California State Board of Horticulture. Thereafter, the program was conducted independently by the State Board and its successor organizations until 1923, when all state activities in this field were transferred to the Agricultural Experiment Station of the University of California, currently with staff and facilities at Riverside (fig. 6–1) and Albany, California.

For many years, the California work was devoted almost exclusively to citrus pest problems, but during the past twenty years increasing attention has been given to a number of important pests of field and deciduous fruit crops.

The early success in the biological control of the cottony-cushion scale in California immediately stimulated interest in this type of control in other citrus-producing countries of the world where that pest, as well as others of major importance, had become established. As a result of this worldwide concentration of effort in the biological control of citrus pest problems, the benefits that have accrued therefrom have far exceeded those attained on any other agricultural crop.

THE PROCEDURES IN BIOLOGICAL CONTROL

When an insect pest of foreign origin becomes established in a new area, through trade channels or by other accidental means, the natural enemies that attack it in the country of origin are usually left behind. As a result of freedom from these controlling influences, it is often able to increase its numbers to a destructive level. The development of a project for control of a pest by the biological method then necessitates, first, the assembling of all available information on its distribution and pest status in other countries and on the natural enemies that are known to attack it. This provides the basis for a decision as to the most promising region in which to undertake the initial search for effective natural enemies. In some cases, the assembled information will pinpoint the native home of the pest and reveal the identity of its

Fig. 6–1. The biological control insectary at the Citrus Research Center and Agricultural Experiment Station, University of California, Riverside.

natural enemies. In other instances, as illustrated by the citrophilus mealybug, the native home is unknown, making necessary a tentative decision as to its origin based upon records of plant importations, volume of plant imports from various regions, the range of plant species which it attacks, and other factors.

Once a decision is reached as to the area for study, the entomological explorer undertakes his investigations there and, if the pest species is present, evaluates insofar as possible the natural enemies that are found and locates sources of adequate material for shipment. In some instances, both the host and its natural enemies may be so scarce that insectary rearing or other methods are necessary to provide sufficient stocks for shipment. Such a situation is in many respects encouraging, as it may indicate that highly effective natural enemies are holding the pest in check.

The mere finding of natural enemies, apparently effective in another country, does not mean that the problem is near solution. They must be adaptable to the conditions prevailing in the country into which they are introduced. Many species are very limited in their adaptability to climatic conditions, usually more so than the pest insect itself. If the initial importations and subsequent releases show that the enemies first found are not effective, then the search must be continued elsewhere. The scale on which such a program may be conducted is illustrated by that on the black scale by California. Most of the tropical and subtropical regions of the world have been searched for effective natural enemies during the past seventy years, and the problem is not yet fully solved. During this period, more than fifty species of primary and secondary parasites were found to attack black scale, as well as a substantial number of predators.

The search for effective parasites cannot be limited strictly to those on the pest insect itself—others of value may be found on related species. For example, the yellow scale race of *Comperiella bifasciata* How., the most effective of the imported enemies of the yellow scale in California, was obtained from related species, *Aonidiella taxus* Leon. and *Chrysomphalus bifasciculatus* Ferris, in Japan.

In the early days, the transport of insect material from one continent to another was only by steamer, the shipments often being in transit for one month or more. Even then, consignments of some types of material could be made successfully under cool storage. In many cases, however, it was necessary to ship growing plants in cages in order that the pest and its natural enemies might reproduce enroute. With present-day air transportation the problem is much simplified and consignments of parasitized host material, or even of the adult parasites and predators themselves, reach their destination within a few days, and with little mortality. This has greatly accelerated the pace of present-day importation programs.

Parasite material received from abroad is always held under strict quarantine until only pure stocks of the wanted species can be released for rearing and field colonization. This procedure ensures the elimination of any living stages of pest insects that may have been present in the shipment, as well as of harmful hyperparasites. Studies on the biology of each of the parasite species is essential during this holding period to differentiate with certainty the primary parasites from those of hyperparasitic habit.

After release from quarantine comes the mass production of the approved species, field colonization, and later the evaluation of results, certain aspects of which are discussed in later sections of this chapter.

PROGRESS IN CONTROL OF SPECIFIC PESTS

The insect pests of citrus comprise many diverse groups, the most important of which are the aphids, scale insects, mealybugs, whiteflies, fruit flies, lepidopterous fruit feeders and leaf miners, coleopterous twig and trunk borers, and the phytophagous mites. In the Asiatic region where citrus is native, there are many native destructive fruit feeders, foliage miners, and twig and trunk borers that are not yet found elsewhere. Thus far, no effort has been made to control them biologically and the prospects of doing so are considered to be slight.

In other parts of the world where citrus is not native but is now grown on a commercial scale, the major pests are of foreign origin and comprise mainly the scale insects, mealybugs, whiteflies, fruit flies, and mites, these being the most readily transported from one country to another in commerce. Success in the biological control of these pests, with the exception of the mites, has been greater than with those of any other crop. This favorable outcome may be attributed to: (1) the crop is grown under tropical or subtropical conditions that provide an optimum climate for development and increase of parasites and predators; (2) a majority of the serious pests are scale insects, mealybugs, and whiteflies that are sessile in habit and are therefore exposed to attack by natural enemies at all times; and (3) these pests almost invariably have a long list of parasites and predators attacking them in the countries of origin, and are available for importation into newly infested countries.

Biological control work on the insect pests of citrus has been under way in California since 1888, and since that time, the majority of the studies have been devoted almost entirely to the scale insects and mealybugs. This work, and the resulting fund of information regarding effective natural enemies of a number of the most destructive species and the development of techniques for handling them, has led other countries to pursue similar programs. Among the more important pests that have been given special attention in many countries of the world are the cottony-cushion scale, California red scale, purple scale, and several species of mealybugs. Included in the long list of these pests is a number of outstanding examples of successful biological control. Some of these problems were solved very quickly, whereas others have been under investigation for sixty years or more, and the end is not yet in sight.

THE FLUTED SCALES (MARGARODIDAE)

Cottony-Cushion Scale, *Icerya purchasi* Mask.

The control of the cottony-cushion scale in California by the biological method, though accomplished early in the 1890's, still stands as the classical example of that type of insect control. It was the first sustained effort in the importation of natural enemies from one country to another for subjugation of an insect pest and, as judged by its later success in virtually all citrus-producing countries of the world, still ranks first in completeness and in value to the industry.

The most complete accounts of this project are presented by Essig (1931) and Doutt (1958), and reveal the intrigues, clashing personalities, and controversies that went to make up, finally, a story without parallel in the field of entomological investigations. By the middle 1880's, the citrus industry of California was threatened with destruction by the scale, first seen in the state at Menlo Park in 1872. Official and private organizations in California petitioned the U.S. Congress in 1887–88 to provide funds for a search for natural enemies of the pest, though at that time its native home was not known with certainty. Nothing came of this, but the objective was attained in a somewhat roundabout way. Although employees of the U.S. Department of Agriculture were at that time denied funds for foreign travel, C. V. Riley, then entomologist of the federal service, arranged to have his agent, Albert Koebele (fig. 6–2), appointed as a representative of the Department of State to the International Exposition at Melbourne, though with no official duties in that capacity. His trip covered the latter portion of 1888 and the first part of 1889.

The occurrence of a dipterous parasite, *Cryptochaetum iceryae* (Will.), in Australia, presumably on the cottony-cushion scale, was known prior to Koebele's trip as a result of Riley's correspondence with collectors in that country. In fact, two small shipments of *Cryptochaetum* were received in California early in 1888 and some adults were liberated in San Mateo County. These were

Fig. 6–2. Albert Koebele (1852–1924), who discovered the ladybird beetle in Australia and sent it to California, where it achieved control of cottony-cushion scale. (Photo from the Brunner Collection.)

probably *C. monophlebi* (Skuse), from a related scale of the genus *Drosicha (Monophlebus)*. Shortly after his arrival in Australia, Koebele forwarded large shipments of *C. iceryae* and very soon discovered the predaceous ladybird beetle *Rodolia cardinalis* (Muls.), commonly known later as the vedalia (fig. 6–3), which was destined to become the lifesaver of the citrus industry in many lands. From his shipments during late 1888 and early 1889, 548 adults of *Cryptochaetum* and 514 of *Rodolia* became available for rearing and release in southern California.

Both species quickly became established and *Rodolia*, within a very few months, so fully demonstrated its capacity to completely control the scale that *Cryptochaetum* was almost entirely ignored. So rapid was the increase and spread of the beetle that control of the scale throughout southern California was achieved within little more than one year. The lifting of the threat to the welfare of the citrus industry was so dramatic that a wave of enthusiasm for biological control swept over the fruit growers of the state, who believed, mistakenly, that a panacea for all their insect problems was at hand.

As a result of the work of *Rodolia*, the cottony-cushion scale became exceedingly scarce in the citrus orchards, it often being difficult to find even a single specimen. This highly satisfactory situation continued until the late 1940's, when the new organic insecticides such as DDT came into general use for control of other citrus pests. These chemicals were highly toxic to *Rodolia*, though not

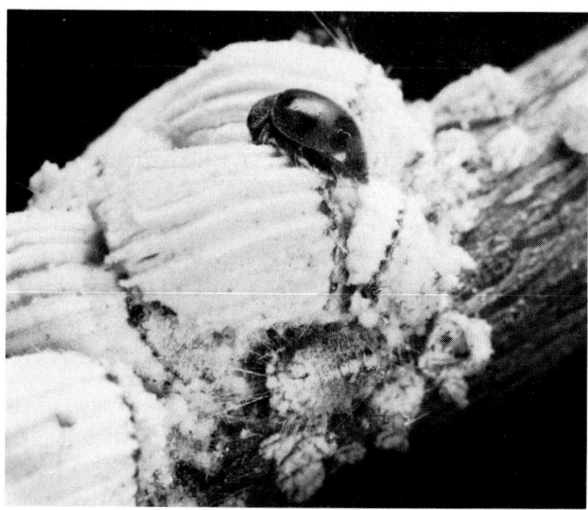

Fig. 6–3. The ladybird beetle *(Rodolia cardinalis)* on cottony-cushion scale.

to the cottony-cushion scale. As a result, heavy infestations appeared once again, especially in Tulare County, California after a lapse of more than fifty years. Fortunately, the insecticide program for citrus has now been modified in such a way as to largely relieve this difficulty.

Although *Cryptochaetum* was completely overshadowed by *Rodolia*, under certain conditions, especially in some coastal areas, it is a highly effective parasite, equal in value to the beetle.

The circumstances surrounding the establishment of the cottony-cushion scale in Florida and its eventual control, as reported by Gossard (1901), are of particular interest. The great success in the biological control of the pest in California had aroused much attention in Florida, as elsewhere, and a firm of nurserymen at Keene made inquiries in 1893 of an unnamed horticultural official in California regarding it. The scale was not present in Florida at that time, and the record is not clear that the nurserymen actually requested that a stock of beetles be forwarded. In any case, such a shipment was sent from California, and it included some live scale material as food for the beetles enroute. The beetles were released and the container discarded near a citrus tree. As a result, the scale became established at Keene, from which point it spread rapidly, whereas the beetle failed to survive.

Because of the heavy infestations that developed in succeeding years, the introduction and establishment of vedalia became imperative. Several shipments from California during 1899 were unsuccessful, as all beetles were dead upon arrival, but the consignments of 1900 brought about establishment and eventual control of the pest.

Gossard was extremely critical of the unnamed California official for including live scale in the 1893 shipment, but this was a standard practice for many years, especially when the period in transit was lengthy, until development of air transport made it unnecessary. The fault in this case was that the recipient was completely without knowledge regarding insects and apparently did not know the cottony-cushion scale or that it was not present in the state.

This unfortunate incident pointed up at an early date the absolute need for proper quarantine handling by competent experts of all insect importations into a new area.

The spread of the cottony-cushion scale from Australia was not limited to the United States but extended to many other countries, so that it now occurs in practically every citrus-producing area of the world. When the spectacular success with *Rodolia* in California became known, steps were taken to introduce it into other countries. As of 1936, it had been imported into and released in forty different countries or geographic areas (fig. 6–4), and at that time it was known to be established in thirty-two of them (Clausen, 1936). Since then, it has been colonized in an additional nineteen areas, and the latest reports indicate establishment in a total of fifty-one countries, areas, or island groups. This is a remarkable record when it is considered that most of the shipments were of only a few dozen beetles, often in transit by steamer for long distances, and the survivors were then released in the orchards, in many cases without their being supplemented by insectary rearing. In general, the control attained has been equal to that in California, though there are exceptions, due mainly to adverse climatic conditions. Granting these exceptions, *Rodolia* has displayed adaptability to a range of conditions, climatic and otherwise, unmatched by any other parasite or predator.

Icerya seychellarum (Westw.)

This insect is a minor pest of citrus in Japan, India, and some other tropical countries and islands. It has been controlled in Japan and several of the islands of Micronesia through the introduction of *Rodolia cardinalis* or *R. pumila* (Weise), but in most of these instances the infestations comprised several species of the genus. On the other hand, *R. cardinalis* proved to be entirely ineffective in Mauritius and the Seychelle Islands. In Mauritius, Moutia and Mamet (1946) found that the *Rodolia* stock in the insectary degenerated when fed on *I. seychellarum* alone and ceased reproduction after three generations. Also, there was no reproduction on this host in the field.

The complete failure of *Rodolia* in Mauritius was in sharp contrast to the results reported from several other countries where the infestations were mixed with other species of the genus and with those of related genera. A clue was provided by Balachowsky (1932) in his studies on *I. purchasi* and the related *Gueriniella serratulae* (F.) in France. The latter species has only a single generation each year and the young larvae enter diapause soon after hatching. In this stage, they are unsuitable as food for *Rodolia*. However, the latter was able to persist because of the presence of a population of *I. purchasi*, and both species were brought under control.

Kuwana's studies (1922) in Japan on *Rodolia* and its relationship to *I. purchasi* and *I. seychellarum* provide the basis on which to explain the seemingly contradictory results mentioned above. In that country, *Rodolia* has eight generations each year, with no diapause stage, and suitable host stages for feeding must therefore be present throughout the year. This requirement is fulfilled

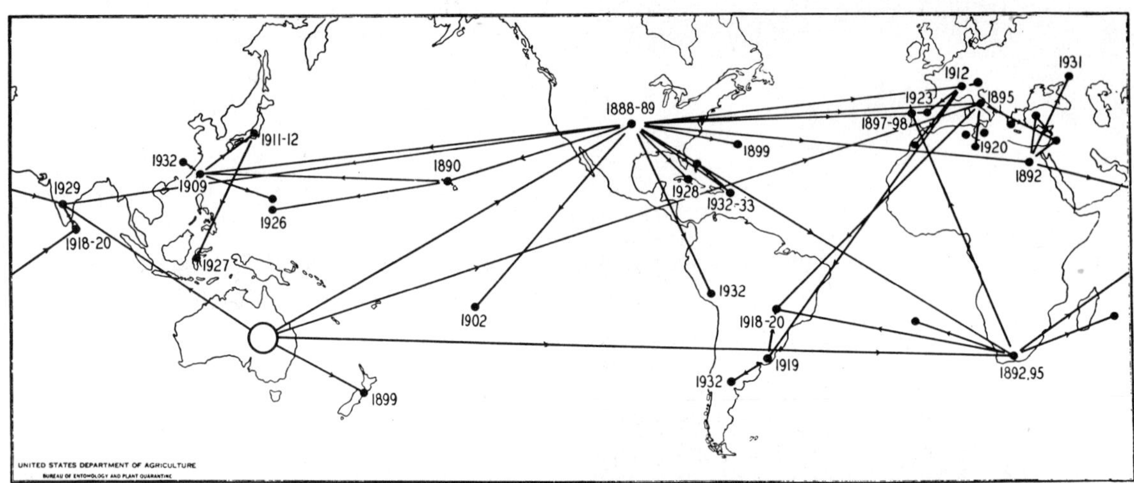

Fig. 6–4. The international movement of the highly effective cottony-cushion scale predator *Rodolia cardinalis* (Muls.), during the 45 years after its initial introduction into California from Australia in 1888–89. (After Clausen, 1936.)

by *I. purchasi*, which has two generations annually, with three in alternate years, and with much overlapping of the broods. *I. seychellarum*, on the contrary, has only a single annual generation, as does *Gueriniella*, with stages suitable for feeding by the predator for only a small portion of the year. This study demonstrated that biological control of *I. seychellarum* can be accomplished only where there is an accompanying infestation of *I. purchasi* or related species of similar habit upon which *Rodolia* may feed and reproduce during the period when suitable stages of *I. seychellarum* are not available.

Other Fluted Scales

While *Icerya purchasi* is by far the best known and most destructive of this group of pests attacking citrus, several other species of minor importance may be mentioned. *I. aegyptiaca* (Doug.), though only an occasional pest of citrus, develops heavy infestations on a number of other fruit trees. It has been adequately controlled on a number of Pacific Islands through the introduction of *Rodolia pumila* Weise from Japan and Formosa (Esaki, 1940; Beardsley, 1955). Partial control was attained in Egypt by *Rodolia cardinalis*, obtained from the United States in 1935–37, while the dipterous internal parasite *Cryptochaetum iceryae* Will. proved most effective in the more humid areas near the coast (Kamal, 1951).

Still another species, *Icerya montserratensis* R. & H., occurs in Central and South America as a minor pest of citrus and other tropical fruits. It is reported to have been controlled in Ecuador by *R. cardinalis*, imported from the United States in 1941 (Rodriguez-Lopez, 1942), but detailed information is lacking.

THE ARMORED SCALES (DIASPIDIDAE)

California Red Scale, *Aonidiella aurantii* (Mask.)

The California red scale was long the most important pest of citrus in southern California and is a major pest in many other subtropical countries, notably South Africa, Australia, and in some areas of the Middle East. Accounts of the work conducted in California on the biological control of this pest have been presented by H. S. Smith (1948) and Compere (1961). The latter author gives a detailed and entertaining recital of all aspects of the problem, with insight into the activities of the many personalities involved, extending from the first importations from Australia by Albert Koebele in 1891 up to 1948. He also evaluates the work, as of the latter date, on biological control of the scale in other countries. Compere paints a rather gloomy picture regarding the supposed progress made to that date and, on the basis of his own observations, challenges the claims that have been made for a substantial degree of control by that means in California, Australia, South Africa, and elsewhere. His conclusions, as applied to the work in California, are unquestionably true as of the date on which his paper was published, but developments during the succeeding period give grounds for hope that substantial progress is being made.

Little need be said regarding the several predators that were introduced into California by Koebele and others during the early days, several of which showed considerable promise for a time. The steely-blue ladybird beetle, *Orcus chalybeus* (Bdv.), imported from Australia in 1892, became very abundant in Santa Barbara County but declined in numbers after a time and can now be found only in certain favorable localities in that county and in a few other coastal areas. Another coccinellid beetle, *Lindorus lophanthae* (Blaisd.), also imported from Australia, is at times an effective aid in the reduction of heavy infestations in some coastal areas of the state.

The red scale-inhabiting race of an internal parasite, *Comperiella bifasciata* How. (fig. 6–5), was repeatedly imported from South China from 1906 onwards, and was finally established as a result of importations made in 1941 (DeBach, 1949). A number of the early attempts to establish *Comperiella* had failed because the stock came from other *Aonidiella* species (Compere and Smith, 1927) and the existence of host-determined races of parasites was not then recognized. More than two million adults of this parasite were reared and colonized in southern California during a fifteen month period. This parasite is now abundant in some inland area orchards and occasionally aids in controlling the infestations. A high degree of control is most frequently attained on dooryard and street trees.

In some areas of southern California, *Comperiella* is a valuable supplement to the several species of *Aphytis* now established on the red scale, as it parasitizes the more mature scales that have developed beyond the stage at which they are subject to attack by the latter.

The prospects for control of the red scale through the use of parasites appeared much enhanced when *Aphytis lingnanensis* Comp. (*Aphytis*

Fig. 6–5. *Comperiella bifasciata* **How., a parasite of the California red scale and yellow scale, imported from Asia into California. (From Smith, H. S., 1948.)**

"A") was obtained from Formosa during 1947–49. This parasite had probably been contained in some of the many shipments of red scale material from South China during the preceding thirty years, but had been confused with the native, or accidentally introduced *Aphytis chrysomphali* (Mercet), long present in California, and little attention was given to it. When it was determined that the two were different, the Formosan species was propagated by the millions in the insectary and distributed throughout the infested areas of the state. It became exceedingly abundant in the coastal areas, bringing about satisfactory control in some orchards, but was less effective in the intermediate climatic areas and failed to persist in any numbers in the hotter interior valleys.

A program was developed for the mass production of *Aphytis lingnanensis* and its periodic release in the intermediate climatic areas to enhance the effectiveness of the field populations there (DeBach and White, 1960). The objective of this program was to produce and release at monthly intervals during the season a total of 400,000 parasites per acre, and at a cost not to exceed that of a standard spray program ($40 per acre per year). This was accomplished and results of field tests were promising, but such a program for periodic release has not come into use commercially.

Since the establishment of *Aphytis lingnanensis* in southern California, additional species of the genus have been imported from India and Pakistan. Of these, the most important is *A. melinus* DeB., which quickly became established and widely distributed. It has displaced *A. lingnanensis* in many areas and has proved to be especially well adapted to the interior and intermediate areas of the state. As a result, the infestations of the California red scale have been substantially reduced in many sections of the citrus-producing areas of the state (DeBach, Landi, and White, 1962; DeBach and Sundby, 1963).

The present occurrence of at least three species of *Aphytis* of similar habit in the citrus orchards of southern California has led to severe competition between them, as a result of which one species usually becomes dominant and the other representatives of the genus decline greatly in numbers. This was noted frequently following the release of *A. lingnanensis*, which in many instances almost completely replaced *A. chrysomphali*, and this species in turn was replaced by *A. melinus*.

In addition to those already mentioned, other parasites of red scale have been introduced into and established in California, among them being *Habrolepis rouxi* Comp. from South Africa and the red scale race of *Prospaltella perniciosi* Tower from Formosa. These two are found only in very localized areas, but *Prospaltella* is at times dominant along the coast.

One interesting parasite of the red scale that has presented a complex problem as regards its introduction into California is *Pteroptrix smithi* (Compere) How. of South China, where it is considered to be an important factor in the natural control of that pest (Flanders, Gressitt, and Fisher, 1958). Repeated shipments of parasitized scale to California yielded large numbers of females but no males, and consequently insectary production was unsuccessful. The habits of *Pteroptrix* were first studied in China by J. L. Gressitt between 1948 and 1950 and then more intensively by S. E. Flanders in 1953-54. Both males and females were found on scale-infested citrus trees, yet not a single male was ever reared from the red scale. This situation led to the conclusion that the *Pteroptrix* males probably are hyperparasitic, as had previously been shown to be the case among several species of *Coccophagus*, parasitic on the black scale, but in some other scale insect, or they may possibly be primary parasites of some widely different host insect.

The solution to the above problem will need to be found before *Pteroptrix* can be successfully reared and released in California, and then only if a suitable host of the males, whatever it may be, is also available in adequate numbers in the orchards.

Yellow Scale, *Aonidiella citrina* (Coq.)

The work on biological control of the yellow scale in California has gone on concurrently with that on the related but more important California red scale, *A. aurantii*. It had been assumed, because of the close relationship of the two species, that any imported natural enemies would attack both equally well, and during the early days the field releases were made with this assumption in mind. As time went on, it developed that certain parasites would breed readily upon one but not upon the other, and that there existed host-determined races of certain species, one attacking the red scale and the other the yellow. This was brought out sharply in the case of the encyrtid parasite *Comperiella bifasciata* How., which had been imported repeatedly from Asia from 1900 onwards.

Rearing tests in California with *C. bifasciata* from Asia, the stock originating from California red scale, showed it to be unable to reproduce on the yellow scale. The yellow scale race of this parasite was first obtained from Japan, where it is a common parasite of *Aonidiella taxus* Leon. and *Chrysomphalus bifasciculatus* Ferris (Flanders, 1948, 1953). The earliest importations of this race were in 1916 and 1922–23, but releases were made only on the red scale and consequently establishment was not attained. Further stocks from *Chrysomphalus* in Japan were obtained in 1925, and field releases resulted in establishment on that host at Pasadena, California. It was then tested on yellow scale and found to be fully adapted to it, whereupon releases were made during 1931 in infestations of that scale in the area of Redlands, California. Definite evidence, not only of establishment, but of control of the pest, was obtained the following year.

In nature, *Comperiella* spreads very slowly, only a few tree rows each year. Following the success at Redlands, releases were made in Ventura County and in the San Joaquin Valley of central California. Control in southern California was most effective under city conditions because of cultural practices that tend to induce a marked overlapping of the stages of the scale insect. In general, the yellow scale is under satisfactory biological control in commercial orchards in southern California except in Ventura County, and in the San Joaquin Valley.

High mortality of the scale results from the feeding by the parasite females on the body fluids of the host, this being in addition to the mortality resulting from direct parasitization. The presence of ants on the trees greatly reduces the effectiveness of *Comperiella*.

Comperiella has not proved to be as effective in the heavy infestations of the commercial orchards of the San Joaquin Valley as in southern California. The uniformity in development of the scale brood there results in the absence at certain times of suitable stages of the scale for parasite attack, whereupon a portion of the adult parasite population largely dies off without reproduction.

Observations by J. K. Holloway on distribution of the yellow scale on the trees may further explain the greater effectiveness of *Comperiella* in the Redlands area than in the San Joaquin Valley. In the former area, the scale is most abundant on the lower sides of the leaves, the habitat favored by the parasite, whereas in the San Joaquin Valley the upper sides of the leaves are most heavily infested.

Florida Red Scale, *Chrysomphalus aonidum* (L.)

The Florida red scale is an important pest of citrus in the Gulf Coast States, especially Florida, and in Mexico. It is also one of the leading pests in some of the Mediterranean countries, where it is known as the black scale.

Biological control work was started in Israel in 1956, when stocks of what was supposed to be *Aphytis lingnanensis* Comp. were obtained from Hong Kong. This species had previously been introduced into California and proved valuable in the control of the California red scale. However, the scale material imported into California was a mixed lot and the parasites were all assumed to be of one species. Later cross-breeding experiments with parasites from the two hosts yielded no progeny, leading to the belief that they were distinct species. Morphological characters were then discovered which distinguished the two forms, and that from the Florida red scale was then described as *Aphytis holoxanthus* DeB. (DeBach, 1960).

Aphytis holoxanthus, obtained directly from Hong Kong, increased very rapidly after its release in the coastal areas of Israel and quickly demonstrated a definite capacity to control the pest.[1] Whether it will prove to be equally effective in the inland plains area remains to be seen.

When the effectiveness of *A. holoxanthus* in Israel became known, stocks were obtained from that country in 1959 for colonization in Florida and Texas, and it was also released in Mexico in 1961. While the Florida red scale is generally rated as one of the important pests of citrus in Florida, Muma (1959) considers it to be under satisfactory natural control, even though outbreaks occur from time to time. The principal native parasite attacking it is the aphelinid, *Pseudhomalopoda prima* Gir. The parasitization by *A. holoxanthus* built up rapidly and gave promise of substantial control.

A related species, the dictyospermum scale, *Chrysomphalus dictyospermi* (Morg.), is also an important citrus pest in the western Mediterranean area. An effort was made in Italy in 1922 to control it biologically, when stocks of *Aspidiotiphagus lounsburyi* (B. & P.) were obtained from Madeira and releases made on the Riviera and in Sicily. Field recoveries were made during the seasons of release, but the parasite apparently did not persist.

Purple Scale, *Lepidosaphes beckii* (Newm.)

The purple scale has long been a major pest of citrus in certain of the coastal areas of southern California, especially Orange County, and rates among the important pests of this crop in many other parts of the world, including Florida, Iran, South Africa, the Mediterranean area, and most of the citrus-producing countries of South America.

Sporadic attempts at biological control of the purple scale have been made in California since the early 1890's, when two coccinellid predators, *Orcus chalybeus* (Bdv.) and *Lindorus lophanthae* (Blaisd.), were imported from Australia and established. They are general feeders on armored scales and apparently prefer the California red scale to the purple scale.

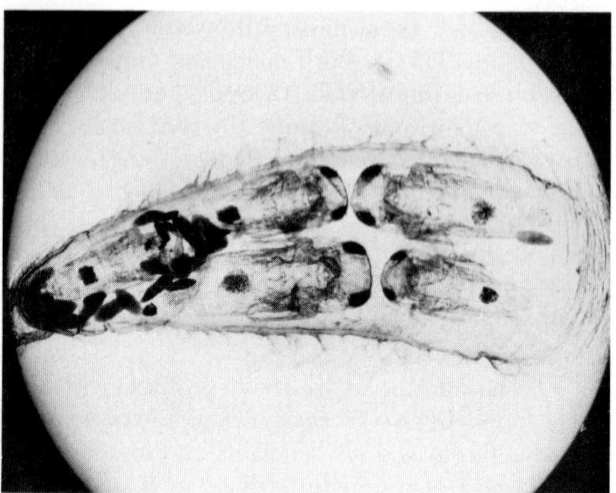

Fig. 6–6. Ventral view of a parasitized purple scale showing five pupae of *Aphytis lepidosaphes* Comp. Much enlarged. (After DeBach and Landi, 1961.)

Various other importations were made during the following fifty years but it was not until 1948–49, when the aphelinid parasite *Aphytis lepidosaphes* Comp. was obtained from South China and Formosa (Flanders, 1950) and *Physcus fulvus* C. & A. from the same region in 1948 and 1950, that prospects became encouraging. *Physcus* is well established at Carlsbad and gives some indication of effectiveness in a few orchards, but major attention has been given to the more promising *Aphytis* (DeBach and Landi, 1961). This parasite develops externally on second- and third-instar female scales and on second-instar prepupal males. Up to eight individuals may develop to maturity on a single female scale (fig. 6–6), though the majority of scales yield only two. The female parasites have the habit of feeding extensively on the body fluids of the scale, thus bringing about high mortality in addition to that effected by direct parasitization.

Aphytis demonstrated a capacity for reducing substantially the infestations of the purple scale, but this was not consistent and led DeBach and Landi (1961) to develop a program of integrated control involving a reduced schedule of insecticide applications (oil sprays) to portions of infested orchards in such a way as to conserve to a large extent the repressive capabilities of the parasite. Alternate two-row strips were treated with an

[1]Personal communication from A. Grünberg to the author, dated January 25, 1959.

oil spray one year and the unsprayed strips then received treatment the following year. Thus, half the orchard was sprayed each year, permitting the natural enemies from the untreated strips to recolonize the adjacent treated strips very soon after the spray application. Test plots handled in this way for a nine-year period showed satisfactory control, with a consequent reduction of about two-thirds in cost over that of a full insecticidal spray program.

Shipments of *Aphytis lepidosaphes* were made to Texas in 1952 and within four years it was reported to have cleaned up the infestations at the original release sites and to have spread seventy miles, while by 1961 the populations were so reduced throughout the Rio Grande Valley that the scale became only a very minor pest.

The situation in Florida is puzzling, as surveys by DeBach indicated definitely that the parasite was not present there in 1950, and M. H. Muma had not encountered it during a six-year survey over the state. It was not intentionally introduced, yet it appeared in collections in 1958 and by then was quite widely distributed. Large-scale collections made throughout the state from 1958 to 1960 showed a mean parasitization of 51.3 per cent (Muma and Clancy, 1961). Concurrently, with this high parasitization there occurred a drastic decline of the purple scale populations, so that it is now rated as only a minor pest.

In recent years, *Aphytis lepidosaphes* has been imported into and released in Chile (1952, 1954), Mexico (1954, 1956), Peru (1958), and Italy (1960), with establishment reported in the first three countries. Final reports are not yet available regarding the degree of control attained.

A number of early writers, including Fawcett (1948), have mentioned several fungi, especially *Sphaerostilbe aurantiicola* (Berk. & Br.) Petch, as contributing to the control of purple scale in Florida. It was a general belief that the application of fungicidal sprays for citrus disease control was responsible for the ensuing increase of purple scale infestations by eliminating the parasitic fungi (Watson, 1912). This matter was investigated by Holloway and Young (1943), who reported that the increases proved to be due to granular residues from spray applications, whether of fungicidal materials or inert, rather than to any adverse influence on the entomogenous fungi.

Later F. E. Fisher and her associates made an intensive study of the relationship of several of these fungi to scale insects and could find no evidence that *S. aurantiicola* or *Nectria diploa* (B. & C.) were parasitic on purple or Florida red scales (Fisher, 1950). Another fungus, *Myiophagus* sp., was determined to be a true parasite and appeared to be of some importance as an enemy of the purple scale. Muma and Clancy (1961) found that the incidence of this fungus declined sharply from the fall of 1958 onwards, concurrently with the buildup of *Aphytis* and the resulting sharp reduction in the scale populations.

It may be of interest here to mention the Manatee snail *Drymaeus dormani* (Binn.) of Florida, which has been widely distributed in that state during the past fifty years or more as an aid in the control of purple and other scale insects and whiteflies. It has not been claimed that the snail is predaceous on these insects, but it contributes to their control by smothering them with its slimy secretions and at the same time providing a substrate that is detrimental to settling of the crawlers (Kramer, n.d.; Norris, 1947). The snails feed mainly on the sooty mold growing in the insect excretions. Foliage and fruit, upon the surface of which the snails have fed, have a highly polished and attractive appearance. Many orchards, especially in Lake County, have for years been commercially clean, without application of insecticides, and the snail is credited with bringing about this condition. A detailed experimental study of the interrelations between the snail and the scale insects and whiteflies would be well worthwhile.

Glover Scale, *Lepidosaphes gloverii* (Pack.)

The Glover scale is of worldwide distribution, but in only a few countries is it an important pest of citrus. It was exceedingly destructive to this crop in Florida a century ago, at which time it threatened to destroy the industry. No parasites were found to attack it, but later one species appeared, apparently an accidental introduction, and brought the pest under reasonably good control (Watson and Berger, 1937). This species has since gone under the name of *Prospaltella aurantii* (How.), a cosmopolitan species recorded from many hosts. Still later, a fungus, *Podonectria coccicola* (E. & E.) appeared and it was credited with aiding further in reducing the infestations. According to Steinhaus (1949), however, some workers believe that this fungus is more probably a secondary parasite or a saprophyte.

Importations of insect parasites into California for control of Glover scale were made from South China in 1948–49, the most important one being *Prospaltella elongata* Doz., which develops internally in the immature scales. Releases were first made in 1948 in a light infestation in Orange County and the species was recovered there in 1950 (Flanders, Gressitt, and DeBach, 1950). *P. elongata* had originally been described from Glover scale from Louisiana. A detailed study of specimens of *Prospaltella* from that host, collected in South China, Louisiana, and Florida showed them to be identical and, accordingly, the record of *P. aurantii* as a parasite of that host must be considered as erroneous.

Yanone Scale, *Unaspis yanonensis* (Kuw.)

The yanone scale occurs as a major pest of citrus only in Japan, where it became established early in the present century. It spread rapidly and its injury to the trees is comparable to that by the purple scale at its worst. Introduction of parasites for its control included *Arrhenophagus* sp. from Hong Kong in 1954 and *Aphytis lingnanensis* Comp. from California in 1955. The latter species is of South China origin also, but had been known up to that time only as an effective parasite of the California red scale. It proved adaptable to the yanone scale and releases in Kyushu resulted in high parasitization (Nishida and Yanai, 1956), but the extent of control attained has not yet been reported.

THE UNARMORED OR SOFT SCALES (COCCIDAE)

Black Scale, *Saissetia oleae* (olivier)

The black scale, more commonly known as the olive scale in the Mediterranean countries, is worldwide in distribution and attacks a wide range of plants, the most important commercially being citrus and olive. For many years, it was rated as the most important of the citrus pests of southern California. In this area, biological control work is complicated by the wide range of climatic conditions in the citrus-producing areas, resulting in the development of only a single generation of the scale each year in the hot interior areas, whereas in the cooler coastal areas there is at least a partial second generation, with all stages present at almost all times of the year.

The importation of natural enemies for control of the black scale in California began before the turn of the century, and the search still continues. Most of the subtropical and tropical countries of the world have been covered in this search, with perhaps the greatest attention to Africa. Reports covering these investigations have been published by H. S. Smith and Compere (1928) and Smith (1948). To date, nine species of parasites and six predators are known to be established as a result of importations from abroad.

One of the first importations was the coccinellid beetle *Rhizobius ventralis* Erich., which was sent from Australia by Albert Koebele in 1888–89 incident to his search for enemies of the cottony-cushion scale, and was established in Santa Barbara County through later shipments in 1891. The beetle increased tremendously in the orchards during the ensuing seasons and aroused strong hopes that control would be attained. This did not materialize, however, and while it is still the most abundant of the lady-beetles attacking the scale, in general *Rhizobius* has since contributed little to control. Three other coccinellid beetles have since been established but have proved to be of little consequence.

Some years later, in 1900–01, a stock of an egg predator, *Scutellista cyanea* Mots., was received from C. P. Lounsbury of South Africa. The eggs of this wasp are laid in the egg chamber of the gravid female scale and the larvae feed upon the eggs and newly hatched young of the scale, and in some cases on the parent female also, in which case the species acts in the role of a parasite of the scale insect itself. *Scutellista* became very abundant in some sections, especially along the coast, but its contribution to control is much less than is indicated by the portion of the scale population that is attacked. This is because of the inability of the larva to consume the entire complement of eggs of the host female, though this may be accomplished when two or more are present. One hundred per cent attack may therefore still leave sufficient unconsumed eggs to maintain a heavy infestation.

The establishment of *Scutellista* in California provides a striking example of the results of competition between two species of similar habit (Flanders, 1958*b*). Prior to the introduction of this egg predator, a presumably native species, *Moranila (Tomocera) californica* (How.), was extremely abundant, and records showed attack upon the scale of up to 75 per cent. Ten years after *Scutellista* became established, it was extremely difficult to find specimens of *Moranila*, and that situation has persisted to the present day. Thus, a highly successful introduction has resulted in no benefit whatsoever so far as control is concerned.

The next introduction was of the gregarious

internal parasite *Metaphycus lounsburyi* (How.), which was established as a result of importations from Australia in 1916. According to H. S. Smith and Compere (1928), the first releases in southern California were on the Limoneira Ranch at Santa Paula and at Alhambra in the fall of 1919. Eight months later a majority of the scales in the Santa Paula orchard were found to be parasitized. This encouraging development led to the early completion of the distribution program throughout southern California.

Metaphycus produces at least three generations annually and requires a continuous supply of suitable hosts for attack in order to perpetuate itself in abundance, and consequently the "uneven hatch" condition of the scale in the coastal areas was most favorable to it. From 1920 to 1924, the pest was so greatly reduced in those areas that fumigation was no longer necessary. This heavy attack soon worked to the disadvantage of the parasite itself, as it brought about an approach to an "even hatch" cycle of the host. On the other hand, the changed situation of the scale greatly facilitated effective control by a single annual fumigation in case such treatment became necessary. One real benefit was the virtual elimination of infestations on the pepper tree *Schinus molle*, which is widely grown as a street and roadside tree in southern California. These trees had previously served as a reservoir from which adjoining orchards quickly became reinfested after insecticidal treatment.

Metaphycus lounsburyi was the most abundant and effective of all parasites of the black scale from 1920 to 1924, and insecticidal treatments became unnecessary in many orchards in the coastal area. Some even-hatch orchards showed parasitization up to 95 per cent or more, yet sufficient young scales were produced to make chemical treatment necessary. The generally favorable situation in the coastal areas failed to persist, however, because of the activities of a secondary parasite, *Quaylea whittieri* (Gir.), which develops as an internal parasite of the larvae of *Aphycus*. The results were disastrous, and *Aphycus* was reduced to an ineffective status, though still persisting in considerable numbers in some localities. *Quaylea* is native to Australia and its intentional introduction into California in 1900–01 constitutes one of the very few mistakes that have been recorded in the history of biological control. At that time the host relationships of the various parasitic groups were not nearly so well known as today, and the biological studies on this species prior to release were not sufficient to reveal its hyperparasitic habit. Today, all imported parasites and predators are subjected to such rigorous quarantine screening and testing that a repetition of this error is virtually impossible.

The consequences of the attack of *Quaylea* upon *Metaphycus* were considered at the time so catastrophic that Smith and Compere were impelled to state: "This parasite is so elastic in its habits that it may even prevent for all time the control of the black scale by the biological method." Fortunately, this dire prognosis failed to hold true. *Quaylea* has shown no tendency to attack the numerous black scale parasites which have been introduced and established since that time. With the decline in most areas of *M. lounsburyi*, its preferred host, and the evening of the black scale broods on citrus, *Quaylea* has virtually disappeared from southern California.

Following the work on *M. lounsburyi* came the introduction and establishment in southern California of a series of five internal parasites of the genus *Coccophagus*, all obtained from South Africa between 1921 and 1937. These were *C. capensis* Comp., *C. cowperi* Grlt., *C. pulvinariae* Comp., *C. rusti* Comp., and *C. trifasciatus* Comp. The establishment of these species were complicated during the early portion of the period by a previously unknown phenomenon in their developmental habits, which was discovered by Flanders (1937, 1952). The females of all species dealt with are primary parasites of the immature stages of the scale, whereas the males are hyperparasitic, developing only on the larvae of their own or a related species present in the same host. Successful colonization was therefore dependent upon repeated releases at the same site, the first of mated females, which would produce only female progeny, followed by one or more releases of unmated females at proper intervals, so that a generation of males could be produced on the female larvae then present in the hosts. None of the above-named species of *Coccophagus* has contributed appreciably to the biological control of black scale on citrus, several of them having shown a preference for other hosts.

A long step forward in the biological control of the black scale was taken in 1937 with the importation of *Metaphycus helvolus* Comp. from South Africa. This parasite usually develops singly in second- and third-instar scales, though occasionally two or three will emerge from a single scale.

Flanders (1942*a*) mentions four attributes of this species that make it especially valuable in control: (1) the females feed extensively on the body fluids of the scale, often effecting a higher mortality by this means than by direct parasitization; (2) they are long lived, with the oviposition period extending through three months or more; (3) the reproductive capacity is high, a female being able to deposit 700 or more eggs; and (4) the developmental cycle is short, requiring only thirteen days from egg to adult.

The first field releases of *Metaphycus helvolus* in southern California were made in 1937, and by 1939 it had demonstrated in several orchards its capacity to control the scale. Two years later it was the dominant parasite attacking the pest and had reduced it to the lowest level on record. In reviewing the situation as of 1947, H. S. Smith (1948) stated that only occasional orchards then required insecticidal treatment. Control was especially good in the coastal areas, while occasional heavy infestations were still to be found in the interior areas. The picture was not so bright after 1948, however, as parasite effectiveness declined and extensive use of insecticides again became necessary. The reasons for this decline are obscure, it being attributed in some years to adverse winter conditions (Flanders, 1949), but milder seasons since then have not brought the parasite back to the level of effectiveness maintained during the 1940's. Thus, although substantial progress has been made, the black scale problem is not yet fully solved, and the search for additional effective natural enemies continues.

Attempts have been made in several other countries to control the black scale by the biological method. The first of these was in western Australia where, according to Wilson (1960), the imported parasites have yielded "a level of control which is regarded as one of the outstanding successes of biological control in the State." This was accomplished by *Metaphycus lounsburyi*, obtained from South Africa, *Moranila (Tomocera) californica* from New South Wales, both in 1902, and *Scutellista cyanea* from California in 1904. There is no reference in the Australian reports as to the outcome of competition between *Moranila* and *Scutellista*, such as occurred in California following the introduction of the latter species there.

Another success with the black scale is reported by Beingolea (1956) from Peru, as a result of the importation of *M. lounsburyi*, *Lecaniobius utilis* Comp., and *Scutellista cyanea* from California in 1936. Effective control was attained in most years, though sporadic local outbreaks still occurred. *Metaphycus helvolus* and *M. stanleyi* were imported in 1958 in the hope that they might further depress the infestations, but information regarding the success of this second effort is not yet available.

Nigra Scale, *Saissetia nigra* (Nietn.)

The cosmopolitan nigra scale is a minor pest of citrus in several countries, but the list of its host plants, as compiled by R. H. Smith (1944) comprises 150 or more plant species, with heavy attack limited largely to a series of ornamental and wild plants. In California, only occasional light infestations have been noted on citrus, but the possibility that it might in time better adapt itself to this host, as has occurred elsewhere, led to efforts for its biological control concurrently with that undertaken on the related and highly important black scale, *Saissetia oleae*.

The first parasite releases in nigra scale infestations were of *Coccophagus cowperi* Grlt. and *C. pulvinariae* Comp. in 1937–38, these having been imported from South Africa the preceding year. While these two species became established, they contributed little to control, and it was not until the large-scale releases of *M. helvolus* (Comp.), likewise obtained from South Africa, from the middle of 1938 onwards that success was assured. The pest was under complete biological control in all areas of parasite release by the spring of 1941. According to Flanders (1959*b*), the nigra scale has been so completely subjugated by the parasite that it is now seldom found in any of the localities of southern California between Santa Barbara and San Diego.

There are several reasons for the greater effectiveness of *M. helvolus* on the nigra scale than has been attained on the black scale. The nigra scale has only a single generation each year, with the adults present during the spring and early summer, yet the females may produce eggs for as long as ten months. The population at any one time may therefore comprise nearly all developmental stages, permitting almost uninterrupted reproduction of the parasite, to the extent of possibly ten generations to one of the host. All larval stages are subject to parasitization. Also, it is able to exert its repressive effect on the scale even when the latter is at a very low population level because of the reservoir of parasites existing in black scale infestations nearby.

Citricola Scale, *Coccus pseudomagnoliarum* (Kuw.)

Since the finding that the citricola scale of California was identical with *Coccus pseudomagnoliarum* of Japan (Clausen, 1923) four attempts have been made to introduce and establish in California a series of parasites from that country. These were in 1922–23, 1936–37, 1951, and 1953. The principal parasites of the scale in Japan are *Coccophagus japonicus* Comp. and *C. yoshidae* Nakay. These two, with *C. hawaiiensis* Timb., *Anicetus annulatus* Timb., and *M. orientalis* Comp., were released at one time or another, but mostly during 1951–52. None of them became established.

Clausen (1923) and Gressitt, Flanders, and Bartlett (1954), in commenting on the status of the scale in Japan, mention that its preferred host plant is trifoliate orange, on which the populations are always low, and that it seldom occurs on commercial varieties of citrus. From this they concluded that the pest is under effective control by its natural enemies. The present writer's observations in Japan in 1953 throw some doubt on this conclusion. True, the scale infestations on trifoliate orange are always low, yet another rutaceous shrub, *Evodia rutaecarpa* H. & T., whenever found in Honshu and Kyushu, was always heavily infested. This shrub is of Chinese origin and was at one time grown commercially for its fruit, but is now seldom seen. It is obviously much preferred over trifoliate orange by the scale and the heavy infestations upon it, despite attack by parasites, indicate strongly that its scarcity on trifoliate orange and commercial varieties of orange is due to some controlling factor other than natural enemies.

The change in status of the citricola scale in southern California since its first appearance there in 1909 is confusing. Heavy infestations built up in the early years, and it was heavily attacked by most of the parasite species occurring on the brown soft scale, the most important of which was *M. luteolus* Timb. These parasites were unable to build up controlling numbers in infestations of citricola scale alone, which has only a single generation annually, whereas they effected a high parasitization in orchards where there was also a sufficient infestation of brown soft scale to permit them to increase during the period in which the citricola scale is immune to attack.

The citricola scale declined to a noneconomic level in southern California during the middle 1930's and has remained so except for occasional sporadic outbreaks in Riverside and San Bernardino counties.

The South African parasite *M. helvolus* (Comp.), which was highly effective in control of the black scale in southern California following its introduction in 1937, proved to be adapted to the citricola scale also. The combined action of *M. helvolus* and *M. luteolus* was responsible for suppression of sporadic outbreaks from that time onwards (Bartlett, 1953).

The situation has not changed in central California, where the scale persists in pest status. *M. helvolus* is not yet established there and *M. luteolus* alone is not able to effect control.

Brown Soft Scale, *Coccus hesperidum* L.

The brown soft scale, now of worldwide distribution, is only a minor pest of citrus in most of the citrus-producing areas of the world, though serious infestations occur periodically in such countries as Australia and South Africa. In California, heavy infestations may be found on single trees or parts of trees, but these are usually of short duration. Here the most important of the parasites attacking it are *M. luteolus* Timb., *Microterys flavus* (How.), and *Coccophagus lycimnia* (Wlkr.).

The early work on biological control of this pest was in Western Australia, where a long series of parasites was introduced from many countries between 1902 and 1909. According to Jenkins (1946), none of them became established. A later review of the subject by Wilson (1960) mentions that one of the parasites introduced in 1902, but not identified, was reported to be effective in controlling the scale in the areas where it was released. *Coccophagus lycimnia*, presumably introduced in 1907, is also said to be established. In general, the scale is now kept under reasonably good control by its natural enemies but, because of the incompleteness of the early records, the contribution of the imported species to this outcome cannot be evaluated.

Microterys flavus, another of the parasites that presumably was introduced into Australia in 1907, was taken to New Zealand in 1920 and is reported to have effected a considerable degree of control there (Dumbleton, 1936).

Under natural conditions, infestations of the brown soft scale are almost invariably heavily attended by ants, and their presence in large numbers on the trees largely inhibits oviposition by some parasite species, such as *Metaphycus luteolus.* The elimination of these honeydew-feeding ants is essential in any control program and their suppression is usually followed by a rapid subsidance of the scale infestations through accelerated parasite attack.

Red Wax Scale, *Ceroplastes rubens* Mask.

The red wax scale is a serious pest of citrus and other fruits and ornamentals in Japan and Australia and is of less importance in several other countries where it occurs. It was first found in Japan in 1897 and soon thereafter spread throughout all citrus-producing areas, becoming the second most serious citrus pest, after the yanone scale. Four species of parasites were imported from Hawaii and California in the 1920's for its control, but none of them became established.

A survey of the parasites attacking the scale in northern Kyushu was undertaken during 1946 and following years, resulting in the finding of a large series of species attacking it, but only one, *Anicetus beneficus* I. & Y., appeared to be of potential value in control (Yasumatsu and Tachikawa, 1949; Yasumatsu, 1951). At the time of the survey its identity was confused with that of *Anicetus annulatus* Timb. and *A. ceroplastis* Ishii. It was found only in Fukuoka and Saga Prefectures, on the island of Kyushu, and effected field parasitization in those areas up to 52 per cent. The scale insect has a single generation each year whereas the parasite has two, through its capacity to attack all larvae except those of the first instar, and the adult females as well.

The high parasitization of the scale in a limited area and its complete absence elsewhere led to the development of a program for its utilization in biological control, especially in Honshu and Shikoku. It was demonstrated by Yasumatsu (1953) that field releases of the parasite resulted at times in full economic control of the pest within three years or less. During a four-year period *Anicetus* was distributed to all infested areas of Japan. While it is now generally established throughout the range of the host, full control has not been obtained in all areas.

In a recent paper, Yasumatsu (1958) has presented an interesting hypothesis to explain the initial appearance of *Anicetus beneficus* in a very restricted area in Japan. He believes it possible that this species may have evolved by mutation from the endemic *A. ceroplastis*, the normal host of which is *Ceroplastes pseudoceriferus* Green. The latter parasite does not attack *C. rubens*, and the two parasite species apparently do not interbreed. Should this explanation be the true one, it will be the first such instance in biological control history and of much evolutionary significance as well as of practical importance. Yasumatsu discounts the possibility that the parasite may be an accidental introduction from abroad, mainly on the basis that, had it been associated with the scale in other countries, such as China, it would have been discovered long before its appearance in Japan. The idea of its originating by mutation is an intriguing one, but until supported by further research the case for foreign origin appears the more plausible.

White Wax Scale, *Ceroplastes destructor* Newst.

The white wax scale is a serious pest of citrus in Australia and importations of natural enemies were made into New South Wales from East Africa and India between 1935 and 1938. This material came from various species of *Ceroplastes* other than *destructor.* Attempts were made to rear some sixteen species of the parasites received but only three reproduced on *C. destructor.* Of these, *Scutellista cyanea* Mots. and *Diversinervus elegans* Silv. were released, but only in small numbers. Neither species became established (Wilson, 1960). *Scutellista* was already present in Australia as a parasite of the black scale but had not been observed to attack *Ceroplastes.* Apparently there are two biological races of this parasite, each restricted in the main to one host genus. *Diversinervus* likewise was already present there on the black scale. Importations are continuing in the effort to obtain parasites effective against *C. destructor.*

Another species of the genus, *Ceroplastes sinensis* Del G., is a pest of citrus in the area of Batum, Russia, and field tests were conducted there to determine the value of spray applications of spores of a parasitic fungus, *Cephalosporium lecanii* Zimm., as a part of the control program. It was found by Evlakhova (1938, 1941) that such applications resulted in mortality of 27.7 to 100 per cent of the nymphs and young adults. The fungus persists through the winter on dead diseased scales on the trees.

Green Shield Scale, *Pulvinaria psidii* Mask.

The green shield scale is a minor pest of citrus in many of the tropical areas of the world, but is of less importance than some other members of the genus. In Puerto Rico, heavy infestations on

Erythrina were brought under control by the coccinellid predator *Cryptolaemus montrouzieri* Muls., which had been introduced mainly for control of mealybugs on sugarcane (Wolcott, 1958).

A campaign for the biological control of *P. psidii* was conducted in Bermuda from 1953 to 1957, when a considerable number of parasites and predators was imported from California, Hawaii, India, and Trinidad (Bennett and Hughes, 1959). Of these, *Aphycus stanleyi* (Comp.), *Microterys kotinskyi* (Full.), *Cryptolaemus montrouzieri*, and *Azya luteipes* (Muls.) became established. *Aphycus stanleyi* became abundant on other scale insects, but was seldom found attacking the green shield scale. The effectiveness of *M. kotinskyi* is reduced because of its habit of often attacking fully mature female scales, which then produce a portion of their eggs before being killed by the parasite. *Cryptolaemus* and *Azya*, the predators, have achieved good control of the scale in several areas, but their effect is reduced by the extensive feeding of tree lizards, *Anolis* spp., upon them and, in fact, their permanent establishment may be endangered thereby.

Fig. 6–7. Adult of *Cryptolaemus montrouzieri* Muls. Both adults and larvae of this beetle are voracious feeders on mealybugs.

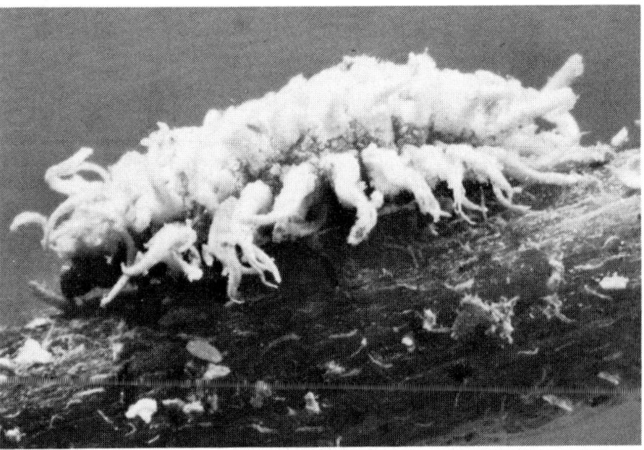

Fig. 6–8. Larva stage of the coccinellid predator *Cryptolaemus montrouzieri* Muls.

THE MEALYBUGS (PSEUDOCOCCIDAE)

Citrus Mealybug, *Planococcus citri* (Risso)

The citrus mealybug is a cosmopolitan species and attacks a wide range of fruit trees and ornamentals. As a pest of citrus it was at one time very destructive in California and is still so in some of the Mediterranean countries, but in most others it is of secondary importance.

Biological control work was started in California as early as 1891–92, when Albert Koebele, on his second trip to Australia, forwarded the coccinellid predator *Cryptolaemus montrouzieri* Muls. Both adults and larvae of this beetle (figs. 6–7 and 6–8) are voracious feeders upon mealybugs of all stages. The adults are the largest of the several species preying upon mealybugs, and are black, with the head, tips of wing covers, and abdomen reddish in color. The larvae may attain a length of nearly one-half inch and are heavily covered with segmental bands of a white waxy secretion.

The species readily became established in the coastal counties of southern California, where the mealybug problem was most severe, and in some instances brought about control. This was not dependable, however, as climatic conditions proved unsuitable for persistence of the beetle in adequate numbers through the winter. Winter mortality was high, and the mealybug infestations reached injurious levels in the spring and early summer before *Cryptolaemus* could increase sufficiently to cope with them.

Some years later, beginning about 1915, the mealybug problem became more acute because of the rapid spread and destructiveness of the citrophilus mealybug, and methods were devised (see p. 308) for mass production of *Cryptolaemus* for use against both species. The basic idea behind this program was that the release of suitable numbers of beetles in infested orchards in spring or early summer, or whenever required, would supplement the existing beetle populations sufficiently to effect control before serious injury occurred. The rate of release was usually ten beetles per tree. This program resulted in reasonably good control of the citrus mealybug, and *Cryptolaemus* is even yet being reared and distributed in considerable numbers by several insectary organizations in Ventura County for use against the occasional outbreaks that still occur.

Importations of other natural enemies of the citrus mealybug have also been made to supplement *Cryptolaemus*. Of these, three parasites have become established in the state: *Leptomastidea abnormis* (Grlt.) from Sicily in 1914, *Pauridia peregrina* Timb. from South China in 1949, and *Allotropa citri* Mues. from the same region in 1950. Also established was a small coccinellid predator, *Scymnus binaevatus* (Muls.), received from South Africa in 1921.

Leptomastidea attacks mainly the first- and second-instar nymphs of the mealybug. It quickly became established throughout the infested area and gave promise of effectiveness in control (H. S. Smith, 1917). The infestations were substantially reduced in severity, though not sufficiently so to permit discontinuation entirely of the *Cryptolaemus release program.*

Pauridia peregrina and another parasite, *Leptomastix dactylopii* How., (fig. 6–9), obtained from Brazil in 1934, have proven of value when released on an annual basis. Many millions of the two species have been produced and colonized annually in Ventura County by private organizations. Even with these large releases over a long period of years, *Leptomastix* is not yet known to be established; winter conditions seem to prevent its survival.

Since its establishment in California, *Cryptolaemus* has been widely distributed over the world for control of various mealybug species. It is known to be established in at least twenty countries or island areas. The most extensive program for its utilization in a periodic release program was in Spain (Gomez-Clemente, 1932). Several insectaries were built and operated solely for the production of *Cryptolaemus*, and results were comparable to those obtained in California.

Fig. 6–9. ***Leptomastix dactylopii*** **How., a parasite of the citrus mealybug. (Photo by T. W. Fisher.)**

Studies were made in Italy during the 1950's on the utilization of a series of parasites obtained from California to supplement the native *Leptomastidea abnormis*, which was not sufficiently effective to hold the infestations in check (Zinna, 1960). The species involved were *Leptomastix dactylopii*, *Pauridia peregrina*, and *Allotropa citri*, as well as several others not fully adapted to this mealybug species. *Leptomastix* proved to be the most effective under the conditions prevailing on the island of Procida, where the tests were made. Field parasitization ranged up to 92 per cent and early season releases brought about control in two to three months. Unfortunately, the parasite was unable to survive the winter season, as was the case in Ventura County, California, thus making it necessary to recolonize at the beginning of each season.

Citrophilus Mealybug, *Pseudococcus fragilis* Brain

The citrophilus mealybug, which is of Australian origin, was first found in southern California in 1913, after which its spread was rapid, and exceedingly heavy infestations developed, far exceeding those of the well-known and more widely distributed citrus mealybug. The first efforts for its control by the biological method consisted of a program for the mass production and periodic release of the coccinellid beetle, *Cryptolaemus montrouzieri* Muls., more extensive even than that developed against the citrus mealybug. This program yielded fairly satisfactory control in most areas, though damaging infestations still occurred, but it was expensive and the cost was an annually recurring one, as the beetles had to be released each season.

It was felt that insect parasites, rather than the predator, might be more effective and less costly, if such species could be found. During this early period, the country of origin of the pest was unknown. It had been described from the British Isles in 1915, but indications were that it was a recent introduction there. An analysis of all pertinent information by H. S. Smith pointed to Australia as the most likely possibility. Accordingly, Harold Compere was delegated to initiate the search for parasites in that country in 1927. On the first day of search in the Botanical Garden in

Sydney, he found a few specimens of *P. fragilis* (=*Pseudococcus gahani* Green), and a few weeks later evidence of parasite attack upon it was observed. The mealybug was exceedingly rare, however, and it was not until several months later, and after insectary rearing had been carried on, that sufficient material became available for shipment. A stock of mealybugs, with the associated parasites, was built up on potato sprouts and transported to California, arriving at Riverside in March, 1928. This reared material was supplemented by a large quantity of parasitized mealybugs obtained from a heavily infested mulberry tree at Pyrmont. Two internal parasites, *Coccophagus gurneyi* Comp. and *Hungariella pretiosa* Timb., were the most important of the series of natural enemies contained in this shipment (Compere and Smith, 1932).

The two parasites and several predators were propagated in the insectary of the Citrus Experiment Station, Riverside, and at several county insectaries, and field releases were begun in late April, 1928. The parasites quickly became established, and by the spring of 1929 there was already a noticeable reduction in the field infestations where the early releases had been made. Completion of the distribution program was rapid, and by the spring of 1930 full economic control had been attained throughout southern California. During this early period, *Coccophagus* was most abundant during the winter, whereas *Hungariella* was dominant during the summer.

In addition to the two parasites mentioned above, a dipterous predator, *Silvestrina koebelei* Felt (*Diplosis* sp.), also became established but contributed nothing to control. Its larvae feed upon the eggs and early larval stages of the mealybug.

In later years, when mealybug populations were at a very low level, *Hungariella pretiosa* became the dominant parasite species, and, rather surprisingly, another species of the genus, *T. peregrinus* Comp., introduced from Brazil in 1934 for control of the long-tailed mealybug, was found to attack the citrophilus mealybug extensively, at times outnumbering the other two species.

The spectacular results of this work on *Pseudococcus fragilis* in California assuredly rates as one of the outstanding examples of biological control of a pest insect, fully comparable in all respects to that of the cottony-cushion scale by *Rodolia cardinalis* Muls. in California and other countries many years before.

An unusual feature of the biological control of this pest is the entire absence of any recurrence of damaging infestations following the application of many of the new organic insecticides for control of other pests. Not a single such instance has been observed; the mealybug consistently remains at such a low population level that it is often difficult to collect even a single specimen in areas that had once been heavily infested, and this regardless of the insecticidal treatments to which the orchards have been subjected.

Since its appearance in California, the citrophilus mealybug has spread to many countries. *Coccophagus gurneyi*, and in some instances *Hungariella pretiosa* also, have been introduced into Chile, South Africa, Russia, and New Zealand. Control comparable to that attained in California is reported in New Zealand, but reports are not available regarding the outcome in other countries.

Long-Tailed Mealybug, *Pseudococcus longispinus* (Targioni-Tazzetti)

The long-tailed mealybug is an occasional injurious pest of citrus as well as other fruit and ornamental trees in southern California and other parts of the world. Three parasites have been imported into and established in California for its control, these being *Anarhopus sydneyensis* (Timb.) from Australia in 1933, *Hungariella peregrina* Comp. from Brazil in 1934, and *Anagyrus fusciventris* (Gir.) from Hawaii in 1936. The first-named species appeared to be the most effective of the three in reducing the pest populations to a noneconomic level in the areas where they were established, though distribution was not complete at the time the report was made (Flanders, 1940). *Anagyrus* proved to be ineffective.

A later study be DeBach, Fleschner, and Dietrick (1949) of the relative abundance of the several members of the natural enemy complex on citrus, conducted in 1947, at which time the infestations were substantially reduced, showed *Anarhopus* to be the dominant parasite, this in spite of heavy attack by a native secondary parasite, *Lygocerus* sp., during the latter part of the season. *Hungariella* had declined to very small numbers, while *Coccophagus gurneyi* Comp., originally imported from Australia in 1928 for control of the citrophilus mealybug, had proved to be well adapted to the long-tailed mealybug and ranked second in importance. While the several species of internal parasites were the most important of the natural enemies during the spring period, the predators were the major factors in the final subjugation of the infestations later in the year. Of these, the brown lacewing, (*Sympherobius californicus* Banks), the green lacewing, (*Chrysopa californica* Coq.), and the exotic coccinellid beetle (*Cryptolaemus montrouzieri* Muls.), were the most important, in the order given.

H. peregrina and *Anagyrus fusciventris* were introduced into Bermuda from California between 1951 and 1953, both becoming established in infestations on various ornamentals rather than on citrus, and brought the pest under satisfactory control (Bennett and Hughes, 1959). The coccinellid predator, *Cryptolaemus montrouzieri*, which has been established in many countries on a number of species of mealybugs, failed to establish itself in Bermuda. This outcome is attributed to the adverse influence of the Argentine ant and to a tree lizard which fed extensively upon the beetles.

Anarhopus sydneyensis and *T. peregrina* were introduced into Israel from the United States in 1953 for control of the same pest and the latter became established. The infestations declined thereafter, though it has not been claimed that this was the result of parasite attack.

Green's Mealybug, *Pseudococcus citriculus* Green

This mealybug is a common pest of citrus, though usually not serious, in the Asiatic region and in the Middle East and in some countries, particularly Japan and Israel, it was long confused with *Pseudococcus comstocki* (Kuw.), which infests mainly deciduous fruit trees and various ornamentals, and elsewhere with *Planococcus citri* (Risso). In Japan, *P. citriculus* and *P. comstocki* are attacked by the same series of parasites, which normally hold them to a noneconomic level. The most important of these natural enemies are *Clausenia purpurea* Ishii, *Pseudaphycus malinus* Gahan, *Allotropa burrelli* Mues., and *Allotropa* sp. The first three have been utilized very effectively in control of *P. comstocki,* a serious pest of apple in the northeastern United States.

Pseudococcus citriculus became highly destructive to citrus in Israel after its establishment in that country. Biological control work was undertaken in 1939, when four species of parasites were imported from Japan, and later a fifth from the United States. These efforts resulted in the establishment of only one of them, *Clausenia purpurea.* It quickly superseded the three indigenous parasites already present in the orchards, even eliminating one or more of them in some localities under observation. The pest was quickly brought under satisfactory control and has remained so since that time (Rivnay, 1946).[2]

Hibiscus Mealybug, *Maconellicoccus hirsutus* (Green)

The hibiscus mealybug is reported by Ebeling (1959) to be the second most important pest of citrus in Egypt, where it also develops damaging infestations on various shade trees and ornamental plants. The importation of parasites from Java was undertaken from 1934 to 1939 in conjunction with work on *Nipaecoccus vastator*, and the parasites received were released in infestations of both pests. According to Moursi (1948), the pest is under control, though sporadic outbreaks still occur, and this result is attributed to an internal parasite, *Anagyrus kamali* Moursi. It is uncertain if this is one of the parasite species imported from Java, inasmuch as it was recognized as new and described by Moursi many years after initial release of the exotic species. Kamal (1951) also mentions the high field parasitization that was attained during the late 1930's, with heavy infestations on various plant hosts wiped out in some areas.

In view of Ebeling's report of the status of *Phenacoccus* as a pest of citrus in Egypt, it would appear that the degree of control mentioned by Moursi and Kamal has not been maintained.

Rastrococcus (Phenacoccus) iceryoides (Green)

This mealybug is a minor pest of citrus in tropical areas extending from Indonesia westwards to East Africa. Biological control work was undertaken in Celebes in 1928, though primarily for control of infestations on coffee. The well-known coccinellid predator *Cryptolaemus montrouzieri* Muls. was imported from Java and releases made in a number of plantations. Field conditions in Celebes proved to be highly favorable to the predator, and the mealybug infestations were satisfactorily suppressed by the end of the season. A single, small outbreak occurred in 1930, which was quickly brought under control, and since that time

[2]Personal communication from A. Grünberg, 1959.

the pest has remained at a low level (van der Goot, 1948). There appears to be some doubt as to the specific identity of this mealybug, as van der Goot mentions that specimens submitted in 1927 to Harold Morrison, an expert on the taxonomy of the mealybugs, were identified as *Phenacoccus spinosus* (Robbins).

THE WHITEFLIES AND BLACKFLIES (ALEYRODIDAE)

The nymphal stages of this group of insects are small and sessile in habit and feed upon the foliage of the host plant in the same manner as do those of the scale insects. The adults of both sexes are winged, some being white and others black, while the nymphs and pupae may be almost transparent, black, or in some cases completely covered by a white waxy secretion, hence the difference in common names. A considerable number of species is known to attack citrus, though relatively few are rated as major pests. Most of them have many natural enemies in the country of origin, and they appear to be exceptionally subject to successful control by the biological method.

Citrus Blackfly, *Aleurocanthus woglumi* Ashby

The citrus blackfly is native to southern Asia, but during the past fifty years has extended its range to the West Indies, Central America, Ecuador, the Seychelle Islands, and South Africa. The number of its favored food plants is unusually large and includes, in addition to all varieties and species of citrus, many fruit and shade trees and ornamental plants such as mango, coffee, and *Ardisia revoluta*. The heavy infestations on citrus and mango in Cuba represented a serious threat to the citrus industry of the United States, especially to nearby Florida, because of the danger of its accidental entry there. This situation prompted the development of a cooperative project between the United States Department of Agriculture and the Cuban Department of Agriculture, Commerce, and Labor for its control on that island by biological means. This was initiated in 1928 and extended through 1932.

The eminent Italian entomologist F. Silvestri (1927) had noted and described several parasites of apparently high effectiveness in southeastern Asia while engaged upon another mission for the University of California in 1925, and this information provided the basis for the parasite collection program. The survey in Asia covered Malaya, Indonesia, Burma, India, and Ceylon and, with the collection and shipment of parasite material to Cuba, extended from 1928 to 1931 (Clausen and Berry, 1932). The blackfly occurs only on citrus in the Asian region, and for that reason infested foliage could not be shipped to Cuba, as that practice would involve risk of introduction of citrus canker into the island. Accordingly, seedlings of other host plants known to be acceptable in Cuba were artificially infested, the parasites established upon the pest stock, and the plants then crated and shipped to Cuba. Later, infested plants in Wardian cages were transported from Cuba to Malaya (fig. 6–10), an adequate stock of the several parasites released in the cages after arrival there, and the entire lot then brought back to Cuba. This method was successful, though the round trip required nearly six months, of which about half was on shipboard.

The survey in Malaya and other countries of tropical Asia revealed the occurrence there of five species of internal parasites attacking the pest, each one being dominant in some portion of the host range and each apparently fully capable of holding the infestations to a very low level under conditions favorable to it.

Of the five parasite and two predator species shipped to Cuba, one parasite, *Eretmocerus serius* Silv., and the two coccinellid beetles, *Catana clauseni* Chapin and *Scymnus smithianus* Silv., became established.

Eretmocerus, the first of the imported natural enemies to be released in Cuba, proved to be perfectly adapted to conditions in that island

Fig. 6–10. Wardian cages containing potted plants infested with citrus blackfly, on shipboard for transport of parasites and predators from Malaya to Cuba. (After Clausen and Berry, 1932.)

and quickly demonstrated its capacity to control the blackfly. A colony of 100 parasites released in the center of a five acre orchard was often sufficient to bring about full economic control in six to nine months. The early success with *Eretmocerus* made unnecessary any further attempts to establish the remaining four species of parasites, and further importations were therefore discontinued.

The coccinellid predator *Catana clauseni* feeds mainly on the eggs and first-instar larvae of the blackfly, and under favorable conditions proved capable of controlling heavy infestations in three to six months, even more rapidly than *Eretmocerus*. Such control, however, was not consistent. While *Catana* was effective in reducing heavy infestations, yet it proved to be of little or no value in holding them at a low level once that stage had been reached. The permanent suppression of the population was due only to the activity of *Eretmocerus*.

After the general disappearance of heavy infestations of the black-fly, *Catana* disappeared from the citrus orchards. In 1938, eight years after its initial release, it could be found only in infestations of other species of Aleyrodidae on papaya and several ornamental plants. An extended search a few years later failed to yield a single specimen, and the species may have disappeared completely from the island.

Very shortly after the effectiveness of *Eretmocerus* in control of the blackfly in Cuba became apparent, it was introduced into and became established in Haiti (1931), Panama (1931), the Bahama Islands (1931), Jamaica (1932), and Costa Rica (1933–34). Adequate control was attained in each case, though this was delayed in the Bahamas but finally accomplished with the aid of *Catana clauseni*, which was introduced there in 1938 (Richardson, 1948).

The citrus blackfly was found on the west coast of Mexico in 1935, and unsuccessful attempts were made to establish *Eretmocerus* there in 1936 and 1938. The rapid spread thereafter and the destructiveness of the pest then led to the development of a cooperative program in biological control between the U. S. Department of Agriculture and the Mexican Secretaria de Agricultura y Fomento comparable to that entered into with Cuba twenty years previously. Additional stocks of *Eretmocerus* were obtained from Panama in 1943 and generally distributed through the infested area, which by that time extended from Colima northwards to the border of Sonora (H. D. Smith, 1945). In view of the high effectiveness of this parasite in Cuba and elsewhere, it had been confidently expected that the same degree of control would be attained in Mexico. This hope, however, was not realized—the parasite proved to be unable to bring about control, apparently because of adverse climatic conditions.

The above situation made necessary an extension of the cooperative program providing for the importation of additional parasite species from southern Asia. It was felt that parasite stocks from northwest India and Pakistan, rather than from Malaya, would be more likely to prove adaptable in Mexico, as climatic conditions are more comparable. The collection and importation of natural enemies from that area was conducted by H. D. Smith of the United States Department of Agriculture during 1949–50, and led to the establishment in Mexico of *Prospaltella smithi* Silv., *P. opulenta* Silv., *P. clypealis* Silv., and *Amitus hesperidum* Silv., these representing the entire complex of effective parasites attacking the blackfly in tropical Asia with the exception of *P. divergens* Silv., which apparently is restricted to the Malayan region.

The establishment of these parasites in Mexico (fig. 6–11) was followed by a collection and distribution program extending over ten years or more that was unparalleled in manpower employed and in cost by any biological control project in any other part of the world. Some states levied a special gasoline tax to defray the cost, and at times upwards of 1,600 men were engaged on the project. During 1952 and 1953, about 242 million adult *Amitus hesperidum* alone were collected from groves showing high parasitization and released throughout the infested areas. Collections and releases of *P. smithi* and *P. opulenta* totaled about three million each, and of *P. clypealis* one million. A great many of the releases of the different species were in groves where they were already established but had not yet effected control. This delay in control was especially noticeable on the West Coast, where suppression of the heavy infestations was not accomplished until several years after initial parasite establishment.

Amitus hesperidum proved to be highly effective against heavy infestations, but was dominated later by *Prospaltella opulenta* and *P. clypealis* as the infestations became lighter. *P. opulenta* (fig. 6–12) is much better adapted to a wide range of climatic conditions than are the other two, and is especially effective in the hot, arid regions of northern Mexico. *P. clypealis*, on the

Fig. 6–11. Citrus orchard near San Luis Potosi, Mexico, which has been seriously infested by citrus blackfly. (Photo courtesy of Harry L. Maltby.)

contrary, is best adapted to the humid areas (Smith, Maltby, and Jimenez-Jimenez, 1964).

Jimenez-Jimenez (1961) records aggregate field parasitization by the four species in practically all infested areas as ranging up to 97 per cent, with few isolated collections showing 50 per cent or less. Commercial control is stated to be attained when the parasitization reaches the 61 to 80 per cent level.

In general, it may be said that the citrus blackfly is under satisfactory control over the entire infested area of Mexico, with only sporadic and localized outbreaks occurring in some sections due to drift of insecticides applied to other crops or to temporary climatic irregularities. The outcome of the program certainly rates as one of the outstanding successes in the biological control of insect pests of citrus trees.

In more recent years, attempts at biological control of the citrus blackfly have been made in other countries, *Eretmocerus serius* having been introduced into the Seychelle Islands in 1955, Kenya in 1958–59, and South Africa in 1959 and 1962, and *Amitus hesperidum* into Ecuador in 1955. Establishment was attained in each instance, but the final outcome has been reported only for Kenya, where satisfactory control was brought about very quickly (Wheatley, 1964), and in the Seychelles, where control was likewise attained.

Spiny Blackfly, *Aleurocanthus spiniferus* (Quaint.)

The spiny blackfly is another of the species of the genus *Aleurocanthus*, native to southern Asia, that is destructive to citrus and has spread to other parts of the world. In its native habitat, it is attacked by the same series of natural enemies that is found upon *A. woglumi*, and in most areas these hold it under reasonable control, though damaging infestations occur at times, especially in India.

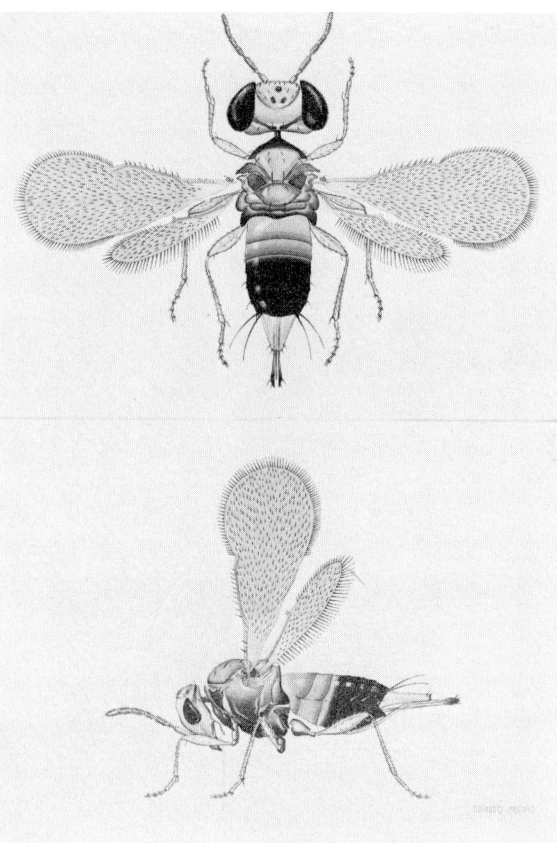

Fig. 6–12. Dorsal and side views of *Prospaltella opulenta* Silv., one of the most effective parasites of citrus blackfly. (Courtesy of U. S. Department of Agriculture.)

Aleurocanthus spiniferus became established in Japan in the vicinity of Nagasaki about 1915 and thereafter spread rapidly to other parts of the island of Kyushu and became exceedingly destructive. The internal parasite *Prospaltella smithi* Silv. was brought to Japan from South China by F. Silvestri in 1925 and, according to Kuwana (1934), quickly brought the pest under full economic control in all infested areas.

The spiny blackfly was found to have established itself on the island of Guam, of the Mariana Islands in the Pacific, in 1951, and steps were immediately taken to import its natural enemies. Five internal parasites, derived from the related *A. woglumi* in Mexico, but originally coming from Malaya and India, were imported in 1952. Two of these, *Prospaltella smithi* and *Amitus hesperidum* Silv., became established. The pest has been fully controlled insofar as the infestations on citrus are concerned, but not to the same extent on other host plants, such as rose and grape (Peterson, 1955). *P. smithi* proved to be the most effective of the two species under the conditions prevailing in the Marianas.

Citrus Whitefly, *Dialeurodes citri* (Ashm.)

The citrus whitefly was at one time a major pest of citrus and various ornamental plants in Florida and is of general distribution, though of little consequence as a pest, throughout tropical Asia. The early attempts at biological control in Florida involved the use of a series of entomogenous fungi, of which the most important were *Aegerita webberi* Fawcett and *Aschersonia aleyrodis* Webber (fig. 6–13). The information regarding these fungi and their employment in the control program has been reviewed by Fawcett (1948) and Steinhaus (1949).

An account of the early studies on these fungi, methods of culture, and application for field control of the whitefly is given by Fawcett (1908), while Berger (1910) and Watson and Berger (1937) discuss further the methods of culture and distribution and the results obtained from their use. The red *Aschersonia aleyrodis* was cultured on sweet-potato strips and these cultures distributed to growers, who prepared a water suspension and applied it as a spray at the rate of one pint of culture per acre. Another method of distribution was that of obtaining a quantity of infested leaves bearing infected whitefly stages, placing them in water, and using the resulting spore suspension as a spray. Watson (1912) mentions that a single commercial spray operator treated 100,000 trees in 1911, and, in addition, supplied fungous material to a large number of growers for their own use.

In its sterile form, the second fungus, *Aegerita webberi,* is brown in color. The perfect

Fig. 6–13. The red Aschersonia fungus *Aschersonia aleyrodis* Webber, on larvae of the citrus whitefly. The fungus pustules have a central mass of red surrounded by a white margin over the larvae after being killed by the penetration of the hyphae.

form has not been found. The stroma covers the entire insect, and during the latter part of the season the marginal hyphae may extend over the entire lower surface of the leaf and may even reach the upper surface. This fungus was first found by H. J. Webber at Manatee, Florida, and proved to be highly effective in control of the whitefly under certain conditions. Since *A. webberi* could not be grown in quantity in pure culture the methods employed for its distribution consisted either of (1) pinning leaves bearing infected larvae onto leaves of trees where control was desired, (2) washing off the pustules in water and applying this suspension as a spray, or (3) planting young trees bearing diseased insects in such a way that the foliage intermingles with that of the infested trees.

An extensive study of the natural control of the whitefly by entomogenous fungi, and an evaluation of the supposed benefits to be derived from artificial dissemination, is given by Morrill and Back (1912). The conclusions reached by these workers are somewhat at variance from those presented by earlier workers. It was concluded that the fungi were fully effective in controlling the pest in low-lying "hammock" orchards such as are found in some parts of Manatee and Lee counties, Florida, and periodically in some other areas. At the time these studies were made, the several species of fungi had become generally distributed over the state, and the field tests reported upon, involving distribution by spraying and other means, indicated that little or no benefit could be expected where the fungi were already present in the orchards, even when at only very low levels. A possible explanation for the contradictory results is offered by Fawcett (1944), to the effect that the experiments by Morrill and Back were conducted during a period of approximate saturation for infection, whereas the earlier work by Berger was at times of unsaturation or of lag in possible infection for the prevailing conditions. If this is the case, it presents considerable difficulties in the practical utilization of these fungi in control programs, as the determination of the proper time for application would be beyond the capabilities of the growers themselves. In any case, the artificial dissemination of the fungi in the citrus orchards of Florida has been discontinued.

Whatever may have been the merits of the program for utilization of the fungi for whitefly control, the fact remains that the status of the whitefly on citrus in Florida has changed greatly during the past forty years. According to Woglum (1913), it was at that time the most serious pest of citrus in the Gulf Coast States and, on the basis of injury and difficulty of control, was the most important obstacle to citrus fruit production in the entire United States. Today it is a relatively minor pest, and the parasitic fungi may well have played an important role in its suppression.

As a part of the biological control program against the whitefly, the importation of insect enemies was undertaken during 1910–11, when Woglum (1913) conducted investigations in India, Pakistan, and other South Asian countries where the pest is presumed to be native. His report mentions the finding of only light infestations on commercial citrus in those countries, heavy infestations being found only where the trees were grown as hedges. Such infestations were also present at times on an ornamental plant, *Jasminium sambac*. Two natural enemies were found, an internal parasite, *Prospaltella lahorensis* How., and a coccinellid predator, *Catana parcesetosa* (Sic.) *Serangiella flavescens* (Motsch.).

Stocks of these two natural enemies were built up and brought back to Florida, arriving there in December, 1911. Unfortunately, all host material then available was in the pupal stage and unsuitable for feeding or reproduction by either parasite or predator. The stocks died out without any field releases having been made. No further attempt has been made to import and establish them. These two species may well be effective in control under more moderate climatic conditions than those prevailing in northwest India and Pakistan, and their importation and release would be well worthwhile in any citrus area where the whitefly persists as an economic pest.

Woolly Whitefly, *Aleurothrixus floccosus* (Mask.)

The woolly whitefly, *Aleurothrixus floccosus* (Mask.) (= *Aleurothrixus howardi* (Quaint.)), is a minor pest of citrus in Florida and occurs also in several countries on the west coast of South America, and is destructive at times in Peru. In 1957, W. Ebeling took stocks of several natural enemies from Florida and elsewhere to that country, these including, according to Beingolea (1959), *Eretmocerus haldemani* How. and the coccinellid predator *Catana clauseni* Chapin. However, A. G. Selhime (personal communication), who assisted in assembling the material in Florida, states that the dominant parasite was *E. portoricensis* Doz. instead, and that the predator was *C. parcesetosa*

Sic., derived from stocks imported from Pakistan. Reports are not yet available regarding their establishment or effectiveness in control.

THE FRUIT FLIES (TEPHRITIDAE) AND OTHER FRUIT FEEDERS

The fruit flies are destructive pests of citrus in practically all parts of the world except the United States. The best known, and those upon which the most effort has been expended in biological control, are the Mediterranean fruit fly *Ceratitis capitata* (Wied.) and the Oriental fruit fly *Dacus dorsalis* Hendel. The fruit fly pests of the West Indies and Central and South America are native species of the genus *Anastrepha*, with the problem aggravated in a few countries by the relatively recent establishment of the Mediterranean fruit fly.

Although there are important fruit feeders among other groups of insects, especially of the Lepidoptera, in subtropical and tropical Asia, they have not spread beyond their original confines, and no efforts have thus far been made to control them by the biological method.

Mediterranean Fruit Fly, *Ceratitis capitata* (Wied.)

Efforts directed towards the biological control of the Mediterranean fruit fly were first initiated in Hawaii in 1912, at which time F. Silvestri was engaged by the Board of Agriculture and Forestry to conduct a worldwide search, with special attention to Africa, for effective natural enemies. His investigations extended to many countries (Silvestri, 1914), and his importations during 1913 resulted in the establishment in Hawaii of two larval parasites, *Opius humilis* Silv. from South Africa and *O. tryoni* (Cam.) from Australia. These two parasites were supplemented in 1914 by *O. fullawayi* (Silv.) and a pupal parasite, *Tetrastichus giffardianus* Silv., both from West Africa, which also became established (Back and Pemberton, 1918).

Opius humilis was the first to be released in June, 1913, and quickly became abundant in the field, effecting parasitization up to 31.5 per cent by 1915, but declined thereafter as *O. tryoni* took over the dominant role. The latter species had become established through the release of only sixteen females, three on Oahu and thirteen on Hawaii, during the summer of 1913. Data are given by Willard and Mason (1937) on field parasitization by the four species for the twenty year period from 1914 to 1933. These figures are from rearings of some forty varieties of fruits and show aggregate annual parasitization ranging up to 56.4 per cent.

The parasitization of fruit fly larvae in different fruits is highly variable, depending in large part on the depth at which the larvae become embedded in the fruit. The larvae in shallow-pulped fruits such as coffee are accessible to the parasites throughout their developmental period, and consequently are subject to heavy attack. The figures for 1924 (Willard and Bissell, 1930), for example, show parasitization of larvae in coffee berries of 45.0 to 74.6 per cent, Indian almond 36.2 to 65.1 per cent, mango 14.8 to 19.4 per cent, and Chinese orange 5.6 to 16.7 per cent.

From the economic point of view, the biological control program in Hawaii was successful only on coffee, where a great reduction in infestation occurred. Infestations in some other fruits were somewhat reduced, though not sufficiently to prevent substantial loss.

The establishment of the three species of *Opius* and their interrelations, which soon became evident in the field, has led to considerable speculation as to the advantage or otherwise of introduction of a single species as against a series of species attacking the same host stage. *O. humilis* was first established and quickly attained a high parasitization, but declined later when in competition with *O. tryoni*. The first-instar of the latter always destroys that of *humilis* when both are contained in a host larva. Pemberton and Willard (1918*a*) believed that *O. humilis* was the most efficient of the three species of *Opius*, and studies relating to the competition between the three in the field led them to the conclusion that the net result of establishment of *O. tryoni* and *O. fullawayi* has been detrimental to the control program.

Total parasitization of larvae in coffee berries in the Kona District on the island of Hawaii ranged from 45.5 per cent in 1914 to 94.4 per cent in 1933. *O. humilis* predominated from 1914 to 1917, after which it declined very sharply, and not a single specimen was reared from that fruit between 1928 and 1933. However, it has persisted in other fruits. A surprising development was the complete disappearance of this parasite from the island of Oahu, the last collection having been made there in the early 1930's.

The Mediterranean fruit fly has become much less of a pest in Hawaii since the establishment of the Oriental fruit fly in the Islands in 1946. The latter has almost completely displaced it at the lower elevations, though it is still destructive to some deciduous fruits at elevations of 2,000 feet or more (Bess, 1953). The Oriental fruit fly parasite *Opius oophilus* Full. proved to be fully adapted to the Mediterranean fruit fly and, to a very large extent superseded *O. tryoni*, which previously had been the most effective parasite attacking it. Further, the field parasitization by *O. oophilus* became substantially higher than that recorded for *O. tryoni* in preceding years.

The early studies on the natural enemies of the Mediterranean fruit fly in Hawaii revealed that, aside from the imported parasites, the big-headed ant *Pheidole megacephala* (F.) is an important controlling agent. Pemberton and Willard (1918*b*) reported that this ant consistently destroys one-third to four-fifths of the fly larvae as they emerge from the fruit to pupate in the soil.

Biological control work against this fruit fly has been carried on in many countries, utilizing not only the parasite species already mentioned, but additional species of parasites and several predators known to attack it. These included a series of parasites established in Hawaii from 1948 to 1951 for control of the Oriental fruit fly. None of these efforts has resulted as yet in any appreciable economic benefit.

Natal Fruit Fly, *Pterandus rosa* (Karsch.)

The Natal fruit fly became established in Mauritius in the early 1950's, and increased greatly during the following year, proving to be a serious pest of citrus as well as other fruits. It largely replaced the Mediterranean fruit fly as the major fruit pest of the island. A series of larval and pupal parasites was introduced from Hawaii between 1957 and 1959, of which the egg-larval parasite *Opius oophilus* Full. and *Syntomosphyrum indicum* Silv., which attacks the full-grown larvae, became established on both pest species (Orian and Moutia, 1960). It is as yet too early to evaluate their effectiveness in control.

Oriental Fruit Fly, *Dacus dorsalis* Hendel

Very soon after the discovery of the Oriental fruit fly in Hawaii in 1946, measures were undertaken for the importation of natural enemies for its control. The foreign exploration was first conducted by the Hawaiian Board of Agriculture and Forestry and joined later by the United States Department of Agriculture and the University of California under a general cooperative program. The importation of natural enemies began in 1947 and continued through 1951, during which period most of the tropical and subtropical areas of the world were surveyed. Shipments of fruit fly puparia to Hawaii comprised more than 60 species and totalled 4.25 million (Clausen, Clancy, and Chock, 1965). The parasites from this material were reared out, some of them propagated in the insectary, and releases made of thirty-two species and varieties (Bess, van den Bosch, and Haramoto, 1961). The total was 890,000 from 1948 to 1952, with 2.5 million released in succeeding years to 1962. The majority of these were larval parasites of the genus *Opius*. Seven species became established on the Oriental fruit fly, of which only *O. longicaudatus* (Ashm.) var. *malaiensis* Full., *O. vandenboschi* Full., and *O. oophilus* Full., in turn, became abundant and of general distribution on the Islands.

The course of events following the establishment of these three species of *Opius* is of particular interest. *Opius longicaudatus* from Malaya was the first of the three to be released in substantial numbers, followed by *O. vandenboschi* and *O. oophilus*, also from Malaya. The ensuing competition resulted in the replacement of *O. longicaudatus* by *O. vandenboschi* in 1949, which was in turn superseded by *O. oophilus* in 1950 (van den Bosch and Haramoto, 1953). The latter species has retained its dominant position since that time, the other two becoming relatively scarce and, in fact, have disappeared from some areas. *O. longicaudatus* oviposits in the second- or third-instar fruit fly larvae, *O. vandenboschi* in those of the early first-instar and *O. oophilus* (fig. 6–14) in the eggs. The latter species is dominant when in competition for individual hosts.

Between 1950 and 1955, the field parasitization of larvae developing in wild guavas, the major reservoir of fruit fly populations, ranged from 60 to 79.1 per cent, with an average of 72 per cent (Bess and Haramoto, 1958, 1961). The field parasitization has remained stabilized at approximately that figure since 1950. Actual mortality through *O. oophilus* was higher than the above figure because of death of many fruit fly eggs from disease transmitted by the parasite at the time of oviposition. Fruit infestation was substantially reduced because of this high parasitization, though the fruit fly still remains a serious pest. Fortunately, it is only a minor pest of citrus, its preferred host fruits being avocado, mango, and papaya.

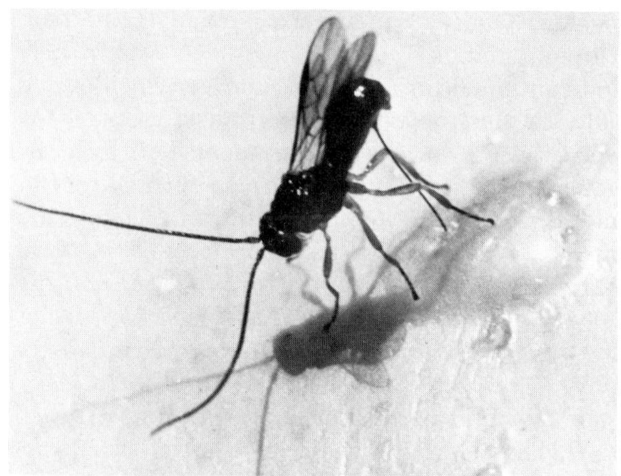

Fig. 6–14. ***Opius oophilus*** **Full., a parasite of the oriental fruit fly imported into Hawaii from Malaya, ovipositing in host eggs beneath the skin of an infested papaya fruit. (Photo by L. D. Christenson.)**

After the effectiveness of certain of the parasites had been domonstrated in Hawaii, nine species of *Opius* and two chalcidoid parasites were imported into Guam, Mariana Islands, from Hawaii between 1949 and 1955 for control of the same pest. Of these, *Syntomosphyrum indicum* is established and five of the species of *Opius* doubtfully so (Peterson, 1957).

Queensland Fruit Fly, *Dacus tryoni* (Frogg.)

This native fruit fly is the most important of the group attacking citrus and many other fruits in Australia. A brief account of the several efforts to control it and the Mediterranean fruit fly by the biological method is given by Wilson (1960). The first importations of natural enemies date back to the period from 1903 to 1907, when a series of ten or more parasites and predators were obtained from Brazil and India. Most of these were released in only small numbers, though the total for *Syntomosphyrum indicum* from 1908 to 1910 was 250,000. None of them became established. From 1928 to 1937, additional parasites were obtained from Hawaii and India for release in New South Wales, these including *Opius humilis* and *O. fullawayi*, but again establishment was not attained.

The most recent importations, beginning in 1952, comprised seven or more species obtained from Hawaii, where several of them had proved to be effective in the partial control of the Oriental fruit fly. The most important of these were *Opius oophilus* Full., *O. longicaudatus* (Ashm.) varieties, and *O. vandenboschi* Full. Relatively small-scale releases of the first two in two areas in New South Wales in 1956–57 failed to achieve establishment, and the program was then changed to provide much larger numbers and for release over a considerably greater area. The 1958–59 releases comprised more than one-half million adults, mainly of *Opius* spp., but including small numbers of three chalcidoid parasites also, and were made at 102 locations in New South Wales, Queensland, western Australia, and on Lord Howe Island.

Reports on the progress of the program have been given by Snowball *et al.* (1962) and Snowball and Lukins (1964). The latest report indicates that *O. oophilus* is well established in eastern Australia, though it disappeared from Lord Howe Islands a few years after release and apparent establishment. This parasite proved to be well adapted to *Dacus tryoni* and also reproduced in the field on several other fruit flies. It has shown a marked range in preference for certain fruit types, parasitization by larvae in *Averrhoa carambola* being much higher than of those in mango and *Citrus* spp. Mean winter temperatures of 60° F or below are highly adverse to the continued maintenance of populations of *O. oophilus*. The extent of parasitization of *D. tryoni* has not been sufficient to influence the level of fruit infestation.

The only other parasite of the series originally imported to become established is *O. longicaudatus*, which has persisted only on Lord Howe Island.

South American Fruit Fly, *Anastrepha fratercula* (Wied.)

This fruit fly is a serious pest of citrus in several countries of South America, especially Argentina, Brazil, and Peru. Importations of parasites into Brazil for its control, and that of the Mediterranean fruit fly also, comprised *Opius tryoni* (Cam.), *O. fletcheri* Silv., and *Tetrastichus giffardianus* Silv., obtained from Hawaii in 1937. The latter species, which attacks the full-grown fruit fly larvae, became established but apparently had little or no effect in controlling the infestations.

A second effort to control this pest was made in 1939 and following years in Argentina, in this instance utilizing the native parasites *Opius tucumana* (Blanch.), *O. anastrephae* Vier., and *Eucoila pelleranoi Brèthes*. These were reared out from infested fruits and distributed widely in the Province of Tucumán, but no benefits from this program have been reported.

A more extensive program for control of *A. fraterculu* and others of that genus was undertaken in Peru in 1942, when 418,000 field-collected puparia of *Anastrepha* were obtained from Tucumán. From these were reared 11,551 adults of the three species of parasites named above (Wille, 1958). Mass-rearing of these parasites was unsuccessful, and the remaining stocks were then released in the field. None became established.

Mexican Fruit Fly, *Anastrepha ludens* (Loew)

This fruit fly is a serious pest of all varieties of citrus except lemon and lime in Mexico, Central America, and northern South America. Importations of natural enemies into Mexico from 1953 to 1956 for its control comprised at least twelve species of larval and pupal parasites derived from the Oriental and Meditterranean fruit flies in Hawaii. Tests showed that some of these species of *Opius* were able to reproduce in *Anastrepha*, but none became established in the field. The chalcidoid parasites, in general, have a much wider host range than do the larval parasites, and one of them, *Syntomosphyrum indicum* Silv., became established on *A. ludens* (Jimenez-Jimenez, 1958).

Southern Green Stink Bug, *Nezara viridula* (L.)

This pentatomid bug, known by various common names in other countries, is widely distributed through many of the tropical and subtropical areas of the world, and feeds upon a wide range of fruit and vegetable crops. It is a minor pest of citrus, at times causing loss through its feeding on the fruit.

Two effective natural enemies of this bug are known, one of which is an egg parasite, *Telenomus basalis* (Woll.) (*Microphanurus megacephalus* [Ashm.]), native to the Mediterranean region, and the other a tachinid fly, *Trichopoda pennipes* (F.), which occurs in North America and the West Indies. The latter attacks the last-instar nymphs and the adults of the bug. The major effort at biological control of *N. viridula* has been in Australia (Wilson, 1960), where the variety *smaragdula* has become a serious pest of many crops. *Telenomus* was imported from Egypt in 1933 and *Trichopoda* from the United States from 1932 onwards. The egg parasite quickly became established in western Australia, and from there it was distributed to all other parts of the country. This parasite was an outstanding success in control of the pest in Western and South Australia and was also effective in the coastal areas of New South Wales. It has been much less effective in the inland areas, possibly because of the lower winter temperatures.

Additional stocks of *Telenomus*, possibly representing different biological races, were imported from Montserrat and Italy in 1953 and 1956, respectively, in the hope that they might be more effective in the inland areas than was the race obtained originally from Egypt. Other egg parasites have since been introduced from Trinidad and Pakistan, but their establishment and effectiveness have not yet been reported upon. Extended releases of *Trichopoda* have failed to effect establishment in any area.

Telenomus has been introduced into several of the islands of the South Pacific, and into South Africa, but the outcome is not known except for Fiji, where it is said to have brought about fair control of the pest (O'Connor, 1950).

THE PLANT-FEEDING MITES (ACARINA)

Citrus Red Mite, *Panonychus citri* (McG.)

Several species of mites of the familes Tetranychidae and Eriophyidae are serious pests of citrus in various parts of the world. *P. citri* now ranks as the most important of all pests of this crop in California. Importation of natural enemies for its control dates back to 1900–01, when several species of predaceous Coccinellidae were obtained from Australia. One of these, *Stethorus vagans* (Blackb.) was recovered during the seasons of release and in 1902, but did not persist. Another species of the genus, *S. gilvifrons* (Muls.), imported from South China in 1950 and Turkey in 1955, was released in considerable numbers in Ventura and San Diego Counties, and field recoveries were made in both areas, yet establishment is still uncertain.

Beginning in 1953 and continuing to the present time, special attention has been given to this problem in California. Collections of numerous natural enemies have been made in many countries, including South China, India, Pakistan, South Africa, the Mediterranean region, Mexico, and Central America. Nine additional species of *Stethorus* have been obtained, also a predaceous dustywing, *Spiliconis picticornis* Banks, and a number of species of predaceous mites of the genus *Typhlodromus*. These latter are often the most effective of the natural enemies of the plant-feeding mites. The imported predators were released in infestations of avocado mites as well as in those of the citrus red mite. To date, none is known to be established.

Because of the increasing seriousness of the mite problem and the difficulties experienced in attaining satisfactory insecticidal control, the search for effective natural enemies is being pressed assiduously.

BIOLOGY OF PARASITIC INSECTS

The parasitic insects show a tremendous range in their biological characteristics to adapt themselves to that mode of life, and knowledge of these characteristics is essential in the rearing and colonization programs of any species being utilized in biological control. Some parasites of scale insects produce females generation after generation without intervention of the male, and thus provide a marked advantage in rearing and in ensuring that the field colonies will not be lost because of widespread dispersal preventing mating. Other species produce only female progeny after mating, or males in varying proportions, dependent upon the temperature under which they are reared. These factors must be taken into account for most effective and economical insectary production.

A very significant discovery that had a direct bearing on the parasite rearing and field release programs for control of several citrus pests was one by Flanders (1937) relating to several species of *Coccophagus* introduced into California for the control of black scale and mealybugs. He found, in several species of that genus, that the males are hyperparasitic, developing not as direct parasites of the scale insect or mealybug, but instead, upon the female larvae of their own or of another parasite species. This habit made necessary a change from the customary method of field release, as a colony of mated females would produce only female progeny which, in the absence of males, would remain unmated, and the colony would therefore fail to establish itself. Several species of *Prospaltella*, parasitic on the citrus blackfly, have a similar habit.

In a further study of this phenomenon, Flanders (1959*a*) mentions the discovery by O. Beingolea in Peru that the females of two species of *Encarsia* develop internally as parasites of whiteflies, whereas the males are produced mainly in the eggs of a leaf-worm infesting the same plants. This rearing of males of scale insect parasites from lepidopterous eggs had been recorded several times previously, but was considered to be more or less accidental rather than the normal habit of the species.

Reference has already been made to *Casca chinensis*, one of the more important of the parasites of the California red scale in South China, that has been introduced into California, though unsuccessfully, on several occasions. The males occur commonly on citrus trees in South China, yet none has ever been reared from the red scale. Extended study and search have failed to reveal the host of the males, and until that becomes known there is no possibility of establishing the species in California or elsewhere.

A different aspect of the problem relates to host-determined races of parasites, in which one race of a species attacks a certain host insect in one part of the world and another race a different host species in another region. Two examples might be cited. *Comperiella bifasciata*, reared from *Aonidiella taxus* in Japan, develops readily in the aspidistra and yellow scales, but not in red scale, whereas the same species from the red scale in South China is equally well adapted to the yellow scale. Also, *Prospaltella perniciosi*, a well-known parasite of the San Jose scale in North America, has never been recorded from the red scale, yet a race of that species, fully adapted to the latter scale, has been obtained from Formosa. They differ biologically in that the San Jose scale race produces hyperparasitic males, whereas populations of the red scale race consist of females only. It may be that these so-called host-determined races are in reality distinct species, but thus far no morphological characters have been discovered to distinguish them.

The few examples cited above illustrate some of the complexities that exist in the reproductive processes of parasitic insects and in their host relationships. Others equally important will undoubtedly be encountered in future work, and it is therefore essential that the basic biological studies be made on each species being introduced in order to give the maximum opportunity for successful rearing and establishment in the field.

ADAPTIVE RACES OF PARASITIC INSECTS

A great many insect parasites have been found to be fully effective over only a small portion of the range of the host insect and therefore of reduced value in field control. This situation is usually due to certain climatic factors, such as extremes of heat or cold. Plant breeders have long been engaged in the production of races of crops adaptable to specific climatic conditions, or having other desirable characteristics, and there would seem to be no insurmountable barrier to the attainment of the same objective with insect parasites.

A start along this line has been made by DeBach (1958) in an attempt to develop a race of *Aphytis lingnanesis*, an imported parasite of the California red scale, which is effective in the coastal areas but adversely affected by the cooler winters and hotter summers of the interior valleys of southern California. Stocks of the parasite have been subjected to irradiation to induce genetic changes, and then selective procedures were employed in rearing them at reduced temperatures, involving not in excess of 50 per cent mortality in each generation. This work, however, is still in the preliminary stage, and it is yet to be seen if a race with the necessary tolerance to cold and heat can be produced and will maintain itself in the field.

Another approach to the problem is by hybridization, whereby a desirable character from one race is introduced into another to produce a form more efficient in control of the pest than either parent. This approach is likewise under study with *Aphytis* spp., but here again only preliminary studies have yet been made.

The high toxicity of the new organic insecticides to many parasites, often resulting in their almost complete elimination from orchards regularly treated for control of various pests, has led to the suggestion that, by a selective process, a race of any given parasite species might be developed that would be tolerant to at least some of these chemicals. Some work has been done along this line, and with encouraging results. It would seem, however, that such "races" would develop in nature in orchards or fields subject to regular insecticidal treatments, just as has occurred with many of the pest insects themselves. Some of the latter have developed almost complete immunity within a relatively short period of time.

SUPERSEDENCE OF PARASITE SPECIES

One of the interesting developments in the biological control of a number of pest insects, including several on citrus, is the replacement of one parasite species by another as a result of competition between them. That this should occur, even when the host population is apparently sufficiently high to support several species of similar habit, and attacking the same host stage, is difficult to explain, yet it unquestionably has occurred in several instances. The first such example to become known involved two egg predators of the black scale in California, *Moranila (Tomocera) californica*, long present and previously abundant in the state, and *Scutellista cyanea*, imported from South Africa in 1900–01. Within ten years after the establishment of *Scutellista*, *Moranila* had almost completely disappeared from the scene. Thus, *Scutellista* usurped the position formerly held by *Moranila*, with no resulting gain in terms of control.

A somewhat similar situation exists today in California with respect to a series of *Aphytis* parasitic on the California red scale. Originally only *A. chrysomphali* was present in the state, but in recent years a number of additional species have been imported and two became established. Interspecific competition has been severe and the situation is not yet stabilized (DeBach and Sundby, 1963), but it appears that climatic conditions indirectly may be the governing factor in determining which species will win in competition and dominate in the several citrus-producing areas.

Another striking example of recent occurrence involves a series of *Opius* species introduced into Hawaii from Malaya for control of the Oriental fruit fly. The first, *O. longicaudatus*, quickly became very abundant and showed great promise, but was supplanted by *O. vandenboschi* the following year. Then came *O. oophilus* to take over the dominant role. This last species has maintained a consistently high rate of parasitization through 1967, whereas the first two have persisted at only a very low level. It was mentioned earlier that this interspecific competition was mainly between species of similar habit, but this is not strictly the case in the present instance. *Opius longicaudatus* oviposits mainly in second- and third-instar larvae, *O. vandenboschi* only in those of the first-instar and *O. oophilus* only in the eggs. Obviously, the last-named species has a decided advantage in that all fruit fly eggs are within its reach for oviposition, whereas a portion of the larvae may be so deeply embedded in the pulp of the fruit as to be inaccessible to the other two species. Also, it is the victor over the other two when in competition in individual fruit fly larvae.

The supersedence of parasite species, so well illustrated in the case of the Oriental fruit fly, is paralleled by that of the Mediterranean fruit fly, also in Hawaii, which has already been discussed. The same parasite, *O. oophilus*, became dominant over *O. tryoni*.

The results of competition thus may have an important bearing upon the outcome of a biological control project. It has been asserted by a number of workers in this field that a single parasite species may be more effective in control than a series of species, all attacking the same host stage. Others are convinced that the combined effect of a series cannot be less than by any one of them alone, and is likely to be greater. This is a question that is extremely difficult to answer, even on the basis of extended field experimentation, and the general practice is still to introduce all promising parasites of a pest in the hope that one of them, or several, will prove to be effective. In the great majority of highly successful biological control projects, one parasite or predator species alone, rather than several, has been responsible for subjugation of the pest.

MASS PRODUCTION OF PARASITES AND PREDATORS

In any biological control program involving the importation of parasites and predators from abroad, it is highly desirable to colonize the natural enemies in adequate numbers throughout the range of the pest insect as soon as possible. Such a program not only reduces the total cost, but ensures that full opportunity is offered for establishment under conditions most favorable to the natural enemies. In many cases, natural enemies will prove to be adaptable to only a portion of the host range. Early determination of this fact is important in shaping the later phases of the program.

The initial importations of any parasite or predator from abroad usually comprise only a relatively small number, at times only a few individuals. This may necessitate insectary production even before the first releases can be made. Then comes the mass production, if the pest being dealt with is of sufficient importance to justify it.

Another type of program is mass production of a parasite or predator that is already well established but, for one reason or other, is not fully effective and therefore requires seasonal or periodic release over a large portion of the host range to reinforce the populations already existing in the fields or orchards. This is illustrated by the use of the well-known Australian ladybird beetle *Cryptolaemus montrouzieri* in control of various mealybug species.

A mass production program may and usually does involve the rearing of millions of a particular species each season. This must be done on an economical basis, and that requirement rules out the rearing of the pest insect and the natural enemy upon potted citrus plants, for example, or any similar procedure, as the cost would be prohibitive. The key to a successful mass production program is almost invariably the production of the pest insect itself in the required numbers; the production of the parasite or predator is then a relatively simple matter, assuming that its biological characteristics have already been determined. The Department of Biological Control of the California Agricultural Experiment Station, in its work on many citrus insects, has been a pioneer in this type of work.

One of the outstanding examples of mass production was that first developed by Branigan (1916) and perfected by H. S. Smith and Armitage (1931) for the rearing of *Cryptolaemus montrouzieri,* and its use seasonally since 1917, for the econtrol of the citrophilus and citrus mealybugs in southern California. It was found that several mealybug species would develop fully as well upon potato sprouts, grown under dim light in the insectary, as on their normal host trees in the orchards. The potatoes were sprouted in shallow trays (fig. 6–15), seeded with mealybugs and then, when the infestation became heavy (fig. 6–16), a generation of *Cryptolaemus* was produced upon them. Individual cage units were unnecessary; instead, room units with a capacity of 120 to 1,000 trays provided highly economical production. The cost of production and distribution in 1967 was approximately $2.50 to $4.00 per thousand beetles, the number required per acre under the recommended schedule of release.

So successful did this program become that by 1927, fifteen insectaries were in operation in

Fig. 6–15. Tiers of trays of sprouted potatoes used in the mass production of mealybug parasites and predators. (Photo by T. W. Fisher.)

southern California solely for the production of this one predator. Some were built and operated by counties and others by cooperative organizations and private, large-scale citrus growers. The largest was the Orange County Insectary (fig. 6–17), comprising twenty-two building units. During the 1927 season, at the peak of activity along this line, more than 42 million beetles were produced and distributed by these insectaries (Essig, 1931). The need for *Cryptolaemus* was very sharply reduced after 1928 because of the high effectiveness of the internal parasites of the citrophilus mealybug that were imported from Australia in that year. The beetle is still being reared in some numbers in Ventura County for use against occasional outbreaks of the citrus mealybug.

Potato sprouts again proved to be useful in a biological control program in California when it was found that the black scale would reproduce satisfactorily upon them. However, the nutritional requirements of the black scale were not identical to those of the mealybugs, and a different variety of potato was required. With some modifications (Flanders, 1942*b*), the original potato sprout method has been employed in the insectary production of millions of a series of black scale parasites imported since 1920 from various parts of the world.

The potato has also proved to be useful in the large-scale production of various armored scales, especially the California red scale, in California. Here it is the tuber itself rather than the sprouts upon which the pest insect is grown. Egg-shaped tubers of the White Rose variety are most satisfactory, and these become heavily encrusted with scale, permitting a high production of parasites with a minimum of space and labor (Flanders, 1947). This method was further refined by Flanders (1951) for the mass production of the golden chalcid *Aphytis chrysomphali* (Mercet) for periodic and inundative releases against the red scale. The cost was estimated at that time to be approximately $100 to $500 per million parasites.

Fig. 6–16. A tray of sprouted potatoes heavily infested with the citrophilus mealybug, for mass production of *Cryptolaemus montrouzieri* Muls. (After Smith and Armitage, 1931.)

Later development in the mass production of red scale parasites is by DeBach and White (1960), and was employed successfully in the propagation of *Aphytis lingnanensis* Comp. and a series of other species of the genus imported in recent years from South China, India, and Pakistan. Several important changes in techniques were adopted: first, the oleander scale *Aspidiotus hederae* (Vallot) was substituted for the red scale as the laboratory host, it having several advantages over the red scale and the parasites reproduced even better upon it; and second, the white banana squash proved to be more satisfactory for year-round scale production than potato tubers. The objective of this study was to develop a method of production that would provide parasites for a periodic release program calling for a total of 400,000 per acre at a cost not to exceed that of the standard spray treatment for the red scale (approximately $40 per acre in 1967). This objective was attained.

In the initial work on the rearing of the many parasites of scale insects and mealybugs imported into California, sleeve cage units (fig. 6–18) have been employed with very satisfactory results, and they have been used also in certain phases of the mass-production programs.

The above examples of mass production have related to scale insects and mealybugs, yet a noteworthy contribution of recent years is that on the Oriental fruit fly in Hawaii. Production of the fruit fly in the fruits themselves presented several difficulties, including unavailability at certain times of the year, premature decay, difficulty of handling, and the labor involved. Efficient production necessitated the development of a synthetic food material for the larvae. The first that was used consisted of blended Hubbard squash (*Cucurbita maxima*), but the results were inconsistent. It was then found by Hagen and Finney (1950) that the addition of a commercial enzymatic hydrolysate of yeast to the food of the adult flies resulted in a substantial increase in fecundity of the females. Later, Finney (1956) developed a blended carrot medium, fortifed with Brewer's yeast and contain-

Fig. 6-17. The Orange County Insectary at Anaheim, California, used for mass-production of a variety of parasites and predators of citrus pests. (Photo courtesy of the U.S. Army Air Corps).

ing chemicals to inhibit growth of fungi and bacteria, that provided all essential food requirements of the larvae and at the same time had certain physical properties that were highly favorable to development of the larvae in their later stages. These various techniques have permitted the production of millions of fruit flies at nominal cost. They have been applied, with modifications, in the production of parasites of several other species of fruit flies.

It was mentioned previously that the oleander scale had been used very efficiently as a substitute or alternate host in the mass rearing of *Aphytis lingnanensis*, a parasite of the California red scale. Other outstanding examples of such use of alternate hosts are known, though not in the citrus insect field. Conspicuous among them are the Angoumois grain moth *Sitotroga cerealella* (Oliv.), for production of the egg parasites; *Trichogramma* spp., employed for control of the sugarcane borer, codling moth, etc.; and the potato tuberworm *Phthorimaea operculella* (Zeller), which was in production of the vast numbers of *Macrocentrus ancylitorus* Roh. released in California during the 1940's for control of the Oriental Fruit moth. The use of such alternate hosts, when possible, permits production of the required number of parasites on a much more economical basis.

EFFECTS OF INSECTICIDES UPON BIOLOGICAL CONTROL

The necessary application of insecticides for the control of the major pests affecting a particular crop always brings up the question of the effect of such applications upon the complex of natural enemies that is normally present in the orchard or field. Such applications against a major pest may have the effect of eliminating the natural enemies of another pest species that is of little or no economic consequence, thus enabling it to increase to serious pest status. Again, such treatments may destroy the natural enemies of a pest, once serious but later brought under full control by introduction of these enemies from abroad, and enable it to regain its previous level of destructiveness. The problem became much more acute with the appearance and widespread use, beginning in the middle 1940's, of the large number of highly

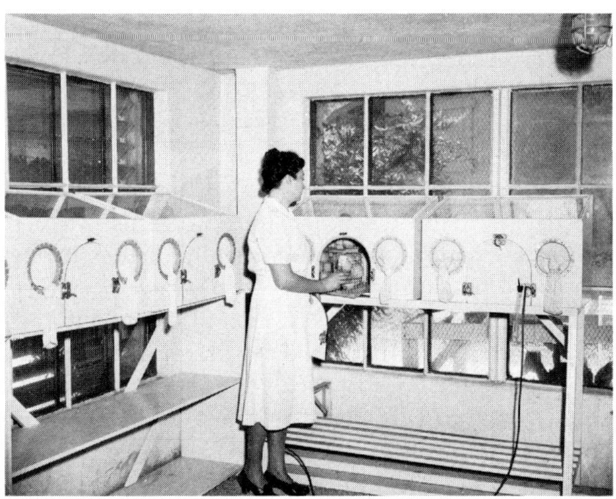

Fig. 6–18. Sleeve cages used in several stages of the insectary production of many imported parasites and predators. (After Flanders, 1951.)

toxic chlorinated hydrocarbons and the organic phosphates. Outbreaks of aphids and mites have been especially numerous and conspicuous following the use of the first group of insecticides in citrus orchards.

Many of the new insecticides are so highly toxic to a wide range of insect life that they virtually eradicate the parasitic and predaceous fauna from the treated orchards and fields. One series, however, classed as the "selective insecticides" has a much reduced detrimental effect on the natural enemies. They are of two types, the first being the ones that are less toxic to the beneficial forms than to the pest insect, and second, those that permit the survival of the natural enemies because of the manner of application, their short residual action, and other factors. The systemic insecticides are especially promising in avoiding high mortality of parasites and predators of sap-feeding insects such as aphids, scale insects, and mites. Ripper, Greenslade, and Hartley (1951), have shown that schradan (bis [dimethlamino] phosphoric anhydride), when applied to foliage, produced little mortality to ladybird beetles, syrphid flies, and an internal parasite, yet effected high mortality of the aphid pest. In general, it has low toxicity to the parasitic and predaceous insects.

The systemic insecticides, applied to the foliage or trunk of the trees, or to the soil about them, are absorbed by the plant and translocated, some in their original form, as in the case of schradan, while others, such as demeton, (*O*, *O*-dimethy O [and S]-2-[ethylthio] ethylphosphoro-dithiates), are transformed into other compounds that are themselves highly toxic. The sap-feeding insects are killed by the ingestion of the poisoned sap that reaches the site at which they are feeding.

All of the new insecticides, when applied directly to the foliage, are destructive to the natural enemies somewhat in proportion to the duration of their residual toxicity. A material that loses its toxicity within seven to ten days usually permits the survival of at least a portion of the parasite and predator populations.

As pointed out by Stern, Smith, van den Bosch, and Hagen (1959), the ideal selective insecticide is not one that eliminates the entire host population while leaving all of the natural enemies unharmed, but instead, shifts the balance in favor of the latter. In other words, it permits the survival of a sufficient number of the pest insect, below the level of economic injury, to enable the proportionately higher numbers of surviving natural enemies to reproduce and thus not only maintain themselves but further suppress the pest population.

A number of instances may be cited of the detrimental effects of insecticide applications against a number of important citrus pests, some normally under full biological control and others only partially so. In the case of the cottony-cushion scale, which is normally held at an exceedingly low level by vedalia, the use of some of the new insecticides has been followed by sharp upsets in the natural balance of that pest. In Tulare County, California, the application of DDT to the trees for control of other pests not only killed all the vedalia then present but, because of its long residual action, prevented reentry of the beetle into the orchards for several months thereafter. As a consequence, the scale was able to build up heavy infestations, the like of which had not been seen in the state for fifty years. Spray applications after July 1 prevented control of the scale by vedalia during the remainder of the season (DeBach, 1947). Application of the insecticide earlier in the season, a change in materials used, and, in some cases, the recolonization of vedalia, have relieved the situation.

In the California desert valleys, such as Coachella and Imperial, the widespread use of the new insecticides, mainly DDT, malathion, and parathion, and the frequent repetition of treatments during the season to various field and vegetable crops, has often resulted in the elimination of vedalia from adjoining citrus orchards (Bartlett and Lagace, 1960). This serious situation has largely been remedied by voluntary cooperation of growers, the measures taken being a shift from air to ground application, greater attention to wind drift, and a change from dust to spray formulations.

The California red scale is often under satisfactory biological control in orchards in the coastal area of southern California, the natural enemies responsible for this condition being *Aphytis chrysomphali* and *A. lingnanensis*, aided to some extent by predators. The extent to which the activities of these natural enemies may be depressed by insecticidal applications was strikingly demonstrated on an experimental basis in two lemon orchards in Santa Barbara County (DeBach and Bartlett, 1951). The test plots received monthly applications over an eleven-month period of a low dosage of DDT that was highly toxic to the parasites and predators but did not retard increase of the scale. The plots were kept under observation for 1½ years after beginning of the treatments. The untreated plots continued to show a very low incidence of scale, whereas in those receiving the light DDT applications the scale increased tremendously.

The lemon orchards in the coastal areas are at times quite heavily infested with the citrus bud mite *Eriophyes sheldoni* Ewing and the citrus red mite *Panonychus citri* (McG.) to the extent that insecticidal treatments are necessary. The problem is, therefore, to control these mite pests and still not upset the favorable balance between the red scale and its natural enemies. Studies toward this end were conducted by DeBach, Landi, and Jeppson (1959). The first step was, of course, the elimination of ants from the plots, and this was followed by application of various acaricides to determine which of them had the least serious effect on the enemies of the red scale. It was found that chlorobenzilate, tedion, and a few others had little toxicity to the parasites and predators. Several applications of these materials each season yielded effective control of the mites yet permitted the natural enemies to hold the red scale below the economic threshold over a three-year period.

Studies have been made in Florida on the effect of oil-DDT applications, used for the control of the little fire ant *Wasmannia auropunctata* (Roger), upon the natural balance of the Florida red scale and other pests occurring in the citrus orchards of that state (Griffiths and Thompson, 1947). Serious outbreaks of the scale and some other pests followed these treatments. The important Florida red scale parasite *Pseudhomalopoda prima* Grlt. was drastically reduced in numbers. In view of these findings, it was concluded that DDT should not be used on citrus in Florida.

An integrated program for control of the purple scale in California, which involves oil spraying of alternate pairs of tree rows in alternate years, has already been discussed (p. 287). This practice provides a continuous reservoir of parasites in the untreated portions of the orchard which can move onto the treated trees very soon after spraying. A similar program might well be practicable against other scale insects and mealybugs, provided additional pests are not present that require applications of chemicals having long-lasting residues for their control.

The application of fungicides in Florida for control of citrus diseases is often followed by a buildup of purple scale infestations, and it was believed by many that this was the result of elimination of the entomogenous fungi attacking it. The problem was investigated by Holloway and Young (1943), who found that the buildup occurred only with materials that left a granular residue on the tree, and that this buildup followed even when totally inert materials such as road dust were applied. The presence of a granular residue enabled a greater portion of the brood of crawlers to settle and to develop successfully. From this it may be inferred that an insecticide leaving a granular residue on the tree, as with some dusts that include a granular diluent, may act in two ways to aid scale buildup: first by destruction of the natural enemies and second, by providing more favorable physical conditions for scale settling and development.

An unusual situation was brought to light by DeBach and Bartlett (1951) in the case of the long-tailed mealybug. Field tests involving application of DDT to infested trees showed an actual increase in parasitization by *Anarhopus sydneyensis* during the months following treatment. This parasite proved to be relatively unaffected by DDT, whereas *Tetracnemus pretiosus* was drastically reduced in numbers. A secondary parasite, *Lygocerus* sp., which normally had destroyed a considerable portion of the *Anarhopus* population, was likewise greatly reduced. *Anarhopus* was thus largely relieved of attack by its secondary parasite and from competition with *Tetracnemus*, and was able to increase its numbers accordingly.

The field status of the various species of mites attacking citrus is often markedly changed following the application of insecticides to the trees. It was found by Holloway, Henderson, and McBurnie (1942) that citrus red mite populations in southern California orchards increased substantially after applications of insecticidal and fungicidal sprays that left a granular residue, even when that residue was inert. In this instance, the increase was not associated with any adverse effect upon the natural enemies. DeBach and Bartlett (1951) report that applications of DDT, cryolite, and zinc sulfate were followed by substantial increases in mite populations and that these increases were correlated with adverse effects upon the predators, most important of which are the ladybird beetle *Stethorus picipes* Casey, dustywings of the genus *Conwentzia*, the lacewing *Chrysopa californica* Coq., and predaceous mites of the genus *Typhlodromus*.

In addition to the detrimental effect of DDT applications on the various natural enemies of the plant-feeding mites, considerable evidence is accumulating to show that this insecticide also serves to stimulate the reproductive activities of these mites, thus compounding the problem.

The term *"integrated control,"* a relatively new name for a long established practice, has come into general use to designate the combination of biological and chemical methods of pest control, whereby the maximum potential of each method is realized. The two methods then become supplementary rather than alternative. Stern *et al.* (1959) have recently presented a detailed account of the basic concepts of this type of control. It applies equally to pest problems where exotic natural enemies have been imported and established, as well as to others where only native enemies are involved. In almost all citrus-producing areas of the world there is at least one pest species sufficiently destructive so that insecticides must be applied to control it. This being so, it is essential that the insecticidal treatment be such as to hold to a minimum its adverse effects upon the complex of natural enemies present in the orchards. This may be accomplished in a number of ways: by a change in material used, a change in formulation or in time of application, strip treatments, etc. To these measures may be added when practicable, the periodic colonization of natural enemies. The use of a "living insecticide" such as *Bacillus thuringiensis,* even when not fully effective in controlling the pest insect, may reduce the pest infestations to such an extent that the natural enemies are able to cope with the remaining population. Any or all of these measures, of course, when applied against scale insects and mealybugs, need to be supplemented by control of ants if they are present in any numbers in the orchards. For control of the Argentine ant in citrus orchards, the use of granular formulations of chlorinated hydrocarbons is least detrimental to the natural enemies attacking pest insects on the trees.

Several examples have already been given of the practical application of integrated control methods for the solution of citrus insect problems, and many others might be cited, but these relate especially to deciduous fruit, field crop, and vegetable insects. It is usually not possible for the individual grower to evaluate the different factors that are involved in developing and applying a program of this type in his own orchard. This situation often leads to what is known as supervised control, wherein a cooperative organization or group of growers engage the services of a qualified entomologist to advise them as to the proper treatments to be applied to the individual orchards. Such organizations have operated successfully in Ventura County, California, for many years, notably the Fillmore Citrus Protection District and the Associates Insectary at Santa Paula.

MICROBIAL CONTROL

The term "microbial control" has come into general use to designate that portion of the biological control field that involves the use of disease-producing microorganisms to control insect pests, as apart from insect parasites and predators. These organisms may be bacteria, fungi, protozoa, microsporidia, or viruses, with which may be included the nematodes. The major citrus pests of the world, and against which the main efforts in biological control have been directed, are the sap-feeding scale insects, mealybugs, and whiteflies, and the fruit flies that feed in the pulp of fruits. With a few conspicuous exceptions, they offer little opportunity for microbial control. The use of entomogenous fungi against the sap-feeders represents the main exception to this generalization.

The parasitic nematodes are found to attack mainly the larval stages of the larger insects such as the Lepidoptera, Coleoptera, and Orthoptera, and the adults of a number of them as well. The bacteria parasitize all of the major orders of insects, and many of them cause widespread epizootics among foliage-feeding caterpillars. One, *Bacillus popilliae* Dutky, has been widely used in control of the Japanese beetle in the eastern United States.

In most cases, the bacterium must be ingested by the host, which explains why very few of them are found as enemies of the sap-feeding scale insects, mealybugs, whiteflies, and mites. Infection by the viruses, as by the bacteria, comes about mainly by ingestion of the organism, though transovarial passage through the egg has been demonstrated in several instances.

The outstanding successes in the use of pathogenic microorganisms in biological control of insect pests, which involved introduction of the organism into one country from another, have been with the viruses. Two of these imported from Europe have brought about spectacular control of the spruce sawfly in Canada and the northeastern United States and of the European pine sawfly in Canada. An unusual feature of these two cases is that the viruses served to hold the pests at a consistently low level after the initial heavy infestations had been reduced.

Mention has already been made of the role of several fungi in control of the citrus whitefly (p. 300 and purple scale (p. 286) in Florida. Speare (1922) called attention to the rapid buildup of infection and mortality of the citrus mealybug during midsummer in that state by *Entomophthora fumosa* Speare, where mortality exceeded 90 per cent. He attributed the low incidence of this pest in Florida, as compared to the heavy infestations in California, to this disease. Fawcett (1948) cited several instances of high mortality of California red scale and citricola scale which resulted presumably from fungus infections, though in each case the causal agent was not definitely determined.

In connection with field studies on the imported parasites of the Oriental fruit fly in Hawaii, it was found that *Opius oophilus*, the most effective of the series, was responsible for transmission of fungus and bacterial diseases of the fruit fly eggs (Bess and Haramoto, 1958). This parasite deposits its own eggs in those of the fruit fly, and it is during this act of oviposition that infection occurs. Both parasitized and unparasitized eggs in the cluster are killed by disease, the mortality from this cause being approximately 73 per cent in the field material that was examined. In view of the very high parasitization normally achieved by *Opius*, even with the loss of a large portion of its eggs through disease, there is considerable question as to the contribution of the disease-producing organisms to reduction of the fruit fly infestations. The survival of all parasitized eggs might well have increased the total mortality in the absence of disease.

The mode of infection by bacteria and viruses is mainly through ingestion of the organisms by the host while feeding, whereas with the fungi the spores, by one means or another, reach the integument of the host, and each one then sends out a germ tube that penetrates into the body cavity. Development of epizootics, or outbreaks, of fungus diseases are governed very largely by prevailing climate, warm and humid or wet conditions being essential in most instances. This requirement explains the frequent occurrence of disease outbreaks on several citrus insects in Florida, and their almost complete absence in California and other semiarid areas of the world.

Unquestionably the pathogenic fungi are responsible for holding many insect pests in check in nature and, under favorable conditions, for reducing heavy infestations. The uncertainty lies in the extent to which they may be manipulated to increase their field efficiency. The saturation point may already have been reached in the field, though at a low level because of adverse climatic conditions. In that situation, no benefit can be expected from artificial distribution of the organism until conditions become more favorable.

With certain exceptions, some of which have been mentioned, the various pathogenic organisms, sometimes called "living insecticides," yield only temporary control and consequently have to be applied periodically, whenever the pest insects reach the point of causing economic injury. This necessitates ready availability of the materials on a commercial basis if they are to come into general use. Only two are as yet (1967) on the market in the United States, these being *Bacillus popilliae* Dutky for use against Japanese beetle larvae and *B. thuringiensis* Berliner as a control of foliage-feeding caterpillars, mainly on vegetable crops, where residues of chemical insecticides are a serious problem.

Difficulties in mass production stand in the way of general use of a number of highly effective organisms. Some fungi and bacteria cannot be grown on any known artificial medium, while with those that can be so produced some decrease in virulence occurs after repeated cultivation on such a medium. The viruses responsible for disease in insects present the most difficult problem, as not a single one has yet been mass-produced on an artificial medium. In exceptional instances, it may be possible to collect a sufficient number of diseased insects in the field to provide the quantity of inoculum needed for a field-control program, but availability by that means alone largely prevents general use.

In summing up, it may be concluded that the possibilities for successful use of disease-producing microorganisms is less against the major pests of citrus than of many other crops. With few exceptions, the organisms attacking them are the fungi, and these flourish only in areas having a warm and humid or wet climate, which precludes their use in many of the main citrus-producing areas. There may be some possibility of use of bacteria such as *Bacillus thuringiensis* against the foliage-feeding caterpillars of the few lepidopterous species known to attack citrus, but field tests upon them have not yet (1967) been made.

THE TIME REQUIRED FOR BIOLOGICAL CONTROL

Growers are always interested in knowing the time interval that must elapse between release of imported natural enemies in the orchard and the attainment of control. It has often been asserted that, because of the small numbers of parasites or predators released in relation to the pest population, a period of years must intervene before any measure of control can be anticipated. This, however, is not the case with parasites or predators that achieve full economic control; it may come about in individual orchards within months rather than years and, at the outside, the outcome is evident within the rather arbitrary limit of three years. The lower portion of that time range has proved to be adequate in the most successful projects for biological control of citrus insects, notably the cottony-cushion scale, citrophilus mealybug, Green's mealybug, citrus blackfly, and spiny blackfly, in the most favorable areas of their host range.

No prediction can be made at the beginning of any biological control project regarding the final outcome, which may range from full economic control to complete failure. However, certain generalizations appear warranted on the basis of past experience. An analysis of all cases of *fully successful and permanent* biological control of insect pests (Clausen, 1951), insofar as the published data are adequate for that purpose, and supplemented by data more recently available, reveals a surprising consistency in the pattern of progress from initial release to ultimate control.

The conclusions that have been drawn in relation to completed projects may be applied with some assurance to projects that are still in the developmental stage. Essential assumptions basic to these conclusions are that the natural enemies have been colonized in all of the main climatic zones occupied by the pest insect and that the biological characteristics of the parasite or predator have been fully determined. The conclusions are: (1) a parasite or predator destined to effect *full and complete economic control* of its host will show definite evidence of such control *in the vicinity of the release points* very quickly, often within months but almost certainly within three years, regardless of the duration of the life cycle of the host; (2) a fully effective parasite is always quickly and easily established, and often through release of very small numbers; and (3) failure of a parasite or predator to become established easily and quickly is an indication that, in the end, it will not be fully effective.

Any highly effective parasite or predator is fully adapted both to its host and to its environment, and, consequently, there is no serious hindrance to the realization of its full reproductive capacity in the field. As a result, its population increase is almost explosive in nature. On the contrary, a partially effective species is not fully adapted, a consequence often of adverse climatic conditions, but in other instances of inherent deficiencies in the parasite itself. Its effectiveness may vary widely from year to year if climate is the controlling factor. In favorable seasons, it may readily become established and effect partial or full control of the host, only to subside to a minor status in following years. Long delay in establishment and increase indicates that, from the start, adverse influences were operating against it. No instance is known of a parasite, long established but ineffective, finally building up its populations and contributing substantially and consistently to control of its host.

The above discussion has dealt with single species of natural enemies in relation to control of the host, rather than with a series of species. Experience has demonstrated that the great majority of highly successful projects have been through a single species of parasite or predator. In those instances where the combined action of several have achieved the same result, each of them is usually strongly dominant over the other in some portion of the pest range. This is especially true of members of a series that attack the same host stage.

In general, it may be said that no single parasite or predator is capable of controlling its host throughout the geographic range of the latter.

The nearest approach to an exception to this generalization is the vedalia beetle, the predaceous enemy of the cottony-cushion scale. Some species are effective in only a small portion of the host range, of which certain parasites of the black scale and California red scale in southern California are good examples. After more than half a century of work upon these two pests, they are not yet under full economic control. Several of the parasites are effective in localized areas, mainly near the coast. The current lack of control in some areas necessitates continued search abroad to complete the series of effective species or races required by the extent of the host range. Under these circumstances, the time required for control is wholly unpredictable and the sought-after parasites may not even exist.

ANTS IN RELATION TO BIOLOGICAL CONTROL

The ants as a group are unquestionably one of the most important of the natural control factors operating to hold many insect pests in check. Many instances are known of the beneficial effects of ants in protecting crops from insect attack. Their actual employment in biological control has been limited, however, by certain obvious objectionable features. For centuries one species, *Oecophylla smaragdina* F., has been used by the citrus growers of South China to protect their trees from various pests, mainly bugs, foliage-feeding caterpillars, and stem and trunkboring beetles. Bamboo runways were even provided to facilitate the movement of the ants from tree to tree. Other species were utilized in the Middle East to protect the date trees from injury by several ant species. In modern times, *Dolichoderus bituberculatus* Mayr has been used in the cocoa plantations of Java to reduce attack upon that crop by sap-feeding bugs of the genus *Helopeltis.* At the present time, much work is being done in Europe with the mound-building ant *Formica rufa* L., and it is being widely distributed through the forests of Italy, Germany, and other countries for protection against various insect pests, especially leaf-feeding caterpillars.

Insofar as the modern citrus industry is concerned, we are more concerned with the harmful effects resulting from ant infestations in the orchards. By their consumption of excess honeydew, direct fostering of the pest insects, and in other ways, they bring about increases in the infestations of many scale insects and mealybugs. A second effect of their presence on the trees is the prevention or hindrance of the activities of the parasitic and predaceous enemies that prey upon these pests. In extreme cases, they may completely nullify the attack of otherwise highly effective parasites, thus making essential either the elimination of the ants or insecticidal treatment for control of the pest. The armored scales do not produce honeydew, while that of some of the unarmored or soft scales and mealybugs, such as the citricola scale, is unattractive to the ants. Regardless of this, ants may be present in abundance on the trees to feed upon honeydew of other insects such as aphids, or at the extrafloral nectaries of the plants, and their activity may promote increased infestations of the unattractive species, as has been conspicuously shown in the case of the California red scale.

The presence of several ant species, but mainly the Argentine ant, *Iridomyrmex humilis* Mayr, in the citrus orchards of California has had a pronounced influence on the effectiveness of many natural enemies in control of several of our most important pests. This detrimental effect has not been consistent, however, as it may be pointed out that the two most conspicuously successful biological control projects have been not at all affected by ant infestations on the trees. They are the cottony-cushion scale, controlled by a ladybird predator supplemented by a dipterous parasite, and the citrophilus mealybug, completely subjugated by two hymenopterous parasites. Not a single instance has been observed of ant interference with these natural enemies to the extent that increases in infestation have occurred, despite the attractiveness of cottony-cushion scale honeydew to ants.

The information relative to the influence of ants on the effectiveness of parasites and predators has been reviewed by Flanders (1958*a*) and Bartlett (1961), with supplementary field data and laboratory tests on a series of parasites attacking the brown soft and the black scale. It is well known that heavy infestations of the brown soft scale develop on trees or parts of trees bearing a high ant population. The honeydew of this scale is highly attractive to the ants, and their presence results in the virtual elimination of parasites, mainly *Aphycus luteolus,* from the trees. Exclusion of ants from such trees is quickly followed by high parasitization and control of the infestation within a very few months. The most effective of the parasites of the black scale, *Aphycus helvolus,* is usually quite scarce on trees heavily infested with ants, and infestations of scale build up rapidly, even in areas where control is normally attained with this parasite.

In his studies on the various factors involved in the interrelations of ants and insect parasites, Bartlett tested fifteen species attacking various scale insects and mealybugs. As had been found by earlier investigators in studies of individual species, a correlation was shown to exist between the time required for oviposition by the parasites and the degree of the adverse effect of the ants upon their activities, though there were some exceptions. In general, the species requiring only a very short period for oviposition were least affected. It was found, however, that the parasite species most valuable in control, such as *Metaphycus luteolus* and *Microterys flavus* on the brown soft scale and *Metaphycus helvolus* on the black scale, require two to three minutes for oviposition, and consequently were the most seriously affected by the presence of ants. A series of six species of *Coccophagus*, requiring only 2 to 67 seconds for oviposition were least affected, but even in the absence of ants these particular species are of little value in control of the scales in citrus orchards.

A number of the most effective of the insect parasites of scale insects have the habit of feeding on the body fluids of their hosts, notably *M. helvolus* on the black scale and *Comperiella bifasciata* and *Aphytis* spp. on the red scale, and interference by ants with this feeding reduces their efficiency in control of the pests.

Infestations of California red scale build up rapidly in the presence of heavy ant populations, and this is attributed to their interference with the activities of the principal parasitic enemy, *Aphytis chrysomphali*, and several predaceous coccinellid beetles (DeBach, Fleschner, and Dietrick, 1953). Extended tests in California, and in South Africa also (Steyn, 1958), have demonstrated that elimination of ants from the citrus trees, either by insecticidal treatment or banding, has resulted in a substantial decline in the red scale infestations.

While most of the natural enemies thus far mentioned have been parasites, it is known that a wide range of predators, including not only the coccinellid beetles but the hover and other flies, lacewings, dustywings, and others are adversely affected by ants. DeBach, Dietrick, and Fleschner (1951) have shown that even the citrus red mite may increase as much as twenty fold as a result of the presence of ants on the trees, as compared with ant-free trees. The effect in this case is entirely on predators, as parasites of this pest are not known.

The evidence at hand clearly indicates that the presence of ants in citrus orchards results consistently in a buildup of insect pests such as scale insects, mealybugs, and mites. This situation warrants a definite program for ant control in any well-managed orchard in which they may become abundant. The measures taken should be other than application of insecticides directly to the trees, as that method of control may have a more serious effect upon the natural enemies than do the ants themselves.

LITERATURE CITED

BACK, E. A., and C. E. PEMBERTON. 1918. The Mediterranean fruit fly in Hawaii. U. S. Dept. Agr. Bul. **536**:188 pp.

BALACHOWSKY, A. 1932. Contribution à l'étude des Coccides de France (6e note). Observations biologiques sur l'adaptation de *Novius cardinalis* Muls. aux dépens de *Gueriniella serratulae* F. Rev. Pathol. Veg. Ent. Agr. **19**:11–17.

BARTLETT, B. R. 1953. Natural control of citricola scale in California. Jour. Econ. Ent. **46**:25–28.

———. 1961. The influence of ants upon parasites, predators, and scale insects. Ann. Ent. Soc. Amer. **54**:643–51.

BARTLETT, B. R., and C. F. LAGACE. 1960. Interference with biological control of cottony-cushion scale by insecticides and attempts to re-establish a favorable natural balance. Jour. Econ. Ent. **53**:1055–58.

BEARDSLEY, J. W., JR. 1955. Fluted scales and their biological control in United States Administered Micronesia. Proc. Hawaiian Ent. Soc. **15**:391–99.

BEINGOLEA G., O. 1956. Estatus actual de la plaga de la quereza negra del olivo (*Saissetia oleae* Bern.) en los valles de Yauca y Ilo. Bol. Trim. Exp. Agropec. (1955) **4**:18–22.

———. 1959. El problema de la "mosca blanca lanuda" de los citricos, en el Peru *Aleurothrixus floccosus* (Homop.: Aleurodidae). Rev. Peruana Ent. Agr. **2**:65–69.

BENNETT, F. D., and T. W. HUGHES. 1959. Biological control of insect pests in Bermuda. Bul. Ent. Res. **50**:423–36.

BERGER, E. W. 1910. Whitefly control. Fla. Agr. Expt. Sta. Bul. **103**:28 pp.

BESS, H. A. 1953. Status of *Ceratitis capitata* in Hawaii following the introduction of *Dacus dorsalis* and its parasites. Proc. Hawaiian Ent. Soc. **15**:221–34.

BESS, H. A., and F. H. HARAMOTO. 1958. Biological control of the oriental fruit fly in Hawaii. Proc. Tenth Intern. Cong. Ent. (1956) **4**:835–40.

———. 1961. Contributions to the biology and ecology of the oriental fruit fly, *Dacus dorsalis* Hendel (Deptera: Tephritidae), in Hawaii. Hawaii Agr. Expt. Sta. Tech. Bul. **44**:30 pp.

BESS, H. A., R. VAN DEN BOSCH, and F. H. HARAMOTO. 1961. Fruit fly parasites and their activities in Hawaii. Proc. Hawaiian Ent. Soc. **17**:367–78.

BRANIGAN, E. J. 1916. A satisfactory method of rearing

mealybugs for use in parasite work. Calif. State Hort. Comm. Mo. Bul. **5**:304–06.

Clausen, C. P. 1923. The citricola scale in Japan and its synonymy. Jour. Econ. Ent. **16**:225–26.

———. 1936. Insect parasitism and biological control. Ann. Ent. Soc. Amer. **29**:201–23.

———. 1951. The time factor in biological control. Jour. Econ. Ent. **44**:1–9.

Clausen, C. P., and P. A. Berry. 1932. The citrus blackfly in tropical Asia, and the importation of its natural enemies into tropical America. U. S. Dept. Agr. Tech. Bul. **320**:58 pp.

Clausen, C.P., D.W. Clancy, and Q.C. Chock. 1965. Biological control of the oriental fruit fly *(Dacus dorsalis* Hendel) and other fruit flies in Hawaii. U.S. Dept. Agr. Tech. Bul. **1322**:102 pp.

Compere, H. 1961. The red scale and its insect parasites. Hilgardia **31**:173–278.

Compere, H., and H. S. Smith. 1927. Notes on the life-history of two oriental chalcidoid parasites of *Chrysomphalus.* Univ. Calif. Pubs. Ent. **4**:63–73.

———. 1932. The control of the citrophilus mealybug, *Pseudococcus gahani,* by Australian parasites. Hilgardia **6**:585–618.

DeBach, P. 1947. Cottony-cushion scale, vedalia, and DDT in central California. Calif. Citrog. **32**:406–407.

———. 1949. The establishment of the Chinese race of *Comperiella bifasciata* on *Aonidiella aurantii* in southern California. Jour. Econ. Ent. **41**:985.

———. 1958. Selective breeding to improve adaptations of parasitic insects. Proc. Tenth Intern. Cong. Ent. (1956) **4**:759–68.

———. 1960. The importance of taxonomy to biological control as illustrated by the cryptic history of *Aphytis holoxanthus* n. sp. (Hymenoptera: Aphelinidae), a parasite of *Chrysomphalus aonidum,* and *Aphytis coheni,* n. sp., a parasite of *Aonidiella aurantii.* Ann. Ent. Soc. Amer. **53**:701–05.

DeBach, P., and B. Bartlett. 1951. Effects of insecticides on biological control of insect pests of citrus. Jour. Econ. Ent. **44**:372–83.

DeBach, P., E. J. Dietrick, and C. A. Fleschner. 1951. Ants and citrus pests. Calif. Agr. **7**:7, 14.

DeBach, P., C. A. Fleschner, and E. J. Dietrick. 1949. Population studies of the long-tailed mealybug and its natural enemies on citrus trees in Southern California. Jour. Econ. Ent. **42**:777–82.

———. 1953. Natural control of the California red scale in untreated citrus orchards in southern California. Proc. Seventh Pac. Sci. Cong. (1950) **4**:236–48.

DeBach, P., and J. Landi. 1961. The introduced purple scale parasite, *Aphytis lepidosaphes* Compere, and a method of integrating chemical with biological control. Hilgardia **31**:459–97.

DeBach, P., J. Landi, and L. Jeppson. 1959. Integrating chemical control of mites with biological control of red scale. Calif. Citrog. **44**:205–09.

DeBach, P., J. Landi, and E. B. White. 1962. Biological control of California red scale. Calif. Citrog. **47**:453–59; **48**:16–20.

DeBach, P., and R. A. Sundby. 1963. Competitive displacement between ecological homologues. Hilgardia **34**:105–66.

DeBach, P., and E. B. White. 1960. Commercial mass culture of the California red scale parasite, *Aphytis lingnanensis.* Calif. Agr. Expt. Sta. Bul. **770**:58 pp.

Doutt, R. L. 1958. Vice, virtue, and vedalia. Bul. Ent. Soc. Amer. **4**:119–123.

Dumbleton, L. J. 1936. Biological control of orchard insect pests. N. Zealand Jour. Sci. Tech. **18**:588–592.

Ebeling. W. 1959. Subtropical fruit pests. Univ. Calif. Div. Agr. Sci., Berkeley. 436 pp.

Esaki, T. 1940. A preliminary report on the entomological survey of the Micronesian Islands under the Japanese Mandate, with special reference to the insects of economic importance. Proc. Sixth Pac. Sci. Cong. (1939) **4**:407–15.

Essig, E. O. 1931. A history of entomology. The Macmillan Co., New York. 1028 pp.

Evlakhova, A. A. 1938. Experiments on the control of *Ceroplastes sinensis* Del Guer. with the fungus *Cephalosporium lecanii* Zimm. [In Russian] *In:* Summary of the scientific research work of the Institute of Plant Protection for the year 1936. III. Viruses and bacterioses, biological method, chemical method and mechanization. Pp. 75–77. Lenin Acad. Agr. Sci. (Abstracted in Rev. Appl. Ent., Ser. A, **27**:308.)

———. 1941. Results of the tests of *Cephalosporium* fungus in the control of scale insects in the citrus groves of the Adjar Aut. Republic in 1939. [In Russian] Bul. Plant Prot., 1941, No. 1: 64–68. (Abstracted in Rev. Appl. Ent., Ser. A, **30**:377.)

Fawcett, H. S. 1908. Fungi parasitic on *Aleyrodes citri.* Univ. Fla. Spec. Studies **1**:41 pp.

———. 1944. Fungus and bacterial diseases of insects as factors in biological control. Bot. Rev. **10**:327–48.

———. 1948. The biological control of citrus insects by parasitic fungi and bacteria. *In:* Batchelor, L.D., and H.J. Webber (eds.). The citrus industry. II: 627–64. Univ. Calif. Press, Berkeley and Los Angeles.

Finney, G. L. 1956. A fortified carrot medium for mass-culture of the oriental fruit fly and certain other Tephritids. Jour. Econ. Ent. **49**:134.

Fisher, F. E. 1950. Entomogenous fungi attacking scale insects and rust mites on citrus in Florida. Jour. Econ. Ent. **43**:305–09.

Flanders S. E. 1937. Ovipositional instincts and developmental sex differences in the genus *Coccophagus.* Univ. Calif. Pubs. Ent. **6**:401–22.

———. 1940. Biological control of the long-tailed mealybug, *Pseudococcus longispinus.* Jour. Econ. Ent. **33**:754–59.

———. 1942*a*. *Metaphycus helvolus,* an encyrtid parasite of the black scale. Jour. Econ. Ent. **35**:690–98.

———. 1942*b*. Propagation of black scale on potato sprouts. Jour. Econ. Ent. **35**:687–89.

———. 1947. Use of the potato tuber in the mass production of diaspine scale insects. Jour. Econ. Ent. **40**:746–47.

———. 1948. Biological control of yellow scale *(Aonidiella citrina).* Calif. Citrog. **34**:56, 76–77.

———. 1949. Cold weather stymied parasites of black scale. Calif. Citrog. **34**:406–07.

———. 1950. An enemy of purple scale recently established in California. Calif. Citrog. **36**:64–65.

———. 1951. Mass culture of California red scale and its golden chalcid parasites. Hilgardia **21**:1–42.

———. 1952. Biological observations on parasites of the black scale. Ann. Ent. Soc. Amer. **45**:543–49.

———. 1953. Hymenopterous parasites of three species of oriental scale insects. Boll. Lab. Zool. Gen. Agr. "Filippo Silvestri" Portici **33**:10–28.

———. 1958*a*. The role of the ant in the biological control of scale insects in California. Proc. Tenth Intern. Cong.

Ent. (1956) **4**:579–84.

———. 1958*b*. *Moranila californica* as a usurped parasite of *Saissetia oleae*. Jour. Econ. Ent. **51**:247.

———. 1959*a*. Differential host relations of the sexes in parasitic Hymenoptera. Ent. Expl. Appl. **2**:125–42.

———. 1959*b*. Biological control of *Saissetia nigra* (Nietn.) in California. Jour. Econ. Ent. **52**:596-600.

FLANDERS, S. E., J. L. GRESSITT, and P DEBACH. 1950. Parasite of Glover's scale established in California. Calif. Citrog. **35**:254–255.

FLANDERS, S. E., J. L. GRESSITT, and T. W. FISHER. 1958. *Casca chinensis*, an internal parasite of California red scale. Hilgardia **28**:65–91.

GOMEZ-CLEMENTE, F. 1932. El *Cryptolaemus montrouzieri* Muls. parasito del *Pseudococcus citri* Risso. Second edition Serv. Agr. Nac., Est. Fitopatol. Agr. Levante, Burjasot, Valencia. 59 pp.

GOSSARD, H. A. 1901. The cottony cushion scale. Fla. Agr. Expt. Sta. Bul. **56**:312–56

GRESSITT, J. L., S. E. FLANDERS, and B. BARTLETT. 1954. Parasites of citricola scale in Japan, and their introduction into California. Pan-Pac. Ent. **30**:5–10.

GRIFFITHS, J. T., JR. and W. L. THOMPSON. 1947. The use of DDT on citrus trees in Florida. Jour. Econ. Ent. **40**:386–88.

GROFF, G. W., and C. W. HOWARD. 1924. The cultured citrus ant of South China. Lingnam Agr. Rev. **2**:108–14.

HAGEN, K. S., and G. L. FINNEY. 1950. A food supplement for effectively increasing the fecundity of certain Tephretid species. Jour. Econ. Ent. **43**:735.

HOLLOWAY, J. K., C. F. HENDERSON, and H. V. MCBURNIE. 1942. Population increase of citrus red mite associated with the use of sprays containing inert granular residues. Jour. Econ. Ent. **35**:348–50.

HOLLOWAY, J. K., and T. R. YOUNG, JR. 1943. The influence of fungicidal sprays on entomogenous fungi and on the purple scale in Florida. Jour. Econ. Ent. **36**: 453–457.

JENKINS, C. F. H. 1946. Biological control in Western Australia. Jour. Roy. Soc. West. Australia **32**:1–17.

JIMÉNEZ—JIMÉNEZ, E. 1958. El *Syntomosphyrum indicum*, un enemigo mortal de la mosca de la fruta (*Anastrepha ludens* Loew.). Fitofilo **11**(21):25–30.

———. 1961. Situación actual de la mosca prieta (*Aleurocanthus woglumi* Ash.), de los citricos en Mexico. Fitofilo **14**(32):39–45.

KAMAL, M. 1951. Biological control projects in Egypt, with a list of introduced parasites and predators. Bul. Soc. Fouad Ier. Ent. **35**:205–20.

KRAMER, F. C. W., JR. [n.d.] My experience with citrus tree snails. Privately printed, Leesburg, Florida, 4 pp.

KUWANA, I. 1922. Studies on Japanese Monophlebinae. Contrib. II. The genus *Icerya*. Imp. Plant Quar. Sta., Yokohama, Japan, Bul. **2**:43 pp.

———. 1934. Notes on a newly imported parasite of the spiny white fly attacking citrus in Japan. Proc. Fifth Pac. Sci. Cong. (1933) **5**:3521–23.

MORRILL, A. W., and E. A. BACK. 1912. Natural control of white flies in Florida. U. S. Dept. Agr. Bur. Ent. Bul. **102**:78 pp.

MOURSI, A. A. 1948. Contributions to the knowledge of the natural enemies of mealybugs. Bul. Soc. Fouad Ier. Ent. **32**:1–40.

MOUTIA, L. A., and R. MAMET. 1946. Review of twenty-five years of economic entomology in the island of Mauritius. Bul. Ent. Res. **36**:439–72.

MUMA, M. H. 1959. Natural control of Florida red scale on citrus in Florida by predators and parasites. Jour. Econ. Ent. **52**:577–86.

MUMA, M. H., and D. W. CLANCY. 1961. Parasitism of purple scale in Florida citrus groves. Fla. Ent. **44**:159–65.

NISHIDA, K., and S. YANAI. 1956. On the adaptability of *Aphytis lingnanensis* Compere to *Unaspis yanonensis* (Kuwana). Fruit Tree Expt. Sta., Kumamoto, Japan. 6 pp. (Processed.)

NORRIS, R. E. 1947. Control of citrus pests by tree snails in Lake County, Fla. Citrus Indus. **3**:10–11.

O'CONNOR, B. A. 1950. *Trichopoda pennipes* F. in Fiji and the British Solomon Islands. Agr. Jour. Fiji **21**:63–71.

ORIAN, A. J. E., and L. A. MOUTIA. 1960. Fruit flies (Trypetidae) of economic importance in Mauritius. Rev. Agr. Sucr. Maurice **39**:142–50.

PEMBERTON, C. E., and H. F. WILLARD. 1918*a*. Interrelations of fruit-fly parasites in Hawaii. Jour. Agr. Res. **12**:285–95.

———. 1918*b*. A contribution to the biology of fruit-fly parasites in Hawaii. Jour. Agr. Res. **15**:419–65.

PETERSON, G. D., JR. 1955. Biological control of the orange spiny whitefly in Guam. Jour. Econ. Ent. **48**:681–83.

———. 1957. An annotated check list of parasites and predators introduced into Guam during the years 1950–1955. Proc. Hawaiian Ent. Soc. **16**: 199-202.

RICHARDSON, H. H. 1948. Present status of the citrus blackfly and its parasite *Eretmocerus serius* at Nassau, Bahamas. Jour. Econ. Ent. **41**:980.

RIPPER, W. E., R. M. GREENSLADE, and G. S. HARTLEY. 1951. Selective insecticides and biological control. Jour. Econ. Ent. **44**:448–59.

RIVNAY, E. 1946. The status of *Clausenia purpurea* Ishii and its competition with other parasites of *Pseudococcus comstocki* Kuw. in Palestine. Bul. Soc. Fouad Ier Ent. **30**:11–19.

RODRIGUEZ-LOPEZ, L. 1942. La "Iceria" plaga de los citricos. Dept. Agr. Ecuador Bol. **17**:10 pp.

SILVESTRI, F. 1914. Report on an expedition to Africa in search of the natural enemies of fruit flies. Hawaii Bd. Agr. For., Div. Ent. Bul. **3**:196 pp.

———. 1927. Contribuzione alla conoscenza degli Aleurodidae (Insecta-Hemiptera) viventi su Citrus in Extremo Oriente e dei loro parassiti. Boll. Lab. Zool. Gen. Agr. Portici **21**:1–60.

SMITH, H. D. 1945. La "Mosca Prieta" de los citricos en la costa occidental de Mexico y la importación y colonizacion de *Eretmocerus serius* Silv. para su control Fitofilo **4**:67–103.

SMITH, H. D., H. L. MALTBY and E. JIMENEZ-JIMENEZ. 1964. Biological control of the citrus blackfly in Mexico. U. S. Dept. Agr. Tech. Bul. **1311**:30 pp.

SMITH, H.S. 1917. On the life-history and successful introduction into the United States of the Sicilian mealy-bug parasite. Jour. Econ. Ent. **10**:262–68.

———. 1948. Biological control of insect pests. *In:* Batchelor, L. D., and H. J. Webber (eds.). The citrus industry. II: 597–625. Univ. Calif. Press, Berkeley and Los Angeles.

SMITH, H. S., and H. M. ARMITAGE. 1931. The biological control of mealybugs attacking citrus. Calif. Agr. Expt. Sta. Bul. **509**:74pp.

SMITH, H. S., and H. COMPERE. 1928. A preliminary report on the insect parasites of the black scale *Saissetia oleae* (Bernard). Univ. Calif. Pubs. Ent. **4**:231–334.

SMITH, R. H. 1944. Bionomics and control of the nigra scale, *Saissetia nigra*. Hilgardia **16**: 225–88.

SNOWBALL, G. J., and R. G. LUKINS. 1964. Status of introduced parasites of Queensland fruit fly (*Strumeta tryoni*),

1960–1962. Austral. Jour. Agr. Res. **15**:586–608.

SNOWBALL, G. J., F. WILSON, T. G. CAMPBELL, and R. G. LUKINS. 1962. The utilization of parasites of oriental fruit fly *(Dacus dorsalis)* against Queensland fruit fly *(Strumeta tryoni)*. Austral. Jour. Agr. Res. **13**:443–60.

SPEARE, A. T. 1922. Natural control of the citrus mealybug in FLorida. U. S. Dept. Agr. Bul. **1117**:18 pp.

STEINHAUS, E. A. 1949. Principles of insect pathology. McGraw-Hill Book Co., New York. 757 pp.

STERN, V. M., R. F. SMITH, R. VAN DEN BOSCH, and K. S. HAGEN. 1959. The integration of chemical and biological control of the spotted alfalfa aphid. The integrated control concept. Hilgardia **29**:81–101.

STEYN, J. J. 1958. The effect of ants on citrus scales at Letaba, South Africa. Proc. Tenth Intern. Cong. Entomol. (1956) **4**:589–94.

VAN DEN BOSCH, R., and F. H. HARAMOTO. 1953. Competition among the parasites of the oriental fruit fly. Proc. Hawaiian Ent. Soc. **15**:201–206.

VAN DER GOOT, P. 1948. Biologische bestrijding van witte luis (*Phenacoccus iceryoides* Gr.) op koffie in de Toradjalanden (Zuid Celebes). [English summary.] Landbouw **20**:107–16.

WATSON, J. R. 1912. Utilization of fungus parasites of Coccidae and Aleurodidae in Florida. Jour. Econ. Ent. **5**:200–04.

WATSON, J. R., and E. W. BERGER. 1937. Citrus insects and their control. Fla. Agr. Ext. Serv. Bul. **88**:135 pp.

WHEATLEY, P. E. 1964. The successful establishment of *Eretmocerus serius* Silv. (Hymenoptera: Eulophidae) in Kenya. E. Africa Agr. For. Jour. **29**:236.

WILLARD, H. F., and T. L. BISSELL. 1930. Parasitism of the Mediterranean fruit fly in Hawaii in 1922–24. U. S. Dept. Agr. Circ. **109**:12 pp.

WILLARD, H. F., and A. C. MASON. 1937. Parasitization of the Mediterranean fruitfly in Hawaii, 1914–33. U. S. Dept. Agr. Circ. **439**:17 pp.

WILLE, J. E. 1958. El control biologico de los insectos agricolas en el Peru. Proc. Tenth Intern. Cong. Ent. (1956) **4**:519–23.

WILSON, F. 1960. A review of the biological control of insects and weeds in Australia and Australian New Guinea. Commonw. Inst. Biol. Cont., Ottawa, Tech. Commun. **1**:102 pp.

WOGLUM, R. S. 1913. Report of a trip to India and the Orient in search of the natural enemies of the citrus whitefly. U. S. Dept. Agr. Bul. **120**:58 pp.

WOLCOTT, G. N. 1958. The evanescence of perfect biological control. Proc. Tenth Intern. Cong. Ent. (1956) **4**:511–13.

YASUMATSU, K. 1951. Further investigations on the hymenopterous parasites of *Ceroplastes rubens* in Japan. Jour. Fac. Agr. Kyushu Univ., Fukuoka **10**:1–27

———. 1953. Preliminary investigations on the activity of a Kyushu race of *Anicetus ceroplastis* Ishii which has been liberated against *Ceroplastes rubens* Maskell in various districts of Japan. Sci. Bul. Fac. Agr. Kyushu Univ., Fukuoka **14**:17–26. [In Japanese, English summary.]

———. 1958. An interesting case of biological control of *Ceroplastes rubens* Maskell in Japan. Proc. Tenth Intern. Cong. Ent. (1956) **4**:771–75.

YASUMATSU, K., and T. TACHIKAWA. 1949. Investigations on the hymenopterous parasites of *Ceroplastes rubens* Maskell in Japan. Jour. Fac. Agr. Kyushu Univ., Fukuoka **9**:99–120.

ZINNA, G. 1960. Esperimenti di lotta biologica contro il cotonello degli agrumi (*Pseudococcus citri* (Risso)) nell'Isola di Procida mediante l'impiego di due parassiti esotica, *Pauridia peregrina* Timb. e *Leptomastix dactylopii* How. Boll. Lab. Ent. Agr. "Filippo Silvestri" Portici **28**:257–84.

CHAPTER 7

Nematodes Attacking Citrus

R. C. BAINES, S. D. VAN GUNDY, and E. P. DuCHARME

NEMATODE PESTS OF CITRUS trees attack only the roots, and thereby interfere with the rate of growth, vigor, and the ability of trees to produce fruit. Sheltered by their habitat on roots, nematodes on citrus escaped detection until 1889 when the root-knot nematode (*Meloidogyne* spp.) was found on citrus in Florida (Neal, 1889). The citrus nematode (*Tylenchulus semipenetrans* Cobb) (Cobb, 1913) was discovered in 1912 in California and later in the same year in Florida, but the importance of nematodes to citriculture was not immediately appreciated. In 1950, Baines showed that the citrus nematode greatly decreased the growth rate of young lemon and orange trees; its causal role in the important citrus replant problem in California was apparent. A little later Suite and DuCharme (1953) reported that the burrowing nematode (*Radopholus similis* (Cobb) (Thorne, 1949) was the causal agent of the serious disease called "spreading decline" in Florida.

These findings led to a number of important investigations on various phases of nematode problems. By 1970, 209 species within 42 genera of plant-parasitic nematodes had been reported in association with citrus roots from the citrus-growing areas of the world. There is evidence that only 16 of the 209 species are important parasites of citrus roots; actual proof of pathogenicity to citrus has been demonstrated for the following nine species: *Belonolaimus longicaudatus* Rau, 1958; *Hemicycliophora arenaria* Raski, 1958; *Pratylenchus brachyurus* (Godfrey, 1929) Filipjev & Schuurmans Stekhoven, 1941; *P. coffeae* (Zimmerman, 1898) Filipjev & Schuurmans Stekhoven, 1941; *P. vulnus* Allen & Jensen, 1951; *Radopholus similis; Trichodorus christiei* Allen, 1957; *T. porosus* Allen, 1957; and *Tylenchulus semipenetrans*. These nematodes will be treated in the order of their economic importance to citrus culture.

Nematodes that attack citrus and other plants are members of the phylum Nemata. They are small round worms, nonsegmented, and usually about 0.4 1.0 mm long. The different species of nematodes that attack citrus differ considerably in shape, size, life history, root tissues attacked, prevalence, and economic importance.

THE CITRUS NEMATODE

The citrus nematode, *Tylenchulus semipenetrans*, occurs in most citrus-growing countries and areas. In the United States it occurs in Arizona, California, Florida, Louisiana, and Texas. It was first observed on orange trees by J. R. Hodges in 1912 in southern California. Soon after, Thomas (1913) reported its occurrence on citrus in Alabama, California, and Florida in 1913. That same year, Cobb (1913) described the nematode and gave additional information on its occurrence on citrus in Australia, Malta, Palestine, Spain, and South America. Thomas (1920) reported that the citrus nematode was widespread in California, and showed that it could injure citrus trees seriously. However, the methods used to demonstrate the detrimental effects of the nematode on the growth of trees may be questioned, since the root washings that he used to infest trees contained not only citrus nematodes but also many other organisms.

Extensive surveys in California reported by Spears (1956) and Alstatt and French (1964) revealed that 92 per cent and 85.6 per cent, respectively, of bearing trees in California were infested with this nematode. Reynolds and O'Bannon (1958) reported that about 50 per cent of the bearing trees in Arizona were infested, and Hannon (1962) reported that 53 per cent of those in Florida were infested. The citrus nematode also occurs on citrus in Algeria, Argentina, Australia, Brazil, China, Egypt, Greece, India, Iran, Iraq, Israel, Italy, Japan, Lebanon, Morocco, Spain, and Taiwan. The wide distribution of this nematode suggests that it has been disseminated by the movement and planting of infested young citrus trees. Alstatt and French (1964) reported that fifteen of twenty citrus nurseries examined in California were infested with the citrus nematode. However, its spread by this means has greatly decreased in recent years.

The citrus nematode does not kill citrus trees but greatly decreases their rate of growth and yield. Young sweet orange (*C. sinensis* (L.) Osbeck), Rough lemon (*C. jambhiri* Lush.), or Troyer citrange rootstocks inoculated with the citrus nematode under controlled conditions weighed between 12 per cent and 60 per cent less than uninoculated trees (fig. 7-2) (Baines, 1950; Baines and Clarke, 1952). The yield of orange trees and young lemon trees frequently decreased by 30 to 50 per cent (fig. 7-3) (Baines and Martin, 1953; Baines, Foote, and Martin, 1956; Baines *et al.*, 1962). The nematode is the principal cause for unthrifty growth and low yield of citrus trees that usually occur when young trees with citrus nematode-susceptible rootstocks are planted on soil infested with nematodes in California and Florida. This condition usually is referred to as the citrus-replant problem.

The extent of decline of mature citrus trees infected with the citrus nematode is related to their vigor and tolerance to the nematode and the degree of root infection. The detrimental effects of the citrus nematode frequently are masked and not readily recognized; trees with genetically-controlled vigor may produce economically satisfactory yields which, in reality are much below their potential. In fact, yields from healthy appearing and high yielding grapefruit, lemon, orange and mandarin trees were increased by 20 to 50 per cent or more after control of the citrus nematodes on their roots.

The causal role of the citrus nematode in the cyclic decline of some mature grapefruit, lemon, or mandarin trees is not completely known. The term "cyclic decline" describes a syndrome in which fairly healthy trees quickly decline in tree condition and vigor, and produce less shoot growth and low yields of small size fruit. Trees may remain in a decline condition for two or more years and then slowly improve. Reynolds and O'Bannon (1963) reported a negative correlation between the population of citrus nematodes in the first foot of soil and the condition of the tops of grapefruit trees and fruit yield in Arizona. However, in California, some mature grapefruit, lemon, or orange trees (20 to 70 years old) that are heavily infected with the citrus nematode have not developed typical decline symptoms, while trees in nearby orchards in the same area have declined (Harding, 1954). In some cases the onset of decline may be rather sudden and apparently is caused by the interaction of a number of factors. Control of the citrus nematode on the roots of decline trees by treatment with nematicides has improved the condition of the trees and increased yield in many orchards. This further indicates the causal role of the citrus nematode in decline of bearing trees (Baines, Stolzy, and Taylor, 1959; Reynolds and O'Bannon, 1958). Hannon (1962) reported that orange trees in coastal areas of Florida showing symptoms of slow decline usually were infected with the citrus nematode; however, he did not demonstrate the causal role of the citrus nematode.

Citrus trees infected by this nematode develop no symptoms on the above-ground parts that are specific for the nematode (figs. 7-2 and 7-3). However, roots infected by the nematode usually appear encrusted, due to soil particles that adhere to the mucus excreted by the female and which envelops the eggs (fig. 7-4). Adhering soil is not readily removed by washing in water. When infected roots are examined at about 30 times magnification, eggs and larvae may be seen around the posterior portion of the mature female nematode protruding from the roots (fig. 7-4).

Nematodes and Mineral Nutrition

The adverse effects of the citrus nematode on the growth rate and vigor of the trees and their fruit production usually are not caused by adverse changes in the mineral nutrition of the tree. Van Gundy and Martin (1961) reported that the citrus nematode slightly decreased the concentration of leaf Mn and Zn of sweet orange seedlings in soils that contained high levels of K or Na. Leaf copper

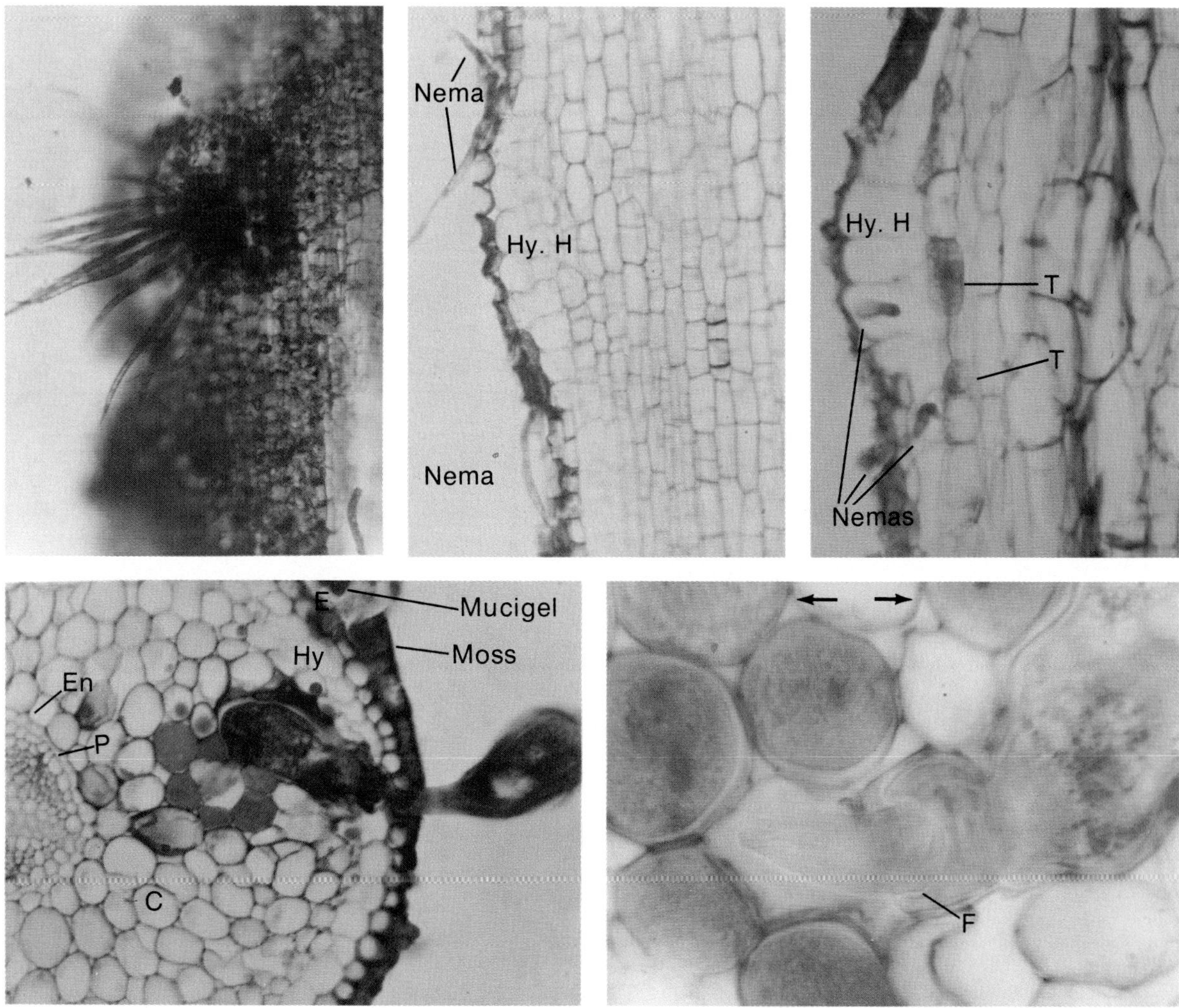

Fig. 7–1. Citrus nematodes on and within citrus roots. Upper left, many citrus nematode larvae (second and third stages) that have penetrated the epidermis in a small area and are on hypodermal cells. Upper center, second stage larvae or males on surface of a root. Upper right, anterior portions of larvae in hypodermal or hypodermal hair cells that have fed on densely stained cortical cells (designated T). Adult female nematode that has penetrated deeply into the cortex of a young (primary stage) sweet orange root. Cortical cells have been killed by penetration of the nematode into the root. The anterior part of the nematode within the root is greatly distorted and the posterior part protruding from the exterior of the root is greatly enlarged. Lower left, note the wound reaction, and the circle of densely stained cells that enclose the head of the nematode. Lower right, view of the head of an adult female and the densely stained cells that have been fed upon (feeding site). (Photos by H. Schneider, 1964.)

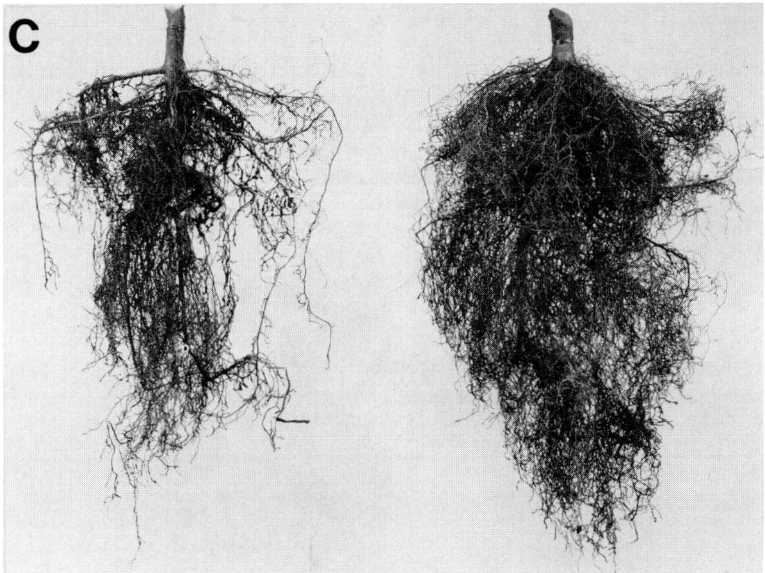

Fig. 7–2. Effect of *T. semipenetrans* on the growth of young lemon and orange trees on standard sour orange rootstock. *A*, left, two noninfected Frost Eureka lemon trees; right, two trees infected with *T. semipenetrans*, 10 months after inoculation. *B*, left, two noninfected Campbell Valencia orange trees; right, two trees infected with *T. semipenetrans*. *C*, left, sour orange roots from Valencia orange tree infected with *T. semipenetrans;* right, noninfected roots.

Fig. 7–3. Growth of orange trees on fumigated and on nonfumigated old citrus soil. Upper left, four-year-old Valencia orange tree on sweet orange rootstock on nontreated soil. Upper right, four-year-old Valencia orange tree on sweet orange rootstock growing in a soil that had been treated before planting with 50 gallons of D-D per acre. Lower left, four-year-old Frost nucellar navel orange on Troyer citrange rootstock on nontreated soil. Lower right, a similar tree on soil that had been treated with 70 gallons of D-D per acre.

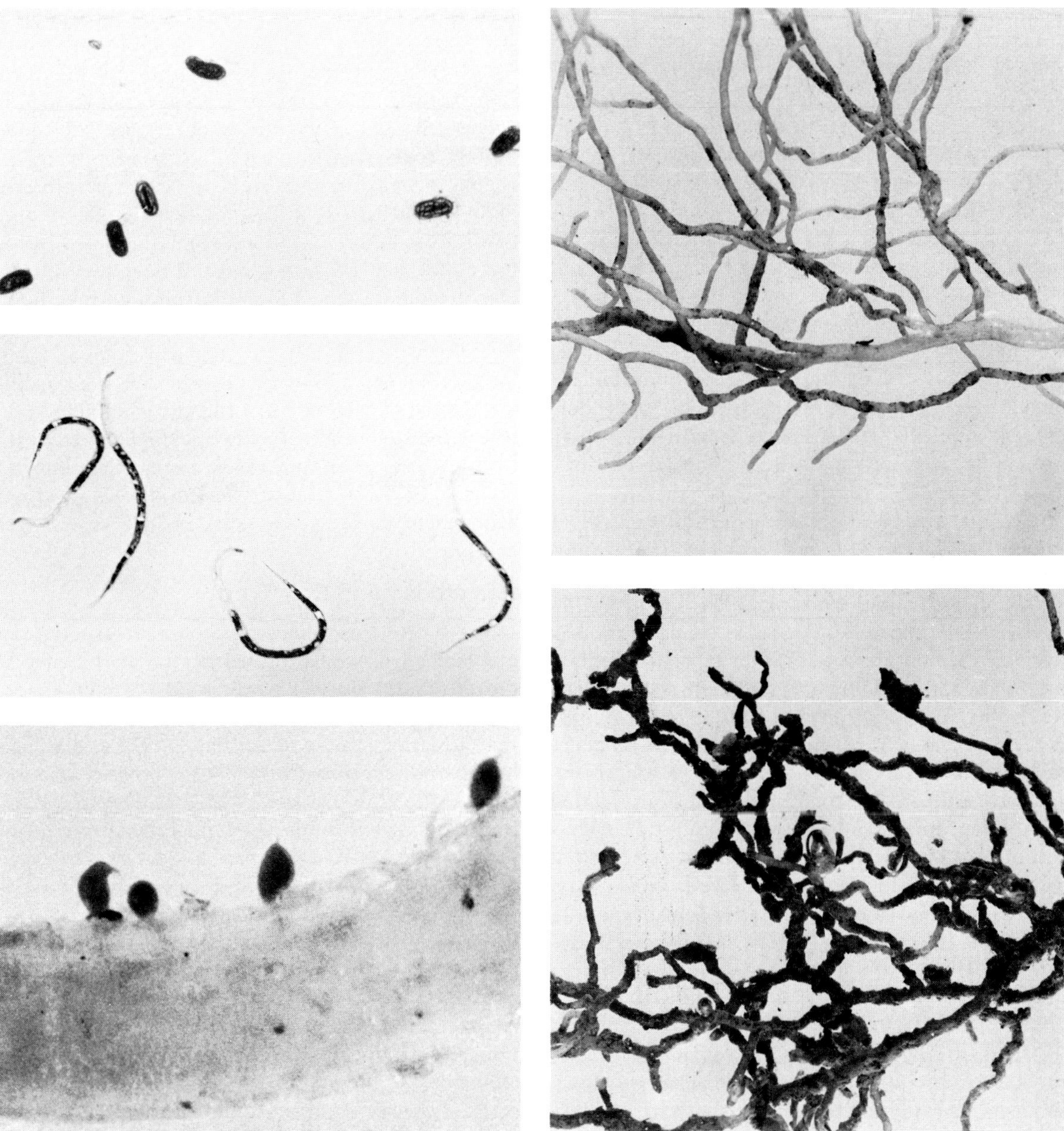

Fig. 7–4. Left, top to bottom: eggs, second stage larvae, and adult female citrus nematodes partially embedded in a sweet orange root. Top right, healthy noninfected sweet orange roots. Lower right, roots heavily infected with the citrus nematode.

was reduced by the citrus nematode in all treatments, but was deficient only in soils that were high in $CaCo_3$, K, or Na. Elgindi *et al.* (1967) reported that light nematode infection (approximately 1 gravid female nematode per 2 cm of feeder roots) decreased the concentration of Mn and Zn by 69 and 46 per cent, respectively, ten weeks after inoculation.

Labanauskas, Baines, and Stolzy (1965) found in two experiments that the differences in concentration of minerals, including Cu, in leaves and roots of both infested and noninfested navel or Valencia orange trees on sweet orange rootstock were too low in magnitude to account for the smaller size of the infested trees. Copper deficiency of citrus trees infected with the citrus nematode is not common in California (Bradford and Harding, 1957; Harding, 1954).

In most cases, deficiencies and excesses of mineral elements are not associated with slow-decline of citrus trees in California. Bradford and Harding (1957), and Harding (1954) found no important differences between the concentration of mineral elements in leaves from trees in 42 high-producing and 30 low-producing orchards. The nematode infestation in 24 of these orchards was determined and, in all but two cases, the concentration of mineral elements was in the range considered adequate for good growth and production (Embleton, Jones, and Labanauskus, 1962). Two of the orchards showed low amounts of copper, yet growth and yield were considered satisfactory. When high concentrations of salts occur in the soil, nematode infection may result in salt concentrations in the leaves that are detrimental to tree growth and production (Baines *et al.*, 1962; Van Gundy and Martin, 1961). The citrus nematode decreases the vigor of trees and apparently makes them more prone to injury from toxic sprays, leading to further debilitation of the trees.

Yields of grapefruit, lemon, and orange trees in both high and low production brackets have been increased greatly by partial control of the citrus nematode with DBCP* (1–2–dibromo-3–chloropropane) (Baines, Stolzy, and Taylor, 1959; Baines, Small, and Stolzy, 1965; O'Bannon and Reynolds, 1963; Reynolds and O'Bannon, 1958, 1963). Analysis of grapefruit and orange leaves in one orchard revealed no changes in the concentration of nutrient elements sufficient to account for the increases in yield and average fruit size obtained by citrus nematode control (Embleton, Jones, and Baines, unpublished data).

The exact nature of the injurious effects of the citrus nematode on citrus trees is not known. It seems that the nematode injects some substance into the roots, possibly an inhibitors of some growth-regulating mechanism, that slows the growth and yield of the trees. Other deleterious effects may result from injury and reduction of the roots. It was thought this might lead to a water deficit within the tree during periods of high transpiration rate; however, unpublished data on rate of water removal in two orchards and of water usage by trees in large tanks failed to support this contention. The insidious nature of the effects of the citrus nematode on tree condition, rate of growth, yield, and size of fruit are very real, and result in many millions of dollars loss in income to the producers of citrus fruits each year.

Nematodes and Soil Types

The citrus nematode occurs on all soil types in which citrus is planted around the world, such as gravelly sand, sand, loamy sands, sandy loams, loams, clay loams, and clay. O'Bannon (1968) found that a higher percentage of larvae infested Rough lemon roots growing in a potted mixture of sand and peat than in just sand. Van Gundy *et al.* (1964) reported that the citrus nematode reproduced most rapidly on Rough lemon and on sweet orange in a potted medium textured sandy loam and less rapidly in sand and clay loam soils. Baines (1974) reported that a higher percentage of nematode larvae infected sweet orange roots in a sandy loam or loamy sand than in coarse sand or in a mixture of coarse sand and peat (2:1 V/V). Under field conditions severe infestation has been observed on sour and sweet orange rootstocks on all soils, except coarse textured sands in California and in Morocco (Villardebo, 1963). Orange roots in sands usually are sparse and appear thick and irregular in shape due to growing between angular particles of sand. Such roots may be less susceptible to the citrus nematode; however, ecological conditions in sand also appear to be less favorable for the citrus nematode than in finer textured soils. Soil acidity between pH 4.9 and 7.6 was most favorable for reproduction of the citrus nematode (Van Gundy and Martin, 1961). A very high level of infection on sweet orange roots in many field soils with pH

*DBCP is no longer authorized, in any chemical or commercial formulation, as an agent in nematode control (effective July, 1977) in California.—Ed

values between 4.5 and 7.8 has been observed. Martin and Van Gundy (1963) found that when P concentration in sweet orange roots increased above 0.2 per cent, the reproduction rate of the nematode decreased. Changes in the concentration of other macro-elements had no direct effect on the nematode.

Nematodes, Soil Moisture, and Oxygen Supply

Soil moisture in the range favorable for the growth of citrus is also favorable for the development and survival of nematodes. High soil moisture content that results in low available oxygen may be unfavorable for the development of both the citrus nematode and citrus roots. Van Gundy, Martin, and Tsao (1964) found that nematode reproduction in sand was favored by low water suction of 0–10 cb; however, in soils containing 13 or 17 per cent clay, reproduction was good at soil-moisture suctions between 0–60 cb on sweet orange seedlings in pots. In studies conducted on a sandy loam in the field and on a loamy sand in large containers outdoors (Labanauskas, Baines, and Stolzy, 1965), the citrus nematode developed equally well at 0–10 cb, and at 60–90 cb water suction. In two other tests, the citrus nematode developed best on sweet orange trees growing under a system in which water was applied only when the suction reached 60 or 70 cb. Since citrus nematode eggs hatch at low soil water tension (0–10 cb), irrigation regimes in which water is applied frequently at low water suction should promote prompter hatching of eggs than when water is applied at less frequent intervals (high suction). This should lead to earlier infection and a more rapid increase of the nematode population when oxygen is not a limiting factor. Frequently, other factors such as aeration and organisms active in the biological control of nematodes are affected by the irrigation regime (Baines, Stolzy and Mankau, unpublished data).

Normal levels of oxygen (oxygen diffusion rate [O.D.R.] of +70 gm $\times$ 10^{-8} $cm^{-2}/min.$) that normally occur in the top two feet of orchard soils are favorable for the development and reproduction of the citrus nematode. At lower levels (O.D.R. of +27), the citrus nematode reproduced at about one half the rate that occurred at O.D.R. 70 (Stolzy *et al.*, 1963). Citrus nematodes survive at depths of from 6 to 8 feet in fine textured soils in California; however, the number of larvae and roots is usually less than occurs in shallower soil.

Effect of Soil Temperature on Infection and Survival

Soil temperatures (see chap. 9, Vol. III) between 25° C and 30° C are most favorable for invasion and development of the citrus nematode on sour orange, sweet orange, or Rough lemon seedlings. Only slight infection occurred at 20° C and 35° C (Baines, 1950; O'Bannon *et al.*, 1966). Soil temperature also affects the longevity or survival of the citrus nematode in soil. Baines (1950) reported that citrus nematode larvae survived for more than one year at 15° C in moist soil that had been steam pasteurized, for one year at 21° C, six and one-half months at 27° C, and for two and one-half months at 33° C. Reynolds *et al.* (1970) reported that larvae and eggs survived for eighteen months in shaded soils in Arizona and Florida. Infective larvae were found to survive in the upper 3 feet of sandy loam soils for five and nine years after mature citrus trees had been removed in California (Baines *et al.*, 1962). In these cases, the citrus nematode appeared to have survived and reproduced on large living citrus roots that occurred in the soil after removal of the trees. However, second stage larvae in eggs may have entered a quiescent state that favored survival. During cropping to nonhosts such as alfalfa, lima beans, or oats for five years, the population of citrus nematodes decreased greatly. Many larvae survived five years' crop rotation and, in fact, soil-fumigation with D-D increased the growth rate and yield of lemon trees. Reynolds and O'Bannon (1963) reported that high soil temperatures (maximum of 39° C at a depth of 50 cm) were unfavorable for development of the citrus nematode, and that only slight infection developed on young citrus trees during the first three years in unshaded soil. During storage in water at 27° C, second stage larvae gradually depleted lipids in their bodies and survived only for three months (Van Gundy, Bird, and Wallace, 1967). Cohen (1966) reported that approximately 70 per cent of citrus nematode larvae survived 24 months *in vitro* at 10° C and that they were as infective, even though vacuolated, as nematodes obtained from fresh citrus roots. Larvae are less active at low soil temperatures and are able to survive for longer periods of time than at high temperatures.

The Nematode's Life Cycle

The specific time required for the citrus nematode to complete its four- to six-week life cycle depends on the temperature and the host

(Cohn, 1965; Macaron, 1972; O'Bannon, Reynolds and Leathers, 1966; Van Gundy, 1958). The citrus nematode molts four times to become a young adult, the first of these molts occurring within the egg. Upon hatching, the second stage larvae molt three times to become young adults (Cobb, 1913; Gutierrez, 1947; Van Gundy, 1958). The larvae feed on the epidermis, hypodermis, and outer cortical cells of rootlets (fig. 7-1) (Cohn, 1965; Schneider, and Baines, 1964; Van Gundy and Kirkpatrick, 1964). This feeding is necessary for larvae to develop and molt. The young female penetrates deeply into the root cortex by feeding upon and passing through one cell after another. Usually the young female does not penetrate in a straight line, but may exit through the side wall of a cell and then turn at right angles to penetrate deeper into the cortex (fig. 7-1). When penetration ceases, the head of the female nematode is positioned in a cortical parenchyma cell, which is killed. The nematode then feeds on the cells that surround the one in which the head is located (fig. 7-1). Cytoplasm in the cells fed upon is dense, fills the lumen, and the nucleus is more prominent than in nonaffected cells. During this process of feeding and penetration, the anterior portion of the nematode within the cortex enlarges, becomes modified, and completely fills the space occupied by the cells through which it passed.

The posterior portion of the nematode that protrudes from the exterior of the root enlarges greatly with development of the reproductive system. Under conditions favorable for development, the first eggs are laid four to six weeks after hatching. They are enveloped in a mucus-like material that is excreted from the excretory pore (Maggenti, 1962) and accumulates in a mass around the female. Waste material also is excreted from the excretory pore and accumulates to form a scale-like encrustation around the pore (Gutierrez, 1947; Alvira and Bello, 1975). Second stage male larvae usually feed, but the young male has only a weak or rudimentary stylet and apparently is unable to feed of roots.

Nematode Hosts

Twenty-six citrus species, twenty-four other plants in the family Rutaceae, and nine noncitrus plants are hosts of the citrus nematode (Baines, Bitters and Clarke, 1960; Cohn, 1966) (Table 7–1).

Many of the plants listed as susceptible are poor hosts in many cases or are not susceptible to all populations or biotypes of *T. semipenetrans*. Thus, olive is susceptible in the United States and South Africa, but not in Israel and Italy. Many selections of *P. trifoliata* are moderately susceptible while others are highly resistant in different citrus regions. *Severinia buxifolia* was not susceptible to two biotypes of the citrus nematode in California, but is susceptible to a slight degree in Florida, and in Israel and South Africa.

Certain selections of *Poncirus trifoliata* are highly resistant to the citrus nematode in Argentina, California, Florida, Israel, and Japan (Baines, Clarke, and Cameron, 1958; Baines, Bitters, and Clarke, 1960; Baines *et al.*, 1969; Cohn, 1965; DuCharme, 1949; Feder, 1968). *P. trifoliata* hybridizes readily with most *Citrus* spp. and a high per cent of F_1 progeny from crossing *Citrus* spp. with *P. trifoliata* were found to be highly resistant to the citrus nematode (Cameron, Baines, and Clarke, 1954). Some F_1 hybrids such as the Carrizo, Troyer, and Uvaldi citranges are highly resistant to certain biotypes of the citrus nematode in California. Biotypes of the citrus nematode, which can be distinguished by their capacity to infect the Troyer citrange and certain selections of *P. trifoliata*, and other noncitrus hosts, occur in California, Florida, Israel, Italy, and Japan (Baines *et al.*, 1969, 1974; Lamberti *et al.*, 1976; O'Bannon *et al.*, 1977). Biotypes of the citrus nematode that differ in pathogenicity on resistant hosts should be considered in the development of satisfactory nematode-resistant rootstocks for citrus by breeding and selection, and in their use.

Differences in Host Resistance.— Differences also occur in the susceptibility of highly susceptible hosts to the nematode. Cohn (1965) reported that the citrus nematode completed its life cycle in a shorter time on Palestine sweet lime than on sour orange. Van Gundy and Kirkpatrick (1964) reported that the resistance of some hosts to the nematode is due chiefly to two factors: (1) a hypersensitive reaction exhibited by immune or highly resistant hosts, such as *Severinia buxifolia* and *Poncirus trifoliata*, to early feeding by larvae; and (2) the formation of wound phelloderm that walls off the nematode and surrounding cortical tissues in moderately resistant hosts, such as the Troyer citrange. Immune and resistant hosts, such as *Severinia* and *Poncirus*, also contained higher concentrations of a water-soluble compound toxic to nematodes than susceptible roots, which may retard or inhibit the development of the nematode and thus enhance the morphological factors for resistance. The susceptibility and resistance of hosts to the nematode also may be due to other factors than these. Recently, Baines (1974) showed that a selection of sour orange was highly tolerant of the citrus nematode.

Nematode Control

Fumigation.—In many soils infested with the citrus nematode, highly resistant rootstocks, such as *P. trifoliata* and its hybrids (citranges), should be used where feasible. When resistant rootstocks are used, it is not necessary to preplant fumigate the soil to kill the citrus nematode. On the other hand, scion trees on rootstocks either slightly or highly susceptible to this pest have benefited from preplanting soil fumigation when soil was infested with a biotype of the citrus nematode that infected young trees. Preplanting soil fumigation has increased both the growth rate and yield of lemon or orange trees on susceptible rootstocks such as Cleopatra mandarin, grapefruit, Rough lemon, sour orange, sweet orange, and Troyer citrange from between 12 per cent and 50 per cent (Baines and Martin, 1953; Baines, Foote, and Martin, 1956; Baines *et al.*, 1962).

For lasting improvement of growth and

TABLE 7–1

CITRUS, RUTACEOUS, AND NONRUTACEOUS SPECIES SUSCEPTIBLE TO *TYLENCHULUS SEMIPENETRANS*

Citrus spp.

C. aurantifolia (Christm.) Swingle
C. aurantium L.
C. celebica var. *southwickii* (Wester) Swingle
C. depressa Hayata
C. erythrosa Hort. ex Tanaka
C. excelsa Wester
C. grandis (L.) Osbeck
C. hystrix D. C.
C. ichangensis Swingle
C. jambhiri Lush.
C. limetta Risso
C. limon Burm f.
C. limonia Osbeck
C. longispina Wester
C. macrophylla Wester
C. medica L.
C. megaloxycarpa Lush
C. mitis Blanco
C. nobilis Lour.
C. paradisi Macford
C. reticulata Blanco
C. sinensis L. Osbeck
C. sunki Hort.
C. tiawanica Tanaka and Shimada
C. webberi Webster

Other Rutaceous Hosts

Afraegle paniculata (Schum.) Engle
Aegle marmelos (L.) Corr.
Atalantia ceylonica (Arn.) Oliv.
A. citroides Pierre ex Guill.
Calodendrum capensis Thunb.
Casamioa edulis La Llave
Citropsis daweana Swing. and M. Kell.
Clausenia anista Willd.
C. Lansium (Lour) Skeel
Cneoridium dumosum Kook.
Eremocitrus glauca (Lindl.) Swing.
Fortunella crassifolia Swing.
F. japonica Thunb.) Swing.
F. marginata (Lour) Swing.
F. obovata Hort.
Gragara capensis Thunb.
Glycosmis pentaphylla (Retz.) Corr
Poncirus triloliata (L.) Raf.
Microcitrus australasica (F. Muell.) Swing.
M. australasica var. *sanguinea* (F. M. Bail) Swing.
Murraya paniculata (L.) Jack
Ruta graveolens L.
Severinia buxifolia (Poir) Tenore
Vepril reflexa Veerdorn

Nonrutaceous Hosts

Andropogon rhisomatus Swallen
Diospyros kaki L.
D. lotus L.
D. virginiana L
Musa textilis Née
Olea europea L.
Syringa vulgaris L.
Vitis vinifera L.
V. belandieri Plancho X *V. ripari* Michaux

Sources: Baines, Bitters, and Clarke, 1960; Baines and Thorne, 1952; Cohn, 1966; Cohn and Milne, 1977; Cohn and Minz, 1961; Lamberti *et al.*, 1976; Nesbitt, 1956; Raski *et al.*, 1956; Seinhurst and Sauer, 1956; Stokes, 1969; and Villardebo and Luc, 1961.

yield of young trees, the entire area or field (overall treatment) should be treated and the nematodes controlled in the top 120 cm (four feet) or more of soil. On shallow soils, the nematode should be killed in the horizon into which the citrus roots will penetrate. Treating a small area around the tree site usually protects the young tree from infection for only a few years, and when the roots extend beyond the treated area into nontreated soil they become infected.

Nematicides.—The 1,3-dichloropropene type of nematicide (D-D[R] and Telone[R]) are highly effective for control of the citrus nematode in most soils. Other compounds such as methyl bromide, chloropicrin, carbon disulfide, Vapam[R] (sodium n-methyl dithiocarbamate) and Vorlex[R] (80 per cent chlorinated C_3 hydrocarbons including dichloropropenes, dichloropropanes, and related chlorinated hydrocarbons and 20 per cent methyl isothiocynate) and others are excellent nematicides when properly applied (Baines, Foote, and Martin, 1965; Baines *et al.*, 1957; Baines, DeWolfe, and Small, 1958; Baines *et al.*, 1966). They are used frequently to disinfest land that is to be planted to citrus. The optimum rate of chemical application for satisfactory control depends on the soil type (per cent clay and organic matter), depth of the root zone, soil structure or profile stratification, and soil moisture content. Some of these compounds also are effective for control of certain soil fungus pathogens such as *Phytophthora* spp. when applied at dosages two or more times that required to kill the citrus nematode (see chap. 1).

Control of the nematode on 50 to 90 per cent of the roots of bearing grapefruit, lemon, orange, and tangerine trees with DBCP (1,2-dibromo-3-chloropropane) has increased yields between 50 and 289 pounds (10 to 93 per cent) of fruit per tree in over thirty tests on different aged trees. The treatments generally increased the average fruit size and were highly profitable. DBCP is moderately toxic to citrus trees and care should be exercised in applying this compound (Baines *et al.*, 1965; Bistline *et al.*, 1963). The minimum dose (34.6 to 86.5 pounds of active ingredient [a.i.] per acre) to give effective control of the citrus nematode on the different soil types should be used (Baines, Stolzy, and Taylor, 1959; Baines, Small, and Stolzy, 1965; O'Bannon and Reynolds, 1963; Otiefa *et al.*, 1965; Reynolds and O'Bannon, 1958, 1963). The low dose is recommended for sands and loamy sands and the high dose for fine sandy loams. Large yield increases have occurred when DBCP was applied on two-thirds or more of the soil surface occupied by the trees. For optimum increases of yield with DBCP, the citrus nematode should be controlled in the top 90 to 120 cm (3 to 4 feet) of soil.

In many Arizona or California orchards that are irrigated by furrows, between 50 and 60 per cent of the soil area occupied by the trees is wetted during irrigation. In arid regions, DBCP need be applied only on the area wetted by the irrigation since roots active in absorption are in this area. In tilled orchards, DBCP should be injected 15 to 17 cm (6 to 7 in.) deep by chisel-shanks spaced 30 cm (12 in.) apart in the open area between the rows of trees. Then furrows should be made and water applied to distribute the DBCP through the soil. DBCP has low vapor pressure (0.8 mm of Hg at 20° C) and moves only slowly in the vapor phase through soil (Johnson and Lear, 1969).

In nontilled orchards that are irrigated by sprinklers, DBCP may be applied 7 to 10 cm (3 to 4 in.) deep by chisels spaced 30 cm (12 in.) apart on the area wetted. Within 72 hours after applying the DBCP, irrigation is done by sprinklers for 24 to 48 hours. Between 10 to 12.5 cm (4 to 5 acre in.) of water should be applied on sandy loam soils. Since DBCP lags behind the water front, larger amounts of water should be applied than in a normal irrigation. DBCP may be injected shallowly in the bottom of permanent furrows and water applied. When the furrows are spaced 90 cm (36 in.) apart, DBCP also should be injected into the ridge between the furrows to insure satisfactory control in this area. Because of this high rate of loss to the atmosphere, DBCP applied in irrigation water usually is not as effective as similar amounts injected into the soil (Baines, Stolzy, and Small, 1963; Hodges and Lear, 1973). However, on coarse textured sandy soils that have a high water infiltration rate, satisfactory control has been obtained with DBCP applied in a large volume of water by furrows, or in basins around the trees. Uneven and poor control frequently has occurred when DBCP was water-applied in permanent furrows when the infiltration rate was low. Loss of DBCP applied by low-head or over-head sprinklers or when sprayed onto the surface of soil has been excessive in many tests, and this method of application is not recommended because of poor and variable control (Baines *et al.*, 1963). Trees should not be treated with DBCP more often than once in three years in the United States because of bromide residue in soil.

Very likely, future use of DBCP for control of the citrus nematode will be definitely restricted by the California Department of Food and Agriculture and the United States Environmental Protection Agency. However, the application of DBCP by deep and shallow injection methods may be permitted. These methods of application would maximize control of the citrus nematode and result in a minimum loss of the compound into the atmosphere.

A number of nonvolatile nematicidal compounds have effectively decreased populations of the citrus nematode, increased yields, and improved the condition of orange trees (Baines *et al.*, 1969, 1977). Compounds such as aldicarb, ethoprop, furadan, and phenamiphos should be incorporated into the soil, and in arid areas irrigated to move the active ingredients to nematodes on tree roots and in the soil. Some of these compounds have systemic properties and also control certain insects. These compounds are highly toxic to warm-blooded animals; however they are nonvolatile at ordinary temperatures. This greatly lessens exposure of applicators to toxic amounts of the chemicals.

Biological Control.—A number of bacteria, fungi, protozoans, predacious nematodes, and microfauna attack plant-parasite nematodes (Boosalis and Mandau, 1965). Many of these organisms, especially nematode-trapping fungi, occur in the rhizosphere of citrus roots and kill many citrus nematodes. However, high levels of biological control of the citrus nematode were not achieved in most cases. Cohn and Mordechai (1974) reported that a predacious nematode *Mylonchulus sigmaturus* (Cobb) Altherr greatly decreased populations of citrus nematode larvae on potted sour orange seedlings. They also reported that *Tagetes patula* L. growing in pots with sour orange had no apparent effect on the development and reproduction of the citrus nematode for fifteen months. The important nematode-parasite *Bacillus penetrans* (Thorne, 1940) Mankau (1975) does not infect the citrus nematode, but infects *Meloidogyne* spp., *P. scribnerii*, *X. elongatum*, and others (Mankau and Imbriani, 1975; Mankau, 1977).

Spreading Decline

History and Distribution.—Spreading decline was recognized as a disease of citrus in Florida about 1930, but the fact that it was caused by the burrowing nematode, *Radopholus similis* (Cobb) Thorne (1949), was not determined until 1953 (DuCharme, 1954; Suite and DuCharme, 1953). Although *R. similis* is distributed throughout the tropical areas of the world and is known to parasitize more than 200 species of tropical and subtropical plants, it is a recognized problem of citrus only in Florida. Approximately 6880 hectares (17,000 acres) of citrus in Florida were infested in 1968, and 2291 hectares (5661 acres) in 1976. The burrowing nematode is also economically important on banana and black pepper in many countries (O'Bannon, 1977; Florida Division of Plant Industry, 1976).

Economic Importance.—Spreading decline constitutes one of the more serious diseases of citrus in Florida. Diseased trees are non-thrifty, lack vigor, and fruit yield is reduced. Loss of production varies from one grove to another, depending on the care the grove receives and the length of time it has been infested. In general, the reduction in yield ranges from 50 to 80 per cent for grapefruit, and 40 to 70 per cent for oranges (DuCharme, 1954; Suit and DuCharme, 1953, 1957; O'Bannon, 1977).

Grove Aspect.—A typical spreading decline area consists of a discrete group of nonthrifty appearing trees. Infested areas gradually increase in extent from year to year. The infested area may occur at any place in the grove and is recognized by the decline aspect of the trees in comparison to adjacent healthy trees.

The infested area increases in size in all directions regardless of rows and direction of cultivation. This measurable spread is a salient and reliable characteristic for diagnosing the disease and led to the name "spreading decline." The rate of spread is approximately 15.25 meters (50 feet) per year on the margin but varies from grove to grove and from year to year in the same grove (DuCharme, 1954; Suit and DuCharme, 1953, 1957). From centers of infection, nematodes cross wide areas into other groves under roads or railroad lines with rights-of-way 30.5 meters (100 feet) wide. These distances between trees are traversed by the nematodes' migrating along roots. At the edges of groves, roots of Rough lemon rootstocks may extend 18 to 21 meters (60 to 70 feet) from the tree trunks.

Since movement of water in sandy soils enhances the spread of nematodes, the spread downhill is greater than uphill in an infected grove (DuCharme, 1955). In one case, the spread downhill amounted to 61 meters (200 feet) in one year while the spread uphill was less than 8 meters (26 feet). The nematodes apparently are not carried freely through the soil in water, but their spread is aided by the flow of water through the soil.

Burrowing nematodes are spread to new locations mainly on infected nursery trees and, occasionally, but ornamental plants adjacent to citrus trees. Machinery for cultivating citrus grove soil may occasionally spread burrowing nematodes within a grove and also to other groves.

Tree Aspect.—Individual trees affected by spreading decline usually are stunted, and have undersized leaves and sparse foliage. Although trees appear to be undernourished, nutritional deficiency symptoms usually are not evident (Feldman *et al.*, 1961). Each flush is weak, has shortened internodes, and bears only three or four smaller-than-normal leaves. Numerous dead twigs are present. A definite change in a tree from a healthy to decline condition usually occurs at the spring flush of growth. The majority of older leaves drop; the flush, if it occurs, is sporadic and may be delayed from two to four weeks. There is a profuse bloom but only a small number of fruits are set. At maturity, the fruit is small although the internal quality is not affected seriously. Such trees remain permanently in a nonthrifty condition but are not killed unless completely neglected.

Decline symptoms in a tree result from the destruction of the feeder roots by the burrowing nematode (fig. 7–5). At depths between 25 and 76 cm (10 and 30 in.), 25 to 30 per cent of the feeder roots are killed; below 76 cm (30 in.), 90 per cent are killed (Ford, 1962). A tree with spreading decline has approximately one half as many functional feeder roots as a healthy tree, and these occur mainly in the upper 60 to 76 cm (24 to 30 in.) of soil.

Parasitized trees wilt more readily during periods of low soil moisture and high transpiration rate, because the reduced root system is unable to supply sufficient water. Adjacent healthy trees usually do not show a need for water under the same conditions. When moisture is again available, the trees make some recovery; but they never resume normal growth because new rootlets soon become infected with nematodes.

Causal Organism.—The burrowing nematode, *Radopholus similis,* was first found in banana roots in the Fiji Islands and was described by Cobb in 1893. Synonyms include: *Tylenchus similis* Cobb 1893; *Tylenchus acutocaudatus* Zimmerman 1898; *Tylenchus biformis* Cobb 1906; *Anguillulina similis* (Cobb, 1893) Goodey 1932; and *Rotylenchulus similis* (Cobb 1893) Filipjev 1936.

Biotypes.—There is a distinct dimorphism between the sexes. On citrus, the females vary from .65 mm to .80 mm long by 20μ to 24μ in diameter. The vulva is located at from 54 per cent to 59 per cent of the distance to the tail. The males, somewhat smaller, range from .5 mm to .65 mm long, and are more slender than the females. The female head is somewhat flat, rounded, supported by a sclerotized cephalic framework, and is offset from the body by a slight constriction. The spherical male head is not supported by a sclerotized framework and is sharply offset from the body by a deep constriction. On both sexes, the tail is elongate-conoid, tapering to an irregular blunt tip where the cuticle is much thickened. The stylet of the female is heavy, 17μ long, and has three distinct basal knobs. The male stylet is weak, short and without basal knobs (Van Weerdt, 1957, 1958).

Two biotypes have been recognized, one that parasitizes banana but not citrus, and the "citrus race," which parasitizes both citrus and banana (DuCharme and Birchfield, 1956). Detailed studies have not been made to determine if other biotypes exist. Adult nematodes from both biotypes did not appear to differ in gross morphologic dimensions and proportions. The race of *R. similis* pathogenic to citrus has been found only in Florida.

Effects of Temperature on Nematode Reproduction.—The optimum temperature range for growth and reproduction of *R. similis* extends from 20°C to 26.5° C and the most rapid population increase occurs at 24° C. The life cycle in citrus roots is completed in 19 to 21 days at 24° C to 26° C. At lower temperatures, the life cycle is extended. The optimum temperature for root invasion is also 24° C (fig. 7–5). The minimum temperature for root invasion and subsequent nematode reproduction is approximately 12° C and the maximum falls between 29.5° C and 32.5° C. In citrus groves on Lakeland fine sand at Lake Alfred, Florida, the monthly mean temperatures at 15 cm range from 15.5° C to 26° C (see chap. 9, vol. III). Although the monthly mean temperatures at 15 cm are within the limits of the extremes for growth and reproduction of *R. similis*, there are times when the soil temperature is either above or below these limits. In this zone, *R. similis* is not found regularly in infested citrus groves. Below 50 cm, which is the zone of greatest rootlet destruction, the monthly mean soil temperatures are close to or within the optimum temperature range for all phases of burrowing nematode activity (DuCharme, 1968). The greatest populations occur at depths

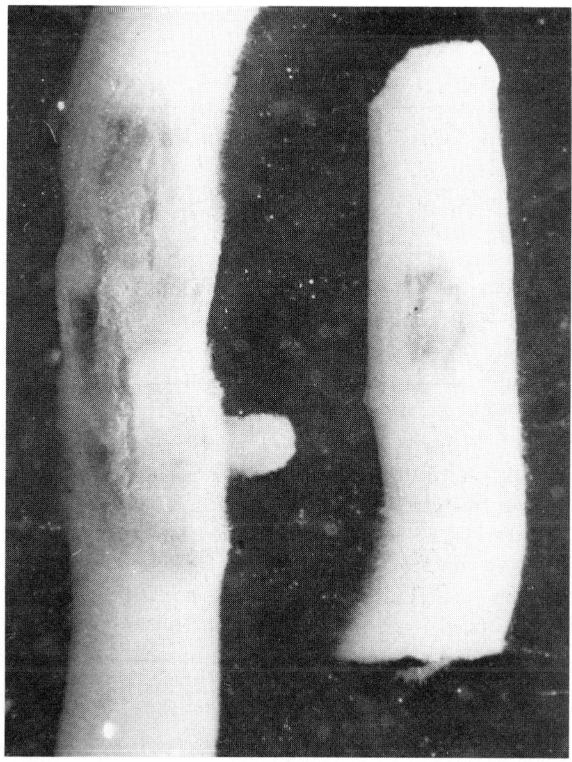

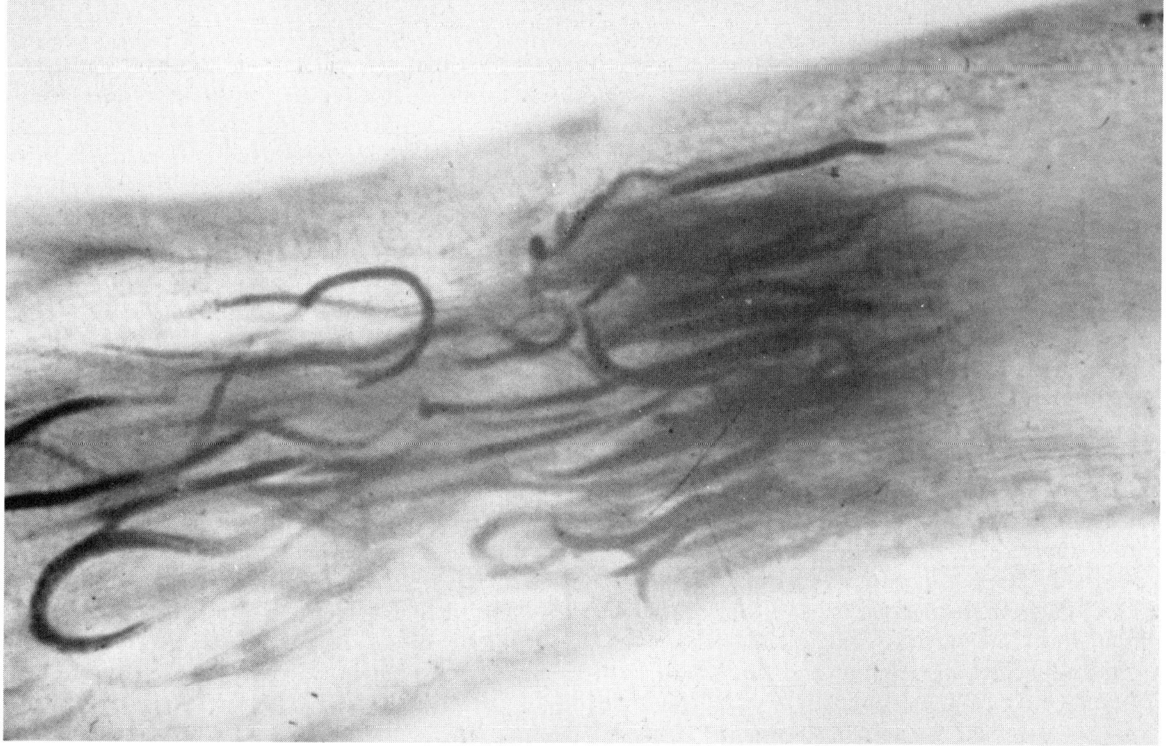

Fig. 7–5. Pathological effects of the burrowing nematode on grapefruit roots. Upper, external appearance of lesions caused by the burrowing nematode on grapefruit roots. Lower, distribution of burrowing nematodes within a citrus feeder root.

between 30 to 180 cm (1 and 6 feet), but also have been found in feeder roots obtained from a depth of 4 meters. The life span of individual *R. similis* is not known, but Tarjan (1961) reported that they have not survived more than 6 months in sandy soil free of citrus rootlets.

In infested orchards, the tips of new feeder roots are parasitized soon after they are produced, and within one month they have rotted and disappeared due to the action of the nematode and other soil micro-organisms, especially at depths below 60 cm. The burrowing nematode does not enter roots which have formed a hardened or suberized epidermis or in which tissue decay has started.

The population of *R. similis* in citrus roots in infested groves in Florida varies from quite high to quite low. The annual recurrence of highest populations takes place from October through December; the lowest populations occur from February through June. In the spring, the population of burrowing nematodes virtually disappears, making it difficult to find them even in groves known to be infested. Although the highest populations always occur during the fall, the precise month when the peak population is reached varies between groves and from year to year (DuCharme, 1967).

Burrowing nematodes are not dispersed uniformly throughout roots, but are aggregated in discrete colonies or lesions within rootlets. The number of nematodes in lesions averages 120 and ranges from just a few to several hundred. Under controlled glasshouse conditions, the population of colonies was much higher than in colonies in rootlets of grove trees (DuCharme and Price, 1966). The ratio of males to females is usually about 1:10; but in some collections, males comprise 40 per cent of the population. Females lay approximately two eggs per day, but can produce up to six eggs per day. This reproductive rate combined with a short life cycle accounts for the rapid population increase that occurs when conditions are favorable.

Method of Infestation.—Burrowing nematodes enter roots in the region of elongation and root hair production (fig. 7–5). To penetrate a rootlet, the female nematode punctures an epidermal cell, then predigests and sucks the dissolved cell contents. It then feeds on and kills adjacent cells in the same manner and gradually burrows into the root, forming cavities and tunnels in the cortex and stele. A female nematode usually enters a root in less than 24 hours. *R. similis* requires living roots for its food supply and normally lives inside rootlets. The nematodes also enter the stele through the passage cells in the endodermis and accumulate in large numbers in the region of the phloem-cambium ring which is often virtually destroyed. In addition, the stele is girdled by a nematode-filled cavity that separates it from the cortex (fig. 7-6). Starch grains disappear from the cells in and adjoining the lesion area. Wound gum accumulates in the invaded tissues, imparting a tan-to-amber color in the older portions of the lesion. Cells exposed to nematode metabolites may become hypertrophied. Hyperplasia and tumor formation from the pericycle occurs when the nematodes establish themselves next to the pericycle. Pericycle tumors are also attacked by the nematodes (DuCharme, 1957, 1959). The mature male nematode has a small rudimentary stylet and has not been observed to enter roots and form cavities.

Eggs are deposited inside the rootlets where the larvae hatch in 3 to 7 days and usually feed on the same or adjacent rootlets. The burrowing nematode spends virtually its entire life within rootlets, feeding and reproducing as long as the tissues remain free of decay. When the lesion is invaded by fungi and bacteria, that portion of the rootlet becomes unsuitable to the nematode. The nematodes then leave in search of new roots. Migration from roots is induced by population pressure and depletion of food. Duration of the migratory period depends on the time required to locate and enter a healthy root tip.

Decline symptoms usually appear about a year after the initial infection, the time required for the nematode population to become large enough to cause extensive root damage. Because of this, parasitized but apparently healthy citrus trees may occur two to three rows in advance of those having visible symptoms.

The respiration rate and catalase activity is lower in the roots of declined trees than in the roots of healthy trees, but is highest in the roots of infected trees before the appearance of visible symptoms (Ford, 1953).

Nematode Effects on Physiology and Mineral Nutrients.—Leaves from citrus trees infected with *R. similis* were found to contain less potassium and nitrogen than leaves from healthy trees. Potassium content was lower in leaves from visibly declined trees than in leaves from infected, but not visibly affected, trees. Potassium levels in leaves of decline trees could be increased by applying high rates of potassium to the soil; however, any improvement in the condition of trees was tempor-

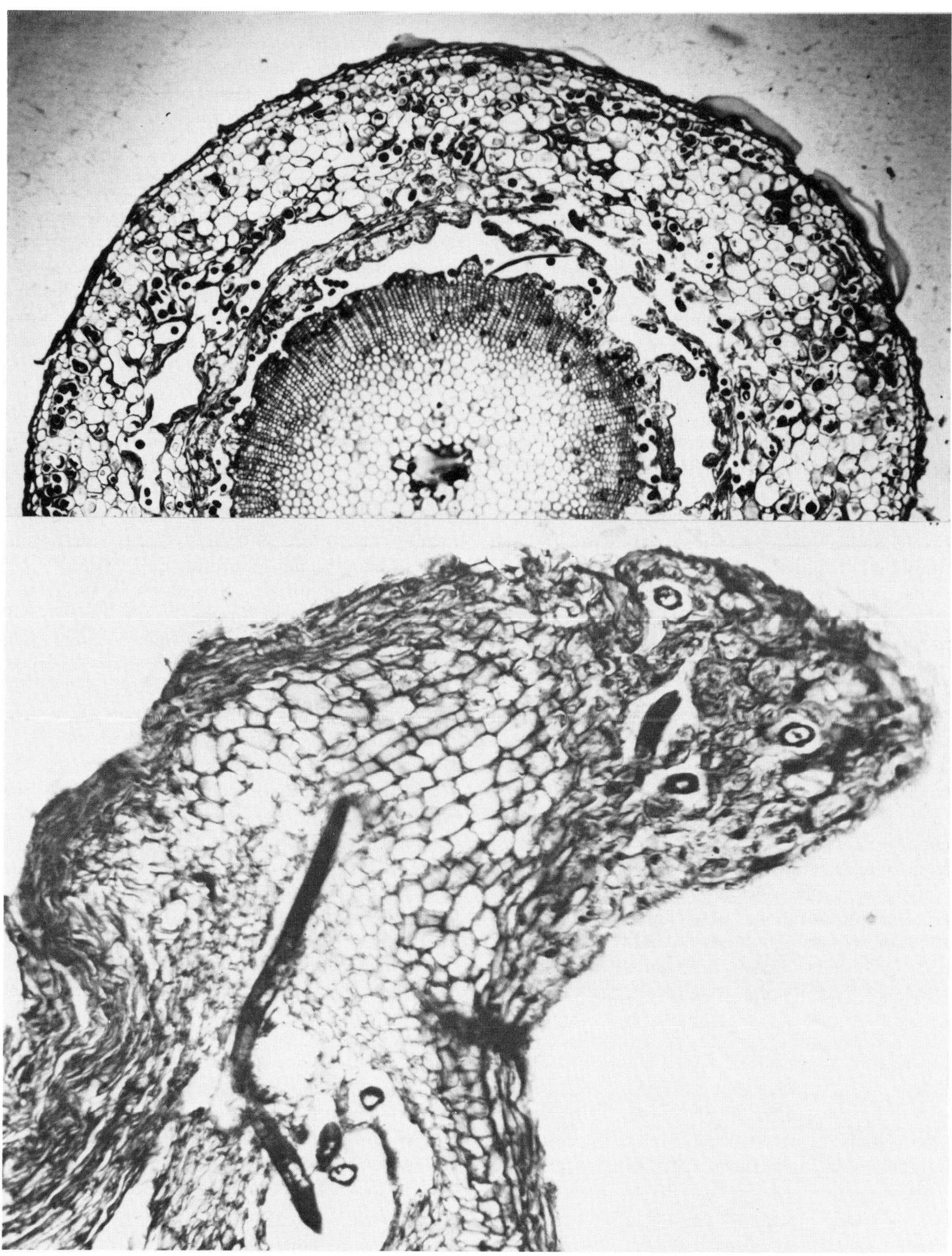

Fig. 7–6. Internal symptoms produced by the burrowing nematode *(R. similis)* in grapefruit roots. Upper, cross section of a grapefruit root in which the phloem-cambium ring has been destroyed by burrowing nematodes. Longitudinal section through a grapefruit root tip parasitized by burrowing nematodes.

ary. No difference was found between levels of phosphorous in decline and healthy trees (Feldman *et al.*, 1961).

Roots of grapefruit seedlings infected with *R. similis* contained up to 400 per cent more total free amino acid than the roots of healthy plants, but the proportion of each of the free amino acids, except arginine, was similar in the roots of diseased and healthy plants (Feldman and Hanks, 1964; Hanks and Feldman, 1963). The accumulation of arginine in the infested roots is characteristic of the biochemical syndrome. Between 39 and 58 per cent more protein amino acids occur in the roots of decline plants than in those of healthy plants, but there is no correlation between the amount of an amino acid in the amino acid pool and the amount in the protein hydrolyzate.

A high concentration of hesperidin occurs in the terminal branches of decline trees and is considered to be a causal factor for the reduced terminal growth of infected trees (Feldman *et al.*, 1966).

Similar phenolic substances were isolated from both healthy and *R. similis*-infected citrus trees. There were no consistent differences in the concentrations of specific free phenolic compounds or total free phenolics in *R. similis*-infected roots of tolerant and susceptible cultivars. However, infected roots of tolerant cultivars contained 27 to 300 per cent more bound phenolics, while roots of susceptible cultivars contained 16 to 34 per cent less bound phenolics than healthy citrus cultivars. No significant change in the quantity of total bound phenolics in leaves from infected tolerant and susceptible trees occurred. Free phenolics in leaves from tolerant cultivars increased from 2 to 7 per cent of total phenolics after infection, while the concentration of free phenolics in susceptible cultivars did not change (Feldman and Hanks, 1968).

The total organic acid content increased in leaves of *R. similis*-infected plants but decreased by 40 per cent in roots. There seemed to be no disproportionate accumulation or decrease of any one organic acid in the infected trees; instead, the entire organic acid system seemed to be affected as a unit (Hanks and Feldman, 1968).

Host Plants.–*Radopholus similis* has been demonstrated to parasitize 1,275 species and varieties of citrus and more than 250 kinds of tropical and subtropical plants (Ford *et al.*, 1960; Ford and Feder, 1962). Attempts to infect citrus with the banana biotype were unsuccessful, but the citrus biotype parasitizes and survives in roots of banana and many other kinds of plants including some of the endemic flora of citrus groves. The nematodes can spread within a grove and from one grove to another through such plants even when the groves are separated by wide strips of land covered only with mixed native vegetation.

Control of Burrowing Nematode

Efforts to control burrowing nematodes with systemic chemicals, high rates of fertilizer, organic matter, and by inoculation of soil with nematode-trapping fungi have not been effective (Feldman and Hanks, 1962; Feldman *et al.*, 1963; Ford, 1956; Suit and Brooks, 1957; Suit *et al.*, 1961; Suit and Feldman, 1961; Tarjan, 1959, 1961; O'Bannon and Tomerlin, 1977).

Burrowing nematodes were effectively eradicated from citrus seedlings in closed containers when the soil was treated with aqueous solutions of DBCP (1,2-dibromo-3-chloropropane), thionazin (0,0-diethyl 0-2 pyrazinyl phosphorothioate), Dasanit[R] (0,0-diethyl 0-[p-(methylsulfinyl) phenyl] phosphorothioate), Temik[R] (2-methyl-2-(methylthio) propionaldehyde 0-(methylcarbamoyl) oxime), Furadan[R] (2,3-dimethyl-2, 2-dihydro-7-benzofuranyl =– N-methylcarbamate), and FCS-13 (0-ethyl-S (N-methoxy-N-methylacetomide)-N-isopropylthio-phosphoramide) (Suit, 1969).

The same chemicals applied to the soil in diseased groves by sprinkler irrigation did not eradicate burrowing nematodes. Only partial control was achieved, and the nematode population regained its former level after one or two years. Some of these chemicals are phytotoxic to citrus and care must be taken in order not to damage the tree excessively and yet still reduce or kill the nematode population.

The "Pull and Treat" Method.—The only control treatment that has been effective is the "pull-and-treat" method, which consists in: eradicating all infected trees plus the noninfected trees from a strip two trees wide around the infested area; then removing all of the roots that can be deep plowed from the area; leveling; and treating the soil with D-D at 561 l/hectare (60 gallons per acre) injected 30 cm (12 in.) into the soil. The treated area is kept free of vegetation for two years before replanting with citrus. This procedure has been effective when carefully followed (Poucher *et al.*, 1967; Suit *et al.*, 1955; Suit and DuCharme, 1957; Suit, 1961). Recently, escapes or buildup of *R. similis* have occurred in some treated areas.

Barriers or buffer zones surrounding infested areas are used to delay or prevent the advance of the burrowing nematode into non-infested areas. A barrier or buffer zone consists of a strip of soil at least 4.9 meters (16 feet) wide treated with D-D or EDB every six months to maintain the zone free of living roots. The surface of the buffer zone is also cultivated regularly or treated with herbicides to prevent the growth of plants (Suit and Brooks, 1957; Suit and Feldman, 1964). One disadvantage of the barrier lies in maintaining an area infested with burrowing nematodes from which they might either migrate or be carried to healthy trees.

The pull-and-treat method and the barrier method have been highly successful, but costly. When they were first established, the Florida State Plant Board paid some of the costs involved; however, due to discontinuation of financial support, few citrus growers are treating and the control program at the orchard level has declined. The nursery certification program is highly effective in preventing or delaying spread of this nematode into new plantings (see chap. 3, pp. 189-96). In 1976 there were 2,291 hectares (5,661 acres) of citrus infested with *R. similis* in Florida, of which 201 hectares (498 acres) were without control (Florida Division of Plant Industry, 1973). This nematode does not occur on citrus in California and quarantine regulations to prevent its introduction are enforced.

Hot water treatment is effective in eradicating burrowing nematodes from infected nursery trees (Birchfield, 1954). The treatment consists in submerging the bare roots of trees in water maintained at 50° C for 10 minutes and then immediately placing the treated trees in cold water for 10 minutes. Trees that have been heat treated require more care and water after planting than nontreated trees.

Resistant Varieties.—Virtually no immunity to *R. similis* has been found within the citrus subtribes Citrinea and Balsamocitrinae, although some species and varieties possess varying degrees of resistance or tolerance (Feder *et al.*, 1958; Ford *et al.*, 1960; Ford and Feder, 1962). Three clonal selections somewhat resistant to *R. similis* are used for replanting in pulled and treated areas. These selections are: 'Milam,' a hybrid of unknown parentage; 'Estes,' a clone of Rough lemon (*C. jambhiri*); and 'Ridge Pineapple,' a variety of sweet orange (*C. sinensis*) (Ford and Feder, 1964).

Other Nematodes Pathogenic on Citrus

In addition to the citrus nematode *T. semipenetrans* and the burrowing nematode *R. similis*, some 40 other genera of nematodes have been found associated with citrus roots and soil in California, Florida, and other world citrus-growing areas.

In California alone some 30 species from 19 genera of plant-parasitic nematodes have been identified from citrus soils. They are: *Criconema*, *Criconemoides*, *Helicotylenchus*, *Hemicycliophora*, *Heterodera*, *Longidorus*, *Meloidogyne*, *Merlinius*, *Paratylenchus*, *Pratylenchus*, *Quinisulcius*, *Rotylenchus*, *Rotylenchulus*, *Scutellonema*, *Sphaeronema*, *Trichodorus*, *Tylenchorhynchus*, *Tylenchulus*, and *Xiphinema* (Siddiqui, Sher, and French, 1973).

Cohn (1972) has listed 22 species of nematodes other than the citrus and burrowing nematodes known to attack citrus. Of these, eight were listed as proven pathogens: *Belonolaimus longicaudatus*, *Hemicycliophora arenaria*, *Meloidogyne* sp., *Pratylenchus brachyurus*, *P. coffeae*, *Trichodorus christiei*, *Xiphinema brevicolle*, and *X. index*. The parasitic nature and importance of many of these nematodes in the citrus decline and replant problems are not known. Others may be potential pathogens of citrus, but have not been studied in detail.

Sheath Nematodes.—Seven species of sheath nematode, members of the genus *Hemicycliophora* have been found in citrus-growing areas. However, only *Hemicycliophora arenaria* and *H. nudata* have been demonstrated to be parasites on citrus roots. *H. nudata* occurs in Australia and produces conspicuous galls on roots of Rough lemon (Colbran, 1963; Meagher, 1969); however, little is known about its biology and pathogenicity (Colbran, 1964). The sheath nematode, *H. arenaria*, was shown to be pathogenic to citrus and to produce distinctive galls at the tips of terminal and lateral roots (Van Gundy, 1957). It is native to the Coachella and Imperial Valleys of California and occurs on a few citrus plantings near Mecca, Niland, and Holtville, California (McElroy *et al.*, 1966; Van Gundy and McElroy, 1969).

The female nematodes are about 1 mm long, have a conspicuous long stylet, a double cuticle, and a degenerate esophagus. Males are not known to feed and are not necessary for reproduction. The life cycle from egg to egg requires about 15–18 days at 28° C to 32° C. The second and third-larval stages survive for only one to two months in fallow soil, but the fourth-stage larvae and adult females are able to survive for at least six months (Van Gundy and Rackham, 1961). *H. arenaria* larvae and adult females feed ectoparasitically on root tips and cause them to swell into small knobs or galls. The swellings at the root tips may be distinguished from root enlargements caused by the root-knot nematode (*Meloidogyne* spp.) since they always occur at the root tips rather than along the root itself (fig. 7–7). Often, the nematodes will remain tightly attached by their stylet and a polysaccharide plug (McElroy and Van Gundy, 1968) to freshly dug roots and appear through a hand lens as fine waving hairs protruding from the galls.

A wide variety of hosts may be attacked, and growth may be reduced by as much as 35 per cent. The nematode infects and reproduces on the roots of plants in the Cucurbitaceae, Leguminoseae, Rutaceae, Solanaceae, and Umbelliferae. *Severinia buxifolia*, *C. jambhiri* (Rough lemon), *C. limettioides* (lime), *C. aurantifolia* (lime), *C. taiwanica*, *C. macrophylla* (alemow), and *C. reticulata* (mandarin) are readily infected. *C., aurantium* (sour orange), *C. paradisi* (grapefruit), *C. sinensis* (sweet orange), *Poncirus trifoliata* (trifoliate orange), and the Troyer and Carrizo citranges are nonhosts (Van Gundy and McElroy, 1969).

The sheath nematode is relatively easy to control because of its exposed nature in the soil and attachment to roots. Results from both laboratory and field tests indicate that 11.4 l per acre (3 gal.) (technical) of 1,2 dibromo-3-chloropropane will effectively kill sheath nematodes around citrus trees in sandy soils. A hot water dip at 46° C for 10 minutes will eradicate the nematodes attached to citrus roots.

Lesion Nematodes.—Seven species of the lesion nematode have been associated with citrus roots and soil. Only *Pratylenchus brachyurus* and *P. coffeae* in Florida, and *P. vulnus* in California and Italy have been shown to be pathogenic on citrus. Lesion nematodes are migratory endoparasites which invade and feed on the cortical parenchyma cells and thereby form cavities or tunnels within the cortex that are similar to those formed by the burrowing nematode.

The pathogenicity of *P. brachyurus* on *C. paradisi* was demonstrated by Brooks and Perry (1967). They found a reduction in both top and root growth of grapefruit seedlings infected by the lesion nematode, and suggested that it may be a factor in reducing yields of citrus trees in Florida. *P. brachyurus* is the most common *Pratylenchus* sp. in citrus in Florida (Tarjan and O'Bannon, 1969). Further reports (O'Bannon *et al.*, 1972, Radewald *et al.*, 1971) indicated that although *P. brachyurus* is common in citrus soils, it reproduced slowly at low soil temperatures. Visible injury was usually confined to young trees in the orchard; as the trees age, the effect of nematode damage appeared to diminish (O'Bannon *et al.*, 1973).

The pathogenicity of *P. coffeae* was demonstrated on Rough lemon seedlings in greenhouse culture and in newly planted orange trees in the field (O'Bannon, 1969; Radewald *et al.*, 1971). In the field, growth reduction of *P. coffeae*-infected young tangelo trees grafted on Rough lemon, sour orange, or mandarin rootstocks was 80, 77, and 49 per cent, respectively, after four years. Yields on noninoculated trees were greater than those on inoculated trees (O'Bannon and Tomerlin, 1973). This nematode also is associated with poor condition of large trees in a few orchards (Tarjan and O'Bannon, 1969). Anatomical studies of host parasite relationships (fig. 7–8) indicated that *P. coffeae* could be a serious threat to citrus production (Radewald *et al.*, 1971). In greenhouse tests, 125 *Citrus* spp. hybrids and three *Citrus* relatives were susceptible to *P. coffeae*. Three *M. australis X M. australasica* hybrids and Rubidoux 70-A5 trifoliate orange were highly resistant to *P. coffeae* (O'Bannon and Esser, 1975).

Jensen (1953) found that *C. paradisi* and *C. sinensis* were suitable hosts for *P. vulnus;* however, in tests by Baines *et al.* (1959) on young Rough lemon and sweet orange trees planted in soil infested with *P. vulnus*, the nematode disappeared after two years. In later tests, *P. vulnus* reproduced on and decreased the growth rate of young Valencia orange trees on trifoliate orange or Troyer citrange rootstock. Inserra and Lamberti (1976) reported that *P. vulnus* decreased the growth of Rough lemon seedlings by 40 per cent and that nematode populations increased on this host.

Sting Nematodes.–*Belonolaimus gracilis* Steiner and *B. longicaudatus* Rau have been found in citrus groves only in Florida (Malo, 1961). Christie (1959) mentioned that sting nematodes were associated with root injury and lack of tree vigor in

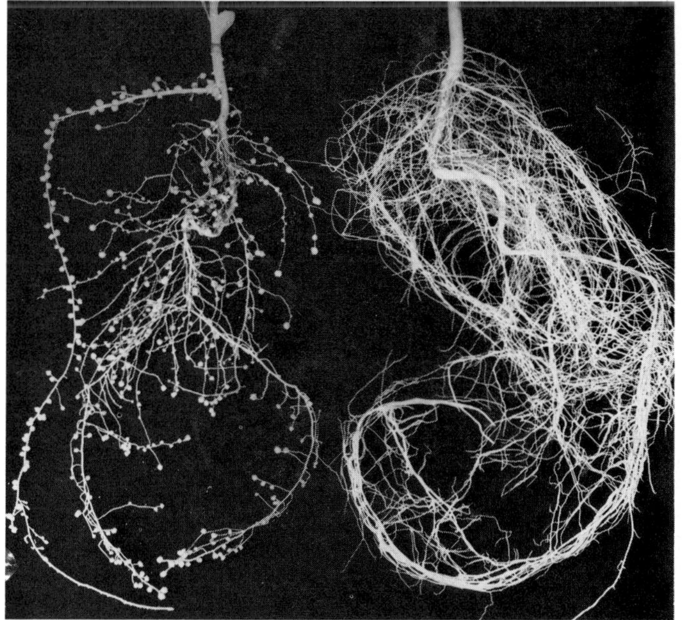

Fig. 7–7. Sheath nematodes *(H. arenaria)* on Rough lemon roots. Upper, numerous large sheath nematodes feeding on the swollen root tips. Lower left, bead-like swollen root tips of a Rough lemon seedling infected with burrowing nematodes. Lower center, healthy roots of a Rough lemon seedling. View of the head ends of two burrowing nematodes attached by means of their long, strong, stylet to a swollen root tip. Note the three cuticles of the nematodes.

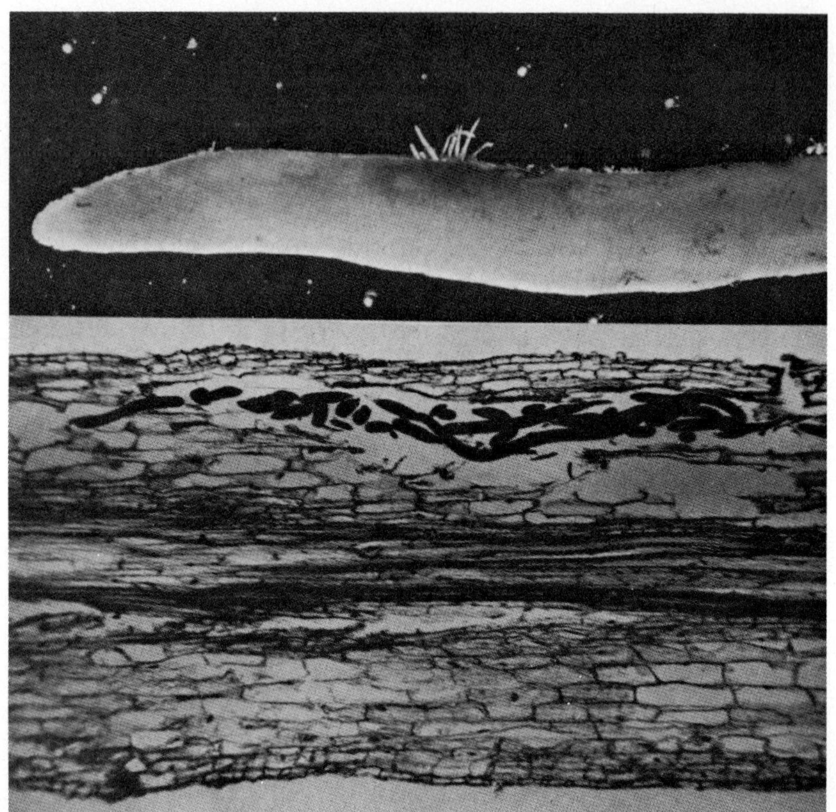

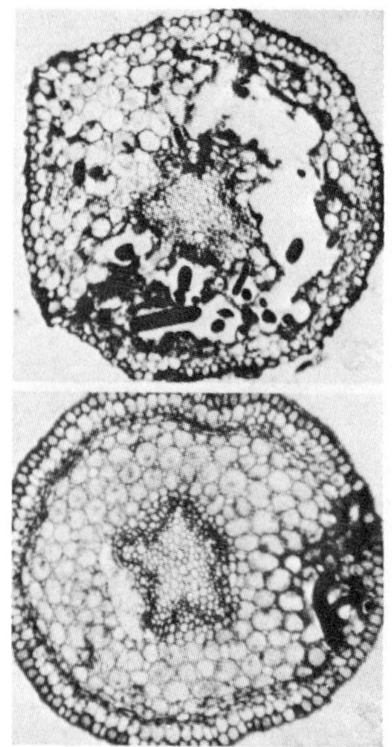

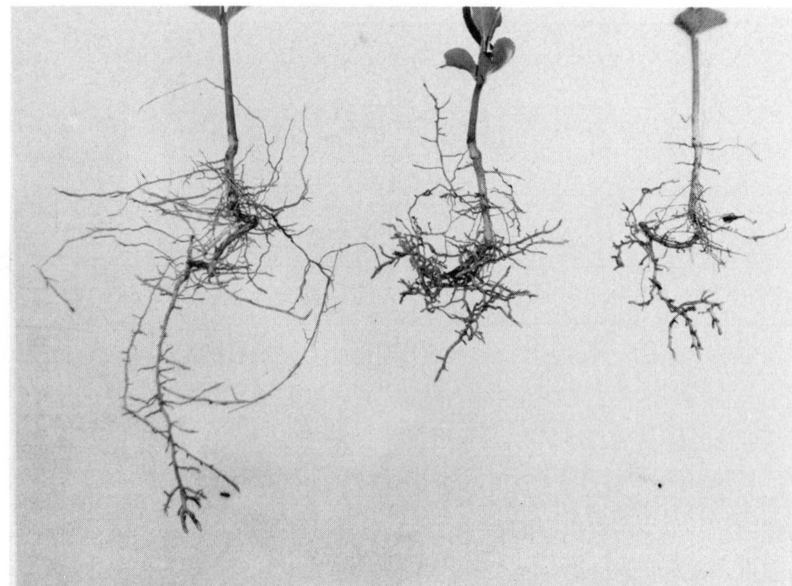

Fig. 7–8. Symptoms of root-lesion nematodes (*P. coffeae*) and of *B. longicaudatus* on Rough lemon roots. Top photo, many lesion nematodes (*P. coffeae*) entering a young root. Second photo from top, longitudinal section of root showing cortical cavity caused by numerous *P. coffeae*. Left, cross sections of young roots that are infected with *P. coffeae*. Lower left, note extensive destruction of cortical tissue in one root and localized lesion in the other root. (Photos by J. D. Radewald *et al.*, 1971.) Lower right, symptoms of sting nematode *B. longicaudatus* on Rough lemon seedlings. Noninfected seedling at left, and two seedlings with sparse stubby roots caused by *B. longicaudatus* feeding upon them. (Photo by F. W. Bistline *et al.*, 1963.)

some Florida citrus plantings. These nematodes can be very damaging to seedlings, transplants, and older plants in sandy soils. Standifer and Perry (1960) found that under greenhouse conditions, *B. longicaudatus* produced lesions at the apex and in the bark of young grapefruit roots (fig. 7–8). Inserra and Lamberti (1976) reported that *P. vulnus* decreased the growth on Rough lemon seedlings by 40 per cent and that nematode populations increased on this host. Nematode feeding caused a general maturation of roots and the production of numerous short, branch roots just back from the root tips. Preplant fumigation trials with a variety of fumigants in citrus groves containing very high populations of *B. longicaudatus* and lower populations of other nematodes controlled the nematode complex and favored a tree growth and yield response initially (Bistline *et al.*, 1963, 1967).

Stubby Root Nematodes.—Nine species of *Trichodorus* have been found associated with citrus in various parts of the world. *Trichodorus aequalis* Allen, *T. christiei* Allen, *T. lobatus* Colbran, *T. porosus* Allen, and *T. proximus* Allen have been found widely distributed in many citrus groves in California (Baines *et al.*, 1959) and Florida (Malo, 1961) in the United States, and in Australia (Colbran, 1964, 1965). They usually occur in small numbers and feed ecto-parasitically. The extent of damage is not known; however, high populations of *T. porosus* have built up in greenhouse experiments and caused a devitalization of the root tips, cessation of growth, and a stubby root type of abnormality. Standifer and Perry (1960) found that injury of grapefruit roots parasitized with *T. christiei* consisted of a maturation of primary root tissues near the root tip, and stimulation of cell division in the pericycle which resulted in the development of new roots. Citrus seedlings grew more rapidly on fumigated nursery soil that controlled *Trichodorus* than on nonfumigated soil in Australia (Meagher, 1969).

Root-knot Nematodes.—Root-knot nematodes do not ordinarily attack citrus roots; however, a few cases of galling of citrus roots and reproduction of the nematode have been reported. Mature females of *M. javanica* on *C. aurantifolia* var. *dulcis* in Israel were reported by Minz (1956). *M. incognita* on a *Citrus* sp. in Australia were reported by Colbran (1958). A new species of *Meloidogyne* on *C. reticulata* var. *Austera*, *C. sinensis*, *C. paradisi*, *C. grandis*, *C. limon*, *C. medica*, *C. aurantifolia*, and *C. aurantium* in India and Taiwan was reported by Chitwood and Tuong (1960), and in Taiwan by Tuong (1962). This nematode was first found in a number of citrus-growing areas of Taiwan and appeared to cause appreciable damage to the fibrous root system. The larvae of *M. javanica*, *M. incognita acrita* Chitwood, and *M. hapla* Chitwood penetrated citrus roots and then died before completing their development in greenhouse tests made in California by Van Gundy *et al.* (1959). However, before they died, small galls were produced on the roots of Troyer citrange and sour orange *(C. aurantium)*, but not on sweet orange *(C. sinensis)*.

Pin Nematodes.–*Paratylenchus* spp. are widespread in California. These relatively small nematodes possess a long, strong stylet and apparently feed on the surface of the root. Rough lemon, sweet orange, and trifoliate orange have been found infested with these nematodes. Baines (unpublished) has found a 20 to 29 per cent increase in the growth of young lemon trees on Rough lemon roots when planted in fumigated soil as compared with infested soil in field trials.

Dagger Nematode.—Dagger nematodes of the genus *Xiphinema* are widespread in California, Florida (Malo, 1961; Tarjan, 1964), Australia (Colbran, 1964), Puerto Rico (Tarjan, 1964), Italy (Martelli *et al.*, 1966), and India (Siddiqi, 1959). Fourteen different species have been associated with citrus plantings. These nematodes generally occur in low numbers; however, high populations of *X. americanum* have been observed in the rhizosphere of citrus roots in the spring and fall in California. Root symptoms consisted of small lesions and swellings near the root tip and necrosis and shriveling farther back on the root. Tarjan (1964) has reported reproduction and maintenance of *X. coxi* Tarjan and *X. vulgare* Tarjan on *C. paradisi* for more than a year under greenhouse conditions.

Cohn and Orion (1970) found that *X. index* and *X. brevicolle* reduced growth of sour orange seedlings in the greenhouse by 46 per cent and 44 per cent, respectively.

Members of the genus *Xiphinema* and *Trichodorus* are vectors of a number of plant viruses. At present, however, no citrus viruses are known to be transmitted by nematodes in either genus. *X. americanum* did not transmit the exocortis virus of citrus in tests made in California (unpublished).

LITERATURE CITED

ALSTATT, G. E., and A. M. FRENCH. 1964. Report of cooperative Federal-state-county burrowing nematode survey in California, 1963–64. California Dept. Agr., Plant Pathology B-64-7:1–8 (6 Tables).

ALVIRA, M. P., and A. BELLO. 1975. Observaciones del poro excretor de la hembra de Tylenchulus semipenetrans Cobb al microscopio electronico de barrido. Nematropica **5**:2–5.

BAINES, R. C. 1950. Nematodes on citrus, soil fumigation and resistant varieties promising as controls. Calif. Agr. **4**:7.

———. 1974. The effect of soil type on movement and infection rate of larvae of *Tylenchulus semipenetrans*. Jour. Nematology **6**:60–62.

———. 1974. Susceptibility and tolerance of eight citrus rootstocks to the citrus nematode, *Tylenchulus semipenetrans*. Jour. Nematology **6**:135 (abstract).

BAINES, R. C., and O. F. CLARKE. 1952. Citrus-root nematode, effects on young lemon and orange trees studied in inoculation tests under controlled conditions. Calif. Agr. **6**:9, 13.

BAINES, R. C., and G. THORNE. 1952. The olive tree as a host of the citrus-root nematode. Phytopathology **42**:77–78.

BAINES, R. C., and J. P. MARTIN. 1953. Effect of soil fumigation on growth and yield of valencia orange trees. Phytopathology **43**:465 (abstract).

BAINES, R. C., F. J. FOOTE, and J. P. MARTIN. 1956. Fumigate soil before replanting citrus for control of the citrus nematode. Calif. Citrog. **41**:427, 448–451.

BAINES, R. C., and R. H. SMALL. 1969. Efficacy of some new compounds for control of the citrus nematode, *Tylenchulus semipenetrans*, on established trees. *In:* Chapman, H. D. (ed.). Proc. 1st Intern. Citrus Symp. **2**:973–77. Univ. of Calif., Riverside, Calif.

BAINES, R. C., R. H. SMALL, T. A. DEWOLFE, J. P. MARTIN, and L. H. STOLZY. 1957. Control of the citrus nematode and *Phytopthora* spp. by Vapam. Plant Dis. Reptr. **41**:405–414.

BAINES, R. C., O. F. CLARKE, and J. W. CAMERON. 1958. A difference in the pathogenicity of the citrus nematode from trifoliate orange and sweet orange roots. Phytopathology **48**:391 (abstract).

BAINES, R. C, L. H. STOLZY, and O. C. TAYLOR. 1959. Nematode control on bearing trees. Calif. Citrog. **43**:328–329.

BAINES, R. C., S. D. VAN GUNDY, and S. A. SHER. 1959. Citrus and avocado nematodes. Calif. Agr. **13**(9):16–18.

BAINES, R. C., S. D. VAN GUNDY, and R. H. SMALL. 1977. Efficacy of some nonfumigant and low volatile nematicides for control of the citrus nematode, and the effect on the yield of navel and Valencia oranges. Jour. Nematology 9:262 (abstract).

BAINES, R. C., W. P. BITTERS, and O. F. CLARKE. 1960. Susceptibility of some species and varieties of citrus and some other rutaceous plants to the citrus nematode. Plant Dis. Reptr. **44**:281–285.

BAINES, R. C., J. P. MARTIN, T. A. DE WOLFE, S. B. BOSWELL, and M. J. GARBER. 1962. Effect of high doses of D-D on soil organisms and the growth and yield of lemon trees. Phytopathology **52**:723 (abstract).

BAINES, R. C., L. H. STOLZY, and R. H. SMALL. 1963. Controlling citrus nematode for increased yield. Calif. Citrog. **48**:186, 207–211.

BAINES, R. C., R. H. SMALL, and L. H. STOLZY. 1965. DBCP recommended for control of citrus nematode on bearing trees. Calif. Citrog. **50**:333, 342, 344, 346.

BAINES, R. C., L. J. KLOTZ, T. A. DE WOLFE, R. H. SMALL, and G. O. TURNER. 1966. Nematocidal and fungicidal properties of some soil fumigants. Phytopathology **56**:691–698.

BAINES, R. C., T. MIYAKAWA, J. W. CAMERON, and R. H. SMALL. 1969. Infectivity of two biotypes of the citrus nematode on citrus and on some other hosts. Jour. Nematology **1**:150–159.

BAINES, R. C., J. W. CAMERON, and R. K. SOOST. 1974. Four biotypes of *Tylenchulus semipenetrans* in California identified, and their importance in the development of resistent citrus rootstocks. Jour. Nematology **6**:63–66.

BIRCHFIELD, W. 1954. The hot-water treatment of nematode infested nursery stock. Proc. Fla. State Hort. Soc. **67**:94–96.

BISTLINE, F. W., B. L. COLLIER, and C. E. DIETER. 1963. The value of nematocides in the replanting of citrus. Down to Earth **19**(1):6–10.

BISTLINE, F. W., B. L. COLLIER, and C. E. DIETER. 1967. Tree and yield response to control of a nematode complex including *Belonolaimus longicaudatus* in replant citrus. Nematologica **13**:137–138 (abstract).

BOOSALIS, M. G., and R. MANKAU. 1965. Parasitism and predation of soil organisms. *In:* Baker, Kenneth F., and William C. Snyder (eds.). Ecology of soil-borne plant pathogens prelude to biological control. Pp. 374–391. Univ. of Calif. Press. 1965.

BRADFORD, G. R., and R. B. HARDING. 1957. A survey of microelements in leaves of forty-three high producing orange orchards in southern California. Proc. Amer. Soc. Hort. Sci. **70**:252–256.

BROOKS, T. L., and V. G. PERRY. 1967. Pathogenicity of *Pratylenchus brachyurus* to citrus. Plant Dis. Reptr. **51**:569–573.

CAMERON, J. W., R. C. BAINES, and O. F. CLARKE. 1954. Resistance of hybrid seedlings of the trifoliate orange to infestation by the citrus nematode. Phytopathology **44**:456–458.

CHRISTIE, J. R. 1959. Plant nematodes, their bionomics and control. Fla. Agr. Expt. Sta., Gainesville. 256 pp.

CHITWOOD, B. G., and MO-CHU TOUNG. 1960. Host-parasite interactions of the Asiatic pyroid citrus nematode. Plant Dis. Reptr. **44**:848–854.

COBB, N; A. 1913. Notes on Mononchus and Tylenchulus. Jour. Washington (D.C.), Acad. Sci. **3**:288–289.

COHN, E., and D. L. MILNE. 1977. New host plants of the citrus nematode from South Africa. Plant Dis. Reptr. **61**:466–67.

COHN, E., and G. MINZ. 1961. Citrus nematode on American persimmon in Israel. Plant Dis. Reptr. **45**:505.

———. 1965. On the feeding and histopathology of the citrus nematode. Nematologica **11**:47–54.

———. 1965. The development of the citrus nematode on some of its hosts. Nematologica **11**:593–600.

———. 1966. Observations on the survival of free-living stages of the citrus nematode. Jour. Nematologica **12**:321–327.

———. 1972. Nematode diseases of citrus, *In:* Webster, J. M. (ed.). Economic Nematology. Pp. 215–244. London, UK. Academic Press.

COHN, E., and M. MORDECHAI. 1974. Experiments in suppressing citrus nematode populations by use of a marigold and a predacious nematode. Menatologia Mediterranea. **2**:43–53.

COHN, E., and D. ORION. 1970. The pathological effect of representative *Xiphinema* and *Longidorus* species on selected host plants. Nematologica **16**:423–428.

COLBRAN, R. C. 1958. Studies of plant and soil nematodes. 2. Queensland host records of root-knot nematodes. (*Meloidogyne* spp.) Qd. Jour. Agr. Sci. **15**:101–135.

———. 1963. Studies of plant and soil nematodes. 6. Two new species from citrus orchards. Qd. Jour. Agr. Sci. **20**:469–474.

———. 1964. Studies of plant and soil nematodes. 7. Queensland records of the Order Tylenchida and the genera *Trichodorus* and *Ziphinema*. Qd. Jour. Agr. Sci. **21**:77–123.

———. 1965. Studies of plant and soil nematodes. 9. *Trichodorus lobatus* n. sp. (Nematoda:Trichodoridae). A stubby-root nematode associated with citrus and peach trees. Qd. Jour. Agr. Agr. Sci. **22**:273–276.

DuCharme, E. P. 1949. Resistance of *Poncirus trifoliata* rootstock to nematode infestation in Argentina. Citrus Indus. **30**:16–17.

———. 1954. Cause and nature of spreading decline of citrus. Proc. Fla. State Hort. Soc. **67**:75–81.

———. 1955. Subsoil drainage as a factor in the spread of the burrowing nematode. Proc. Fla. State Hort. Soc. **68**:29–31.

———. 1957. How burrowing nematodes affect citrus roots. Proc. Fla. State Hort. Soc. **70**:58–60.

———. 1959. Morphogenesis and histopathology of lesions induced on citrus roots by *Radopholus similis*. Phytopathology **49**:388–395.

———. 1967. Annual population periodicity of *Radopholus similis* in Florida citrus groves. Plant Dis. Reptr. **51**:1031–1034.

———. 1968. Temperature in relation to *Radopholus similis* (Nematoda) and spreading decline of citrus. *In:* Chapman, H. D. (ed.) Proc. 1st Intern. Citrus Symp. **2**:979–83. Univ. of Calif., Riverside, Calif.

DuCharme, E. P., and W. Birchfield. 1956. Physiologic races of the burrowing nematode. Phytopathology **46**:615–616.

DuCharme, E. P., and W. C. Price. 1966. Dynamics of multiplication of *Radopholus similis*. Nematologica **12**:113–121.

Elgindi, A. J., S. S. Ahmed, and B. A. Oteifa. 1976. Effects of nonfumigant nematicides on root populations and manganese and zinc levels in Rough lemon seedlings infected with the citrus nematode, *Tylenchulus semipenetrans*. Plant Dis. Reptr. **60**:682–83.

Embleton, T. W., W. W. Jones, and C. K. Labanauskus. 1962. Sampling orange leaves—leaf position important. Calif. Citrog. **47**:382, 396.

Feder, W. A., H. W. Ford, J. Feldmesser, F. E. Gardner, R. F. Suit, A. Pieringer, and P. C. Hutchins. 1958. Citrus varieties, species, and relatives susceptible to attack and damage by the burrowing nematode, *Radopholus similis*. Plant Dis. Reptr. **42**:934–937.

———. 1968. Differential susceptibility of selections of *Poncirus trifoliata* to attack by the citrus nematode, *Tylenchulus semipenetrans*. Israel Jour. Agr. Res. **18**:175–179.

Feldman, A. W., E. P. DuCharme, and R. F. Suit. 1961. N, P, and K in leaves of citrus trees infected with *Radopholus similis*. Plant Dis. Reptr. **45**:564–568.

———. 1963. Attempts to control spreading decline of citrus with high rates of nematocides applied by sprinkler irrigation. Plant Dis. Reptr. **47**:927–931.

Feldman, A. W., and R. W. Hanks. 1962. Evaluation of chemicals for systemic action in citrus seedlings infected with *Radopholus similis*. Plant Dis. Reptr. **46**:430–434.

———. 1964. Quantitative changes in the free and protein amino acids in the roots of healthy, *Radopholus similis*-infected and "recovered" grapefruit seedlings. Phytopathology **54**:1210–1215.

———. 1968. Phenolic content in the roots and leaves of tolerant and susceptible citrus cultivars attacked by *Radopholus similis*. Phytochemistry 7:5–12.

Feldman, A. W., R. W. Hanks, and J. C. Collins. 1966. Modification of growth substances in burrowing nematode infected citrus trees. Phytopathology **56**:1312–1313.

Florida Division Of Plant Industry. 1976. Bureau of Nematology. Triology **16**(7):9.

Ford, H. W. 1953. Changes in rate of respiration and catalase activity assocated with spreading decline of citrus trees. Proc. Amer. Soc. Hort. Sci. **61**:73–76.

———. 1956. Chemicals screened for systemic effects against spreading decline disease of citrus. Plant Dis. Reptr. **40**:861–865.

———. 1962. The effect of spreading decline on the root distribution of citrus. Proc. Fla. State Hort. Soc. **65**:47–50.

Ford, H. W. and W. A. Feder, 1962. Laboratory evaluation of certain citrus rootstock selections for resistance to the burrowing nematode. Jour. Rio Grande Valley Hort. Soc. **16**:35–39.

———. 1964. Three citrus rootstocks recommended for trial in spreading decline areas. Univ. of Fla. Agr. Expt. Sta. Circ. S 151.

Ford, H. W., W. A. Feder, and P. C. Hutchins. 1960. Citrus varieties, hybrids, species and relatives evaluated for resistance to the burrowing nematode, *Radopholus similis*. University of Florida, Citrus Experiment Station Mimeo Series 60–13.

Gutierrez, R. O. 1947. El nematode de las raicillas de los citrus *Tylenchulus semipenetrans* en la Republica Argentina. Rev. Invest. Agric., B. Aires **1**:119–146.

Hanks, R. W., and A. W. Feldman. 1963. Comparison of free amino acids and amides in roots of healthy and *Radopholus similis-infected* grapefruit seedlings. Phytopathology **53**:419–422.

———. 1968. Quantitative changes in organic acids in roots and leaves from grapefruit seedlings infected with *Radopholus similis*. Phytopathology **58**:706–707.

Hannon, C. I. 1962. The occurrence and distribution of the citrus-root nematode, *Tylenchulus semipenetrans* Cobb, in Florida. Plant Dis. Reptr. **46**:451–455.

Harding, R. B. 1954. Exchangeable cations in soils in California orange orchards in relation to yield and size of fruit and leaf composition. Soil Sci. **77**:119–127.

Hodges, L. R., and B. Lear. 1973. Distribution and persistence of 1, 2-Dibromo-3-chloropropane in soil after application by injection and in irrigation water. Nematologica **19**:146–158.

Ichikawa, S. T., J. D. Gilpatrick, and C. W. McBeth. 1955. Soil diffusion pattern of 1,2-Dibromo-3-chloropropane. Phytopathology **45**:576–78.

Inserra, R. N., and V. Vovlas. 1977. Effects of *Pratylenchus vulnus* on the growth of sour orange. Jour. Nematology **9**:154–57.

Jensen, H. J. 1953. Experimental greenhouse host range studies of two root-lesion nematodes. *Pratylenchus vulnus* and *Pratylenchus penetrans*. Plant Dis. Reptr. **37**:384–387.

Johnson, D. E., and B. Lear. 1969. The effect of temperature on the dispersion of 1,2-dibromo-3-chloropropane in soil. Jour. Nematology **1**:116–122.

Labanauskas, C. K., R. C. Baines, and L. H. Stolzy. 1965. Effect of the citrus nematode *Tylenchulus semipenetrans* and two levels of water suction on nutrient concentration in navel orange leaves and roots. Soil Sci. **99**:367–374.

Lamberti, F., N. Vovlas, and A. Tirro. 1976. An Italian biotype of the citrus nematode. Nematologia Mediterranea 4(1):117–120.

MACARON, J. 1972. Contribution à l'étude du nematode phytophage *Tylenchulus semipenetrans* Cobb 1913 (Nematoda-Tylenchida). Academie de Montpellier, University des Science et Techniques du Lanquedoc. Thèse:190.

MAGGENTI, A. R. 1962. The production of the gelatinous matrix and its taxonomic significance in Tylenchulus (Nematoda: Tylenchulinae) Proc. Helminth. Soc. Wash. **29**:139–144.

MALO, S. E. 1961. Nematode populations associated with citrus roots in Central Florida. Plant Dis. Reptr. **45**:20–23.

MANKAU, R. 1975. *Bacillus penetrans* n. comb. causing a virulent disease of plant-parasitic nematodes. Jour. Invert. Path. **26**:333–39.

MANKAU, R., and J. L. IMBRIANI. 1975. The life cycle of an endoparasite in some Tylechid nematodes. Nematologica **21**:89–94.

MANKAU, R., and N. PRASAD. 1977. Infectivity of *Bacillus penetrans* in plant-parasitic nematode. Jour. Nematology **9**:40–45.

MARTELLI, G. P., E. COHN, and A. DALMASSO. 1966. A redescription of *Xiphinema italiae* Meyl, 1953 and its relationship to *Xiphinema arenarium* Luc et Dalmasso, 1963 and *Xiphinema conorum* Siddiqui 1964. Nematologica **12**:183–194.

MARTIN, J. P., and S. D. VAN GUNDY. 1963. Differences of soil P level on the growth of sweet orange seedlings and the activity of the citrus nematode. Soil Sci. **96**:128–135.

MC ELROY, F. C., S. A. SHER and S. D. VAN GUNDY. 1966. The sheath nematode, *Hemicycliophora arenaria*, a native of California soils. Plant Dis. Reptr. **50**:581–583.

MC ELROY, F. D., and S. D. VAN GUNDY. 1968. Observations on the feeding process of *Hemicycliophora arenaria*. Phytopathology **58**:1558–1565.

MEAGHER, J. W. 1969. Nematodes as a factor in citrus production in Australia. *In:* Chapman, H. D. (ed.). Proc. 1st Intern. Citrus Symp. **2**:999–1006. Univ. Calif. Riverside, Calif.

MINZ, G. 1956. The root-knot nematode, *Meloidogyne* spp., in Israel. Plant Dis. Reptr. **40**:798–801.

NEAL, J. C. 1889. The root disease nematode of peach, orange and other plants in Florida due to the work of *Anguillulina*. Bull. U. S. Bur. Ent. **20**:1–31.

NESBITT, R. B. 1956. New host plants of plant parasitic nematodes in California. Plant Dis. Reptr. **40**:276.

O'BANNON, J. H. 1968. The influence of an organic soil amendment on infectivity and reproduction of *Tylenchulus semipenetrans* on two citrus rootstocks. Phytopathology **58**:597–601.

———. 1977. Worldwide dissemination of *Radopholus similis* and its importance in crop production. Jour. Nematology **9**:16–25.

O'BANNON, J. H., V. CHEW, and A. T. TOMERLIN. 1977. Comparison of five populations of *Tylenchulus semipenetrans* to *citrus*, *Poncirus*, and their hybrids. Jour. Nematology **9**:162–65.

O'BANNON, J. H., and R. P. ESSER. 1975. Evaluation of citrus hybrids and relatives as hosts of *Pratylenchus coffeae*, with comments on other hosts. Nematologia Med. **3**:113–22.

O'BANNON, J. H., J. D. RADEWALD, and A. T. TOMERLIN. 1972. Population fluctuation of three parasitic nematodes in Florida Citrus. Jour. Nematol. **4**:194–199.

O'BANNON, J. H., and H. W. REYNOLDS. 1963. Response of navel orange trees to a postplanting application of DBCP for control of the citrus nematode. Plant Dis. Reptr. **47**:401–404.

O'BANNON, J. H., H. W. REYNOLDS, and C. R. LEATHERS. 1966. Effects of temperature on penetration, development, and reproduction of *Tylenchulus semipenetrans*. Nematologica **12**:483–487.

O'BANNON, J. H., A. C. TARJAN, and F. W. BISTLINE. 1973. Control of *Pratylenchus brachyurus* on citrus and tree response to chemical treatment. Proc. Soil and Crop Sci. Soc. Fla., **33**:65–67.

O'BANNON, J. H., and A. T. TOMERLIN. 1969. Population studies on two species of *Pratylenchus* on citrus. Jour. Nematology **1**:299–300.

———. 1973. Citrus tree decline caused by *Pratylenchus brachyrus* on citrus and tree response to chemical treatment. Proc. Soil and Crop Sci. Soc. Fla. **33**:65–67.

———. 1977. Control of the burrowing nematode, *Radopholus similis*, with DBCP and oxamyl. Plant Dis. Reptr. **61**:450–54.

OTIEFA, B. A., and A. T. SHAARAWI. 1962. Observations on the citrus nematode *Tylenchulus semipenetrans* Cobb in United Arab Republic. Nematologica **8**:267–271.

OTIEFA, B. A., F. A. SHAFIEE, and F. M. EISSA. 1965. Efficacy of DBCP flood irrigation in established citrus. Plant Dis. Reptr. **49**:598–599.

POUCHER, C. H., H. W. FORD, R. F. SUIT, and E. P. DU CHARME. 1967. Burrowing nematode in citrus. Fla. Dept. Agr. Div. Plant Ind. Bul. 71–63.

RADEWALD, J. D., J. H. O'BANNON, and A. T. TOMERLIN. 1971. Temperature effects on reproduction and pathogenicity of *Pratylenchus coffeae* and *P. brachyurus* and survival of *P. coffeae* in roots of *Citrus jambhiri*. Jour. Nematol. **3**:390–394.

RADEWALD, J. D., J. H. O'BANNON, and A. T. TOMERLIN. 1971. Anatomical studies of *Citrus jambhiri* roots infected by *Pratylenchus coffeae*. Jour. Nematol. **3**:409–416.

RASKI, D. J., S. A. SHERE, and F. N. JENSEN. 1956. New host records of the citrus nematode in California. Plant Dis. Reptr. **40**:1047–1048.

REYNOLDS, H. W., and J. H. O'BANNON. 1958. The citrus nematode and its control on living citrus in Arizona. Plant Dis. Reptr. **42**:1288–1292.

———. 1963. Decline of grapefruit trees in relation to citrus nematode populations and tree recovery after chemical treatment. Phytopathology **53**:1011–1015.

———. 1963. Factors influencing the citrus nematode and its control on citrus replants in Arizona. Nematologica **9**:337–340.

REYNOLDS, H. W., J. H. O'BANNON, A. T. TOMERLIN, E. L. NIGH, and D. R. RODNEY. 1970. The influence of various ecological factors on survival of *Tylenchulus semipenetrans*. Proc. Soil and Crop Sci. Sco. Fla. **30**:366–370.

SEINHORST, J. W., and M. R. SAUER. 1956. Eelworm attacks on vines in the Murray valley irrigation area. Jour. Austral. Inst. Agr. Sci. **22**:296–299.

SCHNEIDER, H., and R. C. BAINES. 1964. *Tylenchulus semipenetrans*. Parasitism and injury to orange tree roots. Phytopathology **54**:1202–1206.

SIDDIQUI, M. R. 1959. Studies on *Xiphinema* spp. (Nematode: Dorylaimoidea) from Aligarh (North India), with comments on the genus Longidorus Micoletzky, 1922. Proc. Helminth. Soc., Wash. D. C. **26**(2):151–163.

SIDDIQUI, I. A., S. A. SHER, and A. M. FRENCH. 1973. Distribution of plant parasitic nematodes in California. Dept. Food and Agr. Div. Plant Industry, State of California, 324 pp.

SPEARS, J. F. 1956. Report of the burrowing nematode survey of California. Golden Nematode Control Project, Agr. Res.

Serv., U. S. Dept. Agr. (Leaflet):6 pp.

STANDIFER, M. S., and V. G. PERRY. 1960. Some effects of sting and stubby root nematodes on grapefruit roots. Phytopathology **50**:152–156.

STOKES, D. E. 1969. *Andropogon rhizomatus* parasitized by a strain of *Tylenchulus semipenetrans* not parasitic to four citrus rootstocks. Plant Dis. Reptr. **53**:882–85.

STOLZY, L. H., S. D. VAN GUNDY, C. K. LABANAUSKIAS, and T. E. SZUSZKIEWICZ. 1963. Response of *Tylenchulus semipenetrans* infected citrus seedlings to soil-aeration and temperature. Soil Sci. **96**:292–298.

SUIT, R. F., and E. P. DU CHARME. 1953. The burrowing nematode and other plant parasitic nematodes in relation to spreading decline in citrus. Plant Dis. Reptr. **37**:379–383.

SUIT, R. F., E. P. DU CHARME, and T. L. BROOKS. 1955. Effectiveness of the pull-and-treat method for controlling the burrowing nematode on citrus. Proc. Fla. Hort. Soc. **68**:36–38.

SUIT, R. F., and T. L. BROOKS. 1957. Current information relating to barriers for the burrowing nematode. Proc. Fla. State Hort. Soc. **70**:55–57.

SUIT, R. F., and E. P. DU CHARME. 1957. Spreading decline of citrus. State Plant Board of Florida. Pp. 1–24. Vol. 2, Bul. 11.

———. 1961. A comparison of preplant soil treatment chemicals for control of burrowing nematode in citrus groves. Plant Dis. Reptr. **45**:454–456.

SUIT, R. F., E. P. DU CHARME, and A. W. FELDMAN. 1961. Effectiveness of DBCP and fungicides for the control of *Radopholus similis* on citrus trees. Plant Dis. Reptr. **45**:62–66.

SUIT, R. F., and A. W. FELDMAN. 1961. Treatment of citrus trees with cynem for control of *Radopholus similis*. Plant Dis. Reptr. **45**:782–786.

———. 1964. Barriers for spreading decline control. Proc. Fla. State Hort. Soc. **77**:52–56.

———. 1969. Treatment of citrus trees for burrowing nematode control. *In:* Chapman, H. D. (ed.). Proc. 1st Intern. Citrus Symp. **2**:961–968. Univ. of Calif. Riverside, Calif.

TARJAN, A. C. 1959. Pressure injection of chemicals for possible systemic action against burrowing nematodes infecting citrus. Plant Dis. Reptr. **43**:451–458.

———. 1961. Attempts at controlling citrus burrowing nematodes using nematode trapping fungi. Proc. Soil and Crop Sci. Soc. Fla. **21**:17–36.

———. 1961. Longevity of *Radopholus similis* (Cobb) in host-free soil. Nematologica **6**:170–175.

———. 1964. Two new American dagger nematodes (Xiphinema: Dorylaimidae) associated with citrus, with comments on the variability of *X. bakeri* Williams, 1961. Prov. Helminthol. Soc. Wash. D. C. **31**:65–76.

———. 1964. Distribution of plant-parasitic nematodes on citrus and other crops in Puerto Rico. Plant Dis. Reptr. **48**:375–378.

TARJAN, A. C., and J. H. O'BANNON. 1969. Observations on meadow nematodes (*Pratylenchus* spp.) and their relation to declines of citrus in Florida. Plant Dis. Reptr. **58**:683–686.

THOMAS, E. E. 1913. A preliminary report of a nematode observed on citrus roots and its possible relation with mottled appearance of citrus trees. Calif. Agr. Expt. Sta. Circ. **85**:1–14.

THOMAS, E. E. 1920. The citrus nematode, *Tylenchulus semipenetrans*. Univ. of Calif. Agr. Expt. Sta. Tech. Paper **2**:19 (7 pl.).

TOUNG, MO-CHU. 1962. A preliminary survey of some parasitic nematodes in relation to citrus in Taiwan. Jour. Plant Prot. Soc. **4**:59–63.

VAN GUNDY, S. D. 1959. The first report of a species of *Hemicycliophora* attacking citrus roots. Plat Dis. Reptr. **41**:1016–1018.

———. 1958. The life history of the citrus nematode, *Tylenchulus semipenetrans*. Nematologica **3**:283–294.

VAN GUNDY, S. D., I. J. THOMASON, and R. L. RACKHAM. 1959. The reaction of three citrus spp to three *Meloidogyne* spp. Plant Dis. Reptr. **43**:970–971.

VAN GUNDY, S. D., and J. D. KIRKPATRICK. 1964. Nature of resistance in certain citrus rootstocks to citrus nematodes. Phytopathology **54**:419–427.

VAN GUNDY, S. D., and J. P. MARTIN. 1961. Influence of *Tylechulus semipenetrans* on the growth and chemical composition of sweet orange seedlings in soils of various exchangeable cation ratios. Phytopathology **51**:146–151.

VAN GUNDY, S. D., and R. L. RACKHAM. 1961. Studies on the biology and pathogenicity of *Hemicycliophora arenaria*. Phytopathology **51**:393–397.

VAN GUNDY, S. D., J. P. MARTIN, and P. H. TSAO. 1964. Some soil factors influencing reproduction of the citrus nematode and growth of sweet orange seedlings. Phytopathology **54**:294–299.

VAN GUNDY, S. D., J. P. MARTIN, and P. H. TSAO. 1964. Some soil factors influencing reproduction of the citrus nematode and growth reduction of sweet orange seedlings. Phytopathology **54**:294–99.

VAN GUNDY, S. D., A. F. BIRD, and H. R. WALLACE. 1967. Aging and starvation in larvae of *Meloidogyne javanica* and *Tylenchulus semipenetrans*. Phytopathology **57**:559–571.

VAN GUNDY, S. D., and F. D. MCELROY. 1969. Sheath nematode—its biology and contro. *In:* Chapman, H. D. (ed.). Proc. 1st Intern. Citrus Symp. **2**:285–989. Univ. of Calif. Riverside, Calif.

VAN WEERDT, L. G. 1957. Studies on the biology of *Radopholus similis* (Cobb 1893) Thorne 1949. Plant Dis. Reptr. **41**:832–835.

———. 1958. Studies on the biology of *Radopholus similis* (Cobb 1893) Thorne 1949. Part II. Morphological variation within and between progenies of single females. Nematologica III, 184–196.

VILARDEBO, A. 1963. Etude sur *Tylenchulus semipenetrans* Cobb au Maroc. Observations sur le degre d'infestation des vergers. Al Awamia **8**:1–23.

VILARDEBO, A., and M. LUC. 1961. Le (slow decline) des citrus dû au nematode *Tylenchulus semipenetrans* Cobb. Fruits. **16**:445–454.

AUTHORS OF CHAPTERS

LEO J. KLOTZ, PH.D.
Professor of Plant Pathology, Emeritus, Department of Plant Pathology, University of California, Riverside.

JAMES W. WALLACE, PH.D.
Professor of Plant Pathology, Emeritus, Department of Plant Pathology, University of California, Riverside.

E. CLAIR CALAVAN, PH.D.
Professor of Plant Pathology, Department of Plant Pathology, University of California, Riverside; Pathologist, Citrus Research Center and Agricultural Experiment Station, Riverside.

STANLEY M. MATHER, B.S.
Regional Coordinator, State of California Department of Food and Agriculture, Division of Plant Industry, Sacramento, California.

E. H. MCEACHERN, B.S.
Former Chief of Nursery and Seed Services, Division of Plant Industry, State of California Department of Food and Agriculture, Sacramento California.

DAN Y. ROSENBERG, M.S.
Chief of Nursery and Seed Services, Division of Plant Industry, State of California Department of Food and Agriculture, Sacramento, California.

F. LOUIS BLANC, B.S.
Program Supervisor, Pest Detection (Exclusion and Detection Unit), Division of Plant Industry, State of California Department of Food and Agriculture, Sacramento, California.

DANIEL W. ROBINSON, B.S.
Former Principal Staff Entomologist, Division of Plant Industry, State of California Department of Food and Agriculture, Sacramento, California.

H. LEN FOOTE, B.S.
Program Supervisor, Control and Eradication, Division of Plant Industry, State of California Department of Food and Agriculture, Sacramento, California.

MAYNARD W. CUMMINGS, B.S.
Unit Coordinator, Extension, Wildlife, and Sea Grant, University of California, Davis, California.

REX E. MARSH, B.A.
Specialist and Lecturer in Vertebrate Ecology, Division of Wildlife and Fisheries Biology, University of California, Davis, California.

C. P. CLAUSEN, PH.D.
Former Professor of Biological Control and Entomologist Emeritus, Departments of Biological Control and Entomology, University of California, Riverside.

R. C. BAINES
Nematologist Emeritus, Department of Nematology, University of California, Riverside.

S. D. VAN GUNDY, PH.D.
Professor of Nematology, Department of Nematology, University of California, Riverside; Nematologist, Citrus Research Center and Agricultural Experiment Station, Riverside.

E. P. DUCHARME, PH.D.
Professor of Plant Pathology, University of Florida, Agricultural Research Education Center, Institute of Food and Agricultural Sciences, Lake Alfred, Florida.

TABLE I-1

CONVERSION TABLES

TEMPERATURE

To convert a temperature, in either Centigrade (Celsius) or Fahrenheit, to the other scale, find that temperature in the center column, and then find the equivalent temperature in the other scale either in the Centigrade column to the left or in the Fahrenheit column to the right. For example, if the Centigrade temperature is 44°, the equivalent Fahrenheit temperature (in the righthand column) is 111.2°. If the *Fahrenheit* temperature is 44°, the equivalent Centigrade temperature (in the lefthand column) is 6.67°.

On the Centigrade scale the temperature of melting ice is 0° and that of boiling water is 100° at normal atmospheric pressure. On the Fahrenheit scale, the equivalent temperatures are 32° and 212° respectively. The formula for converting Centigrade to Fahrenheit is C = 5/9 F–32, and the formula for converting Fahrenheit to Centigrade is F = 9/5 C + 32.

C	C or F	F	C	C or F	F	C	C or F	F	C	C or F	F
—73.33	**—100**	—148.0	— 6.67	**20**	68.0	15.6	**60**	140.0	43	**110**	230
—70.56	**— 95**	—139.0	— 6.11	**21**	69.8	16.1	**61**	141.8	49	**120**	248
—67.78	**— 90**	—130.0	— 5.56	**22**	71.6	16.7	**62**	143.6	54	**130**	266
—65.00	**— 85**	—121.0	— 5.00	**23**	73.4	17.2	**63**	145.4	60	**140**	284
—62.22	**— 80**	—112.0	— 4.44	**24**	75.2	17.8	**64**	147.2	66	**150**	302
—59.45	**— 75**	—103.0	— 3.89	**25**	77.0	18.3	**65**	149.0	71	**160**	320
—56.67	**— 70**	— 94.0	— 3.33	**26**	78.8	18.9	**66**	150.8	77	**170**	338
—53.89	**— 65**	— 85.0	— 2.78	**27**	80.6	19.4	**67**	152.6	82	**180**	356
—51.11	**— 60**	— 76.0	— 2.22	**28**	82.4	20.0	**68**	154.4	88	**190**	374
—48.34	**— 55**	— 67.0	— 1.67	**29**	84.2	20.6	**69**	156.2	93	**200**	392
—45.56	**— 50**	— 58.0	— 1.11	**30**	86.0	21.1	**70**	158.0	99	**210**	410
—42.78	**— 45**	— 49.0	— 0.56	**31**	87.8	21.7	**71**	159.8	100	**212**	414
—40.0	**— 40**	— 40.0	— 0	**32**	89.6	22.2	**72**	161.6	104	**220**	428
—37.23	**— 35**	— 31.0				22.8	**73**	163.4	110	**230**	446
—34.44	**— 30**	— 22.0	0.56	**33**	91.4	23.3	**74**	165.2	116	**240**	464
—31.67	**— 25**	— 13.0	1.11	**34**	93.2	23.9	**75**	167.0	121	**250**	482
—28.89	**— 20**	— 4.0	1.67	**35**	95.0	24.4	**76**	168.8	127	**260**	500
—26.12	**— 15**	5.0	2.22	**36**	96.8	25.0	**77**	170.6	132	**270**	518
—23.33	**— 10**	14.0	2.78	**37**	98.6	25.6	**78**	172.4	138	**280**	536
—20.56	**— 5**	23.0	3.33	**38**	100.4	26.1	**79**	174.2	143	**290**	554
—17.8	**0**	32.0	3.89	**39**	102.2	26.7	**80**	176.0	149	**300**	572
			4.44	**40**	104.0	27.2	**81**	177.8	154	**310**	590
—17.2	**1**	33.8	5.00	**41**	105.8	27.8	**82**	179.6	160	**320**	608
—16.7	**2**	35.6	5.56	**42**	107.6	28.3	**83**	181.4	166	**330**	626
—16.1	**3**	37.4	6.11	**43**	109.4	28.9	**84**	183.2	171	**340**	644
—15.6	**4**	39.2	6.67	**44**	111.2	29.4	**85**	185.0	177	**350**	662
—15.0	**5**	41.0	7.22	**45**	113.0	30.0	**86**	186.8	182	**360**	680
—14.4	**6**	42.8	7.78	**46**	114.8	30.6	**87**	188.6	188	**370**	698
—13.9	**7**	44.6	8.33	**47**	116.6	31.1	**88**	190.4	193	**380**	716
—13.3	**8**	46.4	8.89	**48**	118.4	31.7	**89**	192.2	199	**390**	734
—12.8	**9**	48.2	9.44	**49**	120.2	32.2	**90**	194.0	204	**400**	752
—12.2	**10**	50.0	10.0	**50**	122.0	32.8	**91**	195.8	210	**410**	770
—11.7	**11**	51.8	10.6	**51**	123.8	33.3	**92**	197.6	216	**420**	788
—11.1	**12**	53.6	11.1	**52**	125.6	33.9	**93**	199.4	221	**430**	806
—10.6	**13**	55.4	11.7	**53**	127.4	34.4	**94**	201.2	227	**440**	824
—10.0	**14**	57.2	12.2	**54**	129.2	35.0	**95**	203.0	232	**450**	842
— 9.44	**15**	59.0	12.8	**55**	131.0	35.6	**96**	204.8	238	**460**	860
— 8.89	**16**	60.8	13.3	**56**	132.8	36.1	**97**	206.6	243	**470**	878
— 8.33	**17**	62.6	13.9	**57**	134.6	36.7	**98**	208.4	249	**480**	896
— 7.78	**18**	64.4	14.4	**58**	136.4	37.2	**99**	210.2	254	**490**	914
— 7.22	**19**	66.2	15.0	**59**	138.2	37.8	**100**	212.0	260	**500**	932

AREA

Metric

1 square centimeter	=	0.155 sq inch
	=	100 sq millimeters
1 square meter	=	1,550 sq inches
	=	10.764 sq feet
	=	1.196 sq yards
	=	10,000 sq centimeters
1 square kilometer	=	0.3861 sq mile
	=	1,000,000 sq meters
1 hectare	=	2.471 acres
	=	10,000 sq meters

Imperial

1 square inch	=	6.452 sq centimeters
	=	1/144 sq foot
	=	1/1296 sq yard
1 square foot	=	929.088 sq centimeters
	=	0.0929 sq meter
1 square yard	=	8,361.3 sq centimeters
	=	0.8361 sq meter
	=	1,296 sq inches
	=	9 sq feet
1 square mile	=	2.59 sq kilometers
	=	640 acres
1 acre	=	0.4047 hectare
	=	43,560 sq feet
	=	4,840 sq yards
	=	4,046.87 sq meters

LENGTH

Metric

1 millimicron	=	0.001 micron
1 micron	=	0.001 millimeter
1 millimeter	=	0.001 meter
	=	0.0394 inch
1 centimeter	=	10 millimeters
	=	0.3937 inch
	=	0.01 meter
1 meter	=	39.37 inches
	=	3.281 feet
	=	1,000 millimeters
	=	100 centimeters
	=	1.2 varas
1 kilometer	=	3,281 feet
	=	1,094 yards
	=	0.621 mile
	=	1,000 meters

Imperial

1 inch	=	25.4 millimeters
	=	2.54 centimeters
1 foot	=	30.48 centimeters
	=	0.3048 meter
	=	12 inches

1 yard	=	0.9144 meter
	=	91.44 centimeters
	=	3 feet
1 mile	=	1,609.347 meters
	=	1.609 kilometers
	=	5,280 feet
	=	1,760 yards

WEIGHT

Metric

1 milligram	=	0.001 gram
	=	0.0154 grain
1 centigram	=	0.01 gram
	=	0.1543 grain
1 gram	=	0.0353 avoirdupois ounce
	=	15.4324 grains
1 kilogram	=	1,000 grams
	=	353 avoirdupois ounces
	=	2.2046 avoirdupois pounds
1 metric ton	=	1,000 kilograms
	=	2,204.6 pounds
	=	1.102 short tons
	=	0.984 long ton

Imperial

1 grain	=	1/700 avoirdupois pound
	=	0.064799 gram
1 ounce (avoirdupois)	=	28.3496 grams
	=	437.5 grains
	=	1/16 pound
1 pound (avoirdupois)	=	453.593 grams
	=	0.45369 kilograms
	=	16 ounces
1 short ton	=	907.184 kilograms
	=	0.9072 metric ton
	=	2,000 pounds

YIELD

Metric

1 kilogram per hectare	=	0.89 pound per acre
1 cubic meter per hectare	=	14.2916 cubic feet per acre

Imperial

1 pound per acre	=	1.121 kilograms per hectare
1 ton (2,000 lb) per acre	=	2.242 metric tons per hectare
1 cubic foot per acre	=	0.0699 cubic meter per hectare
1 bushel (60 lb) per acre	=	67.26 kilograms per hectare

VOLUME

Metric

1 liter	=	1.057 U.S. quarts liquid
	=	0.9081 quart, dry
	=	0.2642 U.S. gallon
	=	0.221 Imperial gallon
	=	1,000 milliliters or cc
	=	0.0353 cubic foot
	=	61.02 cubic inches
	=	0.001 cubic meter
1 cubic meter	=	61,023.38 cubic inches
	=	35.314 cubic feet
	=	1.308 cubic yards
	=	264.17 U.S. gallons
	=	1,000 liters
	=	28.38 U.S. bushels
	=	1,000,000 cu. centimeters
	=	1,000,000,000 cu. millimeters

Imperial

1 fluid ounce	=	1/128 gallon
	=	29.57 cubic centimeters
	=	29.562 milliliters
	=	1.805 cubic inches
	=	0.0625 U.S. pint (liquid)
1 U.S. quart liquid	=	946.3 milliliters
	=	57.75 cubic inches
	=	32 fluid ounces
	=	4 cups
	=	1/4 gallon
	=	2 U.S. pints (liquid)
	=	0.946 liter
1 quart dry	=	1.1012 liters
	=	67.20 cubic inches
	=	2 pints (dry)
	=	0.125 peck
	=	1/32 bushel
1 cubic inch	=	16.387 cubic centimeters
1 cubic foot	=	28,317 cubic centimeters
	=	0.0283 cubic meter
	=	28.316 liters
	=	7.481 U.S. gallons
	=	1,728 cubic inches
1 U.S. gallon	=	16 cups
	=	3.785 liters
	=	231 cubic inches
	=	4 U.S. quarts liquid
	=	8 U.S. pints liquid
	=	8.3453 pounds of water
	=	128 fluid ounces
	=	0.8327 British Imperial gallon
1 British Imperial gallon	=	4.546 liters
	=	1.201 U.S. gallons
	=	277.42 cubic inches
1 U.S. bushel	=	35.24 liters
	=	2,150.42 cubic inches
	=	1.2444 cubic feet
	=	0.03524 cubic meter
	=	2 pecks
	=	32 quarts (dry)
	=	64 pints (dry)

TABLE I-2

NUMBER OF TREES PER ACRE AT GIVEN SPACINGS*

Feet	*No. of Plants*	*Feet*	*No. of Plants*	*Feet*	*No. of Plants*
6 × 1	7,260	10 × 1	4,356	18 × 4	605
6 × 2	3,630	10 × 2	2,178	18 × 6	404
6 × 3	2,420	10 × 3	1,452	18 × 8	303
6 × 4	1,815	10 × 4	1,089	18 × 10	242
6 × 5	1,452	10 × 5	871	18 × 12	202
6 × 6	1,210	10 × 6	726	18 × 14	173
		10 × 7	622	18 × 16	152
7 × 1	6,223	10 × 8	544	18 × 18	132
7 × 2	3,111	10 × 9	484		
7 × 3	2,074	10 × 10	435		
7 × 4	1,556			20 × 8	272
7 × 5	1,244	12 × 2	1,815	20 × 10	218
7 × 6	1,037	12 × 4	907	20 × 12	184
7 × 7	889	12 × 6	605	20 × 14	156
		12 × 7	454	20 × 16	136
8 × 1	5,445	12 × 10	363	20 × 18	121
8 × 2	2,722	12 × 12	302	20 × 20	109
8 × 3	1,815				
8 × 4	1,361	14 × 2	1,556		
8 × 5	1,089	14 × 4	778	24 × 12	151
8 × 6	907	14 × 6	518	24 × 16	114
8 × 7	778	14 × 8	389	24 × 20	92
8 × 8	680	14 × 10	311	24 × 24	76
		14 × 12	259		
9 × 1	4,840	14 × 14	222		
9 × 2	2,420			30 × 20	72
9 × 3	1,613	16 × 2	1,361	30 × 30	48
9 × 4	1,210	16 × 4	680	30 × 40	36
9 × 5	968	16 × 6	454		
9 × 6	807	16 × 8	340		
9 × 7	691	16 × 10	272	40 × 40	27
9 × 8	605	16 × 12	227		
9 × 9	528	16 × 14	194		
		16 × 16	170		

*In order to obtain the number of plants per acre, divide 43,560 by the product of the spacing in the rows expressed in feet.

Table I-3

NUMBER OF TREES PER HECTARE AT GIVEN SPACINGS*

Meters	*No. of Plants*	*Meters*	*No. of Plants*	*Meters*	*No. of Plants*
2 × 0.25	20,000	5 × 1.0	2,000	8 × 1	1,250
2 × 0.50	10,000	5 × 1.5	1,333	8 × 2	555
2 × 0.75	6,666	5 × 2.0	1,000	8 × 3	416
2 × 1.0	5,000	5 × 2.5	800	8 × 4	312
2 × 1.25	4,000	5 × 3.0	666	8 × 5	250
2 × 1.50	3,333	5 × 3.5	571	8 × 6	208
2 × 1.75	2,857	5 × 4.0	500	8 × 7	178
2 × 2.0	2,500	5 × 4.5	444	8 × 8	156
		5 × 5.0	400		
3 × 0.5	6,666				
3 × 1.0	3,333	6 × 1	1,666	9 × 1	1,111
3 × 1.5	2,222	6 × 2	833	9 × 2	555
3 × 2.0	1,666	6 × 3	555	9 × 3	370
3 × 2.5	1,333	6 × 4	416	9 × 4	277
3 × 3.0	1,111	6 × 5	333	9 × 5	222
		6 × 6	277	9 × 6	185
4 × 0.5	5,000			9 × 7	158
4 × 1.0	2,500	7 × 1	1,428	9 × 8	138
4 × 1.5	1,666	7 × 2	714	9 × 9	123
4 × 2.0	1,250	7 × 3	476	9 × 10	111
4 × 2.5	1,000	7 × 4	357		
4 × 3.0	833	7 × 5	285		
4 × 3.5	714	7 × 6	238	10 × 10	100
4 × 4.0	625	7 × 7	204		

*In order to obtain the number of plants per hectare, divide 10,000 by the product of the spacing in the rows expressed in meters.

INDEX

—T—

—U—

—V—

—W—

—X—

—Y—

—Z—